T0198288

Data Structures and Algorithms in Python

Michael T. Goodrich
Department of Computer Science
University of California, Irvine

Roberto Tamassia
Department of Computer Science
Brown University

Michael H. Goldwasser
Department of Mathematics and Computer Science
Saint Louis University

WILEY

VP & PUBLISHER	Don Fowley
EXECUTIVE EDITOR	Beth Lang Golub
EDITORIAL PROGRAM ASSISTANT	Katherine Willis
MARKETING MANAGER	Christopher Ruel
DESIGNER	Kenji Ngieng
SENIOR PRODUCTION MANAGER	Janis Soo
ASSOCIATE PRODUCTION MANAGER	Joyce Poh

This book was set in LaTeX by the authors. Printed and bound by Quad/Graphics. The cover was printed by Quad/Graphics

This book is printed on acid free paper.

Founded in 1807, John Wiley & Sons, Inc. has been a valued source of knowledge and understanding for more than 200 years, helping people around the world meet their needs and fulfill their aspirations. Our company is built on a foundation of principles that include responsibility to the communities we serve and where we live and work. In 2008, we launched a Corporate Citizenship Initiative, a global effort to address the environmental, social, economic, and ethical challenges we face in our business. Among the issues we are addressing are carbon impact, paper specifications and procurement, ethical conduct within our business and among our vendors, and community and charitable support. For more information, please visit our website: www.wiley.com/go/citizenship.

Printed in the United States of America

SKY10037073_101922

To Karen, Paul, Anna, and Jack
– Michael T. Goodrich

To Isabel
– Roberto Tamassia

To Susan, Calista, and Maya
– Michael H. Goldwasser

Preface

The design and analysis of efficient data structures has long been recognized as a vital subject in computing and is part of the core curriculum of computer science and computer engineering undergraduate degrees. *Data Structures and Algorithms in Python* provides an introduction to data structures and algorithms, including their design, analysis, and implementation. This book is designed for use in a beginning-level data structures course, or in an intermediate-level introduction to algorithms course. We discuss its use for such courses in more detail later in this preface.

To promote the development of robust and reusable software, we have tried to take a consistent object-oriented viewpoint throughout this text. One of the main ideas of the object-oriented approach is that data should be presented as being encapsulated with the methods that access and modify them. That is, rather than simply viewing data as a collection of bytes and addresses, we think of data objects as instances of an ***abstract data type*** (***ADT***), which includes a repertoire of methods for performing operations on data objects of this type. We then emphasize that there may be several different implementation strategies for a particular ADT, and explore the relative pros and cons of these choices. We provide complete Python implementations for almost all data structures and algorithms discussed, and we introduce important object-oriented ***design patterns*** as means to organize those implementations into reusable components.

Desired outcomes for readers of our book include that:

- They have knowledge of the most common abstractions for data collections (e.g., stacks, queues, lists, trees, maps).
- They understand algorithmic strategies for producing efficient realizations of common data structures.
- They can analyze algorithmic performance, both theoretically and experimentally, and recognize common trade-offs between competing strategies.
- They can wisely use existing data structures and algorithms found in modern programming language libraries.
- They have experience working with concrete implementations for most foundational data structures and algorithms.
- They can apply data structures and algorithms to solve complex problems.

In support of the last goal, we present many example applications of data structures throughout the book, including the processing of file systems, matching of tags in structured formats such as HTML, simple cryptography, text frequency analysis, automated geometric layout, Huffman coding, DNA sequence alignment, and search engine indexing.

Book Features

This book is based upon the book *Data Structures and Algorithms in Java* by Goodrich and Tamassia, and the related *Data Structures and Algorithms in C++* by Goodrich, Tamassia, and Mount. However, this book is not simply a translation of those other books to Python. In adapting the material for this book, we have significantly redesigned the organization and content of the book as follows:

- The code base has been entirely redesigned to take advantage of the features of Python, such as use of generators for iterating elements of a collection.
- Many algorithms that were presented as pseudo-code in the Java and C++ versions are directly presented as complete Python code.
- In general, ADTs are defined to have consistent interface with Python's built-in data types and those in Python's collections module.
- Chapter 5 provides an in-depth exploration of the dynamic array-based underpinnings of Python's built-in list, tuple, and str classes. New Appendix A serves as an additional reference regarding the functionality of the str class.
- Over 450 illustrations have been created or revised.
- New and revised exercises bring the overall total number to 750.

Online Resources

This book is accompanied by an extensive set of online resources, which can be found at the following Web site:

www.wiley.com/college/goodrich

Students are encouraged to use this site along with the book, to help with exercises and increase understanding of the subject. Instructors are likewise welcome to use the site to help plan, organize, and present their course materials. Included on this Web site is a collection of educational aids that augment the topics of this book, for both students and instructors. Because of their added value, some of these online resources are password protected.

For all readers, and especially for students, we include the following resources:

- All the Python source code presented in this book.
- PDF handouts of Powerpoint slides (four-per-page) provided to instructors.
- A database of hints to *all* exercises, indexed by problem number.

For instructors using this book, we include the following additional teaching aids:

- Solutions to hundreds of the book's exercises.
- Color versions of all figures and illustrations from the book.
- Slides in Powerpoint and PDF (one-per-page) format.

The slides are fully editable, so as to allow an instructor using this book full freedom in customizing his or her presentations. All the online resources are provided at no extra charge to any instructor adopting this book for his or her course.

Contents and Organization

The chapters for this book are organized to provide a pedagogical path that starts with the basics of Python programming and object-oriented design. We then add foundational techniques like algorithm analysis and recursion. In the main portion of the book, we present fundamental data structures and algorithms, concluding with a discussion of memory management (that is, the architectural underpinnings of data structures). Specifically, the chapters for this book are organized as follows:

1. **Python Primer**
2. **Object-Oriented Programming**
3. **Algorithm Analysis**
4. **Recursion**
5. **Array-Based Sequences**
6. **Stacks, Queues, and Deques**
7. **Linked Lists**
8. **Trees**
9. **Priority Queues**
10. **Maps, Hash Tables, and Skip Lists**
11. **Search Trees**
12. **Sorting and Selection**
13. **Text Processing**
14. **Graph Algorithms**
15. **Memory Management and B-Trees**
A. **Character Strings in Python**
B. **Useful Mathematical Facts**

A more detailed table of contents follows this preface, beginning on page xi.

Prerequisites

We assume that the reader is at least vaguely familiar with a high-level programming language, such as C, C++, Python, or Java, and that he or she understands the main constructs from such a high-level language, including:

- Variables and expressions.
- Decision structures (such as if-statements and switch-statements).
- Iteration structures (for loops and while loops).
- Functions (whether stand-alone or object-oriented methods).

For readers who are familiar with these concepts, but not with how they are expressed in Python, we provide a primer on the Python language in Chapter 1. Still, this book is primarily a data structures book, not a Python book; hence, it does not give a comprehensive treatment of Python.

We delay treatment of object-oriented programming in Python until Chapter 2. This chapter is useful for those new to Python, and for those who may be familiar with Python, yet not with object-oriented programming.

In terms of mathematical background, we assume the reader is somewhat familiar with topics from high-school mathematics. Even so, in Chapter 3, we discuss the seven most-important functions for algorithm analysis. In fact, sections that use something other than one of these seven functions are considered optional, and are indicated with a star ($\star$). We give a summary of other useful mathematical facts, including elementary probability, in Appendix B.

Relation to Computer Science Curriculum

To assist instructors in designing a course in the context of the IEEE/ACM 2013 Computing Curriculum, the following table describes curricular knowledge units that are covered within this book.

Knowledge Unit	Relevant Material
AL/Basic Analysis	Chapter 3 and Sections 4.2 & 12.2.4
AL/Algorithmic Strategies	Sections 12.2.1, 13.2.1, 13.3, & 13.4.2
AL/Fundamental Data Structures and Algorithms	Sections 4.1.3, 5.5.2, 9.4.1, 9.3, 10.2, 11.1, 13.2, Chapter 12 & much of Chapter 14
AL/Advanced Data Structures	Sections 5.3, 10.4, 11.2 through 11.6, 12.3.1, 13.5, 14.5.1, & 15.3
AR/Memory System Organization and Architecture	Chapter 15
DS/Sets, Relations and Functions	Sections 10.5.1, 10.5.2, & 9.4
DS/Proof Techniques	Sections 3.4, 4.2, 5.3.2, 9.3.6, & 12.4.1
DS/Basics of Counting	Sections 2.4.2, 6.2.2, 12.2.4, 8.2.2 & Appendix B
DS/Graphs and Trees	Much of Chapters 8 and 14
DS/Discrete Probability	Sections 1.11.1, 10.2, 10.4.2, & 12.3.1
PL/Object-Oriented Programming	Much of the book, yet especially Chapter 2 and Sections 7.4, 9.5.1, 10.1.3, & 11.2.1
PL/Functional Programming	Section 1.10
SDF/Algorithms and Design	Sections 2.1, 3.3, & 12.2.1
SDF/Fundamental Programming Concepts	Chapters 1 & 4
SDF/Fundamental Data Structures	Chapters 6 & 7, Appendix A, and Sections 1.2.1, 5.2, 5.4, 9.1, & 10.1
SDF/Developmental Methods	Sections 1.7 & 2.2
SE/Software Design	Sections 2.1 & 2.1.3

Mapping *IEEE/ACM 2013 Computing Curriculum* knowledge units to coverage in this book.

About the Authors

Michael Goodrich received his Ph.D. in Computer Science from Purdue University in 1987. He is currently a Chancellor's Professor in the Department of Computer Science at University of California, Irvine. Previously, he was a professor at Johns Hopkins University. He is a Fulbright Scholar and a Fellow of the American Association for the Advancement of Science (AAAS), Association for Computing Machinery (ACM), and Institute of Electrical and Electronics Engineers (IEEE). He is a recipient of the IEEE Computer Society Technical Achievement Award, the ACM Recognition of Service Award, and the Pond Award for Excellence in Undergraduate Teaching.

Roberto Tamassia received his Ph.D. in Electrical and Computer Engineering from the University of Illinois at Urbana-Champaign in 1988. He is the Plastech Professor of Computer Science and the Chair of the Department of Computer Science at Brown University. He is also the Director of Brown's Center for Geometric Computing. His research interests include information security, cryptography, analysis, design, and implementation of algorithms, graph drawing and computational geometry. He is a Fellow of the American Association for the Advancement of Science (AAAS), Association for Computing Machinery (ACM) and Institute for Electrical and Electronic Engineers (IEEE). He is also a recipient of the Technical Achievement Award from the IEEE Computer Society.

Michael Goldwasser received his Ph.D. in Computer Science from Stanford University in 1997. He is currently a Professor in the Department of Mathematics and Computer Science at Saint Louis University and the Director of their Computer Science program. Previously, he was a faculty member in the Department of Computer Science at Loyola University Chicago. His research interests focus on the design and implementation of algorithms, having published work involving approximation algorithms, online computation, computational biology, and computational geometry. He is also active in the computer science education community.

Additional Books by These Authors

- M.T. Goodrich and R. Tamassia, *Data Structures and Algorithms in Java*, Wiley.
- M.T. Goodrich, R. Tamassia, and D.M. Mount, *Data Structures and Algorithms in C++*, Wiley.
- M.T. Goodrich and R. Tamassia, *Algorithm Design: Foundations, Analysis, and Internet Examples*, Wiley.
- M.T. Goodrich and R. Tamassia, *Introduction to Computer Security*, Addison-Wesley.
- M.H. Goldwasser and D. Letscher, *Object-Oriented Programming in Python*, Prentice Hall.

Acknowledgments

We have depended greatly upon the contributions of many individuals as part of the development of this book. We begin by acknowledging the wonderful team at Wiley. We are grateful to our editor, Beth Golub, for her enthusiastic support of this project, from beginning to end. The efforts of Elizabeth Mills and Katherine Willis were critical in keeping the project moving, from its early stages as an initial proposal, through the extensive peer review process. We greatly appreciate the attention to detail demonstrated by Julie Kennedy, the copyeditor for this book. Finally, many thanks are due to Joyce Poh for managing the final months of the production process.

We are truly indebted to the outside reviewers and readers for their copious comments, emails, and constructive criticism, which were extremely useful in writing this edition. We therefore thank the following reviewers for their comments and suggestions: Claude Anderson (Rose Hulman Institute of Technology), Alistair Campbell (Hamilton College), Barry Cohen (New Jersey Institute of Technology), Robert Franks (Central College), Andrew Harrington (Loyola University Chicago), Dave Musicant (Carleton College), and Victor Norman (Calvin College). We wish to particularly acknowledge Claude for going above and beyond the call of duty, providing us with an enumeration of 400 detailed corrections or suggestions.

We thank David Mount, of University of Maryland, for graciously sharing the wisdom gained from his experience with the C++ version of this text. We are grateful to Erin Chambers and David Letscher, of Saint Louis University, for their intangible contributions during many hallway conversations about the teaching of data structures, and to David for comments on early versions of the Python code base for this book. We thank David Zampino, a student at Loyola University Chicago, for his feedback while using a draft of this book during an independent study course, and to Andrew Harrington for supervising David's studies.

We also wish to reiterate our thanks to the many research collaborators and teaching assistants whose feedback shaped the previous Java and C++ versions of this material. The benefits of those contributions carry forward to this book.

Finally, we would like to warmly thank Susan Goldwasser, Isabel Cruz, Karen Goodrich, Giuseppe Di Battista, Franco Preparata, Ioannis Tollis, and our parents for providing advice, encouragement, and support at various stages of the preparation of this book, and Calista and Maya Goldwasser for offering their advice regarding the artistic merits of many illustrations. More importantly, we thank all of these people for reminding us that there are things in life beyond writing books.

Michael T. Goodrich
Roberto Tamassia
Michael H. Goldwasser

Contents

Chapter

1

Python Primer

Contents

1.1   Python Overview

Building data structures and algorithms requires that we communicate detailed instructions to a computer. An excellent way to perform such communications is using a high-level computer language, such as Python. The Python programming language was originally developed by Guido van Rossum in the early 1990s, and has since become a prominently used language in industry and education. The second major version of the language, Python 2, was released in 2000, and the third major version, Python 3, released in 2008. We note that there are significant incompatibilities between Python 2 and Python 3. *This book is based on Python 3 (more specifically, Python 3.1 or later).* The latest version of the language is freely available at www.python.org, along with documentation and tutorials.

In this chapter, we provide an overview of the Python programming language, and we continue this discussion in the next chapter, focusing on object-oriented principles. We assume that readers of this book have prior programming experience, although not necessarily using Python. This book does not provide a complete description of the Python language (there are numerous language references for that purpose), but it does introduce all aspects of the language that are used in code fragments later in this book.

1.1.1   The Python Interpreter

Python is formally an *interpreted* language. Commands are executed through a piece of software known as the *Python interpreter*. The interpreter receives a command, evaluates that command, and reports the result of the command. While the interpreter can be used interactively (especially when debugging), a programmer typically defines a series of commands in advance and saves those commands in a plain text file known as *source code* or a *script*. For Python, source code is conventionally stored in a file named with the .py suffix (e.g., demo.py).

On most operating systems, the Python interpreter can be started by typing python from the command line. By default, the interpreter starts in interactive mode with a clean workspace. Commands from a predefined script saved in a file (e.g., demo.py) are executed by invoking the interpreter with the filename as an argument (e.g., python demo.py), or using an additional -i flag in order to execute a script and then enter interactive mode (e.g., python -i demo.py).

Many *integrated development environments* (IDEs) provide richer software development platforms for Python, including one named IDLE that is included with the standard Python distribution. IDLE provides an embedded text-editor with support for displaying and editing Python code, and a basic debugger, allowing step-by-step execution of a program while examining key variable values.

1.1.2 Preview of a Python Program

As a simple introduction, Code Fragment 1.1 presents a Python program that computes the grade-point average (GPA) for a student based on letter grades that are entered by a user. Many of the techniques demonstrated in this example will be discussed in the remainder of this chapter. At this point, we draw attention to a few high-level issues, for readers who are new to Python as a programming language.

Python's syntax relies heavily on the use of whitespace. Individual statements are typically concluded with a newline character, although a command can extend to another line, either with a concluding backslash character (\), or if an opening delimiter has not yet been closed, such as the { character in defining value_map.

Whitespace is also key in delimiting the bodies of control structures in Python. Specifically, a block of code is indented to designate it as the body of a control structure, and nested control structures use increasing amounts of indentation. In Code Fragment 1.1, the body of the **while** loop consists of the subsequent 8 lines, including a nested conditional structure.

Comments are annotations provided for human readers, yet ignored by the Python interpreter. The primary syntax for comments in Python is based on use of the # character, which designates the remainder of the line as a comment.

```python
print('Welcome to the GPA calculator.')
print('Please enter all your letter grades, one per line.')
print('Enter a blank line to designate the end.')
# map from letter grade to point value
points = {'A+':4.0, 'A':4.0, 'A-':3.67, 'B+':3.33, 'B':3.0, 'B-':2.67,
          'C+':2.33, 'C':2.0, 'C':1.67, 'D+':1.33, 'D':1.0, 'F':0.0}
num_courses = 0
total_points = 0
done = False
while not done:
  grade = input( )                          # read line from user
  if grade == '':                           # empty line was entered
    done = True
  elif grade not in points:                 # unrecognized grade entered
    print("Unknown grade '{0}' being ignored".format(grade))
  else:
    num_courses += 1
    total_points += points[grade]
if num_courses > 0:                         # avoid division by zero
  print('Your GPA is {0:.3}'.format(total_points / num_courses))
```

Code Fragment 1.1: A Python program that computes a grade-point average (GPA).

1.2   Objects in Python

Python is an object-oriented language and *classes* form the basis for all data types. In this section, we describe key aspects of Python's object model, and we introduce Python's built-in classes, such as the **int** class for integers, the **float** class for floating-point values, and the **str** class for character strings. A more thorough presentation of object-orientation is the focus of Chapter 2.

1.2.1   Identifiers, Objects, and the Assignment Statement

The most important of all Python commands is an *assignment statement*, such as

>   temperature = 98.6

This command establishes temperature as an *identifier* (also known as a *name*), and then associates it with the *object* expressed on the right-hand side of the equal sign, in this case a floating-point object with value 98.6. We portray the outcome of this assignment in Figure 1.1.

Figure 1.1: The identifier temperature references an instance of the float class having value 98.6.

Identifiers

Identifiers in Python are *case-sensitive*, so temperature and Temperature are distinct names. Identifiers can be composed of almost any combination of letters, numerals, and underscore characters (or more general Unicode characters). The primary restrictions are that an identifier cannot begin with a numeral (thus 9lives is an illegal name), and that there are 33 specially reserved words that cannot be used as identifiers, as shown in Table 1.1.

Reserved Words								
False	as	continue	else	from	in	not	return	yield
None	assert	def	except	global	is	or	try	
True	break	del	finally	if	lambda	pass	while	
and	class	elif	for	import	nonlocal	raise	with	

Table 1.1: A listing of the reserved words in Python. These names cannot be used as identifiers.

For readers familiar with other programming languages, the semantics of a Python identifier is most similar to a reference variable in Java or a pointer variable in C++. Each identifier is implicitly associated with the **memory address** of the object to which it refers. A Python identifier may be assigned to a special object named None, serving a similar purpose to a null reference in Java or C++.

Unlike Java and C++, Python is a **dynamically typed** language, as there is no advance declaration associating an identifier with a particular data type. An identifier can be associated with any type of object, and it can later be reassigned to another object of the same (or different) type. Although an identifier has no declared type, the object to which it refers has a definite type. In our first example, the characters 98.6 are recognized as a floating-point literal, and thus the identifier temperature is associated with an instance of the float class having that value.

A programmer can establish an **alias** by assigning a second identifier to an existing object. Continuing with our earlier example, Figure 1.2 portrays the result of a subsequent assignment, original = temperature.

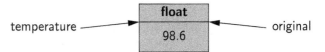

Figure 1.2: Identifiers temperature and original are aliases for the same object.

Once an alias has been established, either name can be used to access the underlying object. If that object supports behaviors that affect its state, changes enacted through one alias will be apparent when using the other alias (because they refer to the same object). However, if one of the *names* is reassigned to a new value using a subsequent assignment statement, that does not affect the aliased object, rather it breaks the alias. Continuing with our concrete example, we consider the command:

temperature = temperature + 5.0

The execution of this command begins with the evaluation of the expression on the right-hand side of the = operator. That expression, temperature + 5.0, is evaluated based on the *existing* binding of the name temperature, and so the result has value 103.6, that is, 98.6 + 5.0. That result is stored as a new floating-point instance, and only then is the name on the left-hand side of the assignment statement, temperature, (re)assigned to the result. The subsequent configuration is diagrammed in Figure 1.3. Of particular note, this last command had no effect on the value of the existing float instance that identifier original continues to reference.

Figure 1.3: The temperature identifier has been assigned to a new value, while original continues to refer to the previously existing value.

1.2.2   Creating and Using Objects

Instantiation

The process of creating a new instance of a class is known as ***instantiation***. In general, the syntax for instantiating an object is to invoke the ***constructor*** of a class. For example, if there were a class named Widget, we could create an instance of that class using a syntax such as w = Widget( ), assuming that the constructor does not require any parameters. If the constructor does require parameters, we might use a syntax such as Widget(a, b, c) to construct a new instance.

Many of Python's built-in classes (discussed in Section 1.2.3) support what is known as a ***literal*** form for designating new instances. For example, the command temperature = 98.6 results in the creation of a new instance of the **float** class; the term 98.6 in that expression is a literal form. We discuss further cases of Python literals in the coming section.

From a programmer's perspective, yet another way to indirectly create a new instance of a class is to call a function that creates and returns such an instance. For example, Python has a built-in function named sorted (see Section 1.5.2) that takes a sequence of comparable elements as a parameter and returns a new instance of the **list** class containing those elements in sorted order.

Calling Methods

Python supports traditional functions (see Section 1.5) that are invoked with a syntax such as sorted(data), in which case data is a parameter sent to the function. Python's classes may also define one or more ***methods*** (also known as ***member functions***), which are invoked on a specific instance of a class using the dot ("·") operator. For example, Python's list class has a method named sort that can be invoked with a syntax such as data.sort( ). This particular method rearranges the contents of the list so that they are sorted.

The expression to the left of the dot identifies the object upon which the method is invoked. Often, this will be an identifier (e.g., data), but we can use the dot operator to invoke a method upon the immediate result of some other operation. For example, if response identifies a string instance (we will discuss strings later in this section), the syntax response.lower( ).startswith('y') first evaluates the method call, response.lower( ), which itself returns a new string instance, and then the startswith('y') method is called on that intermediate string.

When using a method of a class, it is important to understand its behavior. Some methods return information about the state of an object, but do not change that state. These are known as ***accessors***. Other methods, such as the sort method of the list class, do change the state of an object. These methods are known as ***mutators*** or ***update methods***.

1.2.3   Python's Built-In Classes

Table 1.2 provides a summary of commonly used, built-in classes in Python; we take particular note of which classes are mutable and which are immutable. A class is *immutable* if each object of that class has a fixed value upon instantiation that cannot subsequently be changed. For example, the float class is immutable. Once an instance has been created, its value cannot be changed (although an identifier referencing that object can be reassigned to a different value).

Class	Description	Immutable?
bool	Boolean value	✓
int	integer (arbitrary magnitude)	✓
float	floating-point number	✓
list	mutable sequence of objects	
tuple	immutable sequence of objects	✓
str	character string	✓
set	unordered set of distinct objects	
frozenset	immutable form of set class	✓
dict	associative mapping (aka dictionary)	

Table 1.2: Commonly used built-in classes for Python

In this section, we provide an introduction to these classes, discussing their purpose and presenting several means for creating instances of the classes. Literal forms (such as 98.6) exist for most of the built-in classes, and all of the classes support a traditional constructor form that creates instances that are based upon one or more existing values. Operators supported by these classes are described in Section 1.3. More detailed information about these classes can be found in later chapters as follows: lists and tuples (Chapter 5); strings (Chapters 5 and 13, and Appendix A); sets and dictionaries (Chapter 10).

The bool Class

The **bool** class is used to manipulate logical (Boolean) values, and the only two instances of that class are expressed as the literals True and False. The default constructor, bool( ), returns False, but there is no reason to use that syntax rather than the more direct literal form. Python allows the creation of a Boolean value from a nonboolean type using the syntax bool(foo) for value foo. The interpretation depends upon the type of the parameter. Numbers evaluate to False if zero, and True if nonzero. Sequences and other container types, such as strings and lists, evaluate to False if empty and True if nonempty. An important application of this interpretation is the use of a nonboolean value as a condition in a control structure.

The int Class

The **int** and **float** classes are the primary numeric types in Python. The **int** class is designed to represent integer values with arbitrary magnitude. Unlike Java and C++, which support different integral types with different precisions (e.g., int, short, long), Python automatically chooses the internal representation for an integer based upon the magnitude of its value. Typical literals for integers include 0, 137, and -23. In some contexts, it is convenient to express an integral value using binary, octal, or hexadecimal. That can be done by using a prefix of the number 0 and then a character to describe the base. Example of such literals are respectively 0b1011, 0o52, and 0x7f.

The integer constructor, int( ), returns value 0 by default. But this constructor can be used to construct an integer value based upon an existing value of another type. For example, if f represents a floating-point value, the syntax int(f) produces the *truncated* value of f. For example, both int(3.14) and int(3.99) produce the value 3, while int(-3.9) produces the value -3. The constructor can also be used to parse a string that is presumed to represent an integral value (such as one entered by a user). If s represents a string, then int(s) produces the integral value that string represents. For example, the expression int('137') produces the integer value 137. If an invalid string is given as a parameter, as in int('hello'), a ValueError is raised (see Section 1.7 for discussion of Python's exceptions). By default, the string must use base 10. If conversion from a different base is desired, that base can be indicated as a second, optional, parameter. For example, the expression int('7f', 16) evaluates to the integer 127.

The float Class

The **float** class is the sole floating-point type in Python, using a fixed-precision representation. Its precision is more akin to a double in Java or C++, rather than those languages' float type. We have already discussed a typical literal form, 98.6. We note that the floating-point equivalent of an integral number can be expressed directly as 2.0. Technically, the trailing zero is optional, so some programmers might use the expression 2. to designate this floating-point literal. One other form of literal for floating-point values uses scientific notation. For example, the literal 6.022e23 represents the mathematical value 6.022×10^{23}.

The constructor form of float( ) returns 0.0. When given a parameter, the constructor attempts to return the equivalent floating-point value. For example, the call float(2) returns the floating-point value 2.0. If the parameter to the constructor is a string, as with float('3.14'), it attempts to parse that string as a floating-point value, raising a ValueError as an exception.

Sequence Types: The list, tuple, and str Classes

The **list**, **tuple**, and **str** classes are *sequence* types in Python, representing a collection of values in which the order is significant. The list class is the most general, representing a sequence of arbitrary objects (akin to an "array" in other languages). The tuple class is an *immutable* version of the list class, benefiting from a streamlined internal representation. The str class is specially designed for representing an immutable sequence of text characters. We note that Python does not have a separate class for characters; they are just strings with length one.

The list Class

A **list** instance stores a sequence of objects. A list is a *referential* structure, as it technically stores a sequence of *references* to its elements (see Figure 1.4). Elements of a list may be arbitrary objects (including the None object). Lists are *array-based* sequences and are *zero-indexed*, thus a list of length n has elements indexed from 0 to $n-1$ inclusive. Lists are perhaps the most used container type in Python and they will be extremely central to our study of data structures and algorithms. They have many valuable behaviors, including the ability to dynamically expand and contract their capacities as needed. In this chapter, we will discuss only the most basic properties of lists. We revisit the inner working of all of Python's sequence types as the focus of Chapter 5.

Python uses the characters [ ] as delimiters for a list literal, with [ ] itself being an empty list. As another example, ['red', 'green', 'blue'] is a list containing three string instances. The contents of a list literal need not be expressed as literals; if identifiers a and b have been established, then syntax [a, b] is legitimate.

The list( ) constructor produces an empty list by default. However, the constructor will accept any parameter that is of an *iterable* type. We will discuss iteration further in Section 1.8, but examples of iterable types include all of the standard container types (e.g., strings, list, tuples, sets, dictionaries). For example, the syntax list('hello') produces a list of individual characters, ['h', 'e', 'l', 'l', 'o']. Because an existing list is itself iterable, the syntax backup = list(data) can be used to construct a new list instance referencing the same contents as the original.

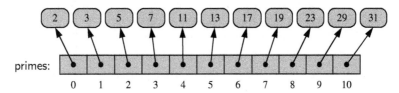

Figure 1.4: Python's internal representation of a list of integers, instantiated as prime = [2, 3, 5, 7, 11, 13, 17, 19, 23, 29, 31]. The implicit indices of the elements are shown below each entry.

The tuple Class

The **tuple** class provides an immutable version of a sequence, and therefore its instances have an internal representation that may be more streamlined than that of a list. While Python uses the [ ] characters to delimit a list, parentheses delimit a tuple, with ( ) being an empty tuple. There is one important subtlety. To express a tuple of length one as a literal, a comma must be placed after the element, but within the parentheses. For example, (17,) is a one-element tuple. The reason for this requirement is that, without the trailing comma, the expression (17) is viewed as a simple parenthesized numeric expression.

The str Class

Python's **str** class is specifically designed to efficiently represent an immutable sequence of characters, based upon the Unicode international character set. Strings have a more compact internal representation than the referential lists and tuples, as portrayed in Figure 1.5.

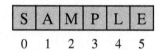

Figure 1.5: A Python string, which is an indexed sequence of characters.

String literals can be enclosed in single quotes, as in 'hello', or double quotes, as in "hello". This choice is convenient, especially when using another of the quotation characters as an actual character in the sequence, as in "Don't worry". Alternatively, the quote delimiter can be designated using a backslash as a so-called *escape character*, as in 'Don\'t worry'. Because the backslash has this purpose, the backslash must itself be escaped to occur as a natural character of the string literal, as in 'C:\\Python\\', for a string that would be displayed as C:\Python\. Other commonly escaped characters are \n for newline and \t for tab. Unicode characters can be included, such as '20\u20AC' for the string 20€.

Python also supports using the delimiter ''' or """ to begin and end a string literal. The advantage of such triple-quoted strings is that newline characters can be embedded naturally (rather than escaped as \n). This can greatly improve the readability of long, multiline strings in source code. For example, at the beginning of Code Fragment 1.1, rather than use separate print statements for each line of introductory output, we can use a single print statement, as follows:

```
print("""Welcome to the GPA calculator.
Please enter all your letter grades, one per line.
Enter a blank line to designate the end.""")
```

The set and frozenset Classes

Python's **set** class represents the mathematical notion of a set, namely a collection of elements, without duplicates, and without an inherent order to those elements. The major advantage of using a set, as opposed to a list, is that it has a highly optimized method for checking whether a specific element is contained in the set. This is based on a data structure known as a ***hash table*** (which will be the primary topic of Chapter 10). However, there are two important restrictions due to the algorithmic underpinnings. The first is that the set does not maintain the elements in any particular order. The second is that only instances of ***immutable*** types can be added to a Python set. Therefore, objects such as integers, floating-point numbers, and character strings are eligible to be elements of a set. It is possible to maintain a set of tuples, but not a set of lists or a set of sets, as lists and sets are mutable. The **frozenset** class is an immutable form of the set type, so it is legal to have a set of frozensets.

Python uses curly braces { and } as delimiters for a set, for example, as {17} or {'red', 'green', 'blue'}. The exception to this rule is that { } does not represent an empty set; for historical reasons, it represents an empty dictionary (see next paragraph). Instead, the constructor syntax set( ) produces an empty set. If an iterable parameter is sent to the constructor, then the set of distinct elements is produced. For example, set('hello') produces {'h', 'e', 'l', 'o'}.

The dict Class

Python's **dict** class represents a ***dictionary***, or ***mapping***, from a set of distinct ***keys*** to associated ***values***. For example, a dictionary might map from unique student ID numbers, to larger student records (such as the student's name, address, and course grades). Python implements a dict using an almost identical approach to that of a set, but with storage of the associated values.

A dictionary literal also uses curly braces, and because dictionaries were introduced in Python prior to sets, the literal form { } produces an empty dictionary. A nonempty dictionary is expressed using a comma-separated series of key:value pairs. For example, the dictionary {'ga' : 'Irish', 'de' : 'German'} maps 'ga' to 'Irish' and 'de' to 'German'.

The constructor for the dict class accepts an existing mapping as a parameter, in which case it creates a new dictionary with identical associations as the existing one. Alternatively, the constructor accepts a sequence of key-value pairs as a parameter, as in dict(pairs) with pairs = [('ga', 'Irish'), ('de', 'German')].

1.3   Expressions, Operators, and Precedence

In the previous section, we demonstrated how names can be used to identify existing objects, and how literals and constructors can be used to create instances of built-in classes. Existing values can be combined into larger syntactic *expressions* using a variety of special symbols and keywords known as *operators*. The semantics of an operator depends upon the type of its operands. For example, when a and b are numbers, the syntax a + b indicates addition, while if a and b are strings, the operator indicates concatenation. In this section, we describe Python's operators in various contexts of the built-in types.

We continue, in Section 1.3.1, by discussing *compound expressions*, such as a + b ∗ c, which rely on the evaluation of two or more operations. The order in which the operations of a compound expression are evaluated can affect the overall value of the expression. For this reason, Python defines a specific order of precedence for evaluating operators, and it allows a programmer to override this order by using explicit parentheses to group subexpressions.

Logical Operators

Python supports the following keyword operators for Boolean values:

not	unary negation
and	conditional and
or	conditional or

The **and** and **or** operators *short-circuit*, in that they do not evaluate the second operand if the result can be determined based on the value of the first operand. This feature is useful when constructing Boolean expressions in which we first test that a certain condition holds (such as a reference not being **None**), and then test a condition that could have otherwise generated an error condition had the prior test not succeeded.

Equality Operators

Python supports the following operators to test two notions of equality:

is	same identity
is not	different identity
==	equivalent
!=	not equivalent

The expression a **is** b evaluates to **True**, precisely when identifiers a and b are aliases for the *same* object. The expression a == b tests a more general notion of equivalence. If identifiers a and b refer to the same object, then a == b should also evaluate to **True**. Yet a == b also evaluates to **True** when the identifiers refer to different objects that happen to have values that are deemed equivalent. The precise notion of equivalence depends on the data type. For example, two strings are considered equivalent if they match character for character. Two sets are equivalent if they have the same contents, irrespective of order. In most programming situations, the equivalence tests == and != are the appropriate operators; use of **is** and **is not** should be reserved for situations in which it is necessary to detect true aliasing.

Comparison Operators

Data types may define a natural order via the following operators:

$$< \quad \text{less than}$$
$$<= \quad \text{less than or equal to}$$
$$> \quad \text{greater than}$$
$$>= \quad \text{greater than or equal to}$$

These operators have expected behavior for numeric types, and are defined lexicographically, and case-sensitively, for strings. An exception is raised if operands have incomparable types, as with $5 <$ 'hello'.

Arithmetic Operators

Python supports the following arithmetic operators:

$$+ \quad \text{addition}$$
$$- \quad \text{subtraction}$$
$$* \quad \text{multiplication}$$
$$/ \quad \text{true division}$$
$$// \quad \text{integer division}$$
$$\% \quad \text{the modulo operator}$$

The use of addition, subtraction, and multiplication is straightforward, noting that if both operands have type int, then the result is an int as well; if one or both operands have type float, the result will be a float.

Python takes more care in its treatment of division. We first consider the case in which both operands have type int, for example, the quantity 27 divided by 4. In mathematical notation, $27 \div 4 = 6\frac{3}{4} = 6.75$. In Python, the / operator designates *true division*, returning the floating-point result of the computation. Thus, 27 / 4 results in the float value 6.75. Python supports the pair of operators // and % to perform the integral calculations, with expression 27 // 4 evaluating to int value 6 (the mathematical *floor* of the quotient), and expression 27 % 4 evaluating to int value 3, the remainder of the integer division. We note that languages such as C, C++, and Java do not support the // operator; instead, the / operator returns the truncated quotient when both operands have integral type, and the result of true division when at least one operand has a floating-point type.

Python carefully extends the semantics of // and % to cases where one or both operands are negative. For the sake of notation, let us assume that variables n and m represent respectively the *dividend* and *divisor* of a quotient $\frac{n}{m}$, and that q = n // m and r = n % m. Python guarantees that q $*$ m $+$ r will equal n. We already saw an example of this identity with positive operands, as $6*4+3 = 27$. When the divisor m is positive, Python further guarantees that $0 \leq r < m$. As a consequence, we find that -27 // 4 evaluates to -7 and -27 % 4 evaluates to 1, as $(-7)*4+1 = -27$. When the divisor is negative, Python guarantees that $m < r \leq 0$. As an example, 27 // -4 is -7 and 27 % -4 is -1, satisfying the identity $27 = (-7)*(-4)+(-1)$.

The conventions for the // and % operators are even extended to floating-point operands, with the expression q = n // m being the integral floor of the quotient, and r = n % m being the "remainder" to ensure that q $*$ m $+$ r equals n. For example, 8.2 // 3.14 evaluates to 2.0 and 8.2 % 3.14 evaluates to 1.92, as $2.0*3.14+1.92 = 8.2$.

Bitwise Operators

Python provides the following bitwise operators for integers:

$\sim$	bitwise complement (prefix unary operator)
&	bitwise and
$\vert$	bitwise or
^	bitwise exclusive-or
<<	shift bits left, filling in with zeros
>>	shift bits right, filling in with sign bit

Sequence Operators

Each of Python's built-in sequence types (**str**, **tuple**, and **list**) support the following operator syntaxes:

s[j]	element at index *j*
s[start:stop]	slice including indices [start,stop)
s[start:stop:step]	slice including indices start, start $+$ step, start $+$ 2$*$step, ..., up to but not equalling or stop
s $+$ t	concatenation of sequences
k $*$ s	shorthand for s $+$ s $+$ s $+$ ... (k times)
val **in** s	containment check
val **not in** s	non-containment check

Python relies on *zero-indexing* of sequences, thus a sequence of length n has elements indexed from 0 to $n-1$ inclusive. Python also supports the use of *negative indices*, which denote a distance from the end of the sequence; index -1 denotes the last element, index -2 the second to last, and so on. Python uses a *slicing* notation to describe subsequences of a sequence. Slices are described as half-open intervals, with a start index that is included, and a stop index that is excluded. For example, the syntax data[3:8] denotes a subsequence including the five indices: 3,4,5,6,7. An optional "step" value, possibly negative, can be indicated as a third parameter of the slice. If a start index or stop index is omitted in the slicing notation, it is presumed to designate the respective extreme of the original sequence.

Because lists are mutable, the syntax s[j] = val can be used to replace an element at a given index. Lists also support a syntax, **del** s[j], that removes the designated element from the list. Slice notation can also be used to replace or delete a sublist.

The notation val **in** s can be used for any of the sequences to see if there is an element equivalent to val in the sequence. For strings, this syntax can be used to check for a single character or for a larger substring, as with 'amp' **in** 'example'.

All sequences define comparison operations based on *lexicographic order*, performing an element by element comparison until the first difference is found. For example, [5, 6, 9] < [5, 7] because of the entries at index 1. Therefore, the following operations are supported by sequence types:

s == t	equivalent (element by element)
s != t	not equivalent
s < t	lexicographically less than
s <= t	lexicographically less than or equal to
s > t	lexicographically greater than
s >= t	lexicographically greater than or equal to

Operators for Sets and Dictionaries

Sets and frozensets support the following operators:

key **in** s	containment check
key **not in** s	non-containment check
s1 == s2	s1 is equivalent to s2
s1 != s2	s1 is not equivalent to s2
s1 <= s2	s1 is subset of s2
s1 < s2	s1 is proper subset of s2
s1 >= s2	s1 is superset of s2
s1 > s2	s1 is proper superset of s2
s1 | s2	the union of s1 and s2
s1 & s2	the intersection of s1 and s2
s1 − s2	the set of elements in s1 but not s2
s1 ^ s2	the set of elements in precisely one of s1 or s2

Note well that sets do not guarantee a particular order of their elements, so the comparison operators, such as <, are not lexicographic; rather, they are based on the mathematical notion of a subset. As a result, the comparison operators define a partial order, but not a total order, as disjoint sets are neither "less than," "equal to," or "greater than" each other. Sets also support many fundamental behaviors through named methods (e.g., add, remove); we will explore their functionality more fully in Chapter 10.

Dictionaries, like sets, do not maintain a well-defined order on their elements. Furthermore, the concept of a subset is not typically meaningful for dictionaries, so the dict class does not support operators such as <. Dictionaries support the notion of equivalence, with d1 == d2 if the two dictionaries contain the same set of key-value pairs. The most widely used behavior of dictionaries is accessing a value associated with a particular key k with the indexing syntax, d[k]. The supported operators are as follows:

d[key]	value associated with given key
d[key] = value	set (or reset) the value associated with given key
del d[key]	remove key and its associated value from dictionary
key **in** d	containment check
key **not in** d	non-containment check
d1 == d2	d1 is equivalent to d2
d1 != d2	d1 is not equivalent to d2

Dictionaries also support many useful behaviors through named methods, which we explore more fully in Chapter 10.

Extended Assignment Operators

Python supports an extended assignment operator for most binary operators, for example, allowing a syntax such as count += 5. By default, this is a shorthand for the more verbose count = count + 5. For an immutable type, such as a number or a string, one should not presume that this syntax changes the value of the existing object, but instead that it will reassign the identifier to a newly constructed value. (See discussion of Figure 1.3.) However, it is possible for a type to redefine such semantics to mutate the object, as the list class does for the += operator.

```
alpha = [1, 2, 3]
beta = alpha                # an alias for alpha
beta += [4, 5]              # extends the original list with two more elements
beta = beta + [6, 7]        # reassigns beta to a new list [1, 2, 3, 4, 5, 6, 7]
print(alpha)               # will be [1, 2, 3, 4, 5]
```

This example demonstrates the subtle difference between the list semantics for the syntax beta += foo versus beta = beta + foo.

1.3.1 Compound Expressions and Operator Precedence

Programming languages must have clear rules for the order in which compound expressions, such as $5 + 2 * 3$, are evaluated. The formal order of precedence for operators in Python is given in Table 1.3. Operators in a category with higher precedence will be evaluated before those with lower precedence, unless the expression is otherwise parenthesized. Therefore, we see that Python gives precedence to multiplication over addition, and therefore evaluates the expression $5 + 2 * 3$ as $5 + (2 * 3)$, with value 11, but the parenthesized expression $(5 + 2) * 3$ evaluates to value 21. Operators within a category are typically evaluated from left to right, thus $5 - 2 + 3$ has value 6. Exceptions to this rule include that unary operators and exponentiation are evaluated from right to left.

Python allows a ***chained assignment***, such as x = y = 0, to assign multiple identifiers to the rightmost value. Python also allows the ***chaining*** of comparison operators. For example, the expression $1 <= x + y <= 10$ is evaluated as the compound $(1 <= x + y)$ **and** $(x + y <= 10)$, but without computing the intermediate value $x + y$ twice.

Operator Precedence		
	Type	**Symbols**
1	member access	expr.member
2	function/method calls container subscripts/slices	expr(...) expr[...]
3	exponentiation	**
4	unary operators	+expr, −expr, ˜expr
5	multiplication, division	*, /, //, %
6	addition, subtraction	+, −
7	bitwise shifting	<<, >>
8	bitwise-and	&
9	bitwise-xor	^
10	bitwise-or	|
11	comparisons containment	**is, is not,** ==, !=, <, <=, >, >= **in, not in**
12	logical-not	**not** expr
13	logical-and	**and**
14	logical-or	**or**
15	conditional	val1 **if** cond **else** val2
16	assignments	=, +=, −=, *=, etc.

Table 1.3: Operator precedence in Python, with categories ordered from highest precedence to lowest precedence. When stated, we use expr to denote a literal, identifier, or result of a previously evaluated expression. All operators without explicit mention of expr are binary operators, with syntax expr1 operator expr2.

1.4 Control Flow

In this section, we review Python's most fundamental control structures: conditional statements and loops. Common to all control structures is the syntax used in Python for defining blocks of code. The colon character is used to delimit the beginning of a block of code that acts as a body for a control structure. If the body can be stated as a single executable statement, it can technically placed on the same line, to the right of the colon. However, a body is more typically typeset as an *indented block* starting on the line following the colon. Python relies on the indentation level to designate the extent of that block of code, or any nested blocks of code within. The same principles will be applied when designating the body of a function (see Section 1.5), and the body of a class (see Section 2.3).

1.4.1 Conditionals

Conditional constructs (also known as **if** statements) provide a way to execute a chosen block of code based on the run-time evaluation of one or more Boolean expressions. In Python, the most general form of a conditional is written as follows:

```
if first_condition:
    first_body
elif second_condition:
    second_body
elif third_condition:
    third_body
else:
    fourth_body
```

Each condition is a Boolean expression, and each body contains one or more commands that are to be executed conditionally. If the first condition succeeds, the first body will be executed; no other conditions or bodies are evaluated in that case. If the first condition fails, then the process continues in similar manner with the evaluation of the second condition. The execution of this overall construct will cause precisely one of the bodies to be executed. There may be any number of **elif** clauses (including zero), and the final **else** clause is optional. As described on page 7, nonboolean types may be evaluated as Booleans with intuitive meanings. For example, if response is a string that was entered by a user, and we want to condition a behavior on this being a nonempty string, we may write

```
if response:
```

as a shorthand for the equivalent,

```
if response != '':
```

As a simple example, a robot controller might have the following logic:

```
if door_is_closed:
    open_door( )
advance( )
```

Notice that the final command, advance( ), is not indented and therefore not part of the conditional body. It will be executed unconditionally (although after opening a closed door).

We may nest one control structure within another, relying on indentation to make clear the extent of the various bodies. Revisiting our robot example, here is a more complex control that accounts for unlocking a closed door.

```
if door_is_closed:
    if door_is_locked:
        unlock_door( )
    open_door( )
advance( )
```

The logic expressed by this example can be diagrammed as a traditional *flowchart*, as portrayed in Figure 1.6.

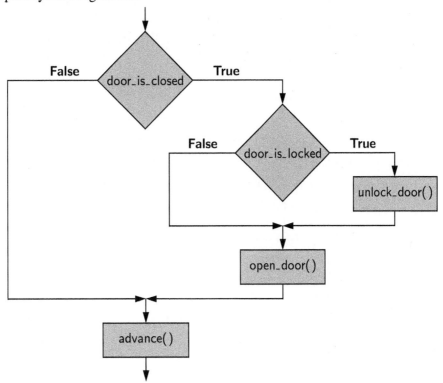

Figure 1.6: A flowchart describing the logic of nested conditional statements.

1.4.2 Loops

Python offers two distinct looping constructs. A **while** loop allows general repetition based upon the repeated testing of a Boolean condition. A **for** loop provides convenient iteration of values from a defined series (such as characters of a string, elements of a list, or numbers within a given range). We discuss both forms in this section.

While Loops

The syntax for a **while** loop in Python is as follows:

```
while condition:
  body
```

As with an **if** statement, *condition* can be an arbitrary Boolean expression, and *body* can be an arbitrary block of code (including nested control structures). The execution of a while loop begins with a test of the Boolean condition. If that condition evaluates to True, the body of the loop is performed. After each execution of the body, the loop condition is retested, and if it evaluates to True, another iteration of the body is performed. When the conditional test evaluates to False (assuming it ever does), the loop is exited and the flow of control continues just beyond the body of the loop.

As an example, here is a loop that advances an index through a sequence of characters until finding an entry with value 'X' or reaching the end of the sequence.

```
j = 0
while j < len(data) and data[j] != 'X':
  j += 1
```

The len function, which we will introduce in Section 1.5.2, returns the length of a sequence such as a list or string. The correctness of this loop relies on the short-circuiting behavior of the **and** operator, as described on page 12. We intentionally test j < len(data) to ensure that j is a valid index, prior to accessing element data[j]. Had we written that compound condition with the opposite order, the evaluation of data[j] would eventually raise an IndexError when 'X' is not found. (See Section 1.7 for discussion of exceptions.)

As written, when this loop terminates, variable j's value will be the index of the leftmost occurrence of 'X', if found, or otherwise the length of the sequence (which is recognizable as an invalid index to indicate failure of the search). It is worth noting that this code behaves correctly, even in the special case when the list is empty, as the condition j < len(data) will initially fail and the body of the loop will never be executed.

For Loops

Python's **for**-loop syntax is a more convenient alternative to a while loop when iterating through a series of elements. The for-loop syntax can be used on any type of *iterable* structure, such as a list, tuple str, set, dict, or file (we will discuss iterators more formally in Section 1.8). Its general syntax appears as follows.

```
for element in iterable:
    body                          # body may refer to 'element' as an identifier
```

For readers familiar with Java, the semantics of Python's for loop is similar to the "for each" loop style introduced in Java 1.5.

As an instructive example of such a loop, we consider the task of computing the sum of a list of numbers. (Admittedly, Python has a built-in function, sum, for this purpose.) We perform the calculation with a for loop as follows, assuming that data identifies the list:

```
total = 0
for val in data:
    total += val                  # note use of the loop variable, val
```

The loop body executes once for each element of the data sequence, with the identifier, val, from the for-loop syntax assigned at the beginning of each pass to a respective element. It is worth noting that val is treated as a standard identifier. If the element of the original data happens to be mutable, the val identifier can be used to invoke its methods. But a reassignment of identifier val to a new value has no affect on the original data, nor on the next iteration of the loop.

As a second classic example, we consider the task of finding the maximum value in a list of elements (again, admitting that Python's built-in max function already provides this support). If we can assume that the list, data, has at least one element, we could implement this task as follows:

```
biggest = data[0]                 # as we assume nonempty list
for val in data:
    if val > biggest:
        biggest = val
```

Although we could accomplish both of the above tasks with a while loop, the for-loop syntax had an advantage of simplicity, as there is no need to manage an explicit index into the list nor to author a Boolean loop condition. Furthermore, we can use a for loop in cases for which a while loop does not apply, such as when iterating through a collection, such as a set, that does not support any direct form of indexing.

Index-Based For Loops

The simplicity of a standard for loop over the elements of a list is wonderful; however, one limitation of that form is that we do not know where an element resides within the sequence. In some applications, we need knowledge of the index of an element within the sequence. For example, suppose that we want to know *where* the maximum element in a list resides.

Rather than directly looping over the elements of the list in that case, we prefer to loop over all possible indices of the list. For this purpose, Python provides a built-in class named range that generates integer sequences. (We will discuss generators in Section 1.8.) In simplest form, the syntax range(n) generates the series of n values from 0 to $n-1$. Conveniently, these are precisely the series of valid indices into a sequence of length n. Therefore, a standard Python idiom for looping through the series of indices of a data sequence uses a syntax,

```
for j in range(len(data)):
```

In this case, identifier j is not an element of the data—it is an integer. But the expression data[j] can be used to retrieve the respective element. For example, we can find the *index* of the maximum element of a list as follows:

```
big_index = 0
for j in range(len(data)):
  if data[j] > data[big_index]:
    big_index = j
```

Break and Continue Statements

Python supports a **break** statement that immediately terminate a while or for loop when executed within its body. More formally, if applied within nested control structures, it causes the termination of the most immediately enclosing loop. As a typical example, here is code that determines whether a target value occurs in a data set:

```
found = False
for item in data:
  if item == target:
    found = True
    break
```

Python also supports a **continue** statement that causes the current *iteration* of a loop body to stop, but with subsequent passes of the loop proceeding as expected.

We recommend that the break and continue statements be used sparingly. Yet, there are situations in which these commands can be effectively used to avoid introducing overly complex logical conditions.

1.5 Functions

In this section, we explore the creation of and use of functions in Python. As we did in Section 1.2.2, we draw a distinction between *functions* and **methods**. We use the general term *function* to describe a traditional, stateless function that is invoked without the context of a particular class or an instance of that class, such as sorted(data). We use the more specific term *method* to describe a member function that is invoked upon a specific object using an object-oriented message passing syntax, such as data.sort(). In this section, we only consider pure functions; methods will be explored with more general object-oriented principles in Chapter 2.

We begin with an example to demonstrate the syntax for defining functions in Python. The following function counts the number of occurrences of a given target value within any form of iterable data set.

```python
def count(data, target):
    n = 0
    for item in data:
        if item == target:        # found a match
            n += 1
    return n
```

The first line, beginning with the keyword **def**, serves as the function's **signature**. This establishes a new identifier as the name of the function (count, in this example), and it establishes the number of parameters that it expects, as well as names identifying those parameters (data and target, in this example). Unlike Java and C++, Python is a dynamically typed language, and therefore a Python signature does not designate the types of those parameters, nor the type (if any) of a return value. Those expectations should be stated in the function's documentation (see Section 2.2.3) and can be enforced within the body of the function, but misuse of a function will only be detected at run-time.

The remainder of the function definition is known as the **body** of the function. As is the case with control structures in Python, the body of a function is typically expressed as an indented block of code. Each time a function is called, Python creates a dedicated **activation record** that stores information relevant to the current call. This activation record includes what is known as a **namespace** (see Section 1.10) to manage all identifiers that have *local scope* within the current call. The namespace includes the function's parameters and any other identifiers that are defined locally within the body of the function. An identifier in the local scope of the function caller has no relation to any identifier with the same name in the caller's scope (although identifiers in different scopes may be aliases to the same object). In our first example, the identifier n has scope that is local to the function call, as does the identifier item, which is established as the loop variable.

Return Statement

A **return** statement is used within the body of a function to indicate that the function should immediately cease execution, and that an expressed value should be returned to the caller. If a return statement is executed without an explicit argument, the None value is automatically returned. Likewise, None will be returned if the flow of control ever reaches the end of a function body without having executed a return statement. Often, a return statement will be the final command within the body of the function, as was the case in our earlier example of a count function. However, there can be multiple return statements in the same function, with conditional logic controlling which such command is executed, if any. As a further example, consider the following function that tests if a value exists in a sequence.

```python
def contains(data, target):
    for item in target:
        if item == target:          # found a match
            return True
    return False
```

If the conditional within the loop body is ever satisfied, the return True statement is executed and the function immediately ends, with True designating that the target value was found. Conversely, if the for loop reaches its conclusion without ever finding the match, the final return False statement will be executed.

1.5.1   Information Passing

To be a successful programmer, one must have clear understanding of the mechanism in which a programming language passes information to and from a function. In the context of a function signature, the identifiers used to describe the expected parameters are known as *formal parameters*, and the objects sent by the caller when invoking the function are the *actual parameters*. Parameter passing in Python follows the semantics of the standard *assignment statement*. When a function is invoked, each identifier that serves as a formal parameter is assigned, in the function's local scope, to the respective actual parameter that is provided by the caller of the function.

For example, consider the following call to our count function from page 23:

```python
prizes = count(grades, 'A')
```

Just before the function body is executed, the actual parameters, grades and 'A', are implicitly assigned to the formal parameters, data and target, as follows:

```python
data = grades
target = 'A'
```

These assignment statements establish identifier data as an alias for grades and target as a name for the string literal 'A'. (See Figure 1.7.)

Figure 1.7: A portrayal of parameter passing in Python, for the function call count(grades, 'A'). Identifiers data and target are formal parameters defined within the local scope of the count function.

The communication of a return value from the function back to the caller is similarly implemented as an assignment. Therefore, with our sample invocation of prizes = count(grades, 'A'), the identifier prizes in the caller's scope is assigned to the object that is identified as n in the return statement within our function body.

An advantage to Python's mechanism for passing information to and from a function is that objects are not copied. This ensures that the invocation of a function is efficient, even in a case where a parameter or return value is a complex object.

Mutable Parameters

Python's parameter passing model has additional implications when a parameter is a mutable object. Because the formal parameter is an alias for the actual parameter, the body of the function may interact with the object in ways that change its state. Considering again our sample invocation of the count function, if the body of the function executes the command data.append('F'), the new entry is added to the end of the list identified as data within the function, which is one and the same as the list known to the caller as grades. As an aside, we note that reassigning a new value to a formal parameter with a function body, such as by setting data = [ ], does not alter the actual parameter; such a reassignment simply breaks the alias.

Our hypothetical example of a count method that appends a new element to a list lacks common sense. There is no reason to expect such a behavior, and it would be quite a poor design to have such an unexpected effect on the parameter. There are, however, many legitimate cases in which a function may be designed (and clearly documented) to modify the state of a parameter. As a concrete example, we present the following implementation of a method named scale that's primary purpose is to multiply all entries of a numeric data set by a given factor.

```python
def scale(data, factor):
    for j in range(len(data)):
        data[j] *= factor
```

Default Parameter Values

Python provides means for functions to support more than one possible calling signature. Such a function is said to be *polymorphic* (which is Greek for "many forms"). Most notably, functions can declare one or more default values for parameters, thereby allowing the caller to invoke a function with varying numbers of actual parameters. As an artificial example, if a function is declared with signature

> **def** foo(a, b=15, c=27):

there are three parameters, the last two of which offer default values. A caller is welcome to send three actual parameters, as in foo(4, 12, 8), in which case the default values are not used. If, on the other hand, the caller only sends one parameter, foo(4), the function will execute with parameters values a=4, b=15, c=27. If a caller sends two parameters, they are assumed to be the first two, with the third being the default. Thus, foo(8, 20) executes with a=8, b=20, c=27. However, it is illegal to define a function with a signature such as bar(a, b=15, c) with b having a default value, yet not the subsequent c; if a default parameter value is present for one parameter, it must be present for all further parameters.

As a more motivating example for the use of a default parameter, we revisit the task of computing a student's GPA (see Code Fragment 1.1). Rather than assume direct input and output with the console, we prefer to design a function that computes and returns a GPA. Our original implementation uses a fixed mapping from each letter grade (such as a B−) to a corresponding point value (such as 2.67). While that point system is somewhat common, it may not agree with the system used by all schools. (For example, some may assign an 'A+' grade a value higher than 4.0.) Therefore, we design a compute_gpa function, given in Code Fragment 1.2, which allows the caller to specify a custom mapping from grades to values, while offering the standard point system as a default.

```
def compute_gpa(grades, points={'A+':4.0, 'A':4.0, 'A-':3.67, 'B+':3.33,
                                'B':3.0, 'B-':2.67,'C+':2.33, 'C':2.0,
                                'C':1.67, 'D+':1.33, 'D':1.0, 'F':0.0}):
    num_courses = 0
    total_points = 0
    for g in grades:
        if g in points:                        # a recognizable grade
            num_courses += 1
            total_points += points[g]
    return total_points / num_courses
```

Code Fragment 1.2: A function that computes a student's GPA with a point value system that can be customized as an optional parameter.

As an additional example of an interesting polymorphic function, we consider Python's support for range. (Technically, this is a constructor for the range class, but for the sake of this discussion, we can treat it as a pure function.) Three calling syntaxes are supported. The one-parameter form, range(n), generates a sequence of integers from 0 up to but not including *n*. A two-parameter form, range(start,stop) generates integers from start up to, but not including, stop. A three-parameter form, range(start, stop, step), generates a similar range as range(start, stop), but with increments of size step rather than 1.

This combination of forms seems to violate the rules for default parameters. In particular, when a single parameter is sent, as in range(n), it serves as the stop value (which is the second parameter); the value of start is effectively 0 in that case. However, this effect can be achieved with some sleight of hand, as follows:

```
def range(start, stop=None, step=1):
    if stop is None:
        stop = start
        start = 0
    ...
```

From a technical perspective, when range(n) is invoked, the actual parameter n will be assigned to formal parameter start. Within the body, if only one parameter is received, the start and stop values are reassigned to provide the desired semantics.

Keyword Parameters

The traditional mechanism for matching the actual parameters sent by a caller, to the formal parameters declared by the function signature is based on the concept of ***positional arguments***. For example, with signature foo(a=10, b=20, c=30), parameters sent by the caller are matched, in the given order, to the formal parameters. An invocation of foo(5) indicates that a=5, while b and c are assigned their default values.

Python supports an alternate mechanism for sending a parameter to a function known as a ***keyword argument***. A keyword argument is specified by explicitly assigning an actual parameter to a formal parameter by name. For example, with the above definition of function foo, a call foo(c=5) will invoke the function with parameters a=10, b=20, c=5.

A function's author can require that certain parameters be sent only through the keyword-argument syntax. We never place such a restriction in our own function definitions, but we will see several important uses of keyword-only parameters in Python's standard libraries. As an example, the built-in max function accepts a keyword parameter, coincidentally named key, that can be used to vary the notion of "maximum" that is used.

By default, max operates based upon the natural order of elements according to the < operator for that type. But the maximum can be computed by comparing some other aspect of the elements. This is done by providing an auxiliary *function* that converts a natural element to some other value for the sake of comparison. For example, if we are interested in finding a numeric value with *magnitude* that is maximal (i.e., considering −35 to be larger than +20), we can use the calling syntax max(a, b, key=abs). In this case, the built-in abs function is itself sent as the value associated with the keyword parameter key. (Functions are first-class objects in Python; see Section 1.10.) When max is called in this way, it will compare abs(a) to abs(b), rather than a to b. The motivation for the keyword syntax as an alternate to positional arguments is important in the case of max. This function is polymorphic in the number of arguments, allowing a call such as max(a,b,c,d); therefore, it is not possible to designate a key function as a traditional positional element. Sorting functions in Python also support a similar key parameter for indicating a nonstandard order. (We explore this further in Section 9.4 and in Section 12.6.1, when discussing sorting algorithms).

1.5.2   Python's Built-In Functions

Table 1.4 provides an overview of common functions that are automatically available in Python, including the previously discussed abs, max, and range. When choosing names for the parameters, we use identifiers x, y, z for arbitrary numeric types, k for an integer, and a, b, and c for arbitrary comparable types. We use the identifier, iterable, to represent an instance of any iterable type (e.g., str, list, tuple, set, dict); we will discuss iterators and iterable data types in Section 1.8. A sequence represents a more narrow category of indexable classes, including str, list, and tuple, but neither set nor dict. Most of the entries in Table 1.4 can be categorized according to their functionality as follows:

Input/Output: print, input, and open will be more fully explained in Section 1.6.

Character Encoding: ord and chr relate characters and their integer code points. For example, ord('A') is 65 and chr(65) is 'A'.

Mathematics: abs, divmod, pow, round, and sum provide common mathematical functionality; an additional math module will be introduced in Section 1.11.

Ordering: max and min apply to any data type that supports a notion of comparison, or to any collection of such values. Likewise, sorted can be used to produce an ordered list of elements drawn from any existing collection.

Collections/Iterations: range generates a new sequence of numbers; len reports the length of any existing collection; functions reversed, all, any, and map operate on arbitrary iterations as well; iter and next provide a general framework for iteration through elements of a collection, and are discussed in Section 1.8.

Common Built-In Functions	
Calling Syntax	**Description**
abs(x)	Return the absolute value of a number.
all(iterable)	Return True if bool(e) is True for each element e.
any(iterable)	Return True if bool(e) is True for at least one element e.
chr(integer)	Return a one-character string with the given Unicode code point.
divmod(x, y)	Return (x // y, x % y) as tuple, if x and y are integers.
hash(obj)	Return an integer hash value for the object (see Chapter 10).
id(obj)	Return the unique integer serving as an "identity" for the object.
input(prompt)	Return a string from standard input; the prompt is optional.
isinstance(obj, cls)	Determine if obj is an instance of the class (or a subclass).
iter(iterable)	Return a new iterator object for the parameter (see Section 1.8).
len(iterable)	Return the number of elements in the given iteration.
map(f, iter1, iter2, ...)	Return an iterator yielding the result of function calls f(e1, e2, ...) for respective elements $e1 \in iter1, e2 \in iter2, ...$
max(iterable)	Return the largest element of the given iteration.
max(a, b, c, ...)	Return the largest of the arguments.
min(iterable)	Return the smallest element of the given iteration.
min(a, b, c, ...)	Return the smallest of the arguments.
next(iterator)	Return the next element reported by the iterator (see Section 1.8).
open(filename, mode)	Open a file with the given name and access mode.
ord(char)	Return the Unicode code point of the given character.
pow(x, y)	Return the value x^y (as an integer if x and y are integers); equivalent to x ** y.
pow(x, y, z)	Return the value $(x^y \bmod z)$ as an integer.
print(obj1, obj2, ...)	Print the arguments, with separating spaces and trailing newline.
range(stop)	Construct an iteration of values $0, 1, ..., stop - 1$.
range(start, stop)	Construct an iteration of values $start, start + 1, ..., stop - 1$.
range(start, stop, step)	Construct an iteration of values $start, start + step, start + 2*step, ...$
reversed(sequence)	Return an iteration of the sequence in reverse.
round(x)	Return the nearest int value (a tie is broken toward the even value).
round(x, k)	Return the value rounded to the nearest 10^{-k} (return-type matches x).
sorted(iterable)	Return a list containing elements of the iterable in sorted order.
sum(iterable)	Return the sum of the elements in the iterable (must be numeric).
type(obj)	Return the class to which the instance obj belongs.

Table 1.4: Commonly used built-in function in Python.

1.6   Simple Input and Output

In this section, we address the basics of input and output in Python, describing standard input and output through the user console, and Python's support for reading and writing text files.

1.6.1   Console Input and Output

The print Function

The built-in function, print, is used to generate standard output to the console. In its simplest form, it prints an arbitrary sequence of arguments, separated by spaces, and followed by a trailing newline character. For example, the command print('maroon', 5) outputs the string 'maroon 5\n'. Note that arguments need not be string instances. A nonstring argument x will be displayed as str(x). Without any arguments, the command print( ) outputs a single newline character.

The print function can be customized through the use of the following keyword parameters (see Section 1.5 for a discussion of keyword parameters):

- By default, the print function inserts a separating space into the output between each pair of arguments. The separator can be customized by providing a desired separating string as a keyword parameter, sep. For example, colon-separated output can be produced as print(a, b, c, sep=':'). The separating string need not be a single character; it can be a longer string, and it can be the empty string, sep='', causing successive arguments to be directly concatenated.
- By default, a trailing newline is output after the final argument. An alternative trailing string can be designated using a keyword parameter, end. Designating the empty string end='' suppresses all trailing characters.
- By default, the print function sends its output to the standard console. However, output can be directed to a file by indicating an output file stream (see Section 1.6.2) using file as a keyword parameter.

The input Function

The primary means for acquiring information from the user console is a built-in function named input. This function displays a prompt, if given as an optional parameter, and then waits until the user enters some sequence of characters followed by the return key. The formal return value of the function is the string of characters that were entered strictly before the return key (i.e., no newline character exists in the returned string).

When reading a numeric value from the user, a programmer must use the input function to get the string of characters, and then use the int or float syntax to construct the numeric value that character string represents. That is, if a call to response = input( ) reports that the user entered the characters, '2013', the syntax int(response) could be used to produce the integer value 2013. It is quite common to combine these operations with a syntax such as

```
year = int(input('In what year were you born? '))
```

if we assume that the user will enter an appropriate response. (In Section 1.7 we discuss error handling in such a situation.)

Because input returns a string as its result, use of that function can be combined with the existing functionality of the string class, as described in Appendix A. For example, if the user enters multiple pieces of information on the same line, it is common to call the split method on the result, as in

```
reply = input('Enter x and y, separated by spaces: ')
pieces = reply.split( )     # returns a list of strings, as separated by spaces
x = float(pieces[0])
y = float(pieces[1])
```

A Sample Program

Here is a simple, but complete, program that demonstrates the use of the input and print functions. The tools for formatting the final output is discussed in Appendix A.

```
age = int(input('Enter your age in years: '))
max_heart_rate = 206.9 − (0.67 * age)    # as per Med Sci Sports Exerc.
target = 0.65 * max_heart_rate
print('Your target fat-burning heart rate is', target)
```

1.6.2 Files

Files are typically accessed in Python beginning with a call to a built-in function, named open, that returns a proxy for interactions with the underlying file. For example, the command, fp = open('sample.txt'), attempts to open a file named sample.txt, returning a proxy that allows read-only access to the text file.

The open function accepts an optional second parameter that determines the access mode. The default mode is 'r' for reading. Other common modes are 'w' for writing to the file (causing any existing file with that name to be overwritten), or 'a' for appending to the end of an existing file. Although we focus on use of text files, it is possible to work with binary files, using access modes such as 'rb' or 'wb'.

When processing a file, the proxy maintains a current position within the file as an offset from the beginning, measured in number of bytes. When opening a file with mode 'r' or 'w', the position is initially 0; if opened in append mode, 'a', the position is initially at the end of the file. The syntax fp.close( ) closes the file associated with proxy fp, ensuring that any written contents are saved. A summary of methods for reading and writing a file is given in Table 1.5

Calling Syntax	Description
fp.read( )	Return the (remaining) contents of a readable file as a string.
fp.read(k)	Return the next *k* bytes of a readable file as a string.
fp.readline( )	Return (remainder of) the current line of a readable file as a string.
fp.readlines( )	Return all (remaining) lines of a readable file as a list of strings.
for line **in** fp:	Iterate all (remaining) lines of a readable file.
fp.seek(k)	Change the current position to be at the kth byte of the file.
fp.tell( )	Return the current position, measured as byte-offset from the start.
fp.write(string)	Write given string at current position of the writable file.
fp.writelines(seq)	Write each of the strings of the given sequence at the current position of the writable file. This command does *not* insert any newlines, beyond those that are embedded in the strings.
print(..., file=fp)	Redirect output of print function to the file.

Table 1.5: Behaviors for interacting with a text file via a file proxy (named fp).

Reading from a File

The most basic command for reading via a proxy is the read method. When invoked on file proxy fp, as fp.read(k), the command returns a string representing the next *k* bytes of the file, starting at the current position. Without a parameter, the syntax fp.read( ) returns the remaining contents of the file in entirety. For convenience, files can be read a line at a time, using the readline method to read one line, or the readlines method to return a list of all remaining lines. Files also support the for-loop syntax, with iteration being line by line (e.g., **for** line **in** fp:).

Writing to a File

When a file proxy is writable, for example, if created with access mode 'w' or 'a', text can be written using methods write or writelines. For example, if we define fp = open('results.txt', 'w'), the syntax fp.write('Hello World.\n') writes a single line to the file with the given string. Note well that write does not explicitly add a trailing newline, so desired newline characters must be embedded directly in the string parameter. Recall that the output of the print method can be redirected to a file using a keyword parameter, as described in Section 1.6.

1.7 Exception Handling

Exceptions are unexpected events that occur during the execution of a program. An exception might result from a logical error or an unanticipated situation. In Python, *exceptions* (also known as *errors*) are objects that are *raised* (or *thrown*) by code that encounters an unexpected circumstance. The Python interpreter can also raise an exception should it encounter an unexpected condition, like running out of memory. A raised error may be *caught* by a surrounding context that "handles" the exception in an appropriate fashion. If uncaught, an exception causes the interpreter to stop executing the program and to report an appropriate message to the console. In this section, we examine the most common error types in Python, the mechanism for catching and handling errors that have been raised, and the syntax for raising errors from within user-defined blocks of code.

Common Exception Types

Python includes a rich hierarchy of exception classes that designate various categories of errors; Table 1.6 shows many of those classes. The Exception class serves as a base class for most other error types. An instance of the various subclasses encodes details about a problem that has occurred. Several of these errors may be raised in exceptional cases by behaviors introduced in this chapter. For example, use of an undefined identifier in an expression causes a NameError, and errant use of the dot notation, as in foo.bar( ), will generate an AttributeError if object foo does not support a member named bar.

Class	Description
Exception	A base class for most error types
AttributeError	Raised by syntax obj.foo, if obj has no member named foo
EOFError	Raised if "end of file" reached for console or file input
IOError	Raised upon failure of I/O operation (e.g., opening file)
IndexError	Raised if index to sequence is out of bounds
KeyError	Raised if nonexistent key requested for set or dictionary
KeyboardInterrupt	Raised if user types ctrl-C while program is executing
NameError	Raised if nonexistent identifier used
StopIteration	Raised by next(iterator) if no element; see Section 1.8
TypeError	Raised when wrong type of parameter is sent to a function
ValueError	Raised when parameter has invalid value (e.g., $\mathrm{sqrt}(-5)$)
ZeroDivisionError	Raised when any division operator used with 0 as divisor

Table 1.6: Common exception classes in Python

Sending the wrong number, type, or value of parameters to a function is another common cause for an exception. For example, a call to abs('hello') will raise a TypeError because the parameter is not numeric, and a call to abs(3, 5) will raise a TypeError because one parameter is expected. A ValueError is typically raised when the correct number and type of parameters are sent, but a value is illegitimate for the context of the function. For example, the int constructor accepts a string, as with int('137'), but a ValueError is raised if that string does not represent an integer, as with int('3.14') or int('hello').

Python's sequence types (e.g., list, tuple, and str) raise an IndexError when syntax such as data[k] is used with an integer k that is not a valid index for the given sequence (as described in Section 1.2.3). Sets and dictionaries raise a KeyError when an attempt is made to access a nonexistent element.

1.7.1 Raising an Exception

An exception is thrown by executing the **raise** statement, with an appropriate instance of an exception class as an argument that designates the problem. For example, if a function for computing a square root is sent a negative value as a parameter, it can raise an exception with the command:

```
raise ValueError('x cannot be negative')
```

This syntax raises a newly created instance of the ValueError class, with the error message serving as a parameter to the constructor. If this exception is not caught within the body of the function, the execution of the function immediately ceases and the exception is propagated to the calling context (and possibly beyond).

When checking the validity of parameters sent to a function, it is customary to first verify that a parameter is of an appropriate type, and then to verify that it has an appropriate value. For example, the sqrt function in Python's math library performs error-checking that might be implemented as follows:

```
def sqrt(x):
  if not isinstance(x, (int, float)):
    raise TypeError('x must be numeric')
  elif x < 0:
    raise ValueError('x cannot be negative')
  # do the real work here...
```

Checking the type of an object can be performed at run-time using the built-in function, isinstance. In simplest form, isinstance(obj, cls) returns True if object, obj, is an instance of class, cls, or any subclass of that type. In the above example, a more general form is used with a tuple of allowable types indicated with the second parameter. After confirming that the parameter is numeric, the function enforces an expectation that the number be nonnegative, raising a ValueError otherwise.

How much error-checking to perform within a function is a matter of debate. Checking the type and value of each parameter demands additional execution time and, if taken to an extreme, seems counter to the nature of Python. Consider the built-in sum function, which computes a sum of a collection of numbers. An implementation with rigorous error-checking might be written as follows:

```
def sum(values):
    if not isinstance(values, collections.Iterable):
        raise TypeError('parameter must be an iterable type')
    total = 0
    for v in values:
        if not isinstance(v, (int, float)):
            raise TypeError('elements must be numeric')
        total = total+ v
    return total
```

The abstract base class, collections.Iterable, includes all of Python's iterable containers types that guarantee support for the for-loop syntax (e.g., list, tuple, set); we discuss iterables in Section 1.8, and the use of modules, such as collections, in Section 1.11. Within the body of the for loop, each element is verified as numeric before being added to the total. A far more direct and clear implementation of this function can be written as follows:

```
def sum(values):
    total = 0
    for v in values:
        total = total + v
    return total
```

Interestingly, this simple implementation performs exactly like Python's built-in version of the function. Even without the explicit checks, appropriate exceptions are raised naturally by the code. In particular, if values is not an iterable type, the attempt to use the for-loop syntax raises a TypeError reporting that the object is not iterable. In the case when a user sends an iterable type that includes a nonnumerical element, such as sum([3.14, 'oops']), a TypeError is naturally raised by the evaluation of expression total + v. The error message

```
unsupported operand type(s) for +:  'float' and 'str'
```

should be sufficiently informative to the caller. Perhaps slightly less obvious is the error that results from sum(['alpha', 'beta']). It will technically report a failed attempt to add an int and str, due to the initial evaluation of total + 'alpha', when total has been initialized to 0.

In the remainder of this book, we tend to favor the simpler implementations in the interest of clean presentation, performing minimal error-checking in most situations.

1.7.2 Catching an Exception

There are several philosophies regarding how to cope with possible exceptional cases when writing code. For example, if a division x/y is to be computed, there is clear risk that a ZeroDivisionError will be raised when variable y has value 0. In an ideal situation, the logic of the program may dictate that y has a nonzero value, thereby removing the concern for error. However, for more complex code, or in a case where the value of y depends on some external input to the program, there remains some possibility of an error.

One philosophy for managing exceptional cases is to *"look before you leap."* The goal is to entirely avoid the possibility of an exception being raised through the use of a proactive conditional test. Revisiting our division example, we might avoid the offending situation by writing:

```
if y != 0:
  ratio = x / y
else:
  ... do something else ...
```

A second philosophy, often embraced by Python programmers, is that *"it is easier to ask for forgiveness than it is to get permission."* This quote is attributed to Grace Hopper, an early pioneer in computer science. The sentiment is that we need not spend extra execution time safeguarding against every possible exceptional case, as long as there is a mechanism for coping with a problem after it arises. In Python, this philosophy is implemented using a *try-except* control structure. Revising our first example, the division operation can be guarded as follows:

```
try:
  ratio = x / y
except ZeroDivisionError:
  ... do something else ...
```

In this structure, the "try" block is the primary code to be executed. Although it is a single command in this example, it can more generally be a larger block of indented code. Following the try-block are one or more "except" cases, each with an identified error type and an indented block of code that should be executed if the designated error is raised within the try-block.

The relative advantage of using a try-except structure is that the non-exceptional case runs efficiently, without extraneous checks for the exceptional condition. However, handling the exceptional case requires slightly more time when using a try-except structure than with a standard conditional statement. For this reason, the try-except clause is best used when there is reason to believe that the exceptional case is relatively unlikely, or when it is prohibitively expensive to proactively evaluate a condition to avoid the exception.

Exception handling is particularly useful when working with user input, or when reading from or writing to files, because such interactions are inherently less predictable. In Section 1.6.2, we suggest the syntax, fp = open('sample.txt'), for opening a file with read access. That command may raise an IOError for a variety of reasons, such as a non-existent file, or lack of sufficient privilege for opening a file. It is significantly easier to attempt the command and catch the resulting error than it is to accurately predict whether the command will succeed.

We continue by demonstrating a few other forms of the try-except syntax. Exceptions are objects that can be examined when caught. To do so, an identifier must be established with a syntax as follows:

```
try:
  fp = open('sample.txt')
except IOError as e:
  print('Unable to open the file:', e)
```

In this case, the name, e, denotes the instance of the exception that was thrown, and printing it causes a detailed error message to be displayed (e.g., "file not found").

A try-statement may handle more than one type of exception. For example, consider the following command from Section 1.6.1:

```
age = int(input('Enter your age in years: '))
```

This command could fail for a variety of reasons. The call to input will raise an EOFError if the console input fails. If the call to input completes successfully, the int constructor raises a ValueError if the user has not entered characters representing a valid integer. If we want to handle two or more types of errors in the same way, we can use a single except-statement, as in the following example:

```
age = -1                        # an initially invalid choice
while age <= 0:
  try:
    age = int(input('Enter your age in years: '))
    if age <= 0:
      print('Your age must be positive')
  except (ValueError, EOFError):
    print('Invalid response')
```

We use the tuple, (ValueError, EOFError), to designate the types of errors that we wish to catch with the except-clause. In this implementation, we catch either error, print a response, and continue with another pass of the enclosing while loop. We note that when an error is raised within the try-block, the remainder of that body is immediately skipped. In this example, if the exception arises within the call to input, or the subsequent call to the int constructor, the assignment to age never occurs, nor the message about needing a positive value. Because the value of age will be unchanged, the while loop will continue. If we preferred to have the while loop continue without printing the 'Invalid response' message, we could have written the exception-clause as

```
except (ValueError, EOFError):
    pass
```

The keyword, **pass**, is a statement that does nothing, yet it can serve syntactically as a body of a control structure. In this way, we quietly catch the exception, thereby allowing the surrounding while loop to continue.

In order to provide different responses to different types of errors, we may use two or more except-clauses as part of a try-structure. In our previous example, an EOFError suggests a more insurmountable error than simply an errant value being entered. In that case, we might wish to provide a more specific error message, or perhaps to allow the exception to interrupt the loop and be propagated to a higher context. We could implement such behavior as follows:

```
age = −1                            # an initially invalid choice
while age <= 0:
  try:
    age = int(input('Enter your age in years: '))
    if age <= 0:
      print('Your age must be positive')
  except ValueError:
    print('That is an invalid age specification')
  except EOFError:
    print('There was an unexpected error reading input.')
    raise                           # let's re-raise this exception
```

In this implementation, we have separate except-clauses for the ValueError and EOFError cases. The body of the clause for handling an EOFError relies on another technique in Python. It uses the raise statement without any subsequent argument, to re-raise the same exception that is currently being handled. This allows us to provide our own response to the exception, and then to interrupt the while loop and propagate the exception upward.

In closing, we note two additional features of try-except structures in Python. It is permissible to have a final except-clause without any identified error types, using syntax **except:**, to catch any other exceptions that occurred. However, this technique should be used sparingly, as it is difficult to suggest how to handle an error of an unknown type. A try-statement can have a **finally** clause, with a body of code that will always be executed in the standard or exceptional cases, even when an uncaught or re-raised exception occurs. That block is typically used for critical cleanup work, such as closing an open file.

1.8 Iterators and Generators

In Section 1.4.2, we introduced the for-loop syntax beginning as:

for *element* **in** *iterable*:

and we noted that there are many types of objects in Python that qualify as being iterable. Basic container types, such as list, tuple, and set, qualify as iterable types. Furthermore, a string can produce an iteration of its characters, a dictionary can produce an iteration of its keys, and a file can produce an iteration of its lines. User-defined types may also support iteration. In Python, the mechanism for iteration is based upon the following conventions:

- An *iterator* is an object that manages an iteration through a series of values. If variable, i, identifies an iterator object, then each call to the built-in function, next(i), produces a subsequent element from the underlying series, with a StopIteration exception raised to indicate that there are no further elements.

- An *iterable* is an object, obj, that produces an *iterator* via the syntax iter(obj).

By these definitions, an instance of a list is an iterable, but not itself an iterator. With data $= [1, 2, 4, 8]$, it is not legal to call next(data). However, an iterator object can be produced with syntax, i $=$ iter(data), and then each subsequent call to next(i) will return an element of that list. The for-loop syntax in Python simply automates this process, creating an iterator for the give iterable, and then repeatedly calling for the next element until catching the StopIteration exception.

More generally, it is possible to create multiple iterators based upon the same iterable object, with each iterator maintaining its own state of progress. However, iterators typically maintain their state with indirect reference back to the original collection of elements. For example, calling iter(data) on a list instance produces an instance of the list_iterator class. That iterator does not store its own copy of the list of elements. Instead, it maintains a current *index* into the original list, representing the next element to be reported. Therefore, if the contents of the original list are modified after the iterator is constructed, but before the iteration is complete, the iterator will be reporting the *updated* contents of the list.

Python also supports functions and classes that produce an implicit iterable series of values, that is, without constructing a data structure to store all of its values at once. For example, the call range(1000000) does *not* return a list of numbers; it returns a range object that is iterable. This object generates the million values one at a time, and only as needed. Such a *lazy evaluation* technique has great advantage. In the case of range, it allows a loop of the form, **for** j **in** range(1000000):, to execute without setting aside memory for storing one million values. Also, if such a loop were to be interrupted in some fashion, no time will have been spent computing unused values of the range.

We see lazy evaluation used in many of Python's libraries. For example, the dictionary class supports methods keys( ), values( ), and items( ), which respectively produce a "view" of all keys, values, or (key,value) pairs within a dictionary. None of these methods produces an explicit list of results. Instead, the views that are produced are iterable objects based upon the actual contents of the dictionary. An explicit list of values from such an iteration can be immediately constructed by calling the list class constructor with the iteration as a parameter. For example, the syntax list(range(1000)) produces a list instance with values from 0 to 999, while the syntax list(d.values( )) produces a list that has elements based upon the current values of dictionary d. We can similarly construct a tuple or set instance based upon a given iterable.

Generators

In Section 2.3.4, we will explain how to define a class whose instances serve as iterators. However, the most convenient technique for creating iterators in Python is through the use of *generators*. A generator is implemented with a syntax that is very similar to a function, but instead of returning values, a **yield** statement is executed to indicate each element of the series. As an example, consider the goal of determining all factors of a positive integer. For example, the number 100 has factors 1, 2, 4, 5, 10, 20, 25, 50, 100. A traditional function might produce and return a list containing all factors, implemented as:

```
def factors(n):              # traditional function that computes factors
    results = [ ]            # store factors in a new list
    for k in range(1,n+1):
        if n % k == 0:       # divides evenly, thus k is a factor
            results.append(k) # add k to the list of factors
    return results           # return the entire list
```

In contrast, an implementation of a *generator* for computing those factors could be implemented as follows:

```
def factors(n):              # generator that computes factors
    for k in range(1,n+1):
        if n % k == 0:       # divides evenly, thus k is a factor
            yield k          # yield this factor as next result
```

Notice use of the keyword **yield** rather than **return** to indicate a result. This indicates to Python that we are defining a generator, rather than a traditional function. It is illegal to combine yield and return statements in the same implementation, other than a zero-argument return statement to cause a generator to end its execution. If a programmer writes a loop such as **for** factor **in** factors(100):, an instance of our generator is created. For each iteration of the loop, Python executes our procedure until a yield statement indicates the next value. At that point, the procedure is temporarily interrupted, only to be resumed when another value is requested. When the flow of control naturally reaches the end of our procedure (or a zero-argument return statement), a StopIteration exception is automatically raised. Although this particular example uses a single yield statement in the source code, a generator can rely on multiple yield statements in different constructs, with the generated series determined by the natural flow of control. For example, we can greatly improve the efficiency of our generator for computing factors of a number, n, by only testing values up to the square root of that number, while reporting the factor $n//k$ that is associated with each k (unless $n//k$ equals k). We might implement such a generator as follows:

```
def factors(n):                  # generator that computes factors
  k = 1
  while k * k < n:               # while k < sqrt(n)
    if n % k == 0:
      yield k
      yield n // k
    k += 1
  if k * k == n:                 # special case if n is perfect square
    yield k
```

We should note that this generator differs from our first version in that the factors are not generated in strictly increasing order. For example, factors(100) generates the series $1, 100, 2, 50, 4, 25, 5, 20, 10$.

In closing, we wish to emphasize the benefits of lazy evaluation when using a generator rather than a traditional function. The results are only computed if requested, and the entire series need not reside in memory at one time. In fact, a generator can effectively produce an infinite series of values. As an example, the Fibonacci numbers form a classic mathematical sequence, starting with value 0, then value 1, and then each subsequent value being the sum of the two preceding values. Hence, the Fibonacci series begins as: $0, 1, 1, 2, 3, 5, 8, 13, \ldots$. The following generator produces this infinite series.

```
def fibonacci():
  a = 0
  b = 1
  while True:                    # keep going...
    yield a                      # report value, a, during this pass
    future = a + b
    a = b                        # this will be next value reported
    b = future                   # and subsequently this
```

1.9   Additional Python Conveniences

In this section, we introduce several features of Python that are particularly convenient for writing clean, concise code. Each of these syntaxes provide functionality that could otherwise be accomplished using functionality that we have introduced earlier in this chapter. However, at times, the new syntax is a more clear and direct expression of the logic.

1.9.1   Conditional Expressions

Python supports a ***conditional expression*** syntax that can replace a simple control structure. The general syntax is an expression of the form:

  expr1 **if** *condition* **else** *expr2*

This compound expression evaluates to *expr1* if the condition is true, and otherwise evaluates to *expr2*. For those familiar with Java or C++, this is equivalent to the syntax, *condition* ? *expr1* : *expr2*, in those languages.

   As an example, consider the goal of sending the absolute value of a variable, n, to a function (and without relying on the built-in abs function, for the sake of example). Using a traditional control structure, we might accomplish this as follows:

```
if n >= 0:
   param = n
else:
   param = −n
result = foo(param)                # call the function
```

With the conditional expression syntax, we can directly assign a value to variable, param, as follows:

```
param = n if n >= 0 else −n        # pick the appropriate value
result = foo(param)                # call the function
```

In fact, there is no need to assign the compound expression to a variable. A conditional expression can itself serve as a parameter to the function, written as follows:

```
result = foo(n if n >= 0 else −n)
```

   Sometimes, the mere shortening of source code is advantageous because it avoids the distraction of a more cumbersome control structure. However, we recommend that a conditional expression be used only when it improves the readability of the source code, and when the first of the two options is the more "natural" case, given its prominence in the syntax. (We prefer to view the alternative value as more exceptional.)

1.9.2 Comprehension Syntax

A very common programming task is to produce one series of values based upon the processing of another series. Often, this task can be accomplished quite simply in Python using what is known as a ***comprehension syntax***. We begin by demonstrating ***list comprehension***, as this was the first form to be supported by Python. Its general form is as follows:

[*expression* **for** *value* **in** *iterable* **if** *condition*]

We note that both *expression* and *condition* may depend on *value*, and that the if-clause is optional. The evaluation of the comprehension is logically equivalent to the following traditional control structure for computing a resulting list:

```
result = [ ]
for value in iterable:
  if condition:
    result.append(expression)
```

As a concrete example, a list of the squares of the numbers from 1 to n, that is $[1, 4, 9, 16, 25, \ldots, n^2]$, can be created by traditional means as follows:

```
squares = [ ]
for k in range(1, n+1):
  squares.append(k*k)
```

With list comprehension, this logic is expressed as follows:

```
squares = [k*k for k in range(1, n+1)]
```

As a second example, Section 1.8 introduced the goal of producing a list of factors for an integer n. That task is accomplished with the following list comprehension:

```
factors = [k for k in range(1,n+1) if n % k == 0]
```

Python supports similar comprehension syntaxes that respectively produce a set, generator, or dictionary. We compare those syntaxes using our example for producing the squares of numbers.

```
[ k*k for k in range(1, n+1) ]          list comprehension
{ k*k for k in range(1, n+1) }          set comprehension
( k*k for k in range(1, n+1) )          generator comprehension
{ k : k*k for k in range(1, n+1) }      dictionary comprehension
```

The generator syntax is particularly attractive when results do not need to be stored in memory. For example, to compute the sum of the first n squares, the generator syntax, total = sum(k*k for k in range(1, n+1)), is preferred to the use of an explicitly instantiated list comprehension as the parameter.

1.9.3 Packing and Unpacking of Sequences

Python provides two additional conveniences involving the treatment of tuples and other sequence types. The first is rather cosmetic. If a series of comma-separated expressions are given in a larger context, they will be treated as a single tuple, even if no enclosing parentheses are provided. For example, the assignment

    data = 2, 4, 6, 8

results in identifier, data, being assigned to the tuple (2, 4, 6, 8). This behavior is called **automatic packing** of a tuple. One common use of packing in Python is when returning multiple values from a function. If the body of a function executes the command,

    return x, y

it will be formally returning a single object that is the tuple (x, y).

As a dual to the packing behavior, Python can automatically **unpack** a sequence, allowing one to assign a series of individual identifiers to the elements of sequence. As an example, we can write

    a, b, c, d = range(7, 11)

which has the effect of assigning a=7, b=8, c=9, and d=10, as those are the four values in the sequence returned by the call to range. For this syntax, the right-hand side expression can be any *iterable* type, as long as the number of variables on the left-hand side is the same as the number of elements in the iteration.

This technique can be used to unpack tuples returned by a function. For example, the built-in function, divmod(a, b), returns the pair of values (a // b, a % b) associated with an integer division. Although the caller can consider the return value to be a single tuple, it is possible to write

    quotient, remainder = divmod(a, b)

to separately identify the two entries of the returned tuple. This syntax can also be used in the context of a for loop, when iterating over a sequence of iterables, as in

    for x, y **in** [(7, 2), (5, 8), (6, 4)]:

In this example, there will be three iterations of the loop. During the first pass, x=7 and y=2, and so on. This style of loop is quite commonly used to iterate through key-value pairs that are returned by the items( ) method of the dict class, as in:

    for k, v **in** mapping.items( ):

Simultaneous Assignments

The combination of automatic packing and unpacking forms a technique known as *simultaneous assignment*, whereby we explicitly assign a series of values to a series of identifiers, using a syntax:

```
x, y, z = 6, 2, 5
```

In effect, the right-hand side of this assignment is automatically packed into a tuple, and then automatically unpacked with its elements assigned to the three identifiers on the left-hand side.

When using a simultaneous assignment, all of the expressions are evaluated on the right-hand side before any of the assignments are made to the left-hand variables. This is significant, as it provides a convenient means for swapping the values associated with two variables:

```
j, k = k, j
```

With this command, j will be assigned to the *old* value of k, and k will be assigned to the *old* value of j. Without simultaneous assignment, a swap typically requires more delicate use of a temporary variable, such as

```
temp = j
j = k
k = temp
```

With the simultaneous assignment, the unnamed tuple representing the packed values on the right-hand side implicitly serves as the temporary variable when performing such a swap.

The use of simultaneous assignments can greatly simplify the presentation of code. As an example, we reconsider the generator on page 41 that produces the Fibonacci series. The original code requires separate initialization of variables a and b to begin the series. Within each pass of the loop, the goal was to reassign a and b, respectively, to the values of b and a+b. At the time, we accomplished this with brief use of a third variable. With simultaneous assignments, that generator can be implemented more directly as follows:

```
def fibonacci():
    a, b = 0, 1
    while True:
        yield a
        a, b = b, a+b
```

1.10 Scopes and Namespaces

When computing a sum with the syntax x + y in Python, the names x and y must have been previously associated with objects that serve as values; a NameError will be raised if no such definitions are found. The process of determining the value associated with an identifier is known as ***name resolution***.

Whenever an identifier is assigned to a value, that definition is made with a specific ***scope***. Top-level assignments are typically made in what is known as ***global*** scope. Assignments made within the body of a function typically have scope that is ***local*** to that function call. Therefore, an assignment, x = 5, within a function has no effect on the identifier, x, in the broader scope.

Each distinct scope in Python is represented using an abstraction known as a ***namespace***. A namespace manages all identifiers that are currently defined in a given scope. Figure 1.8 portrays two namespaces, one being that of a caller to our count function from Section 1.5, and the other being the local namespace during the execution of that function.

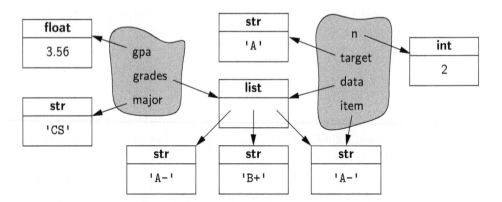

Figure 1.8: A portrayal of the two namespaces associated with a user's call count(grades, 'A'), as defined in Section 1.5. The left namespace is the caller's and the right namespace represents the local scope of the function.

Python implements a namespace with its own dictionary that maps each identifying string (e.g., 'n') to its associated value. Python provides several ways to examine a given namespace. The function, dir, reports the names of the identifiers in a given namespace (i.e., the keys of the dictionary), while the function, vars, returns the full dictionary. By default, calls to dir( ) and vars( ) report on the most locally enclosing namespace in which they are executed.

When an identifier is indicated in a command, Python searches a series of namespaces in the process of name resolution. First, the most locally enclosing scope is searched for a given name. If not found there, the next outer scope is searched, and so on. We will continue our examination of namespaces, in Section 2.5, when discussing Python's treatment of object-orientation. We will see that each object has its own namespace to store its attributes, and that classes each have a namespace as well.

First-Class Objects

In the terminology of programming languages, *first-class objects* are instances of a type that can be assigned to an identifier, passed as a parameter, or returned by a function. All of the data types we introduced in Section 1.2.3, such as int and list, are clearly first-class types in Python. In Python, functions and classes are also treated as first-class objects. For example, we could write the following:

```
scream = print      # assign name 'scream' to the function denoted as 'print'
scream('Hello')     # call that function
```

In this case, we have not created a new function, we have simply defined scream as an alias for the existing print function. While there is little motivation for precisely this example, it demonstrates the mechanism that is used by Python to allow one function to be passed as a parameter to another. On page 28, we noted that the built-in function, max, accepts an optional keyword parameter to specify a non-default order when computing a maximum. For example, a caller can use the syntax, max(a, b, key=abs), to determine which value has the larger absolute value. Within the body of that function, the formal parameter, key, is an identifier that will be assigned to the actual parameter, abs.

In terms of namespaces, an assignment such as scream = print, introduces the identifier, scream, into the current namespace, with its value being the object that represents the built-in function, print. The same mechanism is applied when a user-defined function is declared. For example, our count function from Section 1.5 beings with the following syntax:

```
def count(data, target):
    ...
```

Such a declaration introduces the identifier, count, into the current namespace, with the value being a function instance representing its implementation. In similar fashion, the name of a newly defined class is associated with a representation of that class as its value. (Class definitions will be introduced in the next chapter.)

1.11   Modules and the Import Statement

We have already introduced many functions (e.g., max) and classes (e.g., list) that are defined within Python's built-in namespace. Depending on the version of Python, there are approximately 130–150 definitions that were deemed significant enough to be included in that built-in namespace.

Beyond the built-in definitions, the standard Python distribution includes perhaps tens of thousands of other values, functions, and classes that are organized in additional libraries, known as *modules*, that can be *imported* from within a program. As an example, we consider the math module. While the built-in namespace includes a few mathematical functions (e.g., abs, min, max, round), many more are relegated to the math module (e.g., sin, cos, sqrt). That module also defines approximate values for the mathematical constants, pi and e.

Python's **import** statement loads definitions from a module into the current namespace. One form of an import statement uses a syntax such as the following:

   from math **import** pi, sqrt

This command adds both pi and sqrt, as defined in the math module, into the current namespace, allowing direct use of the identifier, pi, or a call of the function, sqrt(2). If there are many definitions from the same module to be imported, an asterisk may be used as a wild card, as in, **from** math **import** *, but this form should be used sparingly. The danger is that some of the names defined in the module may conflict with names already in the current namespace (or being imported from another module), and the import causes the new definitions to replace existing ones.

Another approach that can be used to access many definitions from the same module is to import the module itself, using a syntax such as:

   import math

Formally, this adds the identifier, math, to the current namespace, with the module as its value. (Modules are also first-class objects in Python.) Once imported, individual definitions from the module can be accessed using a fully-qualified name, such as math.pi or math.sqrt(2).

Creating a New Module

To create a new module, one simply has to put the relevant definitions in a file named with a .py suffix. Those definitions can be imported from any other .py file within the same project directory. For example, if we were to put the definition of our count function (see Section 1.5) into a file named utility.py, we could import that function using the syntax, **from** utility **import** count.

It is worth noting that top-level commands with the module source code are executed when the module is first imported, almost as if the module were its own script. There is a special construct for embedding commands within the module that will be executed if the module is directly invoked as a script, but not when the module is imported from another script. Such commands should be placed in a body of a conditional statement of the following form,

```
if __name__ == '__main__':
```

Using our hypothetical `utility.py` module as an example, such commands will be executed if the interpreter is started with a command `python utility.py`, but not when the utility module is imported into another context. This approach is often used to embed what are known as **unit tests** within the module; we will discuss unit testing further in Section 2.2.4.

1.11.1 Existing Modules

Table 1.7 provides a summary of a few available modules that are relevant to a study of data structures. We have already discussed the math module briefly. In the remainder of this section, we highlight another module that is particularly important for some of the data structures and algorithms that we will study later in this book.

Existing Modules	
Module Name	**Description**
array	Provides compact array storage for primitive types.
collections	Defines additional data structures and abstract base classes involving collections of objects.
copy	Defines general functions for making copies of objects.
heapq	Provides heap-based priority queue functions (see Section 9.3.7).
math	Defines common mathematical constants and functions.
os	Provides support for interactions with the operating system.
random	Provides random number generation.
re	Provides support for processing regular expressions.
sys	Provides additional level of interaction with the Python interpreter.
time	Provides support for measuring time, or delaying a program.

Table 1.7: Some existing Python modules relevant to data structures and algorithms.

Pseudo-Random Number Generation

Python's random module provides the ability to generate pseudo-random numbers, that is, numbers that are statistically random (but not necessarily truly random). A **pseudo-random number generator** uses a deterministic formula to generate the next number in a sequence based upon one or more past numbers that it has generated. Indeed, a simple yet popular pseudo-random number generator chooses its next number based solely on the most recently chosen number and some additional parameters using the following formula.

$$\text{next} = (a*\text{current} + b) \,\%\, n;$$

where a, b, and n are appropriately chosen integers. Python uses a more advanced technique known as a *Mersenne twister*. It turns out that the sequences generated by these techniques can be proven to be statistically uniform, which is usually good enough for most applications requiring random numbers, such as games. For applications, such as computer security settings, where one needs unpredictable random sequences, this kind of formula should not be used. Instead, one should ideally sample from a source that is actually random, such as radio static coming from outer space.

Since the next number in a pseudo-random generator is determined by the previous number(s), such a generator always needs a place to start, which is called its *seed*. The sequence of numbers generated for a given seed will always be the same. One common trick to get a different sequence each time a program is run is to use a seed that will be different for each run. For example, we could use some timed input from a user or the current system time in milliseconds.

Python's random module provides support for pseudo-random number generation by defining a Random class; instances of that class serve as generators with independent state. This allows different aspects of a program to rely on their own pseudo-random number generator, so that calls to one generator do not affect the sequence of numbers produced by another. For convenience, all of the methods supported by the Random class are also supported as stand-alone functions of the random module (essentially using a single generator instance for all top-level calls).

Syntax	Description
seed(hashable)	Initializes the pseudo-random number generator based upon the hash value of the parameter
random( )	Returns a pseudo-random floating-point value in the interval $[0.0, 1.0)$.
randint(a,b)	Returns a pseudo-random integer in the closed interval $[a,b]$.
randrange(start, stop, step)	Returns a pseudo-random integer in the standard Python range indicated by the parameters.
choice(seq)	Returns an element of the given sequence chosen pseudo-randomly.
shuffle(seq)	Reorders the elements of the given sequence pseudo-randomly.

Table 1.8: Methods supported by instances of the Random class, and as top-level functions of the random module.

1.12 Exercises

For help with exercises, please visit the site, www.wiley.com/college/goodrich.

Reinforcement

R-1.1 Write a short Python function, is_multiple(n, m), that takes two integer values and returns True if n is a multiple of m, that is, $n = mi$ for some integer i, and False otherwise.

R-1.2 Write a short Python function, is_even(k), that takes an integer value and returns True if k is even, and **False** otherwise. However, your function cannot use the multiplication, modulo, or division operators.

R-1.3 Write a short Python function, minmax(data), that takes a sequence of one or more numbers, and returns the smallest and largest numbers, in the form of a tuple of length two. Do not use the built-in functions min or max in implementing your solution.

R-1.4 Write a short Python function that takes a positive integer n and returns the sum of the squares of all the positive integers smaller than n.

R-1.5 Give a single command that computes the sum from Exercise R-1.4, relying on Python's comprehension syntax and the built-in sum function.

R-1.6 Write a short Python function that takes a positive integer n and returns the sum of the squares of all the odd positive integers smaller than n.

R-1.7 Give a single command that computes the sum from Exercise R-1.6, relying on Python's comprehension syntax and the built-in sum function.

R-1.8 Python allows negative integers to be used as indices into a sequence, such as a string. If string s has length n, and expression s[k] is used for index $-n \leq k < 0$, what is the equivalent index $j \geq 0$ such that s[j] references the same element?

R-1.9 What parameters should be sent to the range constructor, to produce a range with values 50, 60, 70, 80?

R-1.10 What parameters should be sent to the range constructor, to produce a range with values 8, 6, 4, 2, 0, -2, -4, -6, -8?

R-1.11 Demonstrate how to use Python's list comprehension syntax to produce the list [1, 2, 4, 8, 16, 32, 64, 128, 256].

R-1.12 Python's random module includes a function choice(data) that returns a random element from a non-empty sequence. The random module includes a more basic function randrange, with parameterization similar to the built-in range function, that return a random choice from the given range. Using only the randrange function, implement your own version of the choice function.

Creativity

C-1.13 Write a pseudo-code description of a function that reverses a list of *n* integers, so that the numbers are listed in the opposite order than they were before, and compare this method to an equivalent Python function for doing the same thing.

C-1.14 Write a short Python function that takes a sequence of integer values and determines if there is a distinct pair of numbers in the sequence whose product is odd.

C-1.15 Write a Python function that takes a sequence of numbers and determines if all the numbers are different from each other (that is, they are distinct).

C-1.16 In our implementation of the scale function (page 25), the body of the loop executes the command data[j] *= factor. We have discussed that numeric types are immutable, and that use of the *= operator in this context causes the creation of a new instance (not the mutation of an existing instance). How is it still possible, then, that our implementation of scale changes the actual parameter sent by the caller?

C-1.17 Had we implemented the scale function (page 25) as follows, does it work properly?

```
def scale(data, factor):
    for val in data:
        val *= factor
```

Explain why or why not.

C-1.18 Demonstrate how to use Python's list comprehension syntax to produce the list [0, 2, 6, 12, 20, 30, 42, 56, 72, 90].

C-1.19 Demonstrate how to use Python's list comprehension syntax to produce the list ['a', 'b', 'c', ..., 'z'], but without having to type all 26 such characters literally.

C-1.20 Python's random module includes a function shuffle(data) that accepts a list of elements and randomly reorders the elements so that each possible order occurs with equal probability. The random module includes a more basic function randint(a, b) that returns a uniformly random integer from *a* to *b* (including both endpoints). Using only the randint function, implement your own version of the shuffle function.

C-1.21 Write a Python program that repeatedly reads lines from standard input until an EOFError is raised, and then outputs those lines in reverse order (a user can indicate end of input by typing ctrl-D).

C-1.22 Write a short Python program that takes two arrays a and b of length n storing **int** values, and returns the dot product of a and b. That is, it returns an array c of length n such that $c[i] = a[i] \cdot b[i]$, for $i = 0, \ldots, n-1$.

C-1.23 Give an example of a Python code fragment that attempts to write an element to a list based on an index that may be out of bounds. If that index is out of bounds, the program should catch the exception that results, and print the following error message:
"`Don't try buffer overflow attacks in Python!`"

C-1.24 Write a short Python function that counts the number of vowels in a given character string.

C-1.25 Write a short Python function that takes a string s, representing a sentence, and returns a copy of the string with all punctuation removed. For example, if given the string `"Let's try, Mike."`, this function would return `"Lets try Mike"`.

C-1.26 Write a short program that takes as input three integers, a, b, and c, from the console and determines if they can be used in a correct arithmetic formula (in the given order), like "$a + b = c$," "$a = b - c$," or "$a * b = c$."

C-1.27 In Section 1.8, we provided three different implementations of a generator that computes factors of a given integer. The third of those implementations, from page 41, was the most efficient, but we noted that it did not yield the factors in increasing order. Modify the generator so that it reports factors in increasing order, while maintaining its general performance advantages.

C-1.28 The *p-norm* of a vector $v = (v_1, v_2, \ldots, v_n)$ in n-dimensional space is defined as

$$\|v\| = \sqrt[p]{v_1^p + v_2^p + \cdots + v_n^p}.$$

For the special case of $p = 2$, this results in the traditional *Euclidean norm*, which represents the length of the vector. For example, the Euclidean norm of a two-dimensional vector with coordinates $(4,3)$ has a Euclidean norm of $\sqrt{4^2 + 3^2} = \sqrt{16+9} = \sqrt{25} = 5$. Give an implementation of a function named norm such that norm(v, p) returns the p-norm value of v and norm(v) returns the Euclidean norm of v. You may assume that v is a list of numbers.

Projects

P-1.29 Write a Python program that outputs all possible strings formed by using the characters 'c', 'a', 't', 'd', 'o', and 'g' exactly once.

P-1.30 Write a Python program that can take a positive integer greater than 2 as input and write out the number of times one must repeatedly divide this number by 2 before getting a value less than 2.

P-1.31 Write a Python program that can "make change." Your program should take two numbers as input, one that is a monetary amount charged and the other that is a monetary amount given. It should then return the number of each kind of bill and coin to give back as change for the difference between the amount given and the amount charged. The values assigned to the bills and coins can be based on the monetary system of any current or former government. Try to design your program so that it returns as few bills and coins as possible.

P-1.32 Write a Python program that can simulate a simple calculator, using the console as the exclusive input and output device. That is, each input to the calculator, be it a number, like 12.34 or 1034, or an operator, like + or =, can be done on a separate line. After each such input, you should output to the Python console what would be displayed on your calculator.

P-1.33 Write a Python program that simulates a handheld calculator. Your program should process input from the Python console representing buttons that are "pushed," and then output the contents of the screen after each operation is performed. Minimally, your calculator should be able to process the basic arithmetic operations and a reset/clear operation.

P-1.34 A common punishment for school children is to write out a sentence multiple times. Write a Python stand-alone program that will write out the following sentence one hundred times: "I will never spam my friends again." Your program should number each of the sentences and it should make eight different random-looking typos.

P-1.35 The *birthday paradox* says that the probability that two people in a room will have the same birthday is more than half, provided n, the number of people in the room, is more than 23. This property is not really a paradox, but many people find it surprising. Design a Python program that can test this paradox by a series of experiments on randomly generated birthdays, which test this paradox for $n = 5, 10, 15, 20, \ldots, 100$.

P-1.36 Write a Python program that inputs a list of words, separated by whitespace, and outputs how many times each word appears in the list. You need not worry about efficiency at this point, however, as this topic is something that will be addressed later in this book.

Chapter Notes

The official Python Web site (http://www.python.org) has a wealth of information, including a tutorial and full documentation of the built-in functions, classes, and standard modules. The Python interpreter is itself a useful reference, as the interactive command help(foo) provides documentation for any function, class, or module that foo identifies.

Books providing an introduction to programming in Python include titles authored by Campbell *et al.* [22], Cedar [25], Dawson [32], Goldwasser and Letscher [43], Lutz [72], Perkovic [82], and Zelle [105]. More complete reference books on Python include titles by Beazley [12], and Summerfield [91].

Chapter

2

Object-Oriented Programming

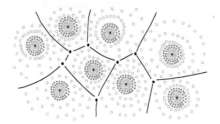

Contents

2.1 Goals, Principles, and Patterns

As the name implies, the main "actors" in the object-oriented paradigm are called *objects*. Each object is an *instance* of a *class*. Each class presents to the outside world a concise and consistent view of the objects that are instances of this class, without going into too much unnecessary detail or giving others access to the inner workings of the objects. The class definition typically specifies *instance variables*, also known as *data members*, that the object contains, as well as the *methods*, also known as *member functions*, that the object can execute. This view of computing is intended to fulfill several goals and incorporate several design principles, which we discuss in this chapter.

2.1.1 Object-Oriented Design Goals

Software implementations should achieve *robustness*, *adaptability*, and *reusability*. (See Figure 2.1.)

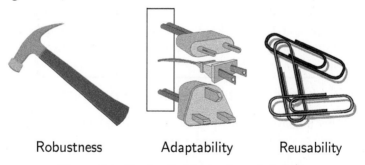

Robustness   Adaptability   Reusability

Figure 2.1: Goals of object-oriented design.

Robustness

Every good programmer wants to develop software that is correct, which means that a program produces the right output for all the anticipated inputs in the program's application. In addition, we want software to be *robust*, that is, capable of handling unexpected inputs that are not explicitly defined for its application. For example, if a program is expecting a positive integer (perhaps representing the price of an item) and instead is given a negative integer, then the program should be able to recover gracefully from this error. More importantly, in *life-critical applications*, where a software error can lead to injury or loss of life, software that is not robust could be deadly. This point was driven home in the late 1980s in accidents involving Therac-25, a radiation-therapy machine, which severely overdosed six patients between 1985 and 1987, some of whom died from complications resulting from their radiation overdose. All six accidents were traced to software errors.

Adaptability

Modern software applications, such as Web browsers and Internet search engines, typically involve large programs that are used for many years. Software, therefore, needs to be able to evolve over time in response to changing conditions in its environment. Thus, another important goal of quality software is that it achieves *adaptability* (also called *evolvability*). Related to this concept is *portability*, which is the ability of software to run with minimal change on different hardware and operating system platforms. An advantage of writing software in Python is the portability provided by the language itself.

Reusability

Going hand in hand with adaptability is the desire that software be reusable, that is, the same code should be usable as a component of different systems in various applications. Developing quality software can be an expensive enterprise, and its cost can be offset somewhat if the software is designed in a way that makes it easily reusable in future applications. Such reuse should be done with care, however, for one of the major sources of software errors in the Therac-25 came from inappropriate reuse of Therac-20 software (which was not object-oriented and not designed for the hardware platform used with the Therac-25).

2.1.2 Object-Oriented Design Principles

Chief among the principles of the object-oriented approach, which are intended to facilitate the goals outlined above, are the following (see Figure 2.2):

- Modularity
- Abstraction
- Encapsulation

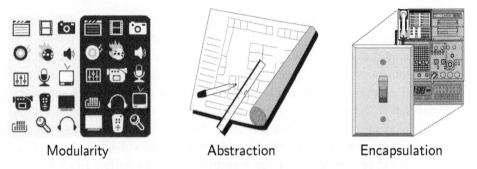

Modularity   Abstraction   Encapsulation

Figure 2.2: Principles of object-oriented design.

Modularity

Modern software systems typically consist of several different components that must interact correctly in order for the entire system to work properly. Keeping these interactions straight requires that these different components be well organized. Modularity refers to an organizing principle in which different components of a software system are divided into separate functional units.

As a real-world analogy, a house or apartment can be viewed as consisting of several interacting units: electrical, heating and cooling, plumbing, and structural. Rather than viewing these systems as one giant jumble of wires, vents, pipes, and boards, the organized architect designing a house or apartment will view them as separate modules that interact in well-defined ways. In so doing, he or she is using modularity to bring a clarity of thought that provides a natural way of organizing functions into distinct manageable units.

In like manner, using modularity in a software system can also provide a powerful organizing framework that brings clarity to an implementation. In Python, we have already seen that a *module* is a collection of closely related functions and classes that are defined together in a single file of source code. Python's standard libraries include, for example, the math module, which provides definitions for key mathematical constants and functions, and the os module, which provides support for interacting with the operating system.

The use of modularity helps support the goals listed in Section 2.1.1. Robustness is greatly increased because it is easier to test and debug separate components before they are integrated into a larger software system. Furthermore, bugs that persist in a complete system might be traced to a particular component, which can be fixed in relative isolation. The structure imposed by modularity also helps enable software reusability. If software modules are written in a general way, the modules can be reused when related need arises in other contexts. This is particularly relevant in a study of data structures, which can typically be designed with sufficient abstraction and generality to be reused in many applications.

Abstraction

The notion of *abstraction* is to distill a complicated system down to its most fundamental parts. Typically, describing the parts of a system involves naming them and explaining their functionality. Applying the abstraction paradigm to the design of data structures gives rise to *abstract data types* (ADTs). An ADT is a mathematical model of a data structure that specifies the type of data stored, the operations supported on them, and the types of parameters of the operations. An ADT specifies *what* each operation does, but not *how* it does it. We will typically refer to the collective set of behaviors supported by an ADT as its *public interface*.

As a programming language, Python provides a great deal of latitude in regard to the specification of an interface. Python has a tradition of treating abstractions implicitly using a mechanism known as *duck typing*. As an interpreted and dynamically typed language, there is no "compile time" checking of data types in Python, and no formal requirement for declarations of abstract base classes. Instead programmers assume that an object supports a set of known behaviors, with the interpreter raising a run-time error if those assumptions fail. The description of this as "duck typing" comes from an adage attributed to poet James Whitcomb Riley, stating that "when I see a bird that walks like a duck and swims like a duck and quacks like a duck, I call that bird a duck."

More formally, Python supports abstract data types using a mechanism known as an *abstract base class* (ABC). An abstract base class cannot be instantiated (i.e., you cannot directly create an instance of that class), but it defines one or more common methods that all implementations of the abstraction must have. An ABC is realized by one or more *concrete classes* that inherit from the abstract base class while providing implementations for those method declared by the ABC. Python's abc module provides formal support for ABCs, although we omit such declarations for simplicity. We will make use of several existing abstract base classes coming from Python's collections module, which includes definitions for several common data structure ADTs, and concrete implementations of some of those abstractions.

Encapsulation

Another important principle of object-oriented design is *encapsulation*. Different components of a software system should not reveal the internal details of their respective implementations. One of the main advantages of encapsulation is that it gives one programmer freedom to implement the details of a component, without concern that other programmers will be writing code that intricately depends on those internal decisions. The only constraint on the programmer of a component is to maintain the public interface for the component, as other programmers will be writing code that depends on that interface. Encapsulation yields robustness and adaptability, for it allows the implementation details of parts of a program to change without adversely affecting other parts, thereby making it easier to fix bugs or add new functionality with relatively local changes to a component.

Throughout this book, we will adhere to the principle of encapsulation, making clear which aspects of a data structure are assumed to be public and which are assumed to be internal details. With that said, Python provides only loose support for encapsulation. By convention, names of members of a class (both data members and member functions) that start with a single underscore character (e.g., _secret) are assumed to be nonpublic and should not be relied upon. Those conventions are reinforced by the intentional omission of those members from automatically generated documentation.

2.1.3   Design Patterns

Object-oriented design facilitates reusable, robust, and adaptable software. Designing good code takes more than simply understanding object-oriented methodologies, however. It requires the effective use of object-oriented design techniques.

Computing researchers and practitioners have developed a variety of organizational concepts and methodologies for designing quality object-oriented software that is concise, correct, and reusable. Of special relevance to this book is the concept of a ***design pattern***, which describes a solution to a "typical" software design problem. A pattern provides a general template for a solution that can be applied in many different situations. It describes the main elements of a solution in an abstract way that can be specialized for a specific problem at hand. It consists of a name, which identifies the pattern; a context, which describes the scenarios for which this pattern can be applied; a template, which describes how the pattern is applied; and a result, which describes and analyzes what the pattern produces.

We present several design patterns in this book, and we show how they can be consistently applied to implementations of data structures and algorithms. These design patterns fall into two groups—patterns for solving algorithm design problems and patterns for solving software engineering problems. The algorithm design patterns we discuss include the following:

- Recursion (Chapter 4)
- Amortization (Sections 5.3 and 11.4)
- Divide-and-conquer (Section 12.2.1)
- Prune-and-search, also known as decrease-and-conquer (Section 12.7.1)
- Brute force (Section 13.2.1)
- Dynamic programming (Section 13.3).
- The greedy method (Sections 13.4.2, 14.6.2, and 14.7)

Likewise, the software engineering design patterns we discuss include:

- Iterator (Sections 1.8 and 2.3.4)
- Adapter (Section 6.1.2)
- Position (Sections 7.4 and 8.1.2)
- Composition (Sections 7.6.1, 9.2.1, and 10.1.4)
- Template method (Sections 2.4.3, 8.4.6, 10.1.3, 10.5.2, and 11.2.1)
- Locator (Section 9.5.1)
- Factory method (Section 11.2.1)

Rather than explain each of these concepts here, however, we introduce them throughout the text as noted above. For each pattern, be it for algorithm engineering or software engineering, we explain its general use and we illustrate it with at least one concrete example.

2.2   Software Development

Traditional software development involves several phases. Three major steps are:

1. Design
2. Implementation
3. Testing and Debugging

In this section, we briefly discuss the role of these phases, and we introduce several good practices for programming in Python, including coding style, naming conventions, formal documentation, and unit testing.

2.2.1   Design

For object-oriented programming, the design step is perhaps the most important phase in the process of developing software. For it is in the design step that we decide how to divide the workings of our program into classes, we decide how these classes will interact, what data each will store, and what actions each will perform. Indeed, one of the main challenges that beginning programmers face is deciding what classes to define to do the work of their program. While general prescriptions are hard to come by, there are some rules of thumb that we can apply when determining how to design our classes:

- *Responsibilities*: Divide the work into different *actors*, each with a different responsibility. Try to describe responsibilities using action verbs. These actors will form the classes for the program.

- *Independence*: Define the work for each class to be as independent from other classes as possible. Subdivide responsibilities between classes so that each class has autonomy over some aspect of the program. Give data (as instance variables) to the class that has jurisdiction over the actions that require access to this data.

- *Behaviors*: Define the behaviors for each class carefully and precisely, so that the consequences of each action performed by a class will be well understood by other classes that interact with it. These behaviors will define the methods that this class performs, and the set of behaviors for a class are the *interface* to the class, as these form the means for other pieces of code to interact with objects from the class.

Defining the classes, together with their instance variables and methods, are key to the design of an object-oriented program. A good programmer will naturally develop greater skill in performing these tasks over time, as experience teaches him or her to notice patterns in the requirements of a program that match patterns that he or she has seen before.

A common tool for developing an initial high-level design for a project is the use of ***CRC cards***. Class-Responsibility-Collaborator (CRC) cards are simple index cards that subdivide the work required of a program. The main idea behind this tool is to have each card represent a component, which will ultimately become a class in the program. We write the name of each component on the top of an index card. On the left-hand side of the card, we begin writing the responsibilities for this component. On the right-hand side, we list the collaborators for this component, that is, the other components that this component will have to interact with to perform its duties.

The design process iterates through an action/actor cycle, where we first identify an action (that is, a responsibility), and we then determine an actor (that is, a component) that is best suited to perform that action. The design is complete when we have assigned all actions to actors. In using index cards for this process (rather than larger pieces of paper), we are relying on the fact that each component should have a small set of responsibilities and collaborators. Enforcing this rule helps keep the individual classes manageable.

As the design takes form, a standard approach to explain and document the design is the use of UML (Unified Modeling Language) diagrams to express the organization of a program. UML diagrams are a standard visual notation to express object-oriented software designs. Several computer-aided tools are available to build UML diagrams. One type of UML figure is known as a ***class diagram***. An example of such a diagram is given in Figure 2.3, for a class that represents a consumer credit card. The diagram has three portions, with the first designating the name of the class, the second designating the recommended instance variables, and the third designating the recommended methods of the class. In Section 2.2.3, we discuss our naming conventions, and in Section 2.3.1, we provide a complete implementation of a Python CreditCard class based on this design.

Class:	CreditCard	
Fields:	_customer _bank _account	_balance _limit
Behaviors:	get_customer( ) get_bank( ) get_account( ) make_payment(amount)	get_balance( ) get_limit( ) charge(price)

Figure 2.3: Class diagram for a proposed CreditCard class.

2.2.2   Pseudo-Code

As an intermediate step before the implementation of a design, programmers are often asked to describe algorithms in a way that is intended for human eyes only. Such descriptions are called ***pseudo-code***. Pseudo-code is not a computer program, but is more structured than usual prose. It is a mixture of natural language and high-level programming constructs that describe the main ideas behind a generic implementation of a data structure or algorithm. Because pseudo-code is designed for a human reader, not a computer, we can communicate high-level ideas, without being burdened with low-level implementation details. At the same time, we should not gloss over important steps. Like many forms of human communication, finding the right balance is an important skill that is refined through practice.

In this book, we rely on a pseudo-code style that we hope will be evident to Python programmers, yet with a mix of mathematical notations and English prose. For example, we might use the phrase "indicate an error" rather than a formal raise statement. Following conventions of Python, we rely on indentation to indicate the extent of control structures and on an indexing notation in which entries of a sequence A with length n are indexed from $A[0]$ to $A[n-1]$. However, we choose to enclose comments within curly braces { like these } in our pseudo-code, rather than using Python's # character.

2.2.3   Coding Style and Documentation

Programs should be made easy to read and understand. Good programmers should therefore be mindful of their coding style, and develop a style that communicates the important aspects of a program's design for both humans and computers. Conventions for coding style tend to vary between different programming communities. The official *Style Guide for Python Code* is available online at

`http://www.python.org/dev/peps/pep-0008/`

The main principles that we adopt are as follows:

- Python code blocks are typically indented by 4 spaces. However, to avoid having our code fragments overrun the book's margins, we use 2 spaces for each level of indentation. It is strongly recommended that tabs be avoided, as tabs are displayed with differing widths across systems, and tabs and spaces are not viewed as identical by the Python interpreter. Many Python-aware editors will automatically replace tabs with an appropriate number of spaces.

- Use meaningful names for identifiers. Try to choose names that can be read aloud, and choose names that reflect the action, responsibility, or data each identifier is naming.

  - Classes (other than Python's built-in classes) should have a name that serves as a singular noun, and should be capitalized (e.g., Date rather than date or Dates). When multiple words are concatenated to form a class name, they should follow the so-called "CamelCase" convention in which the first letter of each word is capitalized (e.g., CreditCard).

  - Functions, including member functions of a class, should be lowercase. If multiple words are combined, they should be separated by under-scores (e.g., make_payment). The name of a function should typically be a verb that describes its affect. However, if the only purpose of the function is to return a value, the function name may be a noun that describes the value (e.g., sqrt rather than calculate_sqrt).

  - Names that identify an individual object (e.g., a parameter, instance variable, or local variable) should be a lowercase noun (e.g., price). Occasionally, we stray from this rule when using a single uppercase letter to designate the name of a data structures (such as tree T).

  - Identifiers that represent a value considered to be a constant are tradi-tionally identified using all capital letters and with underscores to sep-arate words (e.g., MAX_SIZE).

  Recall from our discussion of *encapsulation* that identifiers in any context that begin with a single leading underscore (e.g., _secret) are intended to suggest that they are only for "internal" use to a class or module, and not part of a public interface.

- Use comments that add meaning to a program and explain ambiguous or confusing constructs. In-line comments are good for quick explanations; they are indicated in Python following the # character, as in

  if n % 2 == 1:   # n is odd

  Multiline block comments are good for explaining more complex code sec-tions. In Python, these are technically multiline string literals, typically de-limited with triple quotes ("""), which have no effect when executed. In the next section, we discuss the use of block comments for documentation.

Documentation

Python provides integrated support for embedding formal documentation directly in source code using a mechanism known as a ***docstring***. Formally, any string literal that appears as the *first* statement within the body of a module, class, or function (including a member function of a class) will be considered to be a docstring. By convention, those string literals should be delimited within triple quotes ("""). As an example, our version of the scale function from page 25 could be documented as follows:

```python
def scale(data, factor):
  """Multiply all entries of numeric data list by the given factor."""
  for j in range(len(data)):
    data[j] *= factor
```

It is common to use the triple-quoted string delimiter for a docstring, even when the string fits on a single line, as in the above example. More detailed docstrings should begin with a single line that summarizes the purpose, followed by a blank line, and then further details. For example, we might more clearly document the scale function as follows:

```python
def scale(data, factor):
  """Multiply all entries of numeric data list by the given factor.

  data    an instance of any mutable sequence type (such as a list)
          containing numeric elements

  factor  a number that serves as the multiplicative factor for scaling
  """
  for j in range(len(data)):
    data[j] *= factor
```

A docstring is stored as a field of the module, function, or class in which it is declared. It serves as documentation and can be retrieved in a variety of ways. For example, the command help(x), within the Python interpreter, produces the documentation associated with the identified object x. An external tool named pydoc is distributed with Python and can be used to generate formal documentation as text or as a Web page. Guidelines for *authoring* useful docstrings are available at:

http://www.python.org/dev/peps/pep-0257/

In this book, we will try to present docstrings when space allows. Omitted docstrings can be found in the online version of our source code.

2.2.4   Testing and Debugging

Testing is the process of experimentally checking the correctness of a program, while debugging is the process of tracking the execution of a program and discovering the errors in it. Testing and debugging are often the most time-consuming activity in the development of a program.

Testing

A careful testing plan is an essential part of writing a program. While verifying the correctness of a program over all possible inputs is usually infeasible, we should aim at executing the program on a representative subset of inputs. At the very minimum, we should make sure that every method of a class is tested at least once (method coverage). Even better, each code statement in the program should be executed at least once (statement coverage).

Programs often tend to fail on *special cases* of the input. Such cases need to be carefully identified and tested. For example, when testing a method that sorts (that is, puts in order) a sequence of integers, we should consider the following inputs:

- The sequence has zero length (no elements).
- The sequence has one element.
- All the elements of the sequence are the same.
- The sequence is already sorted.
- The sequence is reverse sorted.

In addition to special inputs to the program, we should also consider special conditions for the structures used by the program. For example, if we use a Python list to store data, we should make sure that boundary cases, such as inserting or removing at the beginning or end of the list, are properly handled.

While it is essential to use handcrafted test suites, it is also advantageous to run the program on a large collection of randomly generated inputs. The random module in Python provides several means for generating random numbers, or for randomizing the order of collections.

The dependencies among the classes and functions of a program induce a hierarchy. Namely, a component A is above a component B in the hierarchy if A depends upon B, such as when function A calls function B, or function A relies on a parameter that is an instance of class B. There are two main testing strategies, *top-down* and *bottom-up*, which differ in the order in which components are tested.

Top-down testing proceeds from the top to the bottom of the program hierarchy. It is typically used in conjunction with *stubbing*, a boot-strapping technique that replaces a lower-level component with a *stub*, a replacement for the component that simulates the functionality of the original. For example, if function A calls function B to get the first line of a file, when testing A we can replace B with a stub that returns a fixed string.

Bottom-up testing proceeds from lower-level components to higher-level components. For example, bottom-level functions, which do not invoke other functions, are tested first, followed by functions that call only bottom-level functions, and so on. Similarly a class that does not depend upon any other classes can be tested before another class that depends on the former. This form of testing is usually described as *unit testing*, as the functionality of a specific component is tested in isolation of the larger software project. If used properly, this strategy better isolates the cause of errors to the component being tested, as lower-level components upon which it relies should have already been thoroughly tested.

Python provides several forms of support for automated testing. When functions or classes are defined in a module, testing for that module can be embedded in the same file. The mechanism for doing so was described in Section 1.11. Code that is shielded in a conditional construct of the form

```
if __name__ == '__main__':
    # perform tests...
```

will be executed when Python is invoked directly on that module, but not when the module is imported for use in a larger software project. It is common to put tests in such a construct to test the functionality of the functions and classes specifically defined in that module.

More robust support for automation of unit testing is provided by Python's unittest module. This framework allows the grouping of individual test cases into larger test suites, and provides support for executing those suites, and reporting or analyzing the results of those tests. As software is maintained, the act of *regression testing* is used, whereby all previous tests are re-executed to ensure that changes to the software do not introduce new bugs in previously tested components.

Debugging

The simplest debugging technique consists of using *print statements* to track the values of variables during the execution of the program. A problem with this approach is that eventually the print statements need to be removed or commented out, so they are not executed when the software is finally released.

A better approach is to run the program within a *debugger*, which is a specialized environment for controlling and monitoring the execution of a program. The basic functionality provided by a debugger is the insertion of *breakpoints* within the code. When the program is executed within the debugger, it stops at each breakpoint. While the program is stopped, the current value of variables can be inspected.

The standard Python distribution includes a module named pdb, which provides debugging support directly within the interpreter. Most IDEs for Python, such as IDLE, provide debugging environments with graphical user interfaces.

2.3 Class Definitions

A class serves as the primary means for abstraction in object-oriented programming. In Python, every piece of data is represented as an instance of some class. A class provides a set of behaviors in the form of *member functions* (also known as *methods*), with implementations that are common to all instances of that class. A class also serves as a blueprint for its instances, effectively determining the way that state information for each instance is represented in the form of *attributes* (also known as *fields*, *instance variables*, or *data members*).

2.3.1 Example: CreditCard Class

As a first example, we provide an implementation of a CreditCard class based on the design we introduced in Figure 2.3 of Section 2.2.1. The instances defined by the CreditCard class provide a simple model for traditional credit cards. They have identifying information about the customer, bank, account number, credit limit, and current balance. The class restricts charges that would cause a card's balance to go over its spending limit, but it does not charge interest or late payments (we revisit such themes in Section 2.4.1).

Our code begins in Code Fragment 2.1 and continues in Code Fragment 2.2. The construct begins with the keyword, **class**, followed by the name of the class, a colon, and then an indented block of code that serves as the body of the class. The body includes definitions for all methods of the class. These methods are defined as functions, using techniques introduced in Section 1.5, yet with a special parameter, named **self**, that serves to identify the particular instance upon which a member is invoked.

The self Identifier

In Python, the self identifier plays a key role. In the context of the CreditCard class, there can presumably be many different CreditCard instances, and each must maintain its own balance, its own credit limit, and so on. Therefore, each instance stores its own instance variables to reflect its current state.

Syntactically, self identifies the instance upon which a method is invoked. For example, assume that a user of our class has a variable, my_card, that identifies an instance of the CreditCard class. When the user calls my_card.get_balance( ), identifier self, within the definition of the get_balance method, refers to the card known as my_card by the caller. The expression, self._balance refers to an instance variable, named _balance, stored as part of that particular credit card's state.

```
 1  class CreditCard:
 2    """A consumer credit card."""
 3
 4    def __init__(self, customer, bank, acnt, limit):
 5      """Create a new credit card instance.
 6
 7      The initial balance is zero.
 8
 9      customer  the name of the customer (e.g., 'John Bowman')
10      bank      the name of the bank (e.g., 'California Savings')
11      acnt      the acount identifier (e.g., '5391 0375 9387 5309')
12      limit     credit limit (measured in dollars)
13      """
14      self._customer = customer
15      self._bank = bank
16      self._account = acnt
17      self._limit = limit
18      self._balance = 0
19
20    def get_customer(self):
21      """Return name of the customer."""
22      return self._customer
23
24    def get_bank(self):
25      """Return the bank's name."""
26      return self._bank
27
28    def get_account(self):
29      """Return the card identifying number (typically stored as a string)."""
30      return self._account
31
32    def get_limit(self):
33      """Return current credit limit."""
34      return self._limit
35
36    def get_balance(self):
37      """Return current balance."""
38      return self._balance
```

Code Fragment 2.1: The beginning of the CreditCard class definition (continued in Code Fragment 2.2).

```
39    def charge(self, price):
40      """Charge given price to the card, assuming sufficient credit limit.
41
42      Return True if charge was processed; False if charge was denied.
43      """
44      if price + self._balance > self._limit:      # if charge would exceed limit,
45        return False                               # cannot accept charge
46      else:
47        self._balance += price
48        return True
49
50    def make_payment(self, amount):
51      """Process customer payment that reduces balance."""
52      self._balance -= amount
```

Code Fragment 2.2: The conclusion of the CreditCard class definition (continued from Code Fragment 2.1). These methods are indented within the class definition.

We draw attention to the difference between the method signature as declared within the class versus that used by a caller. For example, from a user's perspective we have seen that the get_balance method takes zero parameters, yet within the class definition, self is an explicit parameter. Likewise, the charge method is declared within the class having two parameters (self and price), even though this method is called with one parameter, for example, as my_card.charge(200). The interpretter automatically binds the instance upon which the method is invoked to the self parameter.

The Constructor

A user can create an instance of the CreditCard class using a syntax as:

cc = CreditCard('John Doe, '1st Bank', '5391 0375 9387 5309', 1000)

Internally, this results in a call to the specially named __init__ method that serves as the ***constructor*** of the class. Its primary responsibility is to establish the state of a newly created credit card object with appropriate instance variables. In the case of the CreditCard class, each object maintains five instance variables, which we name: _customer, _bank, _account, _limit, and _balance. The initial values for the first four of those five are provided as explicit parameters that are sent by the user when instantiating the credit card, and assigned within the body of the constructor. For example, the command, self._customer = customer, assigns the instance variable self._customer to the parameter customer; note that because customer is ***unqualified*** on the right-hand side, it refers to the parameter in the local namespace.

Encapsulation

By the conventions described in Section 2.2.3, a single leading underscore in the name of a data member, such as _balance, implies that it is intended as ***nonpublic***. Users of a class should not directly access such members.

As a general rule, we will treat all data members as nonpublic. This allows us to better enforce a consistent state for all instances. We can provide accessors, such as get_balance, to provide a user of our class read-only access to a trait. If we wish to allow the user to change the state, we can provide appropriate update methods. In the context of data structures, encapsulating the internal representation allows us greater flexibility to redesign the way a class works, perhaps to improve the efficiency of the structure.

Additional Methods

The most interesting behaviors in our class are charge and make_payment. The charge function typically adds the given price to the credit card balance, to reflect a purchase of said price by the customer. However, before accepting the charge, our implementation verifies that the new purchase would not cause the balance to exceed the credit limit. The make_payment charge reflects the customer sending payment to the bank for the given amount, thereby reducing the balance on the card. We note that in the command, self._balance −= amount, the expression self._balance is qualified with the self identifier because it represents an instance variable of the card, while the unqualified amount represents the local parameter.

Error Checking

Our implementation of the CreditCard class is not particularly robust. First, we note that we did not explicitly check the types of the parameters to charge and make_payment, nor any of the parameters to the constructor. If a user were to make a call such as visa.charge('candy'), our code would presumably crash when attempting to add that parameter to the current balance. If this class were to be widely used in a library, we might use more rigorous techniques to raise a TypeError when facing such misuse (see Section 1.7).

Beyond the obvious type errors, our implementation may be susceptible to logical errors. For example, if a user were allowed to charge a negative price, such as visa.charge(−300), that would serve to *lower* the customer's balance. This provides a loophole for lowering a balance without making a payment. Of course, this might be considered valid usage if modeling the credit received when a customer returns merchandise to a store. We will explore some such issues with the CreditCard class in the end-of-chapter exercises.

Testing the Class

In Code Fragment 2.3, we demonstrate some basic usage of the CreditCard class, inserting three cards into a list named wallet. We use loops to make some charges and payments, and use various accessors to print results to the console.

These tests are enclosed within a conditional, **if** `__name__` == `'__main__'`:, so that they can be embedded in the source code with the class definition. Using the terminology of Section 2.2.4, these tests provide *method coverage*, as each of the methods is called at least once, but it does not provide *statement coverage*, as there is never a case in which a charge is rejected due to the credit limit. This is not a particular advanced from of testing as the output of the given tests must be manually audited in order to determine whether the class behaved as expected. Python has tools for more formal testing (see discussion of the unittest module in Section 2.2.4), so that resulting values can be automatically compared to the predicted outcomes, with output generated only when an error is detected.

```
53  if __name__ == '__main__':
54    wallet = [ ]
55    wallet.append(CreditCard('John Bowman', 'California Savings',
56                             '5391 0375 9387 5309', 2500) )
57    wallet.append(CreditCard('John Bowman', 'California Federal',
58                             '3485 0399 3395 1954', 3500) )
59    wallet.append(CreditCard('John Bowman', 'California Finance',
60                             '5391 0375 9387 5309', 5000) )
61
62    for val in range(1, 17):
63      wallet[0].charge(val)
64      wallet[1].charge(2*val)
65      wallet[2].charge(3*val)
66
67    for c in range(3):
68      print('Customer =', wallet[c].get_customer())
69      print('Bank =', wallet[c].get_bank())
70      print('Account =', wallet[c].get_account())
71      print('Limit =', wallet[c].get_limit())
72      print('Balance =', wallet[c].get_balance())
73      while wallet[c].get_balance( ) > 100:
74        wallet[c].make_payment(100)
75        print('New balance =', wallet[c].get_balance())
76      print( )
```

Code Fragment 2.3: Testing the CreditCard class.

2.3.2   Operator Overloading and Python's Special Methods

Python's built-in classes provide natural semantics for many operators. For example, the syntax a + b invokes addition for numeric types, yet concatenation for sequence types. When defining a new class, we must consider whether a syntax like a + b should be defined when a or b is an instance of that class.

By default, the + operator is undefined for a new class. However, the author of a class may provide a definition using a technique known as *operator overloading*. This is done by implementing a specially named method. In particular, the + operator is overloaded by implementing a method named __add__, which takes the right-hand operand as a parameter and which returns the result of the expression. That is, the syntax, a + b, is converted to a method call on object a of the form, a.__add__(b). Similar specially named methods exist for other operators. Table 2.1 provides a comprehensive list of such methods.

When a binary operator is applied to two instances of different types, as in 3 * 'love me', Python gives deference to the class of the *left* operand. In this example, it would effectively check if the int class provides a sufficient definition for how to multiply an instance by a string, via the __mul__ method. However, if that class does not implement such a behavior, Python checks the class definition for the right-hand operand, in the form of a special method named __rmul__ (i.e., "right multiply"). This provides a way for a new user-defined class to support mixed operations that involve an instance of an existing class (given that the existing class would presumably not have defined a behavior involving this new class). The distinction between __mul__ and __rmul__ also allows a class to define different semantics in cases, such as matrix multiplication, in which an operation is noncommutative (that is, A * x may differ from x * A).

Non-Operator Overloads

In addition to traditional operator overloading, Python relies on specially named methods to control the behavior of various other functionality, when applied to user-defined classes. For example, the syntax, str(foo), is formally a call to the constructor for the string class. Of course, if the parameter is an instance of a user-defined class, the original authors of the string class could not have known how that instance should be portrayed. So the string constructor calls a specially named method, foo.__str__(), that must return an appropriate string representation.

Similar special methods are used to determine how to construct an int, float, or bool based on a parameter from a user-defined class. The conversion to a Boolean value is particularly important, because the syntax, **if** foo:, can be used even when foo is not formally a Boolean value (see Section 1.4.1). For a user-defined class, that condition is evaluated by the special method foo.__bool__().

Common Syntax	Special Method Form
a + b	a.__add__(b); alternatively b.__radd__(a)
a − b	a.__sub__(b); alternatively b.__rsub__(a)
a * b	a.__mul__(b); alternatively b.__rmul__(a)
a / b	a.__truediv__(b); alternatively b.__rtruediv__(a)
a // b	a.__floordiv__(b); alternatively b.__rfloordiv__(a)
a % b	a.__mod__(b); alternatively b.__rmod__(a)
a ** b	a.__pow__(b); alternatively b.__rpow__(a)
a << b	a.__lshift__(b); alternatively b.__rlshift__(a)
a >> b	a.__rshift__(b); alternatively b.__rrshift__(a)
a & b	a.__and__(b); alternatively b.__rand__(a)
a ^ b	a.__xor__(b); alternatively b.__rxor__(a)
a | b	a.__or__(b); alternatively b.__ror__(a)
a += b	a.__iadd__(b)
a −= b	a.__isub__(b)
a *= b	a.__imul__(b)
...	...
+a	a.__pos__()
−a	a.__neg__()
~a	a.__invert__()
abs(a)	a.__abs__()
a < b	a.__lt__(b)
a <= b	a.__le__(b)
a > b	a.__gt__(b)
a >= b	a.__ge__(b)
a == b	a.__eq__(b)
a != b	a.__ne__(b)
v in a	a.__contains__(v)
a[k]	a.__getitem__(k)
a[k] = v	a.__setitem__(k,v)
del a[k]	a.__delitem__(k)
a(arg1, arg2, ...)	a.__call__(arg1, arg2, ...)
len(a)	a.__len__()
hash(a)	a.__hash__()
iter(a)	a.__iter__()
next(a)	a.__next__()
bool(a)	a.__bool__()
float(a)	a.__float__()
int(a)	a.__int__()
repr(a)	a.__repr__()
reversed(a)	a.__reversed__()
str(a)	a.__str__()

Table 2.1: Overloaded operations, implemented with Python's special methods.

Several other top-level functions rely on calling specially named methods. For example, the standard way to determine the size of a container type is by calling the top-level len function. Note well that the calling syntax, len(foo), is not the traditional method-calling syntax with the dot operator. However, in the case of a user-defined class, the top-level len function relies on a call to a specially named __len__ method of that class. That is, the call len(foo) is evaluated through a method call, foo.__len__(). When developing data structures, we will routinely define the __len__ method to return a measure of the size of the structure.

Implied Methods

As a general rule, if a particular special method is not implemented in a user-defined class, the standard syntax that relies upon that method will raise an exception. For example, evaluating the expression, a + b, for instances of a user-defined class without __add__ or __radd__ will raise an error.

However, there are some operators that have default definitions provided by Python, in the absence of special methods, and there are some operators whose definitions are derived from others. For example, the __bool__ method, which supports the syntax **if** foo:, has default semantics so that every object other than None is evaluated as True. However, for container types, the __len__ method is typically defined to return the size of the container. If such a method exists, then the evaluation of bool(foo) is interpreted by default to be True for instances with nonzero length, and False for instances with zero length, allowing a syntax such as **if** waitlist: to be used to test whether there are one or more entries in the waitlist.

In Section 2.3.4, we will discuss Python's mechanism for providing iterators for collections via the special method, __iter__. With that said, if a container class provides implementations for both __len__ and __getitem__, a default iteration is provided automatically (using means we describe in Section 2.3.4). Furthermore, once an iterator is defined, default functionality of __contains__ is provided.

In Section 1.3 we drew attention to the distinction between expression a **is** b and expression a == b, with the former evaluating whether identifiers a and b are aliases for the same object, and the latter testing a notion of whether the two identifiers reference *equivalent* values. The notion of "equivalence" depends upon the context of the class, and semantics is defined with the __eq__ method. However, if no implementation is given for __eq__, the syntax a == b is legal with semantics of a **is** b, that is, an instance is equivalent to itself and no others.

We should caution that some natural implications are *not* automatically provided by Python. For example, the __eq__ method supports syntax a == b, but providing that method does not affect the evaluation of syntax a != b. (The __ne__ method should be provided, typically returning **not** (a == b) as a result.) Similarly, providing a __lt__ method supports syntax a < b, and indirectly b > a, but providing both __lt__ and __eq__ does *not* imply semantics for a <= b.

2.3.3 Example: Multidimensional Vector Class

To demonstrate the use of operator overloading via special methods, we provide an implementation of a Vector class, representing the coordinates of a vector in a multidimensional space. For example, in a three-dimensional space, we might wish to represent a vector with coordinates $\langle 5, -2, 3 \rangle$. Although it might be tempting to directly use a Python list to represent those coordinates, a list does not provide an appropriate abstraction for a geometric vector. In particular, if using lists, the expression [5, −2, 3] + [1, 4, 2] results in the list [5, −2, 3, 1, 4, 2]. When working with vectors, if $u = \langle 5, -2, 3 \rangle$ and $v = \langle 1, 4, 2 \rangle$, one would expect the expression, u + v, to return a three-dimensional vector with coordinates $\langle 6, 2, 5 \rangle$.

We therefore define a Vector class, in Code Fragment 2.4, that provides a better abstraction for the notion of a geometric vector. Internally, our vector relies upon an instance of a list, named _coords, as its storage mechanism. By keeping the internal list encapsulated, we can enforce the desired public interface for instances of our class. A demonstration of supported behaviors includes the following:

```
v = Vector(5)              # construct five-dimensional <0, 0, 0, 0, 0>
v[1] = 23                  # <0, 23, 0, 0, 0> (based on use of __setitem__)
v[−1] = 45                 # <0, 23, 0, 0, 45> (also via __setitem__)
print(v[4])                # print 45 (via __getitem__)
u = v + v                  # <0, 46, 0, 0, 90> (via __add__)
print(u)                   # print <0, 46, 0, 0, 90>
total = 0
for entry in v:            # implicit iteration via __len__ and __getitem__
    total += entry
```

We implement many of the behaviors by trivially invoking a similar behavior on the underlying list of coordinates. However, our implementation of __add__ is customized. Assuming the two operands are vectors with the same length, this method creates a new vector and sets the coordinates of the new vector to be equal to the respective sum of the operands' elements.

It is interesting to note that the class definition, as given in Code Fragment 2.4, automatically supports the syntax u = v + [5, 3, 10, −2, 1], resulting in a new vector that is the element-by-element "sum" of the first vector and the list instance. This is a result of Python's **polymorphism**. Literally, "polymorphism" means "many forms." Although it is tempting to think of the other parameter of our __add__ method as another Vector instance, we never declared it as such. Within the body, the only behaviors we rely on for parameter other is that it supports len(other) and access to other[j]. Therefore, our code executes when the right-hand operand is a list of numbers (with matching length).

```
 1  class Vector:
 2    """Represent a vector in a multidimensional space."""
 3
 4    def __init__(self, d):
 5      """Create d-dimensional vector of zeros."""
 6      self._coords = [0] * d
 7
 8    def __len__(self):
 9      """Return the dimension of the vector."""
10      return len(self._coords)
11
12    def __getitem__(self, j):
13      """Return jth coordinate of vector."""
14      return self._coords[j]
15
16    def __setitem__(self, j, val):
17      """Set jth coordinate of vector to given value."""
18      self._coords[j] = val
19
20    def __add__(self, other):
21      """Return sum of two vectors."""
22      if len(self) != len(other):              # relies on __len__ method
23        raise ValueError('dimensions must agree')
24      result = Vector(len(self))               # start with vector of zeros
25      for j in range(len(self)):
26        result[j] = self[j] + other[j]
27      return result
28
29    def __eq__(self, other):
30      """Return True if vector has same coordinates as other."""
31      return self._coords == other._coords
32
33    def __ne__(self, other):
34      """Return True if vector differs from other."""
35      return not self == other                 # rely on existing __eq__ definition
36
37    def __str__(self):
38      """Produce string representation of vector."""
39      return '<' + str(self._coords)[1:-1] + '>'   # adapt list representation
```

Code Fragment 2.4: Definition of a simple Vector class.

2.3.4 Iterators

Iteration is an important concept in the design of data structures. We introduced Python's mechanism for iteration in Section 1.8. In short, an ***iterator*** for a collection provides one key behavior: It supports a special method named __next__ that returns the next element of the collection, if any, or raises a StopIteration exception to indicate that there are no further elements.

Fortunately, it is rare to have to directly implement an iterator class. Our preferred approach is the use of the ***generator*** syntax (also described in Section 1.8), which automatically produces an iterator of yielded values.

Python also helps by providing an automatic iterator implementation for any class that defines both __len__ and __getitem__. To provide an instructive example of a low-level iterator, Code Fragment 2.5 demonstrates just such an iterator class that works on any collection that supports both __len__ and __getitem__. This class can be instantiated as SequenceIterator(data). It operates by keeping an internal reference to the data sequence, as well as a current index into the sequence. Each time __next__ is called, the index is incremented, until reaching the end of the sequence.

```
 1  class SequenceIterator:
 2    """An iterator for any of Python's sequence types."""
 3
 4    def __init__(self, sequence):
 5      """Create an iterator for the given sequence."""
 6      self._seq = sequence             # keep a reference to the underlying data
 7      self._k = -1                     # will increment to 0 on first call to next
 8
 9    def __next__(self):
10      """Return the next element, or else raise StopIteration error."""
11      self._k += 1                     # advance to next index
12      if self._k < len(self._seq):
13        return(self._seq[self._k])     # return the data element
14      else:
15        raise StopIteration( )         # there are no more elements
16
17    def __iter__(self):
18      """By convention, an iterator must return itself as an iterator."""
19      return self
```

Code Fragment 2.5: An iterator class for any sequence type.

2.3.5   Example: Range Class

As the final example for this section, we develop our own implementation of a class that mimics Python's built-in range class. Before introducing our class, we discuss the history of the built-in version. Prior to Python 3 being released, range was implemented as a function, and it returned a list instance with elements in the specified range. For example, range(2, 10, 2) returned the list [2, 4, 6, 8]. However, a typical use of the function was to support a for-loop syntax, such as **for** k **in** range(10000000). Unfortunately, this caused the instantiation and initialization of a list with the range of numbers. That was an unnecessarily expensive step, in terms of both time and memory usage.

The mechanism used to support ranges in Python 3 is entirely different (to be fair, the "new" behavior existed in Python 2 under the name xrange). It uses a strategy known as *lazy evaluation*. Rather than creating a new list instance, range is a class that can effectively represent the desired range of elements without ever storing them explicitly in memory. To better explore the built-in range class, we recommend that you create an instance as r = range(8, 140, 5). The result is a relatively lightweight object, an instance of the range class, that has only a few behaviors. The syntax len(r) will report the number of elements that are in the given range (27, in our example). A range also supports the __getitem__ method, so that syntax r[15] reports the sixteenth element in the range (as r[0] is the first element). Because the class supports both __len__ and __getitem__, it inherits automatic support for iteration (see Section 2.3.4), which is why it is possible to execute a for loop over a range.

At this point, we are ready to demonstrate our own version of such a class. Code Fragment 2.6 provides a class we name Range (so as to clearly differentiate it from built-in range). The biggest challenge in the implementation is properly computing the number of elements that belong in the range, given the parameters sent by the caller when constructing a range. By computing that value in the constructor, and storing it as self._length, it becomes trivial to return it from the __len__ method. To properly implement a call to __getitem__(k), we simply take the starting value of the range plus k times the step size (i.e., for k=0, we return the start value). There are a few subtleties worth examining in the code:

- To properly support optional parameters, we rely on the technique described on page 27, when discussing a functional version of range.

- We compute the number of elements in the range as
  max(0, (stop − start + step − 1) // step)
  It is worth testing this formula for both positive and negative step sizes.

- The __getitem__ method properly supports negative indices by converting an index −k to len(self)−k before computing the result.

```
1  class Range:
2    """ A class that mimic's the built-in range class."""
3
4    def __init__(self, start, stop=None, step=1):
5      """ Initialize a Range instance.
6
7      Semantics is similar to built-in range class.
8      """
9      if step == 0:
10       raise ValueError('step cannot be 0')
11
12     if stop is None:                     # special case of range(n)
13       start, stop = 0, start             # should be treated as if range(0,n)
14
15     # calculate the effective length once
16     self._length = max(0, (stop - start + step - 1) // step)
17
18     # need knowledge of start and step (but not stop) to support __getitem__
19     self._start = start
20     self._step = step
21
22   def __len__(self):
23     """ Return number of entries in the range."""
24     return self._length
25
26   def __getitem__(self, k):
27     """ Return entry at index k (using standard interpretation if negative)."""
28     if k < 0:
29       k += len(self)                     # attempt to convert negative index
30
31     if not 0 <= k < self._length:
32       raise IndexError('index out of range')
33
34     return self._start + k * self._step
```

Code Fragment 2.6: Our own implementation of a Range class.

2.4   Inheritance

A natural way to organize various structural components of a software package is in a *hierarchical* fashion, with similar abstract definitions grouped together in a level-by-level manner that goes from specific to more general as one traverses up the hierarchy. An example of such a hierarchy is shown in Figure 2.4. Using mathematical notations, the set of houses is a *subset* of the set of buildings, but a *superset* of the set of ranches. The correspondence between levels is often referred to as an *"is a" relationship*, as a house is a building, and a ranch is a house.

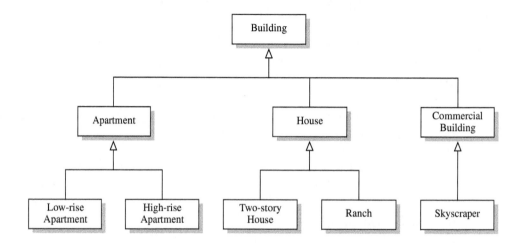

Figure 2.4: An example of an "is a" hierarchy involving architectural buildings.

A hierarchical design is useful in software development, as common functionality can be grouped at the most general level, thereby promoting reuse of code, while differentiated behaviors can be viewed as extensions of the general case, In object-oriented programming, the mechanism for a modular and hierarchical organization is a technique known as *inheritance*. This allows a new class to be defined based upon an existing class as the starting point. In object-oriented terminology, the existing class is typically described as the *base class*, *parent class*, or *superclass*, while the newly defined class is known as the *subclass* or *child class*.

There are two ways in which a subclass can differentiate itself from its superclass. A subclass may *specialize* an existing behavior by providing a new implementation that *overrides* an existing method. A subclass may also *extend* its superclass by providing brand new methods.

Python's Exception Hierarchy

Another example of a rich inheritance hierarchy is the organization of various exception types in Python. We introduced many of those classes in Section 1.7, but did not discuss their relationship with each other. Figure 2.5 illustrates a (small) portion of that hierarchy. The BaseException class is the root of the entire hierarchy, while the more specific Exception class includes most of the error types that we have discussed. Programmers are welcome to define their own special exception classes to denote errors that may occur in the context of their application. Those user-defined exception types should be declared as subclasses of Exception.

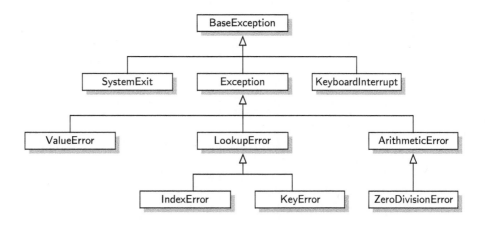

Figure 2.5: A portion of Python's hierarchy of exception types.

2.4.1   Extending the CreditCard Class

To demonstrate the mechanisms for inheritance in Python, we revisit the CreditCard class of Section 2.3, implementing a subclass that, for lack of a better name, we name PredatoryCreditCard. The new class will differ from the original in two ways: (1) if an attempted charge is rejected because it would have exceeded the credit limit, a $5 fee will be charged, and (2) there will be a mechanism for assessing a monthly interest charge on the outstanding balance, based upon an Annual Percentage Rate (APR) specified as a constructor parameter.

In accomplishing this goal, we demonstrate the techniques of specialization and extension. To charge a fee for an invalid charge attempt, we *override* the existing charge method, thereby specializing it to provide the new functionality (although the new version takes advantage of a call to the overridden version). To provide support for charging interest, we extend the class with a new method named process_month.

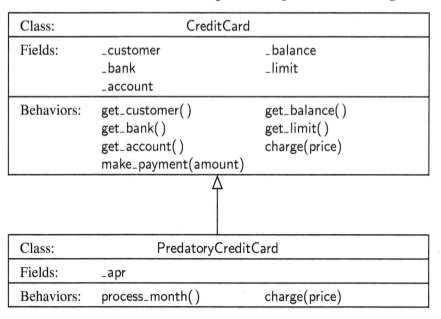

Figure 2.6: Diagram of an inheritance relationship.

Figure 2.6 provides an overview of our use of inheritance in designing the new PredatoryCreditCard class, and Code Fragment 2.7 gives a complete Python implementation of that class.

To indicate that the new class inherits from the existing CreditCard class, our definition begins with the syntax, **class** PredatoryCreditCard(CreditCard). The body of the new class provides three member functions: __init__, charge, and process_month. The __init__ constructor serves a very similar role to the original CreditCard constructor, except that for our new class, there is an extra parameter to specify the annual percentage rate. The body of our new constructor relies upon making a call to the inherited constructor to perform most of the initialization (in fact, everything other than the recording of the percentage rate). The mechanism for calling the inherited constructor relies on the syntax, **super**(). Specifically, at line 15 the command

super().__init__(customer, bank, acnt, limit)

calls the __init__ method that was inherited from the CreditCard superclass. Note well that this method only accepts four parameters. We record the APR value in a new field named _apr.

In similar fashion, our PredatoryCreditCard class provides a new implementation of the charge method that overrides the inherited method. Yet, our implementation of the new method relies on a call to the inherited method, with syntax **super**().charge(price) at line 24. The return value of that call designates whether

```
1  class PredatoryCreditCard(CreditCard):
2    """An extension to CreditCard that compounds interest and fees."""
3
4    def __init__(self, customer, bank, acnt, limit, apr):
5      """Create a new predatory credit card instance.
6
7      The initial balance is zero.
8
9      customer  the name of the customer (e.g., 'John Bowman')
10     bank      the name of the bank (e.g., 'California Savings')
11     acnt      the acount identifier (e.g., '5391 0375 9387 5309')
12     limit     credit limit (measured in dollars)
13     apr       annual percentage rate (e.g., 0.0825 for 8.25% APR)
14     """
15     super().__init__(customer, bank, acnt, limit)    # call super constructor
16     self._apr = apr
17
18   def charge(self, price):
19     """Charge given price to the card, assuming sufficient credit limit.
20
21     Return True if charge was processed.
22     Return False and assess $5 fee if charge is denied.
23     """
24     success = super().charge(price)              # call inherited method
25     if not success:
26       self._balance += 5                         # assess penalty
27     return success                               # caller expects return value
28
29   def process_month(self):
30     """Assess monthly interest on outstanding balance."""
31     if self._balance > 0:
32       # if positive balance, convert APR to monthly multiplicative factor
33       monthly_factor = pow(1 + self._apr, 1/12)
34       self._balance *= monthly_factor
```

Code Fragment 2.7: A subclass of CreditCard that assesses interest and fees.

the charge was successful. We examine that return value to decide whether to assess a fee, and in turn we return that value to the caller of method, so that the new version of charge has a similar outward interface as the original.

The process_month method is a new behavior, so there is no inherited version upon which to rely. In our model, this method should be invoked by the bank, once each month, to add new interest charges to the customer's balance. The most challenging aspect in implementing this method is making sure we have working knowledge of how an annual percentage rate translates to a monthly rate. We do not simply divide the annual rate by twelve to get a monthly rate (that would be too predatory, as it would result in a higher APR than advertised). The correct computation is to take the twelfth-root of $1 + \text{self.\_apr}$, and use that as a multiplicative factor. For example, if the APR is 0.0825 (representing 8.25%), we compute $\sqrt[12]{1.0825} \approx 1.006628$, and therefore charge 0.6628% interest per month. In this way, each $100 of debt will amass $8.25 of compounded interest in a year.

Protected Members

Our PredatoryCreditCard subclass directly accesses the data member self._balance, which was established by the parent CreditCard class. The underscored name, by convention, suggests that this is a *nonpublic* member, so we might ask if it is okay that we access it in this fashion. While general users of the class should not be doing so, our subclass has a somewhat privileged relationship with the superclass. Several object-oriented languages (e.g., Java, C++) draw a distinction for nonpublic members, allowing declarations of *protected* or *private* access modes. Members that are declared as protected are accessible to subclasses, but not to the general public, while members that are declared as private are not accessible to either. In this respect, we are using _balance as if it were protected (but not private).

Python does not support formal access control, but names beginning with a single underscore are conventionally akin to protected, while names beginning with a double underscore (other than special methods) are akin to private. In choosing to use protected data, we have created a dependency in that our PredatoryCreditCard class might be compromised if the author of the CreditCard class were to change the internal design. Note that we could have relied upon the public get_balance( ) method to retrieve the current balance within the process_month method. But the current design of the CreditCard class does not afford an effective way for a subclass to change the balance, other than by direct manipulation of the data member. It may be tempting to use charge to add fees or interest to the balance. However, that method does not allow the balance to go above the customer's credit limit, even though a bank would presumably let interest compound beyond the credit limit, if warranted. If we were to redesign the original CreditCard class, we might add a nonpublic method, _set_balance, that could be used by subclasses to affect a change without directly accessing the data member _balance.

2.4.2 Hierarchy of Numeric Progressions

As a second example of the use of inheritance, we develop a hierarchy of classes for iterating numeric progressions. A numeric progression is a sequence of numbers, where each number depends on one or more of the previous numbers. For example, an ***arithmetic progression*** determines the next number by adding a fixed constant to the previous value, and a ***geometric progression*** determines the next number by multiplying the previous value by a fixed constant. In general, a progression requires a first value, and a way of identifying a new value based on one or more previous values.

To maximize reusability of code, we develop a hierarchy of classes stemming from a general base class that we name Progression (see Figure 2.7). Technically, the Progression class produces the progression of whole numbers: 0, 1, 2, ... However, this class is designed to serve as the base class for other progression types, providing as much common functionality as possible, and thereby minimizing the burden on the subclasses.

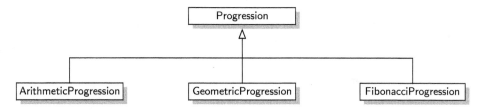

Figure 2.7: Our hierarchy of progression classes.

Our implementation of the basic Progression class is provided in Code Fragment 2.8. The constructor for this class accepts a starting value for the progression (0 by default), and initializes a data member, self._current, to that value.

The Progression class implements the conventions of a Python ***iterator*** (see Section 2.3.4), namely the special __next__ and __iter__ methods. If a user of the class creates a progression as seq = Progression( ), each call to next(seq) will return a subsequent element of the progression sequence. It would also be possible to use a for-loop syntax, **for** value **in** seq:, although we note that our default progression is defined as an infinite sequence.

To better separate the mechanics of the iterator convention from the core logic of advancing the progression, our framework relies on a nonpublic method named _advance to update the value of the self._current field. In the default implementation, _advance adds one to the current value, but our intent is that subclasses will override _advance to provide a different rule for computing the next entry.

For convenience, the Progression class also provides a utility method, named print_progression, that displays the next *n* values of the progression.

```
 1  class Progression:
 2    """Iterator producing a generic progression.
 3
 4    Default iterator produces the whole numbers 0, 1, 2, ...
 5    """
 6
 7    def __init__(self, start=0):
 8      """Initialize current to the first value of the progression."""
 9      self._current = start
10
11    def _advance(self):
12      """Update self._current to a new value.
13
14      This should be overridden by a subclass to customize progression.
15
16      By convention, if current is set to None, this designates the
17      end of a finite progression.
18      """
19      self._current += 1
20
21    def __next__(self):
22      """Return the next element, or else raise StopIteration error."""
23      if self._current is None:          # our convention to end a progression
24        raise StopIteration()
25      else:
26        answer = self._current           # record current value to return
27        self._advance()                  # advance to prepare for next time
28        return answer                    # return the answer
29
30    def __iter__(self):
31      """By convention, an iterator must return itself as an iterator."""
32      return self
33
34    def print_progression(self, n):
35      """Print next n values of the progression."""
36      print(' '.join(str(next(self)) for j in range(n)))
```

Code Fragment 2.8: A general numeric progression class.

An Arithmetic Progression Class

Our first example of a specialized progression is an arithmetic progression. While the default progression increases its value by one in each step, an arithmetic progression adds a fixed constant to one term of the progression to produce the next. For example, using an increment of 4 for an arithmetic progression that starts at 0 results in the sequence $0, 4, 8, 12, \ldots$.

Code Fragment 2.9 presents our implementation of an ArithmeticProgression class, which relies on Progression as its base class. The constructor for this new class accepts both an increment value and a starting value as parameters, although default values for each are provided. By our convention, ArithmeticProgression(4) produces the sequence $0, 4, 8, 12, \ldots$, and ArithmeticProgression(4, 1) produces the sequence $1, 5, 9, 13, \ldots$.

The body of the ArithmeticProgression constructor calls the super constructor to initialize the _current data member to the desired start value. Then it directly establishes the new _increment data member for the arithmetic progression. The only remaining detail in our implementation is to override the _advance method so as to add the increment to the current value.

```
1  class ArithmeticProgression(Progression):          # inherit from Progression
2    """ Iterator producing an arithmetic progression."""
3
4    def __init__(self, increment=1, start=0):
5      """ Create a new arithmetic progression.
6
7      increment   the fixed constant to add to each term (default 1)
8      start         the first term of the progression (default 0)
9      """
10     super().__init__(start)                           # initialize base class
11     self._increment = increment
12
13    def _advance(self):                                 # override inherited version
14      """ Update current value by adding the fixed increment."""
15      self._current += self._increment
```

Code Fragment 2.9: A class that produces an arithmetic progression.

A Geometric Progression Class

Our second example of a specialized progression is a geometric progression, in which each value is produced by multiplying the preceding value by a fixed constant, known as the **base** of the geometric progression. The starting point of a geometric progression is traditionally 1, rather than 0, because multiplying 0 by any factor results in 0. As an example, a geometric progression with base 2 proceeds as $1, 2, 4, 8, 16, \ldots$.

Code Fragment 2.10 presents our implementation of a GeometricProgression class. The constructor uses 2 as a default base and 1 as a default starting value, but either of those can be varied using optional parameters.

```
1   class GeometricProgression(Progression):          # inherit from Progression
2       """Iterator producing a geometric progression."""
3
4       def __init__(self, base=2, start=1):
5           """Create a new geometric progression.
6
7           base        the fixed constant multiplied to each term (default 2)
8           start       the first term of the progression (default 1)
9           """
10          super().__init__(start)
11          self._base = base
12
13      def _advance(self):                            # override inherited version
14          """Update current value by multiplying it by the base value."""
15          self._current *= self._base
```

Code Fragment 2.10: A class that produces a geometric progression.

A Fibonacci Progression Class

As our final example, we demonstrate how to use our progression framework to produce a **Fibonacci progression**. We originally discussed the Fibonacci series on page 41 in the context of generators. Each value of a Fibonacci series is the sum of the two most recent values. To begin the series, the first two values are conventionally 0 and 1, leading to the Fibonacci series $0, 1, 1, 2, 3, 5, 8, \ldots$. More generally, such a series can be generated from any two starting values. For example, if we start with values 4 and 6, the series proceeds as $4, 6, 10, 16, 26, 42, \ldots$.

```
1  class FibonacciProgression(Progression):
2    """Iterator producing a generalized Fibonacci progression."""
3
4    def __init__(self, first=0, second=1):
5      """Create a new fibonacci progression.
6
7      first       the first term of the progression (default 0)
8      second      the second term of the progression (default 1)
9      """
10     super().__init__(first)                # start progression at first
11     self._prev = second − first            # fictitious value preceding the first
12
13   def _advance(self):
14     """Update current value by taking sum of previous two."""
15     self._prev, self._current = self._current, self._prev + self._current
```

Code Fragment 2.11: A class that produces a Fibonacci progression.

We use our progression framework to define a new FibonacciProgression class, as shown in Code Fragment 2.11. This class is markedly different from those for the arithmetic and geometric progressions because we cannot determine the next value of a Fibonacci series solely from the current one. We must maintain knowledge of the two most recent values. The base Progression class already provides storage of the most recent value as the _current data member. Our FibonacciProgression class introduces a new member, named _prev, to store the value that proceeded the current one.

With both previous values stored, the implementation of _advance is relatively straightforward. (We use a simultaneous assignment similar to that on page 45.) However, the question arises as to how to initialize the previous value in the constructor. The desired first and second values are provided as parameters to the constructor. The first should be stored as _current so that it becomes the first one that is reported. Looking ahead, once the first value is reported, we will do an assignment to set the new current value (which will be the second value reported), equal to the first value plus the "previous." By initializing the previous value to (second − first), the initial advancement will set the new current value to first + (second − first) = second, as desired.

Testing Our Progressions

To complete our presentation, Code Fragment 2.12 provides a unit test for all of our progression classes, and Code Fragment 2.13 shows the output of that test.

```
if __name__ == '__main__':
  print('Default progression:')
  Progression().print_progression(10)

  print('Arithmetic progression with increment 5:')
  ArithmeticProgression(5).print_progression(10)

  print('Arithmetic progression with increment 5 and start 2:')
  ArithmeticProgression(5, 2).print_progression(10)

  print('Geometric progression with default base:')
  GeometricProgression().print_progression(10)

  print('Geometric progression with base 3:')
  GeometricProgression(3).print_progression(10)

  print('Fibonacci progression with default start values:')
  FibonacciProgression().print_progression(10)

  print('Fibonacci progression with start values 4 and 6:')
  FibonacciProgression(4, 6).print_progression(10)
```

Code Fragment 2.12: Unit tests for our progression classes.

```
Default progression:
0 1 2 3 4 5 6 7 8 9
Arithmetic progression with increment 5:
0 5 10 15 20 25 30 35 40 45
Arithmetic progression with increment 5 and start 2:
2 7 12 17 22 27 32 37 42 47
Geometric progression with default base:
1 2 4 8 16 32 64 128 256 512
Geometric progression with base 3:
1 3 9 27 81 243 729 2187 6561 19683
Fibonacci progression with default start values:
0 1 1 2 3 5 8 13 21 34
Fibonacci progression with start values 4 and 6:
4 6 10 16 26 42 68 110 178 288
```

Code Fragment 2.13: Output of the unit tests from Code Fragment 2.12.

2.4.3 Abstract Base Classes

When defining a group of classes as part of an inheritance hierarchy, one technique for avoiding repetition of code is to design a base class with common functionality that can be inherited by other classes that need it. As an example, the hierarchy from Section 2.4.2 includes a Progression class, which serves as a base class for three distinct subclasses: ArithmeticProgression, GeometricProgression, and FibonacciProgression. Although it is possible to create an instance of the Progression base class, there is little value in doing so because its behavior is simply a special case of an ArithmeticProgression with increment 1. The real purpose of the Progression class was to centralize the implementations of behaviors that other progressions needed, thereby streamlining the code that is relegated to those subclasses.

In classic object-oriented terminology, we say a class is an ***abstract base class*** if its only purpose is to serve as a base class through inheritance. More formally, an abstract base class is one that cannot be directly instantiated, while a ***concrete class*** is one that can be instantiated. By this definition, our Progression class is technically concrete, although we essentially designed it as an abstract base class.

In statically typed languages such as Java and C++, an abstract base class serves as a formal type that may guarantee one or more ***abstract methods***. This provides support for polymorphism, as a variable may have an abstract base class as its declared type, even though it refers to an instance of a concrete subclass. Because there are no declared types in Python, this kind of polymorphism can be accomplished without the need for a unifying abstract base class. For this reason, there is not as strong a tradition of defining abstract base classes in Python, although Python's abc module provides support for defining a formal abstract base class.

Our reason for focusing on abstract base classes in our study of data structures is that Python's collections module provides several abstract base classes that assist when defining custom data structures that share a common interface with some of Python's built-in data structures. These rely on an object-oriented software design pattern known as the ***template method pattern***. The template method pattern is when an abstract base class provides concrete behaviors that rely upon calls to other abstract behaviors. In that way, as soon as a subclass provides definitions for the missing abstract behaviors, the inherited concrete behaviors are well defined.

As a tangible example, the collections.Sequence abstract base class defines behaviors common to Python's list, str, and tuple classes, as sequences that support element access via an integer index. More so, the collections.Sequence class provides concrete implementations of methods, count, index, and __contains__ that can be inherited by any class that provides concrete implementations of both __len__ and __getitem__. For the purpose of illustration, we provide a sample implementation of such a Sequence abstract base class in Code Fragment 2.14.

```
1    from abc import ABCMeta, abstractmethod          # need these definitions
2
3    class Sequence(metaclass=ABCMeta):
4      """Our own version of collections.Sequence abstract base class."""
5
6      @abstractmethod
7      def __len__(self):
8        """Return the length of the sequence."""
9
10     @abstractmethod
11     def __getitem__(self, j):
12       """Return the element at index j of the sequence."""
13
14     def __contains__(self, val):
15       """Return True if val found in the sequence; False otherwise."""
16       for j in range(len(self)):
17         if self[j] == val:                         # found match
18           return True
19       return False
20
21     def index(self, val):
22       """Return leftmost index at which val is found (or raise ValueError)."""
23       for j in range(len(self)):
24         if self[j] == val:                         # leftmost match
25           return j
26       raise ValueError('value not in sequence')    # never found a match
27
28     def count(self, val):
29       """Return the number of elements equal to given value."""
30       k = 0
31       for j in range(len(self)):
32         if self[j] == val:                         # found a match
33           k += 1
34       return k
```

Code Fragment 2.14: An abstract base class akin to collections.Sequence.

This implementation relies on two advanced Python techniques. The first is that we declare the ABCMeta class of the abc module as a ***metaclass*** of our Sequence class. A metaclass is different from a superclass, in that it provides a template for the class definition itself. Specifically, the ABCMeta declaration assures that the constructor for the class raises an error.

The second advanced technique is the use of the @abstractmethod decorator immediately before the __len__ and __getitem__ methods are declared. That declares these two particular methods to be abstract, meaning that we do not provide an implementation within our Sequence base class, but that we expect any concrete subclasses to support those two methods. Python enforces this expectation, by disallowing instantiation for any subclass that does not override the abstract methods with concrete implementations.

The rest of the Sequence class definition provides tangible implementations for other behaviors, under the assumption that the abstract __len__ and __getitem__ methods will exist in a concrete subclass. If you carefully examine the source code, the implementations of methods __contains__, index, and count do not rely on any assumption about the self instances, other than that syntax len(self) and self[j] are supported (by special methods __len__ and __getitem__, respectively). Support for iteration is automatic as well, as described in Section 2.3.4.

In the remainder of this book, we omit the formality of using the abc module. If we need an "abstract" base class, we simply document the expectation that subclasses provide assumed functionality, without technical declaration of the methods as abstract. But we will make use of the wonderful abstract base classes that are defined within the collections module (such as Sequence). To use such a class, we need only rely on standard inheritance techniques.

For example, our Range class, from Code Fragment 2.6 of Section 2.3.5, is an example of a class that supports the __len__ and __getitem__ methods. But that class does not support methods count or index. Had we originally declared it with Sequence as a superclass, then it would also inherit the count and index methods. The syntax for such a declaration would begin as:

class Range(collections.Sequence):

Finally, we emphasize that if a subclass provides its own implementation of an inherited behaviors from a base class, the new definition overrides the inherited one. This technique can be used when we have the ability to provide a more efficient implementation for a behavior than is achieved by the generic approach. As an example, the general implementation of __contains__ for a sequence is based on a loop used to search for the desired value. For our Range class, there is an opportunity for a more efficient determination of containment. For example, it is evident that the expression, 100000 **in** Range(0, 2000000, 100), should evaluate to True, even without examining the individual elements of the range, because the range starts with zero, has an increment of 100, and goes until 2 million; it must include 100000, as that is a multiple of 100 that is between the start and stop values. Exercise C-2.27 explores the goal of providing an implementation of Range.__contains__ that avoids the use of a (time-consuming) loop.

2.5   Namespaces and Object-Orientation

A *namespace* is an abstraction that manages all of the identifiers that are defined in a particular scope, mapping each name to its associated value. In Python, functions, classes, and modules are all first-class objects, and so the "value" associated with an identifier in a namespace may in fact be a function, class, or module.

In Section 1.10 we explored Python's use of namespaces to manage identifiers that are defined with global scope, versus those defined within the local scope of a function call. In this section, we discuss the important role of namespaces in Python's management of object-orientation.

2.5.1   Instance and Class Namespaces

We begin by exploring what is known as the *instance namespace*, which manages attributes specific to an individual object. For example, each instance of our CreditCard class maintains a distinct balance, a distinct account number, a distinct credit limit, and so on (even though some instances may coincidentally have equivalent balances, or equivalent credit limits). Each credit card will have a dedicated instance namespace to manage such values.

There is a separate *class namespace* for each class that has been defined. This namespace is used to manage members that are to be *shared* by all instances of a class, or used without reference to any particular instance. For example, the make_payment method of the CreditCard class from Section 2.3 is not stored independently by each instance of that class. That member function is stored within the namespace of the CreditCard class. Based on our definition from Code Fragments 2.1 and 2.2, the CreditCard class namespace includes the functions: __init__, get_customer, get_bank, get_account, get_balance, get_limit, charge, and make_payment. Our PredatoryCreditCard class has its own namespace, containing the three methods we defined for that subclass: __init__, charge, and process_month.

Figure 2.8 provides a portrayal of three such namespaces: a class namespace containing methods of the CreditCard class, another class namespace with methods of the PredatoryCreditCard class, and finally a single instance namespace for a sample instance of the PredatoryCreditCard class. We note that there are two different definitions of a function named charge, one in the CreditCard class, and then the overriding method in the PredatoryCreditCard class. In similar fashion, there are two distinct __init__ implementations. However, process_month is a name that is only defined within the scope of the PredatoryCreditCard class. The instance namespace includes all data members for the instance (including the _apr member that is established by the PredatoryCreditCard constructor).

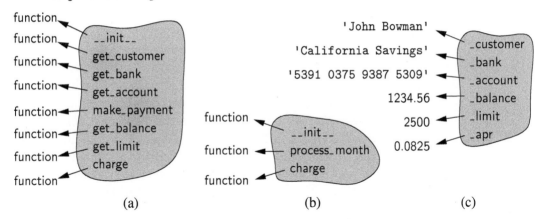

Figure 2.8: Conceptual view of three namespaces: (a) the class namespace for CreditCard; (b) the class namespace for PredatoryCreditCard; (c) the instance namespace for a PredatoryCreditCard object.

How Entries Are Established in a Namespace

It is important to understand why a member such as _balance resides in a credit card's instance namespace, while a member such as make_payment resides in the class namespace. The balance is established within the __init__ method when a new credit card instance is constructed. The original assignment uses the syntax, self._balance = 0, where self is an identifier for the newly constructed instance. The use of self as a qualifier for self._balance in such an assignment causes the _balance identifier to be added directly to the instance namespace.

When inheritance is used, there is still a single *instance namespace* per object. For example, when an instance of the PredatoryCreditCard class is constructed, the _apr attribute as well as attributes such as _balance and _limit all reside in that instance's namespace, because all are assigned using a qualified syntax, such as self._apr.

A *class namespace* includes all declarations that are made directly within the body of the class definition. For example, our CreditCard class definition included the following structure:

```
class CreditCard:
    def make_payment(self, amount):
        ...
```

Because the make_payment function is declared within the scope of the CreditCard class, that function becomes associated with the name make_payment within the CreditCard class namespace. Although member functions are the most typical types of entries that are declared in a class namespace, we next discuss how other types of data values, or even other classes can be declared within a class namespace.

Class Data Members

A class-level data member is often used when there is some value, such as a constant, that is to be shared by all instances of a class. In such a case, it would be unnecessarily wasteful to have each instance store that value in its instance namespace. As an example, we revisit the PredatoryCreditCard introduced in Section 2.4.1. That class assesses a $5 fee if an attempted charge is denied because of the credit limit. Our choice of $5 for the fee was somewhat arbitrary, and our coding style would be better if we used a named variable rather than embedding the literal value in our code. Often, the amount of such a fee is determined by the bank's policy and does not vary for each customer. In that case, we could define and use a class data member as follows:

```python
class PredatoryCreditCard(CreditCard):
    OVERLIMIT_FEE = 5                      # this is a class-level member

    def charge(self, price):
        success = super().charge(price)
        if not success:
            self._balance += PredatoryCreditCard.OVERLIMIT_FEE
        return success
```

The data member, OVERLIMIT_FEE, is entered into the PredatoryCreditCard class namespace because that assignment takes place within the immediate scope of the class definition, and without any qualifying identifier.

Nested Classes

It is also possible to nest one class definition within the scope of another class. This is a useful construct, which we will exploit several times in this book in the implementation of data structures. This can be done by using a syntax such as

```python
class A:          # the outer class
    class B:      # the nested class
        ...
```

In this case, class B is the nested class. The identifier B is entered into the namespace of class A associated with the newly defined class. We note that this technique is unrelated to the concept of inheritance, as class B does not inherit from class A.

Nesting one class in the scope of another makes clear that the nested class exists for support of the outer class. Furthermore, it can help reduce potential name conflicts, because it allows for a similarly named class to exist in another context. For example, we will later introduce a data structure known as a ***linked list*** and will define a nested node class to store the individual components of the list. We will also introduce a data structure known as a ***tree*** that depends upon its own nested node class. These two structures rely on different node definitions, and by nesting those within the respective container classes, we avoid ambiguity.

Another advantage of one class being nested as a member of another is that it allows for a more advanced form of inheritance in which a subclass of the outer class overrides the definition of its nested class. We will make use of that technique in Section 11.2.1 when specializing the nodes of a tree structure.

Dictionaries and the __slots__ Declaration

By default, Python represents each namespace with an instance of the built-in dict class (see Section 1.2.3) that maps identifying names in that scope to the associated objects. While a dictionary structure supports relatively efficient name lookups, it requires additional memory usage beyond the raw data that it stores (we will explore the data structure used to implement dictionaries in Chapter 10).

Python provides a more direct mechanism for representing instance namespaces that avoids the use of an auxiliary dictionary. To use the streamlined representation for all instances of a class, that class definition must provide a class-level member named __slots__ that is assigned to a fixed sequence of strings that serve as names for instance variables. For example, with our CreditCard class, we would declare the following:

```
class CreditCard:
    __slots__ = '_customer', '_bank', '_account', '_balance', '_limit'
```

In this example, the right-hand side of the assignment is technically a tuple (see discussion of automatic packing of tuples in Section 1.9.3).

When inheritance is used, if the base class declares __slots__, a subclass must also declare __slots__ to avoid creation of instance dictionaries. The declaration in the subclass should only include names of supplemental methods that are newly introduced. For example, our PredatoryCreditCard declaration would include the following declaration:

```
class PredatoryCreditCard(CreditCard):
    __slots__ = '_apr'                     # in addition to the inherited members
```

We could choose to use the __slots__ declaration to streamline every class in this book. However, we do not do so because such rigor would be atypical for Python programs. With that said, there are a few classes in this book for which we expect to have a large number of instances, each representing a lightweight construct. For example, when discussing nested classes, we suggest linked lists and trees as data structures that are often comprised of a large number of individual nodes. To promote greater efficiency in memory usage, we will use an explicit __slots__ declaration in any nested classes for which we expect many instances.

2.5.2 Name Resolution and Dynamic Dispatch

In the previous section, we discussed various namespaces, and the mechanism for establishing entries in those namespaces. In this section, we examine the process that is used when *retrieving* a name in Python's object-oriented framework. When the dot operator syntax is used to access an existing member, such as obj.foo, the Python interpreter begins a name resolution process, described as follows:

1. The instance namespace is searched; if the desired name is found, its associated value is used.
2. Otherwise the class namespace, for the class to which the instance belongs, is searched; if the name is found, its associated value is used.
3. If the name was not found in the immediate class namespace, the search continues upward through the inheritance hierarchy, checking the class namespace for each ancestor (commonly by checking the superclass class, then its superclass class, and so on). The first time the name is found, its associate value is used.
4. If the name has still not been found, an AttributeError is raised.

As a tangible example, let us assume that mycard identifies an instance of the PredatoryCreditCard class. Consider the following possible usage patterns.

- mycard._balance (or equivalently, self._balance from within a method body): the _balance method is found within the *instance namespace* for mycard.
- mycard.process_month( ): the search begins in the instance namespace, but the name process_month is not found in that namespace. As a result, the PredatoryCreditCard class namespace is searched; in this case, the name is found and that method is called.
- mycard.make_payment(200): the search for the name, make_payment, fails in the instance namespace and in the PredatoryCreditCard namespace. The name is resolved in the namespace for superclass CreditCard and thus the inherited method is called.
- mycard.charge(50): the search for name charge fails in the instance namespace. The next namespace checked is for the PredatoryCreditCard class, because that is the true type of the instance. There is a definition for a charge function in that class, and so that is the one that is called.

In the last case shown, notice that the existence of a charge function in the PredatoryCreditCard class has the effect of *overriding* the version of that function that exists in the CreditCard namespace. In traditional object-oriented terminology, Python uses what is known as *dynamic dispatch* (or *dynamic binding*) to determine, at run-time, which implementation of a function to call based upon the type of the object upon which it is invoked. This is in contrast to some languages that use *static dispatching*, making a compile-time decision as to which version of a function to call, based upon the declared type of a variable.

2.6 Shallow and Deep Copying

In Chapter 1, we emphasized that an assignment statement foo = bar makes the name foo an *alias* for the object identified as bar. In this section, we consider the task of making a *copy* of an object, rather than an alias. This is necessary in applications when we want to subsequently modify either the original or the copy in an independent manner.

Consider a scenario in which we manage various lists of colors, with each color represented by an instance of a presumed color class. We let identifier warmtones denote an existing list of such colors (e.g., oranges, browns). In this application, we wish to create a new list named palette, which is a copy of the warmtones list. However, we want to subsequently be able to add additional colors to palette, or to modify or remove some of the existing colors, without affecting the contents of warmtones. If we were to execute the command

palette = warmtones

this creates an alias, as shown in Figure 2.9. No new list is created; instead, the new identifier palette references the original list.

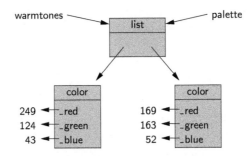

Figure 2.9: Two aliases for the same list of colors.

Unfortunately, this does not meet our desired criteria, because if we subsequently add or remove colors from "palette," we modify the list identified as warmtones.

We can instead create a new instance of the list class by using the syntax:

palette = **list**(warmtones)

In this case, we explicitly call the list constructor, sending the first list as a parameter. This causes a new list to be created, as shown in Figure 2.10; however, it is what is known as a *shallow copy*. The new list is initialized so that its contents are precisely the same as the original sequence. However, Python's lists are *referential* (see page 9 of Section 1.2.3), and so the new list represents a sequence of references to the same elements as in the first.

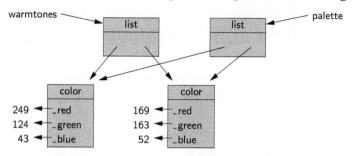

Figure 2.10: A shallow copy of a list of colors.

This is a better situation than our first attempt, as we can legitimately add or remove elements from palette without affecting warmtones. However, if we edit a color instance from the palette list, we effectively change the contents of warmtones. Although palette and warmtones are distinct lists, there remains indirect aliasing, for example, with palette[0] and warmtones[0] as aliases for the same color instance.

We prefer that palette be what is known as a **_deep copy_** of warmtones. In a deep copy, the new copy references its own *copies* of those objects referenced by the original version. (See Figure 2.11.)

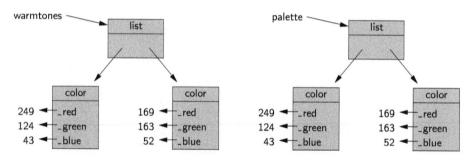

Figure 2.11: A deep copy of a list of colors.

Python's copy Module

To create a deep copy, we could populate our list by explicitly making copies of the original color instances, but this requires that we know how to make copies of colors (rather than aliasing). Python provides a very convenient module, named copy, that can produce both shallow copies and deep copies of arbitrary objects.

This module supports two functions: the copy function creates a shallow copy of its argument, and the deepcopy function creates a deep copy of its argument. After importing the module, we may create a deep copy for our example, as shown in Figure 2.11, using the command:

```
palette = copy.deepcopy(warmtones)
```

2.7 Exercises

For help with exercises, please visit the site, www.wiley.com/college/goodrich.

Reinforcement

R-2.1 Give three examples of life-critical software applications.

R-2.2 Give an example of a software application in which adaptability can mean the difference between a prolonged lifetime of sales and bankruptcy.

R-2.3 Describe a component from a text-editor GUI and the methods that it encapsulates.

R-2.4 Write a Python class, Flower, that has three instance variables of type str, int, and float, that respectively represent the name of the flower, its number of petals, and its price. Your class must include a constructor method that initializes each variable to an appropriate value, and your class should include methods for setting the value of each type, and retrieving the value of each type.

R-2.5 Use the techniques of Section 1.7 to revise the charge and make_payment methods of the CreditCard class to ensure that the caller sends a number as a parameter.

R-2.6 If the parameter to the make_payment method of the CreditCard class were a negative number, that would have the effect of *raising* the balance on the account. Revise the implementation so that it raises a ValueError if a negative value is sent.

R-2.7 The CreditCard class of Section 2.3 initializes the balance of a new account to zero. Modify that class so that a new account can be given a nonzero balance using an optional fifth parameter to the constructor. The four-parameter constructor syntax should continue to produce an account with zero balance.

R-2.8 Modify the declaration of the first for loop in the CreditCard tests, from Code Fragment 2.3, so that it will eventually cause exactly one of the three credit cards to go over its credit limit. Which credit card is it?

R-2.9 Implement the __sub__ method for the Vector class of Section 2.3.3, so that the expression u−v returns a new vector instance representing the difference between two vectors.

R-2.10 Implement the __neg__ method for the Vector class of Section 2.3.3, so that the expression −v returns a new vector instance whose coordinates are all the negated values of the respective coordinates of v.

R-2.11 In Section 2.3.3, we note that our Vector class supports a syntax such as v = u + [5, 3, 10, −2, 1], in which the sum of a vector and list returns a new vector. However, the syntax v = [5, 3, 10, −2, 1] + u is illegal. Explain how the Vector class definition can be revised so that this syntax generates a new vector.

R-2.12 Implement the __mul__ method for the Vector class of Section 2.3.3, so that the expression v * 3 returns a new vector with coordinates that are 3 times the respective coordinates of v.

R-2.13 Exercise R-2.12 asks for an implementation of __mul__, for the Vector class of Section 2.3.3, to provide support for the syntax v * 3. Implement the __rmul__ method, to provide additional support for syntax 3 * v.

R-2.14 Implement the __mul__ method for the Vector class of Section 2.3.3, so that the expression u * v returns a scalar that represents the dot product of the vectors, that is, $\sum_{i=1}^{d} u_i \cdot v_i$.

R-2.15 The Vector class of Section 2.3.3 provides a constructor that takes an integer d, and produces a d-dimensional vector with all coordinates equal to 0. Another convenient form for creating a new vector would be to send the constructor a parameter that is some iterable type representing a sequence of numbers, and to create a vector with dimension equal to the length of that sequence and coordinates equal to the sequence values. For example, Vector([4, 7, 5]) would produce a three-dimensional vector with coordinates <4, 7, 5>. Modify the constructor so that either of these forms is acceptable; that is, if a single integer is sent, it produces a vector of that dimension with all zeros, but if a sequence of numbers is provided, it produces a vector with coordinates based on that sequence.

R-2.16 Our Range class, from Section 2.3.5, relies on the formula
$$max(0, (stop − start + step − 1) \;//\; step)$$
to compute the number of elements in the range. It is not immediately evident why this formula provides the correct calculation, even if assuming a positive step size. Justify this formula, in your own words.

R-2.17 Draw a class inheritance diagram for the following set of classes:

- Class Goat extends object and adds an instance variable _tail and methods milk( ) and jump( ).

- Class Pig extends object and adds an instance variable _nose and methods eat(food) and wallow( ).

- Class Horse extends object and adds instance variables _height and _color, and methods run( ) and jump( ).

- Class Racer extends Horse and adds a method race( ).

- Class Equestrian extends Horse, adding an instance variable _weight and methods trot( ) and is_trained( ).

R-2.18 Give a short fragment of Python code that uses the progression classes from Section 2.4.2 to find the 8th value of a Fibonacci progression that starts with 2 and 2 as its first two values.

R-2.19 When using the ArithmeticProgression class of Section 2.4.2 with an increment of 128 and a start of 0, how many calls to next can we make before we reach an integer of 2^{63} or larger?

R-2.20 What are some potential efficiency disadvantages of having very deep inheritance trees, that is, a large set of classes, A, B, C, and so on, such that B extends A, C extends B, D extends C, etc.?

R-2.21 What are some potential efficiency disadvantages of having very shallow inheritance trees, that is, a large set of classes, A, B, C, and so on, such that all of these classes extend a single class, Z?

R-2.22 The collections.Sequence abstract base class does not provide support for comparing two sequences to each other. Modify our Sequence class from Code Fragment 2.14 to include a definition for the __eq__ method, so that expression seq1 == seq2 will return True precisely when the two sequences are element by element equivalent.

R-2.23 In similar spirit to the previous problem, augment the Sequence class with method __lt__, to support lexicographic comparison seq1 < seq2.

Creativity

C-2.24 Suppose you are on the design team for a new e-book reader. What are the primary classes and methods that the Python software for your reader will need? You should include an inheritance diagram for this code, but you do not need to write any actual code. Your software architecture should at least include ways for customers to buy new books, view their list of purchased books, and read their purchased books.

C-2.25 Exercise R-2.12 uses the __mul__ method to support multiplying a Vector by a number, while Exercise R-2.14 uses the __mul__ method to support computing a dot product of two vectors. Give a single implementation of Vector.__mul__ that uses run-time type checking to support both syntaxes u * v and u * k, where u and v designate vector instances and k represents a number.

C-2.26 The SequenceIterator class of Section 2.3.4 provides what is known as a forward iterator. Implement a class named ReversedSequenceIterator that serves as a reverse iterator for any Python sequence type. The first call to next should return the last element of the sequence, the second call to next should return the second-to-last element, and so forth.

C-2.27 In Section 2.3.5, we note that our version of the Range class has implicit support for iteration, due to its explicit support of both __len__
and __getitem__. The class also receives implicit support of the Boolean
test, "k **in** r" for Range r. This test is evaluated based on a forward iteration through the range, as evidenced by the relative quickness of the test
2 **in** Range(10000000) versus 9999999 **in** Range(10000000). Provide a
more efficient implementation of the __contains__ method to determine
whether a particular value lies within a given range. The running time of
your method should be independent of the length of the range.

C-2.28 The PredatoryCreditCard class of Section 2.4.1 provides a process_month
method that models the completion of a monthly cycle. Modify the class
so that once a customer has made ten calls to charge in the current month,
each additional call to that function results in an additional $1 surcharge.

C-2.29 Modify the PredatoryCreditCard class from Section 2.4.1 so that a customer is assigned a minimum monthly payment, as a percentage of the
balance, and so that a late fee is assessed if the customer does not subsequently pay that minimum amount before the next monthly cycle.

C-2.30 At the close of Section 2.4.1, we suggest a model in which the CreditCard
class supports a nonpublic method, _set_balance(b), that could be used
by subclasses to affect a change to the balance, without directly accessing
the _balance data member. Implement such a model, revising both the
CreditCard and PredatoryCreditCard classes accordingly.

C-2.31 Write a Python class that extends the Progression class so that each value
in the progression is the absolute value of the difference between the previous two values. You should include a constructor that accepts a pair of
numbers as the first two values, using 2 and 200 as the defaults.

C-2.32 Write a Python class that extends the Progression class so that each value
in the progression is the square root of the previous value. (Note that
you can no longer represent each value with an integer.) Your constructor should accept an optional parameter specifying the start value, using
$65,536$ as a default.

Projects

P-2.33 Write a Python program that inputs a polynomial in standard algebraic
notation and outputs the first derivative of that polynomial.

P-2.34 Write a Python program that inputs a document and then outputs a bar-
chart plot of the frequencies of each alphabet character that appears in
that document.

P-2.35 Write a set of Python classes that can simulate an Internet application in which one party, Alice, is periodically creating a set of packets that she wants to send to Bob. An Internet process is continually checking if Alice has any packets to send, and if so, it delivers them to Bob's computer, and Bob is periodically checking if his computer has a packet from Alice, and, if so, he reads and deletes it.

P-2.36 Write a Python program to simulate an ecosystem containing two types of creatures, **bears** and *fish*. The ecosystem consists of a river, which is modeled as a relatively large list. Each element of the list should be a Bear object, a Fish object, or None. In each time step, based on a random process, each animal either attempts to move into an adjacent list location or stay where it is. If two animals of the same type are about to collide in the same cell, then they stay where they are, but they create a new instance of that type of animal, which is placed in a random empty (i.e., previously None) location in the list. If a bear and a fish collide, however, then the fish dies (i.e., it disappears).

P-2.37 Write a simulator, as in the previous project, but add a Boolean gender field and a floating-point strength field to each animal, using an Animal class as a base class. If two animals of the same type try to collide, then they only create a new instance of that type of animal if they are of different genders. Otherwise, if two animals of the same type and gender try to collide, then only the one of larger strength survives.

P-2.38 Write a Python program that simulates a system that supports the functions of an e-book reader. You should include methods for users of your system to "buy" new books, view their list of purchased books, and read their purchased books. Your system should use actual books, which have expired copyrights and are available on the Internet, to populate your set of available books for users of your system to "purchase" and read.

P-2.39 Develop an inheritance hierarchy based upon a Polygon class that has abstract methods area( ) and perimeter( ). Implement classes Triangle, Quadrilateral, Pentagon, Hexagon, and Octagon that extend this base class, with the obvious meanings for the area( ) and perimeter( ) methods. Also implement classes, IsoscelesTriangle, EquilateralTriangle, Rectangle, and Square, that have the appropriate inheritance relationships. Finally, write a simple program that allows users to create polygons of the various types and input their geometric dimensions, and the program then outputs their area and perimeter. For extra effort, allow users to input polygons by specifying their vertex coordinates and be able to test if two such polygons are similar.

Chapter Notes

For a broad overview of developments in computer science and engineering, we refer the reader to *The Computer Science and Engineering Handbook* [96]. For more information about the Therac-25 incident, please see the paper by Leveson and Turner [69].

The reader interested in studying object-oriented programming further, is referred to the books by Booch [17], Budd [20], and Liskov and Guttag [71]. Liskov and Guttag also provide a nice discussion of abstract data types, as does the survey paper by Cardelli and Wegner [23] and the book chapter by Demurjian [33] in the *The Computer Science and Engineering Handbook* [96]. Design patterns are described in the book by Gamma *et al.* [41].

Books with specific focus on object-oriented programming in Python include those by Goldwasser and Letscher [43] at the introductory level, and by Phillips [83] at a more advanced level,

Chapter

3

Algorithm Analysis

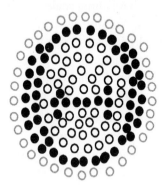

Contents

In a classic story, the famous mathematician Archimedes was asked to determine if a golden crown commissioned by the king was indeed pure gold, and not part silver, as an informant had claimed. Archimedes discovered a way to perform this analysis while stepping into a bath. He noted that water spilled out of the bath in proportion to the amount of him that went in. Realizing the implications of this fact, he immediately got out of the bath and ran naked through the city shouting, "Eureka, eureka!" for he had discovered an analysis tool (displacement), which, when combined with a simple scale, could determine if the king's new crown was good or not. That is, Archimedes could dip the crown and an equal-weight amount of gold into a bowl of water to see if they both displaced the same amount. This discovery was unfortunate for the goldsmith, however, for when Archimedes did his analysis, the crown displaced more water than an equal-weight lump of pure gold, indicating that the crown was not, in fact, pure gold.

In this book, we are interested in the design of "good" data structures and algorithms. Simply put, a ***data structure*** is a systematic way of organizing and accessing data, and an ***algorithm*** is a step-by-step procedure for performing some task in a finite amount of time. These concepts are central to computing, but to be able to classify some data structures and algorithms as "good," we must have precise ways of analyzing them.

The primary analysis tool we will use in this book involves characterizing the running times of algorithms and data structure operations, with space usage also being of interest. Running time is a natural measure of "goodness," since time is a precious resource—computer solutions should run as fast as possible. In general, the running time of an algorithm or data structure operation increases with the input size, although it may also vary for different inputs of the same size. Also, the running time is affected by the hardware environment (e.g., the processor, clock rate, memory, disk) and software environment (e.g., the operating system, programming language) in which the algorithm is implemented and executed. All other factors being equal, the running time of the same algorithm on the same input data will be smaller if the computer has, say, a much faster processor or if the implementation is done in a program compiled into native machine code instead of an interpreted implementation. We begin this chapter by discussing tools for performing experimental studies, yet also limitations to the use of experiments as a primary means for evaluating algorithm efficiency.

Focusing on running time as a primary measure of goodness requires that we be able to use a few mathematical tools. In spite of the possible variations that come from different environmental factors, we would like to focus on the relationship between the running time of an algorithm and the size of its input. We are interested in characterizing an algorithm's running time as a function of the input size. But what is the proper way of measuring it? In this chapter, we "roll up our sleeves" and develop a mathematical way of analyzing algorithms.

3.1 Experimental Studies

If an algorithm has been implemented, we can study its running time by executing it on various test inputs and recording the time spent during each execution. A simple approach for doing this in Python is by using the time function of the time module. This function reports the number of seconds, or fractions thereof, that have elapsed since a benchmark time known as the epoch. The choice of the epoch is not significant to our goal, as we can determine the *elapsed* time by recording the time just before the algorithm and the time just after the algorithm, and computing their difference, as follows:

```
from time import time
start_time = time( )              # record the starting time
run algorithm
end_time = time( )                # record the ending time
elapsed = end_time − start_time   # compute the elapsed time
```

We will demonstrate use of this approach, in Chapter 5, to gather experimental data on the efficiency of Python's list class. An elapsed time measured in this fashion is a decent reflection of the algorithm efficiency, but it is by no means perfect. The time function measures relative to what is known as the "wall clock." Because many processes share use of a computer's *central processing unit* (or *CPU*), the elapsed time will depend on what other processes are running on the computer when the test is performed. A fairer metric is the number of CPU cycles that are used by the algorithm. This can be determined using the clock function of the time module, but even this measure might not be consistent if repeating the identical algorithm on the identical input, and its granularity will depend upon the computer system. Python includes a more advanced module, named timeit, to help automate such evaluations with repetition to account for such variance among trials.

Because we are interested in the general dependence of running time on the size and structure of the input, we should perform independent experiments on many different test inputs of various sizes. We can then visualize the results by plotting the performance of each run of the algorithm as a point with x-coordinate equal to the input size, n, and y-coordinate equal to the running time, t. Figure 3.1 displays such hypothetical data. This visualization may provide some intuition regarding the relationship between problem size and execution time for the algorithm. This may lead to a statistical analysis that seeks to fit the best function of the input size to the experimental data. To be meaningful, this analysis requires that we choose good sample inputs and test enough of them to be able to make sound statistical claims about the algorithm's running time.

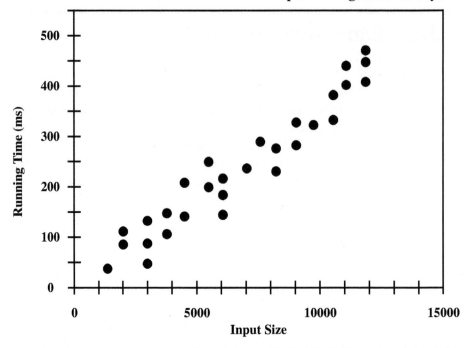

Figure 3.1: Results of an experimental study on the running time of an algorithm. A dot with coordinates (n,t) indicates that on an input of size n, the running time of the algorithm was measured as t milliseconds (ms).

Challenges of Experimental Analysis

While experimental studies of running times are valuable, especially when fine-tuning production-quality code, there are three major limitations to their use for algorithm analysis:

- Experimental running times of two algorithms are difficult to directly compare unless the experiments are performed in the same hardware and software environments.
- Experiments can be done only on a limited set of test inputs; hence, they leave out the running times of inputs not included in the experiment (and these inputs may be important).
- An algorithm must be fully implemented in order to execute it to study its running time experimentally.

This last requirement is the most serious drawback to the use of experimental studies. At early stages of design, when considering a choice of data structures or algorithms, it would be foolish to spend a significant amount of time implementing an approach that could easily be deemed inferior by a higher-level analysis.

3.1.1 Moving Beyond Experimental Analysis

Our goal is to develop an approach to analyzing the efficiency of algorithms that:
1. Allows us to evaluate the relative efficiency of any two algorithms in a way that is independent of the hardware and software environment.
2. Is performed by studying a high-level description of the algorithm without need for implementation.
3. Takes into account all possible inputs.

Counting Primitive Operations

To analyze the running time of an algorithm without performing experiments, we perform an analysis directly on a high-level description of the algorithm (either in the form of an actual code fragment, or language-independent pseudo-code). We define a set of *primitive operations* such as the following:

- Assigning an identifier to an object
- Determining the object associated with an identifier
- Performing an arithmetic operation (for example, adding two numbers)
- Comparing two numbers
- Accessing a single element of a Python list by index
- Calling a function (excluding operations executed within the function)
- Returning from a function.

Formally, a primitive operation corresponds to a low-level instruction with an execution time that is constant. Ideally, this might be the type of basic operation that is executed by the hardware, although many of our primitive operations may be translated to a small number of instructions. Instead of trying to determine the specific execution time of each primitive operation, we will simply count how many primitive operations are executed, and use this number t as a measure of the running time of the algorithm.

This operation count will correlate to an actual running time in a specific computer, for each primitive operation corresponds to a constant number of instructions, and there are only a fixed number of primitive operations. The implicit assumption in this approach is that the running times of different primitive operations will be fairly similar. Thus, the number, t, of primitive operations an algorithm performs will be proportional to the actual running time of that algorithm.

Measuring Operations as a Function of Input Size

To capture the order of growth of an algorithm's running time, we will associate, with each algorithm, a function $f(n)$ that characterizes the number of primitive operations that are performed as a function of the input size n. Section 3.2 will introduce the seven most common functions that arise, and Section 3.3 will introduce a mathematical framework for comparing functions to each other.

Focusing on the Worst-Case Input

An algorithm may run faster on some inputs than it does on others of the same size. Thus, we may wish to express the running time of an algorithm as the function of the input size obtained by taking the average over all possible inputs of the same size. Unfortunately, such an *average-case* analysis is typically quite challenging. It requires us to define a probability distribution on the set of inputs, which is often a difficult task. Figure 3.2 schematically shows how, depending on the input distribution, the running time of an algorithm can be anywhere between the worst-case time and the best-case time. For example, what if inputs are really only of types "A" or "D"?

An average-case analysis usually requires that we calculate expected running times based on a given input distribution, which usually involves sophisticated probability theory. Therefore, for the remainder of this book, unless we specify otherwise, we will characterize running times in terms of the *worst case*, as a function of the input size, n, of the algorithm.

Worst-case analysis is much easier than average-case analysis, as it requires only the ability to identify the worst-case input, which is often simple. Also, this approach typically leads to better algorithms. Making the standard of success for an algorithm to perform well in the worst case necessarily requires that it will do well on *every* input. That is, designing for the worst case leads to stronger algorithmic "muscles," much like a track star who always practices by running up an incline.

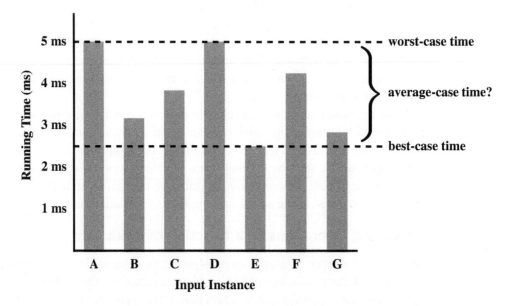

Figure 3.2: The difference between best-case and worst-case time. Each bar represents the running time of some algorithm on a different possible input.

3.2 The Seven Functions Used in This Book

In this section, we briefly discuss the seven most important functions used in the analysis of algorithms. We will use only these seven simple functions for almost all the analysis we do in this book. In fact, a section that uses a function other than one of these seven will be marked with a star ($\star$) to indicate that it is optional. In addition to these seven fundamental functions, Appendix B contains a list of other useful mathematical facts that apply in the analysis of data structures and algorithms.

The Constant Function

The simplest function we can think of is the ***constant function***. This is the function,

$$f(n) = c,$$

for some fixed constant c, such as $c = 5$, $c = 27$, or $c = 2^{10}$. That is, for any argument n, the constant function $f(n)$ assigns the value c. In other words, it does not matter what the value of n is; $f(n)$ will always be equal to the constant value c.

Because we are most interested in integer functions, the most fundamental constant function is $g(n) = 1$, and this is the typical constant function we use in this book. Note that any other constant function, $f(n) = c$, can be written as a constant c times $g(n)$. That is, $f(n) = cg(n)$ in this case.

As simple as it is, the constant function is useful in algorithm analysis, because it characterizes the number of steps needed to do a basic operation on a computer, like adding two numbers, assigning a value to some variable, or comparing two numbers.

The Logarithm Function

One of the interesting and sometimes even surprising aspects of the analysis of data structures and algorithms is the ubiquitous presence of the ***logarithm function***, $f(n) = \log_b n$, for some constant $b > 1$. This function is defined as follows:

$$x = \log_b n \quad \text{if and only if} \quad b^x = n.$$

By definition, $\log_b 1 = 0$. The value b is known as the ***base*** of the logarithm.

The most common base for the logarithm function in computer science is 2, as computers store integers in binary, and because a common operation in many algorithms is to repeatedly divide an input in half. In fact, this base is so common that we will typically omit it from the notation when it is 2. That is, for us,

$$\log n = \log_2 n.$$

We note that most handheld calculators have a button marked LOG, but this is typically for calculating the logarithm base-10, not base-two.

Computing the logarithm function exactly for any integer n involves the use of calculus, but we can use an approximation that is good enough for our purposes without calculus. In particular, we can easily compute the smallest integer greater than or equal to $\log_b n$ (its so-called *ceiling*, $\lceil \log_b n \rceil$). For positive integer, n, this value is equal to the number of times we can divide n by b before we get a number less than or equal to 1. For example, the evaluation of $\lceil \log_3 27 \rceil$ is 3, because $((27/3)/3)/3 = 1$. Likewise, $\lceil \log_4 64 \rceil$ is 3, because $((64/4)/4)/4 = 1$, and $\lceil \log_2 12 \rceil$ is 4, because $(((12/2)/2)/2)/2 = 0.75 \le 1$.

The following proposition describes several important identities that involve logarithms for any base greater than 1.

Proposition 3.1 (Logarithm Rules): *Given real numbers $a > 0$, $b > 1$, $c > 0$ and $d > 1$, we have:*

1. $\log_b(ac) = \log_b a + \log_b c$
2. $\log_b(a/c) = \log_b a - \log_b c$
3. $\log_b(a^c) = c \log_b a$
4. $\log_b a = \log_d a / \log_d b$
5. $b^{\log_d a} = a^{\log_d b}$

By convention, the unparenthesized notation $\log n^c$ denotes the value $\log(n^c)$. We use a notational shorthand, $\log^c n$, to denote the quantity, $(\log n)^c$, in which the result of the logarithm is raised to a power.

The above identities can be derived from converse rules for exponentiation that we will present on page 121. We illustrate these identities with a few examples.

Example 3.2: *We demonstrate below some interesting applications of the logarithm rules from Proposition 3.1 (using the usual convention that the base of a logarithm is 2 if it is omitted).*

- $\log(2n) = \log 2 + \log n = 1 + \log n$, *by rule 1*
- $\log(n/2) = \log n - \log 2 = \log n - 1$, *by rule 2*
- $\log n^3 = 3 \log n$, *by rule 3*
- $\log 2^n = n \log 2 = n \cdot 1 = n$, *by rule 3*
- $\log_4 n = (\log n)/\log 4 = (\log n)/2$, *by rule 4*
- $2^{\log n} = n^{\log 2} = n^1 = n$, *by rule 5.*

As a practical matter, we note that rule 4 gives us a way to compute the base-two logarithm on a calculator that has a base-10 logarithm button, LOG, for

$$\log_2 n = \text{LOG}\, n / \text{LOG}\, 2.$$

The Linear Function

Another simple yet important function is the *linear function*,

$$f(n) = n.$$

That is, given an input value n, the linear function f assigns the value n itself.

This function arises in algorithm analysis any time we have to do a single basic operation for each of n elements. For example, comparing a number x to each element of a sequence of size n will require n comparisons. The linear function also represents the best running time we can hope to achieve for any algorithm that processes each of n objects that are not already in the computer's memory, because reading in the n objects already requires n operations.

The *N*-Log-*N* Function

The next function we discuss in this section is the *n-log-n function*,

$$f(n) = n \log n,$$

that is, the function that assigns to an input n the value of n times the logarithm base-two of n. This function grows a little more rapidly than the linear function and a lot less rapidly than the quadratic function; therefore, we would greatly prefer an algorithm with a running time that is proportional to $n \log n$, than one with quadratic running time. We will see several important algorithms that exhibit a running time proportional to the *n*-log-*n* function. For example, the fastest possible algorithms for sorting n arbitrary values require time proportional to $n \log n$.

The Quadratic Function

Another function that appears often in algorithm analysis is the *quadratic function*,

$$f(n) = n^2.$$

That is, given an input value n, the function f assigns the product of n with itself (in other words, "n squared").

The main reason why the quadratic function appears in the analysis of algorithms is that there are many algorithms that have nested loops, where the inner loop performs a linear number of operations and the outer loop is performed a linear number of times. Thus, in such cases, the algorithm performs $n \cdot n = n^2$ operations.

Nested Loops and the Quadratic Function

The quadratic function can also arise in the context of nested loops where the first iteration of a loop uses one operation, the second uses two operations, the third uses three operations, and so on. That is, the number of operations is

$$1+2+3+\cdots+(n-2)+(n-1)+n.$$

In other words, this is the total number of operations that will be performed by the nested loop if the number of operations performed inside the loop increases by one with each iteration of the outer loop. This quantity also has an interesting history.

In 1787, a German schoolteacher decided to keep his 9- and 10-year-old pupils occupied by adding up the integers from 1 to 100. But almost immediately one of the children claimed to have the answer! The teacher was suspicious, for the student had only the answer on his slate. But the answer, 5050, was correct and the student, Carl Gauss, grew up to be one of the greatest mathematicians of his time. We presume that young Gauss used the following identity.

Proposition 3.3: *For any integer $n \geq 1$, we have:*

$$1+2+3+\cdots+(n-2)+(n-1)+n = \frac{n(n+1)}{2}.$$

We give two "visual" justifications of Proposition 3.3 in Figure 3.3.

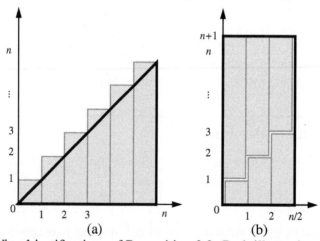

(a)   (b)

Figure 3.3: Visual justifications of Proposition 3.3. Both illustrations visualize the identity in terms of the total area covered by n unit-width rectangles with heights $1, 2, \ldots, n$. In (a), the rectangles are shown to cover a big triangle of area $n^2/2$ (base n and height n) plus n small triangles of area $1/2$ each (base 1 and height 1). In (b), which applies only when n is even, the rectangles are shown to cover a big rectangle of base $n/2$ and height $n+1$.

The lesson to be learned from Proposition 3.3 is that if we perform an algorithm with nested loops such that the operations in the inner loop increase by one each time, then the total number of operations is quadratic in the number of times, n, we perform the outer loop. To be fair, the number of operations is $n^2/2 + n/2$, and so this is just over half the number of operations than an algorithm that uses n operations each time the inner loop is performed. But the order of growth is still quadratic in n.

The Cubic Function and Other Polynomials

Continuing our discussion of functions that are powers of the input, we consider the **cubic function**,

$$f(n) = n^3,$$

which assigns to an input value n the product of n with itself three times. This function appears less frequently in the context of algorithm analysis than the constant, linear, and quadratic functions previously mentioned, but it does appear from time to time.

Polynomials

Most of the functions we have listed so far can each be viewed as being part of a larger class of functions, the **polynomials**. A **polynomial** function has the form,

$$f(n) = a_0 + a_1 n + a_2 n^2 + a_3 n^3 + \cdots + a_d n^d,$$

where $a_0, a_1, \ldots, a_d$ are constants, called the **coefficients** of the polynomial, and $a_d \neq 0$. Integer d, which indicates the highest power in the polynomial, is called the **degree** of the polynomial.

For example, the following functions are all polynomials:

- $f(n) = 2 + 5n + n^2$
- $f(n) = 1 + n^3$
- $f(n) = 1$
- $f(n) = n$
- $f(n) = n^2$

Therefore, we could argue that this book presents just four important functions used in algorithm analysis, but we will stick to saying that there are seven, since the constant, linear, and quadratic functions are too important to be lumped in with other polynomials. Running times that are polynomials with small degree are generally better than polynomial running times with larger degree.

Summations

A notation that appears again and again in the analysis of data structures and algorithms is the *summation*, which is defined as follows:

$$\sum_{i=a}^{b} f(i) = f(a) + f(a+1) + f(a+2) + \cdots + f(b),$$

where a and b are integers and $a \le b$. Summations arise in data structure and algorithm analysis because the running times of loops naturally give rise to summations.

Using a summation, we can rewrite the formula of Proposition 3.3 as

$$\sum_{i=1}^{n} i = \frac{n(n+1)}{2}.$$

Likewise, we can write a polynomial $f(n)$ of degree d with coefficients $a_0, \ldots, a_d$ as

$$f(n) = \sum_{i=0}^{d} a_i n^i.$$

Thus, the summation notation gives us a shorthand way of expressing sums of increasing terms that have a regular structure.

The Exponential Function

Another function used in the analysis of algorithms is the *exponential function*,

$$f(n) = b^n,$$

where b is a positive constant, called the *base*, and the argument n is the *exponent*. That is, function $f(n)$ assigns to the input argument n the value obtained by multiplying the base b by itself n times. As was the case with the logarithm function, the most common base for the exponential function in algorithm analysis is $b = 2$. For example, an integer word containing n bits can represent all the nonnegative integers less than 2^n. If we have a loop that starts by performing one operation and then doubles the number of operations performed with each iteration, then the number of operations performed in the nth iteration is 2^n.

We sometimes have other exponents besides n, however; hence, it is useful for us to know a few handy rules for working with exponents. In particular, the following *exponent rules* are quite helpful.

Proposition 3.4 (Exponent Rules): *Given positive integers a, b, and c, we have*

1. $(b^a)^c = b^{ac}$
2. $b^a b^c = b^{a+c}$
3. $b^a / b^c = b^{a-c}$

For example, we have the following:

- $256 = 16^2 = (2^4)^2 = 2^{4 \cdot 2} = 2^8 = 256$ (Exponent Rule 1)
- $243 = 3^5 = 3^{2+3} = 3^2 3^3 = 9 \cdot 27 = 243$ (Exponent Rule 2)
- $16 = 1024/64 = 2^{10}/2^6 = 2^{10-6} = 2^4 = 16$ (Exponent Rule 3)

We can extend the exponential function to exponents that are fractions or real numbers and to negative exponents, as follows. Given a positive integer k, we define $b^{1/k}$ to be k^{th} root of b, that is, the number r such that $r^k = b$. For example, $25^{1/2} = 5$, since $5^2 = 25$. Likewise, $27^{1/3} = 3$ and $16^{1/4} = 2$. This approach allows us to define any power whose exponent can be expressed as a fraction, for $b^{a/c} = (b^a)^{1/c}$, by Exponent Rule 1. For example, $9^{3/2} = (9^3)^{1/2} = 729^{1/2} = 27$. Thus, $b^{a/c}$ is really just the cth root of the integral exponent b^a.

We can further extend the exponential function to define b^x for any real number x, by computing a series of numbers of the form $b^{a/c}$ for fractions a/c that get progressively closer and closer to x. Any real number x can be approximated arbitrarily closely by a fraction a/c; hence, we can use the fraction a/c as the exponent of b to get arbitrarily close to b^x. For example, the number 2^π is well defined. Finally, given a negative exponent d, we define $b^d = 1/b^{-d}$, which corresponds to applying Exponent Rule 3 with $a = 0$ and $c = -d$. For example, $2^{-3} = 1/2^3 = 1/8$.

Geometric Sums

Suppose we have a loop for which each iteration takes a multiplicative factor longer than the previous one. This loop can be analyzed using the following proposition.

Proposition 3.5: *For any integer $n \geq 0$ and any real number a such that $a > 0$ and $a \neq 1$, consider the summation*

$$\sum_{i=0}^{n} a^i = 1 + a + a^2 + \cdots + a^n$$

(remembering that $a^0 = 1$ if $a > 0$). This summation is equal to

$$\frac{a^{n+1} - 1}{a - 1}.$$

Summations as shown in Proposition 3.5 are called **geometric** summations, because each term is geometrically larger than the previous one if $a > 1$. For example, everyone working in computing should know that

$$1 + 2 + 4 + 8 + \cdots + 2^{n-1} = 2^n - 1,$$

for this is the largest integer that can be represented in binary notation using n bits.

3.2.1   Comparing Growth Rates

To sum up, Table 3.1 shows, in order, each of the seven common functions used in algorithm analysis.

constant	logarithm	linear	n-log-n	quadratic	cubic	exponential
1	$\log n$	n	$n \log n$	n^2	n^3	a^n

Table 3.1: Classes of functions. Here we assume that $a > 1$ is a constant.

Ideally, we would like data structure operations to run in times proportional to the constant or logarithm function, and we would like our algorithms to run in linear or *n*-log-*n* time. Algorithms with quadratic or cubic running times are less practical, and algorithms with exponential running times are infeasible for all but the smallest sized inputs. Plots of the seven functions are shown in Figure 3.4.

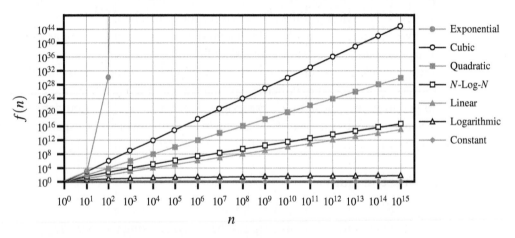

Figure 3.4: Growth rates for the seven fundamental functions used in algorithm analysis. We use base $a = 2$ for the exponential function. The functions are plotted on a log-log chart, to compare the growth rates primarily as slopes. Even so, the exponential function grows too fast to display all its values on the chart.

The Ceiling and Floor Functions

One additional comment concerning the functions above is in order. When discussing logarithms, we noted that the value is generally not an integer, yet the running time of an algorithm is usually expressed by means of an integer quantity, such as the number of operations performed. Thus, the analysis of an algorithm may sometimes involve the use of the *floor function* and *ceiling function*, which are defined respectively as follows:

- $\lfloor x \rfloor$ = the largest integer less than or equal to x.
- $\lceil x \rceil$ = the smallest integer greater than or equal to x.

3.3 Asymptotic Analysis

In algorithm analysis, we focus on the growth rate of the running time as a function of the input size n, taking a "big-picture" approach. For example, it is often enough just to know that the running time of an algorithm *grows proportionally to n*.

We analyze algorithms using a mathematical notation for functions that disregards constant factors. Namely, we characterize the running times of algorithms by using functions that map the size of the input, n, to values that correspond to the main factor that determines the growth rate in terms of n. This approach reflects that each basic step in a pseudo-code description or a high-level language implementation may correspond to a small number of primitive operations. Thus, we can perform an analysis of an algorithm by estimating the number of primitive operations executed up to a constant factor, rather than getting bogged down in language-specific or hardware-specific analysis of the exact number of operations that execute on the computer.

As a tangible example, we revisit the goal of finding the largest element of a Python list; we first used this example when introducing for loops on page 21 of Section 1.4.2. Code Fragment 3.1 presents a function named find_max for this task.

```
1  def find_max(data):
2      """Return the maximum element from a nonempty Python list."""
3      biggest = data[0]              # The initial value to beat
4      for val in data:               # For each value:
5          if val > biggest           # if it is greater than the best so far,
6              biggest = val          # we have found a new best (so far)
7      return biggest                 # When loop ends, biggest is the max
```

Code Fragment 3.1: A function that returns the maximum value of a Python list.

This is a classic example of an algorithm with a running time that grows proportional to n, as the loop executes once for each data element, with some fixed number of primitive operations executing for each pass. In the remainder of this section, we provide a framework to formalize this claim.

3.3.1 The "Big-Oh" Notation

Let $f(n)$ and $g(n)$ be functions mapping positive integers to positive real numbers. We say that $f(n)$ is $O(g(n))$ if there is a real constant $c > 0$ and an integer constant $n_0 \geq 1$ such that

$$f(n) \leq cg(n), \quad \text{for} \quad n \geq n_0.$$

This definition is often referred to as the "big-Oh" notation, for it is sometimes pronounced as "$f(n)$ is *big-Oh* of $g(n)$." Figure 3.5 illustrates the general definition.

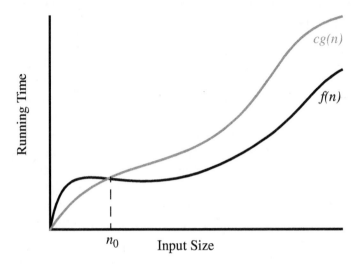

Figure 3.5: Illustrating the "big-Oh" notation. The function $f(n)$ is $O(g(n))$, since $f(n) \leq c \cdot g(n)$ when $n \geq n_0$.

Example 3.6: *The function $8n + 5$ is $O(n)$.*

Justification: By the big-Oh definition, we need to find a real constant $c > 0$ and an integer constant $n_0 \geq 1$ such that $8n + 5 \leq cn$ for every integer $n \geq n_0$. It is easy to see that a possible choice is $c = 9$ and $n_0 = 5$. Indeed, this is one of infinitely many choices available because there is a trade-off between c and n_0. For example, we could rely on constants $c = 13$ and $n_0 = 1$. ∎

The big-Oh notation allows us to say that a function $f(n)$ is "less than or equal to" another function $g(n)$ up to a constant factor and in the *asymptotic* sense as n grows toward infinity. This ability comes from the fact that the definition uses "$\leq$" to compare $f(n)$ to a $g(n)$ times a constant, c, for the asymptotic cases when $n \geq n_0$. However, it is considered poor taste to say "$f(n) \leq O(g(n))$," since the big-Oh already denotes the "less-than-or-equal-to" concept. Likewise, although common, it is not fully correct to say "$f(n) = O(g(n))$," with the usual understanding of the "$=$" relation, because there is no way to make sense of the symmetric statement, "$O(g(n)) = f(n)$." It is best to say,

$$\text{``}f(n) \textbf{ is } O(g(n)).\text{''}$$

Alternatively, we can say "$f(n)$ is **order of** $g(n)$." For the more mathematically inclined, it is also correct to say, "$f(n) \in O(g(n))$," for the big-Oh notation, technically speaking, denotes a whole collection of functions. In this book, we will stick to presenting big-Oh statements as "$f(n)$ **is** $O(g(n))$." Even with this interpretation, there is considerable freedom in how we can use arithmetic operations with the big-Oh notation, and with this freedom comes a certain amount of responsibility.

Characterizing Running Times Using the Big-Oh Notation

The big-Oh notation is used widely to characterize running times and space bounds in terms of some parameter n, which varies from problem to problem, but is always defined as a chosen measure of the "size" of the problem. For example, if we are interested in finding the largest element in a sequence, as with the find_max algorithm, we should let n denote the number of elements in that collection. Using the big-Oh notation, we can write the following mathematically precise statement on the running time of algorithm find_max (Code Fragment 3.1) for *any* computer.

Proposition 3.7: *The algorithm, find_max, for computing the maximum element of a list of n numbers, runs in $O(n)$ time.*

Justification: The initialization before the loop begins requires only a constant number of primitive operations. Each iteration of the loop also requires only a constant number of primitive operations, and the loop executes n times. Therefore, we account for the number of primitive operations being $c' + c'' \cdot n$ for appropriate constants c' and c'' that reflect, respectively, the work performed during initialization and the loop body. Because each primitive operation runs in constant time, we have that the running time of algorithm find_max on an input of size n is at most a constant times n; that is, we conclude that the running time of algorithm find_max is $O(n)$. ∎

Some Properties of the Big-Oh Notation

The big-Oh notation allows us to ignore constant factors and lower-order terms and focus on the main components of a function that affect its growth.

Example 3.8: $5n^4 + 3n^3 + 2n^2 + 4n + 1$ *is* $O(n^4)$.

Justification: Note that $5n^4 + 3n^3 + 2n^2 + 4n + 1 \leq (5 + 3 + 2 + 4 + 1)n^4 = cn^4$, for $c = 15$, when $n \geq n_0 = 1$. ∎

In fact, we can characterize the growth rate of any polynomial function.

Proposition 3.9: *If $f(n)$ is a polynomial of degree d, that is,*

$$f(n) = a_0 + a_1 n + \cdots + a_d n^d,$$

and $a_d > 0$, then $f(n)$ is $O(n^d)$.

Justification: Note that, for $n \geq 1$, we have $1 \leq n \leq n^2 \leq \cdots \leq n^d$; hence,

$$a_0 + a_1 n + a_2 n^2 + \cdots + a_d n^d \leq (|a_0| + |a_1| + |a_2| + \cdots + |a_d|) n^d.$$

We show that $f(n)$ is $O(n^d)$ by defining $c = |a_0| + |a_1| + \cdots + |a_d|$ and $n_0 = 1$. ∎

Thus, the highest-degree term in a polynomial is the term that determines the asymptotic growth rate of that polynomial. We consider some additional properties of the big-Oh notation in the exercises. Let us consider some further examples here, focusing on combinations of the seven fundamental functions used in algorithm design. We rely on the mathematical fact that $\log n \leq n$ for $n \geq 1$.

Example 3.10: $5n^2 + 3n \log n + 2n + 5$ is $O(n^2)$.

Justification: $5n^2 + 3n \log n + 2n + 5 \leq (5 + 3 + 2 + 5)n^2 = cn^2$, for $c = 15$, when $n \geq n_0 = 1$. ∎

Example 3.11: $20n^3 + 10n \log n + 5$ is $O(n^3)$.

Justification: $20n^3 + 10n \log n + 5 \leq 35n^3$, for $n \geq 1$. ∎

Example 3.12: $3 \log n + 2$ is $O(\log n)$.

Justification: $3 \log n + 2 \leq 5 \log n$, for $n \geq 2$. Note that $\log n$ is zero for $n = 1$. That is why we use $n \geq n_0 = 2$ in this case. ∎

Example 3.13: 2^{n+2} is $O(2^n)$.

Justification: $2^{n+2} = 2^n \cdot 2^2 = 4 \cdot 2^n$; hence, we can take $c = 4$ and $n_0 = 1$ in this case. ∎

Example 3.14: $2n + 100 \log n$ is $O(n)$.

Justification: $2n + 100 \log n \leq 102n$, for $n \geq n_0 = 1$; hence, we can take $c = 102$ in this case. ∎

Characterizing Functions in Simplest Terms

In general, we should use the big-Oh notation to characterize a function as closely as possible. While it is true that the function $f(n) = 4n^3 + 3n^2$ is $O(n^5)$ or even $O(n^4)$, it is more accurate to say that $f(n)$ is $O(n^3)$. Consider, by way of analogy, a scenario where a hungry traveler driving along a long country road happens upon a local farmer walking home from a market. If the traveler asks the farmer how much longer he must drive before he can find some food, it may be truthful for the farmer to say, "certainly no longer than 12 hours," but it is much more accurate (and helpful) for him to say, "you can find a market just a few minutes drive up this road." Thus, even with the big-Oh notation, we should strive as much as possible to tell the whole truth.

It is also considered poor taste to include constant factors and lower-order terms in the big-Oh notation. For example, it is not fashionable to say that the function $2n^2$ is $O(4n^2 + 6n \log n)$, although this is completely correct. We should strive instead to describe the function in the big-Oh in *simplest terms*.

The seven functions listed in Section 3.2 are the most common functions used in conjunction with the big-Oh notation to characterize the running times and space usage of algorithms. Indeed, we typically use the names of these functions to refer to the running times of the algorithms they characterize. So, for example, we would say that an algorithm that runs in worst-case time $4n^2 + n\log n$ is a ***quadratic-time*** algorithm, since it runs in $O(n^2)$ time. Likewise, an algorithm running in time at most $5n + 20\log n + 4$ would be called a ***linear-time*** algorithm.

Big-Omega

Just as the big-Oh notation provides an asymptotic way of saying that a function is "less than or equal to" another function, the following notations provide an asymptotic way of saying that a function grows at a rate that is "greater than or equal to" that of another.

Let $f(n)$ and $g(n)$ be functions mapping positive integers to positive real numbers. We say that $f(n)$ is $\Omega(g(n))$, pronounced "$f(n)$ is big-Omega of $g(n)$," if $g(n)$ is $O(f(n))$, that is, there is a real constant $c > 0$ and an integer constant $n_0 \geq 1$ such that

$$f(n) \geq cg(n), \quad \text{for} \quad n \geq n_0.$$

This definition allows us to say asymptotically that one function is greater than or equal to another, up to a constant factor.

Example 3.15: $3n\log n - 2n$ is $\Omega(n\log n)$.

Justification: $3n\log n - 2n = n\log n + 2n(\log n - 1) \geq n\log n$ for $n \geq 2$; hence, we can take $c = 1$ and $n_0 = 2$ in this case. ∎

Big-Theta

In addition, there is a notation that allows us to say that two functions grow at the same rate, up to constant factors. We say that $f(n)$ is $\Theta(g(n))$, pronounced "$f(n)$ is big-Theta of $g(n)$," if $f(n)$ is $O(g(n))$ and $f(n)$ is $\Omega(g(n))$, that is, there are real constants $c' > 0$ and $c'' > 0$, and an integer constant $n_0 \geq 1$ such that

$$c'g(n) \leq f(n) \leq c''g(n), \quad \text{for} \quad n \geq n_0.$$

Example 3.16: $3n\log n + 4n + 5\log n$ is $\Theta(n\log n)$.

Justification: $3n\log n \leq 3n\log n + 4n + 5\log n \leq (3 + 4 + 5)n\log n$ for $n \geq 2$. ∎

3.3.2 Comparative Analysis

Suppose two algorithms solving the same problem are available: an algorithm A, which has a running time of $O(n)$, and an algorithm B, which has a running time of $O(n^2)$. Which algorithm is better? We know that n is $O(n^2)$, which implies that algorithm A is ***asymptotically better*** than algorithm B, although for a small value of n, B may have a lower running time than A.

We can use the big-Oh notation to order classes of functions by asymptotic growth rate. Our seven functions are ordered by increasing growth rate in the following sequence, that is, if a function $f(n)$ precedes a function $g(n)$ in the sequence, then $f(n)$ is $O(g(n))$:

$$1, \quad \log n, \quad n, \quad n\log n, \quad n^2, \quad n^3, \quad 2^n.$$

We illustrate the growth rates of the seven functions in Table 3.2. (See also Figure 3.4 from Section 3.2.1.)

n	$\log n$	n	$n\log n$	n^2	n^3	2^n
8	3	8	24	64	512	256
16	4	16	64	256	4,096	65,536
32	5	32	160	1,024	32,768	4,294,967,296
64	6	64	384	4,096	262,144	1.84×10^{19}
128	7	128	896	16,384	2,097,152	3.40×10^{38}
256	8	256	2,048	65,536	16,777,216	1.15×10^{77}
512	9	512	4,608	262,144	134,217,728	1.34×10^{154}

Table 3.2: Selected values of fundamental functions in algorithm analysis.

We further illustrate the importance of the asymptotic viewpoint in Table 3.3. This table explores the maximum size allowed for an input instance that is processed by an algorithm in 1 second, 1 minute, and 1 hour. It shows the importance of good algorithm design, because an asymptotically slow algorithm is beaten in the long run by an asymptotically faster algorithm, even if the constant factor for the asymptotically faster algorithm is worse.

Running	Maximum Problem Size (n)		
Time (μs)	1 second	1 minute	1 hour
$400n$	2,500	150,000	9,000,000
$2n^2$	707	5,477	42,426
2^n	19	25	31

Table 3.3: Maximum size of a problem that can be solved in 1 second, 1 minute, and 1 hour, for various running times measured in microseconds.

The importance of good algorithm design goes beyond just what can be solved effectively on a given computer, however. As shown in Table 3.4, even if we achieve a dramatic speedup in hardware, we still cannot overcome the handicap of an asymptotically slow algorithm. This table shows the new maximum problem size achievable for any fixed amount of time, assuming algorithms with the given running times are now run on a computer 256 times faster than the previous one.

Running Time	New Maximum Problem Size
$400n$	$256m$
$2n^2$	$16m$
2^n	$m+8$

Table 3.4: Increase in the maximum size of a problem that can be solved in a fixed amount of time, by using a computer that is 256 times faster than the previous one. Each entry is a function of m, the previous maximum problem size.

Some Words of Caution

A few words of caution about asymptotic notation are in order at this point. First, note that the use of the big-Oh and related notations can be somewhat misleading should the constant factors they "hide" be very large. For example, while it is true that the function $10^{100}n$ is $O(n)$, if this is the running time of an algorithm being compared to one whose running time is $10n\log n$, we should prefer the $O(n\log n)$-time algorithm, even though the linear-time algorithm is asymptotically faster. This preference is because the constant factor, 10^{100}, which is called "one googol," is believed by many astronomers to be an upper bound on the number of atoms in the observable universe. So we are unlikely to ever have a real-world problem that has this number as its input size. Thus, even when using the big-Oh notation, we should at least be somewhat mindful of the constant factors and lower-order terms we are "hiding."

The observation above raises the issue of what constitutes a "fast" algorithm. Generally speaking, any algorithm running in $O(n\log n)$ time (with a reasonable constant factor) should be considered efficient. Even an $O(n^2)$-time function may be fast enough in some contexts, that is, when n is small. But an algorithm running in $O(2^n)$ time should almost never be considered efficient.

Exponential Running Times

There is a famous story about the inventor of the game of chess. He asked only that his king pay him 1 grain of rice for the first square on the board, 2 grains for the second, 4 grains for the third, 8 for the fourth, and so on. It is an interesting test of programming skills to write a program to compute exactly the number of grains of rice the king would have to pay.

If we must draw a line between efficient and inefficient algorithms, therefore, it is natural to make this distinction be that between those algorithms running in polynomial time and those running in exponential time. That is, make the distinction between algorithms with a running time that is $O(n^c)$, for some constant $c > 1$, and those with a running time that is $O(b^n)$, for some constant $b > 1$. Like so many notions we have discussed in this section, this too should be taken with a "grain of salt," for an algorithm running in $O(n^{100})$ time should probably not be considered "efficient." Even so, the distinction between polynomial-time and exponential-time algorithms is considered a robust measure of tractability.

3.3.3   Examples of Algorithm Analysis

Now that we have the big-Oh notation for doing algorithm analysis, let us give some examples by characterizing the running time of some simple algorithms using this notation. Moreover, in keeping with our earlier promise, we illustrate below how each of the seven functions given earlier in this chapter can be used to characterize the running time of an example algorithm.

Rather than use pseudo-code in this section, we give complete Python implementations for our examples. We use Python's **list** class as the natural representation for an "array" of values. In Chapter 5, we will fully explore the underpinnings of Python's list class, and the efficiency of the various behaviors that it supports. In this section, we rely on just a few of its behaviors, discussing their efficiencies as introduced.

Constant-Time Operations

Given an instance, named data, of the Python list class, a call to the function, len(data), is evaluated in constant time. This is a very simple algorithm because the list class maintains, for each list, an instance variable that records the current length of the list. This allows it to immediately report that length, rather than take time to iteratively count each of the elements in the list. Using asymptotic notation, we say that this function runs in $O(1)$ time; that is, the running time of this function is independent of the length, n, of the list.

Another central behavior of Python's list class is that it allows access to an arbitrary element of the list using syntax, data[j], for integer index j. Because Python's lists are implemented as ***array-based sequences***, references to a list's elements are stored in a consecutive block of memory. The jth element of the list can be found, not by iterating through the list one element at a time, but by validating the index, and using it as an offset into the underlying array. In turn, computer hardware supports constant-time access to an element based on its memory address. Therefore, we say that the expression data[j] is evaluated in $O(1)$ time for a Python list.

Revisiting the Problem of Finding the Maximum of a Sequence

For our next example, we revisit the find_max algorithm, given in Code Fragment 3.1 on page 123, for finding the largest value in a sequence. Proposition 3.7 on page 125 claimed an $O(n)$ run-time for the find_max algorithm. Consistent with our earlier analysis of syntax data[0], the initialization uses $O(1)$ time. The loop executes n times, and within each iteration, it performs one comparison and possibly one assignment statement (as well as maintenance of the loop variable). Finally, we note that the mechanism for enacting a **return** statement in Python uses $O(1)$ time. Combining these steps, we have that the find_max function runs in $O(n)$ time.

Further Analysis of the Maximum-Finding Algorithm

A more interesting question about find_max is how many times we might update the current "biggest" value. In the worst case, if the data is given to us in increasing order, the biggest value is reassigned $n-1$ times. But what if the input is given to us in random order, with all orders equally likely; what would be the expected number of times we update the biggest value in this case? To answer this question, note that we update the current biggest in an iteration of the loop only if the current element is bigger than all the elements that precede it. If the sequence is given to us in random order, the probability that the jth element is the largest of the first j elements is $1/j$ (assuming uniqueness). Hence, the expected number of times we update the biggest (including initialization) is $H_n = \sum_{j=1}^{n} 1/j$, which is known as the nth **Harmonic number**. It turns out (see Proposition B.16) that H_n is $O(\log n)$. Therefore, the expected number of times the biggest value is updated by find_max on a randomly ordered sequence is $O(\log n)$.

Prefix Averages

The next problem we consider is computing what are known as *prefix averages* of a sequence of numbers. Namely, given a sequence S consisting of n numbers, we want to compute a sequence A such that $A[j]$ is the average of elements $S[0], \ldots, S[j]$, for $j = 0, \ldots, n-1$, that is,

$$A[j] = \frac{\sum_{i=0}^{j} S[i]}{j+1}.$$

Computing prefix averages has many applications in economics and statistics. For example, given the year-by-year returns of a mutual fund, ordered from recent to past, an investor will typically want to see the fund's average annual returns for the most recent year, the most recent three years, the most recent five years, and so on. Likewise, given a stream of daily Web usage logs, a Web site manager may wish to track average usage trends over various time periods. We analyze three different implementations that solve this problem but with rather different running times.

A Quadratic-Time Algorithm

Our first algorithm for computing prefix averages, named prefix_average1, is shown in Code Fragment 3.2. It computes every element of A separately, using an inner loop to compute the partial sum.

```
1  def prefix_average1(S):
2    """Return list such that, for all j, A[j] equals average of S[0], ..., S[j]."""
3    n = len(S)
4    A = [0] * n                    # create new list of n zeros
5    for j in range(n):
6      total = 0                    # begin computing S[0] + ... + S[j]
7      for i in range(j + 1):
8        total += S[i]
9      A[j] = total / (j+1)         # record the average
10   return A
```

Code Fragment 3.2: Algorithm prefix_average1.

In order to analyze the prefix_average1 algorithm, we consider the various steps that are executed.

- The statement, n = len(S), executes in constant time, as described at the beginning of Section 3.3.3.
- The statement, A = [0] * n, causes the creation and initialization of a Python list with length n, and with all entries equal to zero. This uses a constant number of primitive operations per element, and thus runs in $O(n)$ time.
- There are two nested **for** loops, which are controlled, respectively, by counters j and i. The body of the outer loop, controlled by counter j, is executed n times, for $j = 0, \ldots, n-1$. Therefore, statements total = 0 and A[j] = total / (j+1) are executed n times each. This implies that these two statements, plus the management of counter j in the range, contribute a number of primitive operations proportional to n, that is, $O(n)$ time.
- The body of the inner loop, which is controlled by counter i, is executed $j+1$ times, depending on the current value of the outer loop counter j. Thus, statement total += S[i], in the inner loop, is executed $1 + 2 + 3 + \cdots + n$ times. By recalling Proposition 3.3, we know that $1 + 2 + 3 + \cdots + n = n(n+1)/2$, which implies that the statement in the inner loop contributes $O(n^2)$ time. A similar argument can be done for the primitive operations associated with maintaining counter i, which also take $O(n^2)$ time.

The running time of implementation prefix_average1 is given by the sum of three terms. The first and the second terms are $O(n)$, and the third term is $O(n^2)$. By a simple application of Proposition 3.9, the running time of prefix_average1 is $O(n^2)$.

Our second implementation for computing prefix averages, prefix_average2, is presented in Code Fragment 3.3.

```
1  def prefix_average2(S):
2    """Return list such that, for all j, A[j] equals average of S[0], ..., S[j]."""
3    n = len(S)
4    A = [0] * n                      # create new list of n zeros
5    for j in range(n):
6      A[j] = sum(S[0:j+1]) / (j+1)   # record the average
7    return A
```

Code Fragment 3.3: Algorithm prefix_average2.

This approach is essentially the same high-level algorithm as in prefix_average1, but we have replaced the inner loop by using the single expression sum(S[0:j+1]) to compute the partial sum, $S[0] + \cdots + S[j]$. While the use of that function greatly simplifies the presentation of the algorithm, it is worth asking how it affects the efficiency. Asymptotically, this implementation is no better. Even though the expression, sum(S[0:j+1]), seems like a single command, it is a function call and an evaluation of that function takes $O(j+1)$ time in this context. Technically, the computation of the slice, S[0:j+1], also uses $O(j+1)$ time, as it constructs a new list instance for storage. So the running time of prefix_average2 is still dominated by a series of steps that take time proportional to $1+2+3+\cdots+n$, and thus $O(n^2)$.

A Linear-Time Algorithm

Our final algorithm, prefix_averages3, is given in Code Fragment 3.4. Just as with our first two algorithms, we are interested in computing, for each j, the ***prefix sum*** $S[0] + S[1] + \cdots + S[j]$, denoted as total in our code, so that we can then compute the prefix average A[j] =total / (j + 1). However, there is a key difference that results in much greater efficiency.

```
1  def prefix_average3(S):
2    """Return list such that, for all j, A[j] equals average of S[0], ..., S[j]."""
3    n = len(S)
4    A = [0] * n            # create new list of n zeros
5    total = 0              # compute prefix sum as S[0] + S[1] + ...
6    for j in range(n):
7      total += S[j]        # update prefix sum to include S[j]
8      A[j] = total / (j+1)  # compute average based on current sum
9    return A
```

Code Fragment 3.4: Algorithm prefix_average3.

In our first two algorithms, the prefix sum is computed anew for each value of j. That contributed $O(j)$ time for each j, leading to the quadratic behavior. In algorithm prefix_average3, we maintain the current prefix sum dynamically, effectively computing $S[0] + S[1] + \cdots + S[j]$ as total + S[j], where value total is equal to the sum $S[0] + S[1] + \cdots + S[j-1]$ computed by the previous pass of the loop over j. The analysis of the running time of algorithm prefix_average3 follows:

- Initializing variables n and total uses $O(1)$ time.
- Initializing the list A uses $O(n)$ time.
- There is a single **for** loop, which is controlled by counter j. The maintenance of that counter by the range iterator contributes a total of $O(n)$ time.
- The body of the loop is executed n times, for $j = 0, \ldots, n-1$. Thus, statements total += S[j] and A[j] = total / (j+1) are executed n times each. Since each of these statements uses $O(1)$ time per iteration, their overall contribution is $O(n)$ time.

The running time of algorithm prefix_average3 is given by the sum of the four terms. The first is $O(1)$ and the remaining three are $O(n)$. By a simple application of Proposition 3.9, the running time of prefix_average3 is $O(n)$, which is much better than the quadratic time of algorithms prefix_average1 and prefix_average2.

Three-Way Set Disjointness

Suppose we are given three sequences of numbers, A, B, and C. We will assume that no individual sequence contains duplicate values, but that there may be some numbers that are in two or three of the sequences. The ***three-way set disjointness*** problem is to determine if the intersection of the three sequences is empty, namely, that there is no element x such that $x \in A$, $x \in B$, and $x \in C$. A simple Python function to determine this property is given in Code Fragment 3.5.

```
1  def disjoint1(A, B, C):
2    """Return True if there is no element common to all three lists."""
3    for a in A:
4      for b in B:
5        for c in C:
6          if a == b == c:
7            return False         # we found a common value
8    return True                  # if we reach this, sets are disjoint
```

Code Fragment 3.5: Algorithm disjoint1 for testing three-way set disjointness.

This simple algorithm loops through each possible triple of values from the three sets to see if those values are equivalent. If each of the original sets has size n, then the worst-case running time of this function is $O(n^3)$.

We can improve upon the asymptotic performance with a simple observation. Once inside the body of the loop over B, if selected elements a and b do not match each other, it is a waste of time to iterate through all values of C looking for a matching triple. An improved solution to this problem, taking advantage of this observation, is presented in Code Fragment 3.6.

```
1  def disjoint2(A, B, C):
2    """ Return True if there is no element common to all three lists."""
3    for a in A:
4      for b in B:
5        if a == b:              # only check C if we found match from A and B
6          for c in C:
7            if a == c           # (and thus a == b == c)
8              return False       # we found a common value
9    return True                  # if we reach this, sets are disjoint
```

Code Fragment 3.6: Algorithm disjoint2 for testing three-way set disjointness.

In the improved version, it is not simply that we save time if we get lucky. We claim that the *worst-case* running time for disjoint2 is $O(n^2)$. There are quadratically many pairs (a,b) to consider. However, if A and B are each sets of distinct elements, there can be at most $O(n)$ such pairs with a equal to b. Therefore, the innermost loop, over C, executes at most n times.

To account for the overall running time, we examine the time spent executing each line of code. The management of the for loop over A requires $O(n)$ time. The management of the for loop over B accounts for a total of $O(n^2)$ time, since that loop is executed n different times. The test a $==$ b is evaluated $O(n^2)$ times. The rest of the time spent depends upon how many matching (a,b) pairs exist. As we have noted, there are at most n such pairs, and so the management of the loop over C, and the commands within the body of that loop, use at most $O(n^2)$ time. By our standard application of Proposition 3.9, the total time spent is $O(n^2)$.

Element Uniqueness

A problem that is closely related to the three-way set disjointness problem is the ***element uniqueness problem***. In the former, we are given three collections and we presumed that there were no duplicates within a single collection. In the element uniqueness problem, we are given a single sequence S with n elements and asked whether all elements of that collection are distinct from each other.

Our first solution to this problem uses a straightforward iterative algorithm. The unique1 function, given in Code Fragment 3.7, solves the element uniqueness problem by looping through all distinct pairs of indices $j < k$, checking if any of

```
1  def unique1(S):
2    """Return True if there are no duplicate elements in sequence S."""
3    for j in range(len(S)):
4      for k in range(j+1, len(S)):
5        if S[j] == S[k]:
6          return False          # found duplicate pair
7    return True                 # if we reach this, elements were unique
```

Code Fragment 3.7: Algorithm unique1 for testing element uniqueness.

those pairs refer to elements that are equivalent to each other. It does this using two nested for loops, such that the first iteration of the outer loop causes $n - 1$ iterations of the inner loop, the second iteration of the outer loop causes $n - 2$ iterations of the inner loop, and so on. Thus, the worst-case running time of this function is proportional to

$$(n-1) + (n-2) + \cdots + 2 + 1,$$

which we recognize as the familiar $O(n^2)$ summation from Proposition 3.3.

Using Sorting as a Problem-Solving Tool

An even better algorithm for the element uniqueness problem is based on using sorting as a problem-solving tool. In this case, by sorting the sequence of elements, we are guaranteed that any duplicate elements will be placed next to each other. Thus, to determine if there are any duplicates, all we need to do is perform a single pass over the sorted sequence, looking for *consecutive* duplicates. A Python implementation of this algorithm is as follows:

```
1  def unique2(S):
2    """Return True if there are no duplicate elements in sequence S."""
3    temp = sorted(S)            # create a sorted copy of S
4    for j in range(1, len(temp)):
5      if S[j-1] == S[j]:
6        return False            # found duplicate pair
7    return True                 # if we reach this, elements were unique
```

Code Fragment 3.8: Algorithm unique2 for testing element uniqueness.

The built-in function, sorted, as described in Section 1.5.2, produces a copy of the original list with elements in sorted order. It guarantees a worst-case running time of $O(n \log n)$; see Chapter 12 for a discussion of common sorting algorithms. Once the data is sorted, the subsequent loop runs in $O(n)$ time, and so the entire unique2 algorithm runs in $O(n \log n)$ time.

3.4 Simple Justification Techniques

Sometimes, we will want to make claims about an algorithm, such as showing that it is correct or that it runs fast. In order to rigorously make such claims, we must use mathematical language, and in order to back up such claims, we must justify or *prove* our statements. Fortunately, there are several simple ways to do this.

3.4.1 By Example

Some claims are of the generic form, "There is an element x in a set S that has property P." To justify such a claim, we only need to produce a particular x in S that has property P. Likewise, some hard-to-believe claims are of the generic form, "Every element x in a set S has property P." To justify that such a claim is false, we only need to produce a particular x from S that does not have property P. Such an instance is called a *counterexample*.

Example 3.17: *Professor Amongus claims that every number of the form $2^i - 1$ is a prime, when i is an integer greater than 1. Professor Amongus is wrong.*

Justification: To prove Professor Amongus is wrong, we find a counterexample. Fortunately, we need not look too far, for $2^4 - 1 = 15 = 3 \cdot 5$. ∎

3.4.2 The "Contra" Attack

Another set of justification techniques involves the use of the negative. The two primary such methods are the use of the *contrapositive* and the *contradiction*. The use of the contrapositive method is like looking through a negative mirror. To justify the statement "if p is true, then q is true," we establish that "if q is not true, then p is not true" instead. Logically, these two statements are the same, but the latter, which is called the *contrapositive* of the first, may be easier to think about.

Example 3.18: *Let a and b be integers. If ab is even, then a is even or b is even.*

Justification: To justify this claim, consider the contrapositive, "If a is odd and b is odd, then ab is odd." So, suppose $a = 2j + 1$ and $b = 2k + 1$, for some integers j and k. Then $ab = 4jk + 2j + 2k + 1 = 2(2jk + j + k) + 1$; hence, ab is odd. ∎

Besides showing a use of the contrapositive justification technique, the previous example also contains an application of *DeMorgan's Law*. This law helps us deal with negations, for it states that the negation of a statement of the form "p or q" is "not p and not q." Likewise, it states that the negation of a statement of the form "p and q" is "not p or not q."

Contradiction

Another negative justification technique is justification by **contradiction**, which also often involves using DeMorgan's Law. In applying the justification by contradiction technique, we establish that a statement q is true by first supposing that q is false and then showing that this assumption leads to a contradiction (such as $2 \neq 2$ or $1 > 3$). By reaching such a contradiction, we show that no consistent situation exists with q being false, so q must be true. Of course, in order to reach this conclusion, we must be sure our situation is consistent before we assume q is false.

Example 3.19: *Let a and b be integers. If ab is odd, then a is odd and b is odd.*

Justification: Let ab be odd. We wish to show that a is odd and b is odd. So, with the hope of leading to a contradiction, let us assume the opposite, namely, suppose a is even or b is even. In fact, without loss of generality, we can assume that a is even (since the case for b is symmetric). Then $a = 2j$ for some integer j. Hence, $ab = (2j)b = 2(jb)$, that is, ab is even. But this is a contradiction: ab cannot simultaneously be odd and even. Therefore, a is odd and b is odd.   ∎

3.4.3 Induction and Loop Invariants

Most of the claims we make about a running time or a space bound involve an integer parameter n (usually denoting an intuitive notion of the "size" of the problem). Moreover, most of these claims are equivalent to saying some statement $q(n)$ is true "for all $n \geq 1$." Since this is making a claim about an infinite set of numbers, we cannot justify this exhaustively in a direct fashion.

Induction

We can often justify claims such as those above as true, however, by using the technique of **induction**. This technique amounts to showing that, for any particular $n \geq 1$, there is a finite sequence of implications that starts with something known to be true and ultimately leads to showing that $q(n)$ is true. Specifically, we begin a justification by induction by showing that $q(n)$ is true for $n = 1$ (and possibly some other values $n = 2, 3, \ldots, k$, for some constant k). Then we justify that the inductive "step" is true for $n > k$, namely, we show "if $q(j)$ is true for all $j < n$, then $q(n)$ is true." The combination of these two pieces completes the justification by induction.

Proposition 3.20: *Consider the Fibonacci function $F(n)$, which is defined such that $F(1) = 1$, $F(2) = 2$, and $F(n) = F(n-2) + F(n-1)$ for $n > 2$. (See Section 1.8.) We claim that $F(n) < 2^n$.*

Justification: We will show our claim is correct by induction.
Base cases: $(n \leq 2)$. $F(1) = 1 < 2 = 2^1$ and $F(2) = 2 < 4 = 2^2$.
Induction step: $(n > 2)$. Suppose our claim is true for all $n' < n$. Consider $F(n)$. Since $n > 2$, $F(n) = F(n-2) + F(n-1)$. Moreover, since both $n-2$ and $n-1$ are less than n, we can apply the inductive assumption (sometimes called the "inductive hypothesis") to imply that $F(n) < 2^{n-2} + 2^{n-1}$, since

$$2^{n-2} + 2^{n-1} < 2^{n-1} + 2^{n-1} = 2 \cdot 2^{n-1} = 2^n.$$

∎

Let us do another inductive argument, this time for a fact we have seen before.

Proposition 3.21: *(which is the same as Proposition 3.3)*

$$\sum_{i=1}^{n} i = \frac{n(n+1)}{2}.$$

Justification: We will justify this equality by induction.
Base case: $n = 1$. Trivial, for $1 = n(n+1)/2$, if $n = 1$.
Induction step: $n \geq 2$. Assume the claim is true for $n' < n$. Consider n.

$$\sum_{i=1}^{n} i = n + \sum_{i=1}^{n-1} i.$$

By the induction hypothesis, then

$$\sum_{i=1}^{n} i = n + \frac{(n-1)n}{2},$$

which we can simplify as

$$n + \frac{(n-1)n}{2} = \frac{2n + n^2 - n}{2} = \frac{n^2 + n}{2} = \frac{n(n+1)}{2}.$$

∎

We may sometimes feel overwhelmed by the task of justifying something true for *all* $n \geq 1$. We should remember, however, the concreteness of the inductive technique. It shows that, for any particular n, there is a finite step-by-step sequence of implications that starts with something true and leads to the truth about n. In short, the inductive argument is a template for building a sequence of direct justifications.

Loop Invariants

The final justification technique we discuss in this section is the *loop invariant*. To prove some statement $\mathcal{L}$ about a loop is correct, define $\mathcal{L}$ in terms of a series of smaller statements $\mathcal{L}_0, \mathcal{L}_1, \ldots, \mathcal{L}_k$, where:

1. The *initial* claim, $\mathcal{L}_0$, is true before the loop begins.
2. If $\mathcal{L}_{j-1}$ is true before iteration j, then $\mathcal{L}_j$ will be true after iteration j.
3. The final statement, $\mathcal{L}_k$, implies the desired statement $\mathcal{L}$ to be true.

Let us give a simple example of using a loop-invariant argument to justify the correctness of an algorithm. In particular, we use a loop invariant to justify that the function, find (see Code Fragment 3.9), finds the smallest index at which element val occurs in sequence S.

```
1  def find(S, val):
2    """Return index j such that S[j] == val, or -1 if no such element."""
3    n = len(S)
4    j = 0
5    while j < n:
6      if S[j] == val:
7        return j            # a match was found at index j
8      j += 1
9    return −1
```

Code Fragment 3.9: Algorithm for finding the first index at which a given element occurs in a Python list.

To show that find is correct, we inductively define a series of statements, $\mathcal{L}_j$, that lead to the correctness of our algorithm. Specifically, we claim the following is true at the beginning of iteration j of the **while** loop:

$\mathcal{L}_j$: *val* is not equal to any of the first j elements of S.

This claim is true at the beginning of the first iteration of the loop, because j is 0 and there are no elements among the first 0 in S (this kind of a trivially true claim is said to hold *vacuously*). In iteration j, we compare element *val* to element $S[j]$ and return the index j if these two elements are equivalent, which is clearly correct and completes the algorithm in this case. If the two elements *val* and $S[j]$ are not equal, then we have found one more element not equal to *val* and we increment the index j. Thus, the claim $\mathcal{L}_j$ will be true for this new value of j; hence, it is true at the beginning of the next iteration. If the while loop terminates without ever returning an index in S, then we have $j = n$. That is, $\mathcal{L}_n$ is true—there are no elements of S equal to *val*. Therefore, the algorithm correctly returns -1 to indicate that *val* is not in S.

3.5 Exercises

For help with exercises, please visit the site, www.wiley.com/college/goodrich.

Reinforcement

R-3.1 Graph the functions $8n$, $4n\log n$, $2n^2$, n^3, and 2^n using a logarithmic scale for the x- and y-axes; that is, if the function value $f(n)$ is y, plot this as a point with x-coordinate at $\log n$ and y-coordinate at $\log y$.

R-3.2 The number of operations executed by algorithms A and B is $8n\log n$ and $2n^2$, respectively. Determine n_0 such that A is better than B for $n \geq n_0$.

R-3.3 The number of operations executed by algorithms A and B is $40n^2$ and $2n^3$, respectively. Determine n_0 such that A is better than B for $n \geq n_0$.

R-3.4 Give an example of a function that is plotted the same on a log-log scale as it is on a standard scale.

R-3.5 Explain why the plot of the function n^c is a straight line with slope c on a log-log scale.

R-3.6 What is the sum of all the even numbers from 0 to $2n$, for any positive integer n?

R-3.7 Show that the following two statements are equivalent:
(a) The running time of algorithm A is always $O(f(n))$.
(b) In the worst case, the running time of algorithm A is $O(f(n))$.

R-3.8 Order the following functions by asymptotic growth rate.

$$4n\log n + 2n \quad 2^{10} \quad 2^{\log n}$$
$$3n + 100\log n \quad 4n \quad 2^n$$
$$n^2 + 10n \quad n^3 \quad n\log n$$

R-3.9 Show that if $d(n)$ is $O(f(n))$, then $ad(n)$ is $O(f(n))$, for any constant $a > 0$.

R-3.10 Show that if $d(n)$ is $O(f(n))$ and $e(n)$ is $O(g(n))$, then the product $d(n)e(n)$ is $O(f(n)g(n))$.

R-3.11 Show that if $d(n)$ is $O(f(n))$ and $e(n)$ is $O(g(n))$, then $d(n) + e(n)$ is $O(f(n) + g(n))$.

R-3.12 Show that if $d(n)$ is $O(f(n))$ and $e(n)$ is $O(g(n))$, then $d(n) - e(n)$ is **not necessarily** $O(f(n) - g(n))$.

R-3.13 Show that if $d(n)$ is $O(f(n))$ and $f(n)$ is $O(g(n))$, then $d(n)$ is $O(g(n))$.

R-3.14 Show that $O(\max\{f(n), g(n)\}) = O(f(n) + g(n))$.

R-3.15 Show that $f(n)$ is $O(g(n))$ if and only if $g(n)$ is $\Omega(f(n))$.

R-3.16 Show that if $p(n)$ is a polynomial in n, then $\log p(n)$ is $O(\log n)$.

R-3.17 Show that $(n+1)^5$ is $O(n^5)$.

R-3.18 Show that 2^{n+1} is $O(2^n)$.

R-3.19 Show that n is $O(n \log n)$.

R-3.20 Show that n^2 is $\Omega(n \log n)$.

R-3.21 Show that $n \log n$ is $\Omega(n)$.

R-3.22 Show that $\lceil f(n) \rceil$ is $O(f(n))$, if $f(n)$ is a positive nondecreasing function that is always greater than 1.

R-3.23 Give a big-Oh characterization, in terms of n, of the running time of the example1 function shown in Code Fragment 3.10.

R-3.24 Give a big-Oh characterization, in terms of n, of the running time of the example2 function shown in Code Fragment 3.10.

R-3.25 Give a big-Oh characterization, in terms of n, of the running time of the example3 function shown in Code Fragment 3.10.

R-3.26 Give a big-Oh characterization, in terms of n, of the running time of the example4 function shown in Code Fragment 3.10.

R-3.27 Give a big-Oh characterization, in terms of n, of the running time of the example5 function shown in Code Fragment 3.10.

R-3.28 For each function $f(n)$ and time t in the following table, determine the largest size n of a problem P that can be solved in time t if the algorithm for solving P takes $f(n)$ microseconds (one entry is already completed).

	1 Second	1 Hour	1 Month	1 Century
$\log n$	$\approx 10^{300000}$			
n				
$n \log n$				
n^2				
2^n				

R-3.29 Algorithm A executes an $O(\log n)$-time computation for each entry of an n-element sequence. What is its worst-case running time?

R-3.30 Given an n-element sequence S, Algorithm B chooses $\log n$ elements in S at random and executes an $O(n)$-time calculation for each. What is the worst-case running time of Algorithm B?

R-3.31 Given an n-element sequence S of integers, Algorithm C executes an $O(n)$-time computation for each even number in S, and an $O(\log n)$-time computation for each odd number in S. What are the best-case and worst-case running times of Algorithm C?

```
1   def example1(S):
2     """Return the sum of the elements in sequence S."""
3     n = len(S)
4     total = 0
5     for j in range(n):              # loop from 0 to n-1
6       total += S[j]
7     return total
8
9   def example2(S):
10    """Return the sum of the elements with even index in sequence S."""
11    n = len(S)
12    total = 0
13    for j in range(0, n, 2):        # note the increment of 2
14      total += S[j]
15    return total
16
17  def example3(S):
18    """Return the sum of the prefix sums of sequence S."""
19    n = len(S)
20    total = 0
21    for j in range(n):              # loop from 0 to n-1
22      for k in range(1+j):          # loop from 0 to j
23        total += S[k]
24    return total
25
26  def example4(S):
27    """Return the sum of the prefix sums of sequence S."""
28    n = len(S)
29    prefix = 0
30    total = 0
31    for j in range(n):
32      prefix += S[j]
33      total += prefix
34    return total
35
36  def example5(A, B):              # assume that A and B have equal length
37    """Return the number of elements in B equal to the sum of prefix sums in A."""
38    n = len(A)
39    count = 0
40    for i in range(n):              # loop from 0 to n-1
41      total = 0
42      for j in range(n):            # loop from 0 to n-1
43        for k in range(1+j):        # loop from 0 to j
44          total += A[k]
45      if B[i] == total:
46        count += 1
47    return count
```

Code Fragment 3.10: Some sample algorithms for analysis.

R-3.32 Given an n-element sequence S, Algorithm D calls Algorithm E on each element $S[i]$. Algorithm E runs in $O(i)$ time when it is called on element $S[i]$. What is the worst-case running time of Algorithm D?

R-3.33 Al and Bob are arguing about their algorithms. Al claims his $O(n \log n)$-time method is *always* faster than Bob's $O(n^2)$-time method. To settle the issue, they perform a set of experiments. To Al's dismay, they find that if $n < 100$, the $O(n^2)$-time algorithm runs faster, and only when $n \geq 100$ is the $O(n \log n)$-time one better. Explain how this is possible.

R-3.34 There is a well-known city (which will go nameless here) whose inhabitants have the reputation of enjoying a meal only if that meal is the best they have ever experienced in their life. Otherwise, they hate it. Assuming meal quality is distributed uniformly across a person's life, describe the expected number of times inhabitants of this city are happy with their meals?

Creativity

C-3.35 Assuming it is possible to sort n numbers in $O(n \log n)$ time, show that it is possible to solve the three-way set disjointness problem in $O(n \log n)$ time.

C-3.36 Describe an efficient algorithm for finding the ten largest elements in a sequence of size n. What is the running time of your algorithm?

C-3.37 Give an example of a positive function $f(n)$ such that $f(n)$ is neither $O(n)$ nor $\Omega(n)$.

C-3.38 Show that $\sum_{i=1}^{n} i^2$ is $O(n^3)$.

C-3.39 Show that $\sum_{i=1}^{n} i/2^i < 2$. (Hint: Try to bound this sum term by term with a geometric progression.)

C-3.40 Show that $\log_b f(n)$ is $\Theta(\log f(n))$ if $b > 1$ is a constant.

C-3.41 Describe an algorithm for finding both the minimum and maximum of n numbers using fewer than $3n/2$ comparisons. (Hint: First, construct a group of candidate minimums and a group of candidate maximums.)

C-3.42 Bob built a Web site and gave the URL only to his n friends, which he numbered from 1 to n. He told friend number i that he/she can visit the Web site at most i times. Now Bob has a counter, C, keeping track of the total number of visits to the site (but not the identities of who visits). What is the minimum value for C such that Bob can know that one of his friends has visited his/her maximum allowed number of times?

C-3.43 Draw a visual justification of Proposition 3.3 analogous to that of Figure 3.3(b) for the case when n is odd.

C-3.44 Communication security is extremely important in computer networks, and one way many network protocols achieve security is to encrypt messages. Typical *cryptographic* schemes for the secure transmission of messages over such networks are based on the fact that no efficient algorithms are known for factoring large integers. Hence, if we can represent a secret message by a large prime number p, we can transmit, over the network, the number $r = p \cdot q$, where $q > p$ is another large prime number that acts as the *encryption key*. An eavesdropper who obtains the transmitted number r on the network would have to factor r in order to figure out the secret message p.

Using factoring to figure out a message is very difficult without knowing the encryption key q. To understand why, consider the following naive factoring algorithm:

```
for p in range(2,r):
    if r % p == 0:                        # if p divides r
        return 'The secret message is p!'
```

a. Suppose that the eavesdropper uses the above algorithm and has a computer that can carry out in 1 microsecond (1 millionth of a second) a division between two integers of up to 100 bits each. Give an estimate of the time that it will take in the worst case to decipher the secret message p if the transmitted message r has 100 bits.

b. What is the worst-case time complexity of the above algorithm? Since the input to the algorithm is just one large number r, assume that the input size n is the number of bytes needed to store r, that is, $n = \lfloor (\log_2 r)/8 \rfloor + 1$, and that each division takes time $O(n)$.

C-3.45 A sequence S contains $n-1$ unique integers in the range $[0, n-1]$, that is, there is one number from this range that is not in S. Design an $O(n)$-time algorithm for finding that number. You are only allowed to use $O(1)$ additional space besides the sequence S itself.

C-3.46 Al says he can prove that all sheep in a flock are the same color:

Base case: One sheep. It is clearly the same color as itself.

Induction step: A flock of n sheep. Take a sheep, a, out. The remaining $n-1$ are all the same color by induction. Now put sheep a back in and take out a different sheep, b. By induction, the $n-1$ sheep (now with a) are all the same color. Therefore, all the sheep in the flock are the same color. What is wrong with Al's "justification"?

C-3.47 Let S be a set of n lines in the plane such that no two are parallel and no three meet in the same point. Show, by induction, that the lines in S determine $\Theta(n^2)$ intersection points.

C-3.48 Consider the following "justification" that the Fibonacci function, $F(n)$ (see Proposition 3.20) is $O(n)$:
Base case $(n \leq 2)$: $F(1) = 1$ and $F(2) = 2$.
Induction step $(n > 2)$: Assume claim true for $n' < n$. Consider n. $F(n) = F(n-2) + F(n-1)$. By induction, $F(n-2)$ is $O(n-2)$ and $F(n-1)$ is $O(n-1)$. Then, $F(n)$ is $O((n-2) + (n-1))$, by the identity presented in Exercise R-3.11. Therefore, $F(n)$ is $O(n)$.
What is wrong with this "justification"?

C-3.49 Consider the Fibonacci function, $F(n)$ (see Proposition 3.20). Show by induction that $F(n)$ is $\Omega((3/2)^n)$.

C-3.50 Let $p(x)$ be a polynomial of degree n, that is, $p(x) = \sum_{i=0}^{n} a_i x^i$.
(a) Describe a simple $O(n^2)$-time algorithm for computing $p(x)$.
(b) Describe an $O(n \log n)$-time algorithm for computing $p(x)$, based upon a more efficient calculation of x^i.
(c) Now consider a rewriting of $p(x)$ as

$$p(x) = a_0 + x(a_1 + x(a_2 + x(a_3 + \cdots + x(a_{n-1} + x a_n) \cdots))),$$

which is known as ***Horner's method***. Using the big-Oh notation, characterize the number of arithmetic operations this method executes.

C-3.51 Show that the summation $\sum_{i=1}^{n} \log i$ is $O(n \log n)$.

C-3.52 Show that the summation $\sum_{i=1}^{n} \log i$ is $\Omega(n \log n)$.

C-3.53 An evil king has n bottles of wine, and a spy has just poisoned one of them. Unfortunately, they do not know which one it is. The poison is very deadly; just one drop diluted even a billion to one will still kill. Even so, it takes a full month for the poison to take effect. Design a scheme for determining exactly which one of the wine bottles was poisoned in just one month's time while expending $O(\log n)$ taste testers.

C-3.54 A sequence S contains n integers taken from the interval $[0, 4n]$, with repetitions allowed. Describe an efficient algorithm for determining an integer value k that occurs the most often in S. What is the running time of your algorithm?

Projects

P-3.55 Perform an experimental analysis of the three algorithms prefix_average1, prefix_average2, and prefix_average3, from Section 3.3.3. Visualize their running times as a function of the input size with a log-log chart.

P-3.56 Perform an experimental analysis that compares the relative running times of the functions shown in Code Fragment 3.10.

P-3.57 Perform experimental analysis to test the hypothesis that Python's sorted method runs in $O(n \log n)$ time on average.

P-3.58 For each of the three algorithms, unique1, unique2, and unique3, which solve the element uniqueness problem, perform an experimental analysis to determine the largest value of n such that the given algorithm runs in one minute or less.

Chapter Notes

The big-Oh notation has prompted several comments about its proper use [19, 49, 63]. Knuth [64, 63] defines it using the notation $f(n) = O(g(n))$, but says this "equality" is only "one way." We have chosen to take a more standard view of equality and view the big-Oh notation as a set, following Brassard [19]. The reader interested in studying average-case analysis is referred to the book chapter by Vitter and Flajolet [101]. For some additional mathematical tools, please refer to Appendix B.

Chapter 4

Recursion

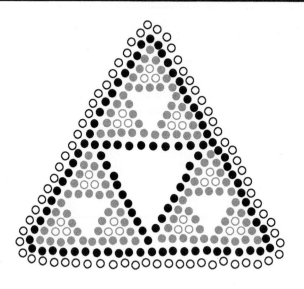

Contents

One way to describe repetition within a computer program is the use of loops, such as Python's while-loop and for-loop constructs described in Section 1.4.2. An entirely different way to achieve repetition is through a process known as *recursion*.

Recursion is a technique by which a function makes one or more calls to itself during execution, or by which a data structure relies upon smaller instances of the very same type of structure in its representation. There are many examples of recursion in art and nature. For example, fractal patterns are naturally recursive. A physical example of recursion used in art is in the Russian Matryoshka dolls. Each doll is either made of solid wood, or is hollow and contains another Matryoshka doll inside it.

In computing, recursion provides an elegant and powerful alternative for performing repetitive tasks. In fact, a few programming languages (e.g., Scheme, Smalltalk) do not explicitly support looping constructs and instead rely directly on recursion to express repetition. Most modern programming languages support functional recursion using the identical mechanism that is used to support traditional forms of function calls. When one invocation of the function make a recursive call, that invocation is suspended until the recursive call completes.

Recursion is an important technique in the study of data structures and algorithms. We will use it prominently in several later chapters of this book (most notably, Chapters 8 and 12). In this chapter, we begin with the following four illustrative examples of the use of recursion, providing a Python implementation for each.

- The *factorial function* (commonly denoted as $n!$) is a classic mathematical function that has a natural recursive definition.

- An *English ruler* has a recursive pattern that is a simple example of a fractal structure.

- *Binary search* is among the most important computer algorithms. It allows us to efficiently locate a desired value in a data set with upwards of billions of entries.

- The *file system* for a computer has a recursive structure in which directories can be nested arbitrarily deeply within other directories. Recursive algorithms are widely used to explore and manage these file systems.

We then describe how to perform a formal analysis of the running time of a recursive algorithm and we discuss some potential pitfalls when defining recursions. In the balance of the chapter, we provide many more examples of recursive algorithms, organized to highlight some common forms of design.

4.1   Illustrative Examples

4.1.1   The Factorial Function

To demonstrate the mechanics of recursion, we begin with a simple mathematical example of computing the value of the *factorial function*. The factorial of a positive integer n, denoted $n!$, is defined as the product of the integers from 1 to n. If $n = 0$, then $n!$ is defined as 1 by convention. More formally, for any integer $n \geq 0$,

$$n! = \begin{cases} 1 & \text{if } n = 0 \\ n \cdot (n-1) \cdot (n-2) \cdots 3 \cdot 2 \cdot 1 & \text{if } n \geq 1. \end{cases}$$

For example, $5! = 5 \cdot 4 \cdot 3 \cdot 2 \cdot 1 = 120$. The factorial function is important because it is known to equal the number of ways in which n distinct items can be arranged into a sequence, that is, the number of *permutations* of n items. For example, the three characters a, b, and c can be arranged in $3! = 3 \cdot 2 \cdot 1 = 6$ ways: abc, acb, bac, bca, cab, and cba.

There is a natural recursive definition for the factorial function. To see this, observe that $5! = 5 \cdot (4 \cdot 3 \cdot 2 \cdot 1) = 5 \cdot 4!$. More generally, for a positive integer n, we can define $n!$ to be $n \cdot (n-1)!$. This *recursive definition* can be formalized as

$$n! = \begin{cases} 1 & \text{if } n = 0 \\ n \cdot (n-1)! & \text{if } n \geq 1. \end{cases}$$

This definition is typical of many recursive definitions. First, it contains one or more *base cases*, which are defined nonrecursively in terms of fixed quantities. In this case, $n = 0$ is the base case. It also contains one or more *recursive cases*, which are defined by appealing to the definition of the function being defined.

A Recursive Implementation of the Factorial Function

Recursion is not just a mathematical notation; we can use recursion to design a Python implementation of a factorial function, as shown in Code Fragment 4.1.

```
1  def factorial(n):
2    if n == 0:
3      return 1
4    else:
5      return n * factorial(n−1)
```

Code Fragment 4.1: A recursive implementation of the factorial function.

This function does not use any explicit loops. Repetition is provided by the repeated recursive invocations of the function. There is no circularity in this definition, because each time the function is invoked, its argument is smaller by one, and when a base case is reached, no further recursive calls are made.

We illustrate the execution of a recursive function using a ***recursion trace***. Each entry of the trace corresponds to a recursive call. Each new recursive function call is indicated by a downward arrow to a new invocation. When the function returns, an arrow showing this return is drawn and the return value may be indicated alongside this arrow. An example of such a trace for the factorial function is shown in Figure 4.1.

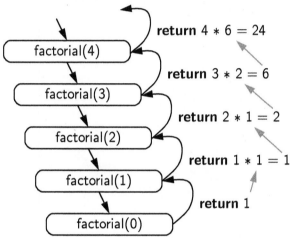

Figure 4.1: A recursion trace for the call factorial(5).

A recursion trace closely mirrors the programming language's execution of the recursion. In Python, each time a function (recursive or otherwise) is called, a structure known as an ***activation record*** or ***frame*** is created to store information about the progress of that invocation of the function. This activation record includes a namespace for storing the function call's parameters and local variables (see Section 1.10 for a discussion of namespaces), and information about which command in the body of the function is currently executing.

When the execution of a function leads to a nested function call, the execution of the former call is suspended and its activation record stores the place in the source code at which the flow of control should continue upon return of the nested call. This process is used both in the standard case of one function calling a different function, or in the recursive case in which a function invokes itself. The key point is that there is a different activation record for each active call.

4.1.2   Drawing an English Ruler

In the case of computing a factorial, there is no compelling reason for preferring recursion over a direct iteration with a loop. As a more complex example of the use of recursion, consider how to draw the markings of a typical English ruler. For each inch, we place a tick with a numeric label. We denote the length of the tick designating a whole inch as the ***major tick length***. Between the marks for whole inches, the ruler contains a series of ***minor ticks***, placed at intervals of 1/2 inch, 1/4 inch, and so on. As the size of the interval decreases by half, the tick length decreases by one. Figure 4.2 demonstrates several such rulers with varying major tick lengths (although not drawn to scale).

```
    ---- 0              ----- 0              --- 0
    -                   -                    -
    --                  --                   --
    -                   -                    -
    ---                 ---                  --- 1
    -                   -                    -
    --                  --                   --
    -                   -                    -
    ---- 1              ----                 --- 2
    -                   -                    -
    --                  --                   --
    -                   -                    -
    ---                 ---                  --- 3
    -                   -
    --                  --
    -                   -
    ---- 2              ----- 1

    (a)                 (b)                  (c)
```

Figure 4.2: Three sample outputs of an English ruler drawing: (a) a 2-inch ruler with major tick length 4; (b) a 1-inch ruler with major tick length 5; (c) a 3-inch ruler with major tick length 3.

A Recursive Approach to Ruler Drawing

The English ruler pattern is a simple example of a *fractal*, that is, a shape that has a self-recursive structure at various levels of magnification. Consider the rule with major tick length 5 shown in Figure 4.2(b). Ignoring the lines containing 0 and 1, let us consider how to draw the sequence of ticks lying between these lines. The central tick (at 1/2 inch) has length 4. Observe that the two patterns of ticks above and below this central tick are identical, and each has a central tick of length 3.

In general, an interval with a central tick length $L \geq 1$ is composed of:

- An interval with a central tick length $L - 1$
- A single tick of length L
- An interval with a central tick length $L - 1$

Although it is possible to draw such a ruler using an iterative process (see Exercise P-4.25), the task is considerably easier to accomplish with recursion. Our implementation consists of three functions, as shown in Code Fragment 4.2. The main function, draw_ruler, manages the construction of the entire ruler. Its arguments specify the total number of inches in the ruler and the major tick length. The utility function, draw_line, draws a single tick with a specified number of dashes (and an optional string label, that is printed after the tick).

The interesting work is done by the recursive draw_interval function. This function draws the sequence of minor ticks within some interval, based upon the length of the interval's central tick. We rely on the intuition shown at the top of this page, and with a base case when $L = 0$ that draws nothing. For $L \geq 1$, the first and last steps are performed by recursively calling draw_interval($L - 1$). The middle step is performed by calling the function draw_line(L).

```
 1  def draw_line(tick_length, tick_label=''):
 2    """Draw one line with given tick length (followed by optional label)."""
 3    line = '-' * tick_length
 4    if tick_label:
 5      line += ' ' + tick_label
 6    print(line)
 7
 8  def draw_interval(center_length):
 9    """Draw tick interval based upon a central tick length."""
10    if center_length > 0:                    # stop when length drops to 0
11      draw_interval(center_length - 1)       # recursively draw top ticks
12      draw_line(center_length)               # draw center tick
13      draw_interval(center_length - 1)       # recursively draw bottom ticks
14
15  def draw_ruler(num_inches, major_length):
16    """Draw English ruler with given number of inches, major tick length."""
17    draw_line(major_length, '0')             # draw inch 0 line
18    for j in range(1, 1 + num_inches):
19      draw_interval(major_length - 1)        # draw interior ticks for inch
20      draw_line(major_length, str(j))        # draw inch j line and label
```

Code Fragment 4.2: A recursive implementation of a function that draws a ruler.

Illustrating Ruler Drawing Using a Recursion Trace

The execution of the recursive draw_interval function can be visualized using a recursion trace. The trace for draw_interval is more complicated than in the factorial example, however, because each instance makes two recursive calls. To illustrate this, we will show the recursion trace in a form that is reminiscent of an outline for a document. See Figure 4.3.

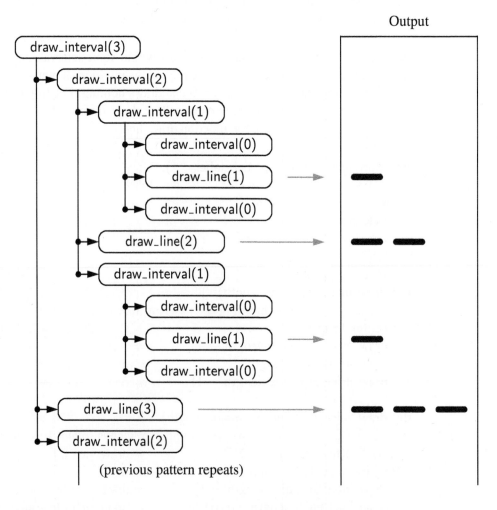

Figure 4.3: A partial recursion trace for the call draw_interval(3). The second pattern of calls for draw_interval(2) is not shown, but it is identical to the first.

4.1.3 Binary Search

In this section, we describe a classic recursive algorithm, **binary search**, that is used to efficiently locate a target value within a sorted sequence of n elements. This is among the most important of computer algorithms, and it is the reason that we so often store data in sorted order (as in Figure 4.4).

0	1	2	3	4	5	6	7	8	9	10	11	12	13	14	15
2	4	5	7	8	9	12	14	17	19	22	25	27	28	33	37

Figure 4.4: Values stored in sorted order within an indexable sequence, such as a Python list. The numbers at top are the indices.

When the sequence is **unsorted**, the standard approach to search for a target value is to use a loop to examine every element, until either finding the target or exhausting the data set. This is known as the **sequential search** algorithm. This algorithm runs in $O(n)$ time (i.e., linear time) since every element is inspected in the worst case.

When the sequence is **sorted** and **indexable**, there is a much more efficient algorithm. (For intuition, think about how you would accomplish this task by hand!) For any index j, we know that all the values stored at indices $0, \ldots, j-1$ are less than or equal to the value at index j, and all the values stored at indices $j+1, \ldots, n-1$ are greater than or equal to that at index j. This observation allows us to quickly "home in" on a search target using a variant of the children's game "high-low." We call an element of the sequence a **candidate** if, at the current stage of the search, we cannot rule out that this item matches the target. The algorithm maintains two parameters, low and high, such that all the candidate entries have index at least low and at most high. Initially, low $= 0$ and high $= n-1$. We then compare the target value to the median candidate, that is, the item data[mid] with index

$$\text{mid} = \lfloor (\text{low} + \text{high})/2 \rfloor.$$

We consider three cases:

- If the target equals data[mid], then we have found the item we are looking for, and the search terminates successfully.
- If target $<$ data[mid], then we recur on the first half of the sequence, that is, on the interval of indices from low to mid -1.
- If target $>$ data[mid], then we recur on the second half of the sequence, that is, on the interval of indices from mid $+1$ to high.

An unsuccessful search occurs if low $>$ high, as the interval [low, high] is empty.

This algorithm is known as **binary search**. We give a Python implementation in Code Fragment 4.3, and an illustration of the execution of the algorithm in Figure 4.5. Whereas sequential search runs in $O(n)$ time, the more efficient binary search runs in $O(\log n)$ time. This is a significant improvement, given that if n is one billion, $\log n$ is only 30. (We defer our formal analysis of binary search's running time to Proposition 4.2 in Section 4.2.)

```
1  def binary_search(data, target, low, high):
2    """Return True if target is found in indicated portion of a Python list.
3
4    The search only considers the portion from data[low] to data[high] inclusive.
5    """
6    if low > high:
7      return False                              # interval is empty; no match
8    else:
9      mid = (low + high) // 2
10     if target == data[mid]:                    # found a match
11       return True
12     elif target < data[mid]:
13       # recur on the portion left of the middle
14       return binary_search(data, target, low, mid − 1)
15     else:
16       # recur on the portion right of the middle
17       return binary_search(data, target, mid + 1, high)
```

Code Fragment 4.3: An implementation of the binary search algorithm.

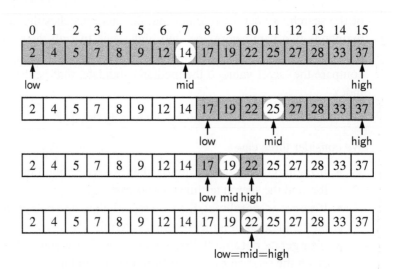

Figure 4.5: Example of a binary search for target value 22.

4.1.4 File Systems

Modern operating systems define file-system directories (which are also sometimes called "folders") in a recursive way. Namely, a file system consists of a top-level directory, and the contents of this directory consists of files and other directories, which in turn can contain files and other directories, and so on. The operating system allows directories to be nested arbitrarily deep (as long as there is enough space in memory), although there must necessarily be some base directories that contain only files, not further subdirectories. A representation of a portion of such a file system is given in Figure 4.6.

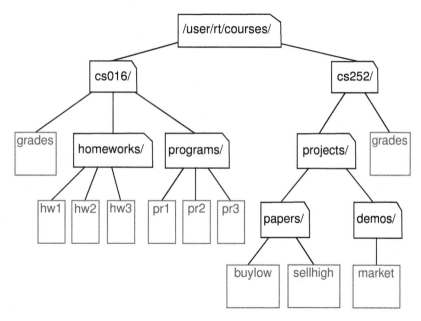

Figure 4.6: A portion of a file system demonstrating a nested organization.

Given the recursive nature of the file-system representation, it should not come as a surprise that many common behaviors of an operating system, such as copying a directory or deleting a directory, are implemented with recursive algorithms. In this section, we consider one such algorithm: computing the total disk usage for all files and directories nested within a particular directory.

For illustration, Figure 4.7 portrays the disk space being used by all entries in our sample file system. We differentiate between the *immediate* disk space used by each entry and the *cumulative* disk space used by that entry and all nested features. For example, the cs016 directory uses only 2K of immediate space, but a total of 249K of cumulative space.

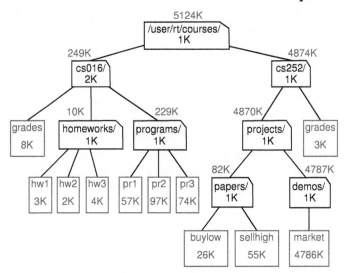

Figure 4.7: The same portion of a file system given in Figure 4.6, but with additional annotations to describe the amount of disk space that is used. Within the icon for each file or directory is the amount of space directly used by that artifact. Above the icon for each directory is an indication of the *cumulative* disk space used by that directory and all its (recursive) contents.

The cumulative disk space for an entry can be computed with a simple recursive algorithm. It is equal to the immediate disk space used by the entry plus the sum of the *cumulative* disk space usage of any entries that are stored directly within the entry. For example, the cumulative disk space for cs016 is 249K because it uses 2K itself, 8K cumulatively in grades, 10K cumulatively in homeworks, and 229K cumulatively in programs. Pseudo-code for this algorithm is given in Code Fragment 4.4.

Algorithm DiskUsage(path):

    Input: A string designating a path to a file-system entry

    Output: The cumulative disk space used by that entry and any nested entries

    total = size(path)   {immediate disk space used by the entry}

    if path represents a directory **then**

       for each child entry stored within directory path **do**

          total = total + DiskUsage(child)   {recursive call}

    return *total*

Code Fragment 4.4: An algorithm for computing the cumulative disk space usage nested at a file-system entry. Function size returns the immediate disk space of an entry.

Python's os Module

To provide a Python implementation of a recursive algorithm for computing disk usage, we rely on Python's os module, which provides robust tools for interacting with the operating system during the execution of a program. This is an extensive library, but we will only need the following four functions:

- **os.path.getsize(path)**
  Return the immediate disk usage (measured in bytes) for the file or directory that is identified by the string path (e.g., /user/rt/courses).

- **os.path.isdir(path)**
  Return True if entry designated by string path is a directory; False otherwise.

- **os.listdir(path)**
  Return a list of strings that are the names of all entries within a directory designated by string path. In our sample file system, if the parameter is /user/rt/courses, this returns the list ['cs016', 'cs252'].

- **os.path.join(path, filename)**
  Compose the path string and filename string using an appropriate operating system separator between the two (e.g., the / character for a Unix/Linux system, and the \ character for Windows). Return the string that represents the full path to the file.

Python Implementation

With use of the os module, we now convert the algorithm from Code Fragment 4.4 into the Python implementation of Code Fragment 4.5.

```
 1  import os
 2
 3  def disk_usage(path):
 4    """Return the number of bytes used by a file/folder and any descendents."""
 5    total = os.path.getsize(path)                      # account for direct usage
 6    if os.path.isdir(path):                            # if this is a directory,
 7      for filename in os.listdir(path):                # then for each child:
 8        childpath = os.path.join(path, filename)       # compose full path to child
 9        total += disk_usage(childpath)                 # add child's usage to total
10
11    print ('{0:<7}'.format(total), path)               # descriptive output (optional)
12    return total                                       # return the grand total
```

Code Fragment 4.5: A recursive function for reporting disk usage of a file system.

Recursion Trace

To produce a different form of a recursion trace, we have included an extraneous print statement within our Python implementation (line 11 of Code Fragment 4.5). The precise format of that output intentionally mirrors output that is produced by a classic Unix/Linux utility named du (for "disk usage"). It reports the amount of disk space used by a directory and all contents nested within, and can produce a verbose report, as given in Figure 4.8.

Our implementation of the disk_usage function produces an identical result, when executed on the sample file system portrayed in Figure 4.7. During the execution of the algorithm, exactly one recursive call is made for each entry in the portion of the file system that is considered. Because the print statement is made just before returning from a recursive call, the output shown in Figure 4.8 reflects the order in which the recursive calls are completed. In particular, we begin and end a recursive call for each entry that is nested below another entry, computing the nested cumulative disk space before we can compute and report the cumulative disk space for the containing entry. For example, we do not know the cumulative total for entry /user/rt/courses/cs016 until after the recursive calls regarding contained entries grades, homeworks, and programs complete.

```
8        /user/rt/courses/cs016/grades
3        /user/rt/courses/cs016/homeworks/hw1
2        /user/rt/courses/cs016/homeworks/hw2
4        /user/rt/courses/cs016/homeworks/hw3
10       /user/rt/courses/cs016/homeworks
57       /user/rt/courses/cs016/programs/pr1
97       /user/rt/courses/cs016/programs/pr2
74       /user/rt/courses/cs016/programs/pr3
229      /user/rt/courses/cs016/programs
249      /user/rt/courses/cs016
26       /user/rt/courses/cs252/projects/papers/buylow
55       /user/rt/courses/cs252/projects/papers/sellhigh
82       /user/rt/courses/cs252/projects/papers
4786     /user/rt/courses/cs252/projects/demos/market
4787     /user/rt/courses/cs252/projects/demos
4870     /user/rt/courses/cs252/projects
3        /user/rt/courses/cs252/grades
4874     /user/rt/courses/cs252
5124     /user/rt/courses/
```

Figure 4.8: A report of the disk usage for the file system shown in Figure 4.7, as generated by the Unix/Linux utility du (with command-line options -ak), or equivalently by our disk_usage function from Code Fragment 4.5.

4.2 Analyzing Recursive Algorithms

In Chapter 3, we introduced mathematical techniques for analyzing the efficiency of an algorithm, based upon an estimate of the number of primitive operations that are executed by the algorithm. We use notations such as big-Oh to summarize the relationship between the number of operations and the input size for a problem. In this section, we demonstrate how to perform this type of running-time analysis to recursive algorithms.

With a recursive algorithm, we will account for each operation that is performed based upon the particular **activation** of the function that manages the flow of control at the time it is executed. Stated another way, for each invocation of the function, we only account for the number of operations that are performed within the body of that activation. We can then account for the overall number of operations that are executed as part of the recursive algorithm by taking the sum, over all activations, of the number of operations that take place during each individual activation. (As an aside, this is also the way we analyze a nonrecursive function that calls other functions from within its body.)

To demonstrate this style of analysis, we revisit the four recursive algorithms presented in Sections 4.1.1 through 4.1.4: factorial computation, drawing an English ruler, binary search, and computation of the cumulative size of a file system. In general, we may rely on the intuition afforded by a *recursion trace* in recognizing how many recursive activations occur, and how the parameterization of each activation can be used to estimate the number of primitive operations that occur within the body of that activation. However, each of these recursive algorithms has a unique structure and form.

Computing Factorials

It is relatively easy to analyze the efficiency of our function for computing factorials, as described in Section 4.1.1. A sample recursion trace for our factorial function was given in Figure 4.1. To compute factorial(n), we see that there are a total of $n+1$ activations, as the parameter decreases from n in the first call, to $n-1$ in the second call, and so on, until reaching the base case with parameter 0.

It is also clear, given an examination of the function body in Code Fragment 4.1, that each individual activation of factorial executes a constant number of operations. Therefore, we conclude that the overall number of operations for computing factorial(n) is $O(n)$, as there are $n+1$ activations, each of which accounts for $O(1)$ operations.

Drawing an English Ruler

In analyzing the English ruler application from Section 4.1.2, we consider the fundamental question of how many total lines of output are generated by an initial call to draw_interval(c), where c denotes the center length. This is a reasonable benchmark for the overall efficiency of the algorithm as each line of output is based upon a call to the draw_line utility, and each recursive call to draw_interval with nonzero parameter makes exactly one direct call to draw_line.

Some intuition may be gained by examining the source code and the recursion trace. We know that a call to draw_interval(c) for $c > 0$ spawns two calls to draw_interval(c−1) and a single call to draw_line. We will rely on this intuition to prove the following claim.

Proposition 4.1: *For $c \geq 0$, a call to draw_interval(c) results in precisely $2^c - 1$ lines of output.*

Justification: We provide a formal proof of this claim by *induction* (see Section 3.4.3). In fact, induction is a natural mathematical technique for proving the correctness and efficiency of a recursive process. In the case of the ruler, we note that an application of draw_interval(0) generates no output, and that $2^0 - 1 = 1 - 1 = 0$. This serves as a base case for our claim.

More generally, the number of lines printed by draw_interval(c) is one more than twice the number generated by a call to draw_interval(c−1), as one center line is printed between two such recursive calls. By induction, we have that the number of lines is thus $1 + 2 \cdot (2^{c-1} - 1) = 1 + 2^c - 2 = 2^c - 1$.   ∎

This proof is indicative of a more mathematically rigorous tool, known as a *recurrence equation* that can be used to analyze the running time of a recursive algorithm. That technique is discussed in Section 12.2.4, in the context of recursive sorting algorithms.

Performing a Binary Search

Considering the running time of the binary search algorithm, as presented in Section 4.1.3, we observe that a constant number of primitive operations are executed at each recursive call of method of a binary search. Hence, the running time is proportional to the number of recursive calls performed. We will show that at most $\lfloor \log n \rfloor + 1$ recursive calls are made during a binary search of a sequence having n elements, leading to the following claim.

Proposition 4.2: *The binary search algorithm runs in $O(\log n)$ time for a sorted sequence with n elements.*

Justification: To prove this claim, a crucial fact is that with each recursive call the number of candidate entries still to be searched is given by the value

$$\text{high} - \text{low} + 1.$$

Moreover, the number of remaining candidates is reduced by at least one half with each recursive call. Specifically, from the definition of mid, the number of remaining candidates is either

$$(\text{mid} - 1) - \text{low} + 1 = \left\lfloor \frac{\text{low} + \text{high}}{2} \right\rfloor - \text{low} \leq \frac{\text{high} - \text{low} + 1}{2}$$

or

$$\text{high} - (\text{mid} + 1) + 1 = \text{high} - \left\lfloor \frac{\text{low} + \text{high}}{2} \right\rfloor \leq \frac{\text{high} - \text{low} + 1}{2}.$$

Initially, the number of candidates is n; after the first call in a binary search, it is at most $n/2$; after the second call, it is at most $n/4$; and so on. In general, after the jth call in a binary search, the number of candidate entries remaining is at most $n/2^j$. In the worst case (an unsuccessful search), the recursive calls stop when there are no more candidate entries. Hence, the maximum number of recursive calls performed, is the smallest integer r such that

$$\frac{n}{2^r} < 1.$$

In other words (recalling that we omit a logarithm's base when it is 2), $r > \log n$. Thus, we have
$$r = \lfloor \log n \rfloor + 1,$$

which implies that binary search runs in $O(\log n)$ time. ∎

Computing Disk Space Usage

Our final recursive algorithm from Section 4.1 was that for computing the overall disk space usage in a specified portion of a file system. To characterize the "problem size" for our analysis, we let n denote the number of file-system entries in the portion of the file system that is considered. (For example, the file system portrayed in Figure 4.6 has $n = 19$ entries.)

To characterize the cumulative time spent for an initial call to the disk_usage function, we must analyze the total number of recursive invocations that are made, as well as the number of operations that are executed within those invocations.

We begin by showing that there are precisely n recursive invocations of the function, in particular, one for each entry in the relevant portion of the file system. Intuitively, this is because a call to disk_usage for a particular entry e of the file system is only made from within the for loop of Code Fragment 4.5 when processing the entry for the unique directory that contains e, and that entry will only be explored once.

To formalize this argument, we can define the ***nesting level*** of each entry such that the entry on which we begin has nesting level 0, entries stored directly within it have nesting level 1, entries stored within those entries have nesting level 2, and so on. We can prove by induction that there is exactly one recursive invocation of disk_usage upon each entry at nesting level k. As a base case, when $k = 0$, the only recursive invocation made is the initial one. As the inductive step, once we know there is exactly one recursive invocation for each entry at nesting level k, we can claim that there is exactly one invocation for each entry e at nesting level k, made within the for loop for the entry at level k that contains e.

Having established that there is one recursive call for each entry of the file system, we return to the question of the overall computation time for the algorithm. It would be great if we could argue that we spend $O(1)$ time in any single invocation of the function, but that is not the case. While there are a constant number of steps reflect in the call to os.path.getsize to compute the disk usage directly at that entry, when the entry is a directory, the body of the disk_usage function includes a for loop that iterates over all entries that are contained within that directory. In the worst case, it is possible that one entry includes $n - 1$ others.

Based on this reasoning, we could conclude that there are $O(n)$ recursive calls, each of which runs in $O(n)$ time, leading to an overall running time that is $O(n^2)$. While this upper bound is technically true, it is not a tight upper bound. Remarkably, we can prove the stronger bound that the recursive algorithm for disk_usage completes in $O(n)$ time! The weaker bound was pessimistic because it assumed a worst-case number of entries for each directory. While it is possible that some directories contain a number of entries proportional to n, they cannot all contain that many. To prove the stronger claim, we choose to consider the *overall* number of iterations of the for loop across all recursive calls. We claim there are precisely $n - 1$ such iteration of that loop overall. We base this claim on the fact that each iteration of that loop makes a recursive call to disk_usage, and yet we have already concluded that there are a total of n calls to disk_usage (including the original call). We therefore conclude that there are $O(n)$ recursive calls, each of which uses $O(1)$ time outside the loop, and that the *overall* number of operations due to the loop is $O(n)$. Summing all of these bounds, the overall number of operations is $O(n)$.

The argument we have made is more advanced than with the earlier examples of recursion. The idea that we can sometimes get a tighter bound on a series of operations by considering the cumulative effect, rather than assuming that each achieves a worst case is a technique called ***amortization***; we will see a further example of such analysis in Section 5.3. Furthermore, a file system is an implicit example of a data structure known as a ***tree***, and our disk usage algorithm is really a manifestation of a more general algorithm known as a ***tree traversal***. Trees will be the focus of Chapter 8, and our argument about the $O(n)$ running time of the disk usage algorithm will be generalized for tree traversals in Section 8.4.

4.3 Recursion Run Amok

Although recursion is a very powerful tool, it can easily be misused in various ways. In this section, we examine several problems in which a poorly implemented recursion causes drastic inefficiency, and we discuss some strategies for recognizing and avoid such pitfalls.

We begin by revisiting the ***element uniqueness problem***, defined on page 135 of Section 3.3.3. We can use the following recursive formulation to determine if all n elements of a sequence are unique. As a base case, when $n = 1$, the elements are trivially unique. For $n \geq 2$, the elements are unique if and only if the first $n - 1$ elements are unique, the last $n - 1$ items are unique, and the first and last elements are different (as that is the only pair that was not already checked as a subcase). A recursive implementation based on this idea is given in Code Fragment 4.6, named unique3 (to differentiate it from unique1 and unique2 from Chapter 3).

```
1  def unique3(S, start, stop):
2      """Return True if there are no duplicate elements in slice S[start:stop]."""
3      if stop − start <= 1: return True          # at most one item
4      elif not unique(S, start, stop−1): return False   # first part has duplicate
5      elif not unique(S, start+1, stop): return False   # second part has duplicate
6      else: return S[start] != S[stop−1]         # do first and last differ?
```

Code Fragment 4.6: Recursive unique3 for testing element uniqueness.

Unfortunately, this is a terribly inefficient use of recursion. The nonrecursive part of each call uses $O(1)$ time, so the overall running time will be proportional to the total number of recursive invocations. To analyze the problem, we let n denote the number of entries under consideration, that is, let n= stop − start.

If $n = 1$, then the running time of unique3 is $O(1)$, since there are no recursive calls for this case. In the general case, the important observation is that a single call to unique3 for a problem of size n may result in two recursive calls on problems of size $n - 1$. Those two calls with size $n - 1$ could in turn result in four calls (two each) with a range of size $n - 2$, and thus eight calls with size $n - 3$ and so on. Thus, in the worst case, the total number of function calls is given by the geometric summation

$$1 + 2 + 4 + \cdots + 2^{n-1},$$

which is equal to $2^n - 1$ by Proposition 3.5. Thus, the running time of function unique3 is $O(2^n)$. This is an incredibly inefficient function for solving the element uniqueness problem. Its inefficiency comes not from the fact that it uses recursion—it comes from the fact that it uses recursion poorly, which is something we address in Exercise C-4.11.

An Inefficient Recursion for Computing Fibonacci Numbers

In Section 1.8, we introduced a process for generating the Fibonacci numbers, which can be defined recursively as follows:

$$
\begin{aligned}
F_0 &= 0 \\
F_1 &= 1 \\
F_n &= F_{n-2} + F_{n-1} \quad \text{for } n > 1.
\end{aligned}
$$

Ironically, a direct implementation based on this definition results in the function bad_fibonacci shown in Code Fragment 4.7, which computes the sequence of Fibonacci numbers by making two recursive calls in each non-base case.

```
1  def bad_fibonacci(n):
2    """Return the nth Fibonacci number."""
3    if n <= 1:
4      return n
5    else:
6      return bad_fibonacci(n-2) + bad_fibonacci(n-1)
```

Code Fragment 4.7: Computing the nth Fibonacci number using binary recursion.

Unfortunately, such a direct implementation of the Fibonacci formula results in a terribly inefficient function. Computing the nth Fibonacci number in this way requires an exponential number of calls to the function. Specifically, let c_n denote the number of calls performed in the execution of bad_fibonacci(n). Then, we have the following values for the c_n's:

$$
\begin{aligned}
c_0 &= 1 \\
c_1 &= 1 \\
c_2 &= 1 + c_0 + c_1 = 1 + 1 + 1 = 3 \\
c_3 &= 1 + c_1 + c_2 = 1 + 1 + 3 = 5 \\
c_4 &= 1 + c_2 + c_3 = 1 + 3 + 5 = 9 \\
c_5 &= 1 + c_3 + c_4 = 1 + 5 + 9 = 15 \\
c_6 &= 1 + c_4 + c_5 = 1 + 9 + 15 = 25 \\
c_7 &= 1 + c_5 + c_6 = 1 + 15 + 25 = 41 \\
c_8 &= 1 + c_6 + c_7 = 1 + 25 + 41 = 67
\end{aligned}
$$

If we follow the pattern forward, we see that the number of calls more than doubles for each two consecutive indices. That is, c_4 is more than twice c_2, c_5 is more than twice c_3, c_6 is more than twice c_4, and so on. Thus, $c_n > 2^{n/2}$, which means that bad_fibonacci(n) makes a number of calls that is exponential in n.

An Efficient Recursion for Computing Fibonacci Numbers

We were tempted into using the bad recursion formulation because of the way the nth Fibonacci number, F_n, depends on the two previous values, F_{n-2} and F_{n-1}. But notice that after computing F_{n-2}, the call to compute F_{n-1} requires its own recursive call to compute F_{n-2}, as it does not have knowledge of the value of F_{n-2} that was computed at the earlier level of recursion. That is duplicative work. Worse yet, both of those calls will need to (re)compute the value of F_{n-3}, as will the computation of F_{n-1}. This snowballing effect is what leads to the exponential running time of bad_recursion.

We can compute F_n much more efficiently using a recursion in which each invocation makes only one recursive call. To do so, we need to redefine the expectations of the function. Rather than having the function return a single value, which is the nth Fibonacci number, we define a recursive function that returns a pair of consecutive Fibonacci numbers (F_n, F_{n-1}), using the convention $F_{-1} = 0$. Although it seems to be a greater burden to report two consecutive Fibonacci numbers instead of one, passing this extra information from one level of the recursion to the next makes it much easier to continue the process. (It allows us to avoid having to recompute the second value that was already known within the recursion.) An implementation based on this strategy is given in Code Fragment 4.8.

```
1  def good_fibonacci(n):
2    """Return pair of Fibonacci numbers, F(n) and F(n-1)."""
3    if n <= 1:
4      return (n,0)
5    else:
6      (a, b) = good_fibonacci(n−1)
7      return (a+b, a)
```

Code Fragment 4.8: Computing the nth Fibonacci number using linear recursion.

In terms of efficiency, the difference between the bad recursion and the good recursion for this problem is like night and day. The bad_fibonacci function uses exponential time. We claim that the execution of function good_fibonacci(n) takes $O(n)$ time. Each recursive call to good_fibonacci decreases the argument n by 1; therefore, a recursion trace includes a series of n function calls. Because the nonrecursive work for each call uses constant time, the overall computation executes in $O(n)$ time.

4.3.1 Maximum Recursive Depth in Python

Another danger in the misuse of recursion is known as *infinite recursion*. If each recursive call makes another recursive call, without ever reaching a base case, then we have an infinite series of such calls. This is a fatal error. An infinite recursion can quickly swamp computing resources, not only due to rapid use of the CPU, but because each successive call creates an activation record requiring additional memory. A blatant example of an ill-formed recursion is the following:

```python
def fib(n):
  return fib(n)                    # fib(n) equals fib(n)
```

However, there are far more subtle errors that can lead to an infinite recursion. Revisiting our implementation of binary search in Code Fragment 4.3, in the final case (line 17) we make a recursive call on the right portion of the sequence, in particular going from index mid+1 to high. Had that line instead been written as

```python
        return binary_search(data, target, mid, high)    # note the use of mid
```

this could result in an infinite recursion. In particular, when searching a range of two elements, it becomes possible to make a recursive call on the identical range.

A programmer should ensure that each recursive call is in some way progressing toward a base case (for example, by having a parameter value that decreases with each call). However, to combat against infinite recursions, the designers of Python made an intentional decision to limit the overall number of function activations that can be simultaneously active. The precise value of this limit depends upon the Python distribution, but a typical default value is 1000. If this limit is reached, the Python interpreter raises a RuntimeError with a message, `maximum recursion depth exceeded`.

For many legitimate applications of recursion, a limit of 1000 nested function calls suffices. For example, our binary_search function (Section 4.1.3) has $O(\log n)$ recursive depth, and so for the default recursive limit to be reached, there would need to be 2^{1000} elements (far, far more than the estimated number of atoms in the universe). However, in the next section we discuss several algorithms that have recursive depth proportional to n. Python's artificial limit on the recursive depth could disrupt such otherwise legitimate computations.

Fortunately, the Python interpreter can be dynamically reconfigured to change the default recursive limit. This is done through use of a module named sys, which supports a getrecursionlimit function and a setrecursionlimit. Sample usage of those functions is demonstrated as follows:

```python
import sys
old = sys.getrecursionlimit( )         # perhaps 1000 is typical
sys.setrecursionlimit(1000000)         # change to allow 1 million nested calls
```

4.4 Further Examples of Recursion

In the remainder of this chapter, we provide additional examples of the use of recursion. We organize our presentation by considering the maximum number of recursive calls that may be started from within the body of a single activation.

- If a recursive call starts at most one other, we call this a *linear recursion*.
- If a recursive call may start two others, we call this a *binary recursion*.
- If a recursive call may start three or more others, this is *multiple recursion*.

4.4.1 Linear Recursion

If a recursive function is designed so that each invocation of the body makes at most one new recursive call, this is know as *linear recursion*. Of the recursions we have seen so far, the implementation of the factorial function (Section 4.1.1) and the good_fibonacci function (Section 4.3) are clear examples of linear recursion. More interestingly, the binary search algorithm (Section 4.1.3) is also an example of *linear recursion*, despite the "binary" terminology in the name. The code for binary search (Code Fragment 4.3) includes a case analysis with two branches that lead to recursive calls, but only one of those calls can be reached during a particular execution of the body.

A consequence of the definition of linear recursion is that any recursion trace will appear as a single sequence of calls, as we originally portrayed for the factorial function in Figure 4.1 of Section 4.1.1. Note that the *linear recursion* terminology reflects the structure of the recursion trace, not the asymptotic analysis of the running time; for example, we have seen that binary search runs in $O(\log n)$ time.

Summing the Elements of a Sequence Recursively

Linear recursion can be a useful tool for processing a data sequence, such as a Python list. Suppose, for example, that we want to compute the sum of a sequence, S, of n integers. We can solve this summation problem using linear recursion by observing that the sum of all n integers in S is trivially 0, if $n = 0$, and otherwise that it is the sum of the first $n-1$ integers in S plus the last element in S. (See Figure 4.9.)

0	1	2	3	4	5	6	7	8	9	10	11	12	13	14	15
4	3	6	2	8	9	3	2	8	5	1	7	2	8	3	7

Figure 4.9: Computing the sum of a sequence recursively, by adding the last number to the sum of the first $n-1$.

A recursive algorithm for computing the sum of a sequence of numbers based on this intuition is implemented in Code Fragment 4.9.

```
1  def linear_sum(S, n):
2    """Return the sum of the first n numbers of sequence S."""
3    if n == 0:
4      return 0
5    else:
6      return linear_sum(S, n−1) + S[n−1]
```

Code Fragment 4.9: Summing the elements of a sequence using linear recursion.

A recursion trace of the linear_sum function for a small example is given in Figure 4.10. For an input of size n, the linear_sum algorithm makes $n+1$ function calls. Hence, it will take $O(n)$ time, because it spends a constant amount of time performing the nonrecursive part of each call. Moreover, we can also see that the memory space used by the algorithm (in addition to the sequence S) is also $O(n)$, as we use a constant amount of memory space for each of the $n+1$ activation records in the trace at the time we make the final recursive call (with $n = 0$).

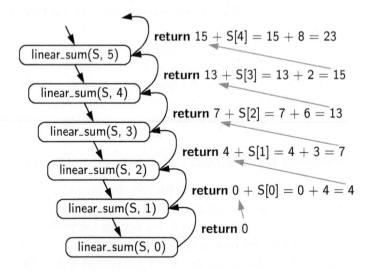

Figure 4.10: Recursion trace for an execution of linear_sum(S, 5) with input parameter S = [4, 3, 6, 2, 8].

Reversing a Sequence with Recursion

Next, let us consider the problem of reversing the *n* elements of a sequence, *S*, so that the first element becomes the last, the second element becomes second to the last, and so on. We can solve this problem using linear recursion, by observing that the reversal of a sequence can be achieved by swapping the first and last elements and then recursively reversing the remaining elements. We present an implementation of this algorithm in Code Fragment 4.10, using the convention that the first time we call this algorithm we do so as reverse(S, 0, len(S)).

```
1  def reverse(S, start, stop):
2      """Reverse elements in implicit slice S[start:stop]."""
3      if start < stop − 1:                            # if at least 2 elements:
4          S[start], S[stop−1] = S[stop−1], S[start]   # swap first and last
5          reverse(S, start+1, stop−1)                 # recur on rest
```

Code Fragment 4.10: Reversing the elements of a sequence using linear recursion.

Note that there are two implicit base case scenarios: When start == stop, the implicit range is empty, and when start == stop−1, the implicit range has only one element. In either of these cases, there is no need for action, as a sequence with zero elements or one element is trivially equal to its reversal. When otherwise invoking recursion, we are guaranteed to make progress towards a base case, as the difference, stop−start, decreases by two with each call (see Figure 4.11). If *n* is even, we will eventually reach the start == stop case, and if *n* is odd, we will eventually reach the start == stop − 1 case.

The above argument implies that the recursive algorithm of Code Fragment 4.10 is guaranteed to terminate after a total of $1 + \lfloor \frac{n}{2} \rfloor$ recursive calls. Since each call involves a constant amount of work, the entire process runs in $O(n)$ time.

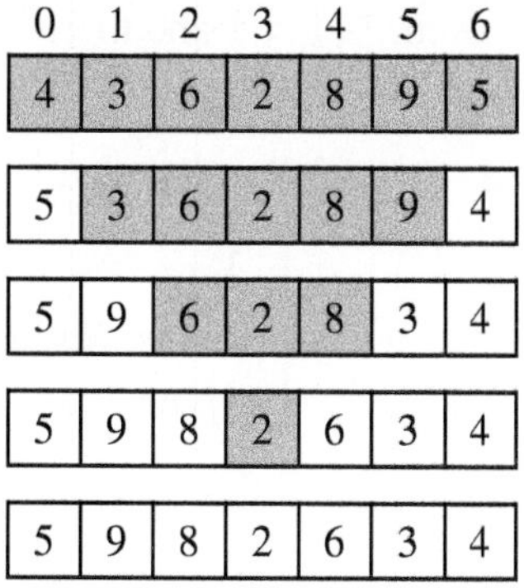

Figure 4.11: A trace of the recursion for reversing a sequence. The shaded portion has yet to be reversed.

Recursive Algorithms for Computing Powers

As another interesting example of the use of linear recursion, we consider the problem of raising a number x to an arbitrary nonnegative integer, n. That is, we wish to compute the **power function**, defined as $power(x, n) = x^n$. (We use the name "power" for this discussion, to differentiate from the built-in function pow that provides such functionality.) We will consider two different recursive formulations for the problem that lead to algorithms with very different performance.

A trivial recursive definition follows from the fact that $x^n = x \cdot x^{n-1}$ for $n > 0$.

$$power(x, n) = \begin{cases} 1 & \text{if } n = 0 \\ x \cdot power(x, n - 1) & \text{otherwise.} \end{cases}$$

This definition leads to a recursive algorithm shown in Code Fragment 4.11.

```
1  def power(x, n):
2    """Compute the value x**n for integer n."""
3    if n == 0:
4      return 1
5    else:
6      return x * power(x, n−1)
```

Code Fragment 4.11: Computing the power function using trivial recursion.

A recursive call to this version of $power(x, n)$ runs in $O(n)$ time. Its recursion trace has structure very similar to that of the factorial function from Figure 4.1, with the parameter decreasing by one with each call, and constant work performed at each of $n + 1$ levels.

However, there is a much faster way to compute the power function using an alternative definition that employs a squaring technique. Let $k = \left\lfloor \frac{n}{2} \right\rfloor$ denote the floor of the division (expressed as n // 2 in Python). We consider the expression $\left(x^k\right)^2$. When n is even, $\left\lfloor \frac{n}{2} \right\rfloor = \frac{n}{2}$ and therefore $\left(x^k\right)^2 = \left(x^{\frac{n}{2}}\right)^2 = x^n$. When n is odd, $\left\lfloor \frac{n}{2} \right\rfloor = \frac{n-1}{2}$ and $\left(x^k\right)^2 = x^{n-1}$, and therefore $x^n = x \cdot \left(x^k\right)^2$, just as $2^{13} = 2 \cdot 2^6 \cdot 2^6$. This analysis leads to the following recursive definition:

$$power(x, n) = \begin{cases} 1 & \text{if } n = 0 \\ x \cdot \left(power\left(x, \left\lfloor \frac{n}{2} \right\rfloor\right)\right)^2 & \text{if } n > 0 \text{ is odd} \\ \left(power\left(x, \left\lfloor \frac{n}{2} \right\rfloor\right)\right)^2 & \text{if } n > 0 \text{ is even} \end{cases}$$

If we were to implement this recursion making *two* recursive calls to compute $power(x, \left\lfloor \frac{n}{2} \right\rfloor) \cdot power(x, \left\lfloor \frac{n}{2} \right\rfloor)$, a trace of the recursion would demonstrate $O(n)$ calls. We can perform significantly fewer operations by computing $power(x, \left\lfloor \frac{n}{2} \right\rfloor)$ as a partial result, and then multiplying it by itself. An implementation based on this recursive definition is given in Code Fragment 4.12.

```
1   def power(x, n):
2     """Compute the value x**n for integer n."""
3     if n == 0:
4       return 1
5     else:
6       partial = power(x, n // 2)              # rely on truncated division
7       result = partial * partial
8       if n % 2 == 1:                          # if n odd, include extra factor of x
9         result *= x
10      return result
```

Code Fragment 4.12: Computing the power function using repeated squaring.

To illustrate the execution of our improved algorithm, Figure 4.12 provides a recursion trace of the computation power(2, 13).

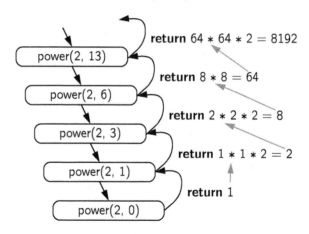

Figure 4.12: Recursion trace for an execution of power(2, 13).

To analyze the running time of the revised algorithm, we observe that the exponent in each recursive call of function power(x,n) is at most half of the preceding exponent. As we saw with the analysis of binary search, the number of times that we can divide n in half before getting to one or less is $O(\log n)$. Therefore, our new formulation of the power function results in $O(\log n)$ recursive calls. Each individual activation of the function uses $O(1)$ operations (excluding the recursive calls), and so the total number of operations for computing power(x,n) is $O(\log n)$. This is a significant improvement over the original $O(n)$-time algorithm.

The improved version also provides significant saving in reducing the memory usage. The first version has a recursive depth of $O(n)$, and therefore $O(n)$ activation records are simultaneous stored in memory. Because the recursive depth of the improved version is $O(\log n)$, its memory usages is $O(\log n)$ as well.

4.4.2   Binary Recursion

When a function makes two recursive calls, we say that it uses ***binary recursion***. We have already seen several examples of binary recursion, most notably when drawing the English ruler (Section 4.1.2), or in the bad_fibonacci function of Section 4.3. As another application of binary recursion, let us revisit the problem of summing the n elements of a sequence, S, of numbers. Computing the sum of one or zero elements is trivial. With two or more elements, we can recursively compute the sum of the first half, and the sum of the second half, and add these sums together. Our implementation of such an algorithm, in Code Fragment 4.13, is initially invoked as binary_sum(A, 0, len(A)).

```
1  def binary_sum(S, start, stop):
2    """Return the sum of the numbers in implicit slice S[start:stop]."""
3    if start >= stop:                       # zero elements in slice
4      return 0
5    elif start == stop−1:                   # one element in slice
6      return S[start]
7    else:                                   # two or more elements in slice
8      mid = (start + stop) // 2
9      return binary_sum(S, start, mid) + binary_sum(S, mid, stop)
```

Code Fragment 4.13: Summing the elements of a sequence using binary recursion.

To analyze algorithm binary_sum, we consider, for simplicity, the case where n is a power of two. Figure 4.13 shows the recursion trace of an execution of binary_sum(0, 8). We label each box with the values of parameters start:stop for that call. The size of the range is divided in half at each recursive call, and so the depth of the recursion is $1 + \log_2 n$. Therefore, binary_sum uses $O(\log n)$ amount of additional space, which is a big improvement over the $O(n)$ space used by the linear_sum function of Code Fragment 4.9. However, the running time of binary_sum is $O(n)$, as there are $2n - 1$ function calls, each requiring constant time.

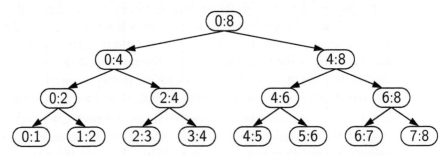

Figure 4.13: Recursion trace for the execution of binary_sum(0, 8).

4.4.3 Multiple Recursion

Generalizing from binary recursion, we define ***multiple recursion*** as a process in which a function may make more than two recursive calls. Our recursion for analyzing the disk space usage of a file system (see Section 4.1.4) is an example of multiple recursion, because the number of recursive calls made during one invocation was equal to the number of entries within a given directory of the file system.

Another common application of multiple recursion is when we want to enumerate various configurations in order to solve a combinatorial puzzle. For example, the following are all instances of what are known as ***summation puzzles***:

$$pot + pan = bib$$
$$dog + cat = pig$$
$$boy + girl = baby$$

To solve such a puzzle, we need to assign a unique digit (that is, $0, 1, \ldots, 9$) to each letter in the equation, in order to make the equation true. Typically, we solve such a puzzle by using our human observations of the particular puzzle we are trying to solve to eliminate configurations (that is, possible partial assignments of digits to letters) until we can work though the feasible configurations left, testing for the correctness of each one.

If the number of possible configurations is not too large, however, we can use a computer to simply enumerate all the possibilities and test each one, without employing any human observations. In addition, such an algorithm can use multiple recursion to work through the configurations in a systematic way. We show pseudocode for such an algorithm in Code Fragment 4.14. To keep the description general enough to be used with other puzzles, the algorithm enumerates and tests all k-length sequences without repetitions of the elements of a given universe U. We build the sequences of k elements by the following steps:

1. Recursively generating the sequences of $k - 1$ elements
2. Appending to each such sequence an element not already contained in it.

Throughout the execution of the algorithm, we use a set U to keep track of the elements not contained in the current sequence, so that an element e has not been used yet if and only if e is in U.

Another way to look at the algorithm of Code Fragment 4.14 is that it enumerates every possible size-k ordered subset of U, and tests each subset for being a possible solution to our puzzle.

For summation puzzles, $U = \{0, 1, 2, 3, 4, 5, 6, 7, 8, 9\}$ and each position in the sequence corresponds to a given letter. For example, the first position could stand for b, the second for o, the third for y, and so on.

Algorithm PuzzleSolve(k,S,U):

    Input: An integer k, sequence S, and set U

    Output: An enumeration of all k-length extensions to S using elements in U
        without repetitions

    for each e in U **do**

        Add e to the end of S

        Remove e from U   {e is now being used}

        if k == 1 **then**

            Test whether S is a configuration that solves the puzzle

            if S solves the puzzle **then**

                return "Solution found: " S

        else

            PuzzleSolve(k−1,S,U)   {a recursive call}

        Remove e from the end of S

        Add e back to U   {e is now considered as unused}

Code Fragment 4.14: Solving a combinatorial puzzle by enumerating and testing all possible configurations.

In Figure 4.14, we show a recursion trace of a call to PuzzleSolve$(3, S, U)$, where S is empty and $U = \{a, b, c\}$. During the execution, all the permutations of the three characters are generated and tested. Note that the initial call makes three recursive calls, each of which in turn makes two more. If we had executed PuzzleSolve$(3, S, U)$ on a set U consisting of four elements, the initial call would have made four recursive calls, each of which would have a trace looking like the one in Figure 4.14.

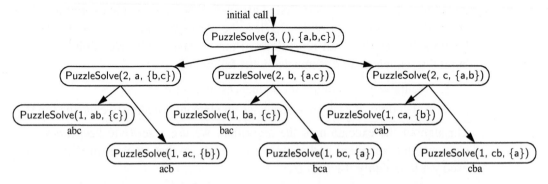

Figure 4.14: Recursion trace for an execution of PuzzleSolve$(3, S, U)$, where S is empty and $U = \{a, b, c\}$. This execution generates and tests all permutations of $a, b,$ and c. We show the permutations generated directly below their respective boxes.

4.5 Designing Recursive Algorithms

In general, an algorithm that uses recursion typically has the following form:

- *Test for base cases.* We begin by testing for a set of base cases (there should be at least one). These base cases should be defined so that every possible chain of recursive calls will eventually reach a base case, and the handling of each base case should not use recursion.

- *Recur.* If not a base case, we perform one or more recursive calls. This recursive step may involve a test that decides which of several possible recursive calls to make. We should define each possible recursive call so that it makes progress towards a base case.

Parameterizing a Recursion

To design a recursive algorithm for a given problem, it is useful to think of the different ways we might define subproblems that have the same general structure as the original problem. If one has difficulty finding the repetitive structure needed to design a recursive algorithm, it is sometimes useful to work out the problem on a few concrete examples to see how the subproblems should be defined.

A successful recursive design sometimes requires that we redefine the original problem to facilitate similar-looking subproblems. Often, this involved reparameterizing the signature of the function. For example, when performing a binary search in a sequence, a natural function signature for a caller would appear as binary_search(data, target). However, in Section 4.1.3, we defined our function with calling signature binary_search(data, target, low, high), using the additional parameters to demarcate sublists as the recursion proceeds. This change in parameterization is critical for binary search. If we had insisted on the cleaner signature, binary_search(data, target), the only way to invoke a search on half the list would have been to make a new list instance with only those elements to send as the first parameter. However, making a copy of half the list would already take $O(n)$ time, negating the whole benefit of the binary search algorithm.

If we wished to provide a cleaner public interface to an algorithm like binary search, without bothering a user with the extra parameters, a standard technique is to make one function for public use with the cleaner interface, such as binary_search(data, target), and then having its body invoke a nonpublic utility function having the desired recursive parameters.

You will see that we similarly reparameterized the recursion in several other examples of this chapter (e.g., reverse, linear_sum, binary_sum). We saw a different approach to redefining a recursion in our good_fibonacci implementation, by intentionally strengthening the expectation of what is returned (in that case, returning a pair of numbers rather than a single number).

4.6   Eliminating Tail Recursion

The main benefit of a recursive approach to algorithm design is that it allows us to succinctly take advantage of a repetitive structure present in many problems. By making our algorithm description exploit the repetitive structure in a recursive way, we can often avoid complex case analyses and nested loops. This approach can lead to more readable algorithm descriptions, while still being quite efficient.

However, the usefulness of recursion comes at a modest cost. In particular, the Python interpreter must maintain activation records that keep track of the state of each nested call. When computer memory is at a premium, it is useful in some cases to be able to derive nonrecursive algorithms from recursive ones.

In general, we can use the stack data structure, which we will introduce in Section 6.1, to convert a recursive algorithm into a nonrecursive algorithm by managing the nesting of the recursive structure ourselves, rather than relying on the interpreter to do so. Although this only shifts the memory usage from the interpreter to our stack, we may be able to reduce the memory usage by storing only the minimal information necessary.

Even better, some forms of recursion can be eliminated without any use of axillary memory. A notable such form is known as *tail recursion*. A recursion is a tail recursion if any recursive call that is made from one context is the very last operation in that context, with the return value of the recursive call (if any) immediately returned by the enclosing recursion. By necessity, a tail recursion must be a linear recursion (since there is no way to make a second recursive call if you must immediately return the result of the first).

Of the recursive functions demonstrated in this chapter, the binary_search function of Code Fragment 4.3 and the reverse function of Code Fragment 4.10 are examples of tail recursion. Several others of our linear recursions are almost like tail recursion, but not technically so. For example, our factorial function of Code Fragment 4.1 is *not* a tail recursion. It concludes with the command:

return n * factorial(n−1)

This is not a tail recursion because an additional multiplication is performed after the recursive call is completed. For similar reasons, the linear_sum function of Code Fragment 4.9 and the good_fibonacci function of Code Fragment 4.7 fail to be tail recursions.

Any tail recursion can be reimplemented nonrecursively by enclosing the body in a loop for repetition, and replacing a recursive call with new parameters by a reassignment of the existing parameters to those values. As a tangible example, our binary_search function can be reimplemented as shown in Code Fragment 4.15. We initialize variables low and high, just prior to our while loop, to represent the full extent of the sequence. Then, during each pass of the loop, we either find

```
 1  def binary_search_iterative(data, target):
 2    """Return True if target is found in the given Python list."""
 3    low = 0
 4    high = len(data)−1
 5    while low <= high:
 6      mid = (low + high) // 2
 7      if target == data[mid]:          # found a match
 8        return True
 9      elif target < data[mid]:
10        high = mid − 1                 # only consider values left of mid
11      else:
12        low = mid + 1                  # only consider values right of mid
13    return False                       # loop ended without success
```

Code Fragment 4.15: A nonrecursive implementation of binary search.

the target, or we narrow the range of the candidate subsequence. Where we made the recursive call binary_search(data, target, low, mid −1) in the original version, we simply replace high = mid − 1 in our new version and then continue to the next iteration of the loop. Our original base case condition of low > high has simply been replaced by the opposite loop condition **while** low <= high. In our new implementation, we return False to designate a failed search if the while loop ends (that is, without having ever returned True from within).

We can similarly develop a nonrecursive implementation (Code Fragment 4.16) of the original recursive reverse method of Code Fragment 4.10.

```
 1  def reverse_iterative(S):
 2    """Reverse elements in sequence S."""
 3    start, stop = 0, len(S)
 4    while start < stop − 1:
 5      S[start], S[stop−1] = S[stop−1], S[start]    # swap first and last
 6      start, stop = start + 1, stop − 1            # narrow the range
```

Code Fragment 4.16: Reversing the elements of a sequence using iteration.

In this new version, we update the values start and stop during each pass of the loop, exiting once we reach the case of having one or less elements in that range.

Many other linear recursions can be expressed quite efficiently with iteration, even if they were not formally tail recursions. For example, there are trivial nonrecursive implementations for computing factorials, summing elements of a sequence, or computing Fibonacci numbers efficiently. In fact, our implementation of a Fibonacci generator, from Section 1.8, produces each subsequent value in $O(1)$ time, and thus takes $O(n)$ time to generate the nth entry in the series.

4.7 Exercises

For help with exercises, please visit the site, www.wiley.com/college/goodrich.

Reinforcement

R-4.1 Describe a recursive algorithm for finding the maximum element in a sequence, S, of n elements. What is your running time and space usage?

R-4.2 Draw the recursion trace for the computation of *power*$(2,5)$, using the traditional function implemented in Code Fragment 4.11.

R-4.3 Draw the recursion trace for the computation of *power*$(2,18)$, using the repeated squaring algorithm, as implemented in Code Fragment 4.12.

R-4.4 Draw the recursion trace for the execution of function reverse(S, 0, 5) (Code Fragment 4.10) on S = [4, 3, 6, 2, 6].

R-4.5 Draw the recursion trace for the execution of function PuzzleSolve$(3,S,U)$ (Code Fragment 4.14), where S is empty and $U = \{a,b,c,d\}$.

R-4.6 Describe a recursive function for computing the nth **Harmonic number**, $H_n = \sum_{i=1}^{n} 1/i$.

R-4.7 Describe a recursive function for converting a string of digits into the integer it represents. For example, '13531' represents the integer $13,531$.

R-4.8 Isabel has an interesting way of summing up the values in a sequence A of n integers, where n is a power of two. She creates a new sequence B of half the size of A and sets $B[i] = A[2i] + A[2i+1]$, for $i = 0, 1, \ldots, (n/2) - 1$. If B has size 1, then she outputs $B[0]$. Otherwise, she replaces A with B, and repeats the process. What is the running time of her algorithm?

Creativity

C-4.9 Write a short recursive Python function that finds the minimum and maximum values in a sequence without using any loops.

C-4.10 Describe a recursive algorithm to compute the integer part of the base-two logarithm of n using only addition and integer division.

C-4.11 Describe an efficient recursive function for solving the element uniqueness problem, which runs in time that is at most $O(n^2)$ in the worst case without using sorting.

C-4.12 Give a recursive algorithm to compute the product of two positive integers, m and n, using only addition and subtraction.

C-4.13 In Section 4.2 we prove by induction that the number of *lines* printed by a call to draw_interval(c) is $2^c - 1$. Another interesting question is how many *dashes* are printed during that process. Prove by induction that the number of dashes printed by draw_interval(c) is $2^{c+1} - c - 2$.

C-4.14 In the ***Towers of Hanoi*** puzzle, we are given a platform with three pegs, a, b, and c, sticking out of it. On peg a is a stack of n disks, each larger than the next, so that the smallest is on the top and the largest is on the bottom. The puzzle is to move all the disks from peg a to peg c, moving one disk at a time, so that we never place a larger disk on top of a smaller one. See Figure 4.15 for an example of the case $n = 4$. Describe a recursive algorithm for solving the Towers of Hanoi puzzle for arbitrary n. (Hint: Consider first the subproblem of moving all but the nth disk from peg a to another peg using the third as "temporary storage.")

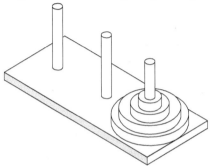

Figure 4.15: An illustration of the Towers of Hanoi puzzle.

C-4.15 Write a recursive function that will output all the subsets of a set of n elements (without repeating any subsets).

C-4.16 Write a short recursive Python function that takes a character string s and outputs its reverse. For example, the reverse of 'pots&pans' would be 'snap&stop'.

C-4.17 Write a short recursive Python function that determines if a string s is a palindrome, that is, it is equal to its reverse. For example, 'racecar' and 'gohangasalamiimalasagnahog' are palindromes.

C-4.18 Use recursion to write a Python function for determining if a string s has more vowels than consonants.

C-4.19 Write a short recursive Python function that rearranges a sequence of integer values so that all the even values appear before all the odd values.

C-4.20 Given an unsorted sequence, S, of integers and an integer k, describe a recursive algorithm for rearranging the elements in S so that all elements less than or equal to k come before any elements larger than k. What is the running time of your algorithm on a sequence of n values?

C-4.21 Suppose you are given an n-element sequence, S, containing distinct integers that are listed in increasing order. Given a number k, describe a recursive algorithm to find two integers in S that sum to k, if such a pair exists. What is the running time of your algorithm?

C-4.22 Develop a nonrecursive implementation of the version of power from Code Fragment 4.12 that uses repeated squaring.

Projects

P-4.23 Implement a recursive function with signature find(path, filename) that reports all entries of the file system rooted at the given path having the given file name.

P-4.24 Write a program for solving summation puzzles by enumerating and testing all possible configurations. Using your program, solve the three puzzles given in Section 4.4.3.

P-4.25 Provide a nonrecursive implementation of the draw_interval function for the English ruler project of Section 4.1.2. There should be precisely $2^c - 1$ lines of output if c represents the length of the center tick. If incrementing a counter from 0 to $2^c - 2$, the number of dashes for each tick line should be exactly one more than the number of consecutive 1's at the end of the binary representation of the counter.

P-4.26 Write a program that can solve instances of the Tower of Hanoi problem (from Exercise C-4.14).

P-4.27 Python's os module provides a function with signature walk(path) that is a generator yielding the tuple (dirpath, dirnames, filenames) for each subdirectory of the directory identified by string path, such that string dirpath is the full path to the subdirectory, dirnames is a list of the names of the subdirectories within dirpath, and filenames is a list of the names of non-directory entries of dirpath. For example, when visiting the cs016 subdirectory of the file system shown in Figure 4.6, the walk would yield ('/user/rt/courses/cs016', ['homeworks', 'programs'], ['grades']). Give your own implementation of such a walk function.

Chapter Notes

The use of recursion in programs belongs to the folkore of computer science (for example, see the article of Dijkstra [36]). It is also at the heart of functional programming languages (for example, see the classic book by Abelson, Sussman, and Sussman [1]). Interestingly, binary search was first published in 1946, but was not published in a fully correct form until 1962. For further discussions on lessons learned, please see papers by Bentley [14] and Lesuisse [68].

Chapter

5

Array-Based Sequences

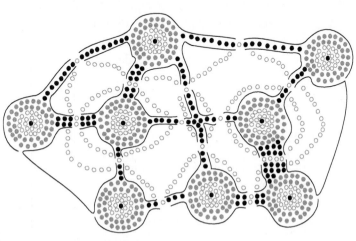

Contents

5.1   Python's Sequence Types

In this chapter, we explore Python's various "sequence" classes, namely the built-in **list**, **tuple**, and **str** classes. There is significant commonality between these classes, most notably: each supports indexing to access an individual element of a sequence, using a syntax such as seq[k], and each uses a low-level concept known as an *array* to represent the sequence. However, there are significant differences in the abstractions that these classes represent, and in the way that instances of these classes are represented internally by Python. Because these classes are used so widely in Python programs, and because they will become building blocks upon which we will develop more complex data structures, it is imperative that we establish a clear understanding of both the public behavior and inner workings of these classes.

Public Behaviors

A proper understanding of the outward semantics for a class is a necessity for a good programmer. While the basic usage of lists, strings, and tuples may seem straightforward, there are several important subtleties regarding the behaviors associated with these classes (such as what it means to make a copy of a sequence, or to take a slice of a sequence). Having a misunderstanding of a behavior can easily lead to inadvertent bugs in a program. Therefore, we establish an accurate mental model for each of these classes. These images will help when exploring more advanced usage, such as representing a multidimensional data set as a list of lists.

Implementation Details

A focus on the internal implementations of these classes seems to go against our stated principles of object-oriented programming. In Section 2.1.2, we emphasized the principle of *encapsulation*, noting that the user of a class need not know about the internal details of the implementation. While it is true that one only needs to understand the syntax and semantics of a class's public interface in order to be able to write legal and correct code that uses instances of the class, the efficiency of a program depends greatly on the efficiency of the components upon which it relies.

Asymptotic and Experimental Analyses

In describing the efficiency of various operations for Python's sequence classes, we will rely on the formal *asymptotic analysis* notations established in Chapter 3. We will also perform experimental analyses of the primary operations to provide empirical evidence that is consistent with the more theoretical asymptotic analyses.

5.2 Low-Level Arrays

To accurately describe the way in which Python represents the sequence types, we must first discuss aspects of the low-level computer architecture. The primary memory of a computer is composed of bits of information, and those bits are typically grouped into larger units that depend upon the precise system architecture. Such a typical unit is a ***byte***, which is equivalent to 8 bits.

A computer system will have a huge number of bytes of memory, and to keep track of what information is stored in what byte, the computer uses an abstraction known as a ***memory address***. In effect, each byte of memory is associated with a unique number that serves as its address (more formally, the binary representation of the number serves as the address). In this way, the computer system can refer to the data in "byte #2150" versus the data in "byte #2157," for example. Memory addresses are typically coordinated with the physical layout of the memory system, and so we often portray the numbers in sequential fashion. Figure 5.1 provides such a diagram, with the designated memory address for each byte.

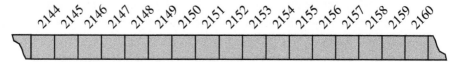

Figure 5.1: A representation of a portion of a computer's memory, with individual bytes labeled with consecutive memory addresses.

Despite the sequential nature of the numbering system, computer hardware is designed, in theory, so that any byte of the main memory can be efficiently accessed based upon its memory address. In this sense, we say that a computer's main memory performs as ***random access memory (RAM)***. That is, it is just as easy to retrieve byte #8675309 as it is to retrieve byte #309. (In practice, there are complicating factors including the use of caches and external memory; we address some of those issues in Chapter 15.) Using the notation for asymptotic analysis, we say that any individual byte of memory can be stored or retrieved in $O(1)$ time.

In general, a programming language keeps track of the association between an identifier and the memory address in which the associated value is stored. For example, identifier x might be associated with one value stored in memory, while y is associated with another value stored in memory. A common programming task is to keep track of a sequence of related objects. For example, we may want a video game to keep track of the top ten scores for that game. Rather than use ten different variables for this task, we would prefer to use a single name for the group and use index numbers to refer to the high scores in that group.

A group of related variables can be stored one after another in a contiguous portion of the computer's memory. We will denote such a representation as an *array*. As a tangible example, a text string is stored as an ordered sequence of individual characters. In Python, each character is represented using the Unicode character set, and on most computing systems, Python internally represents each Unicode character with 16 bits (i.e., 2 bytes). Therefore, a six-character string, such as 'SAMPLE', would be stored in 12 consecutive bytes of memory, as diagrammed in Figure 5.2.

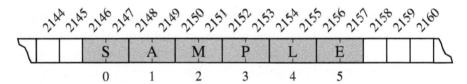

Figure 5.2: A Python string embedded as an array of characters in the computer's memory. We assume that each Unicode character of the string requires two bytes of memory. The numbers below the entries are indices into the string.

We describe this as an *array of six characters*, even though it requires 12 bytes of memory. We will refer to each location within an array as a *cell*, and will use an integer *index* to describe its location within the array, with cells numbered starting with 0, 1, 2, and so on. For example, in Figure 5.2, the cell of the array with index 4 has contents L and is stored in bytes 2154 and 2155 of memory.

Each cell of an array must use the same number of bytes. This requirement is what allows an arbitrary cell of the array to be accessed in constant time based on its index. In particular, if one knows the memory address at which an array starts (e.g., 2146 in Figure 5.2), the number of bytes per element (e.g., 2 for a Unicode character), and a desired index within the array, the appropriate memory address can be computed using the calculation, start + cellsize * index. By this formula, the cell at index 0 begins precisely at the start of the array, the cell at index 1 begins precisely cellsize bytes beyond the start of the array, and so on. As an example, cell 4 of Figure 5.2 begins at memory location $2146 + 2 \cdot 4 = 2146 + 8 = 2154$.

Of course, the arithmetic for calculating memory addresses within an array can be handled automatically. Therefore, a programmer can envision a more typical high-level abstraction of an array of characters as diagrammed in Figure 5.3.

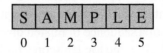

Figure 5.3: A higher-level abstraction for the string portrayed in Figure 5.2.

5.2.1 Referential Arrays

As another motivating example, assume that we want a medical information system to keep track of the patients currently assigned to beds in a certain hospital. If we assume that the hospital has 200 beds, and conveniently that those beds are numbered from 0 to 199, we might consider using an array-based structure to maintain the names of the patients currently assigned to those beds. For example, in Python we might use a list of names, such as:

['Rene', 'Joseph', 'Janet', 'Jonas', 'Helen', 'Virginia', ...]

To represent such a list with an array, Python must adhere to the requirement that each cell of the array use the same number of bytes. Yet the elements are strings, and strings naturally have different lengths. Python could attempt to reserve enough space for each cell to hold the *maximum* length string (not just of currently stored strings, but of any string we might ever want to store), but that would be wasteful.

Instead, Python represents a list or tuple instance using an internal storage mechanism of an array of object *references*. At the lowest level, what is stored is a consecutive sequence of memory addresses at which the elements of the sequence reside. A high-level diagram of such a list is shown in Figure 5.4.

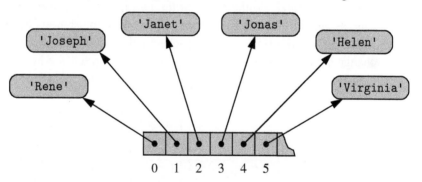

Figure 5.4: An array storing references to strings.

Although the relative size of the individual elements may vary, the number of bits used to store the memory address of each element is fixed (e.g., 64-bits per address). In this way, Python can support constant-time access to a list or tuple element based on its index.

In Figure 5.4, we characterize a list of strings that are the names of the patients in a hospital. It is more likely that a medical information system would manage more comprehensive information on each patient, perhaps represented as an instance of a Patient class. From the perspective of the list implementation, the same principle applies: The list will simply keep a sequence of references to those objects. Note as well that a reference to the **None** object can be used as an element of the list to represent an empty bed in the hospital.

The fact that lists and tuples are referential structures is significant to the semantics of these classes. A single list instance may include multiple references to the same object as elements of the list, and it is possible for a single object to be an element of two or more lists, as those lists simply store references back to that object. As an example, when you compute a slice of a list, the result is a new list instance, but that new list has references to the same elements that are in the original list, as portrayed in Figure 5.5.

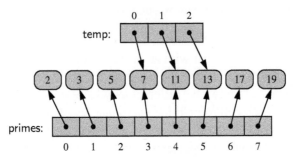

Figure 5.5: The result of the command temp = primes[3:6].

When the elements of the list are immutable objects, as with the integer instances in Figure 5.5, the fact that the two lists share elements is not that significant, as neither of the lists can cause a change to the shared object. If, for example, the command temp[2] = 15 were executed from this configuration, that does not change the existing integer object; it changes the reference in cell 2 of the temp list to reference a different object. The resulting configuration is shown in Figure 5.6.

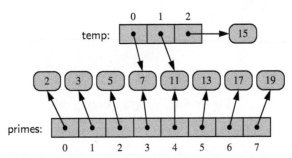

Figure 5.6: The result of the command temp[2] = 15 upon the configuration portrayed in Figure 5.5.

The same semantics is demonstrated when making a new list as a copy of an existing one, with a syntax such as backup = **list**(primes). This produces a new list that is a ***shallow copy*** (see Section 2.6), in that it references the same elements as in the first list. With immutable elements, this point is moot. If the contents of the list were of a mutable type, a ***deep copy***, meaning a new list with *new* elements, can be produced by using the deepcopy function from the copy module.

As a more striking example, it is a common practice in Python to initialize an array of integers using a syntax such as counters = [0] * 8. This syntax produces a list of length eight, with all eight elements being the value zero. Technically, all eight cells of the list reference the *same* object, as portrayed in Figure 5.7.

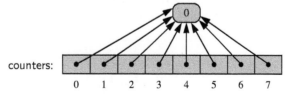

Figure 5.7: The result of the command data = [0] * 8.

At first glance, the extreme level of aliasing in this configuration may seem alarming. However, we rely on the fact that the referenced integer is immutable. Even a command such as counters[2] += 1 does not technically change the value of the existing integer instance. This computes a new integer, with value $0 + 1$, and sets cell 2 to reference the newly computed value. The resulting configuration is shown in Figure 5.8.

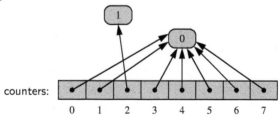

Figure 5.8: The result of command data[2] += 1 upon the list from Figure 5.7.

As a final manifestation of the referential nature of lists, we note that the extend command is used to add all elements from one list to the end of another list. The extended list does not receive copies of those elements, it receives references to those elements. Figure 5.9 portrays the effect of a call to extend.

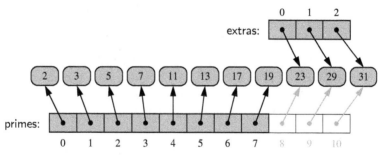

Figure 5.9: The effect of command primes.extend(extras), shown in light gray.

5.2.2   Compact Arrays in Python

In the introduction to this section, we emphasized that strings are represented using an array of characters (not an array of references). We will refer to this more direct representation as a ***compact array*** because the array is storing the bits that represent the primary data (characters, in the case of strings).

Compact arrays have several advantages over referential structures in terms of computing performance. Most significantly, the overall memory usage will be much lower for a compact structure because there is no overhead devoted to the explicit storage of the sequence of memory references (in addition to the primary data). That is, a referential structure will typically use 64-bits for the memory address stored in the array, on top of whatever number of bits are used to represent the object that is considered the element. Also, each Unicode character stored in a compact array within a string typically requires 2 bytes. If each character were stored independently as a one-character string, there would be significantly more bytes used.

As another case study, suppose we wish to store a sequence of one million, 64-bit integers. In theory, we might hope to use only 64 million bits. However, we estimate that a Python list will use *four to five times as much memory*. Each element of the list will result in a 64-bit memory address being stored in the primary array, and an **int** instance being stored elsewhere in memory. Python allows you to query the actual number of bytes being used for the primary storage of any object. This is done using the getsizeof function of the sys module. On our system, the size of a typical int object requires 14 bytes of memory (well beyond the 4 bytes needed for representing the actual 64-bit number). In all, the list will be using 18 bytes per entry, rather than the 4 bytes that a compact list of integers would require.

Another important advantage to a compact structure for high-performance computing is that the primary data are stored consecutively in memory. Note well that this is not the case for a referential structure. That is, even though a list maintains careful ordering of the sequence of memory addresses, where those elements reside in memory is not determined by the list. Because of the workings of the cache and memory hierarchies of computers, it is often advantageous to have data stored in memory near other data that might be used in the same computations.

Despite the apparent inefficiencies of referential structures, we will generally be content with the convenience of Python's lists and tuples in this book. The only place in which we consider alternatives will be in Chapter 15, which focuses on the impact of memory usage on data structures and algorithms. Python provides several means for creating compact arrays of various types.

Primary support for compact arrays is in a module named array. That module defines a class, also named array, providing compact storage for arrays of primitive data types. A portrayal of such an array of integers is shown in Figure 5.10.

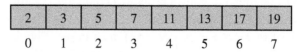

Figure 5.10: Integers stored compactly as elements of a Python array.

The public interface for the array class conforms mostly to that of a Python list. However, the constructor for the array class requires a *type code* as a first parameter, which is a character that designates the type of data that will be stored in the array. As a tangible example, the type code, 'i', designates an array of (signed) integers, typically represented using at least 16-bits each. We can declare the array shown in Figure 5.10 as,

primes = array('i', [2, 3, 5, 7, 11, 13, 17, 19])

The type code allows the interpreter to determine precisely how many bits are needed per element of the array. The type codes supported by the array module, as shown in Table 5.1, are formally based upon the native data types used by the C programming language (the language in which the the most widely used distribution of Python is implemented). The precise number of bits for the C data types is system-dependent, but typical ranges are shown in the table.

Code	C Data Type	Typical Number of Bytes
'b'	signed char	1
'B'	unsigned char	1
'u'	Unicode char	2 or 4
'h'	signed short int	2
'H'	unsigned short int	2
'i'	signed int	2 or 4
'I'	unsigned int	2 or 4
'l'	signed long int	4
'L'	unsigned long int	4
'f'	float	4
'd'	float	8

Table 5.1: Type codes supported by the array module.

The array module does not provide support for making compact arrays of user-defined data types. Compact arrays of such structures can be created with the lower-level support of a module named ctypes. (See Section 5.3.1 for more discussion of the ctypes module.)

5.3   Dynamic Arrays and Amortization

When creating a low-level array in a computer system, the precise size of that array must be explicitly declared in order for the system to properly allocate a consecutive piece of memory for its storage. For example, Figure 5.11 displays an array of 12 bytes that might be stored in memory locations 2146 through 2157.

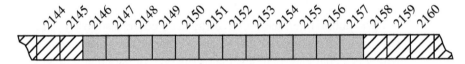

Figure 5.11: An array of 12 bytes allocated in memory locations 2146 through 2157.

Because the system might dedicate neighboring memory locations to store other data, the capacity of an array cannot trivially be increased by expanding into subsequent cells. In the context of representing a Python tuple or str instance, this constraint is no problem. Instances of those classes are immutable, so the correct size for an underlying array can be fixed when the object is instantiated.

Python's list class presents a more interesting abstraction. Although a list has a particular length when constructed, the class allows us to add elements to the list, with no apparent limit on the overall capacity of the list. To provide this abstraction, Python relies on an algorithmic sleight of hand known as a ***dynamic array***.

The first key to providing the semantics of a dynamic array is that a list instance maintains an underlying array that often has greater capacity than the current length of the list. For example, while a user may have created a list with five elements, the system may have reserved an underlying array capable of storing eight object references (rather than only five). This extra capacity makes it easy to append a new element to the list by using the next available cell of the array.

If a user continues to append elements to a list, any reserved capacity will eventually be exhausted. In that case, the class requests a new, larger array from the system, and initializes the new array so that its prefix matches that of the existing smaller array. At that point in time, the old array is no longer needed, so it is reclaimed by the system. Intuitively, this strategy is much like that of the hermit crab, which moves into a larger shell when it outgrows its previous one.

We give empirical evidence that Python's list class is based upon such a strategy. The source code for our experiment is displayed in Code Fragment 5.1, and a sample output of that program is given in Code Fragment 5.2. We rely on a function named getsizeof that is available from the sys module. This function reports the number of bytes that are being used to store an object in Python. For a list, it reports the number of bytes devoted to the array and other instance variables of the list, but *not* any space devoted to elements referenced by the list.

```
1  import sys                                    # provides getsizeof function
2  data = [ ]
3  for k in range(n):                            # NOTE: must fix choice of n
4    a = len(data)                               # number of elements
5    b = sys.getsizeof(data)                     # actual size in bytes
6    print('Length: {0:3d}; Size in bytes: {1:4d}'.format(a, b))
7    data.append(None)                           # increase length by one
```

Code Fragment 5.1: An experiment to explore the relationship between a list's length and its underlying size in Python.

```
Length:  0; Size in bytes:   72
Length:  1; Size in bytes:  104
Length:  2; Size in bytes:  104
Length:  3; Size in bytes:  104
Length:  4; Size in bytes:  104
Length:  5; Size in bytes:  136
Length:  6; Size in bytes:  136
Length:  7; Size in bytes:  136
Length:  8; Size in bytes:  136
Length:  9; Size in bytes:  200
Length: 10; Size in bytes:  200
Length: 11; Size in bytes:  200
Length: 12; Size in bytes:  200
Length: 13; Size in bytes:  200
Length: 14; Size in bytes:  200
Length: 15; Size in bytes:  200
Length: 16; Size in bytes:  200
Length: 17; Size in bytes:  272
Length: 18; Size in bytes:  272
Length: 19; Size in bytes:  272
Length: 20; Size in bytes:  272
Length: 21; Size in bytes:  272
Length: 22; Size in bytes:  272
Length: 23; Size in bytes:  272
Length: 24; Size in bytes:  272
Length: 25; Size in bytes:  272
Length: 26; Size in bytes:  352
```

Code Fragment 5.2: Sample output from the experiment of Code Fragment 5.1.

In evaluating the results of the experiment, we draw attention to the first line of output from Code Fragment 5.2. We see that an empty list instance already requires a certain number of bytes of memory (72 on our system). In fact, each object in Python maintains some state, for example, a reference to denote the class to which it belongs. Although we cannot directly access private instance variables for a list, we can speculate that in some form it maintains state information akin to:

_n	The number of actual elements currently stored in the list.
_capacity	The maximum number of elements that could be stored in the currently allocated array.
_A	The reference to the currently allocated array (initially None).

As soon as the first element is inserted into the list, we detect a change in the underlying size of the structure. In particular, we see the number of bytes jump from 72 to 104, an increase of exactly 32 bytes. Our experiment was run on a 64-bit machine architecture, meaning that each memory address is a 64-bit number (i.e., 8 bytes). We speculate that the increase of 32 bytes reflects the allocation of an underlying array capable of storing four object references. This hypothesis is consistent with the fact that we do not see any underlying change in the memory usage after inserting the second, third, or fourth element into the list.

After the fifth element has been added to the list, we see the memory usage jump from 104 bytes to 136 bytes. If we assume the original base usage of 72 bytes for the list, the total of 136 suggests an additional $64 = 8 \times 8$ bytes that provide capacity for up to eight object references. Again, this is consistent with the experiment, as the memory usage does not increase again until the ninth insertion. At that point, the 200 bytes can be viewed as the original 72 plus an additional 128-byte array to store 16 object references. The 17th insertion pushes the overall memory usage to $272 = 72 + 200 = 72 + 25 \times 8$, hence enough to store up to 25 element references.

Because a list is a referential structure, the result of getsizeof for a list instance only includes the size for representing its primary structure; it does not account for memory used by the *objects* that are elements of the list. In our experiment, we repeatedly append None to the list, because we do not care about the contents, but we could append any type of object without affecting the number of bytes reported by getsizeof(data).

If we were to continue such an experiment for further iterations, we might try to discern the pattern for how large of an array Python creates each time the capacity of the previous array is exhausted (see Exercises R-5.2 and C-5.13). Before exploring the precise sequence of capacities used by Python, we continue in this section by describing a general approach for implementing dynamic arrays and for performing an asymptotic analysis of their performance.

5.3.1 Implementing a Dynamic Array

Although the Python list class provides a highly optimized implementation of dynamic arrays, upon which we rely for the remainder of this book, it is instructive to see how such a class might be implemented.

The key is to provide means to grow the array A that stores the elements of a list. Of course, we cannot actually grow that array, as its capacity is fixed. If an element is appended to a list at a time when the underlying array is full, we perform the following steps:

1. Allocate a new array B with larger capacity.
2. Set $B[i] = A[i]$, for $i = 0, \ldots, n-1$, where n denotes current number of items.
3. Set $A = B$, that is, we henceforth use B as the array supporting the list.
4. Insert the new element in the new array.

An illustration of this process is shown in Figure 5.12.

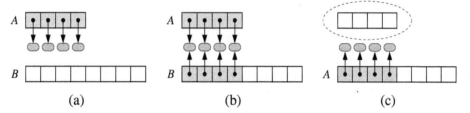

| (a) | (b) | (c) |

Figure 5.12: An illustration of the three steps for "growing" a dynamic array: (a) create new array B; (b) store elements of A in B; (c) reassign reference A to the new array. Not shown is the future garbage collection of the old array, or the insertion of the new element.

The remaining issue to consider is how large of a new array to create. A commonly used rule is for the new array to have twice the capacity of the existing array that has been filled. In Section 5.3.2, we will provide a mathematical analysis to justify such a choice.

In Code Fragment 5.3, we offer a concrete implementation of dynamic arrays in Python. Our DynamicArray class is designed using ideas described in this section. While consistent with the interface of a Python list class, we provide only limited functionality in the form of an append method, and accessors __len__ and __getitem__. Support for creating low-level arrays is provided by a module named ctypes. Because we will not typically use such a low-level structure in the remainder of this book, we omit a detailed explanation of the ctypes module. Instead, we wrap the necessary command for declaring the raw array within a private utility method _make_array. The hallmark expansion procedure is performed in our nonpublic _resize method.

```
1  import ctypes                                   # provides low-level arrays
2
3  class DynamicArray:
4    """A dynamic array class akin to a simplified Python list."""
5
6    def __init__(self):
7      """Create an empty array."""
8      self._n = 0                                 # count actual elements
9      self._capacity = 1                          # default array capacity
10     self._A = self._make_array(self._capacity)  # low-level array
11
12   def __len__(self):
13     """Return number of elements stored in the array."""
14     return self._n
15
16   def __getitem__(self, k):
17     """Return element at index k."""
18     if not 0 <= k < self._n:
19       raise IndexError('invalid index')
20     return self._A[k]                            # retrieve from array
21
22   def append(self, obj):
23     """Add object to end of the array."""
24     if self._n == self._capacity:               # not enough room
25       self._resize(2 * self._capacity)          # so double capacity
26     self._A[self._n] = obj
27     self._n += 1
28
29   def _resize(self, c):                          # nonpublic utility
30     """Resize internal array to capacity c."""
31     B = self._make_array(c)                      # new (bigger) array
32     for k in range(self._n):                     # for each existing value
33       B[k] = self._A[k]
34     self._A = B                                  # use the bigger array
35     self._capacity = c
36
37   def _make_array(self, c):                      # nonpublic utility
38     """Return new array with capacity c."""
39     return (c * ctypes.py_object)()              # see ctypes documentation
```

Code Fragment 5.3: An implementation of a DynamicArray class, using a raw array from the ctypes module as storage.

5.3.2 Amortized Analysis of Dynamic Arrays

In this section, we perform a detailed analysis of the running time of operations on dynamic arrays. We use the big-Omega notation introduced in Section 3.3.1 to give an asymptotic lower bound on the running time of an algorithm or step within it.

The strategy of replacing an array with a new, larger array might at first seem slow, because a single append operation may require $\Omega(n)$ time to perform, where n is the current number of elements in the array. However, notice that by doubling the capacity during an array replacement, our new array allows us to add n new elements before the array must be replaced again. In this way, there are many simple append operations for each expensive one (see Figure 5.13). This fact allows us to show that performing a series of operations on an initially empty dynamic array is efficient in terms of its total running time.

Using an algorithmic design pattern called ***amortization***, we can show that performing a sequence of such append operations on a dynamic array is actually quite efficient. To perform an ***amortized analysis***, we use an accounting technique where we view the computer as a coin-operated appliance that requires the payment of one ***cyber-dollar*** for a constant amount of computing time. When an operation is executed, we should have enough cyber-dollars available in our current "bank account" to pay for that operation's running time. Thus, the total amount of cyber-dollars spent for any computation will be proportional to the total time spent on that computation. The beauty of using this analysis method is that we can overcharge some operations in order to save up cyber-dollars to pay for others.

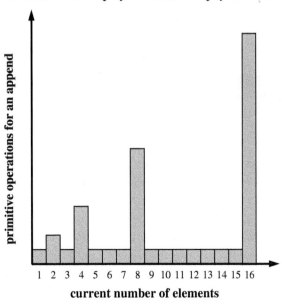

Figure 5.13: Running times of a series of append operations on a dynamic array.

Proposition 5.1: *Let S be a sequence implemented by means of a dynamic array with initial capacity one, using the strategy of doubling the array size when full. The total time to perform a series of n append operations in S, starting from S being empty, is $O(n)$.*

Justification: Let us assume that one cyber-dollar is enough to pay for the execution of each append operation in S, excluding the time spent for growing the array. Also, let us assume that growing the array from size k to size $2k$ requires k cyber-dollars for the time spent initializing the new array. We shall charge each append operation three cyber-dollars. Thus, we overcharge each append operation that does not cause an overflow by two cyber-dollars. Think of the two cyber-dollars profited in an insertion that does not grow the array as being "stored" with the cell in which the element was inserted. An overflow occurs when the array S has 2^i elements, for some integer $i \geq 0$, and the size of the array used by the array representing S is 2^i. Thus, doubling the size of the array will require 2^i cyber-dollars. Fortunately, these cyber-dollars can be found stored in cells 2^{i-1} through $2^i - 1$. (See Figure 5.14.) Note that the previous overflow occurred when the number of elements became larger than 2^{i-1} for the first time, and thus the cyber-dollars stored in cells 2^{i-1} through $2^i - 1$ have not yet been spent. Therefore, we have a valid amortization scheme in which each operation is charged three cyber-dollars and all the computing time is paid for. That is, we can pay for the execution of n append operations using $3n$ cyber-dollars. In other words, the amortized running time of each append operation is $O(1)$; hence, the total running time of n append operations is $O(n)$. ∎

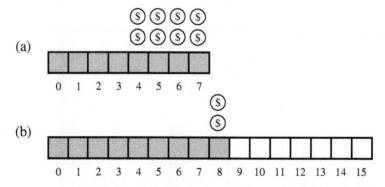

Figure 5.14: Illustration of a series of append operations on a dynamic array: (a) an 8-cell array is full, with two cyber-dollars "stored" at cells 4 through 7; (b) an append operation causes an overflow and a doubling of capacity. Copying the eight old elements to the new array is paid for by the cyber-dollars already stored in the table. Inserting the new element is paid for by one of the cyber-dollars charged to the current append operation, and the two cyber-dollars profited are stored at cell 8.

Geometric Increase in Capacity

Although the proof of Proposition 5.1 relies on the array being doubled each time we expand, the $O(1)$ amortized bound per operation can be proven for any geometrically increasing progression of array sizes (see Section 2.4.2 for discussion of geometric progressions). When choosing the geometric base, there exists a trade-off between run-time efficiency and memory usage. With a base of 2 (i.e., doubling the array), if the last insertion causes a resize event, the array essentially ends up twice as large as it needs to be. If we instead increase the array by only 25% of its current size (i.e., a geometric base of 1.25), we do not risk wasting as much memory in the end, but there will be more intermediate resize events along the way. Still it is possible to prove an $O(1)$ amortized bound, using a constant factor greater than the 3 cyber-dollars per operation used in the proof of Proposition 5.1 (see Exercise C-5.15). The key to the performance is that the amount of additional space is proportional to the current size of the array.

Beware of Arithmetic Progression

To avoid reserving too much space at once, it might be tempting to implement a dynamic array with a strategy in which a constant number of additional cells are reserved each time an array is resized. Unfortunately, the overall performance of such a strategy is significantly worse. At an extreme, an increase of only one cell causes each append operation to resize the array, leading to a familiar $1 + 2 + 3 + \cdots + n$ summation and $\Omega(n^2)$ overall cost. Using increases of 2 or 3 at a time is slightly better, as portrayed in Figure 5.13, but the overall cost remains quadratic.

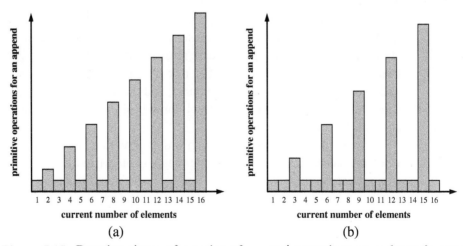

Figure 5.15: Running times of a series of append operations on a dynamic array using arithmetic progression of sizes. (a) Assumes increase of 2 in size of the array, while (b) assumes increase of 3.

Using a *fixed* increment for each resize, and thus an arithmetic progression of intermediate array sizes, results in an overall time that is quadratic in the number of operations, as shown in the following proposition. Intuitively, even an increase in 1000 cells per resize will become insignificant for large data sets.

Proposition 5.2: *Performing a series of n append operations on an initially empty dynamic array using a fixed increment with each resize takes $\Omega(n^2)$ time.*

Justification: Let $c > 0$ represent the fixed increment in capacity that is used for each resize event. During the series of n append operations, time will have been spent initializing arrays of size $c, 2c, 3c, \ldots, mc$ for $m = \lceil n/c \rceil$, and therefore, the overall time would be proportional to $c + 2c + 3c + \cdots + mc$. By Proposition 3.3, this sum is

$$\sum_{i=1}^{m} ci = c \cdot \sum_{i=1}^{m} i = c\frac{m(m+1)}{2} \geq c\frac{\frac{n}{c}\left(\frac{n}{c}+1\right)}{2} \geq \frac{n^2}{2c}.$$

Therefore, performing the n append operations takes $\Omega(n^2)$ time.   ∎

A lesson to be learned from Propositions 5.1 and 5.2 is that a subtle difference in an algorithm design can produce drastic differences in the asymptotic performance, and that a careful analysis can provide important insights into the design of a data structure.

Memory Usage and Shrinking an Array

Another consequence of the rule of a geometric increase in capacity when appending to a dynamic array is that the final array size is guaranteed to be proportional to the overall number of elements. That is, the data structure uses $O(n)$ memory. This is a very desirable property for a data structure.

If a container, such as a Python list, provides operations that cause the removal of one or more elements, greater care must be taken to ensure that a dynamic array guarantees $O(n)$ memory usage. The risk is that repeated insertions may cause the underlying array to grow arbitrarily large, and that there will no longer be a proportional relationship between the actual number of elements and the array capacity after many elements are removed.

A robust implementation of such a data structure will shrink the underlying array, on occasion, while maintaining the $O(1)$ amortized bound on individual operations. However, care must be taken to ensure that the structure cannot rapidly oscillate between growing and shrinking the underlying array, in which case the amortized bound would not be achieved. In Exercise C-5.16, we explore a strategy in which the array capacity is halved whenever the number of actual element falls below one fourth of that capacity, thereby guaranteeing that the array capacity is at most four times the number of elements; we explore the amortized analysis of such a strategy in Exercises C-5.17 and C-5.18.

5.3.3 Python's List Class

The experiments of Code Fragment 5.1 and 5.2, at the beginning of Section 5.3, provide empirical evidence that Python's list class is using a form of dynamic arrays for its storage. Yet, a careful examination of the intermediate array capacities (see Exercises R-5.2 and C-5.13) suggests that Python is not using a pure geometric progression, nor is it using an arithmetic progression.

With that said, it is clear that Python's implementation of the append method exhibits amortized constant-time behavior. We can demonstrate this fact experimentally. A single append operation typically executes so quickly that it would be difficult for us to accurately measure the time elapsed at that granularity, although we should notice some of the more expensive operations in which a resize is performed. We can get a more accurate measure of the amortized cost per operation by performing a series of n append operations on an initially empty list and determining the *average* cost of each. A function to perform that experiment is given in Code Fragment 5.4.

```
1  from time import time             # import time function from time module
2  def compute_average(n):
3    """Perform n appends to an empty list and return average time elapsed."""
4    data = [ ]
5    start = time( )                  # record the start time (in seconds)
6    for k in range(n):
7      data.append(None)
8    end = time( )                    # record the end time (in seconds)
9    return (end − start) / n         # compute average per operation
```

Code Fragment 5.4: Measuring the amortized cost of append for Python's list class.

Technically, the time elapsed between the start and end includes the time to manage the iteration of the for loop, in addition to the append calls. The empirical results of the experiment, for increasingly large values of n, are shown in Table 5.2. We see higher average cost for the smaller data sets, perhaps in part due to the overhead of the loop range. There is also natural variance in measuring the amortized cost in this way, because of the impact of the final resize event relative to n. Taken as a whole, there seems clear evidence that the amortized time for each append is independent of n.

n	100	1,000	10,000	100,000	1,000,000	10,000,000	100,000,000
μs	0.219	0.158	0.164	0.151	0.147	0.147	0.149

Table 5.2: Average running time of append, measured in microseconds, as observed over a sequence of n calls, starting with an empty list.

5.4   Efficiency of Python's Sequence Types

In the previous section, we began to explore the underpinnings of Python's list class, in terms of implementation strategies and efficiency. We continue in this section by examining the performance of all of Python's sequence types.

5.4.1   Python's List and Tuple Classes

The *nonmutating* behaviors of the list class are precisely those that are supported by the tuple class. We note that tuples are typically more memory efficient than lists because they are immutable; therefore, there is no need for an underlying dynamic array with surplus capacity. We summarize the asymptotic efficiency of the nonmutating behaviors of the list and tuple classes in Table 5.3. An explanation of this analysis follows.

Operation	Running Time
len(data)	$O(1)$
data[j]	$O(1)$
data.count(value)	$O(n)$
data.index(value)	$O(k+1)$
value **in** data	$O(k+1)$
data1 == data2 (similarly !=, <, <=, >, >=)	$O(k+1)$
data[j:k]	$O(k-j+1)$
data1 + data2	$O(n_1+n_2)$
c * data	$O(cn)$

Table 5.3: Asymptotic performance of the nonmutating behaviors of the list and tuple classes. Identifiers data, data1, and data2 designate instances of the list or tuple class, and n, n_1, and n_2 their respective lengths. For the containment check and index method, k represents the index of the leftmost occurrence (with $k = n$ if there is no occurrence). For comparisons between two sequences, we let k denote the leftmost index at which they disagree or else $k = \min(n_1, n_2)$.

Constant-Time Operations

The length of an instance is returned in constant time because an instance explicitly maintains such state information. The constant-time efficiency of syntax data[j] is assured by the underlying access into an array.

Searching for Occurrences of a Value

Each of the count, index, and __contains__ methods proceed through iteration of the sequence from left to right. In fact, Code Fragment 2.14 of Section 2.4.3 demonstrates how those behaviors might be implemented. Notably, the loop for computing the count must proceed through the entire sequence, while the loops for checking containment of an element or determining the index of an element immediately exit once they find the leftmost occurrence of the desired value, if one exists. So while count always examines the n elements of the sequence, index and __contains__ examine n elements in the worst case, but may be faster. Empirical evidence can be found by setting data = list(range(10000000)) and then comparing the relative efficiency of the test, 5 **in** data, relative to the test, 9999995 **in** data, or even the failed test, −5 **in** data.

Lexicographic Comparisons

Comparisons between two sequences are defined lexicographically. In the worst case, evaluating such a condition requires an iteration taking time proportional to the length of the *shorter* of the two sequences (because when one sequence ends, the lexicographic result can be determined). However, in some cases the result of the test can be evaluated more efficiently. For example, if evaluating [7, 3, ...] < [7, 5, ...], it is clear that the result is True without examining the remainders of those lists, because the second element of the left operand is strictly less than the second element of the right operand.

Creating New Instances

The final three behaviors in Table 5.3 are those that construct a new instance based on one or more existing instances. In all cases, the running time depends on the construction and initialization of the new result, and therefore the asymptotic behavior is proportional to the *length* of the result. Therefore, we find that slice data[6000000:6000008] can be constructed almost immediately because it has only eight elements, while slice data[6000000:7000000] has one million elements, and thus is more time-consuming to create.

Mutating Behaviors

The efficiency of the mutating behaviors of the list class are described in Table 5.3. The simplest of those behaviors has syntax data[j] = val, and is supported by the special __setitem__ method. This operation has worst-case $O(1)$ running time because it simply replaces one element of a list with a new value. No other elements are affected and the size of the underlying array does not change. The more interesting behaviors to analyze are those that add or remove elements from the list.

Operation	Running Time
data[j] = val	$O(1)$
data.append(value)	$O(1)^*$
data.insert(k, value)	$O(n-k+1)^*$
data.pop( )	$O(1)^*$
data.pop(k) **del** data[k]	$O(n-k)^*$
data.remove(value)	$O(n)^*$
data1.extend(data2) data1 += data2	$O(n_2)^*$
data.reverse( )	$O(n)$
data.sort( )	$O(n\log n)$

*amortized

Table 5.4: Asymptotic performance of the mutating behaviors of the list class. Identifiers data, data1, and data2 designate instances of the list class, and n, n_1, and n_2 their respective lengths.

Adding Elements to a List

In Section 5.3 we fully explored the append method. In the worst case, it requires $\Omega(n)$ time because the underlying array is resized, but it uses $O(1)$ time in the amortized sense. Lists also support a method, with signature insert(k, value), that inserts a given value into the list at index $0 \leq k \leq n$ while shifting all subsequent elements back one slot to make room. For the purpose of illustration, Code Fragment 5.5 provides an implementation of that method, in the context of our DynamicArray class introduced in Code Fragment 5.3. There are two complicating factors in analyzing the efficiency of such an operation. First, we note that the addition of one element may require a resizing of the dynamic array. That portion of the work requires $\Omega(n)$ worst-case time but only $O(1)$ amortized time, as per append. The other expense for insert is the shifting of elements to make room for the new item. The time for

```
1    def insert(self, k, value):
2        """Insert value at index k, shifting subsequent values rightward."""
3        # (for simplicity, we assume 0 <= k <= n in this verion)
4        if self._n == self._capacity:          # not enough room
5            self._resize(2 * self._capacity)   # so double capacity
6        for j in range(self._n, k, -1):        # shift rightmost first
7            self._A[j] = self._A[j-1]
8        self._A[k] = value                     # store newest element
9        self._n += 1
```

Code Fragment 5.5: Implementation of insert for our DynamicArray class.

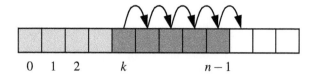

Figure 5.16: Creating room to insert a new element at index k of a dynamic array.

that process depends upon the index of the new element, and thus the number of other elements that must be shifted. That loop copies the reference that had been at index $n-1$ to index n, then the reference that had been at index $n-2$ to $n-1$, continuing until copying the reference that had been at index k to $k+1$, as illustrated in Figure 5.16. Overall this leads to an amortized $O(n-k+1)$ performance for inserting at index k.

When exploring the efficiency of Python's append method in Section 5.3.3, we performed an experiment that measured the average cost of repeated calls on varying sizes of lists (see Code Fragment 5.4 and Table 5.2). We have repeated that experiment with the insert method, trying three different access patterns:

- In the first case, we repeatedly insert at the beginning of a list,
  ```
  for n in range(N):
      data.insert(0, None)
  ```

- In a second case, we repeatedly insert near the middle of a list,
  ```
  for n in range(N):
      data.insert(n // 2, None)
  ```

- In a third case, we repeatedly insert at the end of the list,
  ```
  for n in range(N):
      data.insert(n, None)
  ```

The results of our experiment are given in Table 5.5, reporting the *average* time per operation (not the total time for the entire loop). As expected, we see that inserting at the beginning of a list is most expensive, requiring linear time per operation. Inserting at the middle requires about half the time as inserting at the beginning, yet is still $\Omega(n)$ time. Inserting at the end displays $O(1)$ behavior, akin to append.

	N				
	100	1,000	10,000	100,000	1,000,000
$k=0$	0.482	0.765	4.014	36.643	351.590
$k=n//2$	0.451	0.577	2.191	17.873	175.383
$k=n$	0.420	0.422	0.395	0.389	0.397

Table 5.5: Average running time of insert(k, val), measured in microseconds, as observed over a sequence of N calls, starting with an empty list. We let n denote the size of the current list (as opposed to the final list).

Removing Elements from a List

Python's list class offers several ways to remove an element from a list. A call to pop( ) removes the last element from a list. This is most efficient, because all other elements remain in their original location. This is effectively an $O(1)$ operation, but the bound is amortized because Python will occasionally shrink the underlying dynamic array to conserve memory.

The parameterized version, pop(k), removes the element that is at index $k < n$ of a list, shifting all subsequent elements leftward to fill the gap that results from the removal. The efficiency of this operation is $O(n - k)$, as the amount of shifting depends upon the choice of index k, as illustrated in Figure 5.17. Note well that this implies that pop(0) is the most expensive call, using $\Omega(n)$ time. (see experiments in Exercise R-5.8.)

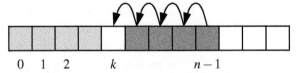

$$0 \quad 1 \quad 2 \qquad k \qquad\qquad n-1$$

Figure 5.17: Removing an element at index k of a dynamic array.

The list class offers another method, named remove, that allows the caller to specify the *value* that should be removed (not the *index* at which it resides). Formally, it removes only the first occurrence of such a value from a list, or raises a ValueError if no such value is found. An implementation of such behavior is given in Code Fragment 5.6, again using our DynamicArray class for illustration.

Interestingly, there is no "efficient" case for remove; every call requires $\Omega(n)$ time. One part of the process searches from the beginning until finding the value at index k, while the rest iterates from k to the end in order to shift elements leftward. This linear behavior can be observed experimentally (see Exercise C-5.24).

```python
def remove(self, value):
    """Remove first occurrence of value (or raise ValueError)."""
    # note: we do not consider shrinking the dynamic array in this version
    for k in range(self._n):
        if self._A[k] == value:              # found a match!
            for j in range(k, self._n - 1):  # shift others to fill gap
                self._A[j] = self._A[j+1]
            self._A[self._n - 1] = None      # help garbage collection
            self._n -= 1                     # we have one less item
            return                           # exit immediately
    raise ValueError('value not found')      # only reached if no match
```

Code Fragment 5.6: Implementation of remove for our DynamicArray class.

Extending a List

Python provides a method named extend that is used to add all elements of one list to the end of a second list. In effect, a call to data.extend(other) produces the same outcome as the code,

```
for element in other:
    data.append(element)
```

In either case, the running time is proportional to the length of the other list, and amortized because the underlying array for the first list may be resized to accommodate the additional elements.

In practice, the extend method is preferable to repeated calls to append because the constant factors hidden in the asymptotic analysis are significantly smaller. The greater efficiency of extend is threefold. First, there is always some advantage to using an appropriate Python method, because those methods are often implemented natively in a compiled language (rather than as interpreted Python code). Second, there is less overhead to a single function call that accomplishes all the work, versus many individual function calls. Finally, increased efficiency of extend comes from the fact that the resulting size of the updated list can be calculated in advance. If the second data set is quite large, there is some risk that the underlying dynamic array might be resized multiple times when using repeated calls to append. With a single call to extend, at most one resize operation will be performed. Exercise C-5.22 explores the relative efficiency of these two approaches experimentally.

Constructing New Lists

There are several syntaxes for constructing new lists. In almost all cases, the asymptotic efficiency of the behavior is linear in the length of the list that is created. However, as with the case in the preceding discussion of extend, there are significant differences in the practical efficiency.

Section 1.9.2 introduces the topic of *list comprehension*, using an example such as squares = [k*k **for** k **in** range(1, n+1)] as a shorthand for

```
squares = [ ]
for k in range(1, n+1):
    squares.append(k*k)
```

Experiments should show that the list comprehension syntax is significantly faster than building the list by repeatedly appending (see Exercise C-5.23).

Similarly, it is a common Python idiom to initialize a list of constant values using the multiplication operator, as in [0] * n to produce a list of length n with all values equal to zero. Not only is this succinct for the programmer; it is more efficient than building such a list incrementally.

5.4.2   Python's String Class

Strings are very important in Python. We introduced their use in Chapter 1, with a discussion of various operator syntaxes in Section 1.3. A comprehensive summary of the named methods of the class is given in Tables A.1 through A.4 of Appendix A. We will not formally analyze the efficiency of each of those behaviors in this section, but we do wish to comment on some notable issues. In general, we let n denote the length of a string. For operations that rely on a second string as a pattern, we let m denote the length of that pattern string.

The analysis for many behaviors is quite intuitive. For example, methods that produce a new string (e.g., capitalize, center, strip) require time that is linear in the length of the string that is produced. Many of the behaviors that test Boolean conditions of a string (e.g., islower) take $O(n)$ time, examining all n characters in the worst case, but short circuiting as soon as the answer becomes evident (e.g., islower can immediately return False if the first character is uppercased). The comparison operators (e.g., ==, <) fall into this category as well.

Pattern Matching

Some of the most interesting behaviors, from an algorithmic point of view, are those that in some way depend upon finding a string pattern within a larger string; this goal is at the heart of methods such as __contains__, find, index, count, replace, and split. String algorithms will be the topic of Chapter 13, and this particular problem known as ***pattern matching*** will be the focus of Section 13.2. A naive implementation runs in $O(mn)$ time case, because we consider the $n - m + 1$ possible starting indices for the pattern, and we spend $O(m)$ time at each starting position, checking if the pattern matches. However, in Section 13.2, we will develop an algorithm for finding a pattern of length m within a longer string of length n in $O(n)$ time.

Composing Strings

Finally, we wish to comment on several approaches for composing large strings. As an academic exercise, assume that we have a large string named document, and our goal is to produce a new string, letters, that contains only the alphabetic characters of the original string (e.g., with spaces, numbers, and punctuation removed). It may be tempting to compose a result through repeated concatenation, as follows.

```
# WARNING: do not do this
letters = ''                          # start with empty string
for c in document:
  if c.isalpha():
    letters += c                      # concatenate alphabetic character
```

While the preceding code fragment accomplishes the goal, it may be terribly inefficient. Because strings are immutable, the command, letters += c, would presumably compute the concatenation, letters + c, as a new string instance and then reassign the identifier, letters, to that result. Constructing that new string would require time proportional to its length. If the final result has n characters, the series of concatenations would take time proportional to the familiar sum $1 + 2 + 3 + \cdots + n$, and therefore $O(n^2)$ time.

Inefficient code of this type is widespread in Python, perhaps because of the somewhat natural appearance of the code, and mistaken presumptions about how the += operator is evaluated with strings. Some later implementations of the Python interpreter have developed an optimization to allow such code to complete in linear time, but this is not guaranteed for all Python implementations. The optimization is as follows. The reason that a command, letters += c, causes a new string instance to be created is that the original string must be left unchanged if another variable in a program refers to that string. On the other hand, if Python knew that there were no other references to the string in question, it could implement += more efficiently by directly mutating the string (as a dynamic array). As it happens, the Python interpreter already maintains what are known as **reference counts** for each object; this count is used in part to determine if an object can be garbage collected. (See Section 15.1.2.) But in this context, it provides a means to detect when no other references exist to a string, thereby allowing the optimization.

A more standard Python idiom to guarantee linear time composition of a string is to use a temporary list to store individual pieces, and then to rely on the join method of the str class to compose the final result. Using this technique with our previous example would appear as follows:

```
temp = [ ]                        # start with empty list
for c in document:
  if c.isalpha( ):
    temp.append(c)                # append alphabetic character
letters = ''.join(temp)           # compose overall result
```

This approach is guaranteed to run in $O(n)$ time. First, we note that the series of up to n append calls will require a total of $O(n)$ time, as per the definition of the amortized cost of that operation. The final call to join also guarantees that it takes time that is linear in the final length of the composed string.

As we discussed at the end of the previous section, we can further improve the practical execution time by using a list comprehension syntax to build up the temporary list, rather than by repeated calls to append. That solution appears as,

```
letters = ''.join([c for c in document if c.isalpha( )])
```

Better yet, we can entirely avoid the temporary list with a generator comprehension:

```
letters = ''.join(c for c in document if c.isalpha( ))
```

5.5 Using Array-Based Sequences

5.5.1 Storing High Scores for a Game

The first application we study is storing a sequence of high score entries for a video game. This is representative of many applications in which a sequence of objects must be stored. We could just as easily have chosen to store records for patients in a hospital or the names of players on a football team. Nevertheless, let us focus on storing high score entries, which is a simple application that is already rich enough to present some important data-structuring concepts.

To begin, we consider what information to include in an object representing a high score entry. Obviously, one component to include is an integer representing the score itself, which we identify as _score. Another useful thing to include is the name of the person earning this score, which we identify as _name. We could go on from here, adding fields representing the date the score was earned or game statistics that led to that score. However, we omit such details to keep our example simple. A Python class, GameEntry, representing a game entry, is given in Code Fragment 5.7.

```python
1  class GameEntry:
2    """Represents one entry of a list of high scores."""
3
4    def __init__(self, name, score):
5      self._name = name
6      self._score = score
7
8    def get_name(self):
9      return self._name
10
11   def get_score(self):
12     return self._score
13
14   def __str__(self):
15     return '({0}, {1})'.format(self._name, self._score)  # e.g., '(Bob, 98)'
```

Code Fragment 5.7: Python code for a simple GameEntry class. We include methods for returning the name and score for a game entry object, as well as a method for returning a string representation of this entry.

A Class for High Scores

To maintain a sequence of high scores, we develop a class named Scoreboard. A scoreboard is limited to a certain number of high scores that can be saved; once that limit is reached, a new score only qualifies for the scoreboard if it is strictly higher than the lowest "high score" on the board. The length of the desired scoreboard may depend on the game, perhaps 10, 50, or 500. Since that limit may vary depending on the game, we allow it to be specified as a parameter to our Scoreboard constructor.

Internally, we will use a Python list named _board in order to manage the GameEntry instances that represent the high scores. Since we expect the scoreboard to eventually reach full capacity, we initialize the list to be large enough to hold the maximum number of scores, but we initially set all entries to None. By allocating the list with maximum capacity initially, it never needs to be resized. As entries are added, we will maintain them from highest to lowest score, starting at index 0 of the list. We illustrate a typical state of the data structure in Figure 5.18.

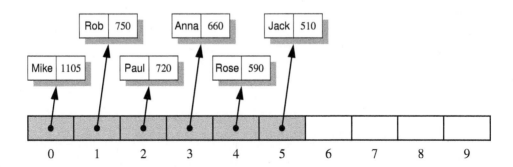

Figure 5.18: An illustration of an ordered list of length ten, storing references to six GameEntry objects in the cells from index 0 to 5, with the rest being None.

A complete Python implementation of the Scoreboard class is given in Code Fragment 5.8. The constructor is rather simple. The command

    self._board = [**None**] * capacity

creates a list with the desired length, yet all entries equal to None. We maintain an additional instance variable, _n, that represents the number of actual entries currently in our table. For convenience, our class supports the __getitem__ method to retrieve an entry at a given index with a syntax board[i] (or None if no such entry exists), and we support a simple __str__ method that returns a string representation of the entire scoreboard, with one entry per line.

```
1   class Scoreboard:
2      """Fixed-length sequence of high scores in nondecreasing order."""
3
4      def __init__(self, capacity=10):
5         """Initialize scoreboard with given maximum capacity.
6
7         All entries are initially None.
8         """
9         self._board = [None] * capacity       # reserve space for future scores
10        self._n = 0                           # number of actual entries
11
12     def __getitem__(self, k):
13        """Return entry at index k."""
14        return self._board[k]
15
16     def __str__(self):
17        """Return string representation of the high score list."""
18        return '\n'.join(str(self._board[j]) for j in range(self._n))
19
20     def add(self, entry):
21        """Consider adding entry to high scores."""
22        score = entry.get_score()
23
24        # Does new entry qualify as a high score?
25        # answer is yes if board not full or score is higher than last entry
26        good = self._n < len(self._board) or score > self._board[-1].get_score()
27
28        if good:
29           if self._n < len(self._board):      # no score drops from list
30              self._n += 1                      # so overall number increases
31
32           # shift lower scores rightward to make room for new entry
33           j = self._n - 1
34           while j > 0 and self._board[j-1].get_score() < score:
35              self._board[j] = self._board[j-1]    # shift entry from j-1 to j
36              j -= 1                               # and decrement j
37           self._board[j] = entry                  # when done, add new entry
```

Code Fragment 5.8: Python code for a Scoreboard class that maintains an ordered series of scores as GameEntry objects.

Adding an Entry

The most interesting method of the Scoreboard class is add, which is responsible for considering the addition of a new entry to the scoreboard. Keep in mind that every entry will not necessarily qualify as a high score. If the board is not yet full, any new entry will be retained. Once the board is full, a new entry is only retained if it is strictly better than one of the other scores, in particular, the last entry of the scoreboard, which is the lowest of the high scores.

When a new score is considered, we begin by determining whether it qualifies as a high score. If so, we increase the count of active scores, _n, unless the board is already at full capacity. In that case, adding a new high score causes some other entry to be dropped from the scoreboard, so the overall number of entries remains the same.

To correctly place a new entry within the list, the final task is to shift any inferior scores one spot lower (with the least score being dropped entirely when the scoreboard is full). This process is quite similar to the implementation of the insert method of the list class, as described on pages 204–205. In the context of our scoreboard, there is no need to shift any None references that remain near the end of the array, so the process can proceed as diagrammed in Figure 5.19.

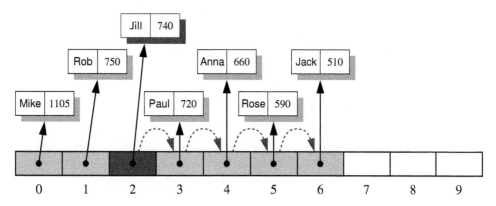

Figure 5.19: Adding a new GameEntry for Jill to the scoreboard. In order to make room for the new reference, we have to shift the references for game entries with smaller scores than the new one to the right by one cell. Then we can insert the new entry with index 2.

To implement the final stage, we begin by considering index j = self._n − 1, which is the index at which the last GameEntry instance will reside, after completing the operation. Either j is the correct index for the newest entry, or one or more immediately before it will have lesser scores. The while loop at line 34 checks the compound condition, shifting references rightward and decrementing j, as long as there is another entry at index $j − 1$ with a score less than the new score.

5.5.2 Sorting a Sequence

In the previous subsection, we considered an application for which we added an object to a sequence at a given position while shifting other elements so as to keep the previous order intact. In this section, we use a similar technique to solve the *sorting* problem, that is, starting with an unordered sequence of elements and rearranging them into nondecreasing order.

The Insertion-Sort Algorithm

We study several sorting algorithms in this book, most of which are described in Chapter 12. As a warm-up, in this section we describe a nice, simple sorting algorithm known as *insertion-sort*. The algorithm proceeds as follows for an array-based sequence. We start with the first element in the array. One element by itself is already sorted. Then we consider the next element in the array. If it is smaller than the first, we swap them. Next we consider the third element in the array. We swap it leftward until it is in its proper order with the first two elements. We then consider the fourth element, and swap it leftward until it is in the proper order with the first three. We continue in this manner with the fifth element, the sixth, and so on, until the whole array is sorted. We can express the insertion-sort algorithm in pseudo-code, as shown in Code Fragment 5.9.

Algorithm InsertionSort(A):
    Input: An array A of n comparable elements
    Output: The array A with elements rearranged in nondecreasing order
    for k from 1 to n − 1 **do**
        Insert A[k] at its proper location within A[0], A[1], ..., A[k].

Code Fragment 5.9: High-level description of the insertion-sort algorithm.

This is a simple, high-level description of insertion-sort. If we look back to Code Fragment 5.8 of Section 5.5.1, we see that the task of inserting a new entry into the list of high scores is almost identical to the task of inserting a newly considered element in insertion-sort (except that game scores were ordered from high to low). We provide a Python implementation of insertion-sort in Code Fragment 5.10, using an outer loop to consider each element in turn, and an inner loop that moves a newly considered element to its proper location relative to the (sorted) subarray of elements that are to its left. We illustrate an example run of the insertion-sort algorithm in Figure 5.20.

The nested loops of insertion-sort lead to an $O(n^2)$ running time in the worst case. The most work is done if the array is initially in reverse order. On the other hand, if the initial array is nearly sorted or perfectly sorted, insertion-sort runs in $O(n)$ time because there are few or no iterations of the inner loop.

```
1  def insertion_sort(A):
2    """Sort list of comparable elements into nondecreasing order."""
3    for k in range(1, len(A)):          # from 1 to n-1
4      cur = A[k]                         # current element to be inserted
5      j = k                             # find correct index j for current
6      while j > 0 and A[j−1] > cur:      # element A[j-1] must be after current
7        A[j] = A[j−1]
8        j −= 1
9      A[j] = cur                        # cur is now in the right place
```

Code Fragment 5.10: Python code for performing insertion-sort on a list.

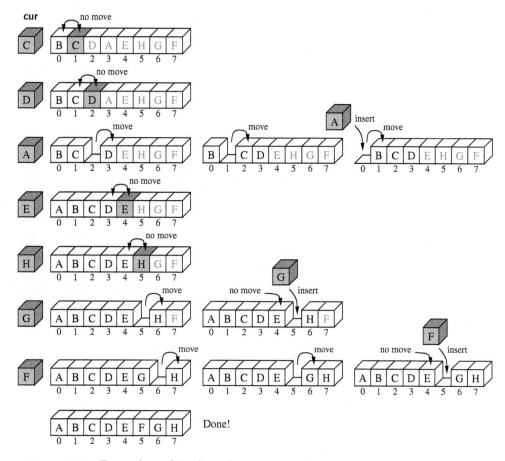

Figure 5.20: Execution of the insertion-sort algorithm on an array of eight characters. Each row corresponds to an iteration of the outer loop, and each copy of the sequence in a row corresponds to an iteration of the inner loop. The current element that is being inserted is highlighted in the array, and shown as the cur value.

5.5.3   Simple Cryptography

An interesting application of strings and lists is *cryptography*, the science of secret messages and their applications. This field studies ways of performing *encryption*, which takes a message, called the *plaintext*, and converts it into a scrambled message, called the *ciphertext*. Likewise, cryptography also studies corresponding ways of performing *decryption*, which takes a ciphertext and turns it back into its original plaintext.

Arguably the earliest encryption scheme is the *Caesar cipher*, which is named after Julius Caesar, who used this scheme to protect important military messages. (All of Caesar's messages were written in Latin, of course, which already makes them unreadable for most of us!) The Caesar cipher is a simple way to obscure a message written in a language that forms words with an alphabet.

The Caesar cipher involves replacing each letter in a message with the letter that is a certain number of letters after it in the alphabet. So, in an English message, we might replace each A with D, each B with E, each C with F, and so on, if shifting by three characters. We continue this approach all the way up to W, which is replaced with Z. Then, we let the substitution pattern *wrap around*, so that we replace X with A, Y with B, and Z with C.

Converting Between Strings and Character Lists

Given that strings are immutable, we cannot directly edit an instance to encrypt it. Instead, our goal will be to generate a new string. A convenient technique for performing string transformations is to create an equivalent list of characters, edit the list, and then reassemble a (new) string based on the list. The first step can be performed by sending the string as a parameter to the constructor of the list class. For example, the expression list('bird') produces the result ['b', 'i', 'r', 'd']. Conversely, we can use a list of characters to build a string by invoking the join method on an empty string, with the list of characters as the parameter. For example, the call ''.join(['b', 'i', 'r', 'd']) returns the string 'bird'.

Using Characters as Array Indices

If we were to number our letters like array indices, so that A is 0, B is 1, C is 2, and so on, then we can write the Caesar cipher with a rotation of r as a simple formula: Replace each letter i with the letter $(i + r) \bmod 26$, where mod is the *modulo* operator, which returns the remainder after performing an integer division. This operator is denoted with % in Python, and it is exactly the operator we need to easily perform the wrap around at the end of the alphabet. For 26 mod 26 is 0, 27 mod 26 is 1, and 28 mod 26 is 2. The decryption algorithm for the Caesar cipher is just the opposite—we replace each letter with the one r places before it, with wrap around (that is, letter i is replaced by letter $(i - r) \bmod 26$).

We can represent a replacement rule using another string to describe the translation. As a concrete example, suppose we are using a Caesar cipher with a three-character rotation. We can precompute a string that represents the replacements that should be used for each character from A to Z. For example, A should be replaced by D, B replaced by E, and so on. The 26 replacement characters in order are 'DEFGHIJKLMNOPQRSTUVWXYZABC'. We can subsequently use this translation string as a guide to encrypt a message. The remaining challenge is how to quickly locate the replacement for each character of the original message.

Fortunately, we can rely on the fact that characters are represented in Unicode by integer code points, and the code points for the uppercase letters of the Latin alphabet are consecutive (for simplicity, we restrict our encryption to uppercase letters). Python supports functions that convert between integer code points and one-character strings. Specifically, the function ord(c) takes a one-character string as a parameter and returns the integer code point for that character. Conversely, the function chr(j) takes an integer and returns its associated one-character string.

In order to find a replacement for a character in our Caesar cipher, we need to map the characters 'A' to 'Z' to the respective numbers 0 to 25. The formula for doing that conversion is $j = \text{ord}(c) - \text{ord}('A')$. As a sanity check, if character c is 'A', we have that $j = 0$. When c is 'B', we will find that its ordinal value is precisely one more than that for 'A', so their difference is 1. In general, the integer j that results from such a calculation can be used as an index into our precomputed translation string, as illustrated in Figure 5.21.

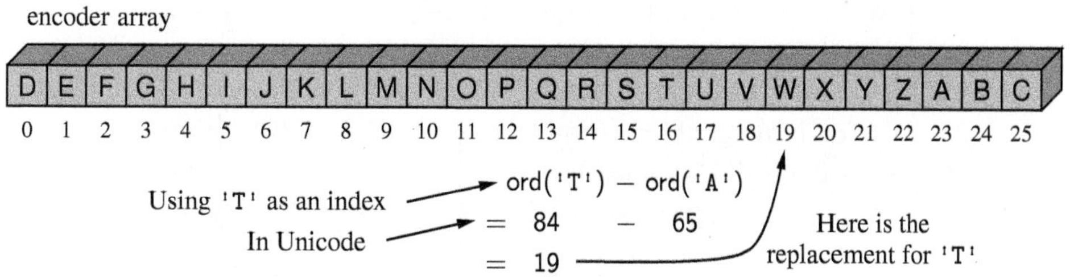

encoder array

Figure 5.21: Illustrating the use of uppercase characters as indices, in this case to perform the replacement rule for Caesar cipher encryption.

In Code Fragment 5.11, we develop a Python class for performing the Caesar cipher with an arbitrary rotational shift, and demonstrate its use. When we run this program (to perform a simple test), we get the following output.

```
Secret:  WKH HDJOH LV LQ SODB; PHHW DW MRH'V.
Message: THE EAGLE IS IN PLAY; MEET AT JOE'S.
```

The constructor for the class builds the forward and backward translation strings for the given rotation. With those in hand, the encryption and decryption algorithms are essentially the same, and so we perform both by means of a nonpublic utility method named _transform.

```
1   class CaesarCipher:
2     """Class for doing encryption and decryption using a Caesar cipher."""
3
4     def __init__(self, shift):
5       """Construct Caesar cipher using given integer shift for rotation."""
6       encoder = [None] * 26                      # temp array for encryption
7       decoder = [None] * 26                      # temp array for decryption
8       for k in range(26):
9         encoder[k] = chr((k + shift) % 26 + ord('A'))
10        decoder[k] = chr((k - shift) % 26 + ord('A'))
11      self._forward = ''.join(encoder)           # will store as string
12      self._backward = ''.join(decoder)          # since fixed
13
14    def encrypt(self, message):
15      """Return string representing encripted message."""
16      return self._transform(message, self._forward)
17
18    def decrypt(self, secret):
19      """Return decrypted message given encrypted secret."""
20      return self._transform(secret, self._backward)
21
22    def _transform(self, original, code):
23      """Utility to perform transformation based on given code string."""
24      msg = list(original)
25      for k in range(len(msg)):
26        if msg[k].isupper():
27          j = ord(msg[k]) - ord('A')             # index from 0 to 25
28          msg[k] = code[j]                        # replace this character
29      return ''.join(msg)
30
31  if __name__ == '__main__':
32    cipher = CaesarCipher(3)
33    message = "THE EAGLE IS IN PLAY; MEET AT JOE'S."
34    coded = cipher.encrypt(message)
35    print('Secret: ', coded)
36    answer = cipher.decrypt(coded)
37    print('Message:', answer)
```

Code Fragment 5.11: A complete Python class for the Caesar cipher.

5.6 Multidimensional Data Sets

Lists, tuples, and strings in Python are one-dimensional. We use a single index to access each element of the sequence. Many computer applications involve multidimensional data sets. For example, computer graphics are often modeled in either two or three dimensions. Geographic information may be naturally represented in two dimensions, medical imaging may provide three-dimensional scans of a patient, and a company's valuation is often based upon a high number of independent financial measures that can be modeled as multidimensional data. A two-dimensional array is sometimes also called a *matrix*. We may use two indices, say i and j, to refer to the cells in the matrix. The first index usually refers to a row number and the second to a column number, and these are traditionally zero-indexed in computer science. Figure 5.22 illustrates a two-dimensional data set with integer values. This data might, for example, represent the number of stores in various regions of Manhattan.

	0	1	2	3	4	5	6	7	8	9
0	22	18	709	5	33	10	4	56	82	440
1	45	32	830	120	750	660	13	77	20	105
2	4	880	45	66	61	28	650	7	510	67
3	940	12	36	3	20	100	306	590	0	500
4	50	65	42	49	88	25	70	126	83	288
5	398	233	5	83	59	232	49	8	365	90
6	33	58	632	87	94	5	59	204	120	829
7	62	394	3	4	102	140	183	390	16	26

Figure 5.22: Illustration of a two-dimensional integer data set, which has 8 rows and 10 columns. The rows and columns are zero-indexed. If this data set were named stores, the value of stores[3][5] is 100 and the value of stores[6][2] is 632.

A common representation for a two-dimensional data set in Python is as a list of lists. In particular, we can represent a two-dimensional array as a list of rows, with each row itself being a list of values. For example, the two-dimensional data

$$
\begin{array}{ccccc}
22 & 18 & 709 & 5 & 33 \\
45 & 32 & 830 & 120 & 750 \\
4 & 880 & 45 & 66 & 61
\end{array}
$$

might be stored in Python as follows.

    data = [[22, 18, 709, 5, 33], [45, 32, 830, 120, 750], [4, 880, 45, 66, 61]]

An advantage of this representation is that we can naturally use a syntax such as data[1][3] to represent the value that has row index 1 and column index 3, as data[1], the second entry in the outer list, is itself a list, and thus indexable.

Constructing a Multidimensional List

To quickly initialize a one-dimensional list, we generally rely on a syntax such as data = [0] * n to create a list of n zeros. On page 189, we emphasized that from a technical perspective, this creates a list of length n with all entries referencing the same integer instance, but that there was no meaningful consequence of such aliasing because of the immutability of the int class in Python.

We have to be considerably more careful when creating a list of lists. If our goal were to create the equivalent of a two-dimensional list of integers, with r rows and c columns, and to initialize all values to zero, a flawed approach might be to try the command

```
data = ([0] * c) * r            # Warning: this is a mistake
```

While([0] * c) is indeed a list of c zeros, multiplying that list by r unfortunately creates a single list with length $r \cdot c$, just as [2,4,6] * 2 results in list [2, 4, 6, 2, 4, 6].

A better, yet still flawed attempt is to make a list that contains the list of c zeros as its only element, and then to multiply that list by r. That is, we could try the command

```
data = [ [0] * c ] * r          # Warning: still a mistake
```

This is much closer, as we actually do have a structure that is formally a list of lists. The problem is that all r entries of the list known as data are references to the same instance of a list of c zeros. Figure 5.23 provides a portrayal of such aliasing.

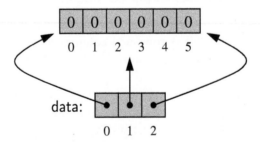

Figure 5.23: A flawed representation of a 3×6 data set as a list of lists, created with the command data = [[0] * 6] * 3. (For simplicity, we overlook the fact that the values in the secondary list are referential.)

This is truly a problem. Setting an entry such as data[2][0] = 100 would change the first entry of the secondary list to reference a new value, 100. Yet that cell of the secondary list also represents the value data[0][0], because "row" data[0] and "row" data[2] refer to the same secondary list.

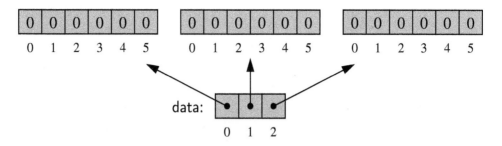

Figure 5.24: A valid representation of a 3×6 data set as a list of lists. (For simplicity, we overlook the fact that the values in the secondary lists are referential.)

To properly initialize a two-dimensional list, we must ensure that each cell of the primary list refers to an *independent* instance of a secondary list. This can be accomplished through the use of Python's list comprehension syntax.

data = [[0] * c for j in range(r)]

This command produces a valid configuration, similar to the one shown in Figure 5.24. By using list comprehension, the expression [0] * c is reevaluated for each pass of the embedded for loop. Therefore, we get r distinct secondary lists, as desired. (We note that the variable j in that command is irrelevant; we simply need a for loop that iterates r times.)

Two-Dimensional Arrays and Positional Games

Many computer games, be they strategy games, simulation games, or first-person conflict games, involve objects that reside in a two-dimensional space. Software for such **positional games** need a way of representing such a two-dimensional "board," and in Python the list of lists is a natural choice.

Tic-Tac-Toe

As most school children know, **Tic-Tac-Toe** is a game played in a three-by-three board. Two players—X and O—alternate in placing their respective marks in the cells of this board, starting with player X. If either player succeeds in getting three of his or her marks in a row, column, or diagonal, then that player wins.

This is admittedly not a sophisticated positional game, and it's not even that much fun to play, since a good player O can always force a tie. Tic-Tac-Toe's saving grace is that it is a nice, simple example showing how two-dimensional arrays can be used for positional games. Software for more sophisticated positional games, such as checkers, chess, or the popular simulation games, are all based on the same approach we illustrate here for using a two-dimensional array for Tic-Tac-Toe.

Our representation of a 3×3 board will be a list of lists of characters, with 'X' or 'O' designating a player's move, or ' ' designating an empty space. For example, the board configuration

will be stored internally as

[['O', 'X', 'O'], [' ', 'X', ' '], [' ', 'O', 'X']]

We develop a complete Python class for maintaining a Tic-Tac-Toe board for two players. That class will keep track of the moves and report a winner, but it does not perform any strategy or allow someone to play Tic-Tac-Toe against the computer. The details of such a program are beyond the scope of this chapter, but it might nonetheless make a good course project (see Exercise P-8.68).

Before presenting the implementation of the class, we demonstrate its public interface with a simple test in Code Fragment 5.12.

```
 1    game = TicTacToe()
 2    # X moves:              # O moves:
 3    game.mark(1, 1);        game.mark(0, 2)
 4    game.mark(2, 2);        game.mark(0, 0)
 5    game.mark(0, 1);        game.mark(2, 1)
 6    game.mark(1, 2);        game.mark(1, 0)
 7    game.mark(2, 0)
 8
 9    print(game)
10    winner = game.winner()
11    if winner is None:
12       print('Tie')
13    else:
14       print(winner, 'wins')
```

Code Fragment 5.12: A simple test for our Tic-Tac-Toe class.

The basic operations are that a new game instance represents an empty board, that the mark(i,j) method adds a mark at the given position for the current player (with the software managing the alternating of turns), and that the game board can be printed and the winner determined. The complete source code for the TicTacToe class is given in Code Fragment 5.13. Our mark method performs error checking to make sure that valid indices are sent, that the position is not already occupied, and that no further moves are made after someone wins the game.

```
1   class TicTacToe:
2     """Management of a Tic-Tac-Toe game (does not do strategy)."""
3
4     def __init__(self):
5       """Start a new game."""
6       self._board = [ [' '] * 3 for j in range(3) ]
7       self._player = 'X'
8
9     def mark(self, i, j):
10      """Put an X or O mark at position (i,j) for next player's turn."""
11      if not (0 <= i <= 2 and 0 <= j <= 2):
12        raise ValueError('Invalid board position')
13      if self._board[i][j] != ' ':
14        raise ValueError('Board position occupied')
15      if self.winner( ) is not None:
16        raise ValueError('Game is already complete')
17      self._board[i][j] = self._player
18      if self._player == 'X':
19        self._player = 'O'
20      else:
21        self._player = 'X'
22
23    def _is_win(self, mark):
24      """Check whether the board configuration is a win for the given player."""
25      board = self._board                                    # local variable for shorthand
26      return (mark == board[0][0] == board[0][1] == board[0][2] or    # row 0
27              mark == board[1][0] == board[1][1] == board[1][2] or    # row 1
28              mark == board[2][0] == board[2][1] == board[2][2] or    # row 2
29              mark == board[0][0] == board[1][0] == board[2][0] or    # column 0
30              mark == board[0][1] == board[1][1] == board[2][1] or    # column 1
31              mark == board[0][2] == board[1][2] == board[2][2] or    # column 2
32              mark == board[0][0] == board[1][1] == board[2][2] or    # diagonal
33              mark == board[0][2] == board[1][1] == board[2][0])      # rev diag
34
35    def winner(self):
36      """Return mark of winning player, or None to indicate a tie."""
37      for mark in 'XO':
38        if self._is_win(mark):
39          return mark
40      return None
41
42    def __str__(self):
43      """Return string representation of current game board."""
44      rows = ['|'.join(self._board[r]) for r in range(3)]
45      return '\n-----\n'.join(rows)
```

Code Fragment 5.13: A complete Python class for managing a Tic-Tac-Toe game.

5.7 Exercises

For help with exercises, please visit the site, www.wiley.com/college/goodrich.

Reinforcement

R-5.1 Execute the experiment from Code Fragment 5.1 and compare the results on your system to those we report in Code Fragment 5.2.

R-5.2 In Code Fragment 5.1, we perform an experiment to compare the length of a Python list to its underlying memory usage. Determining the sequence of array sizes requires a manual inspection of the output of that program. Redesign the experiment so that the program outputs only those values of k at which the existing capacity is exhausted. For example, on a system consistent with the results of Code Fragment 5.2, your program should output that the sequence of array capacities are 0, 4, 8, 16, 25, ...

R-5.3 Modify the experiment from Code Fragment 5.1 in order to demonstrate that Python's list class occasionally shrinks the size of its underlying array when elements are popped from a list.

R-5.4 Our DynamicArray class, as given in Code Fragment 5.3, does not support use of negative indices with __getitem__. Update that method to better match the semantics of a Python list.

R-5.5 Redo the justification of Proposition 5.1 assuming that the the cost of growing the array from size k to size $2k$ is $3k$ cyber-dollars. How much should each append operation be charged to make the amortization work?

R-5.6 Our implementation of insert for the DynamicArray class, as given in Code Fragment 5.5, has the following inefficiency. In the case when a resize occurs, the resize operation takes time to copy all the elements from an old array to a new array, and then the subsequent loop in the body of insert shifts many of those elements. Give an improved implementation of the insert method, so that, in the case of a resize, the elements are shifted into their final position during that operation, thereby avoiding the subsequent shifting.

R-5.7 Let A be an array of size $n \geq 2$ containing integers from 1 to $n-1$, inclusive, with exactly one repeated. Describe a fast algorithm for finding the integer in A that is repeated.

R-5.8 Experimentally evaluate the efficiency of the pop method of Python's list class when using varying indices as a parameter, as we did for insert on page 205. Report your results akin to Table 5.5.

R-5.9 Explain the changes that would have to be made to the program of Code Fragment 5.11 so that it could perform the Caesar cipher for messages that are written in an alphabet-based language other than English, such as Greek, Russian, or Hebrew.

R-5.10 The constructor for the CaesarCipher class in Code Fragment 5.11 can be implemented with a two-line body by building the forward and backward strings using a combination of the join method and an appropriate comprehension syntax. Give such an implementation.

R-5.11 Use standard control structures to compute the sum of all numbers in an $n \times n$ data set, represented as a list of lists.

R-5.12 Describe how the built-in sum function can be combined with Python's comprehension syntax to compute the sum of all numbers in an $n \times n$ data set, represented as a list of lists.

Creativity

C-5.13 In the experiment of Code Fragment 5.1, we begin with an empty list. If data were initially constructed with nonempty length, does this affect the sequence of values at which the underlying array is expanded? Perform your own experiments, and comment on any relationship you see between the initial length and the expansion sequence.

C-5.14 The shuffle method, supported by the random module, takes a Python list and rearranges it so that every possible ordering is equally likely. Implement your own version of such a function. You may rely on the randrange(n) function of the random module, which returns a random number between 0 and $n-1$ inclusive.

C-5.15 Consider an implementation of a dynamic array, but instead of copying the elements into an array of double the size (that is, from N to $2N$) when its capacity is reached, we copy the elements into an array with $\lceil N/4 \rceil$ additional cells, going from capacity N to capacity $N + \lceil N/4 \rceil$. Prove that performing a sequence of n append operations still runs in $O(n)$ time in this case.

C-5.16 Implement a pop method for the DynamicArray class, given in Code Fragment 5.3, that removes the last element of the array, and that shrinks the capacity, N, of the array by half any time the number of elements in the array goes below $N/4$.

C-5.17 Prove that when using a dynamic array that grows and shrinks as in the previous exercise, the following series of $2n$ operations takes $O(n)$ time: n append operations on an initially empty array, followed by n pop operations.

C-5.18 Give a formal proof that any sequence of n append or pop operations on an initially empty dynamic array takes $O(n)$ time, if using the strategy described in Exercise C-5.16.

C-5.19 Consider a variant of Exercise C-5.16, in which an array of capacity N is resized to capacity precisely that of the number of elements, any time the number of elements in the array goes strictly below $N/4$. Give a formal proof that any sequence of n append or pop operations on an initially empty dynamic array takes $O(n)$ time.

C-5.20 Consider a variant of Exercise C-5.16, in which an array of capacity N, is resized to capacity precisely that of the number of elements, any time the number of elements in the array goes strictly below $N/2$. Show that there exists a sequence of n operations that requires $\Omega(n^2)$ time to execute.

C-5.21 In Section 5.4.2, we described four different ways to compose a long string: (1) repeated concatenation, (2) appending to a temporary list and then joining, (3) using list comprehension with join, and (4) using generator comprehension with join. Develop an experiment to test the efficiency of all four of these approaches and report your findings.

C-5.22 Develop an experiment to compare the relative efficiency of the extend method of Python's list class versus using repeated calls to append to accomplish the equivalent task.

C-5.23 Based on the discussion of page 207, develop an experiment to compare the efficiency of Python's list comprehension syntax versus the construction of a list by means of repeated calls to append.

C-5.24 Perform experiments to evaluate the efficiency of the remove method of Python's list class, as we did for insert on page 205. Use known values so that all removals occur either at the beginning, middle, or end of the list. Report your results akin to Table 5.5.

C-5.25 The syntax data.remove(value) for Python list data removes only the first occurrence of element value from the list. Give an implementation of a function, with signature remove_all(data, value), that removes *all* occurrences of value from the given list, such that the worst-case running time of the function is $O(n)$ on a list with n elements. Not that it is not efficient enough in general to rely on repeated calls to remove.

C-5.26 Let B be an array of size $n \geq 6$ containing integers from 1 to $n-5$, inclusive, with exactly five repeated. Describe a good algorithm for finding the five integers in B that are repeated.

C-5.27 Given a Python list L of n positive integers, each represented with $k = \lceil \log n \rceil + 1$ bits, describe an $O(n)$-time method for finding a k-bit integer not in L.

C-5.28 Argue why any solution to the previous problem must run in $\Omega(n)$ time.

C-5.29 A useful operation in databases is the ***natural join***. If we view a database as a list of *ordered* pairs of objects, then the natural join of databases A and B is the list of all ordered triples (x,y,z) such that the pair (x,y) is in A and the pair (y,z) is in B. Describe and analyze an efficient algorithm for computing the natural join of a list A of n pairs and a list B of m pairs.

C-5.30 When Bob wants to send Alice a message M on the Internet, he breaks M into n ***data packets***, numbers the packets consecutively, and injects them into the network. When the packets arrive at Alice's computer, they may be out of order, so Alice must assemble the sequence of n packets in order before she can be sure she has the entire message. Describe an efficient scheme for Alice to do this, assuming that she knows the value of n. What is the running time of this algorithm?

C-5.31 Describe a way to use recursion to add all the numbers in an $n \times n$ data set, represented as a list of lists.

Projects

P-5.32 Write a Python function that takes two three-dimensional numeric data sets and adds them componentwise.

P-5.33 Write a Python program for a matrix class that can add and multiply two-dimensional arrays of numbers, assuming the dimensions agree appropriately for the operation.

P-5.34 Write a program that can perform the Caesar cipher for English messages that include both upper- and lowercase characters.

P-5.35 Implement a class, SubstitutionCipher, with a constructor that takes a string with the 26 uppercase letters in an arbitrary order and uses that for the forward mapping for encryption (akin to the self._forward string in our CaesarCipher class of Code Fragment 5.11). You should derive the backward mapping from the forward version.

P-5.36 Redesign the CaesarCipher class as a subclass of the SubstitutionCipher from the previous problem.

P-5.37 Design a RandomCipher class as a subclass of the SubstitutionCipher from Exercise P-5.35, so that each instance of the class relies on a random permutation of letters for its mapping.

Chapter Notes

The fundamental data structures of arrays belong to the folklore of computer science. They were first chronicled in the computer science literature by Knuth in his seminal book on *Fundamental Algorithms* [64].

Chapter

6

Stacks, Queues, and Deques

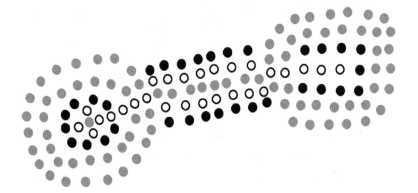

Contents

6.1 Stacks

A *stack* is a collection of objects that are inserted and removed according to the *last-in, first-out* (*LIFO*) principle. A user may insert objects into a stack at any time, but may only access or remove the most recently inserted object that remains (at the so-called "top" of the stack). The name "stack" is derived from the metaphor of a stack of plates in a spring-loaded, cafeteria plate dispenser. In this case, the fundamental operations involve the "pushing" and "popping" of plates on the stack. When we need a new plate from the dispenser, we "pop" the top plate off the stack, and when we add a plate, we "push" it down on the stack to become the new top plate. Perhaps an even more amusing example is a PEZ® candy dispenser, which stores mint candies in a spring-loaded container that "pops" out the topmost candy in the stack when the top of the dispenser is lifted (see Figure 6.1). Stacks are a fundamental data structure. They are used in many applications, including the following.

Example 6.1: *Internet Web browsers store the addresses of recently visited sites in a stack. Each time a user visits a new site, that site's address is "pushed" onto the stack of addresses. The browser then allows the user to "pop" back to previously visited sites using the "back" button.*

Example 6.2: *Text editors usually provide an "undo" mechanism that cancels recent editing operations and reverts to former states of a document. This undo operation can be accomplished by keeping text changes in a stack.*

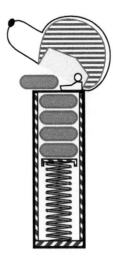

Figure 6.1: A schematic drawing of a PEZ® dispenser; a physical implementation of the stack ADT. (PEZ® is a registered trademark of PEZ Candy, Inc.)

6.1.1   The Stack Abstract Data Type

Stacks are the simplest of all data structures, yet they are also among the most important. They are used in a host of different applications, and as a tool for many more sophisticated data structures and algorithms. Formally, a stack is an abstract data type (ADT) such that an instance S supports the following two methods:

S.push(e): Add element e to the top of stack S.

S.pop( ): Remove and return the top element from the stack S; an error occurs if the stack is empty.

Additionally, let us define the following accessor methods for convenience:

S.top( ): Return a reference to the top element of stack S, without removing it; an error occurs if the stack is empty.

S.is_empty( ): Return True if stack S does not contain any elements.

len(S): Return the number of elements in stack S; in Python, we implement this with the special method __len__.

By convention, we assume that a newly created stack is empty, and that there is no a priori bound on the capacity of the stack. Elements added to the stack can have arbitrary type.

Example 6.3: *The following table shows a series of stack operations and their effects on an initially empty stack S of integers.*

Operation	Return Value	Stack Contents
S.push(5)	–	[5]
S.push(3)	–	[5, 3]
len(S)	2	[5, 3]
S.pop( )	3	[5]
S.is_empty( )	False	[5]
S.pop( )	5	[ ]
S.is_empty( )	True	[ ]
S.pop( )	"error"	[ ]
S.push(7)	–	[7]
S.push(9)	–	[7, 9]
S.top( )	9	[7, 9]
S.push(4)	–	[7, 9, 4]
len(S)	3	[7, 9, 4]
S.pop( )	4	[7, 9]
S.push(6)	–	[7, 9, 6]
S.push(8)	–	[7, 9, 6, 8]
S.pop( )	8	[7, 9, 6]

6.1.2 Simple Array-Based Stack Implementation

We can implement a stack quite easily by storing its elements in a Python list. The list class already supports adding an element to the end with the append method, and removing the last element with the pop method, so it is natural to align the top of the stack at the end of the list, as shown in Figure 6.2.

Figure 6.2: Implementing a stack with a Python list, storing the top element in the rightmost cell.

Although a programmer could directly use the list class in place of a formal stack class, lists also include behaviors (e.g., adding or removing elements from arbitrary positions) that would break the abstraction that the stack ADT represents. Also, the terminology used by the list class does not precisely align with traditional nomenclature for a stack ADT, in particular the distinction between append and push. Instead, we demonstrate how to use a list for internal storage while providing a public interface consistent with a stack.

The Adapter Pattern

The *adapter* design pattern applies to any context where we effectively want to modify an existing class so that its methods match those of a related, but different, class or interface. One general way to apply the adapter pattern is to define a new class in such a way that it contains an instance of the existing class as a hidden field, and then to implement each method of the new class using methods of this hidden instance variable. By applying the adapter pattern in this way, we have created a new class that performs some of the same functions as an existing class, but repackaged in a more convenient way. In the context of the stack ADT, we can adapt Python's list class using the correspondences shown in Table 6.1.

Stack Method	*Realization with Python list*
S.push(e)	L.append(e)
S.pop()	L.pop()
S.top()	L[−1]
S.is_empty()	len(L) == 0
len(S)	len(L)

Table 6.1: Realization of a stack S as an adaptation of a Python list L.

Implementing a Stack Using a Python List

We use the adapter design pattern to define an ArrayStack class that uses an underlying Python list for storage. (We choose the name ArrayStack to emphasize that the underlying storage is inherently array based.) One question that remains is what our code should do if a user calls pop or top when the stack is empty. Our ADT suggests that an error occurs, but we must decide what type of error. When pop is called on an empty Python list, it formally raises an IndexError, as lists are index-based sequences. That choice does not seem appropriate for a stack, since there is no assumption of indices. Instead, we can define a new exception class that is more appropriate. Code Fragment 6.1 defines such an Empty class as a trivial subclass of the Python Exception class.

```python
class Empty(Exception):
  """Error attempting to access an element from an empty container."""
  pass
```

Code Fragment 6.1: Definition for an Empty exception class.

The formal definition for our ArrayStack class is given in Code Fragment 6.2. The constructor establishes the member self._data as an initially empty Python list, for internal storage. The rest of the public stack behaviors are implemented, using the corresponding adaptation that was outlined in Table 6.1.

Example Usage

Below, we present an example of the use of our ArrayStack class, mirroring the operations at the beginning of Example 6.3 on page 230.

```python
S = ArrayStack( )         # contents: [ ]
S.push(5)                 # contents: [5]
S.push(3)                 # contents: [5, 3]
print(len(S))             # contents: [5, 3];        outputs 2
print(S.pop())            # contents: [5];           outputs 3
print(S.is_empty())       # contents: [5];           outputs False
print(S.pop())            # contents: [ ];           outputs 5
print(S.is_empty())       # contents: [ ];           outputs True
S.push(7)                 # contents: [7]
S.push(9)                 # contents: [7, 9]
print(S.top())            # contents: [7, 9];        outputs 9
S.push(4)                 # contents: [7, 9, 4]
print(len(S))             # contents: [7, 9, 4];     outputs 3
print(S.pop())            # contents: [7, 9];        outputs 4
S.push(6)                 # contents: [7, 9, 6]
```

```
 1  class ArrayStack:
 2    """LIFO Stack implementation using a Python list as underlying storage."""
 3
 4    def __init__(self):
 5      """Create an empty stack."""
 6      self._data = [ ]                          # nonpublic list instance
 7
 8    def __len__(self):
 9      """Return the number of elements in the stack."""
10      return len(self._data)
11
12    def is_empty(self):
13      """Return True if the stack is empty."""
14      return len(self._data) == 0
15
16    def push(self, e):
17      """Add element e to the top of the stack."""
18      self._data.append(e)                     # new item stored at end of list
19
20    def top(self):
21      """Return (but do not remove) the element at the top of the stack.
22
23      Raise Empty exception if the stack is empty.
24      """
25      if self.is_empty():
26        raise Empty('Stack is empty')
27      return self._data[-1]                     # the last item in the list
28
29    def pop(self):
30      """Remove and return the element from the top of the stack (i.e., LIFO).
31
32      Raise Empty exception if the stack is empty.
33      """
34      if self.is_empty():
35        raise Empty('Stack is empty')
36      return self._data.pop( )                  # remove last item from list
```

Code Fragment 6.2: Implementing a stack using a Python list as storage.

Analyzing the Array-Based Stack Implementation

Table 6.2 shows the running times for our ArrayStack methods. The analysis directly mirrors the analysis of the list class given in Section 5.3. The implementations for top, is_empty, and len use constant time in the worst case. The $O(1)$ time for push and pop are **amortized** bounds (see Section 5.3.2); a typical call to either of these methods uses constant time, but there is occasionally an $O(n)$-time worst case, where n is the current number of elements in the stack, when an operation causes the list to resize its internal array. The space usage for a stack is $O(n)$.

Operation	Running Time
S.push(e)	$O(1)^*$
S.pop()	$O(1)^*$
S.top()	$O(1)$
S.is_empty()	$O(1)$
len(S)	$O(1)$

*amortized

Table 6.2: Performance of our array-based stack implementation. The bounds for push and pop are amortized due to similar bounds for the list class. The space usage is $O(n)$, where n is the current number of elements in the stack.

Avoiding Amortization by Reserving Capacity

In some contexts, there may be additional knowledge that suggests a maximum size that a stack will reach. Our implementation of ArrayStack from Code Fragment 6.2 begins with an empty list and expands as needed. In the analysis of lists from Section 5.4.1, we emphasized that it is more efficient in practice to construct a list with initial length n than it is to start with an empty list and append n items (even though both approaches run in $O(n)$ time).

As an alternate model for a stack, we might wish for the constructor to accept a parameter specifying the maximum capacity of a stack and to initialize the _data member to a list of that length. Implementing such a model requires significant changes relative to Code Fragment 6.2. The size of the stack would no longer be synonymous with the length of the list, and pushes and pops of the stack would not require changing the length of the list. Instead, we suggest maintaining a separate integer as an instance variable that denotes the current number of elements in the stack. Details of such an implementation are left as Exercise C-6.17.

6.1.3 Reversing Data Using a Stack

As a consequence of the LIFO protocol, a stack can be used as a general tool to reverse a data sequence. For example, if the values 1, 2, and 3 are pushed onto a stack in that order, they will be popped from the stack in the order 3, 2, and then 1.

This idea can be applied in a variety of settings. For example, we might wish to print lines of a file in reverse order in order to display a data set in decreasing order rather than increasing order. This can be accomplished by reading each line and pushing it onto a stack, and then writing the lines in the order they are popped. An implementation of such a process is given in Code Fragment 6.3.

```
1  def reverse_file(filename):
2    """Overwrite given file with its contents line-by-line reversed."""
3    S = ArrayStack( )
4    original = open(filename)
5    for line in original:
6      S.push(line.rstrip('\n'))        # we will re-insert newlines when writing
7    original.close( )
8
9    # now we overwrite with contents in LIFO order
10   output = open(filename, 'w')       # reopening file overwrites original
11   while not S.is_empty( ):
12     output.write(S.pop( ) + '\n')   # re-insert newline characters
13   output.close( )
```

Code Fragment 6.3: A function that reverses the order of lines in a file.

One technical detail worth noting is that we intentionally strip trailing newlines from lines as they are read, and then re-insert newlines after each line when writing the resulting file. Our reason for doing this is to handle a special case in which the original file does not have a trailing newline for the final line. If we exactly echoed the lines read from the file in reverse order, then the original last line would be followed (without newline) by the original second-to-last line. In our implementation, we ensure that there will be a separating newline in the result.

The idea of using a stack to reverse a data set can be applied to other types of sequences. For example, Exercise R-6.5 explores the use of a stack to provide yet another solution for reversing the contents of a Python list (a recursive solution for this goal was discussed in Section 4.4.1). A more challenging task is to reverse the order in which elements are stored within a stack. If we were to move them from one stack to another, they would be reversed, but if we were to then replace them into the original stack, they would be reversed again, thereby reverting to their original order. Exercise C-6.18 explores a solution for this task.

6.1.4   Matching Parentheses and HTML Tags

In this subsection, we explore two related applications of stacks, both of which involve testing for pairs of matching delimiters. In our first application, we consider arithmetic expressions that may contain various pairs of grouping symbols, such as

- Parentheses: "(" and ")"
- Braces: "{" and "}"
- Brackets: "[" and "]"

Each opening symbol must match its corresponding closing symbol. For example, a left bracket, "[," must match a corresponding right bracket, "]," as in the expression [(5+x)-(y+z)]. The following examples further illustrate this concept:

- Correct: ()(()){([()])}
- Correct: ((()(()){([()])}))
- Incorrect:)(()){([()])}
- Incorrect: ({[])}
- Incorrect: (

We leave the precise definition of a matching group of symbols to Exercise R-6.6.

An Algorithm for Matching Delimiters

An important task when processing arithmetic expressions is to make sure their delimiting symbols match up correctly. Code Fragment 6.4 presents a Python implementation of such an algorithm. A discussion of the code follows.

```
1  def is_matched(expr):
2    """Return True if all delimiters are properly match; False otherwise."""
3    lefty = '({['                          # opening delimiters
4    righty = ')}]'                         # respective closing delims
5    S = ArrayStack()
6    for c in expr:
7      if c in lefty:
8        S.push(c)                          # push left delimiter on stack
9      elif c in righty:
10       if S.is_empty():
11         return False                     # nothing to match with
12       if righty.index(c) != lefty.index(S.pop()):
13         return False                     # mismatched
14   return S.is_empty()                    # were all symbols matched?
```

Code Fragment 6.4: Function for matching delimiters in an arithmetic expression.

We assume the input is a sequence of characters, such as ' [(5+x)-(y+z)] '. We perform a left-to-right scan of the original sequence, using a stack S to facilitate the matching of grouping symbols. Each time we encounter an opening symbol, we push that symbol onto S, and each time we encounter a closing symbol, we pop a symbol from the stack S (assuming S is not empty), and check that these two symbols form a valid pair. If we reach the end of the expression and the stack is empty, then the original expression was properly matched. Otherwise, there must be an opening delimiter on the stack without a matching symbol.

If the length of the original expression is n, the algorithm will make at most n calls to push and n calls to pop. Those calls run in a total of $O(n)$ time, even considering the amortized nature of the $O(1)$ time bound for those methods. Given that our selection of possible delimiters, ({[, has constant size, auxiliary tests such as c in lefty and righty.index(c) each run in $O(1)$ time. Combining these operations, the matching algorithm on a sequence of length n runs in $O(n)$ time.

Matching Tags in a Markup Language

Another application of matching delimiters is in the validation of markup languages such as HTML or XML. HTML is the standard format for hyperlinked documents on the Internet and XML is an extensible markup language used for a variety of structured data sets. We show a sample HTML document and a possible rendering in Figure 6.3.

```
<body>
<center>
<h1> The Little Boat </h1>
</center>
<p> The storm tossed the little
boat like a cheap sneaker in an
old washing machine.  The three
drunken fishermen were used to
such treatment, of course, but
not the tree salesman, who even as
a stowaway now felt that he
had overpaid for the voyage. </p>
<ol>
<li> Will the salesman die? </li>
<li> What color is the boat? </li>
<li> And what about Naomi? </li>
</ol>
</body>
```

(a)

The Little Boat

The storm tossed the little boat like a cheap sneaker in an old washing machine. The three drunken fishermen were used to such treatment, of course, but not the tree salesman, who even as a stowaway now felt that he had overpaid for the voyage.

1. Will the salesman die?
2. What color is the boat?
3. And what about Naomi?

(b)

Figure 6.3: Illustrating HTML tags. (a) An HTML document; (b) its rendering.

In an HTML document, portions of text are delimited by *HTML tags*. A simple opening HTML tag has the form "<name>" and the corresponding closing tag has the form "</name>". For example, we see the <body> tag on the first line of Figure 6.3(a), and the matching </body> tag at the close of that document. Other commonly used HTML tags that are used in this example include:

- body: document body
- h1: section header
- center: center justify
- p: paragraph
- ol: numbered (ordered) list
- li: list item

Ideally, an HTML document should have matching tags, although most browsers tolerate a certain number of mismatching tags. In Code Fragment 6.5, we give a Python function that matches tags in a string representing an HTML document. We make a left-to-right pass through the raw string, using index j to track our progress and the find method of the str class to locate the '<' and '>' characters that define the tags. Opening tags are pushed onto the stack, and matched against closing tags as they are popped from the stack, just as we did when matching delimiters in Code Fragment 6.4. By similar analysis, this algorithm runs in $O(n)$ time, where n is the number of characters in the raw HTML source.

```python
1  def is_matched_html(raw):
2    """Return True if all HTML tags are properly match; False otherwise."""
3    S = ArrayStack()
4    j = raw.find('<')                        # find first '<' character (if any)
5    while j != -1:
6      k = raw.find('>', j+1)                 # find next '>' character
7      if k == -1:
8        return False                         # invalid tag
9      tag = raw[j+1:k]                        # strip away < >
10     if not tag.startswith('/'):            # this is opening tag
11       S.push(tag)
12     else:                                  # this is closing tag
13       if S.is_empty():
14         return False                       # nothing to match with
15       if tag[1:] != S.pop():
16         return False                       # mismatched delimiter
17     j = raw.find('<', k+1)                 # find next '<' character (if any)
18   return S.is_empty()                      # were all opening tags matched?
```

Code Fragment 6.5: Function for testing if an HTML document has matching tags.

6.2 Queues

Another fundamental data structure is the *queue*. It is a close "cousin" of the stack, as a queue is a collection of objects that are inserted and removed according to the *first-in, first-out* (*FIFO*) principle. That is, elements can be inserted at any time, but only the element that has been in the queue the longest can be next removed.

We usually say that elements enter a queue at the back and are removed from the front. A metaphor for this terminology is a line of people waiting to get on an amusement park ride. People waiting for such a ride enter at the back of the line and get on the ride from the front of the line. There are many other applications of queues (see Figure 6.4). Stores, theaters, reservation centers, and other similar services typically process customer requests according to the FIFO principle. A queue would therefore be a logical choice for a data structure to handle calls to a customer service center, or a wait-list at a restaurant. FIFO queues are also used by many computing devices, such as a networked printer, or a Web server responding to requests.

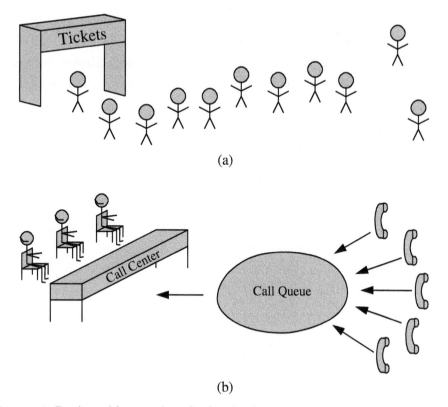

(a)

(b)

Figure 6.4: Real-world examples of a first-in, first-out queue. (a) People waiting in line to purchase tickets; (b) phone calls being routed to a customer service center.

6.2.1 The Queue Abstract Data Type

Formally, the queue abstract data type defines a collection that keeps objects in a sequence, where element access and deletion are restricted to the *first* element in the queue, and element insertion is restricted to the back of the sequence. This restriction enforces the rule that items are inserted and deleted in a queue according to the first-in, first-out (FIFO) principle. The *queue* abstract data type (ADT) supports the following two fundamental methods for a queue Q:

Q.enqueue(e): Add element e to the back of queue Q.

Q.dequeue( ): Remove and return the first element from queue Q; an error occurs if the queue is empty.

The queue ADT also includes the following supporting methods (with first being analogous to the stack's top method):

Q.first( ): Return a reference to the element at the front of queue Q, without removing it; an error occurs if the queue is empty.

Q.is_empty( ): Return True if queue Q does not contain any elements.

len(Q): Return the number of elements in queue Q; in Python, we implement this with the special method __len__.

By convention, we assume that a newly created queue is empty, and that there is no a priori bound on the capacity of the queue. Elements added to the queue can have arbitrary type.

Example 6.4: *The following table shows a series of queue operations and their effects on an initially empty queue Q of integers.*

Operation	Return Value	first ← Q ← last
Q.enqueue(5)	–	[5]
Q.enqueue(3)	–	[5, 3]
len(Q)	2	[5, 3]
Q.dequeue( )	5	[3]
Q.is_empty( )	False	[3]
Q.dequeue( )	3	[ ]
Q.is_empty( )	True	[ ]
Q.dequeue( )	"error"	[ ]
Q.enqueue(7)	–	[7]
Q.enqueue(9)	–	[7, 9]
Q.first( )	7	[7, 9]
Q.enqueue(4)	–	[7, 9, 4]
len(Q)	3	[7, 9, 4]
Q.dequeue( )	7	[9, 4]

6.2.2 Array-Based Queue Implementation

For the stack ADT, we created a very simple adapter class that used a Python list as the underlying storage. It may be very tempting to use a similar approach for supporting the queue ADT. We could enqueue element e by calling append(e) to add it to the end of the list. We could use the syntax pop(0), as opposed to pop( ), to intentionally remove the *first* element from the list when dequeuing.

As easy as this would be to implement, it is tragically inefficient. As we discussed in Section 5.4.1, when pop is called on a list with a non-default index, a loop is executed to shift all elements beyond the specified index to the left, so as to fill the hole in the sequence caused by the pop. Therefore, a call to pop(0) always causes the worst-case behavior of $\Theta(n)$ time.

We can improve on the above strategy by avoiding the call to pop(0) entirely. We can replace the dequeued entry in the array with a reference to None, and maintain an explicit variable f to store the index of the element that is currently at the front of the queue. Such an algorithm for dequeue would run in $O(1)$ time. After several dequeue operations, this approach might lead to the configuration portrayed in Figure 6.5.

Figure 6.5: Allowing the front of the queue to drift away from index 0.

Unfortunately, there remains a drawback to the revised approach. In the case of a stack, the length of the list was precisely equal to the size of the stack (even if the underlying array for the list was slightly larger). With the queue design that we are considering, the situation is worse. We can build a queue that has relatively few elements, yet which are stored in an arbitrarily large list. This occurs, for example, if we repeatedly enqueue a new element and then dequeue another (allowing the front to drift rightward). Over time, the size of the underlying list would grow to $O(m)$ where m is the *total* number of enqueue operations since the creation of the queue, rather than the current number of elements in the queue.

This design would have detrimental consequences in applications in which queues have relatively modest size, but which are used for long periods of time. For example, the wait-list for a restaurant might never have more than 30 entries at one time, but over the course of a day (or a week), the overall number of entries would be significantly larger.

Using an Array Circularly

In developing a more robust queue implementation, we allow the front of the queue to drift rightward, and we allow the contents of the queue to "wrap around" the end of an underlying array. We assume that our underlying array has fixed length N that is greater that the actual number of elements in the queue. New elements are enqueued toward the "end" of the current queue, progressing from the front to index $N-1$ and continuing at index 0, then 1. Figure 6.6 illustrates such a queue with first element E and last element M.

Figure 6.6: Modeling a queue with a circular array that wraps around the end.

Implementing this circular view is not difficult. When we dequeue an element and want to "advance" the front index, we use the arithmetic $f = (f + 1) \% N$. Recall that the $\%$ operator in Python denotes the ***modulo*** operator, which is computed by taking the remainder after an integral division. For example, 14 divided by 3 has a quotient of 4 with remainder 2, that is, $\frac{14}{3} = 4\frac{2}{3}$. So in Python, 14 // 3 evaluates to the quotient 4, while 14 % 3 evaluates to the remainder 2. The modulo operator is ideal for treating an array circularly. As a concrete example, if we have a list of length 10, and a front index 7, we can advance the front by formally computing (7+1) % 10, which is simply 8, as 8 divided by 10 is 0 with a remainder of 8. Similarly, advancing index 8 results in index 9. But when we advance from index 9 (the last one in the array), we compute (9+1) % 10, which evaluates to index 0 (as 10 divided by 10 has a remainder of zero).

A Python Queue Implementation

A complete implementation of a queue ADT using a Python list in circular fashion is presented in Code Fragments 6.6 and 6.7. Internally, the queue class maintains the following three instance variables:

> **_data:** is a reference to a list instance with a fixed capacity.
>
> **_size:** is an integer representing the current number of elements stored in the queue (as opposed to the length of the _data list).
>
> **_front:** is an integer that represents the index within _data of the first element of the queue (assuming the queue is not empty).

We initially reserve a list of moderate size for storing data, although the queue formally has size zero. As a technicality, we initialize the _front index to zero.

When front or dequeue are called with no elements in the queue, we raise an instance of the Empty exception, defined in Code Fragment 6.1 for our stack.

```
1   class ArrayQueue:
2     """FIFO queue implementation using a Python list as underlying storage."""
3     DEFAULT_CAPACITY = 10          # moderate capacity for all new queues
4
5     def __init__(self):
6       """Create an empty queue."""
7       self._data = [None] * ArrayQueue.DEFAULT_CAPACITY
8       self._size = 0
9       self._front = 0
10
11    def __len__(self):
12      """Return the number of elements in the queue."""
13      return self._size
14
15    def is_empty(self):
16      """Return True if the queue is empty."""
17      return self._size == 0
18
19    def first(self):
20      """Return (but do not remove) the element at the front of the queue.
21
22      Raise Empty exception if the queue is empty.
23      """
24      if self.is_empty():
25        raise Empty('Queue is empty')
26      return self._data[self._front]
27
28    def dequeue(self):
29      """Remove and return the first element of the queue (i.e., FIFO).
30
31      Raise Empty exception if the queue is empty.
32      """
33      if self.is_empty():
34        raise Empty('Queue is empty')
35      answer = self._data[self._front]
36      self._data[self._front] = None                    # help garbage collection
37      self._front = (self._front + 1) % len(self._data)
38      self._size -= 1
39      return answer
```

Code Fragment 6.6: Array-based implementation of a queue (continued in Code Fragment 6.7).

```
40    def enqueue(self, e):
41        """Add an element to the back of queue."""
42        if self._size == len(self._data):
43            self._resize(2 * len(self.data))        # double the array size
44        avail = (self._front + self._size) % len(self._data)
45        self._data[avail] = e
46        self._size += 1
47
48    def _resize(self, cap):                         # we assume cap >= len(self)
49        """Resize to a new list of capacity >= len(self)."""
50        old = self._data                            # keep track of existing list
51        self._data = [None] * cap                   # allocate list with new capacity
52        walk = self._front
53        for k in range(self._size):                 # only consider existing elements
54            self._data[k] = old[walk]               # intentionally shift indices
55            walk = (1 + walk) % len(old)            # use old size as modulus
56        self._front = 0                             # front has been realigned
```

Code Fragment 6.7: Array-based implementation of a queue (continued from Code Fragment 6.6).

The implementation of __len__ and is_empty are trivial, given knowledge of the size. The implementation of the front method is also simple, as the _front index tells us precisely where the desired element is located within the _data list, assuming that list is not empty.

Adding and Removing Elements

The goal of the enqueue method is to add a new element to the back of the queue. We need to determine the proper index at which to place the new element. Although we do not explicitly maintain an instance variable for the back of the queue, we compute the location of the next opening based on the formula:

$$\text{avail} = (\text{self.\_front} + \text{self.\_size}) \% \text{len(self.\_data)}$$

Note that we are using the size of the queue as it exists *prior* to the addition of the new element. For example, consider a queue with capacity 10, current size 3, and first element at index 5. The three elements of such a queue are stored at indices 5, 6, and 7. The new element should be placed at index $(\text{front} + \text{size}) = 8$. In a case with wrap-around, the use of the modular arithmetic achieves the desired circular semantics. For example, if our hypothetical queue had 3 elements with the first at index 8, our computation of $(8+3) \% 10$ evaluates to 1, which is perfect since the three existing elements occupy indices 8, 9, and 0.

When the dequeue method is called, the current value of self._front designates the index of the value that is to be removed and returned. We keep a local reference to the element that will be returned, setting answer = self._data[self._front] just prior to removing the reference to that object from the list, with the assignment self._data[self._front] = None. Our reason for the assignment to None relates to Python's mechanism for reclaiming unused space. Internally, Python maintains a count of the number of references that exist to each object. If that count reaches zero, the object is effectively inaccessible, thus the system may reclaim that memory for future use. (For more details, see Section 15.1.2.) Since we are no longer responsible for storing a dequeued element, we remove the reference to it from our list so as to reduce that element's reference count.

The second significant responsibility of the dequeue method is to update the value of _front to reflect the removal of the element, and the presumed promotion of the second element to become the new first. In most cases, we simply want to increment the index by one, but because of the possibility of a wrap-around configuration, we rely on modular arithmetic as originally described on page 242.

Resizing the Queue

When enqueue is called at a time when the size of the queue equals the size of the underlying list, we rely on a standard technique of doubling the storage capacity of the underlying list. In this way, our approach is similar to the one used when we implemented a DynamicArray in Section 5.3.1.

However, more care is needed in the queue's _resize utility than was needed in the corresponding method of the DynamicArray class. After creating a temporary reference to the old list of values, we allocate a new list that is twice the size and copy references from the old list to the new list. While transferring the contents, we intentionally realign the front of the queue with index 0 in the new array, as shown in Figure 6.7. This realignment is not purely cosmetic. Since the modular arithmetic depends on the size of the array, our state would be flawed had we transferred each element to its same index in the new array.

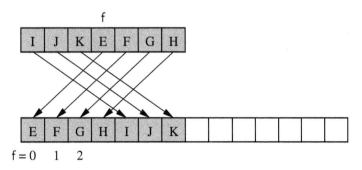

Figure 6.7: Resizing the queue, while realigning the front element with index 0.

Shrinking the Underlying Array

A desirable property of a queue implementation is to have its space usage be $\Theta(n)$ where n is the current number of elements in the queue. Our ArrayQueue implementation, as given in Code Fragments 6.6 and 6.7, does not have this property. It expands the underlying array when enqueue is called with the queue at full capacity, but the dequeue implementation never shrinks the underlying array. As a consequence, the capacity of the underlying array is proportional to the maximum number of elements that have ever been stored in the queue, not the current number of elements.

We discussed this very issue on page 200, in the context of dynamic arrays, and in subsequent Exercises C-5.16 through C-5.20 of that chapter. A robust approach is to reduce the array to half of its current size, whenever the number of elements stored in it falls below *one fourth* of its capacity. We can implement this strategy by adding the following two lines of code in our dequeue method, just after reducing self._size at line 38 of Code Fragment 6.6, to reflect the loss of an element.

```
if 0 < self._size < len(self._data) // 4:
    self._resize(len(self._data) // 2)
```

Analyzing the Array-Based Queue Implementation

Table 6.3 describes the performance of our array-based implementation of the queue ADT, assuming the improvement described above for occasionally shrinking the size of the array. With the exception of the _resize utility, all of the methods rely on a constant number of statements involving arithmetic operations, comparisons, and assignments. Therefore, each method runs in worst-case $O(1)$ time, except for enqueue and dequeue, which have ***amortized*** bounds of $O(1)$ time, for reasons similar to those given in Section 5.3.

Operation	Running Time
Q.enqueue(e)	$O(1)^*$
Q.dequeue( )	$O(1)^*$
Q.first( )	$O(1)$
Q.is_empty( )	$O(1)$
len(Q)	$O(1)$

*amortized

Table 6.3: Performance of an array-based implementation of a queue. The bounds for enqueue and dequeue are amortized due to the resizing of the array. The space usage is $O(n)$, where n is the current number of elements in the queue.

6.3 Double-Ended Queues

We next consider a queue-like data structure that supports insertion and deletion at both the front and the back of the queue. Such a structure is called a ***double-ended queue***, or ***deque***, which is usually pronounced "deck" to avoid confusion with the dequeue method of the regular queue ADT, which is pronounced like the abbreviation "D.Q."

The deque abstract data type is more general than both the stack and the queue ADTs. The extra generality can be useful in some applications. For example, we described a restaurant using a queue to maintain a waitlist. Occassionally, the first person might be removed from the queue only to find that a table was not available; typically, the restaurant will re-insert the person at the *first* position in the queue. It may also be that a customer at the end of the queue may grow impatient and leave the restaurant. (We will need an even more general data structure if we want to model customers leaving the queue from other positions.)

6.3.1 The Deque Abstract Data Type

To provide a symmetrical abstraction, the deque ADT is defined so that deque D supports the following methods:

D.add_first(e): Add element e to the front of deque D.

D.add_last(e): Add element e to the back of deque D.

D.delete_first( ): Remove and return the first element from deque D; an error occurs if the deque is empty.

D.delete_last( ): Remove and return the last element from deque D; an error occurs if the deque is empty.

Additionally, the deque ADT will include the following accessors:

D.first( ): Return (but do not remove) the first element of deque D; an error occurs if the deque is empty.

D.last( ): Return (but do not remove) the last element of deque D; an error occurs if the deque is empty.

D.is_empty( ): Return True if deque D does not contain any elements.

len(D): Return the number of elements in deque D; in Python, we implement this with the special method __len__.

Example 6.5: *The following table shows a series of operations and their effects on an initially empty deque D of integers.*

Operation	Return Value	Deque
D.add_last(5)	–	[5]
D.add_first(3)	–	[3, 5]
D.add_first(7)	–	[7, 3, 5]
D.first()	7	[7, 3, 5]
D.delete_last()	5	[7, 3]
len(D)	2	[7, 3]
D.delete_last()	3	[7]
D.delete_last()	7	[ ]
D.add_first(6)	–	[6]
D.last()	6	[6]
D.add_first(8)	–	[8, 6]
D.is_empty()	False	[8, 6]
D.last()	6	[8, 6]

6.3.2 Implementing a Deque with a Circular Array

We can implement the deque ADT in much the same way as the ArrayQueue class provided in Code Fragments 6.6 and 6.7 of Section 6.2.2 (so much so that we leave the details of an ArrayDeque implementation to Exercise P-6.32). We recommend maintaining the same three instance variables: _data, _size, and _front. Whenever we need to know the index of the back of the deque, or the first available slot beyond the back of the deque, we use modular arithmetic for the computation. For example, our implementation of the last() method uses the index

back = (self._front + self._size − 1) % len(self._data)

Our implementation of the ArrayDeque.add_last method is essentially the same as that for ArrayQueue.enqueue, including the reliance on a _resize utility. Likewise, the implementation of the ArrayDeque.delete_first method is the same as ArrayQueue.dequeue. Implementations of add_first and delete_last use similar techniques. One subtlety is that a call to add_first may need to wrap around the beginning of the array, so we rely on modular arithmetic to circularly *decrement* the index, as

self._front = (self._front − 1) % len(self._data)   # cyclic shift

The efficiency of an ArrayDeque is similar to that of an ArrayQueue, with all operations having $O(1)$ running time, but with that bound being amortized for operations that may change the size of the underlying list.

6.3.3 Deques in the Python Collections Module

An implementation of a deque class is available in Python's standard collections module. A summary of the most commonly used behaviors of the collections.deque class is given in Table 6.4. It uses more asymmetric nomenclature than our ADT.

Our Deque ADT	collections.deque	Description
len(D)	len(D)	number of elements
D.add_first( )	D.appendleft( )	add to beginning
D.add_last( )	D.append( )	add to end
D.delete_first( )	D.popleft( )	remove from beginning
D.delete_last( )	D.pop( )	remove from end
D.first( )	D[0]	access first element
D.last( )	D[-1]	access last element
	D[j]	access arbitrary entry by index
	D[j] = val	modify arbitrary entry by index
	D.clear( )	clear all contents
	D.rotate(k)	circularly shift rightward k steps
	D.remove(e)	remove first matching element
	D.count(e)	count number of matches for e

Table 6.4: Comparison of our deque ADT and the collections.deque class.

The collections.deque interface was chosen to be consistent with established naming conventions of Python's list class, for which append and pop are presumed to act at the end of the list. Therefore, appendleft and popleft designate an operation at the beginning of the list. The library deque also mimics a list in that it is an indexed sequence, allowing arbitrary access or modification using the D[j] syntax.

The library deque constructor also supports an optional maxlen parameter to force a fixed-length deque. However, if a call to append at either end is invoked when the deque is full, it does not throw an error; instead, it causes one element to be dropped from the opposite side. That is, calling appendleft when the deque is full causes an implicit pop from the right side to make room for the new element.

The current Python distribution implements collections.deque with a hybrid approach that uses aspects of circular arrays, but organized into blocks that are themselves organized in a doubly linked list (a data structure that we will introduce in the next chapter). The deque class is formally documented to guarantee $O(1)$-time operations at either end, but $O(n)$-time worst-case operations when using index notation near the middle of the deque.

6.4   Exercises

For help with exercises, please visit the site, www.wiley.com/college/goodrich.

Reinforcement

R-6.1 What values are returned during the following series of stack operations, if executed upon an initially empty stack? push(5), push(3), pop(), push(2), push(8), pop(), pop(), push(9), push(1), pop(), push(7), push(6), pop(), pop(), push(4), pop(), pop().

R-6.2 Suppose an initially empty stack S has executed a total of 25 push operations, 12 top operations, and 10 pop operations, 3 of which raised Empty errors that were caught and ignored. What is the current size of S?

R-6.3 Implement a function with signature transfer(S, T) that transfers all elements from stack S onto stack T, so that the element that starts at the top of S is the first to be inserted onto T, and the element at the bottom of S ends up at the top of T.

R-6.4 Give a recursive method for removing all the elements from a stack.

R-6.5 Implement a function that reverses a list of elements by pushing them onto a stack in one order, and writing them back to the list in reversed order.

R-6.6 Give a precise and complete definition of the concept of matching for grouping symbols in an arithmetic expression. Your definition may be recursive.

R-6.7 What values are returned during the following sequence of queue operations, if executed on an initially empty queue? enqueue(5), enqueue(3), dequeue(), enqueue(2), enqueue(8), dequeue(), dequeue(), enqueue(9), enqueue(1), dequeue(), enqueue(7), enqueue(6), dequeue(), dequeue(), enqueue(4), dequeue(), dequeue().

R-6.8 Suppose an initially empty queue Q has executed a total of 32 enqueue operations, 10 first operations, and 15 dequeue operations, 5 of which raised Empty errors that were caught and ignored. What is the current size of Q?

R-6.9 Had the queue of the previous problem been an instance of ArrayQueue that used an initial array of capacity 30, and had its size never been greater than 30, what would be the final value of the _front instance variable?

R-6.10 Consider what happens if the loop in the ArrayQueue._resize method at lines 53–55 of Code Fragment 6.7 had been implemented as:

```
for k in range(self._size):
    self._data[k] = old[k]                    # rather than old[walk]
```

Give a clear explanation of what could go wrong.

R-6.11 Give a simple adapter that implements our queue ADT while using a collections.deque instance for storage.

R-6.12 What values are returned during the following sequence of deque ADT operations, on initially empty deque? add_first(4), add_last(8), add_last(9), add_first(5), back( ), delete_first( ), delete_last( ), add_last(7), first( ), last( ), add_last(6), delete_first( ), delete_first( ).

R-6.13 Suppose you have a deque D containing the numbers $(1,2,3,4,5,6,7,8)$, in this order. Suppose further that you have an initially empty queue Q. Give a code fragment that uses only D and Q (and no other variables) and results in D storing the elements in the order $(1,2,3,5,4,6,7,8)$.

R-6.14 Repeat the previous problem using the deque D and an initially empty stack S.

Creativity

C-6.15 Suppose Alice has picked three distinct integers and placed them into a stack S in random order. Write a short, straight-line piece of pseudo-code (with no loops or recursion) that uses only one comparison and only one variable x, yet that results in variable x storing the largest of Alice's three integers with probability $2/3$. Argue why your method is correct.

C-6.16 Modify the ArrayStack implementation so that the stack's capacity is limited to maxlen elements, where maxlen is an optional parameter to the constructor (that defaults to None). If push is called when the stack is at full capacity, throw a Full exception (defined similarly to Empty).

C-6.17 In the previous exercise, we assume that the underlying list is initially empty. Redo that exercise, this time preallocating an underlying list with length equal to the stack's maximum capacity.

C-6.18 Show how to use the transfer function, described in Exercise R-6.3, and two temporary stacks, to replace the contents of a given stack S with those same elements, but in reversed order.

C-6.19 In Code Fragment 6.5 we assume that opening tags in HTML have form `<name>`, as with `<li>`. More generally, HTML allows optional attributes to be expressed as part of an opening tag. The general form used is `<name attribute1="value1" attribute2="value2">`; for example, a table can be given a border and additional padding by using an opening tag of `<table border="3" cellpadding="5">`. Modify Code Fragment 6.5 so that it can properly match tags, even when an opening tag may include one or more such attributes.

C-6.20 Describe a nonrecursive algorithm for enumerating all permutations of the numbers $\{1,2,\ldots,n\}$ using an explicit stack.

C-6.21 Show how to use a stack S and a queue Q to generate all possible subsets of an n-element set T nonrecursively.

C-6.22 *Postfix notation* is an unambiguous way of writing an arithmetic expression without parentheses. It is defined so that if "$(exp_1) \, \mathbf{op} \, (exp_2)$" is a normal, fully parenthesized expression whose operation is **op**, the postfix version of this is "$pexp_1 \, pexp_2 \, \mathbf{op}$", where $pexp_1$ is the postfix version of exp_1 and $pexp_2$ is the postfix version of exp_2. The postfix version of a single number or variable is just that number or variable. For example, the postfix version of "$((5+2)*(8-3))/4$" is "$5 \, 2 + 8 \, 3 - * 4 \, /$". Describe a nonrecursive way of evaluating an expression in postfix notation.

C-6.23 Suppose you have three nonempty stacks R, S, and T. Describe a sequence of operations that results in S storing all elements originally in T below all of S's original elements, with both sets of those elements in their original order. The final configuration for R should be the same as its original configuration. For example, if $R = [1,2,3]$, $S = [4,5]$, and $T = [6,7,8,9]$, the final configuration should have $R = [1,2,3]$ and $S = [6,7,8,9,4,5]$.

C-6.24 Describe how to implement the stack ADT using a single queue as an instance variable, and only constant additional local memory within the method bodies. What is the running time of the push(), pop(), and top() methods for your design?

C-6.25 Describe how to implement the queue ADT using two stacks as instance variables, such that all queue operations execute in amortized $O(1)$ time. Give a formal proof of the amortized bound.

C-6.26 Describe how to implement the double-ended queue ADT using two stacks as instance variables. What are the running times of the methods?

C-6.27 Suppose you have a stack S containing n elements and a queue Q that is initially empty. Describe how you can use Q to scan S to see if it contains a certain element x, with the additional constraint that your algorithm must return the elements back to S in their original order. You may only use S, Q, and a constant number of other variables.

C-6.28 Modify the ArrayQueue implementation so that the queue's capacity is limited to maxlen elements, where maxlen is an optional parameter to the constructor (that defaults to None). If enqueue is called when the queue is at full capacity, throw a Full exception (defined similarly to Empty).

C-6.29 In certain applications of the queue ADT, it is common to repeatedly dequeue an element, process it in some way, and then immediately enqueue the same element. Modify the ArrayQueue implementation to include a rotate() method that has semantics identical to the combination, Q.enqueue(Q.dequeue()). However, your implementation should be more efficient than making two separate calls (for example, because there is no need to modify _size).

C-6.30 Alice has two queues, Q and R, which can store integers. Bob gives Alice 50 odd integers and 50 even integers and insists that she store all 100 integers in Q and R. They then play a game where Bob picks Q or R at random and then applies the round-robin scheduler, described in the chapter, to the chosen queue a random number of times. If the last number to be processed at the end of this game was odd, Bob wins. Otherwise, Alice wins. How can Alice allocate integers to queues to optimize her chances of winning? What is her chance of winning?

C-6.31 Suppose Bob has four cows that he wants to take across a bridge, but only one yoke, which can hold up to two cows, side by side, tied to the yoke. The yoke is too heavy for him to carry across the bridge, but he can tie (and untie) cows to it in no time at all. Of his four cows, Mazie can cross the bridge in 2 minutes, Daisy can cross it in 4 minutes, Crazy can cross it in 10 minutes, and Lazy can cross it in 20 minutes. Of course, when two cows are tied to the yoke, they must go at the speed of the slower cow. Describe how Bob can get all his cows across the bridge in 34 minutes.

Projects

P-6.32 Give a complete ArrayDeque implementation of the double-ended queue ADT as sketched in Section 6.3.2.

P-6.33 Give an array-based implementation of a double-ended queue supporting all of the public behaviors shown in Table 6.4 for the collections.deque class, including use of the maxlen optional parameter. When a length-limited deque is full, provide semantics similar to the collections.deque class, whereby a call to insert an element on one end of a deque causes an element to be lost from the opposite side.

P-6.34 Implement a program that can input an expression in postfix notation (see Exercise C-6.22) and output its value.

P-6.35 The introduction of Section 6.1 notes that stacks are often used to provide "undo" support in applications like a Web browser or text editor. While support for undo can be implemented with an unbounded stack, many applications provide only *limited* support for such an undo history, with a fixed-capacity stack. When push is invoked with the stack at full capacity, rather than throwing a Full exception (as described in Exercise C-6.16), a more typical semantic is to accept the pushed element at the top while "leaking" the oldest element from the bottom of the stack to make room.

Give an implementation of such a LeakyStack abstraction, using a circular array with appropriate storage capacity. This class should have a public interface similar to the bounded-capacity stack in Exercise C-6.16, but with the desired leaky semantics when full.

P-6.36 When a share of common stock of some company is sold, the *capital gain* (or, sometimes, loss) is the difference between the share's selling price and the price originally paid to buy it. This rule is easy to understand for a single share, but if we sell multiple shares of stock bought over a long period of time, then we must identify the shares actually being sold. A standard accounting principle for identifying which shares of a stock were sold in such a case is to use a FIFO protocol—the shares sold are the ones that have been held the longest (indeed, this is the default method built into several personal finance software packages). For example, suppose we buy 100 shares at $20 each on day 1, 20 shares at $24 on day 2, 200 shares at $36 on day 3, and then sell 150 shares on day 4 at $30 each. Then applying the FIFO protocol means that of the 150 shares sold, 100 were bought on day 1, 20 were bought on day 2, and 30 were bought on day 3. The capital gain in this case would therefore be $100 \cdot 10 + 20 \cdot 6 + 30 \cdot (-6)$, or $940. Write a program that takes as input a sequence of transactions of the form "buy x share(s) at $\$y$ each" or "sell x share(s) at $\$y$ each," assuming that the transactions occur on consecutive days and the values x and y are integers. Given this input sequence, the output should be the total capital gain (or loss) for the entire sequence, using the FIFO protocol to identify shares.

P-6.37 Design an ADT for a two-color, double-stack ADT that consists of two stacks—one "red" and one "blue"—and has as its operations color-coded versions of the regular stack ADT operations. For example, this ADT should support both a red push operation and a blue push operation. Give an efficient implementation of this ADT using a single array whose capacity is set at some value N that is assumed to always be larger than the sizes of the red and blue stacks combined.

Chapter Notes

We were introduced to the approach of defining data structures first in terms of their ADTs and then in terms of concrete implementations by the classic books by Aho, Hopcroft, and Ullman [5, 6]. Exercises C-6.30, and C-6.31 are similar to interview questions said to be from a well-known software company. For further study of abstract data types, see Liskov and Guttag [71], Cardelli and Wegner [23], or Demurjian [33].

Chapter

7

Linked Lists

Contents

In Chapter 5 we carefully examined Python's array-based list class, and in Chapter 6 we demonstrated use of that class in implementing the classic stack, queue, and dequeue ADTs. Python's list class is highly optimized, and often a great choice for storage. With that said, there are some notable disadvantages:

1. The length of a dynamic array might be longer than the actual number of elements that it stores.

2. Amortized bounds for operations may be unacceptable in real-time systems.

3. Insertions and deletions at interior positions of an array are expensive.

In this chapter, we introduce a data structure known as a ***linked list***, which provides an alternative to an array-based sequence (such as a Python list). Both array-based sequences and linked lists keep elements in a certain order, but using a very different style. An array provides the more centralized representation, with one large chunk of memory capable of accommodating references to many elements. A linked list, in contrast, relies on a more distributed representation in which a lightweight object, known as a ***node***, is allocated for each element. Each node maintains a reference to its element and one or more references to neighboring nodes in order to collectively represent the linear order of the sequence.

We will demonstrate a trade-off of advantages and disadvantages when contrasting array-based sequences and linked lists. Elements of a linked list cannot be efficiently accessed by a numeric index k, and we cannot tell just by examining a node if it is the second, fifth, or twentieth node in the list. However, linked lists avoid the three disadvantages noted above for array-based sequences.

7.1 Singly Linked Lists

A ***singly linked list***, in its simplest form, is a collection of ***nodes*** that collectively form a linear sequence. Each node stores a reference to an object that is an element of the sequence, as well as a reference to the next node of the list (see Figures 7.1 and 7.2).

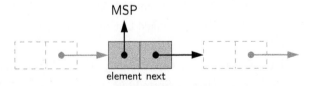

Figure 7.1: Example of a node instance that forms part of a singly linked list. The node's element member references an arbitrary object that is an element of the sequence (the airport code MSP, in this example), while the next member references the subsequent node of the linked list (or None if there is no further node).

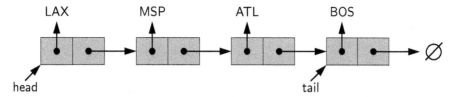

Figure 7.2: Example of a singly linked list whose elements are strings indicating airport codes. The list instance maintains a member named head that identifies the first node of the list, and in some applications another member named tail that identifies the last node of the list. The **None** object is denoted as Ø.

The first and last node of a linked list are known as the ***head*** and ***tail*** of the list, respectively. By starting at the head, and moving from one node to another by following each node's next reference, we can reach the tail of the list. We can identify the tail as the node having None as its next reference. This process is commonly known as ***traversing*** the linked list. Because the next reference of a node can be viewed as a ***link*** or ***pointer*** to another node, the process of traversing a list is also known as ***link hopping*** or ***pointer hopping***.

A linked list's representation in memory relies on the collaboration of many objects. Each node is represented as a unique object, with that instance storing a reference to its element and a reference to the next node (or None). Another object represents the linked list as a whole. Minimally, the linked list instance must keep a reference to the head of the list. Without an explicit reference to the head, there would be no way to locate that node (or indirectly, any others). There is not an absolute need to store a direct reference to the tail of the list, as it could otherwise be located by starting at the head and traversing the rest of the list. However, storing an explicit reference to the tail node is a common convenience to avoid such a traversal. In similar regard, it is common for the linked list instance to keep a count of the total number of nodes that comprise the list (commonly described as the ***size*** of the list), to avoid the need to traverse the list to count the nodes.

For the remainder of this chapter, we continue to illustrate nodes as objects, and each node's "next" reference as a pointer. However, for the sake of simplicity, we illustrate a node's element embedded directly within the node structure, even though the element is, in fact, an independent object. For example, Figure 7.3 is a more compact illustration of the linked list from Figure 7.2.

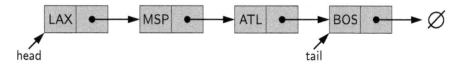

Figure 7.3: A compact illustration of a singly linked list, with elements embedded in the nodes (rather than more accurately drawn as references to external objects).

Inserting an Element at the Head of a Singly Linked List

An important property of a linked list is that it does not have a predetermined fixed size; it uses space proportionally to its current number of elements. When using a singly linked list, we can easily insert an element at the head of the list, as shown in Figure 7.4, and described with pseudo-code in Code Fragment 7.1. The main idea is that we create a new node, set its element to the new element, set its next link to refer to the current head, and then set the list's head to point to the new node.

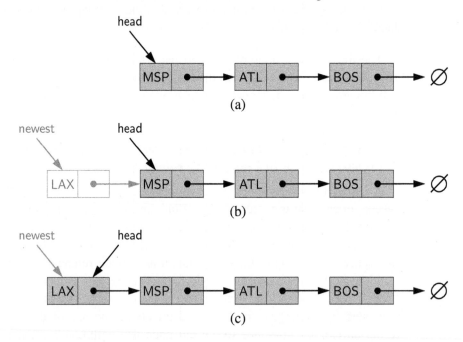

Figure 7.4: Insertion of an element at the head of a singly linked list: (a) before the insertion; (b) after creation of a new node; (c) after reassignment of the head reference.

Algorithm add_first(L, e):
    newest = Node(e) {create new node instance storing reference to element e}
    newest.next = L.head   {set new node's next to reference the old head node}
    L.head = newest   {set variable head to reference the new node}
    L.size = L.size + 1   {increment the node count}

Code Fragment 7.1: Inserting a new element at the beginning of a singly linked list L. Note that we set the next pointer of the new node *before* we reassign variable L.head to it. If the list were initially empty (i.e., L.head is None), then a natural consequence is that the new node has its next reference set to None.

Inserting an Element at the Tail of a Singly Linked List

We can also easily insert an element at the tail of the list, provided we keep a reference to the tail node, as shown in Figure 7.5. In this case, we create a new node, assign its next reference to None, set the next reference of the tail to point to this new node, and then update the tail reference itself to this new node. We give the details in Code Fragment 7.2.

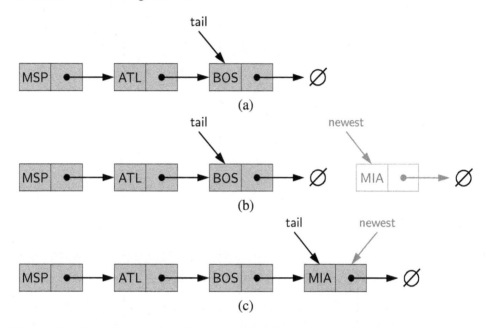

(a)

(b)

(c)

Figure 7.5: Insertion at the tail of a singly linked list: (a) before the insertion; (b) after creation of a new node; (c) after reassignment of the tail reference. Note that we must set the next link of the tail in (b) before we assign the tail variable to point to the new node in (c).

Algorithm add_last(L,e):
    newest = Node(e) {create new node instance storing reference to element e}
    newest.next = None   {set new node's next to reference the None object}
    L.tail.next = newest   {make old tail node point to new node}
    L.tail = newest   {set variable tail to reference the new node}
    L.size = L.size + 1   {increment the node count}

Code Fragment 7.2: Inserting a new node at the end of a singly linked list. Note that we set the next pointer for the old tail node *before* we make variable tail point to the new node. This code would need to be adjusted for inserting onto an empty list, since there would not be an existing tail node.

Removing an Element from a Singly Linked List

Removing an element from the ***head*** of a singly linked list is essentially the reverse operation of inserting a new element at the head. This operation is illustrated in Figure 7.6 and given in detail in Code Fragment 7.3.

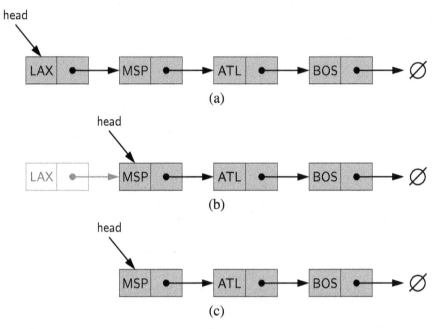

Figure 7.6: Removal of an element at the head of a singly linked list: (a) before the removal; (b) after "linking out" the old head; (c) final configuration.

Algorithm remove_first(L):
    if L.head is None **then**
      Indicate an error: the list is empty.
    L.head = L.head.next   {make head point to next node (or None)}
    L.size = L.size − 1   {decrement the node count}

Code Fragment 7.3: Removing the node at the beginning of a singly linked list.

Unfortunately, we cannot easily delete the last node of a singly linked list. Even if we maintain a tail reference directly to the last node of the list, we must be able to access the node ***before*** the last node in order to remove the last node. But we cannot reach the node before the tail by following next links from the tail. The only way to access this node is to start from the head of the list and search all the way through the list. But such a sequence of link-hopping operations could take a long time. If we want to support such an operation efficiently, we will need to make our list ***doubly linked*** (as we do in Section 7.3).

7.1.1 Implementing a Stack with a Singly Linked List

In this section, we demonstrate use of a singly linked list by providing a complete Python implementation of the stack ADT (see Section 6.1). In designing such an implementation, we need to decide whether to model the top of the stack at the head or at the tail of the list. There is clearly a best choice here; we can efficiently insert and delete elements in constant time only at the head. Since all stack operations affect the top, we orient the top of the stack at the head of our list.

To represent individual nodes of the list, we develop a lightweight _Node class. This class will never be directly exposed to the user of our stack class, so we will formally define it as a nonpublic, nested class of our eventual LinkedStack class (see Section 2.5.1 for discussion of nested classes). The definition of the _Node class is shown in Code Fragment 7.4.

```python
class _Node:
    """Lightweight, nonpublic class for storing a singly linked node."""
    __slots__ = '_element', '_next'          # streamline memory usage

    def __init__(self, element, next):        # initialize node's fields
        self._element = element                # reference to user's element
        self._next = next                      # reference to next node
```

Code Fragment 7.4: A lightweight _Node class for a singly linked list.

A node has only two instance variables: _element and _next. We intentionally define __slots__ to streamline the memory usage (see page 99 of Section 2.5.1 for discussion), because there may potentially be many node instances in a single list. The constructor of the _Node class is designed for our convenience, allowing us to specify initial values for both fields of a newly created node.

A complete implementation of our LinkedStack class is given in Code Fragments 7.5 and 7.6. Each stack instance maintains two variables. The _head member is a reference to the node at the head of the list (or None, if the stack is empty). We keep track of the current number of elements with the _size instance variable, for otherwise we would be forced to traverse the entire list to count the number of elements when reporting the size of the stack.

The implementation of push essentially mirrors the pseudo-code for insertion at the head of a singly linked list as outlined in Code Fragment 7.1. When we push a new element e onto the stack, we accomplish the necessary changes to the linked structure by invoking the constructor of the _Node class as follows:

```python
self._head = self._Node(e, self._head)    # create and link a new node
```

Note that the _next field of the new node is set to the *existing* top node, and then self._head is reassigned to the new node.

```
1   class LinkedStack:
2     """LIFO Stack implementation using a singly linked list for storage."""
3
4     #-------------------------- nested _Node class --------------------------
5     class _Node:
6       """Lightweight, nonpublic class for storing a singly linked node."""
7       __slots__ = '_element', '_next'          # streamline memory usage
8
9       def __init__(self, element, next):       # initialize node's fields
10         self._element = element                # reference to user's element
11         self._next = next                      # reference to next node
12
13     #----------------------------- stack methods -----------------------------
14     def __init__(self):
15       """Create an empty stack."""
16       self._head = None                        # reference to the head node
17       self._size = 0                           # number of stack elements
18
19     def __len__(self):
20       """Return the number of elements in the stack."""
21       return self._size
22
23     def is_empty(self):
24       """Return True if the stack is empty."""
25       return self._size == 0
26
27     def push(self, e):
28       """Add element e to the top of the stack."""
29       self._head = self._Node(e, self._head)   # create and link a new node
30       self._size += 1
31
32     def top(self):
33       """Return (but do not remove) the element at the top of the stack.
34
35       Raise Empty exception if the stack is empty.
36       """
37       if self.is_empty():
38         raise Empty('Stack is empty')
39       return self._head._element               # top of stack is at head of list
```

Code Fragment 7.5: Implementation of a stack ADT using a singly linked list (continued in Code Fragment 7.6).

```
40    def pop(self):
41        """Remove and return the element from the top of the stack (i.e., LIFO).
42
43        Raise Empty exception if the stack is empty.
44        """
45        if self.is_empty():
46            raise Empty('Stack is empty')
47        answer = self._head._element
48        self._head = self._head._next        # bypass the former top node
49        self._size -= 1
50        return answer
```

Code Fragment 7.6: Implementation of a stack ADT using a singly linked list (continued from Code Fragment 7.5).

When implementing the top method, the goal is to return the ***element*** that is at the top of the stack. When the stack is empty, we raise an Empty exception, as originally defined in Code Fragment 6.1 of Chapter 6. When the stack is nonempty, self._head is a reference to the first ***node*** of the linked list. The top element can be identified as self._head._element.

Our implementation of pop essentially mirrors the pseudo-code given in Code Fragment 7.3, except that we maintain a local reference to the element that is stored at the node that is being removed, and we return that element to the caller of pop.

The analysis of our LinkedStack operations is given in Table 7.1. We see that all of the methods complete in ***worst-case*** constant time. This is in contrast to the amortized bounds for the ArrayStack that were given in Table 6.2.

Operation	Running Time
S.push(e)	$O(1)$
S.pop()	$O(1)$
S.top()	$O(1)$
len(S)	$O(1)$
S.is_empty()	$O(1)$

Table 7.1: Performance of our LinkedStack implementation. All bounds are worst-case and our space usage is $O(n)$, where n is the current number of elements in the stack.

7.1.2 Implementing a Queue with a Singly Linked List

As we did for the stack ADT, we can use a singly linked list to implement the queue ADT while supporting worst-case $O(1)$-time for all operations. Because we need to perform operations on both ends of the queue, we will explicitly maintain both a _head reference and a _tail reference as instance variables for each queue. The natural orientation for a queue is to align the front of the queue with the head of the list, and the back of the queue with the tail of the list, because we must be able to enqueue elements at the back, and dequeue them from the front. (Recall from the introduction of Section 7.1 that we are unable to efficiently remove elements from the tail of a singly linked list.) Our implementation of a LinkedQueue class is given in Code Fragments 7.7 and 7.8.

```
1  class LinkedQueue:
2    """FIFO queue implementation using a singly linked list for storage."""
3
4    class _Node:
5      """Lightweight, nonpublic class for storing a singly linked node."""
6      (omitted here; identical to that of LinkedStack._Node)
7
8    def __init__(self):
9      """Create an empty queue."""
10     self._head = None
11     self._tail = None
12     self._size = 0                          # number of queue elements
13
14    def __len__(self):
15      """Return the number of elements in the queue."""
16      return self._size
17
18    def is_empty(self):
19      """Return True if the queue is empty."""
20      return self._size == 0
21
22    def first(self):
23      """Return (but do not remove) the element at the front of the queue."""
24      if self.is_empty():
25        raise Empty('Queue is empty')
26      return self._head._element             # front aligned with head of list
```

Code Fragment 7.7: Implementation of a queue ADT using a singly linked list (continued in Code Fragment 7.8).

```
27    def dequeue(self):
28      """Remove and return the first element of the queue (i.e., FIFO).
29
30      Raise Empty exception if the queue is empty.
31      """
32      if self.is_empty():
33        raise Empty('Queue is empty')
34      answer = self._head._element
35      self._head = self._head._next
36      self._size -= 1
37      if self.is_empty():                      # special case as queue is empty
38        self._tail = None                      # removed head had been the tail
39      return answer
40
41    def enqueue(self, e):
42      """Add an element to the back of queue."""
43      newest = self._Node(e, None)             # node will be new tail node
44      if self.is_empty():
45        self._head = newest                    # special case: previously empty
46      else:
47        self._tail._next = newest
48      self._tail = newest                      # update reference to tail node
49      self._size += 1
```

Code Fragment 7.8: Implementation of a queue ADT using a singly linked list (continued from Code Fragment 7.7).

Many aspects of our implementation are similar to that of the LinkedStack class, such as the definition of the nested _Node class. Our implementation of dequeue for LinkedQueue is similar to that of pop for LinkedStack, as both remove the head of the linked list. However, there is a subtle difference because our queue must accurately maintain the _tail reference (no such variable was maintained for our stack). In general, an operation at the head has no effect on the tail, but when dequeue is invoked on a queue with one element, we are simultaneously removing the tail of the list. We therefore set self._tail to None for consistency.

There is a similar complication in our implementation of enqueue. The newest node always becomes the new tail. Yet a distinction is made depending on whether that new node is the only node in the list. In that case, it also becomes the new head; otherwise the new node must be linked immediately after the existing tail node.

In terms of performance, the LinkedQueue is similar to the LinkedStack in that all operations run in worst-case constant time, and the space usage is linear in the current number of elements.

7.2   Circularly Linked Lists

In Section 6.2.2, we introduced the notion of a "circular" array and demonstrated its use in implementing the queue ADT. In reality, the notion of a circular array was artificial, in that there was nothing about the representation of the array itself that was circular in structure. It was our use of modular arithmetic when "advancing" an index from the last slot to the first slot that provided such an abstraction.

In the case of linked lists, there is a more tangible notion of a circularly linked list, as we can have the tail of the list use its next reference to point back to the head of the list, as shown in Figure 7.7. We call such a structure a *circularly linked list*.

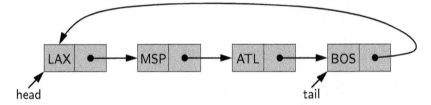

Figure 7.7: Example of a singly linked list with circular structure.

A circularly linked list provides a more general model than a standard linked list for data sets that are cyclic, that is, which do not have any particular notion of a beginning and end. Figure 7.8 provides a more symmetric illustration of the same circular list structure as Figure 7.7.

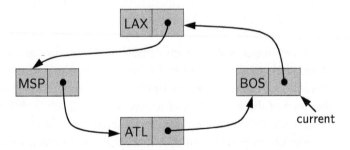

Figure 7.8: Example of a circular linked list, with current denoting a reference to a select node.

A circular view similar to Figure 7.8 could be used, for example, to describe the order of train stops in the Chicago loop, or the order in which players take turns during a game. Even though a circularly linked list has no beginning or end, per se, we must maintain a reference to a particular node in order to make use of the list. We use the identifier *current* to describe such a designated node. By setting current = current.next, we can effectively advance through the nodes of the list.

7.2.1 Round-Robin Schedulers

To motivate the use of a circularly linked list, we consider a *round-robin* scheduler, which iterates through a collection of elements in a circular fashion and "services" each element by performing a given action on it. Such a scheduler is used, for example, to fairly allocate a resource that must be shared by a collection of clients. For instance, round-robin scheduling is often used to allocate slices of CPU time to various applications running concurrently on a computer.

A round-robin scheduler could be implemented with the general queue ADT, by repeatedly performing the following steps on queue Q (see Figure 7.9):

1. $e = Q$.dequeue()
2. Service element e
3. Q.enqueue(e)

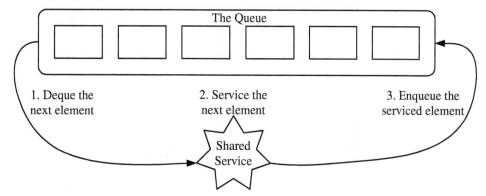

Figure 7.9: The three iterative steps for round-robin scheduling using a queue.

If we use of the LinkedQueue class of Section 7.1.2 for such an application, there is unnecessary effort in the combination of a dequeue operation followed soon after by an enqueue of the same element. One node is removed from the list, with appropriate adjustments to the head of the list and the size decremented, and then a new node is created to reinsert at the tail of the list and the size is incremented.

If using a circularly linked list, the effective transfer of an item from the "head" of the list to the "tail" of the list can be accomplished by advancing a reference that marks the boundary of the queue. We will next provide an implementation of a CircularQueue class that supports the entire queue ADT, together with an additional method, rotate( ), that moves the first element of the queue to the back. (A similar method is supported by the deque class of Python's collections module; see Table 6.4.) With this operation, a round-robin schedule can more efficiently be implemented by repeatedly performing the following steps:

1. Service element Q.front()
2. Q.rotate()

7.2.2 Implementing a Queue with a Circularly Linked List

To implement the queue ADT using a circularly linked list, we rely on the intuition of Figure 7.7, in which the queue has a head and a tail, but with the next reference of the tail linked to the head. Given such a model, there is no need for us to explicitly store references to both the head and the tail; as long as we keep a reference to the tail, we can always find the head by following the tail's next reference.

Code Fragments 7.9 and 7.10 provide an implementation of a CircularQueue class based on this model. The only two instance variables are _tail, which is a reference to the tail node (or None when empty), and _size, which is the current number of elements in the queue. When an operation involves the front of the queue, we recognize self._tail._next as the head of the queue. When enqueue is called, a new node is placed just after the tail but before the current head, and then the new node becomes the tail.

In addition to the traditional queue operations, the CircularQueue class supports a rotate method that more efficiently enacts the combination of removing the front element and reinserting it at the back of the queue. With the circular representation, we simply set self._tail = self._tail._next to make the old head become the new tail (with the node after the old head becoming the new head).

```python
1  class CircularQueue:
2    """Queue implementation using circularly linked list for storage."""
3
4    class _Node:
5      """Lightweight, nonpublic class for storing a singly linked node."""
6      (omitted here; identical to that of LinkedStack._Node)
7
8    def __init__(self):
9      """Create an empty queue."""
10     self._tail = None               # will represent tail of queue
11     self._size = 0                  # number of queue elements
12
13   def __len__(self):
14     """Return the number of elements in the queue."""
15     return self._size
16
17   def is_empty(self):
18     """Return True if the queue is empty."""
19     return self._size == 0
```

Code Fragment 7.9: Implementation of a CircularQueue class, using a circularly linked list as storage (continued in Code Fragment 7.10).

```
20    def first(self):
21        """Return (but do not remove) the element at the front of the queue.
22
23        Raise Empty exception if the queue is empty.
24        """
25        if self.is_empty():
26            raise Empty('Queue is empty')
27        head = self._tail._next
28        return head._element
29
30    def dequeue(self):
31        """Remove and return the first element of the queue (i.e., FIFO).
32
33        Raise Empty exception if the queue is empty.
34        """
35        if self.is_empty():
36            raise Empty('Queue is empty')
37        oldhead = self._tail._next
38        if self._size == 1:                    # removing only element
39            self._tail = None                  # queue becomes empty
40        else:
41            self._tail._next = oldhead._next   # bypass the old head
42        self._size -= 1
43        return oldhead._element
44
45    def enqueue(self, e):
46        """Add an element to the back of queue."""
47        newest = self._Node(e, None)           # node will be new tail node
48        if self.is_empty():
49            newest._next = newest              # initialize circularly
50        else:
51            newest._next = self._tail._next    # new node points to head
52            self._tail._next = newest          # old tail points to new node
53        self._tail = newest                    # new node becomes the tail
54        self._size += 1
55
56    def rotate(self):
57        """Rotate front element to the back of the queue."""
58        if self._size > 0:
59            self._tail = self._tail._next      # old head becomes new tail
```

Code Fragment 7.10: Implementation of a CircularQueue class, using a circularly linked list as storage (continued from Code Fragment 7.9).

7.3   Doubly Linked Lists

In a singly linked list, each node maintains a reference to the node that is immediately after it. We have demonstrated the usefulness of such a representation when managing a sequence of elements. However, there are limitations that stem from the asymmetry of a singly linked list. In the opening of Section 7.1, we emphasized that we can efficiently insert a node at either end of a singly linked list, and can delete a node at the head of a list, but we are unable to efficiently delete a node at the tail of the list. More generally, we cannot efficiently delete an arbitrary node from an interior position of the list if only given a reference to that node, because we cannot determine the node that immediately *precedes* the node to be deleted (yet, that node needs to have its next reference updated).

To provide greater symmetry, we define a linked list in which each node keeps an explicit reference to the node before it and a reference to the node after it. Such a structure is known as a ***doubly linked list***. These lists allow a greater variety of $O(1)$-time update operations, including insertions and deletions at arbitrary positions within the list. We continue to use the term "next" for the reference to the node that follows another, and we introduce the term "prev" for the reference to the node that precedes it.

Header and Trailer Sentinels

In order to avoid some special cases when operating near the boundaries of a doubly linked list, it helps to add special nodes at both ends of the list: a ***header*** node at the beginning of the list, and a ***trailer*** node at the end of the list. These "dummy" nodes are known as ***sentinels*** (or guards), and they do not store elements of the primary sequence. A doubly linked list with such sentinels is shown in Figure 7.10.

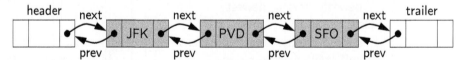

Figure 7.10: A doubly linked list representing the sequence { JFK, PVD, SFO }, using sentinels header and trailer to demarcate the ends of the list.

When using sentinel nodes, an empty list is initialized so that the next field of the header points to the trailer, and the prev field of the trailer points to the header; the remaining fields of the sentinels are irrelevant (presumably None, in Python). For a nonempty list, the header's next will refer to a node containing the first real element of a sequence, just as the trailer's prev references the node containing the last element of a sequence.

Advantage of Using Sentinels

Although we could implement a doubly linked list without sentinel nodes (as we did with our singly linked list in Section 7.1), the slight extra space devoted to the sentinels greatly simplifies the logic of our operations. Most notably, the header and trailer nodes never change—only the nodes between them change. Furthermore, we can treat all insertions in a unified manner, because a new node will always be placed between a pair of existing nodes. In similar fashion, every element that is to be deleted is guaranteed to be stored in a node that has neighbors on each side.

For contrast, look back at our LinkedQueue implementation from Section 7.1.2. Its enqueue method, given in Code Fragment 7.8, adds a new node to the end of the list. However, its implementation required a conditional to manage the special case of inserting into an empty list. In the general case, the new node was linked after the existing tail. But when adding to an empty list, there is no existing tail; instead it is necessary to reassign self._head to reference the new node. The use of a sentinel node in that implementation would eliminate the special case, as there would always be an existing node (possibly the header) before a new node.

Inserting and Deleting with a Doubly Linked List

Every insertion into our doubly linked list representation will take place between a pair of existing nodes, as diagrammed in Figure 7.11. For example, when a new element is inserted at the front of the sequence, we will simply add the new node *between* the header and the node that is currently after the header. (See Figure 7.12.)

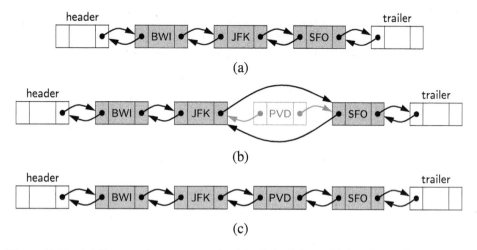

Figure 7.11: Adding an element to a doubly linked list with header and trailer sentinels: (a) before the operation; (b) after creating the new node; (c) after linking the neighbors to the new node.

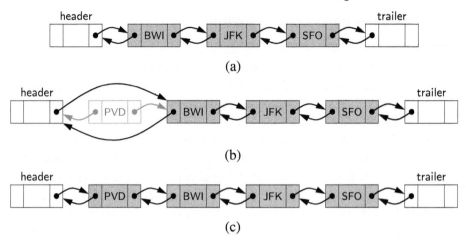

Figure 7.12: Adding an element to the front of a sequence represented by a doubly linked list with header and trailer sentinels: (a) before the operation; (b) after creating the new node; (c) after linking the neighbors to the new node.

The deletion of a node, portrayed in Figure 7.13, proceeds in the opposite fashion of an insertion. The two neighbors of the node to be deleted are linked directly to each other, thereby bypassing the original node. As a result, that node will no longer be considered part of the list and it can be reclaimed by the system. Because of our use of sentinels, the same implementation can be used when deleting the first or the last element of a sequence, because even such an element will be stored at a node that lies between two others.

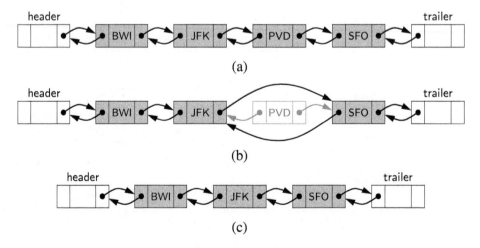

Figure 7.13: Removing the element PVD from a doubly linked list: (a) before the removal; (b) after linking out the old node; (c) after the removal (and garbage collection).

7.3.1 Basic Implementation of a Doubly Linked List

We begin by providing a preliminary implementation of a doubly linked list, in the form of a class named _DoublyLinkedBase. We intentionally name the class with a leading underscore because we do not intend for it to provide a coherent public interface for general use. We will see that linked lists can support general insertions and deletions in $O(1)$ worst-case time, but only if the location of an operation can be succinctly identified. With array-based sequences, an integer index was a convenient means for describing a position within a sequence. However, an index is not convenient for linked lists as there is no efficient way to find the jth element; it would seem to require a traversal of a portion of the list.

When working with a linked list, the most direct way to describe the location of an operation is by identifying a relevant node of the list. However, we prefer to encapsulate the inner workings of our data structure to avoid having users directly access nodes of a list. In the remainder of this chapter, we will develop two public classes that inherit from our _DoublyLinkedBase class to provide more coherent abstractions. Specifically, in Section 7.3.2, we provide a LinkedDeque class that implements the double-ended queue ADT introduced in Section 6.3; that class only supports operations at the ends of the queue, so there is no need for a user to identify an interior position within the list. In Section 7.4, we introduce a new PositionalList abstraction that provides a public interface that allows arbitrary insertions and deletions from a list.

Our low-level _DoublyLinkedBase class relies on the use of a nonpublic _Node class that is similar to that for a singly linked list, as given in Code Fragment 7.4, except that the doubly linked version includes a _prev attribute, in addition to the _next and _element attributes, as shown in Code Fragment 7.11.

```python
class _Node:
    """Lightweight, nonpublic class for storing a doubly linked node."""
    __slots__ = '_element', '_prev', '_next'      # streamline memory

    def __init__(self, element, prev, next):      # initialize node's fields
        self._element = element                    # user's element
        self._prev = prev                          # previous node reference
        self._next = next                          # next node reference
```

Code Fragment 7.11: A Python _Node class for use in a doubly linked list.

The remainder of our _DoublyLinkedBase class is given in Code Fragment 7.12. The constructor instantiates the two sentinel nodes and links them directly to each other. We maintain a _size member and provide public support for __len__ and is_empty so that these behaviors can be directly inherited by the subclasses.

```python
1   class _DoublyLinkedBase:
2     """A base class providing a doubly linked list representation."""
3
4     class _Node:
5       """Lightweight, nonpublic class for storing a doubly linked node."""
6       (omitted here; see previous code fragment)
7
8     def __init__(self):
9       """Create an empty list."""
10      self._header = self._Node(None, None, None)
11      self._trailer = self._Node(None, None, None)
12      self._header._next = self._trailer        # trailer is after header
13      self._trailer._prev = self._header        # header is before trailer
14      self._size = 0                            # number of elements
15
16    def __len__(self):
17      """Return the number of elements in the list."""
18      return self._size
19
20    def is_empty(self):
21      """Return True if list is empty."""
22      return self._size == 0
23
24    def _insert_between(self, e, predecessor, successor):
25      """Add element e between two existing nodes and return new node."""
26      newest = self._Node(e, predecessor, successor)   # linked to neighbors
27      predecessor._next = newest
28      successor._prev = newest
29      self._size += 1
30      return newest
31
32    def _delete_node(self, node):
33      """Delete nonsentinel node from the list and return its element."""
34      predecessor = node._prev
35      successor = node._next
36      predecessor._next = successor
37      successor._prev = predecessor
38      self._size -= 1
39      element = node._element                       # record deleted element
40      node._prev = node._next = node._element = None  # deprecate node
41      return element                                # return deleted element
```

Code Fragment 7.12: A base class for managing a doubly linked list.

The other two methods of our class are the nonpublic utilities, _insert_between and _delete_node. These provide generic support for insertions and deletions, respectively, but require one or more node references as parameters. The implementation of the _insert_between method is modeled upon the algorithm that was previously portrayed in Figure 7.11. It creates a new node, with that node's fields initialized to link to the specified neighboring nodes. Then the fields of the neighboring nodes are updated to include the newest node in the list. For later convenience, the method returns a reference to the newly created node.

The implementation of the _delete_node method is modeled upon the algorithm portrayed in Figure 7.13. The neighbors of the node to be deleted are linked directly to each other, thereby bypassing the deleted node from the list. As a formality, we intentionally reset the _prev, _next, and _element fields of the deleted node to None (after recording the element to be returned). Although the deleted node will be ignored by the rest of the list, setting its fields to None is advantageous as it may help Python's garbage collection, since unnecessary links to the other nodes and the stored element are eliminated. We will also rely on this configuration to recognize a node as "deprecated" when it is no longer part of the list.

7.3.2 Implementing a Deque with a Doubly Linked List

The double-ended queue (deque) ADT was introduced in Section 6.3. With an array-based implementation, we achieve all operations in *amortized* $O(1)$ time, due to the occasional need to resize the array. With an implementation based upon a doubly linked list, we can achieve all deque operation in *worst-case* $O(1)$ time.

We provide an implementation of a LinkedDeque class (Code Fragment 7.13) that inherits from the _DoublyLinkedBase class of the preceding section. We do not provide an explicit __init__ method for the LinkedDeque class, as the inherited version of that method suffices to initialize a new instance. We also rely on the inherited methods __len__ and is_empty in meeting the deque ADT.

With the use of sentinels, the key to our implementation is to remember that the header does not store the first element of the deque—it is the node just *after* the header that stores the first element (assuming the deque is nonempty). Similarly, the node just *before* the trailer stores the last element of the deque.

We use the inherited _insert_between method to insert at either end of the deque. To insert an element at the front of the deque, we place it immediately between the header and the node just after the header. An insertion at the end of deque is placed immediately before the trailer node. Note that these operations succeed, even when the deque is empty; in such a situation, the new node is placed between the two sentinels. When deleting an element from a nonempty deque, we rely upon the inherited _delete_node method, knowing that the designated node is assured to have neighbors on each side.

```
1   class LinkedDeque(_DoublyLinkedBase):              # note the use of inheritance
2     """Double-ended queue implementation based on a doubly linked list."""
3
4     def first(self):
5       """Return (but do not remove) the element at the front of the deque."""
6       if self.is_empty():
7         raise Empty("Deque is empty")
8       return self._header._next._element              # real item just after header
9
10    def last(self):
11      """Return (but do not remove) the element at the back of the deque."""
12      if self.is_empty():
13        raise Empty("Deque is empty")
14      return self._trailer._prev._element             # real item just before trailer
15
16    def insert_first(self, e):
17      """Add an element to the front of the deque."""
18      self._insert_between(e, self._header, self._header._next)   # after header
19
20    def insert_last(self, e):
21      """Add an element to the back of the deque."""
22      self._insert_between(e, self._trailer._prev, self._trailer)   # before trailer
23
24    def delete_first(self):
25      """Remove and return the element from the front of the deque.
26
27      Raise Empty exception if the deque is empty.
28      """
29      if self.is_empty():
30        raise Empty("Deque is empty")
31      return self._delete_node(self._header._next)    # use inherited method
32
33    def delete_last(self):
34      """Remove and return the element from the back of the deque.
35
36      Raise Empty exception if the deque is empty.
37      """
38      if self.is_empty():
39        raise Empty("Deque is empty")
40      return self._delete_node(self._trailer._prev)   # use inherited method
```

Code Fragment 7.13: Implementation of a LinkedDeque class that inherits from the _DoublyLinkedBase class.

7.4   The Positional List ADT

The abstract data types that we have considered thus far, namely stacks, queues, and double-ended queues, only allow update operations that occur at one end of a sequence or the other. We wish to have a more general abstraction. For example, although we motivated the FIFO semantics of a queue as a model for customers who are waiting to speak with a customer service representative, or fans who are waiting in line to buy tickets to a show, the queue ADT is too limiting. What if a waiting customer decides to hang up before reaching the front of the customer service queue? Or what if someone who is waiting in line to buy tickets allows a friend to "cut" into line at that position? We would like to design an abstract data type that provides a user a way to refer to elements anywhere in a sequence, and to perform arbitrary insertions and deletions.

When working with array-based sequences (such as a Python list), integer in-dices provide an excellent means for describing the location of an element, or the location at which an insertion or deletion should take place. However, numeric in-dices are not a good choice for describing positions within a linked list because we cannot efficiently access an entry knowing only its index; finding an element at a given index within a linked list requires traversing the list incrementally from its beginning or end, counting elements as we go.

Furthermore, indices are not a good abstraction for describing a local position in some applications, because the index of an entry changes over time due to inser-tions or deletions that happen earlier in the sequence. For example, it may not be convenient to describe the location of a person waiting in line by knowing precisely how far away that person is from the front of the line. We prefer an abstraction, as characterized in Figure 7.14, in which there is some other means for describing a position. We then wish to model situations such as when an identified person leaves the line before reaching the front, or in which a new person is added to a line immediately behind another identified person.

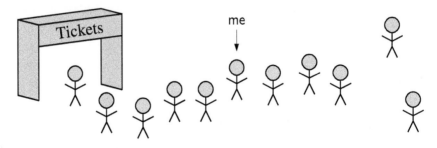

Figure 7.14: We wish to be able to identify the position of an element in a sequence without the use of an integer index.

As another example, a text document can be viewed as a long sequence of characters. A word processor uses the abstraction of a *cursor* to describe a position within the document without explicit use of an integer index, allowing operations such as "delete the character at the cursor" or "insert a new character just after the cursor." Furthermore, we may be able to refer to an inherent position within a document, such as the beginning of a particular section, without relying on a character index (or even a section number) that may change as the document evolves.

A Node Reference as a Position?

One of the great benefits of a linked list structure is that it is possible to perform $O(1)$-time insertions and deletions at arbitrary positions of the list, as long as we are given a reference to a relevant node of the list. It is therefore very tempting to develop an ADT in which a node reference serves as the mechanism for describing a position. In fact, our _DoublyLinkedBase class of Section 7.3.1 has methods _insert_between and _delete_node that accept node references as parameters.

However, such direct use of nodes would violate the object-oriented design principles of abstraction and encapsulation that were introduced in Chapter 2. There are several reasons to prefer that we encapsulate the nodes of a linked list, for both our sake and for the benefit of users of our abstraction.

- It will be simpler for users of our data structure if they are not bothered with unnecessary details of our implementation, such as low-level manipulation of nodes, or our reliance on the use of sentinel nodes. Notice that to use the _insert_between method of our _DoublyLinkedBase class to add a node at the beginning of a sequence, the header sentinel must be sent as a parameter.
- We can provide a more robust data structure if we do not permit users to directly access or manipulate the nodes. In that way, we ensure that users cannot invalidate the consistency of a list by mismanaging the linking of nodes. A more subtle problem arises if a user were allowed to call the _insert_between or _delete_node method of our _DoublyLinkedBase class, sending a node that does not belong to the given list as a parameter. (Go back and look at that code and see why it causes a problem!)
- By better encapsulating the internal details of our implementation, we have greater flexibility to redesign the data structure and improve its performance. In fact, with a well-designed abstraction, we can provide a notion of a nonnumeric position, even if using an array-based sequence.

For these reasons, instead of relying directly on nodes, we introduce an independent *position* abstraction to denote the location of an element within a list, and then a complete *positional list ADT* that can encapsulate a doubly linked list (or even an array-based sequence; see Exercise P-7.46).

7.4.1 The Positional List Abstract Data Type

To provide for a general abstraction of a sequence of elements with the ability to identify the location of an element, we define a *positional list ADT* as well as a simpler *position* abstract data type to describe a location within a list. A position acts as a marker or token within the broader positional list. A position *p* is unaffected by changes elsewhere in a list; the only way in which a position becomes invalid is if an explicit command is issued to delete it.

A position instance is a simple object, supporting only the following method:

p.element( ): Return the element stored at position p.

In the context of the positional list ADT, positions serve as parameters to some methods and as return values from other methods. In describing the behaviors of a positional list, we being by presenting the accessor methods supported by a list L:

L.first( ): Return the position of the first element of L, or None if L is empty.

L.last( ): Return the position of the last element of L, or None if L is empty.

L.before(p): Return the position of L immediately before position p, or None if p is the first position.

L.after(p): Return the position of L immediately after position p, or None if p is the last position.

L.is_empty( ): Return True if list L does not contain any elements.

len(L): Return the number of elements in the list.

iter(L): Return a forward iterator for the *elements* of the list. See Section 1.8 for discussion of iterators in Python.

The positional list ADT also includes the following *update* methods:

L.add_first(e): Insert a new element e at the front of L, returning the position of the new element.

L.add_last(e): Insert a new element e at the back of L, returning the position of the new element.

L.add_before(p, e): Insert a new element e just before position p in L, returning the position of the new element.

L.add_after(p, e): Insert a new element e just after position p in L, returning the position of the new element.

L.replace(p, e): Replace the element at position p with element e, returning the element formerly at position p.

L.delete(p): Remove and return the element at position p in L, invalidating the position.

For those methods of the ADT that accept a position p as a parameter, an error occurs if p is not a valid position for list L.

Note well that the first( ) and last( ) methods of the positional list ADT return the associated *positions*, not the *elements*. (This is in contrast to the corresponding first and last methods of the deque ADT.) The first element of a positional list can be determined by subsequently invoking the element method on that position, as L.first( ).element( ). The advantage of receiving a position as a return value is that we can use that position to navigate the list. For example, the following code fragment prints all elements of a positional list named data.

```
cursor = data.first()
while cursor is not None:
    print(cursor.element())      # print the element stored at the position
    cursor = data.after(cursor)  # advance to the next position (if any)
```

This code relies on the stated convention that the None object is returned when after is called upon the last position. That return value is clearly distinguishable from any legitimate position. The positional list ADT similarly indicates that the None value is returned when the before method is invoked at the front of the list, or when first or last methods are called upon an empty list. Therefore, the above code fragment works correctly even if the data list is empty.

Because the ADT includes support for Python's iter function, users may rely on the traditional for-loop syntax for such a forward traversal of a list named data.

```
for e in data:
    print(e)
```

More general navigational and update methods of the positional list ADT are shown in the following example.

Example 7.1: *The following table shows a series of operations on an initially empty positional list L. To identify position instances, we use variables such as p and q. For ease of exposition, when displaying the list contents, we use subscript notation to denote its positions.*

Operation	Return Value	L
L.add_last(8)	p	8_p
L.first()	p	8_p
L.add_after(p, 5)	q	$8_p, 5_q$
L.before(q)	p	$8_p, 5_q$
L.add_before(q, 3)	r	$8_p, 3_r, 5_q$
r.element()	3	$8_p, 3_r, 5_q$
L.after(p)	r	$8_p, 3_r, 5_q$
L.before(p)	None	$8_p, 3_r, 5_q$
L.add_first(9)	s	$9_s, 8_p, 3_r, 5_q$
L.delete(L.last())	5	$9_s, 8_p, 3_r$
L.replace(p, 7)	8	$9_s, 7_p, 3_r$

7.4.2 Doubly Linked List Implementation

In this section, we present a complete implementation of a PositionalList class using a doubly linked list that satisfies the following important proposition.

Proposition 7.2: *Each method of the positional list ADT runs in worst-case $O(1)$ time when implemented with a doubly linked list.*

We rely on the _DoublyLinkedBase class from Section 7.3.1 for our low-level representation; the primary responsibility of our new class is to provide a public interface in accordance with the positional list ADT. We begin our class definition in Code Fragment 7.14 with the definition of the public Position class, nested within our PositionalList class. Position instances will be used to represent the locations of elements within the list. Our various PositionalList methods may end up creating redundant Position instances that reference the same underlying node (for example, when first and last are the same). For that reason, our Position class defines the __eq__ and __ne__ special methods so that a test such as p == q evaluates to True when two positions refer to the same node.

Validating Positions

Each time a method of the PositionalList class accepts a position as a parameter, we want to verify that the position is valid, and if so, to determine the underlying node associated with the position. This functionality is implemented by a non-public method named _validate. Internally, a position maintains a reference to the associated node of the linked list, and also a reference to the list instance that contains the specified node. With the container reference, we can robustly detect when a caller sends a position instance that does not belong to the indicated list.

We are also able to detect a position instance that belongs to the list, but that refers to a node that is no longer part of that list. Recall that the _delete_node of the base class sets the previous and next references of a deleted node to None; we can recognize that condition to detect a deprecated node.

Access and Update Methods

The access methods of the PositionalList class are given in Code Fragment 7.15 and the update methods are given in Code Fragment 7.16. All of these methods trivially adapt the underlying doubly linked list implementation to support the public interface of the positional list ADT. Those methods rely on the _validate utility to "unwrap" any position that is sent. They also rely on a _make_position utility to "wrap" nodes as Position instances to return to the user, making sure never to return a position referencing a sentinel. For convenience, we have overridden the inherited _insert_between utility method so that ours returns a *position* associated with the newly created node (whereas the inherited version returns the node itself).

```
1   class PositionalList(_DoublyLinkedBase):
2     """A sequential container of elements allowing positional access."""
3
4     #------------------------- nested Position class -------------------------
5     class Position:
6       """An abstraction representing the location of a single element."""
7
8       def __init__(self, container, node):
9         """Constructor should not be invoked by user."""
10        self._container = container
11        self._node = node
12
13      def element(self):
14        """Return the element stored at this Position."""
15        return self._node._element
16
17      def __eq__(self, other):
18        """Return True if other is a Position representing the same location."""
19        return type(other) is type(self) and other._node is self._node
20
21      def __ne__(self, other):
22        """Return True if other does not represent the same location."""
23        return not (self == other)            # opposite of __eq__
24
25    #------------------------------ utility method ------------------------------
26    def _validate(self, p):
27      """Return position's node, or raise appropriate error if invalid."""
28      if not isinstance(p, self.Position):
29        raise TypeError('p must be proper Position type')
30      if p._container is not self:
31        raise ValueError('p does not belong to this container')
32      if p._node._next is None:                    # convention for deprecated nodes
33        raise ValueError('p is no longer valid')
34      return p._node
```

Code Fragment 7.14: A PositionalList class based on a doubly linked list. (Continues in Code Fragments 7.15 and 7.16.)

```
35    #------------------------------ utility method ------------------------------
36    def _make_position(self, node):
37      """Return Position instance for given node (or None if sentinel)."""
38      if node is self._header or node is self._trailer:
39        return None                              # boundary violation
40      else:
41        return self.Position(self, node)          # legitimate position
42
43    #------------------------------ accessors ------------------------------
44    def first(self):
45      """Return the first Position in the list (or None if list is empty)."""
46      return self._make_position(self._header._next)
47
48    def last(self):
49      """Return the last Position in the list (or None if list is empty)."""
50      return self._make_position(self._trailer._prev)
51
52    def before(self, p):
53      """Return the Position just before Position p (or None if p is first)."""
54      node = self._validate(p)
55      return self._make_position(node._prev)
56
57    def after(self, p):
58      """Return the Position just after Position p (or None if p is last)."""
59      node = self._validate(p)
60      return self._make_position(node._next)
61
62    def __iter__(self):
63      """Generate a forward iteration of the elements of the list."""
64      cursor = self.first()
65      while cursor is not None:
66        yield cursor.element()
67        cursor = self.after(cursor)
```

Code Fragment 7.15: A PositionalList class based on a doubly linked list. (Continued from Code Fragment 7.14; continues in Code Fragment 7.16.)

```
68    #------------------------------ mutators ------------------------------
69    # override inherited version to return Position, rather than Node
70    def _insert_between(self, e, predecessor, successor):
71      """Add element between existing nodes and return new Position."""
72      node = super()._insert_between(e, predecessor, successor)
73      return self._make_position(node)
74
75    def add_first(self, e):
76      """Insert element e at the front of the list and return new Position."""
77      return self._insert_between(e, self._header, self._header._next)
78
79    def add_last(self, e):
80      """Insert element e at the back of the list and return new Position."""
81      return self._insert_between(e, self._trailer._prev, self._trailer)
82
83    def add_before(self, p, e):
84      """Insert element e into list before Position p and return new Position."""
85      original = self._validate(p)
86      return self._insert_between(e, original._prev, original)
87
88    def add_after(self, p, e):
89      """Insert element e into list after Position p and return new Position."""
90      original = self._validate(p)
91      return self._insert_between(e, original, original._next)
92
93    def delete(self, p):
94      """Remove and return the element at Position p."""
95      original = self._validate(p)
96      return self._delete_node(original)        # inherited method returns element
97
98    def replace(self, p, e):
99      """Replace the element at Position p with e.
100
101     Return the element formerly at Position p.
102     """
103     original = self._validate(p)
104     old_value = original._element             # temporarily store old element
105     original._element = e                      # replace with new element
106     return old_value                          # return the old element value
```

Code Fragment 7.16: A PositionalList class based on a doubly linked list. (Continued from Code Fragments 7.14 and 7.15.)

7.5 Sorting a Positional List

In Section 5.5.2, we introduced the ***insertion-sort*** algorithm, in the context of an array-based sequence. In this section, we develop an implementation that operates on a PositionalList, relying on the same high-level algorithm in which each element is placed relative to a growing collection of previously sorted elements.

We maintain a variable named marker that represents the rightmost position of the currently sorted portion of a list. During each pass, we consider the position just past the marker as the pivot and consider where the pivot's element belongs relative to the sorted portion; we use another variable, named walk, to move leftward from the marker, as long as there remains a preceding element with value larger than the pivot's. A typical configuration of these variables is diagrammed in Figure 7.15. A Python implementation of this strategy is given in Code 7.17.

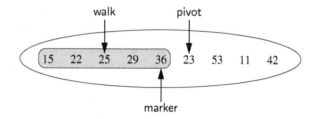

Figure 7.15: Overview of one step of our insertion-sort algorithm. The shaded elements, those up to and including marker, have already been sorted. In this step, the pivot's element should be relocated immediately before the walk position.

```
1  def insertion_sort(L):
2    """Sort PositionalList of comparable elements into nondecreasing order."""
3    if len(L) > 1:                        # otherwise, no need to sort it
4      marker = L.first()
5      while marker != L.last():
6        pivot = L.after(marker)           # next item to place
7        value = pivot.element()
8        if value > marker.element():      # pivot is already sorted
9          marker = pivot                  # pivot becomes new marker
10       else:                             # must relocate pivot
11         walk = marker                   # find leftmost item greater than value
12         while walk != L.first() and L.before(walk).element() > value:
13           walk = L.before(walk)
14         L.delete(pivot)
15         L.add_before(walk, value)       # reinsert value before walk
```

Code Fragment 7.17: Python code for performing insertion-sort on a positional list.

7.6   Case Study: Maintaining Access Frequencies

The positional list ADT is useful in a number of settings. For example, a program
that simulates a game of cards could model each person's hand as a positional list
(Exercise P-7.47). Since most people keep cards of the same suit together, inserting
and removing cards from a person's hand could be implemented using the methods
of the positional list ADT, with the positions being determined by a natural order
of the suits. Likewise, a simple text editor embeds the notion of positional insertion
and deletion, since such editors typically perform all updates relative to a *cursor*,
which represents the current position in the list of characters of text being edited.

In this section, we consider maintaining a collection of elements while keeping
track of the number of times each element is accessed. Keeping such access counts
allows us to know which elements are among the most popular. Examples of such
scenarios include a Web browser that keeps track of a user's most accessed URLs,
or a music collection that maintains a list of the most frequently played songs for
a user. We model this with a new *favorites list ADT* that supports the len and
is_empty methods as well as the following:

> access(**e**): Access the element e, incrementing its access count, and
> adding it to the favorites list if it is not already present.

> remove(**e**): Remove element e from the favorites list, if present.

> top(**k**): Return an iteration of the k most accessed elements.

7.6.1   Using a Sorted List

Our first approach for managing a list of favorites is to store elements in a linked
list, keeping them in nonincreasing order of access counts. We access or remove
an element by searching the list from the most frequently accessed to the least
frequently accessed. Reporting the top *k* most accessed elements is easy, as they
are the first *k* entries of the list.

To maintain the invariant that elements are stored in nonincreasing order of
access counts, we must consider how a single access operation may affect the order.
The accessed element's count increases by one, and so it may become larger than
one or more of its preceding neighbors in the list, thereby violating the invariant.

Fortunately, we can reestablish the sorted invariant using a technique similar to
a single pass of the insertion-sort algorithm, introduced in the previous section. We
can perform a backward traversal of the list, starting at the position of the element
whose access count has increased, until we locate a valid position after which the
element can be relocated.

Using the Composition Pattern

We wish to implement a favorites list by making use of a PositionalList for storage. If elements of the positional list were simply elements of the favorites list, we would be challenged to maintain access counts and to keep the proper count with the associated element as the contents of the list are reordered. We use a general object-oriented design pattern, the ***composition pattern***, in which we define a single object that is composed of two or more other objects. Specifically, we define a nonpublic nested class, _Item, that stores the element and its access count as a single instance. We then maintain our favorites list as a PositionalList of *item* instances, so that the access count for a user's element is embedded alongside it in our representation. (An _Item is never exposed to a user of a FavoritesList.)

```python
 1  class FavoritesList:
 2    """List of elements ordered from most frequently accessed to least."""
 3
 4    #-------------------------- nested _Item class ----------------------------
 5    class _Item:
 6      __slots__ = '_value', '_count'            # streamline memory usage
 7      def __init__(self, e):
 8        self._value = e                         # the user's element
 9        self._count = 0                         # access count initially zero
10
11    #-------------------------- nonpublic utilities ---------------------------
12    def _find_position(self, e):
13      """Search for element e and return its Position (or None if not found)."""
14      walk = self._data.first()
15      while walk is not None and walk.element()._value != e:
16        walk = self._data.after(walk)
17      return walk
18
19    def _move_up(self, p):
20      """Move item at Position p earlier in the list based on access count."""
21      if p != self._data.first():               # consider moving...
22        cnt = p.element()._count
23        walk = self._data.before(p)
24        if cnt > walk.element()._count:         # must shift forward
25          while (walk != self._data.first() and
26                 cnt > self._data.before(walk).element()._count):
27            walk = self._data.before(walk)
28          self._data.add_before(walk, self._data.delete(p))  # delete/reinsert
```

Code Fragment 7.18: Class FavoritesList. (Continues in Code Fragment 7.19.)

```
29    #------------------------------ public methods ------------------------------
30    def __init__(self):
31      """Create an empty list of favorites."""
32      self._data = PositionalList( )              # will be list of _Item instances
33
34    def __len__(self):
35      """Return number of entries on favorites list."""
36      return len(self._data)
37
38    def is_empty(self):
39      """Return True if list is empty."""
40      return len(self._data) == 0
41
42    def access(self, e):
43      """Access element e, thereby increasing its access count."""
44      p = self._find_position(e)                  # try to locate existing element
45      if p is None:
46        p = self._data.add_last(self._Item(e))    # if new, place at end
47      p.element()._count += 1                      # always increment count
48      self._move_up(p)                             # consider moving forward
49
50    def remove(self, e):
51      """Remove element e from the list of favorites."""
52      p = self._find_position(e)                  # try to locate existing element
53      if p is not None:
54        self._data.delete(p)                      # delete, if found
55
56    def top(self, k):
57      """Generate sequence of top k elements in terms of access count."""
58      if not 1 <= k <= len(self):
59        raise ValueError('Illegal value for k')
60      walk = self._data.first( )
61      for j in range(k):
62        item = walk.element( )                     # element of list is _Item
63        yield item._value                          # report user's element
64        walk = self._data.after(walk)
```

Code Fragment 7.19: Class FavoritesList. (Continued from Code Fragment 7.18.)

7.6.2 Using a List with the Move-to-Front Heuristic

The previous implementation of a favorites list performs the access(e) method in time proportional to the index of e in the favorites list. That is, if e is the kth most popular element in the favorites list, then accessing it takes $O(k)$ time. In many real-life access sequences (e.g., Web pages visited by a user), once an element is accessed it is more likely to be accessed again in the near future. Such scenarios are said to possess *locality of reference*.

A *heuristic*, or rule of thumb, that attempts to take advantage of the locality of reference that is present in an access sequence is the *move-to-front heuristic*. To apply this heuristic, each time we access an element we move it all the way to the front of the list. Our hope, of course, is that this element will be accessed again in the near future. Consider, for example, a scenario in which we have n elements and the following series of n^2 accesses:

- element 1 is accessed n times
- element 2 is accessed n times
- $\cdots$
- element n is accessed n times.

If we store the elements sorted by their access counts, inserting each element the first time it is accessed, then

- each access to element 1 runs in $O(1)$ time
- each access to element 2 runs in $O(2)$ time
- $\cdots$
- each access to element n runs in $O(n)$ time.

Thus, the total time for performing the series of accesses is proportional to

$$n + 2n + 3n + \cdots + n \cdot n = n(1 + 2 + 3 + \cdots + n) = n \cdot \frac{n(n+1)}{2},$$

which is $O(n^3)$.

On the other hand, if we use the move-to-front heuristic, inserting each element the first time it is accessed, then

- each subsequent access to element 1 takes $O(1)$ time
- each subsequent access to element 2 takes $O(1)$ time
- $\cdots$
- each subsequent access to element n runs in $O(1)$ time.

So the running time for performing all the accesses in this case is $O(n^2)$. Thus, the move-to-front implementation has faster access times for this scenario. Still, the move-to-front approach is just a heuristic, for there are access sequences where using the move-to-front approach is slower than simply keeping the favorites list ordered by access counts.

The Trade-Offs with the Move-to-Front Heuristic

If we no longer maintain the elements of the favorites list ordered by their access counts, when we are asked to find the k most accessed elements, we need to search for them. We will implement the top(k) method as follows:

1. We copy all entries of our favorites list into another list, named temp.

2. We scan the temp list k times. In each scan, we find the entry with the largest access count, remove this entry from temp, and report it in the results.

This implementation of method top takes $O(kn)$ time. Thus, when k is a constant, method top runs in $O(n)$ time. This occurs, for example, when we want to get the "top ten" list. However, if k is proportional to n, then top runs in $O(n^2)$ time. This occurs, for example, when we want a "top 25%" list.

In Chapter 9 we will introduce a data structure that will allow us to implement top in $O(n + k \log n)$ time (see Exercise P-9.54), and more advanced techniques could be used to perform top in $O(n + k \log k)$ time.

We could easily achieve $O(n \log n)$ time if we use a standard sorting algorithm to reorder the temporary list before reporting the top k (see Chapter 12); this approach would be preferred to the original in the case that k is $\Omega(\log n)$. (Recall the big-Omega notation introduced in Section 3.3.1 to give an asymptotic lower bound on the running time of an algorithm.) There is a more specialized sorting algorithm (see Section 12.4.2) that can take advantage of the fact that access counts are integers in order to achieve $O(n)$ time for top, for any value of k.

Implementing the Move-to-Front Heuristic in Python

We give an implementation of a favorites list using the move-to-front heuristic in Code Fragment 7.20. The new FavoritesListMTF class inherits most of its functionality from the original FavoritesList as a base class.

By our original design, the access method of the original class relies on a non-public utility named _move_up to enact the potential shifting of an element forward in the list, after its access count had been incremented. Therefore, we implement the move-to-front heuristic by simply overriding the _move_up method so that each accessed element is moved directly to the front of the list (if not already there). This action is easily implemented by means of the positional list ADT.

The more complex portion of our FavoritesListMTF class is the new definition for the top method. We rely on the first of the approaches outlined above, inserting copies of the items into a temporary list and then repeatedly finding, reporting, and removing an element that has the largest access count of those remaining.

```
1   class FavoritesListMTF(FavoritesList):
2     """List of elements ordered with move-to-front heuristic."""
3
4     # we override _move_up to provide move-to-front semantics
5     def _move_up(self, p):
6       """Move accessed item at Position p to front of list."""
7       if p != self._data.first( ):
8         self._data.add_first(self._data.delete(p))        # delete/reinsert
9
10    # we override top because list is no longer sorted
11    def top(self, k):
12      """Generate sequence of top k elements in terms of access count."""
13      if not 1 <= k <= len(self):
14        raise ValueError('Illegal value for k')
15
16      # we begin by making a copy of the original list
17      temp = PositionalList( )
18      for item in self._data:                    # positional lists support iteration
19        temp.add_last(item)
20
21      # we repeatedly find, report, and remove element with largest count
22      for j in range(k):
23        # find and report next highest from temp
24        highPos = temp.first( )
25        walk = temp.after(highPos)
26        while walk is not None:
27          if walk.element( )._count > highPos.element( )._count:
28            highPos = walk
29          walk = temp.after(walk)
30        # we have found the element with highest count
31        yield highPos.element( )._value              # report element to user
32        temp.delete(highPos)                         # remove from temp list
```

Code Fragment 7.20: Class FavoritesListMTF implementing the move-to-front heuristic. This class extends FavoritesList (Code Fragments 7.18 and 7.19) and overrides methods _move_up and top.

7.7   Link-Based vs. Array-Based Sequences

We close this chapter by reflecting on the relative pros and cons of array-based and link-based data structures that have been introduced thus far. The dichotomy between these approaches presents a common design decision when choosing an appropriate implementation of a data structure. There is not a one-size-fits-all solution, as each offers distinct advantages and disadvantages.

Advantages of Array-Based Sequences

- *Arrays provide $O(1)$-time access to an element based on an integer index.* The ability to access the kth element for any k in $O(1)$ time is a hallmark advantage of arrays (see Section 5.2). In contrast, locating the kth element in a linked list requires $O(k)$ time to traverse the list from the beginning, or possibly $O(n-k)$ time, if traversing backward from the end of a doubly linked list.

- *Operations with equivalent asymptotic bounds typically run a constant factor more efficiently with an array-based structure versus a linked structure.* As an example, consider the typical enqueue operation for a queue. Ignoring the issue of resizing an array, this operation for the ArrayQueue class (see Code Fragment 6.7) involves an arithmetic calculation of the new index, an increment of an integer, and storing a reference to the element in the array. In contrast, the process for a LinkedQueue (see Code Fragment 7.8) requires the instantiation of a node, appropriate linking of nodes, and an increment of an integer. While this operation completes in $O(1)$ time in either model, the actual number of CPU operations will be more in the linked version, especially given the instantiation of the new node.

- *Array-based representations typically use proportionally less memory than linked structures.* This advantage may seem counterintuitive, especially given that the length of a dynamic array may be longer than the number of elements that it stores. Both array-based lists and linked lists are referential structures, so the primary memory for storing the actual objects that are elements is the same for either structure. What differs is the auxiliary amounts of memory that are used by the two structures. For an array-based container of n elements, a typical worst case may be that a recently resized dynamic array has allocated memory for $2n$ object references. With linked lists, memory must be devoted not only to store a reference to each contained object, but also explicit references that link the nodes. So a singly linked list of length n already requires $2n$ references (an element reference and next reference for each node). With a doubly linked list, there are $3n$ references.

Advantages of Link-Based Sequences

- *Link-based structures provide worst-case time bounds for their operations.* This is in contrast to the amortized bounds associated with the expansion or contraction of a dynamic array (see Section 5.3).

  When many individual operations are part of a larger computation, and we only care about the total time of that computation, an amortized bound is as good as a worst-case bound precisely because it gives a guarantee on the sum of the time spent on the individual operations.

  However, if data structure operations are used in a real-time system that is designed to provide more immediate responses (e.g., an operating system, Web server, air traffic control system), a long delay caused by a single (amortized) operation may have an adverse effect.

- *Link-based structures support $O(1)$-time insertions and deletions at arbitrary positions.* The ability to perform a constant-time insertion or deletion with the PositionalList class, by using a Position to efficiently describe the location of the operation, is perhaps the most significant advantage of the linked list.

  This is in stark contrast to an array-based sequence. Ignoring the issue of resizing an array, inserting or deleting an element from the end of an array-based list can be done in constant time. However, more general insertions and deletions are expensive. For example, with Python's array-based list class, a call to insert or pop with index k uses $O(n - k + 1)$ time because of the loop to shift all subsequent elements (see Section 5.4).

  As an example application, consider a text editor that maintains a document as a sequence of characters. Although users often add characters to the end of the document, it is also possible to use the cursor to insert or delete one or more characters at an arbitrary position within the document. If the character sequence were stored in an array-based sequence (such as a Python list), each such edit operation may require linearly many characters to be shifted, leading to $O(n)$ performance for each edit operation. With a linked-list representation, an arbitrary edit operation (insertion or deletion of a character at the cursor) can be performed in $O(1)$ worst-case time, assuming we are given a position that represents the location of the cursor.

7.8   Exercises

For help with exercises, please visit the site, www.wiley.com/college/goodrich.

Reinforcement

R-7.1 Give an algorithm for finding the second-to-last node in a singly linked list in which the last node is indicated by a next reference of None.

R-7.2 Describe a good algorithm for concatenating two singly linked lists L and M, given only references to the first node of each list, into a single list L' that contains all the nodes of L followed by all the nodes of M.

R-7.3 Describe a recursive algorithm that counts the number of nodes in a singly linked list.

R-7.4 Describe in detail how to swap two nodes x and y (and not just their contents) in a singly linked list L given references only to x and y. Repeat this exercise for the case when L is a doubly linked list. Which algorithm takes more time?

R-7.5 Implement a function that counts the number of nodes in a circularly linked list.

R-7.6 Suppose that x and y are references to nodes of circularly linked lists, although not necessarily the same list. Describe a fast algorithm for telling if x and y belong to the same list.

R-7.7 Our CircularQueue class of Section 7.2.2 provides a rotate( ) method that has semantics equivalent to Q.enqueue(Q.dequeue( )), for a nonempty queue. Implement such a method for the LinkedQueue class of Section 7.1.2 without the creation of any new nodes.

R-7.8 Describe a nonrecursive method for finding, by link hopping, the middle node of a doubly linked list with header and trailer sentinels. In the case of an even number of nodes, report the node slightly left of center as the "middle." (Note: This method must only use link hopping; it cannot use a counter.) What is the running time of this method?

R-7.9 Give a fast algorithm for concatenating two doubly linked lists L and M, with header and trailer sentinel nodes, into a single list L'.

R-7.10 There seems to be some redundancy in the repertoire of the positional list ADT, as the operation L.add_first(e) could be enacted by the alternative L.add_before(L.first( ), e). Likewise, L.add_last(e) might be performed as L.add_after(L.last( ), e). Explain why the methods add_first and add_last are necessary.

R-7.11 Implement a function, with calling syntax max(L), that returns the maximum element from a PositionalList instance L containing comparable elements.

R-7.12 Redo the previously problem with max as a method of the PositionalList class, so that calling syntax L.max( ) is supported.

R-7.13 Update the PositionalList class to support an additional method find(e), which returns the position of the (first occurrence of) element e in the list (or None if not found).

R-7.14 Repeat the previous process using recursion. Your method should not contain any loops. How much space does your method use in addition to the space used for L?

R-7.15 Provide support for a __reversed__ method of the PositionalList class that is similar to the given __iter__, but that iterates the elements in *reversed* order.

R-7.16 Describe an implementation of the PositionalList methods add_last and add_before realized by using only methods in the set {is_empty, first, last, prev, next, add_after, and add_first}.

R-7.17 In the FavoritesListMTF class, we rely on public methods of the positional list ADT to move an element of a list at position p to become the first element of the list, while keeping the relative order of the remaining elements unchanged. Internally, that combination of operations causes one node to be removed and a new node to be inserted. Augment the PositionalList class to support a new method, move_to_front(p), that accomplishes this goal more directly, by relinking the existing node.

R-7.18 Given the set of element $\{a,b,c,d,e,f\}$ stored in a list, show the final state of the list, assuming we use the move-to-front heuristic and access the elements according to the following sequence: $(a,b,c,d,e,f,a,c,f,b,d,e)$.

R-7.19 Suppose that we have made kn total accesses to the elements in a list L of n elements, for some integer $k \geq 1$. What are the minimum and maximum number of elements that have been accessed fewer than k times?

R-7.20 Let L be a list of n items maintained according to the move-to-front heuristic. Describe a series of $O(n)$ accesses that will reverse L.

R-7.21 Suppose we have an n-element list L maintained according to the move-to-front heuristic. Describe a sequence of n^2 accesses that is guaranteed to take $\Omega(n^3)$ time to perform on L.

R-7.22 Implement a clear( ) method for the FavoritesList class that returns the list to empty.

R-7.23 Implement a reset_counts( ) method for the FavoritesList class that resets all elements' access counts to zero (while leaving the order of the list unchanged).

Creativity

C-7.24 Give a complete implementation of the stack ADT using a singly linked list that includes a header sentinel.

C-7.25 Give a complete implementation of the queue ADT using a singly linked list that includes a header sentinel.

C-7.26 Implement a method, concatenate(Q2) for the LinkedQueue class that takes all elements of LinkedQueue Q2 and appends them to the end of the original queue. The operation should run in $O(1)$ time and should result in Q2 being an empty queue.

C-7.27 Give a recursive implementation of a singly linked list class, such that an instance of a nonempty list stores its first element and a reference to a list of remaining elements.

C-7.28 Describe a fast recursive algorithm for reversing a singly linked list.

C-7.29 Describe in detail an algorithm for reversing a singly linked list L using only a constant amount of additional space and not using any recursion.

C-7.30 Exercise P-6.35 describes a LeakyStack abstraction. Implement that ADT using a *singly* linked list for storage.

C-7.31 Design a *forward list* ADT that abstracts the operations on a singly linked list, much as the positional list ADT abstracts the use of a doubly linked list. Implement a ForwardList class that supports such an ADT.

C-7.32 Design a circular positional list ADT that abstracts a circularly linked list in the same way that the positional list ADT abstracts a doubly linked list, with a notion of a designated "cursor" position within the list.

C-7.33 Modify the _DoublyLinkedBase class to include a reverse method that reverses the order of the list, yet without creating or destroying any nodes.

C-7.34 Modify the PositionalList class to support a method swap(p, q) that causes the underlying nodes referenced by positions p and q to be exchanged for each other. Relink the existing nodes; do not create any new nodes.

C-7.35 To implement the iter method of the PositionalList class, we relied on the convenience of Python's generator syntax and the yield statement. Give an alternative implementation of iter by designing a nested iterator class. (See Section 2.3.4 for discussion of iterators.)

C-7.36 Give a complete implementation of the positional list ADT using a doubly linked list that does not include any sentinel nodes.

C-7.37 Implement a function that accepts a PositionalList L of n integers sorted in nondecreasing order, and another value V, and determines in $O(n)$ time if there are two elements of L that sum precisely to V. The function should return a pair of positions of such elements, if found, or None otherwise.

C-7.38 There is a simple, but inefficient, algorithm, called ***bubble-sort***, for sorting a list L of n comparable elements. This algorithm scans the list $n-1$ times, where, in each scan, the algorithm compares the current element with the next one and swaps them if they are out of order. Implement a bubble_sort function that takes a positional list L as a parameter. What is the running time of this algorithm, assuming the positional list is implemented with a doubly linked list?

C-7.39 To better model a FIFO queue in which entries may be deleted before reaching the front, design a PositionalQueue class that supports the complete queue ADT, yet with enqueue returning a position instance and support for a new method, delete(p), that removes the element associated with position p from the queue. You may use the adapter design pattern (Section 6.1.2), using a PositionalList as your storage.

C-7.40 Describe an efficient method for maintaining a favorites list L, with move-to-front heuristic, such that elements that have not been accessed in the most recent n accesses are automatically purged from the list.

C-7.41 Exercise C-5.29 introduces the notion of a ***natural join*** of two databases. Describe and analyze an efficient algorithm for computing the natural join of a linked list A of n pairs and a linked list B of m pairs.

C-7.42 Write a Scoreboard class that maintains the top 10 scores for a game application using a singly linked list, rather than the array that was used in Section 5.5.1.

C-7.43 Describe a method for performing a ***card shuffle*** of a list of $2n$ elements, by converting it into two lists. A card shuffle is a permutation where a list L is cut into two lists, L_1 and L_2, where L_1 is the first half of L and L_2 is the second half of L, and then these two lists are merged into one by taking the first element in L_1, then the first element in L_2, followed by the second element in L_1, the second element in L_2, and so on.

Projects

P-7.44 Write a simple text editor that stores and displays a string of characters using the positional list ADT, together with a cursor object that highlights a position in this string. A simple interface is to print the string and then to use a second line of output to underline the position of the cursor. Your editor should support the following operations:

- left: Move cursor left one character (do nothing if at beginning).
- right: Move cursor right one character (do nothing if at end).
- insert c: Insert the character c just after the cursor.
- delete: Delete the character just after the cursor (do nothing at end).

P-7.45 An array A is *sparse* if most of its entries are empty (i.e., None). A list L can be used to implement such an array efficiently. In particular, for each nonempty cell $A[i]$, we can store an entry (i,e) in L, where e is the element stored at $A[i]$. This approach allows us to represent A using $O(m)$ storage, where m is the number of nonempty entries in A. Provide such a SparseArray class that minimally supports methods __getitem__(j) and __setitem__(j, e) to provide standard indexing operations. Analyze the efficiency of these methods.

P-7.46 Although we have used a doubly linked list to implement the positional list ADT, it is possible to support the ADT with an array-based implementation. The key is to use the composition pattern and store a sequence of position items, where each item stores an element as well as that element's current index in the array. Whenever an element's place in the array is changed, the recorded index in the position must be updated to match. Given a complete class providing such an array-based implementation of the positional list ADT. What is the efficiency of the various operations?

P-7.47 Implement a CardHand class that supports a person arranging a group of cards in his or her hand. The simulator should represent the sequence of cards using a single positional list ADT so that cards of the same suit are kept together. Implement this strategy by means of four "fingers" into the hand, one for each of the suits of hearts, clubs, spades, and diamonds, so that adding a new card to the person's hand or playing a correct card from the hand can be done in constant time. The class should support the following methods:

- add_card(r, s): Add a new card with rank r and suit s to the hand.
- play(s): Remove and return a card of suit s from the player's hand; if there is no card of suit s, then remove and return an arbitrary card from the hand.
- __iter__( ): Iterate through all cards currently in the hand.
- all_of_suit(s): Iterate through all cards of suit s that are currently in the hand.

Chapter Notes

A view of data structures as collections (and other principles of object-oriented design) can be found in object-oriented design books by Booch [17], Budd [20], Goldberg and Robson [42], and Liskov and Guttag [71]. Our positional list ADT is derived from the "position" abstraction introduced by Aho, Hopcroft, and Ullman [6], and the list ADT of Wood [104]. Implementations of linked lists are discussed by Knuth [64].

Chapter

8

Trees

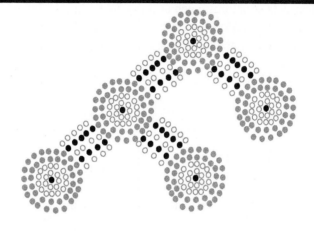

Contents

8.1   General Trees

Productivity experts say that breakthroughs come by thinking "nonlinearly." In this chapter, we discuss one of the most important nonlinear data structures in computing—*trees*. Tree structures are indeed a breakthrough in data organization, for they allow us to implement a host of algorithms much faster than when using linear data structures, such as array-based lists or linked lists. Trees also provide a natural organization for data, and consequently have become ubiquitous structures in file systems, graphical user interfaces, databases, Web sites, and other computer systems.

It is not always clear what productivity experts mean by "nonlinear" thinking, but when we say that trees are "nonlinear," we are referring to an organizational relationship that is richer than the simple "before" and "after" relationships between objects in sequences. The relationships in a tree are *hierarchical*, with some objects being "above" and some "below" others. Actually, the main terminology for tree data structures comes from family trees, with the terms "parent," "child," "ancestor," and "descendant" being the most common words used to describe relationships. We show an example of a family tree in Figure 8.1.

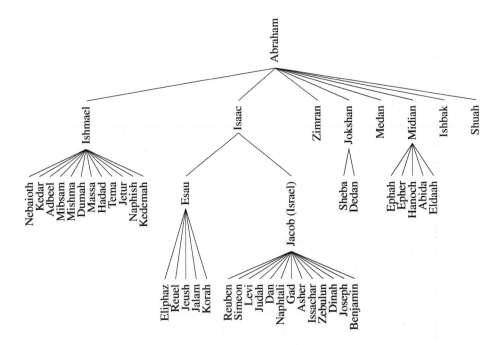

Figure 8.1: A family tree showing some descendants of Abraham, as recorded in Genesis, chapters 25–36.

8.1.1 Tree Definitions and Properties

A *tree* is an abstract data type that stores elements hierarchically. With the exception of the top element, each element in a tree has a *parent* element and zero or more *children* elements. A tree is usually visualized by placing elements inside ovals or rectangles, and by drawing the connections between parents and children with straight lines. (See Figure 8.2.) We typically call the top element the *root* of the tree, but it is drawn as the highest element, with the other elements being connected below (just the opposite of a botanical tree).

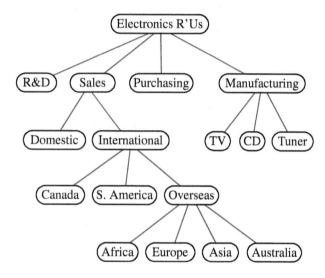

Figure 8.2: A tree with 17 nodes representing the organization of a fictitious corporation. The root stores *Electronics R'Us*. The children of the root store *R&D*, *Sales*, *Purchasing*, and *Manufacturing*. The internal nodes store *Sales*, *International*, *Overseas*, *Electronics R'Us*, and *Manufacturing*.

Formal Tree Definition

Formally, we define a *tree* T as a set of *nodes* storing elements such that the nodes have a *parent-child* relationship that satisfies the following properties:

- If T is nonempty, it has a special node, called the *root* of T, that has no parent.
- Each node v of T different from the root has a unique *parent* node w; every node with parent w is a *child* of w.

Note that according to our definition, a tree can be empty, meaning that it does not have any nodes. This convention also allows us to define a tree recursively such that a tree T is either empty or consists of a node r, called the root of T, and a (possibly empty) set of subtrees whose roots are the children of r.

Other Node Relationships

Two nodes that are children of the same parent are *siblings*. A node v is *external* if v has no children. A node v is *internal* if it has one or more children. External nodes are also known as *leaves*.

Example 8.1: *In Section 4.1.4, we discussed the hierarchical relationship between files and directories in a computer's file system, although at the time we did not emphasize the nomenclature of a file system as a tree. In Figure 8.3, we revisit an earlier example. We see that the internal nodes of the tree are associated with directories and the leaves are associated with regular files. In the UNIX and Linux operating systems, the root of the tree is appropriately called the "root directory," and is represented by the symbol "/."*

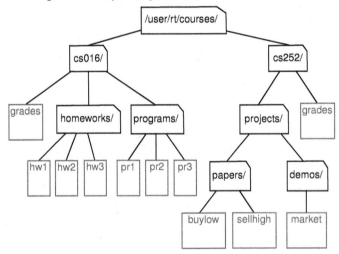

Figure 8.3: Tree representing a portion of a file system.

A node u is an *ancestor* of a node v if $u = v$ or u is an ancestor of the parent of v. Conversely, we say that a node v is a *descendant* of a node u if u is an ancestor of v. For example, in Figure 8.3, cs252/ is an ancestor of papers/, and pr3 is a descendant of cs016/. The *subtree* of T *rooted* at a node v is the tree consisting of all the descendants of v in T (including v itself). In Figure 8.3, the subtree rooted at cs016/ consists of the nodes cs016/, grades, homeworks/, programs/, hw1, hw2, hw3, pr1, pr2, and pr3.

Edges and Paths in Trees

An *edge* of tree T is a pair of nodes (u,v) such that u is the parent of v, or vice versa. A *path* of T is a sequence of nodes such that any two consecutive nodes in the sequence form an edge. For example, the tree in Figure 8.3 contains the path (cs252/, projects/, demos/, market).

Example 8.2: *The inheritance relation between classes in a Python program forms a tree when single inheritance is used. For example, in Section 2.4 we provided a summary of the hierarchy for Python's exception types, as portrayed in Figure 8.4 (originally Figure 2.5). The BaseException class is the root of that hierarchy, while all user-defined exception classes should conventionally be declared as descendants of the more specific Exception class. (See, for example, the Empty class we introduced in Code Fragment 6.1 of Chapter 6.)*

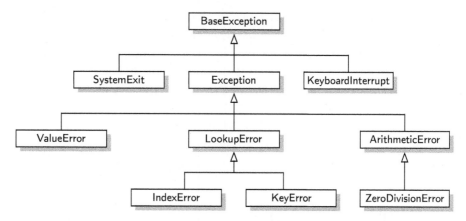

Figure 8.4: A portion of Python's hierarchy of exception types.

In Python, all classes are organized into a single hierarchy, as there exists a built-in class named object as the ultimate base class. It is a direct or indirect base class of all other types in Python (even if not declared as such when defining a new class). Therefore, the hierarchy pictured in Figure 8.4 is only a portion of Python's complete class hierarchy.

As a preview of the remainder of this chapter, Figure 8.5 portrays our own hierarchy of classes for representing various forms of a tree.

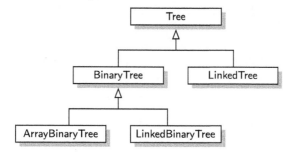

Figure 8.5: Our own inheritance hierarchy for modeling various abstractions and implementations of tree data structures. In the remainder of this chapter, we provide implementations of Tree, BinaryTree, and LinkedBinaryTree classes, and high-level sketches for how LinkedTree and ArrayBinaryTree might be designed.

Ordered Trees

A tree is *ordered* if there is a meaningful linear order among the children of each node; that is, we purposefully identify the children of a node as being the first, second, third, and so on. Such an order is usually visualized by arranging siblings left to right, according to their order.

Example 8.3: *The components of a structured document, such as a book, are hierarchically organized as a tree whose internal nodes are parts, chapters, and sections, and whose leaves are paragraphs, tables, figures, and so on. (See Figure 8.6.) The root of the tree corresponds to the book itself. We could, in fact, consider expanding the tree further to show paragraphs consisting of sentences, sentences consisting of words, and words consisting of characters. Such a tree is an example of an ordered tree, because there is a well-defined order among the children of each node.*

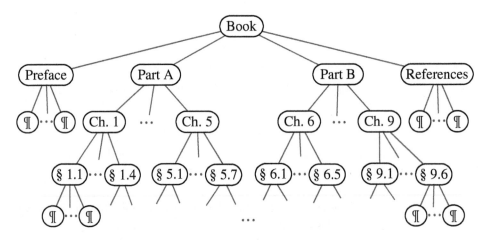

Figure 8.6: An ordered tree associated with a book.

Let's look back at the other examples of trees that we have described thus far, and consider whether the order of children is significant. A family tree that describes generational relationships, as in Figure 8.1, is often modeled as an ordered tree, with siblings ordered according to their birth.

In contrast, an organizational chart for a company, as in Figure 8.2, is typically considered an unordered tree. Likewise, when using a tree to describe an inheritance hierarchy, as in Figure 8.4, there is no particular significance to the order among the subclasses of a parent class. Finally, we consider the use of a tree in modeling a computer's file system, as in Figure 8.3. Although an operating system often displays entries of a directory in a particular order (e.g., alphabetical, chronological), such an order is not typically inherent to the file system's representation.

8.1.2 The Tree Abstract Data Type

As we did with positional lists in Section 7.4, we define a tree ADT using the concept of a *position* as an abstraction for a node of a tree. An element is stored at each position, and positions satisfy parent-child relationships that define the tree structure. A position object for a tree supports the method:

p.element( ): Return the element stored at position p.

The tree ADT then supports the following *accessor methods*, allowing a user to navigate the various positions of a tree:

T.root( ): Return the position of the root of tree T, or None if T is empty.

T.is_root(p): Return True if position p is the root of Tree T.

T.parent(p): Return the position of the parent of position p, or None if p is the root of T.

T.num_children(p): Return the number of children of position p.

T.children(p): Generate an iteration of the children of position p.

T.is_leaf(p): Return True if position p does not have any children.

len(T): Return the number of positions (and hence elements) that are contained in tree T.

T.is_empty( ): Return True if tree T does not contain any positions.

T.positions( ): Generate an iteration of all *positions* of tree T.

iter(T): Generate an iteration of all *elements* stored within tree T.

Any of the above methods that accepts a position as an argument should generate a ValueError if that position is invalid for T.

If a tree T is ordered, then T.children(p) reports the children of p in the natural order. If p is a leaf, then T.children(p) generates an empty iteration. In similar regard, if tree T is empty, then both T.positions( ) and iter(T) generate empty iterations. We will discuss general means for iterating through all positions of a tree in Sections 8.4.

We do not define any methods for creating or modifying trees at this point. We prefer to describe different tree update methods in conjunction with specific implementations of the tree interface, and specific applications of trees.

A Tree Abstract Base Class in Python

In discussing the object-oriented design principle of abstraction in Section 2.1.2, we noted that a public interface for an abstract data type is often managed in Python via **duck typing**. For example, we defined the notion of the public interface for a queue ADT in Section 6.2, and have since presented several classes that implement the queue interface (e.g., ArrayQueue in Section 6.2.2, LinkedQueue in Section 7.1.2, CircularQueue in Section 7.2.2). However, we never gave any formal definition of the queue ADT in Python; all of the concrete implementations were self-contained classes that just happen to adhere to the same public interface. A more formal mechanism to designate the relationships between different implementations of the same abstraction is through the definition of one class that serves as an **abstract base class**, via inheritance, for one or more **concrete classes**. (See Section 2.4.3.)

We choose to define a Tree class, in Code Fragment 8.1, that serves as an abstract base class corresponding to the tree ADT. Our reason for doing so is that there is quite a bit of useful code that we can provide, even at this level of abstraction, allowing greater code reuse in the concrete tree implementations we later define. The Tree class provides a definition of a nested Position class (which is also abstract), and declarations of many of the accessor methods included in the tree ADT.

However, our Tree class does not define any internal representation for storing a tree, and five of the methods given in that code fragment remain **abstract** (root, parent, num_children, children, and __len__); each of these methods raises a NotImplementedError. (A more formal approach for defining abstract base classes and abstract methods, using Python's abc module, is described in Section 2.4.3.) The subclasses are responsible for overriding abstract methods, such as children, to provide a working implementation for each behavior, based on their chosen internal representation.

Although the Tree class is an abstract base class, it includes several **concrete** methods with implementations that rely on calls to the abstract methods of the class. In defining the tree ADT in the previous section, we declare ten accessor methods. Five of those are the ones we left as abstract, in Code Fragment 8.1. The other five can be implemented based on the former. Code Fragment 8.2 provides concrete implementations for methods is_root, is_leaf, and is_empty. In Section 8.4, we will explore general algorithms for traversing a tree that can be used to provide concrete implementations of the positions and __iter__ methods within the Tree class. The beauty of this design is that the concrete methods defined within the Tree abstract base class will be inherited by all subclasses. This promotes greater code reuse, as there will be no need for those subclasses to reimplement such behaviors.

We note that, with the Tree class being abstract, there is no reason to create a direct instance of it, nor would such an instance be useful. The class exists to serve as a base for inheritance, and users will create instances of concrete subclasses.

```
1  class Tree:
2    """Abstract base class representing a tree structure."""
3
4    #------------------------------ nested Position class ------------------------------
5    class Position:
6      """An abstraction representing the location of a single element."""
7
8      def element(self):
9        """Return the element stored at this Position."""
10       raise NotImplementedError('must be implemented by subclass')
11
12     def __eq__(self, other):
13       """Return True if other Position represents the same location."""
14       raise NotImplementedError('must be implemented by subclass')
15
16     def __ne__(self, other):
17       """Return True if other does not represent the same location."""
18       return not (self == other)              # opposite of __eq__
19
20   # ---------- abstract methods that concrete subclass must support ----------
21   def root(self):
22     """Return Position representing the tree's root (or None if empty)."""
23     raise NotImplementedError('must be implemented by subclass')
24
25   def parent(self, p):
26     """Return Position representing p's parent (or None if p is root)."""
27     raise NotImplementedError('must be implemented by subclass')
28
29   def num_children(self, p):
30     """Return the number of children that Position p has."""
31     raise NotImplementedError('must be implemented by subclass')
32
33   def children(self, p):
34     """Generate an iteration of Positions representing p's children."""
35     raise NotImplementedError('must be implemented by subclass')
36
37   def __len__(self):
38     """Return the total number of elements in the tree."""
39     raise NotImplementedError('must be implemented by subclass')
```

Code Fragment 8.1: A portion of our Tree abstract base class (continued in Code Fragment 8.2).

```
40    # ---------- concrete methods implemented in this class ----------
41    def is_root(self, p):
42      """Return True if Position p represents the root of the tree."""
43      return self.root( ) == p
44
45    def is_leaf(self, p):
46      """Return True if Position p does not have any children."""
47      return self.num_children(p) == 0
48
49    def is_empty(self):
50      """Return True if the tree is empty."""
51      return len(self) == 0
```

Code Fragment 8.2: Some concrete methods of our Tree abstract base class.

8.1.3 Computing Depth and Height

Let p be the position of a node of a tree T. The ***depth*** of p is the number of ancestors of p, excluding p itself. For example, in the tree of Figure 8.2, the node storing *International* has depth 2. Note that this definition implies that the depth of the root of T is 0. The depth of p can also be recursively defined as follows:

- If p is the root, then the depth of p is 0.
- Otherwise, the depth of p is one plus the depth of the parent of p.

Based on this definition, we present a simple, recursive algorithm, depth, in Code Fragment 8.3, for computing the depth of a position p in Tree T. This method calls itself recursively on the parent of p, and adds 1 to the value returned.

```
52    def depth(self, p):
53      """Return the number of levels separating Position p from the root."""
54      if self.is_root(p):
55        return 0
56      else:
57        return 1 + self.depth(self.parent(p))
```

Code Fragment 8.3: Method depth of the Tree class.

The running time of T.depth(p) for position p is $O(d_p + 1)$, where d_p denotes the depth of p in the tree T, because the algorithm performs a constant-time recursive step for each ancestor of p. Thus, algorithm T.depth(p) runs in $O(n)$ worst-case time, where n is the total number of positions of T, because a position of T may have depth $n - 1$ if all nodes form a single branch. Although such a running time is a function of the input size, it is more informative to characterize the running time in terms of the parameter d_p, as this parameter may be much smaller than n.

Height

The *height* of a position p in a tree T is also defined recursively:
- If p is a leaf, then the height of p is 0.
- Otherwise, the height of p is one more than the maximum of the heights of p's children.

The *height* of a nonempty tree T is the height of the root of T. For example, the tree of Figure 8.2 has height 4. In addition, height can also be viewed as follows.

Proposition 8.4: *The height of a nonempty tree T is equal to the maximum of the depths of its leaf positions.*

We leave the justification of this fact to an exercise (R-8.3). We present an algorithm, height1, implemented in Code Fragment 8.4 as a nonpublic method _height1 of the Tree class. It computes the height of a nonempty tree T based on Proposition 8.4 and the algorithm depth from Code Fragment 8.3.

```
58    def _height1(self):                    # works, but O(n^2) worst-case time
59        """Return the height of the tree."""
60        return max(self.depth(p) for p in self.positions( ) if self.is_leaf(p))
```

Code Fragment 8.4: Method _height1 of the Tree class. Note that this method calls the depth method.

Unfortunately, algorithm height1 is not very efficient. We have not yet defined the positions( ) method; we will see that it can be implemented to run in $O(n)$ time, where n is the number of positions of T. Because height1 calls algorithm depth(p) on each leaf of T, its running time is $O(n + \sum_{p \in L}(d_p + 1))$, where L is the set of leaf positions of T. In the worst case, the sum $\sum_{p \in L}(d_p + 1)$ is proportional to n^2. (See Exercise C-8.33.) Thus, algorithm height1 runs in $O(n^2)$ worst-case time.

We can compute the height of a tree more efficiently, in $O(n)$ worst-case time, by relying instead on the original recursive definition. To do this, we will parameterize a function based on a position within the tree, and calculate the height of the subtree rooted at that position. Algorithm height2, shown as nonpublic method _height2 in Code Fragment 8.5, computes the height of tree T in this way.

```
61    def _height2(self, p):                    # time is linear in size of subtree
62        """Return the height of the subtree rooted at Position p."""
63        if self.is_leaf(p):
64            return 0
65        else:
66            return 1 + max(self._height2(c) for c in self.children(p))
```

Code Fragment 8.5: Method _height2 for computing the height of a subtree rooted at a position p of a Tree.

It is important to understand why algorithm height2 is more efficient than height1. The algorithm is recursive, and it progresses in a top-down fashion. If the method is initially called on the root of T, it will eventually be called once for each position of T. This is because the root eventually invokes the recursion on each of its children, which in turn invokes the recursion on each of their children, and so on.

We can determine the running time of the height2 algorithm by summing, over all the positions, the amount of time spent on the nonrecursive part of each call. (Review Section 4.2 for analyses of recursive processes.) In our implementation, there is a constant amount of work per position, plus the overhead of computing the maximum over the iteration of children. Although we do not yet have a concrete implementation of children(p), we assume that such an iteration is generated in $O(c_p + 1)$ time, where c_p denotes the number of children of p. Algorithm height2 spends $O(c_p + 1)$ time at each position p to compute the maximum, and its overall running time is $O(\sum_p (c_p + 1)) = O(n + \sum_p c_p)$. In order to complete the analysis, we make use of the following property.

Proposition 8.5: *Let T be a tree with n positions, and let c_p denote the number of children of a position p of T. Then, summing over the positions of T, $\sum_p c_p = n - 1$.*

Justification: Each position of T, with the exception of the root, is a child of another position, and thus contributes one unit to the above sum.   ■

By Proposition 8.5, the running time of algorithm height2, when called on the root of T, is $O(n)$, where n is the number of positions of T.

Revisiting the public interface for our Tree class, the ability to compute heights of subtrees is beneficial, but a user might expect to be able to compute the height of the entire tree without explicitly designating the tree root. We can wrap the non-public _height2 in our implementation with a public height method that provides a default interpretation when invoked on tree T with syntax T.height( ). Such an implementation is given in Code Fragment 8.6.

```
67    def height(self, p=None):
68       """Return the height of the subtree rooted at Position p.
69
70       If p is None, return the height of the entire tree.
71       """
72       if p is None:
73          p = self.root()
74       return self._height2(p)              # start _height2 recursion
```

Code Fragment 8.6: Public method Tree.height that computes the height of the entire tree by default, or a subtree rooted at given position, if specified.

8.2 Binary Trees

A *binary tree* is an ordered tree with the following properties:
1. Every node has at most two children.
2. Each child node is labeled as being either a *left child* or a *right child*.
3. A left child precedes a right child in the order of children of a node.

The subtree rooted at a left or right child of an internal node v is called a *left subtree* or *right subtree*, respectively, of v. A binary tree is *proper* if each node has either zero or two children. Some people also refer to such trees as being *full* binary trees. Thus, in a proper binary tree, every internal node has exactly two children. A binary tree that is not proper is *improper*.

Example 8.6: *An important class of binary trees arises in contexts where we wish to represent a number of different outcomes that can result from answering a series of yes-or-no questions. Each internal node is associated with a question. Starting at the root, we go to the left or right child of the current node, depending on whether the answer to the question is "Yes" or "No." With each decision, we follow an edge from a parent to a child, eventually tracing a path in the tree from the root to a leaf. Such binary trees are known as* **decision trees,** *because a leaf position p in such a tree represents a decision of what to do if the questions associated with p's ancestors are answered in a way that leads to p. A decision tree is a proper binary tree. Figure 8.7 illustrates a decision tree that provides recommendations to a prospective investor.*

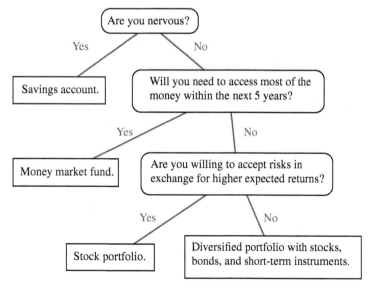

Figure 8.7: A decision tree providing investment advice.

Example 8.7: *An arithmetic expression can be represented by a binary tree whose leaves are associated with variables or constants, and whose internal nodes are associated with one of the operators $+$, $-$, $\times$, and $/$. (See Figure 8.8.) Each node in such a tree has a value associated with it.*

- *If a node is leaf, then its value is that of its variable or constant.*
- *If a node is internal, then its value is defined by applying its operation to the values of its children.*

An arithmetic expression tree is a proper binary tree, since each operator $+$, $-$, $\times$, and $/$ takes exactly two operands. Of course, if we were to allow unary operators, like negation $(-)$, as in "$-x$," then we could have an improper binary tree.

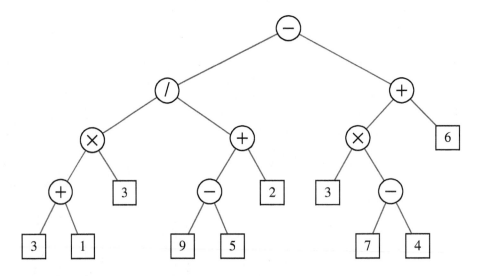

Figure 8.8: A binary tree representing an arithmetic expression. This tree represents the expression $((((3+1) \times 3)/((9-5)+2)) - ((3 \times (7-4))+6))$. The value associated with the internal node labeled "$/$" is 2.

A Recursive Binary Tree Definition

Incidentally, we can also define a binary tree in a recursive way such that a binary tree is either empty or consists of:

- A node r, called the root of T, that stores an element
- A binary tree (possibly empty), called the left subtree of T
- A binary tree (possibly empty), called the right subtree of T

8.2.1 The Binary Tree Abstract Data Type

As an abstract data type, a binary tree is a specialization of a tree that supports three additional accessor methods:

T.left(p): Return the position that represents the left child of p, or None if p has no left child.

T.right(p): Return the position that represents the right child of p, or None if p has no right child.

T.sibling(p): Return the position that represents the sibling of p, or None if p has no sibling.

Just as in Section 8.1.2 for the tree ADT, we do not define specialized update methods for binary trees here. Instead, we will consider some possible update methods when we describe specific implementations and applications of binary trees.

The BinaryTree Abstract Base Class in Python

Just as Tree was defined as an abstract base class in Section 8.1.2, we define a new BinaryTree class associated with the binary tree ADT. We rely on inheritance to define the BinaryTree class based upon the existing Tree class. However, our BinaryTree class remains *abstract*, as we still do not provide complete specifications for how such a structure will be represented internally, nor implementations for some necessary behaviors.

Our Python implementation of the BinaryTree class is given in Code Fragment 8.7. By using inheritance, a binary tree supports all the functionality that was defined for general trees (e.g., parent, is_leaf, root). Our new class also inherits the nested Position class that was originally defined within the Tree class definition. In addition, the new class provides declarations for new abstract methods left and right that should be supported by concrete subclasses of BinaryTree.

Our new class also provides two concrete implementations of methods. The new sibling method is derived from the combination of left, right, and parent. Typically, we identify the sibling of a position p as the "other" child of p's parent. However, if p is the root, it has no parent, and thus no sibling. Also, p may be the only child of its parent, and thus does not have a sibling.

Finally, Code Fragment 8.7 provides a concrete implementation of the children method; this method is abstract in the Tree class. Although we have still not specified how the children of a node will be stored, we derive a generator for the ordered children based upon the implied behavior of abstract methods left and right.

```
 1  class BinaryTree(Tree):
 2    """Abstract base class representing a binary tree structure."""
 3
 4    # ---------------------- additional abstract methods ----------------------
 5    def left(self, p):
 6      """Return a Position representing p's left child.
 7
 8      Return None if p does not have a left child.
 9      """
10      raise NotImplementedError('must be implemented by subclass')
11
12    def right(self, p):
13      """Return a Position representing p's right child.
14
15      Return None if p does not have a right child.
16      """
17      raise NotImplementedError('must be implemented by subclass')
18
19    # ---------- concrete methods implemented in this class ----------
20    def sibling(self, p):
21      """Return a Position representing p's sibling (or None if no sibling)."""
22      parent = self.parent(p)
23      if parent is None:                      # p must be the root
24        return None                           # root has no sibling
25      else:
26        if p == self.left(parent):
27          return self.right(parent)           # possibly None
28        else:
29          return self.left(parent)            # possibly None
30
31    def children(self, p):
32      """Generate an iteration of Positions representing p's children."""
33      if self.left(p) is not None:
34        yield self.left(p)
35      if self.right(p) is not None:
36        yield self.right(p)
```

Code Fragment 8.7: A BinaryTree abstract base class that extends the existing Tree abstract base class from Code Fragments 8.1 and 8.2.

8.2.2 Properties of Binary Trees

Binary trees have several interesting properties dealing with relationships between their heights and number of nodes. We denote the set of all nodes of a tree T at the same depth d as **level** d of T. In a binary tree, level 0 has at most one node (the root), level 1 has at most two nodes (the children of the root), level 2 has at most four nodes, and so on. (See Figure 8.9.) In general, level d has at most 2^d nodes.

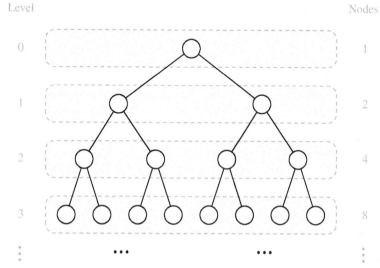

Figure 8.9: Maximum number of nodes in the levels of a binary tree.

We can see that the maximum number of nodes on the levels of a binary tree grows exponentially as we go down the tree. From this simple observation, we can derive the following properties relating the height of a binary tree T with its number of nodes. A detailed justification of these properties is left as Exercise R-8.8.

Proposition 8.8: *Let T be a nonempty binary tree, and let n, n_E, n_I and h denote the number of nodes, number of external nodes, number of internal nodes, and height of T, respectively. Then T has the following properties:*

1. $h+1 \leq n \leq 2^{h+1} - 1$
2. $1 \leq n_E \leq 2^h$
3. $h \leq n_I \leq 2^h - 1$
4. $\log(n+1) - 1 \leq h \leq n - 1$

Also, if T is proper, then T has the following properties:

1. $2h+1 \leq n \leq 2^{h+1} - 1$
2. $h+1 \leq n_E \leq 2^h$
3. $h \leq n_I \leq 2^h - 1$
4. $\log(n+1) - 1 \leq h \leq (n-1)/2$

Relating Internal Nodes to External Nodes in a Proper Binary Tree

In addition to the earlier binary tree properties, the following relationship exists between the number of internal nodes and external nodes in a proper binary tree.

Proposition 8.9: *In a nonempty proper binary tree* T, *with* n_E *external nodes and* n_I *internal nodes, we have* $n_E = n_I + 1$.

Justification: We justify this proposition by removing nodes from T and dividing them up into two "piles," an internal-node pile and an external-node pile, until T becomes empty. The piles are initially empty. By the end, we will show that the external-node pile has one more node than the internal-node pile. We consider two cases:

Case 1: If T has only one node v, we remove v and place it on the external-node pile. Thus, the external-node pile has one node and the internal-node pile is empty.

Case 2: Otherwise (T has more than one node), we remove from T an (arbitrary) external node w and its parent v, which is an internal node. We place w on the external-node pile and v on the internal-node pile. If v has a parent u, then we reconnect u with the former sibling z of w, as shown in Figure 8.10. This operation, removes one internal node and one external node, and leaves the tree being a proper binary tree.

Repeating this operation, we eventually are left with a final tree consisting of a single node. Note that the same number of external and internal nodes have been removed and placed on their respective piles by the sequence of operations leading to this final tree. Now, we remove the node of the final tree and we place it on the external-node pile. Thus, the the external-node pile has one more node than the internal-node pile. ∎

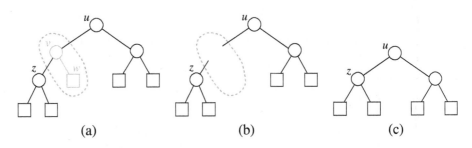

Figure 8.10: Operation that removes an external node and its parent node, used in the justification of Proposition 8.9.

Note that the above relationship does not hold, in general, for improper binary trees and nonbinary trees, although there are other interesting relationships that do hold. (See Exercises C-8.32 through C-8.34.)

8.3 Implementing Trees

The Tree and BinaryTree classes that we have defined thus far in this chapter are both formally **abstract base classes**. Although they provide a great deal of support, neither of them can be directly instantiated. We have not yet defined key implementation details for how a tree will be represented internally, and how we can effectively navigate between parents and children. Specifically, a concrete implementation of a tree must provide methods root, parent, num_children, children, __len__, and in the case of BinaryTree, the additional accessors left and right.

There are several choices for the internal representation of trees. We describe the most common representations in this section. We begin with the case of a **binary tree**, since its shape is more narrowly defined.

8.3.1 Linked Structure for Binary Trees

A natural way to realize a binary tree T is to use a **linked structure**, with a node (see Figure 8.11a) that maintains references to the element stored at a position p and to the nodes associated with the children and parent of p. If p is the root of T, then the parent field of p is None. Likewise, if p does not have a left child (respectively, right child), the associated field is None. The tree itself maintains an instance variable storing a reference to the root node (if any), and a variable, called size, that represents the overall number of nodes of T. We show such a linked structure representation of a binary tree in Figure 8.11b.

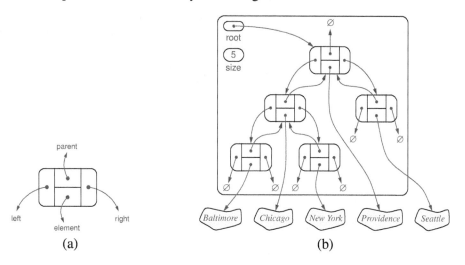

(a)   (b)

Figure 8.11: A linked structure for representing: (a) a single node; (b) a binary tree.

Python Implementation of a Linked Binary Tree Structure

In this section, we define a concrete LinkedBinaryTree class that implements the binary tree ADT by subclassing the BinaryTree class. Our general approach is very similar to what we used when developing the PositionalList in Section 7.4: We define a simple, nonpublic _Node class to represent a node, and a public Position class that wraps a node. We provide a _validate utility for robustly checking the validity of a given position instance when unwrapping it, and a _make_position utility for wrapping a node as a position to return to a caller.

Those definitions are provided in Code Fragment 8.8. As a formality, the new Position class is declared to inherit immediately from BinaryTree.Position. Technically, the BinaryTree class definition (see Code Fragment 8.7) does not formally declare such a nested class; it trivially inherits it from Tree.Position. A minor benefit from this design is that our position class inherits the __ne__ special method so that syntax p != q is derived appropriately relative to __eq__.

Our class definition continues, in Code Fragment 8.9, with a constructor and with concrete implementations for the methods that remain abstract in the Tree and BinaryTree classes. The constructor creates an empty tree by initializing _root to None and _size to zero. These accessor methods are implemented with careful use of the _validate and _make_position utilities to safeguard against boundary cases.

Operations for Updating a Linked Binary Tree

Thus far, we have provided functionality for examining an existing binary tree. However, the constructor for our LinkedBinaryTree class results in an empty tree and we have not provided any means for changing the structure or content of a tree.

We chose not to declare update methods as part of the Tree or BinaryTree abstract base classes for several reasons. First, although the principle of encapsulation suggests that the outward behaviors of a class need not depend on the internal representation, the *efficiency* of the operations depends greatly upon the representation. We prefer to have each concrete implementation of a tree class offer the most suitable options for updating a tree.

The second reason we do not provide update methods in the base class is that we may not want such update methods to be part of a public interface. There are many applications of trees, and some forms of update operations that are suitable for one application may be unacceptable in another. However, if we place an update method in a base class, any class that inherits from that base will inherit the update method. Consider, for example, the possibility of a method T.replace(p, e) that replaces the element stored at position *p* with another element *e*. Such a general method may be unacceptable in the context of an ***arithmetic expression tree*** (see Example 8.7 on page 312, and a later case study in Section 8.5), because we may want to enforce that internal nodes store only operators as elements.

For linked binary trees, a reasonable set of update methods to support for general usage are the following:

T.add_root(e): Create a root for an empty tree, storing e as the element, and return the position of that root; an error occurs if the tree is not empty.

T.add_left(p, e): Create a new node storing element e, link the node as the left child of position p, and return the resulting position; an error occurs if p already has a left child.

T.add_right(p, e): Create a new node storing element e, link the node as the right child of position p, and return the resulting position; an error occurs if p already has a right child.

T.replace(p, e): Replace the element stored at position p with element e, and return the previously stored element.

T.delete(p): Remove the node at position p, replacing it with its child, if any, and return the element that had been stored at p; an error occurs if p has two children.

T.attach(p, T1, T2): Attach the internal structure of trees T1 and T2, respectively, as the left and right subtrees of leaf position p of T, and reset T1 and T2 to empty trees; an error condition occurs if p is not a leaf.

We have specifically chosen this collection of operations because each can be implemented in $O(1)$ worst-case time with our linked representation. The most complex of these are delete and attach, due to the case analyses involving the various parent-child relationships and boundary conditions, yet there remains only a constant number of operations to perform. (The implementation of both methods could be greatly simplified if we used a tree representation with a sentinel node, akin to our treatment of positional lists; see Exercise C-8.40).

To avoid the problem of undesirable update methods being inherited by subclasses of LinkedBinaryTree, we have chosen an implementation in which none of the above methods are publicly supported. Instead, we provide *nonpublic* versions of each, for example, providing the underscored _delete in lieu of a public delete. Our implementations of these six update methods are provided in Code Fragments 8.10 and 8.11.

In particular applications, subclasses of LinkedBinaryTree can invoke the nonpublic methods internally, while preserving a public interface that is appropriate for the application. A subclass may also choose to wrap one or more of the nonpublic update methods with a public method to expose it to the user. We leave as an exercise (R-8.15), the task of defining a MutableLinkedBinaryTree subclass that provides public methods wrapping each of these six update methods.

```
1   class LinkedBinaryTree(BinaryTree):
2     """Linked representation of a binary tree structure."""
3
4     class _Node:          # Lightweight, nonpublic class for storing a node.
5       __slots__ = '_element', '_parent', '_left', '_right'
6       def __init__(self, element, parent=None, left=None, right=None):
7         self._element = element
8         self._parent = parent
9         self._left = left
10        self._right = right
11
12    class Position(BinaryTree.Position):
13      """An abstraction representing the location of a single element."""
14
15      def __init__(self, container, node):
16        """Constructor should not be invoked by user."""
17        self._container = container
18        self._node = node
19
20      def element(self):
21        """Return the element stored at this Position."""
22        return self._node._element
23
24      def __eq__(self, other):
25        """Return True if other is a Position representing the same location."""
26        return type(other) is type(self) and other._node is self._node
27
28    def _validate(self, p):
29      """Return associated node, if position is valid."""
30      if not isinstance(p, self.Position):
31        raise TypeError('p must be proper Position type')
32      if p._container is not self:
33        raise ValueError('p does not belong to this container')
34      if p._node._parent is p._node:          # convention for deprecated nodes
35        raise ValueError('p is no longer valid')
36      return p._node
37
38    def _make_position(self, node):
39      """Return Position instance for given node (or None if no node)."""
40      return self.Position(self, node) if node is not None else None
```

Code Fragment 8.8: The beginning of our LinkedBinaryTree class (continued in Code Fragments 8.9 through 8.11).

```
41    #------------------------ binary tree constructor ------------------------
42    def __init__(self):
43      """Create an initially empty binary tree."""
44      self._root = None
45      self._size = 0
46
47    #------------------------ public accessors ------------------------
48    def __len__(self):
49      """Return the total number of elements in the tree."""
50      return self._size
51
52    def root(self):
53      """Return the root Position of the tree (or None if tree is empty)."""
54      return self._make_position(self._root)
55
56    def parent(self, p):
57      """Return the Position of p's parent (or None if p is root)."""
58      node = self._validate(p)
59      return self._make_position(node._parent)
60
61    def left(self, p):
62      """Return the Position of p's left child (or None if no left child)."""
63      node = self._validate(p)
64      return self._make_position(node._left)
65
66    def right(self, p):
67      """Return the Position of p's right child (or None if no right child)."""
68      node = self._validate(p)
69      return self._make_position(node._right)
70
71    def num_children(self, p):
72      """Return the number of children of Position p."""
73      node = self._validate(p)
74      count = 0
75      if node._left is not None:        # left child exists
76        count += 1
77      if node._right is not None:       # right child exists
78        count += 1
79      return count
```

Code Fragment 8.9: Public accessors for our LinkedBinaryTree class. The class begins in Code Fragment 8.8 and continues in Code Fragments 8.10 and 8.11.

```
80    def _add_root(self, e):
81      """Place element e at the root of an empty tree and return new Position.
82
83      Raise ValueError if tree nonempty.
84      """
85      if self._root is not None: raise ValueError('Root exists')
86      self._size = 1
87      self._root = self._Node(e)
88      return self._make_position(self._root)
89
90    def _add_left(self, p, e):
91      """Create a new left child for Position p, storing element e.
92
93      Return the Position of new node.
94      Raise ValueError if Position p is invalid or p already has a left child.
95      """
96      node = self._validate(p)
97      if node._left is not None: raise ValueError('Left child exists')
98      self._size += 1
99      node._left = self._Node(e, node)             # node is its parent
100     return self._make_position(node._left)
101
102   def _add_right(self, p, e):
103     """Create a new right child for Position p, storing element e.
104
105     Return the Position of new node.
106     Raise ValueError if Position p is invalid or p already has a right child.
107     """
108     node = self._validate(p)
109     if node._right is not None: raise ValueError('Right child exists')
110     self._size += 1
111     node._right = self._Node(e, node)            # node is its parent
112     return self._make_position(node._right)
113
114   def _replace(self, p, e):
115     """Replace the element at position p with e, and return old element."""
116     node = self._validate(p)
117     old = node._element
118     node._element = e
119     return old
```

Code Fragment 8.10: Nonpublic update methods for the LinkedBinaryTree class (continued in Code Fragment 8.11).

```
120    def _delete(self, p):
121      """Delete the node at Position p, and replace it with its child, if any.
122
123      Return the element that had been stored at Position p.
124      Raise ValueError if Position p is invalid or p has two children.
125      """
126      node = self._validate(p)
127      if self.num_children(p) == 2: raise ValueError('p has two children')
128      child = node._left if node._left else node._right      # might be None
129      if child is not None:
130        child._parent = node._parent      # child's grandparent becomes parent
131      if node is self._root:
132        self._root = child                 # child becomes root
133      else:
134        parent = node._parent
135        if node is parent._left:
136          parent._left = child
137        else:
138          parent._right = child
139      self._size -= 1
140      node._parent = node                  # convention for deprecated node
141      return node._element
142
143    def _attach(self, p, t1, t2):
144      """Attach trees t1 and t2 as left and right subtrees of external p."""
145      node = self._validate(p)
146      if not self.is_leaf(p): raise ValueError('position must be leaf')
147      if not type(self) is type(t1) is type(t2):   # all 3 trees must be same type
148        raise TypeError('Tree types must match')
149      self._size += len(t1) + len(t2)
150      if not t1.is_empty():                # attached t1 as left subtree of node
151        t1._root._parent = node
152        node._left = t1._root
153        t1._root = None                    # set t1 instance to empty
154        t1._size = 0
155      if not t2.is_empty():                # attached t2 as right subtree of node
156        t2._root._parent = node
157        node._right = t2._root
158        t2._root = None                    # set t2 instance to empty
159        t2._size = 0
```

Code Fragment 8.11: Nonpublic update methods for the LinkedBinaryTree class (continued from Code Fragment 8.10).

Performance of the Linked Binary Tree Implementation

To summarize the efficiencies of the linked structure representation, we analyze the running times of the LinkedBinaryTree methods, including derived methods that are inherited from the Tree and BinaryTree classes:

- The len method, implemented in LinkedBinaryTree, uses an instance variable storing the number of nodes of T and takes $O(1)$ time. Method is_empty, inherited from Tree, relies on a single call to len and thus takes $O(1)$ time.

- The accessor methods root, left, right, parent, and num_children are implemented directly in LinkedBinaryTree and take $O(1)$ time. The sibling and children methods are derived in BinaryTree based on a constant number of calls to these other accessors, so they run in $O(1)$ time as well.

- The is_root and is_leaf methods, from the Tree class, both run in $O(1)$ time, as is_root calls root and then relies on equivalence testing of positions, while is_leaf calls left and right and verifies that None is returned by both.

- Methods depth and height were each analyzed in Section 8.1.3. The depth method at position p runs in $O(d_p + 1)$ time where d_p is its depth; the height method on the root of the tree runs in $O(n)$ time.

- The various update methods add_root, add_left, add_right, replace, delete, and attach (that is, their nonpublic implementations) each run in $O(1)$ time, as they involve relinking only a constant number of nodes per operation.

Table 8.1 summarizes the performance of the linked structure implementation of a binary tree.

Operation	Running Time
len, is_empty	$O(1)$
root, parent, left, right, sibling, children, num_children	$O(1)$
is_root, is_leaf	$O(1)$
depth(p)	$O(d_p + 1)$
height	$O(n)$
add_root, add_left, add_right, replace, delete, attach	$O(1)$

Table 8.1: Running times for the methods of an n-node binary tree implemented with a linked structure. The space usage is $O(n)$.

8.3.2 Array-Based Representation of a Binary Tree

An alternative representation of a binary tree T is based on a way of numbering the positions of T. For every position p of T, let $f(p)$ be the integer defined as follows.

- If p is the root of T, then $f(p) = 0$.
- If p is the left child of position q, then $f(p) = 2f(q) + 1$.
- If p is the right child of position q, then $f(p) = 2f(q) + 2$.

The numbering function f is known as a ***level numbering*** of the positions in a binary tree T, for it numbers the positions on each level of T in increasing order from left to right. (See Figure 8.12.) Note well that the level numbering is based on *potential* positions within the tree, not actual positions of a given tree, so they are not necessarily consecutive. For example, in Figure 8.12(b), there are no nodes with level numbering 13 or 14, because the node with level numbering 6 has no children.

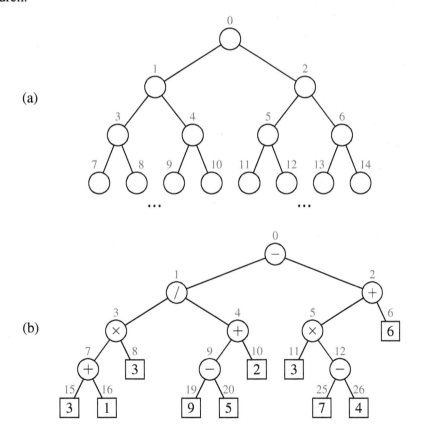

Figure 8.12: Binary tree level numbering: (a) general scheme; (b) an example.

The level numbering function f suggests a representation of a binary tree T by means of an array-based structure A (such as a Python list), with the element at position p of T stored at index $f(p)$ of the array. We show an example of an array-based representation of a binary tree in Figure 8.13.

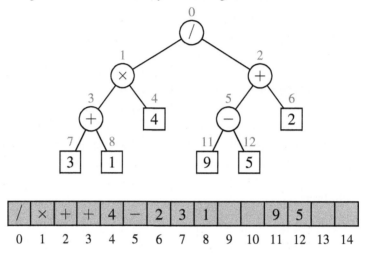

Figure 8.13: Representation of a binary tree by means of an array.

One advantage of an array-based representation of a binary tree is that a position p can be represented by the single integer $f(p)$, and that position-based methods such as root, parent, left, and right can be implemented using simple arithmetic operations on the number $f(p)$. Based on our formula for the level numbering, the left child of p has index $2f(p)+1$, the right child of p has index $2f(p)+2$, and the parent of p has index $\lfloor (f(p)-1)/2 \rfloor$. We leave the details of a complete implementation as an exercise (R-8.18).

The space usage of an array-based representation depends greatly on the shape of the tree. Let n be the number of nodes of T, and let f_M be the maximum value of $f(p)$ over all the nodes of T. The array A requires length $N = 1 + f_M$, since elements range from $A[0]$ to $A[f_M]$. Note that A may have a number of empty cells that do not refer to existing nodes of T. In fact, in the worst case, $N = 2^n - 1$, the justification of which is left as an exercise (R-8.16). In Section 9.3, we will see a class of binary trees, called "heaps" for which $N = n$. Thus, in spite of the worst-case space usage, there are applications for which the array representation of a binary tree is space efficient. Still, for general binary trees, the exponential worst-case space requirement of this representation is prohibitive.

Another drawback of an array representation is that some update operations for trees cannot be efficiently supported. For example, deleting a node and promoting its child takes $O(n)$ time because it is not just the child that moves locations within the array, but all descendants of that child.

8.3.3 Linked Structure for General Trees

When representing a binary tree with a linked structure, each node explicitly maintains fields left and right as references to individual children. For a general tree, there is no a priori limit on the number of children that a node may have. A natural way to realize a general tree T as a linked structure is to have each node store a single *container* of references to its children. For example, a children field of a node can be a Python list of references to the children of the node (if any). Such a linked representation is schematically illustrated in Figure 8.14.

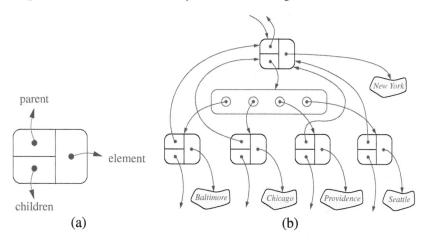

Figure 8.14: The linked structure for a general tree: (a) the structure of a node; (b) a larger portion of the data structure associated with a node and its children.

Table 8.2 summarizes the performance of the implementation of a general tree using a linked structure. The analysis is left as an exercise (R-8.14), but we note that, by using a collection to store the children of each position p, we can implement children(p) by simply iterating that collection.

Operation	Running Time
len, is_empty	$O(1)$
root, parent, is_root, is_leaf	$O(1)$
children(p)	$O(c_p + 1)$
depth(p)	$O(d_p + 1)$
height	$O(n)$

Table 8.2: Running times of the accessor methods of an n-node general tree implemented with a linked structure. We let c_p denote the number of children of a position p. The space usage is $O(n)$.

8.4   Tree Traversal Algorithms

A *traversal* of a tree T is a systematic way of accessing, or "visiting," all the positions of T. The specific action associated with the "visit" of a position p depends on the application of this traversal, and could involve anything from incrementing a counter to performing some complex computation for p. In this section, we describe several common traversal schemes for trees, implement them in the context of our various tree classes, and discuss several common applications of tree traversals.

8.4.1   Preorder and Postorder Traversals of General Trees

In a *preorder traversal* of a tree T, the root of T is visited first and then the subtrees rooted at its children are traversed recursively. If the tree is ordered, then the subtrees are traversed according to the order of the children. The pseudo-code for the preorder traversal of the subtree rooted at a position p is shown in Code Fragment 8.12.

Algorithm preorder(T, p):
    perform the "visit" action for position p
    for each child c in T.children(p) **do**
        preorder(T, c)   {recursively traverse the subtree rooted at c}

Code Fragment 8.12: Algorithm preorder for performing the preorder traversal of a subtree rooted at position p of a tree T.

Figure 8.15 portrays the order in which positions of a sample tree are visited during an application of the preorder traversal algorithm.

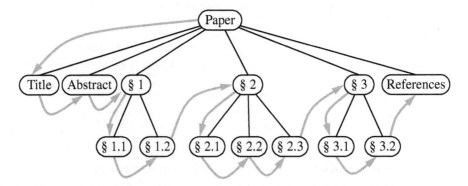

Figure 8.15: Preorder traversal of an ordered tree, where the children of each position are ordered from left to right.

Postorder Traversal

Another important tree traversal algorithm is the ***postorder traversal***. In some sense, this algorithm can be viewed as the opposite of the preorder traversal, because it recursively traverses the subtrees rooted at the children of the root first, and then visits the root (hence, the name "postorder"). Pseudo-code for the postorder traversal is given in Code Fragment 8.13, and an example of a postorder traversal is portrayed in Figure 8.16.

Algorithm postorder(T, p):
    for each child c in T.children(p) **do**
        postorder(T, c)   {recursively traverse the subtree rooted at c}
    perform the "visit" action for position p

Code Fragment 8.13: Algorithm postorder for performing the postorder traversal of a subtree rooted at position p of a tree T.

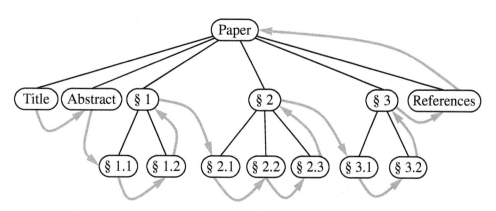

Figure 8.16: Postorder traversal of the ordered tree of Figure 8.15.

Running-Time Analysis

Both preorder and postorder traversal algorithms are efficient ways to access all the positions of a tree. The analysis of either of these traversal algorithms is similar to that of algorithm height2, given in Code Fragment 8.5 of Section 8.1.3. At each position p, the nonrecursive part of the traversal algorithm requires time $O(c_p+1)$, where c_p is the number of children of p, under the assumption that the "visit" itself takes $O(1)$ time. By Proposition 8.5, the overall running time for the traversal of tree T is $O(n)$, where n is the number of positions in the tree. This running time is asymptotically optimal since the traversal must visit all the n positions of the tree.

8.4.2   Breadth-First Tree Traversal

Although the preorder and postorder traversals are common ways of visiting the positions of a tree, another common approach is to traverse a tree so that we visit all the positions at depth d before we visit the positions at depth $d+1$. Such an algorithm is known as a ***breadth-first traversal***.

A breadth-first traversal is a common approach used in software for playing games. A ***game tree*** represents the possible choices of moves that might be made by a player (or computer) during a game, with the root of the tree being the initial configuration for the game. For example, Figure 8.17 displays a partial game tree for Tic-Tac-Toe.

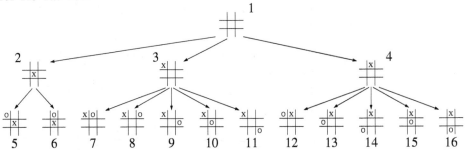

Figure 8.17: Partial game tree for Tic-Tac-Toe, with annotations displaying the order in which positions are visited in a breadth-first traversal.

A breadth-first traversal of such a game tree is often performed because a computer may be unable to explore a complete game tree in a limited amount of time. So the computer will consider all moves, then responses to those moves, going as deep as computational time allows.

Pseudo-code for a breadth-first traversal is given in Code Fragment 8.14. The process is not recursive, since we are not traversing entire subtrees at once. We use a queue to produce a FIFO (i.e., first-in first-out) semantics for the order in which we visit nodes. The overall running time is $O(n)$, due to the n calls to enqueue and n calls to dequeue.

Algorithm breadthfirst(T):
    Initialize queue Q to contain T.root( )
    while Q not empty **do**
        p = Q.dequeue( )   {p is the oldest entry in the queue}
        perform the "visit" action for position p
        for each child c in T.children(p) **do**
            Q.enqueue(c)   {add p's children to the end of the queue for later visits}

Code Fragment 8.14: Algorithm for performing a breadth-first traversal of a tree.

8.4.3   Inorder Traversal of a Binary Tree

The standard preorder, postorder, and breadth-first traversals that were introduced for general trees, can be directly applied to binary trees. In this section, we introduce another common traversal algorithm specifically for a binary tree.

During an ***inorder traversal***, we visit a position between the recursive traversals of its left and right subtrees. The inorder traversal of a binary tree T can be informally viewed as visiting the nodes of T "from left to right." Indeed, for every position p, the inorder traversal visits p after all the positions in the left subtree of p and before all the positions in the right subtree of p. Pseudo-code for the inorder traversal algorithm is given in Code Fragment 8.15, and an example of an inorder traversal is portrayed in Figure 8.18.

Algorithm inorder(p):

   if p has a left child lc **then**
      inorder(lc)   {recursively traverse the left subtree of p}
   perform the "visit" action for position p
   if p has a right child rc **then**
      inorder(rc)   {recursively traverse the right subtree of p}

Code Fragment 8.15: Algorithm inorder for performing an inorder traversal of a subtree rooted at position p of a binary tree.

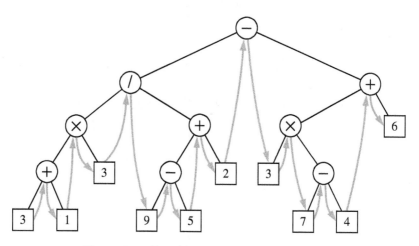

Figure 8.18: Inorder traversal of a binary tree.

The inorder traversal algorithm has several important applications. When using a binary tree to represent an arithmetic expression, as in Figure 8.18, the inorder traversal visits positions in a consistent order with the standard representation of the expression, as in $3 + 1 \times 3/9 - 5 + 2\ldots$ (albeit without parentheses).

Binary Search Trees

An important application of the inorder traversal algorithm arises when we store an ordered sequence of elements in a binary tree, defining a structure we call a ***binary search tree***. Let S be a set whose unique elements have an order relation. For example, S could be a set of integers. A binary search tree for S is a binary tree T such that, for each position p of T:

- Position p stores an element of S, denoted as $e(p)$.
- Elements stored in the left subtree of p (if any) are less than $e(p)$.
- Elements stored in the right subtree of p (if any) are greater than $e(p)$.

An example of a binary search tree is shown in Figure 8.19. The above properties assure that an inorder traversal of a binary search tree T visits the elements in nondecreasing order.

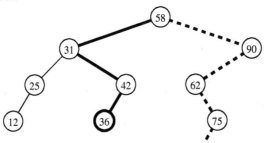

Figure 8.19: A binary search tree storing integers. The solid path is traversed when searching (successfully) for 36. The dashed path is traversed when searching (unsuccessfully) for 70.

We can use a binary search tree T for set S to find whether a given search value v is in S, by traversing a path down the tree T, starting at the root. At each internal position p encountered, we compare our search value v with the element $e(p)$ stored at p. If $v < e(p)$, then the search continues in the left subtree of p. If $v = e(p)$, then the search terminates successfully. If $v > e(p)$, then the search continues in the right subtree of p. Finally, if we reach an empty subtree, the search terminates unsuccessfully. In other words, a binary search tree can be viewed as a binary decision tree (recall Example 8.6), where the question asked at each internal node is whether the element at that node is less than, equal to, or larger than the element being searched for. We illustrate several examples of the search operation in Figure 8.19.

Note that the running time of searching in a binary search tree T is proportional to the height of T. Recall from Proposition 8.8 that the height of a binary tree with n nodes can be as small as $\log(n+1) - 1$ or as large as $n - 1$. Thus, binary search trees are most efficient when they have small height. Chapter 11 is devoted to the study of search trees.

8.4.4   Implementing Tree Traversals in Python

When first defining the tree ADT in Section 8.1.2, we stated that tree T should include support for the following methods:

> **T.positions( ):** Generate an iteration of all *positions* of tree T.

> **iter(T):** Generate an iteration of all *elements* stored within tree T.

At that time, we did not make any assumption about the order in which these iterations report their results. In this section, we demonstrate how any of the tree traversal algorithms we have introduced could be used to produce these iterations.

To begin, we note that it is easy to produce an iteration of all elements of a tree, if we rely on a presumed iteration of all positions. Therefore, support for the iter(T) syntax can be formally provided by a concrete implementation of the special method __iter__ within the abstract base class Tree. We rely on Python's generator syntax as the mechanism for producing iterations. (See Section 1.8.) Our implementation of Tree.__iter__ is given in Code Fragment 8.16.

```
75   def __iter__(self):
76       """Generate an iteration of the tree's elements."""
77       for p in self.positions( ):          # use same order as positions()
78           yield p.element( )                # but yield each element
```

Code Fragment 8.16: Iterating all elements of a Tree instance, based upon an iteration of the positions of the tree. This code should be included in the body of the Tree class.

To implement the positions method, we have a choice of tree traversal algorithms. Given that there are advantages to each of those traversal orders, we will provide independent implementations of each strategy that can be called directly by a user of our class. We can then trivially adapt one of those as a default order for the positions method of the tree ADT.

Preorder Traversal

We begin by considering the ***preorder traversal*** algorithm. We will support a public method with calling signature T.preorder( ) for tree T, which generates a preorder iteration of all positions within the tree. However, the recursive algorithm for generating a preorder traversal, as originally described in Code Fragment 8.12, must be parameterized by a specific position within the tree that serves as the root of a subtree to traverse. A standard solution for such a circumstance is to define a non-public utility method with the desired recursive parameterization, and then to have the public method preorder invoke the nonpublic method upon the root of the tree. Our implementation of such a design is given in Code Fragment 8.17.

```
79    def preorder(self):
80        """Generate a preorder iteration of positions in the tree."""
81        if not self.is_empty():
82            for p in self._subtree_preorder(self.root()):      # start recursion
83                yield p
84
85    def _subtree_preorder(self, p):
86        """Generate a preorder iteration of positions in subtree rooted at p."""
87        yield p                                    # visit p before its subtrees
88        for c in self.children(p):                 # for each child c
89            for other in self._subtree_preorder(c):   # do preorder of c's subtree
90                yield other                        # yielding each to our caller
```

Code Fragment 8.17: Support for performing a preorder traversal of a tree. This code should be included in the body of the Tree class.

Formally, both preorder and the utility _subtree_preorder are generators. Rather than perform a "visit" action from within this code, we yield each position to the caller and let the caller decide what action to perform at that position.

The _subtree_preorder method is the recursive one. However, because we are relying on generators rather than traditional functions, the recursion has a slightly different form. In order to yield all positions within the subtree of child c, we loop over the positions yielded by the recursive call self._subtree_preorder(c), and re-yield each position in the outer context. Note that if p is a leaf, the for loop over self.children(p) is trivial (this is the base case for our recursion).

We rely on a similar technique in the public preorder method to re-yield all positions that are generated by the recursive process starting at the root of the tree; if the tree is empty, nothing is yielded. At this point, we have provided full support for the preorder generator. A user of the class can therefore write code such as

```
for p in T.preorder():
    # "visit" position p
```

The official tree ADT requires that all trees support a positions method as well. To use a preorder traversal as the default order of iteration, we include the definition shown in Code Fragment 8.18 within our Tree class. Rather than loop over the results returned by the preorder call, we return the entire iteration as an object.

```
91    def positions(self):
92        """Generate an iteration of the tree's positions."""
93        return self.preorder()                  # return entire preorder iteration
```

Code Fragment 8.18: An implementation of the positions method for the Tree class that relies on a preorder traversal to generate the results.

Postorder Traversal

We can implement a postorder traversal using very similar technique as with a preorder traversal. The only difference is that within the recursive utility for a postorder we wait to yield position *p* until *after* we have recursively yield the positions in its subtrees. An implementation is given in Code Fragment 8.19.

```
94   def postorder(self):
95     """Generate a postorder iteration of positions in the tree."""
96     if not self.is_empty():
97       for p in self._subtree_postorder(self.root()):     # start recursion
98         yield p
99
100  def _subtree_postorder(self, p):
101    """Generate a postorder iteration of positions in subtree rooted at p."""
102    for c in self.children(p):                   # for each child c
103      for other in self._subtree_postorder(c):   # do postorder of c's subtree
104        yield other                              # yielding each to our caller
105    yield p                                      # visit p after its subtrees
```

Code Fragment 8.19: Support for performing a postorder traversal of a tree. This code should be included in the body of the Tree class.

Breadth-First Traversal

In Code Fragment 8.20, we provide an implementation of the breadth-first traversal algorithm in the context of our Tree class. Recall that the breadth-first traversal algorithm is not recursive; it relies on a queue of positions to manage the traversal process. Our implementation uses the LinkedQueue class from Section 7.1.2, although any implementation of the queue ADT would suffice.

Inorder Traversal for Binary Trees

The preorder, postorder, and breadth-first traversal algorithms are applicable to all trees, and so we include their implementations within the Tree abstract base class. Those methods are inherited by the abstract BinaryTree class, the concrete LinkedBinaryTree class, and any other dependent tree classes we might develop.

The inorder traversal algorithm, because it explicitly relies on the notion of a left and right child of a node, only applies to binary trees. We therefore include its definition within the body of the BinaryTree class. We use a similar technique to implement an inorder traversal (Code Fragment 8.21) as we did with preorder and postorder traversals.

```
106   def breadthfirst(self):
107     """Generate a breadth-first iteration of the positions of the tree."""
108     if not self.is_empty():
109       fringe = LinkedQueue()                # known positions not yet yielded
110       fringe.enqueue(self.root())           # starting with the root
111       while not fringe.is_empty():
112         p = fringe.dequeue()                # remove from front of the queue
113         yield p                             # report this position
114         for c in self.children(p):
115           fringe.enqueue(c)                 # add children to back of queue
```

Code Fragment 8.20: An implementation of a breadth-first traversal of a tree. This code should be included in the body of the Tree class.

```
37    def inorder(self):
38      """Generate an inorder iteration of positions in the tree."""
39      if not self.is_empty():
40        for p in self._subtree_inorder(self.root()):
41          yield p
42
43    def _subtree_inorder(self, p):
44      """Generate an inorder iteration of positions in subtree rooted at p."""
45      if self.left(p) is not None:        # if left child exists, traverse its subtree
46        for other in self._subtree_inorder(self.left(p)):
47          yield other
48      yield p                             # visit p between its subtrees
49      if self.right(p) is not None:       # if right child exists, traverse its subtree
50        for other in self._subtree_inorder(self.right(p)):
51          yield other
```

Code Fragment 8.21: Support for performing an inorder traversal of a binary tree. This code should be included in the BinaryTree class (given in Code Fragment 8.7).

For many applications of binary trees, an inorder traversal provides a natural iteration. We could make it the default for the BinaryTree class by overriding the positions method that was inherited from the Tree class (see Code Fragment 8.22).

```
52    # override inherited version to make inorder the default
53    def positions(self):
54      """Generate an iteration of the tree's positions."""
55      return self.inorder()               # make inorder the default
```

Code Fragment 8.22: Defining the BinaryTree.position method so that positions are reported using inorder traversal.

8.4.5 Applications of Tree Traversals

In this section, we demonstrate several representative applications of tree traversals, including some customizations of the standard traversal algorithms.

Table of Contents

When using a tree to represent the hierarchical structure of a document, a preorder traversal of the tree can naturally be used to produce a table of contents for the document. For example, the table of contents associated with the tree from Figure 8.15 is displayed in Figure 8.20. Part (a) of that figure gives a simple presentation with one element per line; part (b) shows a more attractive presentation produced by indenting each element based on its depth within the tree. A similar presentation could be used to display the contents of a computer's file system, based on its tree representation (as in Figure 8.3).

```
Paper                   Paper
Title                     Title
Abstract                  Abstract
§1                        §1
§1.1                        §1.1
§1.2                        §1.2
§2                        §2
§2.1                        §2.1
...                       ...

      (a)                      (b)
```

Figure 8.20: Table of contents for a document represented by the tree in Figure 8.15: (a) without indentation; (b) with indentation based on depth within the tree.

The unindented version of the table of contents, given a tree T, can be produced with the following code:

```
for p in T.preorder():
    print(p.element())
```

To produce the presentation of Figure 8.20(b), we indent each element with a number of spaces equal to twice the element's depth in the tree (hence, the root element was unindented). Although we could replace the body of the above loop with the statement print(2*T.depth(p)*' ' + str(p.element())), such an approach is unnecessarily inefficient. Although the work to produce the preorder traversal runs in $O(n)$ time, based on the analysis of Section 8.4.1, the calls to depth incur a hidden cost. Making a call to depth from every position of the tree results in $O(n^2)$ worst-case time, as noted when analyzing the algorithm height1 in Section 8.1.3.

A preferred approach to producing an indented table of contents is to redesign a top-down recursion that includes the current depth as an additional parameter. Such an implementation is provided in Code Fragment 8.23. This implementation runs in worst-case $O(n)$ time (except, technically, the time it takes to print strings of increasing lengths).

```
1  def preorder_indent(T, p, d):
2    """Print preorder representation of subtree of T rooted at p at depth d."""
3    print(2*d*' ' + str(p.element()))          # use depth for indentation
4    for c in T.children(p):
5      preorder_indent(T, c, d+1)               # child depth is d+1
```

Code Fragment 8.23: Efficient recursion for printing indented version of a pre-order traversal. On a complete tree T, the recursion should be started with form preorder_indent(T, T.root(), 0).

In the example of Figure 8.20, we were fortunate in that the numbering was embedded within the elements of the tree. More generally, we might be interested in using a preorder traversal to display the structure of a tree, with indentation and also explicit numbering that was not present in the tree. For example, we might display the tree from Figure 8.2 beginning as:

```
Electronics R'Us
   1 R&D
   2 Sales
      2.1 Domestic
      2.2 International
         2.2.1 Canada
         2.2.2 S. America
```

This is more challenging, because the numbers used as labels are implicit in the structure of the tree. A label depends on the index of each position, relative to its siblings, along the path from the root to the current position. To accomplish the task, we add a representation of that path as an additional parameter to the recursive signature. Specifically, we use a list of zero-indexed numbers, one for each position along the downward path, other than the root. (We convert those numbers to one-indexed form when printing.)

At the implementation level, we wish to avoid the inefficiency of duplicating such lists when sending a new parameter from one level of the recursion to the next. A standard solution is to share the same list instance throughout the recursion. At one level of the recursion, a new entry is temporarily added to the end of the list before making further recursive calls. In order to "leave no trace," that same block of code must remove the extraneous entry from the list before completing its task. An implementation based on this approach is given in Code Fragment 8.24.

```
1   def preorder_label(T, p, d, path):
2     """Print labeled representation of subtree of T rooted at p at depth d."""
3     label = '.'.join(str(j+1) for j in path)    # displayed labels are one-indexed
4     print(2*d*' ' + label, p.element())
5     path.append(0)                               # path entries are zero-indexed
6     for c in T.children(p):
7       preorder_label(T, c, d+1, path)            # child depth is d+1
8       path[-1] += 1
9     path.pop()
```

Code Fragment 8.24: Efficient recursion for printing an indented and *labeled* presentation of a preorder traversal.

Parenthetic Representations of a Tree

It is not possible to reconstruct a general tree, given only the preorder sequence of elements, as in Figure 8.20(a). Some additional context is necessary for the structure of the tree to be well defined. The use of indentation or numbered labels provides such context, with a very human-friendly presentation. However, there are more concise string representations of trees that are computer-friendly.

In this section, we explore one such representation. The ***parenthetic string representation*** $P(T)$ of tree T is recursively defined as follows. If T consists of a single position p, then

$$P(T) = \text{str}(p.\text{element}()).$$

Otherwise, it is defined recursively as,

$$P(T) = \text{str}(p.\text{element}()) + \text{'('} + P(T_1) + \text{', '} + \cdots + \text{', '} + P(T_k) + \text{')'}$$

where p is the root of T and $T_1, T_2, \ldots, T_k$ are the subtrees rooted at the children of p, which are given in order if T is an ordered tree. We are using "+" here to denote string concatenation. As an example, the parenthetic representation of the tree of Figure 8.2 would appear as follows (line breaks are cosmetic):

```
Electronics R'Us (R&D, Sales (Domestic, International (Canada,
S. America, Overseas (Africa, Europe, Asia, Australia)))),
Purchasing, Manufacturing (TV, CD, Tuner))
```

Although the parenthetic representation is essentially a preorder traversal, we cannot easily produce the additional punctuation using the formal implementation of preorder, as given in Code Fragment 8.17. The opening parenthesis must be produced just before the loop over a position's children and the closing parenthesis must be produced just after that loop. Furthermore, the separating commas must be produced. The Python function parenthesize, shown in Code Fragment 8.25, is a custom traversal that prints such a parenthetic string representation of a tree T.

```
1  def parenthesize(T, p):
2    """Print parenthesized representation of subtree of T rooted at p."""
3    print(p.element( ), end='')              # use of end avoids trailing newline
4    if not T.is_leaf(p):
5      first_time = True
6      for c in T.children(p):
7        sep = ' (' if first_time else ', '    # determine proper separator
8        print(sep, end='')
9        first_time = False                    # any future passes will not be the first
10       parenthesize(T, c)                    # recur on child
11     print(')', end='')                      # include closing parenthesis
```

Code Fragment 8.25: Function that prints parenthetic string representation of a tree.

Computing Disk Space

In Example 8.1, we considered the use of a tree as a model for a file-system structure, with internal positions representing directories and leaves representing files. In fact, when introducing the use of recursion back in Chapter 4, we specifically examined the topic of file systems (see Section 4.1.4). Although we did not explicitly model it as a tree at that time, we gave an implementation of an algorithm for computing the disk usage (Code Fragment 4.5).

The recursive computation of disk space is emblematic of a *postorder* traversal, as we cannot effectively compute the total space used by a directory until *after* we know the space that is used by its children directories. Unfortunately, the formal implementation of postorder, as given in Code Fragment 8.19 does not suffice for this purpose. As it visits the position of a directory, there is no easy way to discern which of the previous positions represent children of that directory, nor how much recursive disk space was allocated.

We would like to have a mechanism for children to return information to the parent as part of the traversal process. A custom solution to the disk space problem, with each level of recursion providing a return value to the (parent) caller, is provided in Code Fragment 8.26.

```
1  def disk_space(T, p):
2    """Return total disk space for subtree of T rooted at p."""
3    subtotal = p.element( ).space( )          # space used at position p
4    for c in T.children(p):
5      subtotal += disk_space(T, c)            # add child's space to subtotal
6    return subtotal
```

Code Fragment 8.26: Recursive computation of disk space for a tree. We assume that a space( ) method of each tree element reports the local space used at that position.

8.4.6 Euler Tours and the Template Method Pattern ⋆

The various applications described in Section 8.4.5 demonstrate the great power of recursive tree traversals. Unfortunately, they also show that the specific implementations of the preorder and postorder methods of our Tree class, or the inorder method of the BinaryTree class, are not general enough to capture the range of computations we desire. In some cases, we need more of a blending of the approaches, with initial work performed before recurring on subtrees, additional work performed after those recursions, and in the case of a binary tree, work performed between the two possible recursions. Furthermore, in some contexts it was important to know the depth of a position, or the complete path from the root to that position, or to return information from one level of the recursion to another. For each of the previous applications, we were able to develop a custom implementation to properly adapt the recursive ideas, but the great principles of object-oriented programming introduced in Section 2.1.1 include **adaptability** and **reusability**.

In this section, we develop a more general framework for implementing tree traversals based on a concept known as an **Euler tour traversal**. The Euler tour traversal of a general tree T can be informally defined as a "walk" around T, where we start by going from the root toward its leftmost child, viewing the edges of T as being "walls" that we always keep to our left. (See Figure 8.21.)

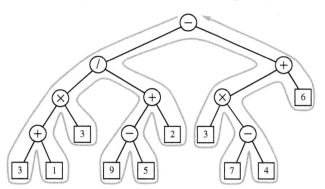

Figure 8.21: Euler tour traversal of a tree.

The complexity of the walk is $O(n)$, because it progresses exactly two times along each of the $n-1$ edges of the tree—once going downward along the edge, and later going upward along the edge. To unify the concept of preorder and postorder traversals, we can think of there being two notable "visits" to each position p:

- A "pre visit" occurs when first reaching the position, that is, when the walk passes immediately left of the node in our visualization.
- A "post visit" occurs when the walk later proceeds upward from that position, that is, when the walk passes to the right of the node in our visualization.

The process of an Euler tour can easily be viewed recursively. In between the "pre visit" and "post visit" of a given position will be a recursive tour of each of its subtrees. Looking at Figure 8.21 as an example, there is a contiguous portion of the entire tour that is itself an Euler tour of the subtree of the node with element "/". That tour contains two contiguous subtours, one traversing that position's left subtree and another traversing the right subtree. The pseudo-code for an Euler tour traversal of a subtree rooted at a position p is shown in Code Fragment 8.27.

Algorithm eulertour(T, p):

    perform the "pre visit" action for position p
    for each child c in T.children(p) **do**
       eulertour(T, c)   {recursively tour the subtree rooted at c}
    perform the "post visit" action for position p

Code Fragment 8.27: Algorithm eulertour for performing an Euler tour traversal of a subtree rooted at position p of a tree.

The Template Method Pattern

To provide a framework that is reusable and adaptable, we rely on an interesting object-oriented software design pattern, the ***template method pattern***. The template method pattern describes a generic computation mechanism that can be specialized for a particular application by redefining certain steps. To allow customization, the primary algorithm calls auxiliary functions known as ***hooks*** at designated steps of the process.

In the context of an Euler tour traversal, we define two separate hooks, a previsit hook that is called before the subtrees are traversed, and a postvisit hook that is called after the completion of the subtree traversals. Our implementation will take the form of an EulerTour class that manages the process, and defines trivial definitions for the hooks that do nothing. The traversal can be customized by defining a subclass of EulerTour and overriding one or both hooks to provide specialized behavior.

Python Implementation

Our implementation of an EulerTour class is provided in Code Fragment 8.28. The primary recursive process is defined in the nonpublic _tour method. A tour instance is created by sending a reference to a specific tree to the constructor, and then by calling the public execute method, which beings the tour and returns a final result of the computation.

```
1  class EulerTour:
2    """Abstract base class for performing Euler tour of a tree.
3
4    _hook_previsit and _hook_postvisit may be overridden by subclasses.
5    """
6    def __init__(self, tree):
7      """Prepare an Euler tour template for given tree."""
8      self._tree = tree
9
10   def tree(self):
11     """Return reference to the tree being traversed."""
12     return self._tree
13
14   def execute(self):
15     """Perform the tour and return any result from post visit of root."""
16     if len(self._tree) > 0:
17       return self._tour(self._tree.root( ), 0, [ ])      # start the recursion
18
19   def _tour(self, p, d, path):
20     """Perform tour of subtree rooted at Position p.
21
22     p        Position of current node being visited
23     d        depth of p in the tree
24     path     list of indices of children on path from root to p
25     """
26     self._hook_previsit(p, d, path)                        # "pre visit" p
27     results = [ ]
28     path.append(0)          # add new index to end of path before recursion
29     for c in self._tree.children(p):
30       results.append(self._tour(c, d+1, path))      # recur on child's subtree
31       path[-1] += 1               # increment index
32     path.pop( )                   # remove extraneous index from end of path
33     answer = self._hook_postvisit(p, d, path, results)        # "post visit" p
34     return answer
35
36   def _hook_previsit(self, p, d, path):                   # can be overridden
37     pass
38
39   def _hook_postvisit(self, p, d, path, results):         # can be overridden
40     pass
```

Code Fragment 8.28: An EulerTour base class providing a framework for performing Euler tour traversals of a tree.

Based on our experience of customizing traversals for sample applications Section 8.4.5, we build support into the primary EulerTour for maintaining the recursive depth and the representation of the recursive path through a tree, using the approach that we introduced in Code Fragment 8.24. We also provide a mechanism for one recursive level to return a value to another when post-processing. Formally, our framework relies on the following two hooks that can be specialized:

- method _hook_previsit(p, d, path)
  This function is called once for each position, immediately before its subtrees (if any) are traversed. Parameter p is a position in the tree, d is the depth of that position, and path is a list of indices, using the convention described in the discussion of Code Fragment 8.24. No return value is expected from this function.

- method _hook_postvisit(p, d, path, results)
  This function is called once for each position, immediately after its subtrees (if any) are traversed. The first three parameters use the same convention as did _hook_previsit. The final parameter is a list of objects that were provided as return values from the post visits of the respective subtrees of p. Any value returned by this call will be available to the parent of p during its postvisit.

For more complex tasks, subclasses of EulerTour may also choose to initialize and maintain additional state in the form of instance variables that can be accessed within the bodies of the hooks.

Using the Euler Tour Framework

To demonstrate the flexibility of our Euler tour framework, we revisit the sample applications from Section 8.4.5. As a simple example, an indented preorder traversal, akin to that originally produced by Code Fragment 8.23, can be generated with the simple subclass given in Code Fragment 8.29.

```
1  class PreorderPrintIndentedTour(EulerTour):
2    def _hook_previsit(self, p, d, path):
3      print(2*d*' ' + str(p.element()))
```

Code Fragment 8.29: A subclass of EulerTour that produces an indented preorder list of a tree's elements.

Such a tour would be started by creating an instance of the subclass for a given tree T, and invoking its execute method. This could be expressed as follows:

```
tour = PreorderPrintIndentedTour(T)
tour.execute()
```

A labeled version of an indented, preorder presentation, akin to Code Fragment 8.24, could be generated by the new subclass of EulerTour shown in Code Fragment 8.30.

```
1  class PreorderPrintIndentedLabeledTour(EulerTour):
2    def _hook_previsit(self, p, d, path):
3      label = '.'.join(str(j+1) for j in path)   # labels are one-indexed
4      print(2*d*' ' + label, p.element())
```

Code Fragment 8.30: A subclass of EulerTour that produces a labeled and indented, preorder list of a tree's elements.

To produce the parenthetic string representation, originally achieved with Code Fragment 8.25, we define a subclass that overrides both the previsit and postvisit hooks. Our new implementation is given in Code Fragment 8.31.

```
1   class ParenthesizeTour(EulerTour):
2     def _hook_previsit(self, p, d, path):
3       if path and path[-1] > 0:              # p follows a sibling
4         print(', ', end='')                  # so preface with comma
5       print(p.element(), end='')             # then print element
6       if not self.tree().is_leaf(p):         # if p has children
7         print(' (', end='')                  # print opening parenthesis
8
9     def _hook_postvisit(self, p, d, path, results):
10      if not self.tree().is_leaf(p):         # if p has children
11        print(')', end='')                   # print closing parenthesis
```

Code Fragment 8.31: A subclass of EulerTour that prints a parenthetic string representation of a tree.

Notice that in this implementation, we need to invoke a method on the tree instance that is being traversed from within the hooks. The public tree( ) method of the EulerTour class serves as an accessor for that tree.

Finally, the task of computing disk space, as originally implemented in Code Fragment 8.26, can be performed quite easily with the EulerTour subclass shown in Code Fragment 8.32. The postvisit result of the root will be returned by the call to execute( ).

```
1  class DiskSpaceTour(EulerTour):
2    def _hook_postvisit(self, p, d, path, results):
3      # we simply add space associated with p to that of its subtrees
4      return p.element().space() + sum(results)
```

Code Fragment 8.32: A subclass of EulerTour that computes disk space for a tree.

The Euler Tour Traversal of a Binary Tree

In Section 8.4.6, we introduced the concept of an Euler tour traversal of a general graph, using the template method pattern in designing the EulerTour class. That class provided methods _hook_previsit and _hook_postvisit that could be overridden to customize a tour. In Code Fragment 8.33 we provide a BinaryEulerTour specialization that includes an additional _hook_invisit that is called once for each position—after its left subtree is traversed, but before its right subtree is traversed.

Our implementation of BinaryEulerTour replaces the original _tour utility to specialize to the case in which a node has at most two children. If a node has only one child, a tour differentiates between whether that is a left child or a right child, with the "in visit" taking place after the visit of a sole left child, but before the visit of a sole right child. In the case of a leaf, the three hooks are called in succession.

```
 1  class BinaryEulerTour(EulerTour):
 2    """Abstract base class for performing Euler tour of a binary tree.
 3
 4    This version includes an additional _hook_invisit that is called after the tour
 5    of the left subtree (if any), yet before the tour of the right subtree (if any).
 6
 7    Note: Right child is always assigned index 1 in path, even if no left sibling.
 8    """
 9    def _tour(self, p, d, path):
10      results = [None, None]              # will update with results of recursions
11      self._hook_previsit(p, d, path)                          # "pre visit" for p
12      if self._tree.left(p) is not None:                     # consider left child
13        path.append(0)
14        results[0] = self._tour(self._tree.left(p), d+1, path)
15        path.pop()
16      self._hook_invisit(p, d, path)                          # "in visit" for p
17      if self._tree.right(p) is not None:                   # consider right child
18        path.append(1)
19        results[1] = self._tour(self._tree.right(p), d+1, path)
20        path.pop()
21      answer = self._hook_postvisit(p, d, path, results)       # "post visit" p
22      return answer
23
24    def _hook_invisit(self, p, d, path): pass                 # can be overridden
```

Code Fragment 8.33: A BinaryEulerTour base class providing a specialized tour for binary trees. The original EulerTour base class was given in Code Fragment 8.28.

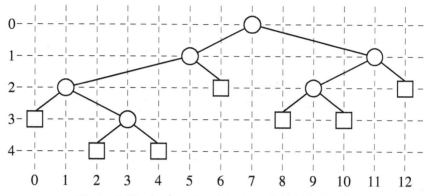

Figure 8.22: An inorder drawing of a binary tree.

To demonstrate use of the BinaryEulerTour framework, we develop a subclass that computes a graphical layout of a binary tree, as shown in Figure 8.22. The geometry is determined by an algorithm that assigns x- and y-coordinates to each position p of a binary tree T using the following two rules:

- $x(p)$ is the number of positions visited before p in an inorder traversal of T.
- $y(p)$ is the depth of p in T.

In this application, we take the convention common in computer graphics that x-coordinates increase left to right and y-coordinates increase top to bottom. So the origin is in the upper left corner of the computer screen.

Code Fragment 8.34 provides an implementation of a BinaryLayout subclass that implements the above algorithm for assigning (x,y) coordinates to the element stored at each position of a binary tree. We adapt the BinaryEulerTour framework by introducing additional state in the form of a _count instance variable that represents the number of "in visits" that we have performed. The x-coordinate for each position is set according to that counter.

```
1  class BinaryLayout(BinaryEulerTour):
2    """Class for computing (x,y) coordinates for each node of a binary tree."""
3    def __init__(self, tree):
4      super().__init__(tree)              # must call the parent constructor
5      self._count = 0                     # initialize count of processed nodes
6
7    def _hook_invisit(self, p, d, path):
8      p.element().setX(self._count)       # x-coordinate serialized by count
9      p.element().setY(d)                 # y-coordinate is depth
10     self._count += 1                    # advance count of processed nodes
```

Code Fragment 8.34: A BinaryLayout class that computes coordinates at which to draw positions of a binary tree. We assume that the element type for the original tree supports setX and setY methods.

8.5   Case Study: An Expression Tree

In Example 8.7, we introduced the use of a binary tree to represent the structure of an arithmetic expression. In this section, we define a new ExpressionTree class that provides support for constructing such trees, and for displaying and evaluating the arithmetic expression that such a tree represents. Our ExpressionTree class is defined as a subclass of LinkedBinaryTree, and we rely on the nonpublic mutators to construct such trees. Each internal node must store a string that defines a binary operator (e.g., '+'), and each leaf must store a numeric value (or a string representing a numeric value).

Our eventual goal is to build arbitrarily complex expression trees for compound arithmetic expressions such as $(((3+1) \times 4)/((9-5)+2))$. However, it suffices for the ExpressionTree class to support two basic forms of initialization:

ExpressionTree(value): Create a tree storing the given value at the root.

ExpressionTree(op, E_1, E_2): Create a tree storing string op at the root (e.g., +), and with the structures of existing ExpressionTree instances E_1 and E_2 as the left and right subtrees of the root, respectively.

Such a constructor for the ExpressionTree class is given in Code Fragment 8.35. The class formally inherits from LinkedBinaryTree, so it has access to all the non-public update methods that were defined in Section 8.3.1. We use _add_root to create an initial root of the tree storing the token provided as the first parameter. Then we perform run-time checking of the parameters to determine whether the caller invoked the one-parameter version of the constructor (in which case, we are done), or the three-parameter form. In that case, we use the inherited _attach method to incorporate the structure of the existing trees as subtrees of the root.

Composing a Parenthesized String Representation

A string representation of an existing expression tree instance, for example, as '(((3+1)x4)/((9-5)+2))', can be produced by displaying tree elements using an inorder traversal, but with opening and closing parentheses inserted with a preorder and postorder step, respectively. In the context of an ExpressionTree class, we support a special __str__ method (see Section 2.3.2) that returns the appropriate string. Because it is more efficient to first build a sequence of individual strings to be joined together (see discussion of "Composing Strings" in Section 5.4.2), the implementation of __str__ relies on a nonpublic, recursive method named _parenthesize_recur that appends a series of strings to a list. These methods are included in Code 8.35.

```
1   class ExpressionTree(LinkedBinaryTree):
2     """An arithmetic expression tree."""
3
4     def __init__(self, token, left=None, right=None):
5       """Create an expression tree.
6
7       In a single parameter form, token should be a leaf value (e.g., '42'),
8       and the expression tree will have that value at an isolated node.
9
10      In a three-parameter version, token should be an operator,
11      and left and right should be existing ExpressionTree instances
12      that become the operands for the binary operator.
13      """
14      super().__init__()                     # LinkedBinaryTree initialization
15      if not isinstance(token, str):
16        raise TypeError('Token must be a string')
17      self._add_root(token)                  # use inherited, nonpublic method
18      if left is not None:                   # presumably three-parameter form
19        if token not in '+-*x/':
20          raise ValueError('token must be valid operator')
21        self._attach(self.root(), left, right)  # use inherited, nonpublic method
22
23    def __str__(self):
24      """Return string representation of the expression."""
25      pieces = [ ]                           # sequence of piecewise strings to compose
26      self._parenthesize_recur(self.root(), pieces)
27      return ''.join(pieces)
28
29    def _parenthesize_recur(self, p, result):
30      """Append piecewise representation of p's subtree to resulting list."""
31      if self.is_leaf(p):
32        result.append(str(p.element()))                  # leaf value as a string
33      else:
34        result.append('(')                               # opening parenthesis
35        self._parenthesize_recur(self.left(p), result)   # left subtree
36        result.append(p.element())                       # operator
37        self._parenthesize_recur(self.right(p), result)  # right subtree
38        result.append(')')                               # closing parenthesis
```

Code Fragment 8.35: The beginning of an ExpressionTree class.

Expression Tree Evaluation

The numeric evaluation of an expression tree can be accomplished with a simple application of a postorder traversal. If we know the values represented by the two subtrees of an internal position, we can calculate the result of the computation that position designates. Pseudo-code for the recursive evaluation of the value represented by a subtree rooted at position *p* is given in Code Fragment 8.36.

Algorithm evaluate_recur(p):
   if p is a leaf **then**
      return the value stored at p
   else
      let ○ be the operator stored at p
      x = evaluate_recur(left(p))
      y = evaluate_recur(right(p))
      return x ○ y

Code Fragment 8.36: Algorithm evaluate_recur for evaluating the expression represented by a subtree of an arithmetic expression tree rooted at position p.

To implement this algorithm in the context of a Python ExpressionTree class, we provide a public evaluate method that is invoked on instance T as T.evaluate( ). Code Fragment 8.37 provides such an implementation, relying on a nonpublic _evaluate_recur method that computes the value of a designated subtree.

```
39    def evaluate(self):
40       """Return the numeric result of the expression."""
41       return self._evaluate_recur(self.root())
42
43    def _evaluate_recur(self, p):
44       """Return the numeric result of subtree rooted at p."""
45       if self.is_leaf(p):
46          return float(p.element())        # we assume element is numeric
47       else:
48          op = p.element()
49          left_val = self._evaluate_recur(self.left(p))
50          right_val = self._evaluate_recur(self.right(p))
51          if op == '+': return left_val + right_val
52          elif op == '-': return left_val - right_val
53          elif op == '/': return left_val / right_val
54          else: return left_val * right_val       # treat 'x' or '*' as multiplication
```

Code Fragment 8.37: Support for evaluating an ExpressionTree instance.

Building an Expression Tree

The constructor for the ExpressionTree class, from Code Fragment 8.35, provides basic functionality for combining existing trees to build larger expression trees. However, the question still remains how to construct a tree that represents an expression for a given string, such as '(((3+1)x4)/((9−5)+2))'.

To automate this process, we rely on a bottom-up construction algorithm, assuming that a string can first be tokenized so that multidigit numbers are treated atomically (see Exercise R-8.30), and that the expression is fully parenthesized. The algorithm uses a stack S while scanning tokens of the input expression E to find values, operators, and right parentheses. (Left parentheses are ignored.)

- When we see an operator ○, we push that string on the stack.
- When we see a literal value v, we create a single-node expression tree T storing v, and push T on the stack.
- When we see a right parenthesis, ')', we pop the top three items from the stack S, which represent a subexpression $(E_1 \circ E_2)$. We then construct a tree T using trees for E_1 and E_2 as subtrees of the root storing ○, and push the resulting tree T back on the stack.

We repeat this until the expression E has been processed, at which time the top element on the stack is the expression tree for E. The total running time is $O(n)$.

An implementation of this algorithm is given in Code Fragment 8.38 in the form of a stand-alone function named build_expression_tree, which produces and returns an appropriate ExpressionTree instance, assuming the input has been tokenized.

```
1  def build_expression_tree(tokens):
2    """Returns an ExpressionTree based upon by a tokenized expression."""
3    S = [ ]                                      # we use Python list as stack
4    for t in tokens:
5      if t in '+-x*/':                           # t is an operator symbol
6        S.append(t)                              # push the operator symbol
7      elif t not in '()':                        # consider t to be a literal
8        S.append(ExpressionTree(t))              # push trivial tree storing value
9      elif t == ')':            # compose a new tree from three constituent parts
10       right = S.pop( )                          # right subtree as per LIFO
11       op = S.pop( )                             # operator symbol
12       left = S.pop( )                           # left subtree
13       S.append(ExpressionTree(op, left, right)) # repush tree
14     # we ignore a left parenthesis
15   return S.pop()
```

Code Fragment 8.38: Implementation of a build_expression_tree that produces an ExpressionTree from a sequence of tokens representing an arithmetic expression.

8.6   Exercises

For help with exercises, please visit the site, www.wiley.com/college/goodrich.

Reinforcement

R-8.1 The following questions refer to the tree of Figure 8.3.

    a. Which node is the root?

    b. What are the internal nodes?

    c. How many descendants does node cs016/ have?

    d. How many ancestors does node cs016/ have?

    e. What are the siblings of node homeworks/?

    f. Which nodes are in the subtree rooted at node projects/?

    g. What is the depth of node papers/?

    h. What is the height of the tree?

R-8.2 Show a tree achieving the worst-case running time for algorithm depth.

R-8.3 Give a justification of Proposition 8.4.

R-8.4 What is the running time of a call to T._height2(p) when called on a position p distinct from the root of T? (See Code Fragment 8.5.)

R-8.5 Describe an algorithm, relying only on the BinaryTree operations, that counts the number of leaves in a binary tree that are the *left* child of their respective parent.

R-8.6 Let T be an n-node binary tree that may be improper. Describe how to represent T by means of a ***proper*** binary tree T' with $O(n)$ nodes.

R-8.7 What are the minimum and maximum number of internal and external nodes in an improper binary tree with n nodes?

R-8.8 Answer the following questions so as to justify Proposition 8.8.

    a. What is the minimum number of external nodes for a proper binary tree with height h? Justify your answer.

    b. What is the maximum number of external nodes for a proper binary tree with height h? Justify your answer.

    c. Let T be a proper binary tree with height h and n nodes. Show that

$$\log(n+1) - 1 \le h \le (n-1)/2.$$

    d. For which values of n and h can the above lower and upper bounds on h be attained with equality?

R-8.9 Give a proof by induction of Proposition 8.9.

R-8.10 Give a direct implementation of the num_children method within the class BinaryTree.

R-8.11 Find the value of the arithmetic expression associated with each subtree of the binary tree of Figure 8.8.

R-8.12 Draw an arithmetic expression tree that has four external nodes, storing the numbers 1, 5, 6, and 7 (with each number stored in a distinct external node, but not necessarily in this order), and has three internal nodes, each storing an operator from the set $\{+, -, \times, /\}$, so that the value of the root is 21. The operators may return and act on fractions, and an operator may be used more than once.

R-8.13 Draw the binary tree representation of the following arithmetic expression: "$(((5 + 2) * (2 - 1))/((2 + 9) + ((7 - 2) - 1)) * 8)$".

R-8.14 Justify Table 8.2, summarizing the running time of the methods of a tree represented with a linked structure, by providing, for each method, a description of its implementation, and an analysis of its running time.

R-8.15 The LinkedBinaryTree class provides only nonpublic versions of the update methods discussed on page 319. Implement a simple subclass named MutableLinkedBinaryTree that provides public wrapper functions for each of the inherited nonpublic update methods.

R-8.16 Let T be a binary tree with n nodes, and let $f()$ be the level numbering function of the positions of T, as given in Section 8.3.2.

    a. Show that, for every position p of T, $f(p) \leq 2^n - 2$.

    b. Show an example of a binary tree with seven nodes that attains the above upper bound on $f(p)$ for some position p.

R-8.17 Show how to use the Euler tour traversal to compute the level number $f(p)$, as defined in Section 8.3.2, of each position in a binary tree T.

R-8.18 Let T be a binary tree with n positions that is realized with an array representation A, and let $f()$ be the level numbering function of the positions of T, as given in Section 8.3.2. Give pseudo-code descriptions of each of the methods root, parent, left, right, is_leaf, and is_root.

R-8.19 Our definition of the level numbering function $f(p)$, as given in Section 8.3.2, began with the root having number 0. Some authors prefer to use a level numbering $g(p)$ in which the root is assigned number 1, because it simplifies the arithmetic for finding neighboring positions. Redo Exercise R-8.18, but assuming that we use a level numbering $g(p)$ in which the root is assigned number 1.

R-8.20 Draw a binary tree T that simultaneously satisfies the following:

- Each internal node of T stores a single character.
- A *preorder* traversal of T yields EXAMFUN.
- An *inorder* traversal of T yields MAFXUEN.

R-8.21 In what order are positions visited during a preorder traversal of the tree of Figure 8.8?

R-8.22 In what order are positions visited during a postorder traversal of the tree of Figure 8.8?

R-8.23 Let T be an ordered tree with more than one node. Is it possible that the preorder traversal of T visits the nodes in the same order as the postorder traversal of T? If so, give an example; otherwise, explain why this cannot occur. Likewise, is it possible that the preorder traversal of T visits the nodes in the reverse order of the postorder traversal of T? If so, give an example; otherwise, explain why this cannot occur.

R-8.24 Answer the previous question for the case when T is a proper binary tree with more than one node.

R-8.25 Consider the example of a breadth-first traversal given in Figure 8.17. Using the annotated numbers from that figure, describe the contents of the queue before each pass of the while loop in Code Fragment 8.14. To get started, the queue has contents $\{1\}$ before the first pass, and contents $\{2,3,4\}$ before the second pass.

R-8.26 The collections.deque class supports an extend method that adds a collection of elements to the end of the queue at once. Reimplement the breadthfirst method of the Tree class to take advantage of this feature.

R-8.27 Give the output of the function parenthesize(T, T.root()), as described in Code Fragment 8.25, when T is the tree of Figure 8.8.

R-8.28 What is the running time of parenthesize(T, T.root()), as given in Code Fragment 8.25, for a tree T with n nodes?

R-8.29 Describe, in pseudo-code, an algorithm for computing the number of descendants of each node of a binary tree. The algorithm should be based on the Euler tour traversal.

R-8.30 The build_expression_tree method of the ExpressionTree class requires input that is an iterable of string tokens. We used a convenient example, '(((3+1)x4)/((9-5)+2))', in which each character is its own token, so that the string itself sufficed as input to build_expression_tree. In general, a string, such as '(35 + 14)', must be explicitly tokenized into list ['(', '35', '+', '14', ')'] so as to ignore whitespace and to recognize multidigit numbers as a single token. Write a utility method, tokenize(raw), that returns such a list of tokens for a raw string.

Creativity

C-8.31 Define the *internal path length*, $I(T)$, of a tree T to be the sum of the depths of all the internal positions in T. Likewise, define the *external path length*, $E(T)$, of a tree T to be the sum of the depths of all the external positions in T. Show that if T is a proper binary tree with n positions, then $E(T) = I(T) + n - 1$.

C-8.32 Let T be a (not necessarily proper) binary tree with n nodes, and let D be the sum of the depths of all the external nodes of T. Show that if T has the minimum number of external nodes possible, then D is $O(n)$ and if T has the maximum number of external nodes possible, then D is $O(n \log n)$.

C-8.33 Let T be a (possibly improper) binary tree with n nodes, and let D be the sum of the depths of all the external nodes of T. Describe a configuration for T such that D is $\Omega(n^2)$. Such a tree would be the worst case for the asymptotic running time of method _height1 (Code Fragment 8.4).

C-8.34 For a tree T, let n_I denote the number of its internal nodes, and let n_E denote the number of its external nodes. Show that if every internal node in T has exactly 3 children, then $n_E = 2n_I + 1$.

C-8.35 Two ordered trees T' and T'' are said to be *isomorphic* if one of the following holds:

- Both T' and T'' are empty.
- The roots of T' and T'' have the same number $k \geq 0$ of subtrees, and the ith such subtree of T' is isomorphic to the ith such subtree of T'' for $i = 1, \ldots, k$.

Design an algorithm that tests whether two given ordered trees are isomorphic. What is the running time of your algorithm?

C-8.36 Show that there are more than 2^n improper binary trees with n internal nodes such that no pair are isomorphic (see Exercise C-8.35).

C-8.37 If we exclude isomorphic trees (see Exercise C-8.35), exactly how many proper binary trees exist with exactly 4 leaves?

C-8.38 Add support in LinkedBinaryTree for a method, _delete_subtree(p), that removes the entire subtree rooted at position p, making sure to maintain the count on the size of the tree. What is the running time of your implementation?

C-8.39 Add support in LinkedBinaryTree for a method, _swap(p,q), that has the effect of restructuring the tree so that the node referenced by p takes the place of the node referenced by q, and vice versa. Make sure to properly handle the case when the nodes are adjacent.

C-8.40 We can simplify parts of our LinkedBinaryTree implementation if we make use of of a single sentinel node, referenced as the _sentinel member of the tree instance, such that the sentinel is the parent of the real root of the tree, and the root is referenced as the left child of the sentinel. Furthermore, the sentinel will take the place of None as the value of the _left or _right member for a node without such a child. Give a new implementation of the update methods _delete and _attach, assuming such a representation.

C-8.41 Describe how to clone a LinkedBinaryTree instance representing a proper binary tree, with use of the _attach method.

C-8.42 Describe how to clone a LinkedBinaryTree instance representing a (not necessarily proper) binary tree, with use of the _add_left and add_right methods.

C-8.43 We can define a *binary tree representation* T' for an ordered general tree T as follows (see Figure 8.23):

- For each position p of T, there is an associated position p' of T'.
- If p is a leaf of T, then p' in T' does not have a left child; otherwise the left child of p' is q', where q is the first child of p in T.
- If p has a sibling q ordered immediately after it in T, then q' is the right child of p' in T; otherwise p' does not have a right child.

Given such a representation T' of a general ordered tree T, answer each of the following questions:

- a. Is a preorder traversal of T' equivalent to a preorder traversal of T?
- b. Is a postorder traversal of T' equivalent to a postorder traversal of T?
- c. Is an inorder traversal of T' equivalent to one of the standard traversals of T? If so, which one?

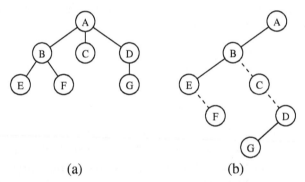

(a)   (b)

Figure 8.23: Representation of a tree with a binary tree: (a) tree T; (b) binary tree T' for T. The dashed edges connect nodes of T' that are siblings in T.

C-8.44 Give an efficient algorithm that computes and prints, for every position p of a tree T, the element of p followed by the height of p's subtree.

C-8.45 Give an $O(n)$-time algorithm for computing the depths of all positions of a tree T, where n is the number of nodes of T.

C-8.46 The *path length* of a tree T is the sum of the depths of all positions in T. Describe a linear-time method for computing the path length of a tree T.

C-8.47 The *balance factor* of an internal position p of a proper binary tree is the difference between the heights of the right and left subtrees of p. Show how to specialize the Euler tour traversal of Section 8.4.6 to print the balance factors of all the internal nodes of a proper binary tree.

C-8.48 Given a proper binary tree T, define the *reflection* of T to be the binary tree T' such that each node v in T is also in T', but the left child of v in T is v's right child in T' and the right child of v in T is v's left child in T'. Show that a preorder traversal of a proper binary tree T is the same as the postorder traversal of T's reflection, but in reverse order.

C-8.49 Let the *rank* of a position p during a traversal be defined such that the first element visited has rank 1, the second element visited has rank 2, and so on. For each position p in a tree T, let $\text{pre}(p)$ be the rank of p in a preorder traversal of T, let $\text{post}(p)$ be the rank of p in a postorder traversal of T, let $\text{depth}(p)$ be the depth of p, and let $\text{desc}(p)$ be the number of descendants of p, including p itself. Derive a formula defining $\text{post}(p)$ in terms of $\text{desc}(p)$, $\text{depth}(p)$, and $\text{pre}(p)$, for each node p in T.

C-8.50 Design algorithms for the following operations for a binary tree T:
- preorder_next(p): Return the position visited after p in a preorder traversal of T (or None if p is the last node visited).
- inorder_next(p): Return the position visited after p in an inorder traversal of T (or None if p is the last node visited).
- postorder_next(p): Return the position visited after p in a postorder traversal of T (or None if p is the last node visited).

What are the worst-case running times of your algorithms?

C-8.51 To implement the preorder method of the LinkedBinaryTree class, we relied on the convenience of Python's generator syntax and the yield statement. Give an alternative implementation of preorder that returns an explicit instance of a nested iterator class. (See Section 2.3.4 for discussion of iterators.)

C-8.52 Algorithm preorder_draw draws a binary tree T by assigning x- and y-coordinates to each position p such that $x(p)$ is the number of nodes preceding p in the preorder traversal of T and $y(p)$ is the depth of p in T.
  a. Show that the drawing of T produced by preorder_draw has no pairs of crossing edges.
  b. Redraw the binary tree of Figure 8.22 using preorder_draw.

C-8.53 Redo the previous problem for the algorithm postorder_draw that is similar to preorder_draw except that it assigns $x(p)$ to be the number of nodes preceding position p in the postorder traversal.

C-8.54 Design an algorithm for drawing *general* trees, using a style similar to the inorder traversal approach for drawing binary trees.

C-8.55 Exercise P-4.27 described the walk function of the os module. This function performs a traversal of the implicit tree represented by the file system. Read the formal documentation for the function, and in particular its use of an optional Boolean parameter named topdown. Describe how its behavior relates to tree traversal algorithms described in this chapter.

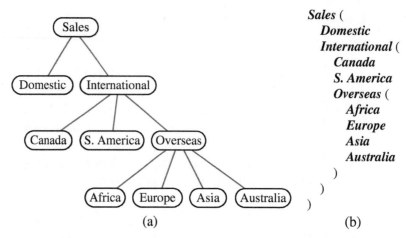

Figure 8.24: (a) Tree T; (b) indented parenthetic representation of T.

C-8.56 The *indented parenthetic representation* of a tree T is a variation of the parenthetic representation of T (see Code Fragment 8.25) that uses indentation and line breaks as illustrated in Figure 8.24. Give an algorithm that prints this representation of a tree.

C-8.57 Let T be a binary tree with n positions. Define a *Roman position* to be a position p in T, such that the number of descendants in p's left subtree differ from the number of descendants in p's right subtree by at most 5. Describe a linear-time method for finding each position p of T, such that p is not a Roman position, but all of p's descendants are Roman.

C-8.58 Let T be a tree with n positions. Define the *lowest common ancestor* (LCA) between two positions p and q as the lowest position in T that has both p and q as descendants (where we allow a position to be a descendant of itself). Given two positions p and q, describe an efficient algorithm for finding the LCA of p and q. What is the running time of your algorithm?

C-8.59 Let T be a binary tree with n positions, and, for any position p in T, let d_p denote the depth of p in T. The *distance* between two positions p and q in T is $d_p + d_q - 2d_a$, where a is the lowest common ancestor (LCA) of p and q. The *diameter* of T is the maximum distance between two positions in T. Describe an efficient algorithm for finding the diameter of T. What is the running time of your algorithm?

C-8.60 Suppose each position p of a binary tree T is labeled with its value $f(p)$ in a level numbering of T. Design a fast method for determining $f(a)$ for the lowest common ancestor (LCA), a, of two positions p and q in T, given $f(p)$ and $f(q)$. You do not need to find position a, just value $f(a)$.

C-8.61 Give an alternative implementation of the build_expression_tree method of the ExpressionTree class that relies on recursion to perform an implicit Euler tour of the tree that is being built.

C-8.62 Note that the build_expression_tree function of the ExpressionTree class is written in such a way that a leaf token can be any string; for example, it parses the expression '(a*(b+c))'. However, within the evaluate method, an error would occur when attempting to convert a leaf token to a number. Modify the evaluate method to accept an optional Python dictionary that can be used to map such string variables to numeric values, with a syntax such as T.evaluate({'a':3, 'b':1, 'c':5}). In this way, the same algebraic expression can be evaluated using different values.

C-8.63 As mentioned in Exercise C-6.22, *postfix notation* is an unambiguous way of writing an arithmetic expression without parentheses. It is defined so that if "(exp_1) **op** (exp_2)" is a normal (infix) fully parenthesized expression with operation **op**, then its postfix equivalent is "$pexp_1$ $pexp_2$ **op**", where $pexp_1$ is the postfix version of exp_1 and $pexp_2$ is the postfix version of exp_2. The postfix version of a single number or variable is just that number or variable. So, for example, the postfix version of the infix expression "$((5+2)*(8-3))/4$" is "$5\ 2+8\ 3-*4\ /$". Implement a postfix method of the ExpressionTree class of Section 8.5 that produces the postfix notation for the given expression.

Projects

P-8.64 Implement the binary tree ADT using the array-based representation described in Section 8.3.2.

P-8.65 Implement the tree ADT using a linked structure as described in Section 8.3.3. Provide a reasonable set of update methods for your tree.

P-8.66 The memory usage for the LinkedBinaryTree class can be streamlined by removing the parent reference from each node, and instead having each Position instance keep a member, _path, that is a list of nodes representing the entire path from the root to that position. (This generally saves memory because there are typically relatively few stored position instances.) Reimplement the LinkedBinaryTree class using this strategy.

P-8.67 A *slicing floor plan* divides a rectangle with horizontal and vertical sides using horizontal and vertical *cuts*. (See Figure 8.25a.) A slicing floor plan can be represented by a proper binary tree, called a *slicing tree*, whose internal nodes represent the cuts, and whose external nodes represent the *basic rectangles* into which the floor plan is decomposed by the cuts. (See Figure 8.25b.) The *compaction problem* for a slicing floor plan is defined as follows. Assume that each basic rectangle of a slicing floor plan is assigned a minimum width w and a minimum height h. The compaction problem is to find the smallest possible height and width for each rectangle of the slicing floor plan that is compatible with the minimum dimensions

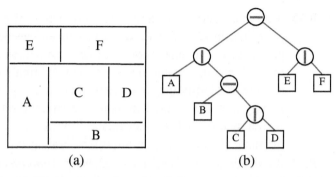

(a)   (b)

Figure 8.25: (a) Slicing floor plan; (b) slicing tree associated with the floor plan.

of the basic rectangles. Namely, this problem requires the assignment of values $h(p)$ and $w(p)$ to each position p of the slicing tree such that:

$$w(p) = \begin{cases} w & \text{if } p \text{ is a leaf whose basic rectangle has minimum width } w \\[1.5em] \max(w(\ell), w(r)) & \text{if } p \text{ is an internal position, associated with a horizontal cut, with left child } \ell \text{ and right child } r \\[1.5em] w(\ell) + w(r) & \text{if } p \text{ is an internal position, associated with a vertical cut, with left child } \ell \text{ and right child } r \end{cases}$$

$$h(p) = \begin{cases} h & \text{if } p \text{ is a leaf node whose basic rectangle has minimum height } h \\[1.5em] h(\ell) + h(r) & \text{if } p \text{ is an internal position, associated with a horizontal cut, with left child } \ell \text{ and right child } r \\[1.5em] \max(h(\ell), h(r)) & \text{if } p \text{ is an internal position, associated with a vertical cut, with left child } \ell \text{ and right child } r \end{cases}$$

Design a data structure for slicing floor plans that supports the operations:

- Create a floor plan consisting of a single basic rectangle.
- Decompose a basic rectangle by means of a horizontal cut.
- Decompose a basic rectangle by means of a vertical cut.
- Assign minimum height and width to a basic rectangle.
- Draw the slicing tree associated with the floor plan.
- Compact and draw the floor plan.

P-8.68 Write a program that can play Tic-Tac-Toe effectively. (See Section 5.6.) To do this, you will need to create a *game tree* T, which is a tree where each position corresponds to a *game configuration*, which, in this case, is a representation of the Tic-Tac-Toe board. (See Section 8.4.2.) The root corresponds to the initial configuration. For each internal position p in T, the children of p correspond to the game states we can reach from p's game state in a single legal move for the appropriate player, A (the first player) or B (the second player). Positions at even depths correspond to moves for A and positions at odd depths correspond to moves for B. Leaves are either final game states or are at a depth beyond which we do not want to explore. We score each leaf with a value that indicates how good this state is for player A. In large games, like chess, we have to use a heuristic scoring function, but for small games, like Tic-Tac-Toe, we can construct the entire game tree and score leaves as $+1$, 0, -1, indicating whether player A has a win, draw, or lose in that configuration. A good algorithm for choosing moves is *minimax*. In this algorithm, we assign a score to each internal position p in T, such that if p represents A's turn, we compute p's score as the maximum of the scores of p's children (which corresponds to A's optimal play from p). If an internal node p represents B's turn, then we compute p's score as the minimum of the scores of p's children (which corresponds to B's optimal play from p).

P-8.69 Implement the tree ADT using the binary tree representation described in Exercise C-8.43. You may adapt the LinkedBinaryTree implementation.

P-8.70 Write a program that takes as input a general tree T and a position p of T and converts T to another tree with the same set of position adjacencies, but now with p as its root.

Chapter Notes

Discussions of the classic preorder, inorder, and postorder tree traversal methods can be found in Knuth's *Fundamental Algorithms* book [64]. The Euler tour traversal technique comes from the parallel algorithms community; it is introduced by Tarjan and Vishkin [93] and is discussed by JáJá [54] and by Karp and Ramachandran [58]. The algorithm for drawing a tree is generally considered to be a part of the "folklore" of graph-drawing algorithms. The reader interested in graph drawing is referred to the book by Di Battista, Eades, Tamassia, and Tollis [34] and the survey by Tamassia and Liotta [92]. The puzzle in Exercise R-8.12 was communicated by Micha Sharir.

Chapter 9

Priority Queues

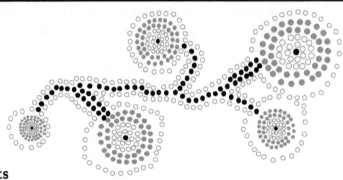

Contents

9.1 The Priority Queue Abstract Data Type

9.1.1 Priorities

In Chapter 6, we introduced the queue ADT as a collection of objects that are added and removed according to the *first-in, first-out* (*FIFO*) principle. A company's customer call center embodies such a model in which waiting customers are told "calls will be answered in the order that they were received." In that setting, a new call is added to the back of the queue, and each time a customer service representative becomes available, he or she is connected with the call that is removed from the front of the call queue.

In practice, there are many applications in which a queue-like structure is used to manage objects that must be processed in some way, but for which the first-in, first-out policy does not suffice. Consider, for example, an air-traffic control center that has to decide which flight to clear for landing from among many approaching the airport. This choice may be influenced by factors such as each plane's distance from the runway, time spent waiting in a holding pattern, or amount of remaining fuel. It is unlikely that the landing decisions are based purely on a FIFO policy.

There are other situations in which a "first come, first serve" policy might seem reasonable, yet for which other priorities come into play. To use another airline analogy, suppose a certain flight is fully booked an hour prior to departure. Because of the possibility of cancellations, the airline maintains a queue of standby passengers hoping to get a seat. Although the priority of a standby passenger is influenced by the check-in time of that passenger, other considerations include the fare paid and frequent-flyer status. So it may be that an available seat is given to a passenger who has arrived *later* than another, if such a passenger is assigned a better priority by the airline agent.

In this chapter, we introduce a new abstract data type known as a *priority queue*. This is a collection of prioritized elements that allows arbitrary element insertion, and allows the removal of the element that has first priority. When an element is added to a priority queue, the user designates its priority by providing an associated *key*. The element with the *minimum* key will be the next to be removed from the queue (thus, an element with key 1 will be given priority over an element with key 2). Although it is quite common for priorities to be expressed numerically, any Python object may be used as a key, as long as the object type supports a consistent meaning for the test a < b, for any instances a and b, so as to define a natural order of the keys. With such generality, applications may develop their own notion of priority for each element. For example, different financial analysts may assign different ratings (i.e., priorities) to a particular asset, such as a share of stock.

9.1.2   The Priority Queue ADT

Formally, we model an element and its priority as a key-value pair. We define the priority queue ADT to support the following methods for a priority queue P:

P.add(k, v): Insert an item with key k and value v into priority queue P.

P.min( ): Return a tuple, (k,v), representing the key and value of an item in priority queue P with minimum key (but do not remove the item); an error occurs if the priority queue is empty.

P.remove_min( ): Remove an item with minimum key from priority queue P, and return a tuple, (k,v), representing the key and value of the removed item; an error occurs if the priority queue is empty.

P.is_empty( ): Return True if priority queue P does not contain any items.

len(P): Return the number of items in priority queue P.

A priority queue may have multiple entries with equivalent keys, in which case methods min and remove_min may report an arbitrary choice of item having minimum key. Values may be any type of object.

In our initial model for a priority queue, we assume that an element's key remains fixed once it has been added to a priority queue. In Section 9.5, we consider an extension that allows a user to update an element's key within the priority queue.

Example 9.1: *The following table shows a series of operations and their effects on an initially empty priority queue P. The "Priority Queue" column is somewhat deceiving since it shows the entries as tuples and sorted by key. Such an internal representation is not required of a priority queue.*

Operation	Return Value	Priority Queue
P.add(5,A)		{(5,A)}
P.add(9,C)		{(5,A), (9,C)}
P.add(3,B)		{(3,B), (5,A), (9,C)}
P.add(7,D)		{(3,B), (5,A), (7,D), (9,C)}
P.min( )	(3,B)	{(3,B), (5,A), (7,D), (9,C)}
P.remove_min( )	(3,B)	{(5,A), (7,D), (9,C)}
P.remove_min( )	(5,A)	{(7,D), (9,C)}
len(P)	2	{(7,D), (9,C)}
P.remove_min( )	(7,D)	{(9,C)}
P.remove_min( )	(9,C)	{ }
P.is_empty( )	True	{ }
P.remove_min( )	"error"	{ }

9.2 Implementing a Priority Queue

In this section, we show how to implement a priority queue by storing its entries in a positional list L. (See Section 7.4.) We provide two realizations, depending on whether or not we keep the entries in L sorted by key.

9.2.1 The Composition Design Pattern

One challenge in implementing a priority queue is that we must keep track of both an element and its key, even as items are relocated within our data structure. This is reminiscent of a case study from Section 7.6 in which we maintain access counts with each element. In that setting, we introduced the *composition design pattern*, defining an _Item class that assured that each element remained paired with its associated count in our primary data structure.

For priority queues, we will use composition to store items internally as pairs consisting of a key k and a value v. To implement this concept for all priority queue implementations, we provide a PriorityQueueBase class (see Code Fragment 9.1) that includes a definition for a nested class named _Item. We define the syntax a < b, for item instances a and b, to be based upon the keys.

```
1  class PriorityQueueBase:
2    """Abstract base class for a priority queue."""
3
4    class _Item:
5      """Lightweight composite to store priority queue items."""
6      __slots__ = '_key', '_value'
7
8      def __init__(self, k, v):
9        self._key = k
10       self._value = v
11
12     def __lt__(self, other):
13       return self._key < other._key      # compare items based on their keys
14
15   def is_empty(self):                    # concrete method assuming abstract len
16     """Return True if the priority queue is empty."""
17     return len(self) == 0
```

Code Fragment 9.1: A PriorityQueueBase class with a nested _Item class that composes a key and a value into a single object. For convenience, we provide a concrete implementation of is_empty that is based on a presumed __len__ impelementation.

9.2.2   Implementation with an Unsorted List

In our first concrete implementation of a priority queue, we store entries within an *unsorted list*. Our UnsortedPriorityQueue class is given in Code Fragment 9.2, inheriting from the PriorityQueueBase class introduced in Code Fragment 9.1. For internal storage, key-value pairs are represented as composites, using instances of the inherited _Item class. These items are stored within a PositionalList, identified as the _data member of our class. We assume that the positional list is implemented with a doubly-linked list, as in Section 7.4, so that all operations of that ADT execute in $O(1)$ time.

We begin with an empty list when a new priority queue is constructed. At all times, the size of the list equals the number of key-value pairs currently stored in the priority queue. For this reason, our priority queue __len__ method simply returns the length of the internal _data list. By the design of our PriorityQueueBase class, we inherit a concrete implementation of the is_empty method that relies on a call to our __len__ method.

Each time a key-value pair is added to the priority queue, via the add method, we create a new _Item composite for the given key and value, and add that item to the end of the list. Such an implementation takes $O(1)$ time.

The remaining challenge is that when min or remove_min is called, we must locate the item with minimum key. Because the items are not sorted, we must inspect all entries to find one with a minimum key. For convenience, we define a nonpublic _find_min utility that returns the *position* of an item with minimum key. Knowledge of the position allows the remove_min method to invoke the delete method on the positional list. The min method simply uses the position to retrieve the item when preparing a key-value tuple to return. Due to the loop for finding the minimum key, both min and remove_min methods run in $O(n)$ time, where n is the number of entries in the priority queue.

A summary of the running times for the UnsortedPriorityQueue class is given in Table 9.1.

Operation	Running Time
len	$O(1)$
is_empty	$O(1)$
add	$O(1)$
min	$O(n)$
remove_min	$O(n)$

Table 9.1: Worst-case running times of the methods of a priority queue of size n, realized by means of an unsorted, doubly linked list. The space requirement is $O(n)$.

```
1   class UnsortedPriorityQueue(PriorityQueueBase):  # base class defines _Item
2     """A min-oriented priority queue implemented with an unsorted list."""
3
4     def _find_min(self):                        # nonpublic utility
5       """Return Position of item with minimum key."""
6       if self.is_empty():                       # is_empty inherited from base class
7         raise Empty('Priority queue is empty')
8       small = self._data.first()
9       walk = self._data.after(small)
10      while walk is not None:
11        if walk.element() < small.element():
12          small = walk
13        walk = self._data.after(walk)
14      return small
15
16    def __init__(self):
17      """Create a new empty Priority Queue."""
18      self._data = PositionalList()
19
20    def __len__(self):
21      """Return the number of items in the priority queue."""
22      return len(self._data)
23
24    def add(self, key, value):
25      """Add a key-value pair."""
26      self._data.add_last(self._Item(key, value))
27
28    def min(self):
29      """Return but do not remove (k,v) tuple with minimum key."""
30      p = self._find_min()
31      item = p.element()
32      return (item._key, item._value)
33
34    def remove_min(self):
35      """Remove and return (k,v) tuple with minimum key."""
36      p = self._find_min()
37      item = self._data.delete(p)
38      return (item._key, item._value)
```

Code Fragment 9.2: An implementation of a priority queue using an unsorted list. The parent class PriorityQueueBase is given in Code Fragment 9.1, and the PositionalList class is from Section 7.4.

9.2.3   Implementation with a Sorted List

An alternative implementation of a priority queue uses a positional list, yet maintaining entries sorted by nondecreasing keys. This ensures that the first element of the list is an entry with the smallest key.

Our SortedPriorityQueue class is given in Code Fragment 9.3. The implementation of min and remove_min are rather straightforward given knowledge that the first element of a list has a minimum key. We rely on the first method of the positional list to find the position of the first item, and the delete method to remove the entry from the list. Assuming that the list is implemented with a doubly linked list, operations min and remove_min take $O(1)$ time.

This benefit comes at a cost, however, for method add now requires that we scan the list to find the appropriate position to insert the new item. Our implementation starts at the end of the list, walking backward until the new key is smaller than an existing item; in the worst case, it progresses until reaching the front of the list. Therefore, the add method takes $O(n)$ worst-case time, where n is the number of entries in the priority queue at the time the method is executed. In summary, when using a sorted list to implement a priority queue, insertion runs in linear time, whereas finding and removing the minimum can be done in constant time.

Comparing the Two List-Based Implementations

Table 9.2 compares the running times of the methods of a priority queue realized by means of a sorted and unsorted list, respectively. We see an interesting trade-off when we use a list to implement the priority queue ADT. An unsorted list supports fast insertions but slow queries and deletions, whereas a sorted list allows fast queries and deletions, but slow insertions.

Operation	Unsorted List	Sorted List
len	$O(1)$	$O(1)$
is_empty	$O(1)$	$O(1)$
add	$O(1)$	$O(n)$
min	$O(n)$	$O(1)$
remove_min	$O(n)$	$O(1)$

Table 9.2: Worst-case running times of the methods of a priority queue of size n, realized by means of an unsorted or sorted list, respectively. We assume that the list is implemented by a doubly linked list. The space requirement is $O(n)$.

```
1  class SortedPriorityQueue(PriorityQueueBase):  # base class defines _Item
2    """A min-oriented priority queue implemented with a sorted list."""
3
4    def __init__(self):
5      """Create a new empty Priority Queue."""
6      self._data = PositionalList()
7
8    def __len__(self):
9      """Return the number of items in the priority queue."""
10     return len(self._data)
11
12   def add(self, key, value):
13     """Add a key-value pair."""
14     newest = self._Item(key, value)              # make new item instance
15     walk = self._data.last()          # walk backward looking for smaller key
16     while walk is not None and newest < walk.element():
17       walk = self._data.before(walk)
18     if walk is None:
19       self._data.add_first(newest)               # new key is smallest
20     else:
21       self._data.add_after(walk, newest)         # newest goes after walk
22
23   def min(self):
24     """Return but do not remove (k,v) tuple with minimum key."""
25     if self.is_empty():
26       raise Empty('Priority queue is empty.')
27     p = self._data.first()
28     item = p.element()
29     return (item._key, item._value)
30
31   def remove_min(self):
32     """Remove and return (k,v) tuple with minimum key."""
33     if self.is_empty():
34       raise Empty('Priority queue is empty.')
35     item = self._data.delete(self._data.first())
36     return (item._key, item._value)
```

Code Fragment 9.3: An implementation of a priority queue using a sorted list. The parent class PriorityQueueBase is given in Code Fragment 9.1, and the PositionalList class is from Section 7.4.

9.3   Heaps

The two strategies for implementing a priority queue ADT in the previous section demonstrate an interesting trade-off. When using an *unsorted* list to store entries, we can perform insertions in $O(1)$ time, but finding or removing an element with minimum key requires an $O(n)$-time loop through the entire collection. In contrast, if using a *sorted* list, we can trivially find or remove the minimum element in $O(1)$ time, but adding a new element to the queue may require $O(n)$ time to restore the sorted order.

In this section, we provide a more efficient realization of a priority queue using a data structure called a ***binary heap***. This data structure allows us to perform both insertions and removals in logarithmic time, which is a significant improvement over the list-based implementations discussed in Section 9.2. The fundamental way the heap achieves this improvement is to use the structure of a binary tree to find a compromise between elements being entirely unsorted and perfectly sorted.

9.3.1   The Heap Data Structure

A heap (see Figure 9.1) is a binary tree T that stores a collection of items at its positions and that satisfies two additional properties: a relational property defined in terms of the way keys are stored in T and a structural property defined in terms of the shape of T itself. The relational property is the following:

Heap-Order Property: In a heap T, for every position p other than the root, the key stored at p is greater than or equal to the key stored at p's parent.

As a consequence of the heap-order property, the keys encountered on a path from the root to a leaf of T are in nondecreasing order. Also, a minimum key is always stored at the root of T. This makes it easy to locate such an item when min or remove_min is called, as it is informally said to be "at the top of the heap" (hence, the name "heap" for the data structure). By the way, the heap data structure defined here has nothing to do with the memory heap (Section 15.1.1) used in the run-time environment supporting a programming language like Python.

For the sake of efficiency, as will become clear later, we want the heap T to have as small a height as possible. We enforce this requirement by insisting that the heap T satisfy an additional structural property—it must be what we term ***complete***.

Complete Binary Tree Property: A heap T with height h is a ***complete*** binary tree if levels $0, 1, 2, \ldots, h-1$ of T have the maximum number of nodes possible (namely, level i has 2^i nodes, for $0 \leq i \leq h-1$) and the remaining nodes at level h reside in the leftmost possible positions at that level.

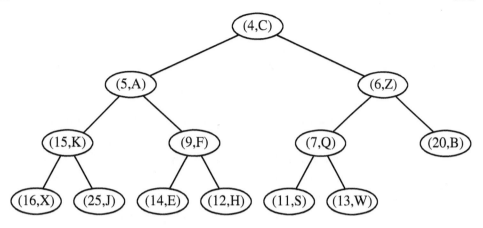

Figure 9.1: Example of a heap storing 13 entries with integer keys. The last position is the one storing entry $(13, W)$.

The tree in Figure 9.1 is complete because levels 0, 1, and 2 are full, and the six nodes in level 3 are in the six leftmost possible positions at that level. In formalizing what we mean by the leftmost possible positions, we refer to the discussion of *level numbering* from Section 8.3.2, in the context of an array-based representation of a binary tree. (In fact, in Section 9.3.3 we will discuss the use of an array to represent a heap.) A complete binary tree with n elements is one that has positions with level numbering 0 through $n - 1$. For example, in an array-based representation of the above tree, its 13 entries would be stored consecutively from $A[0]$ to $A[12]$.

The Height of a Heap

Let h denote the height of T. Insisting that T be complete also has an important consequence, as shown in Proposition 9.2.

Proposition 9.2: *A heap T storing n entries has height $h = \lfloor \log n \rfloor$.*

Justification: From the fact that T is complete, we know that the number of nodes in levels 0 through $h - 1$ of T is precisely $1 + 2 + 4 + \cdots + 2^{h-1} = 2^h - 1$, and that the number of nodes in level h is at least 1 and at most 2^h. Therefore

$$n \geq 2^h - 1 + 1 = 2^h \quad \text{and} \quad n \leq 2^h - 1 + 2^h = 2^{h+1} - 1.$$

By taking the logarithm of both sides of inequality $2^h \leq n$, we see that height $h \leq \log n$. By rearranging terms and taking the logarithm of both sides of inequality $n \leq 2^{h+1} - 1$, we see that $\log(n + 1) - 1 \leq h$. Since h is an integer, these two inequalities imply that $h = \lfloor \log n \rfloor$. ∎

9.3.2   Implementing a Priority Queue with a Heap

Proposition 9.2 has an important consequence, for it implies that if we can perform update operations on a heap in time proportional to its height, then those operations will run in logarithmic time. Let us therefore turn to the problem of how to efficiently perform various priority queue methods using a heap.

We will use the composition pattern from Section 9.2.1 to store key-value pairs as items in the heap. The len and is_empty methods can be implemented based on examination of the tree, and the min operation is equally trivial because the heap property assures that the element at the root of the tree has a minimum key. The interesting algorithms are those for implementing the add and remove_min methods.

Adding an Item to the Heap

Let us consider how to perform add(k,v) on a priority queue implemented with a heap T. We store the pair (k, v) as an item at a new node of the tree. To maintain the *complete binary tree property*, that new node should be placed at a position p just beyond the rightmost node at the bottom level of the tree, or as the leftmost position of a new level, if the bottom level is already full (or if the heap is empty).

Up-Heap Bubbling After an Insertion

After this action, the tree T is complete, but it may violate the *heap-order property*. Hence, unless position p is the root of T (that is, the priority queue was empty before the insertion), we compare the key at position p to that of p's parent, which we denote as q. If key $k_p \geq k_q$, the heap-order property is satisfied and the algorithm terminates. If instead $k_p < k_q$, then we need to restore the heap-order property, which can be locally achieved by swapping the entries stored at positions p and q. (See Figure 9.2c and d.) This swap causes the new item to move up one level. Again, the heap-order property may be violated, so we repeat the process, going up in T until no violation of the heap-order property occurs. (See Figure 9.2e and h.)

The upward movement of the newly inserted entry by means of swaps is conventionally called *up-heap bubbling*. A swap either resolves the violation of the heap-order property or propagates it one level up in the heap. In the worst case, up-heap bubbling causes the new entry to move all the way up to the root of heap T. Thus, in the worst case, the number of swaps performed in the execution of method add is equal to the height of T. By Proposition 9.2, that bound is $\lfloor \log n \rfloor$.

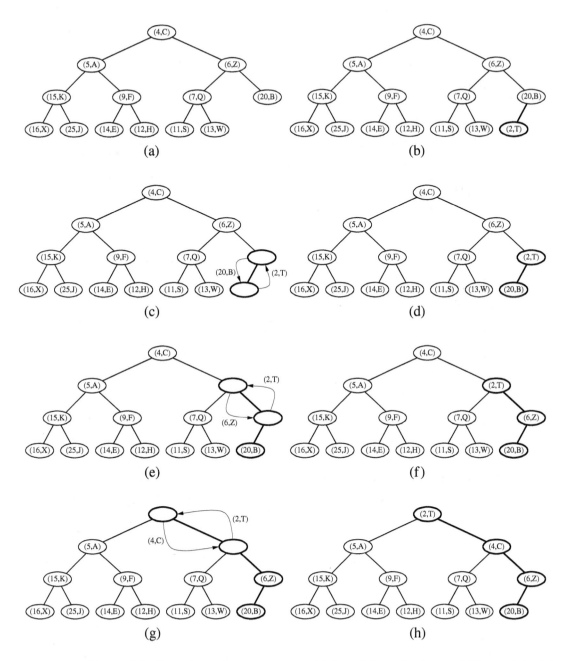

Figure 9.2: Insertion of a new entry with key 2 into the heap of Figure 9.1: (a) initial heap; (b) after performing operation add; (c and d) swap to locally restore the partial order property; (e and f) another swap; (g and h) final swap.

Removing the Item with Minimum Key

Let us now turn to method remove_min of the priority queue ADT. We know that an entry with the smallest key is stored at the root r of T (even if there is more than one entry with smallest key). However, in general we cannot simply delete node r, because this would leave two disconnected subtrees.

Instead, we ensure that the shape of the heap respects the ***complete binary tree property*** by deleting the leaf at the *last* position p of T, defined as the rightmost position at the bottommost level of the tree. To preserve the item from the last position p, we copy it to the root r (in place of the item with minimum key that is being removed by the operation). Figure 9.3a and b illustrates an example of these steps, with minimal item $(4, C)$ being removed from the root and replaced by item $(13, W)$ from the last position. The node at the last position is removed from the tree.

Down-Heap Bubbling After a Removal

We are not yet done, however, for even though T is now complete, it likely violates the heap-order property. If T has only one node (the root), then the heap-order property is trivially satisfied and the algorithm terminates. Otherwise, we distinguish two cases, where p initially denotes the root of T:

- If p has no right child, let c be the left child of p.
- Otherwise (p has both children), let c be a child of p with minimal key.

If key $k_p \leq k_c$, the heap-order property is satisfied and the algorithm terminates. If instead $k_p > k_c$, then we need to restore the heap-order property. This can be locally achieved by swapping the entries stored at p and c. (See Figure 9.3c and d.) It is worth noting that when p has two children, we intentionally consider the *smaller* key of the two children. Not only is the key of c smaller than that of p, it is at least as small as the key at c's sibling. This ensures that the heap-order property is locally restored when that smaller key is promoted above the key that had been at p and that at c's sibling.

Having restored the heap-order property for node p relative to its children, there may be a violation of this property at c; hence, we may have to continue swapping down T until no violation of the heap-order property occurs. (See Figure 9.3e–h.) This downward swapping process is called ***down-heap bubbling***. A swap either resolves the violation of the heap-order property or propagates it one level down in the heap. In the worst case, an entry moves all the way down to the bottom level. (See Figure 9.3.) Thus, the number of swaps performed in the execution of method remove_min is, in the worst case, equal to the height of heap T, that is, it is $\lfloor \log n \rfloor$ by Proposition 9.2.

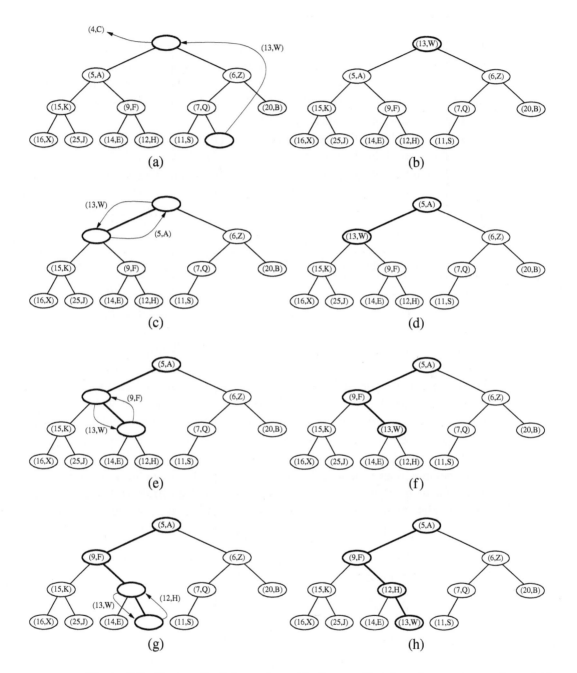

Figure 9.3: Removal of the entry with the smallest key from a heap: (a and b) deletion of the last node, whose entry gets stored into the root; (c and d) swap to locally restore the heap-order property; (e and f) another swap; (g and h) final swap.

9.3.3   Array-Based Representation of a Complete Binary Tree

The array-based representation of a binary tree (Section 8.3.2) is especially suitable for a complete binary tree T. We recall that in this implementation, the elements of T are stored in an array-based list A such that the element at position p in T is stored in A with index equal to the level number $f(p)$ of p, defined as follows:

- If p is the root of T, then $f(p) = 0$.
- If p is the left child of position q, then $f(p) = 2f(q) + 1$.
- If p is the right child of position q, then $f(p) = 2f(q) + 2$.

With this implementation, the elements of T have contiguous indices in the range $[0, n-1]$ and the last position of T is always at index $n-1$, where n is the number of positions of T. For example, Figure 9.4 illustrates the array-based representation of the heap structure originally portrayed in Figure 9.1.

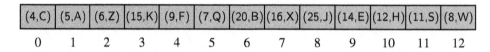

Figure 9.4: An array-based representation of the heap from Figure 9.1.

Implementing a priority queue using an array-based heap representation allows us to avoid some complexities of a node-based tree structure. In particular, the add and remove_min operations of a priority queue both depend on locating the last index of a heap of size n. With the array-based representation, the last position is at index $n-1$ of the array. Locating the last position of a complete binary tree implemented with a linked structure requires more effort. (See Exercise C-9.34.)

If the size of a priority queue is not known in advance, use of an array-based representation does introduce the need to dynamically resize the array on occasion, as is done with a Python list. The space usage of such an array-based representation of a complete binary tree with n nodes is $O(n)$, and the time bounds of methods for adding or removing elements become *amortized*. (See Section 5.3.1.)

9.3.4   Python Heap Implementation

We provide a Python implementation of a heap-based priority queue in Code Fragments 9.4 and 9.5. We use an array-based representation, maintaining a Python list of item composites. Although we do not formally use the binary tree ADT, Code Fragment 9.4 includes nonpublic utility functions that compute the level numbering of a parent or child of another. This allows us to describe the rest of our algorithms using tree-like terminology of *parent*, *left*, and *right*. However, the relevant variables are integer indexes (not "position" objects). We use recursion to implement the repetition in the _upheap and _downheap utilities.

```
1   class HeapPriorityQueue(PriorityQueueBase):  # base class defines _Item
2     """A min-oriented priority queue implemented with a binary heap."""
3     #---------------------------- nonpublic behaviors ----------------------------
4     def _parent(self, j):
5       return (j−1) // 2
6
7     def _left(self, j):
8       return 2*j + 1
9
10    def _right(self, j):
11      return 2*j + 2
12
13    def _has_left(self, j):
14      return self._left(j) < len(self._data)     # index beyond end of list?
15
16    def _has_right(self, j):
17      return self._right(j) < len(self._data)    # index beyond end of list?
18
19    def _swap(self, i, j):
20      """Swap the elements at indices i and j of array."""
21      self._data[i], self._data[j] = self._data[j], self._data[i]
22
23    def _upheap(self, j):
24      parent = self._parent(j)
25      if j > 0 and self._data[j] < self._data[parent]:
26        self._swap(j, parent)
27        self._upheap(parent)                    # recur at position of parent
28
29    def _downheap(self, j):
30      if self._has_left(j):
31        left = self._left(j)
32        small_child = left                      # although right may be smaller
33        if self._has_right(j):
34          right = self._right(j)
35          if self._data[right] < self._data[left]:
36            small_child = right
37        if self._data[small_child] < self._data[j]:
38          self._swap(j, small_child)
39          self._downheap(small_child)           # recur at position of small child
```

Code Fragment 9.4: An implementation of a priority queue using an array-based heap (continued in Code Fragment 9.5). The extends the PriorityQueueBase class from Code Fragment 9.1.

```
40    #----------------------------- public behaviors -----------------------------
41    def __init__(self):
42      """Create a new empty Priority Queue."""
43      self._data = [ ]
44
45    def __len__(self):
46      """Return the number of items in the priority queue."""
47      return len(self._data)
48
49    def add(self, key, value):
50      """Add a key-value pair to the priority queue."""
51      self._data.append(self._Item(key, value))
52      self._upheap(len(self._data) − 1)            # upheap newly added position
53
54    def min(self):
55      """Return but do not remove (k,v) tuple with minimum key.
56
57      Raise Empty exception if empty.
58      """
59      if self.is_empty():
60        raise Empty('Priority queue is empty.')
61      item = self._data[0]
62      return (item._key, item._value)
63
64    def remove_min(self):
65      """Remove and return (k,v) tuple with minimum key.
66
67      Raise Empty exception if empty.
68      """
69      if self.is_empty():
70        raise Empty('Priority queue is empty.')
71      self._swap(0, len(self._data) − 1)           # put minimum item at the end
72      item = self._data.pop( )                      # and remove it from the list;
73      self._downheap(0)                             # then fix new root
74      return (item._key, item._value)
```

Code Fragment 9.5: An implementation of a priority queue using an array-based heap (continued from Code Fragment 9.4).

9.3.5 Analysis of a Heap-Based Priority Queue

Table 9.3 shows the running time of the priority queue ADT methods for the heap implementation of a priority queue, assuming that two keys can be compared in $O(1)$ time and that the heap T is implemented with an array-based or linked-based tree representation.

In short, each of the priority queue ADT methods can be performed in $O(1)$ or in $O(\log n)$ time, where n is the number of entries at the time the method is executed. The analysis of the running time of the methods is based on the following:

- The heap T has n nodes, each storing a reference to a key-value pair.

- The height of heap T is $O(\log n)$, since T is complete (Proposition 9.2).

- The min operation runs in $O(1)$ because the root of the tree contains such an element.

- Locating the last position of a heap, as required for add and remove_min, can be performed in $O(1)$ time for an array-based representation, or $O(\log n)$ time for a linked-tree representation. (See Exercise C-9.34.)

- In the worst case, up-heap and down-heap bubbling perform a number of swaps equal to the height of T.

Operation	Running Time
len(P), P.is_empty( )	$O(1)$
P.min( )	$O(1)$
P.add( )	$O(\log n)^*$
P.remove_min( )	$O(\log n)^*$

*amortized, if array-based

Table 9.3: Performance of a priority queue, P, realized by means of a heap. We let n denote the number of entries in the priority queue at the time an operation is executed. The space requirement is $O(n)$. The running time of operations min and remove_min are amortized for an array-based representation, due to occasional resizing of a dynamic array; those bounds are worst case with a linked tree structure.

We conclude that the heap data structure is a very efficient realization of the priority queue ADT, independent of whether the heap is implemented with a linked structure or an array. The heap-based implementation achieves fast running times for both insertion and removal, unlike the implementations that were based on using an unsorted or sorted list.

9.3.6   Bottom-Up Heap Construction ⋆

If we start with an initially empty heap, n successive calls to the add operation will run in $O(n \log n)$ time in the worst case. However, if all n key-value pairs to be stored in the heap are given in advance, such as during the first phase of the heap-sort algorithm, there is an alternative ***bottom-up*** construction method that runs in $O(n)$ time. (Heap-sort, however, still requires $\Theta(n \log n)$ time because of the second phase in which we repeatedly remove the remaining element with smallest key.)

In this section, we describe the bottom-up heap construction, and provide an implementation that can be used by the constructor of a heap-based priority queue.

For simplicity of exposition, we describe this bottom-up heap construction assuming the number of keys, n, is an integer such that $n = 2^{h+1} - 1$. That is, the heap is a complete binary tree with every level being full, so the heap has height $h = \log(n+1) - 1$. Viewed nonrecursively, bottom-up heap construction consists of the following $h + 1 = \log(n+1)$ steps:

1. In the first step (see Figure 9.5b), we construct $(n+1)/2$ elementary heaps storing one entry each.

2. In the second step (see Figure 9.5c–d), we form $(n+1)/4$ heaps, each storing three entries, by joining pairs of elementary heaps and adding a new entry. The new entry is placed at the root and may have to be swapped with the entry stored at a child to preserve the heap-order property.

3. In the third step (see Figure 9.5e–f), we form $(n+1)/8$ heaps, each storing 7 entries, by joining pairs of 3-entry heaps (constructed in the previous step) and adding a new entry. The new entry is placed initially at the root, but may have to move down with a down-heap bubbling to preserve the heap-order property.

$\vdots$

i. In the generic i^{th} step, $2 \le i \le h$, we form $(n+1)/2^i$ heaps, each storing $2^i - 1$ entries, by joining pairs of heaps storing $(2^{i-1} - 1)$ entries (constructed in the previous step) and adding a new entry. The new entry is placed initially at the root, but may have to move down with a down-heap bubbling to preserve the heap-order property.

$\vdots$

$h+1$. In the last step (see Figure 9.5g–h), we form the final heap, storing all the n entries, by joining two heaps storing $(n-1)/2$ entries (constructed in the previous step) and adding a new entry. The new entry is placed initially at the root, but may have to move down with a down-heap bubbling to preserve the heap-order property.

We illustrate bottom-up heap construction in Figure 9.5 for $h = 3$.

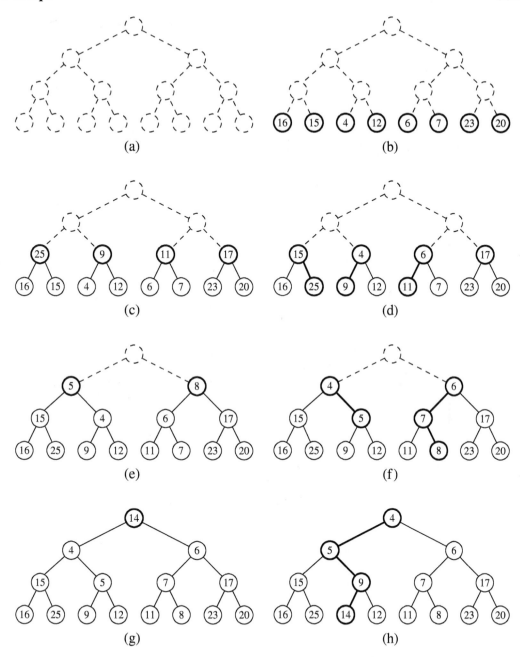

Figure 9.5: Bottom-up construction of a heap with 15 entries: (a and b) we begin by constructing 1-entry heaps on the bottom level; (c and d) we combine these heaps into 3-entry heaps, and then (e and f) 7-entry heaps, until (g and h) we create the final heap. The paths of the down-heap bubblings are highlighted in (d, f, and h). For simplicity, we only show the key within each node instead of the entire entry.

Python Implementation of a Bottom-Up Heap Construction

Implementing a bottom-up heap construction is quite easy, given the existence of a "down-heap" utility function. The "merging" of two equally sized heaps that are subtrees of a common position p, as described in the opening of this section, can be accomplished simply by down-heaping p's entry. For example, that is what happened to the key 14 in going from Figure 9.5(f) to (g).

With our array-based representation of a heap, if we initially store all n items in arbitrary order within the array, we can implement the bottom-up heap construction process with a single loop that makes a call to _downheap from each position of the tree, as long as those calls are ordered starting with the *deepest* level and ending with the root of the tree. In fact, that loop can start with the deepest nonleaf, since there is no effect when down-heap is called at a leaf position.

In Code Fragment 9.6, we augment the original HeapPriorityQueue class from Section 9.3.4 to provide support for the bottom-up construction of an initial collection. We introduce a nonpublic utility method, _heapify, that calls _downheap on each nonleaf position, beginning with the deepest and concluding with a call at the root of the tree. We have redesigned the constructor of the class to accept an optional parameter that can be any sequence of (k,v) tuples. Rather than initializing self._data to an empty list, we use a list comprehension syntax (see Section 1.9.2) to create an initial list of item composites based on the given contents. We declare an empty sequence as the default parameter value so that the default syntax HeapPriorityQueue() continues to result in an empty priority queue.

```python
def __init__(self, contents=()):
  """Create a new priority queue.

  By default, queue will be empty. If contents is given, it should be as an
  iterable sequence of (k,v) tuples specifying the initial contents.
  """
    self._data = [ self._Item(k,v) for k,v in contents ]     # empty by default
    if len(self._data) > 1:
      self._heapify()

def _heapify(self):
    start = self._parent(len(self) - 1)      # start at PARENT of last leaf
    for j in range(start, -1, -1):           # going to and including the root
      self._downheap(j)
```

Code Fragment 9.6: Revision to the HeapPriorityQueue class of Code Fragments 9.4 and 9.5 to support a linear-time construction given an initial sequence of entries.

Asymptotic Analysis of Bottom-Up Heap Construction

Bottom-up heap construction is asymptotically faster than incrementally inserting n keys into an initially empty heap. Intuitively, we are performing a single down-heap operation at each position in the tree, rather than a single up-heap operation from each. Since more nodes are closer to the bottom of a tree than the top, the sum of the downward paths is linear, as shown in the following proposition.

Proposition 9.3: *Bottom-up construction of a heap with n entries takes $O(n)$ time, assuming two keys can be compared in $O(1)$ time.*

Justification: The primary cost of the construction is due to the down-heap steps performed at each nonleaf position. Let π_v denote the path of T from nonleaf node v to its "inorder successor" leaf, that is, the path that starts at v, goes to the right child of v, and then goes down leftward until it reaches a leaf. Although, π_v is not necessarily the path followed by the down-heap bubbling step from v, the length $\|\pi_v\|$ (its number of edges) is proportional to the height of the subtree rooted at v, and thus a bound on the complexity of the down-heap operation at v. We can bound the total running time of the bottom-up heap construction algorithm based on the sum of the sizes of paths, $\sum_v \|\pi_v\|$. For intuition, Figure 9.6 illustrates the justification "visually," marking each edge with the label of the nonleaf node v whose path π_v contains that edge.

We claim that the paths π_v for all nonleaf v are edge-disjoint, and thus the sum of the path lengths is bounded by the number of total edges in the tree, hence $O(n)$. To show this, we consider what we term "right-leaning" and "left-leaning" edges (i.e., those going from a parent to a right, respectively left, child). A particular right-leaning edge e can only be part of the path π_v for node v that is the parent in the relationship represented by e. Left-leaning edges can be partitioned by considering the leaf that is reached if continuing down leftward until reaching a leaf. Each nonleaf node only uses left-leaning edges in the group leading to that nonleaf node's inorder successor. Since each nonleaf node must have a different inorder successor, no two such paths can contain the same left-leaning edge. We conclude that the bottom-up construction of heap T takes $O(n)$ time. ∎

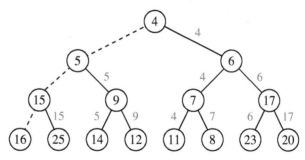

Figure 9.6: Visual justification of the linear running time of bottom-up heap construction. Each edge e is labeled with a node v for which π_v contains e (if any).

9.3.7   Python's heapq Module

Python's standard distribution includes a heapq module that provides support for heap-based priority queues. That module does not provide any priority queue class; instead it provides functions that allow a standard Python list to be managed as a heap. Its model is essentially the same as our own, with n elements stored in list cells $L[0]$ through $L[n-1]$, based on the level-numbering indices with the smallest element at the root in $L[0]$. We note that heapq does not separately manage associated values; elements serve as their own key.

The heapq module supports the following functions, all of which presume that existing list L satisfies the heap-order property prior to the call:

heappush(L, e): Push element e onto list L and restore the heap-order property. The function executes in $O(\log n)$ time.

heappop(L): Pop and return the element with smallest value from list L, and reestablish the heap-order property. The operation executes in $O(\log n)$ time.

heappushpop(L, e): Push element e on list L and then pop and return the smallest item. The time is $O(\log n)$, but it is slightly more efficient than separate calls to push and pop because the size of the list never changes. If the newly pushed element becomes the smallest, it is immediately returned. Otherwise, the new element takes the place of the popped element at the root and a down-heap is performed.

heapreplace(L, e): Similar to heappushpop, but equivalent to the pop being performed before the push (in other words, the new element cannot be returned as the smallest). Again, the time is $O(\log n)$, but it is more efficient that two separate operations.

The module supports additional functions that operate on sequences that do not previously satisfy the heap-order property.

heapify(L): Transform unordered list to satisfy the heap-order property. This executes in $O(n)$ time by using the bottom-up construction algorithm.

nlargest(k, iterable): Produce a list of the k largest values from a given iterable. This can be implemented to run in $O(n + k\log n)$ time, where we use n to denote the length of the iterable (see Exercise C-9.42).

nsmallest(k, iterable): Produce a list of the k smallest values from a given iterable. This can be implemented to run in $O(n + k\log n)$ time, using similar technique as with nlargest.

9.4 Sorting with a Priority Queue

In defining the priority queue ADT, we noted that any type of object can be used as a key, but that any pair of keys must be comparable to each other, and that the set of keys be naturally ordered. In Python, it is common to rely on the $<$ operator to define such an order, in which case the following properties must be satisfied:

- **Irreflexive property**: $k \not< k$.
- **Transitive property**: if $k_1 < k_2$ and $k_2 < k_3$, then $k_1 < k_3$.

Formally, such a relationship defines what is known as a ***strict weak order***, as it allows for keys to be considered equal to each other, but the broader equivalence classes are ***totally ordered***, as they can be uniquely arranged from smallest to largest due to the transitive property.

As our first application of priority queues, we demonstrate how they can be used to sort a collection C of comparable elements. That is, we can produce a sequence of elements of C in increasing order (or at least in nondecreasing order if there are duplicates). The algorithm is quite simple—we insert all elements into an initially empty priority queue, and then we repeatedly call remove_min to retrieve the elements in nondecreasing order.

An implementation of this algorithm is given in Code Fragment 9.7, assuming that C is a positional list. (See Chapter 7.4.) We use an original element of the collection as both a key and value when calling P.add(element, element).

```
1  def pq_sort(C):
2    """Sort a collection of elements stored in a positional list."""
3    n = len(C)
4    P = PriorityQueue()
5    for j in range(n):
6      element = C.delete(C.first())
7      P.add(element, element)          # use element as key and value
8    for j in range(n):
9      (k,v) = P.remove_min()
10     C.add_last(v)                    # store smallest remaining element in C
```

Code Fragment 9.7: An implementation of the pq_sort function, assuming an appropriate implementation of a PriorityQueue class. Note that each element of the input list C serves as its own key in the priority queue P.

With a minor modification to this code, we can provide more general support, sorting elements according to an ordering other than the default. For example, when working with strings, the $<$ operator defines a ***lexicographic ordering***, which is an extension of the alphabetic ordering to Unicode. For example, we have that '12' $<$ '4' because of the order of the first character of each string, just as 'apple' < 'banana'. Suppose that we have an application in which we have a list of strings that are all known to represent integral values (e.g., '12'), and our goal is to sort the strings according to those integral values.

In Python, the standard approach for customizing the order for a sorting algorithm is to provide, as an optional parameter to the sorting function, an object that is itself a one-parameter function that computes a key for a given element. (See Sections 1.5 and 1.10 for a discussion of this approach in the context of the built-in max function.) For example, with a list of (numeric) strings, we might wish to use the value of int(s) as a key for a string s of the list. In this case, the constructor for the int class can serve as the one-parameter function for computing a key. In that way, the string '4' will be ordered before string '12' because its key int('4') < int('12'). We leave it as an exercise to support such an optional key parameter for the pq_sort function. (See Exercise C-9.46.)

9.4.1 Selection-Sort and Insertion-Sort

Our pq_sort function works correctly given any valid implementation of the priority queue class. However, the running time of the sorting algorithm depends on the running times of the operations add and remove_min for the given priority queue class. We next discuss a choice of priority queue implementations that in effect cause the pq_sort computation to behave as one of several classic sorting algorithms.

Selection-Sort

If we implement P with an unsorted list, then Phase 1 of pq_sort takes $O(n)$ time, for we can add each element in $O(1)$ time. In Phase 2, the running time of each remove_min operation is proportional to the size of P. Thus, the bottleneck computation is the repeated "selection" of the minimum element in Phase 2. For this reason, this algorithm is better known as *selection-sort*. (See Figure 9.7.)

As noted above, the bottleneck is in Phase 2 where we repeatedly remove an entry with smallest key from the priority queue P. The size of P starts at n and incrementally decreases with each remove_min until it becomes 0. Thus, the first operation takes time $O(n)$, the second one takes time $O(n-1)$, and so on. Therefore, the total time needed for the second phase is

$$O(n + (n-1) + \cdots + 2 + 1) = O\left(\sum_{i=1}^{n} i\right).$$

By Proposition 3.3, we have $\sum_{i=1}^{n} i = n(n+1)/2$. Thus, Phase 2 takes time $O(n^2)$, as does the entire selection-sort algorithm.

		Collection C	Priority Queue P
Input		$(7,4,8,2,5,3)$	$()$
Phase 1	(a)	$(4,8,2,5,3)$	(7)
	(b)	$(8,2,5,3)$	$(7,4)$
	⋮	⋮	⋮
	(f)	$()$	$(7,4,8,2,5,3)$
Phase 2	(a)	(2)	$(7,4,8,5,3)$
	(b)	$(2,3)$	$(7,4,8,5)$
	(c)	$(2,3,4)$	$(7,8,5)$
	(d)	$(2,3,4,5)$	$(7,8)$
	(e)	$(2,3,4,5,7)$	(8)
	(f)	$(2,3,4,5,7,8)$	$()$

Figure 9.7: Execution of selection-sort on collection $C = (7,4,8,2,5,3)$.

Insertion-Sort

If we implement the priority queue P using a sorted list, then we improve the running time of Phase 2 to $O(n)$, for each remove_min operation on P now takes $O(1)$ time. Unfortunately, Phase 1 becomes the bottleneck for the running time, since, in the worst case, each add operation takes time proportional to the current size of P. This sorting algorithm is better known as ***insertion-sort*** (see Figure 9.8); in fact, our implementation for adding an element to a priority queue is almost identical to a step of insertion-sort as presented in Section 7.5.

The worst-case running time of Phase 1 of insertion-sort is

$$O(1+2+\ldots+(n-1)+n) = O\left(\sum_{i=1}^{n} i\right).$$

Again, by Proposition 3.3, this implies a worst-case $O(n^2)$ time for Phase 1, and thus, the entire insertion-sort algorithm. However, unlike selection-sort, insertion-sort has a *best-case* running time of $O(n)$.

		Collection C	Priority Queue P
Input		$(7,4,8,2,5,3)$	$()$
Phase 1	(a)	$(4,8,2,5,3)$	(7)
	(b)	$(8,2,5,3)$	$(4,7)$
	(c)	$(2,5,3)$	$(4,7,8)$
	(d)	$(5,3)$	$(2,4,7,8)$
	(e)	(3)	$(2,4,5,7,8)$
	(f)	$()$	$(2,3,4,5,7,8)$
Phase 2	(a)	(2)	$(3,4,5,7,8)$
	(b)	$(2,3)$	$(4,5,7,8)$
	⋮	⋮	⋮
	(f)	$(2,3,4,5,7,8)$	$()$

Figure 9.8: Execution of insertion-sort on collection $C = (7,4,8,2,5,3)$.

9.4.2   Heap-Sort

As we have previously observed, realizing a priority queue with a heap has the advantage that all the methods in the priority queue ADT run in logarithmic time or better. Hence, this realization is suitable for applications where fast running times are sought for all the priority queue methods. Therefore, let us again consider the pq_sort scheme, this time using a heap-based implementation of the priority queue.

During Phase 1, the ith add operation takes $O(\log i)$ time, since the heap has i entries after the operation is performed. Therefore this phase takes $O(n \log n)$ time. (It could be improved to $O(n)$ with the bottom-up heap construction described in Section 9.3.6.)

During the second phase of pq_sort, the jth remove_min operation runs in $O(\log(n - j + 1))$, since the heap has $n - j + 1$ entries at the time the operation is performed. Summing over all j, this phase takes $O(n \log n)$ time, so the entire priority-queue sorting algorithm runs in $O(n \log n)$ time when we use a heap to implement the priority queue. This sorting algorithm is better known as ***heap-sort***, and its performance is summarized in the following proposition.

Proposition 9.4: *The heap-sort algorithm sorts a collection C of n elements in $O(n \log n)$ time, assuming two elements of C can be compared in $O(1)$ time.*

Let us stress that the $O(n \log n)$ running time of heap-sort is considerably better than the $O(n^2)$ running time of selection-sort and insertion-sort (Section 9.4.1).

Implementing Heap-Sort In-Place

If the collection C to be sorted is implemented by means of an array-based sequence, most notably as a Python list, we can speed up heap-sort and reduce its space requirement by a constant factor using a portion of the list itself to store the heap, thus avoiding the use of an auxiliary heap data structure. This is accomplished by modifying the algorithm as follows:

1. We redefine the heap operations to be a *maximum-oriented* heap, with each position's key being at least as *large* as its children. This can be done by recoding the algorithm, or by adjusting the notion of keys to be negatively oriented. At any time during the execution of the algorithm, we use the left portion of C, up to a certain index $i - 1$, to store the entries of the heap, and the right portion of C, from index i to $n - 1$, to store the elements of the sequence. Thus, the first i elements of C (at indices $0, \ldots, i - 1$) provide the array-list representation of the heap.

2. In the first phase of the algorithm, we start with an empty heap and move the boundary between the heap and the sequence from left to right, one step at a time. In step i, for $i = 1, \ldots, n$, we expand the heap by adding the element at index $i - 1$.

3. In the second phase of the algorithm, we start with an empty sequence and move the boundary between the heap and the sequence from right to left, one step at a time. At step i, for $i = 1, \ldots, n$, we remove a maximum element from the heap and store it at index $n - i$.

In general, we say that a sorting algorithm is *in-place* if it uses only a small amount of memory in addition to the sequence storing the objects to be sorted. The variation of heap-sort above qualifies as in-place; instead of transferring elements out of the sequence and then back in, we simply rearrange them. We illustrate the second phase of in-place heap-sort in Figure 9.9.

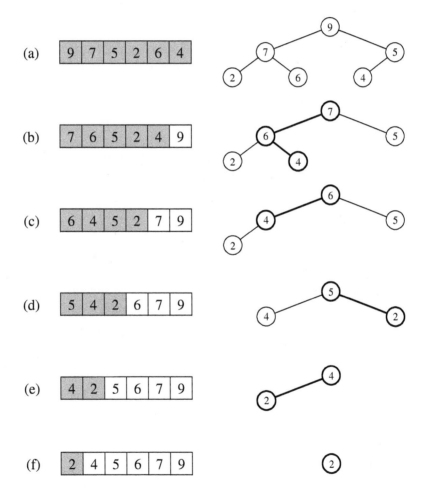

Figure 9.9: Phase 2 of an in-place heap-sort. The heap portion of each sequence representation is highlighted. The binary tree that each sequence (implicitly) represents is diagrammed with the most recent path of down-heap bubbling highlighted.

9.5   Adaptable Priority Queues

The methods of the priority queue ADT given in Section 9.1.2 are sufficient for most basic applications of priority queues, such as sorting. However, there are situations in which additional methods would be useful, as shown by the scenarios below involving the standby airline passenger application.

- A standby passenger with a pessimistic attitude may become tired of waiting and decide to leave ahead of the boarding time, requesting to be removed from the waiting list. Thus, we would like to remove from the priority queue the entry associated with this passenger. Operation remove_min does not suffice since the passenger leaving does not necessarily have first priority. Instead, we want a new operation, remove, that removes an arbitrary entry.

- Another standby passenger finds her gold frequent-flyer card and shows it to the agent. Thus, her priority has to be modified accordingly. To achieve this change of priority, we would like to have a new operation update allowing us to replace the key of an existing entry with a new key.

We will see another application of adaptable priority queues when implementing certain graph algorithms in Sections 14.6.2 and 14.7.1.

In this section, we develop an ***adaptable priority queue*** ADT and demonstrate how to implement this abstraction as an extension to our heap-based priority queue.

9.5.1   Locators

In order to implement methods update and remove efficiently, we need a mechanism for finding a user's element within a priority queue that avoids performing a linear search through the entire collection. To support our goal, when a new element is added to the priority queue, we return a special object known as a ***locator*** to the caller. We then require the user to provide an appropriate locator as a parameter when invoking the update or remove method, as follows, for a priority queue P:

P.update(loc, k, v): Replace key and value for the item identified by locator loc.

P.remove(loc): Remove the item identified by locator loc from the priority queue and return its (key,value) pair.

The locator abstraction is somewhat akin to the Position abstraction used in our positional list ADT from Section 7.4, and our tree ADT from Chapter 8. However, we differentiate between a locator and a position because a locator for a priority queue does not represent a tangible placement of an element within the structure. In our priority queue, an element may be relocated within our data structure during an operation that does not seem directly relevant to that element. A locator for an item will remain valid, as long as that item remains somewhere in the queue.

9.5.2 Implementing an Adaptable Priority Queue

In this section, we provide a Python implementation of an adaptable priority queue as an extension of our HeapPriorityQueue class from Section 9.3.4. To implement a Locator class, we will extend the existing _Item composite to add an additional field designating the current index of the element within the array-based representation of our heap, as shown in Figure 9.10.

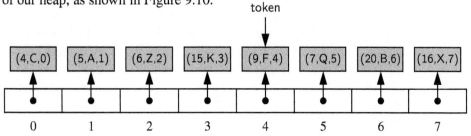

Figure 9.10: Representing a heap using a sequence of locators. The third element of each locator instance corresponds to the index of the item within the array. Identifier token is presumed to be a locator reference in the user's scope.

The list is a sequence of references to locator instances, each of which stores a key, value, and the current index of the item within the list. The user will be given a reference to the Locator instance for each inserted element, as portrayed by the token identifier in Figure 9.10.

When we perform priority queue operations on our heap, and items are relocated within our structure, we reposition the locator instances within the list and we update the third field of each locator to reflect its new index within the list. As an example, Figure 9.11 shows the state of the above heap after a call to remove_min( ). The heap operation caused the minimum entry, (4,C), to be removed, and the entry, (16,X), to be temporarily moved from the last position to the root, followed by a down-heap bubble phase. During the down-heap, element (16,X) was swapped

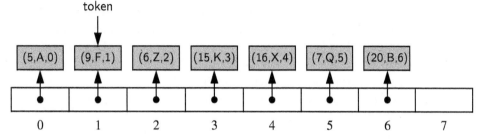

Figure 9.11: The result of a call to remove_min( ) on the heap originally portrayed in Figure 9.10. Identifier token continues to reference the same locator instance as in the original configuration, but the placement of that locator in the list has changed, as has the third field of the locator.

with its left child, (5,A), at index 1 of the list, then swapped with its right child, (9,F), at index 4 of the list. In the final configuration, the locator instances for all affected elements have been modified to reflect their new location.

It is important to emphasize that the locator instances have not changed identity. The user's token reference, portrayed in Figures 9.10 and 9.11, continues to reference the same instance; we have simply changed the third field of that instance, and we have changed where that instance is referenced within the list sequence.

With this new representation, providing the additional support for the adaptable priority queue ADT is rather straightforward. When a locator instance is sent as a parameter to update or remove, we may rely on the third field of that structure to designate where the element resides in the heap. With that knowledge, the update of a key may simply require an up-heap or down-heap bubbling step to reestablish the heap-order property. (The complete binary tree property remains intact.) To implement the removal of an arbitrary element, we move the element at the last position to the vacated location, and again perform an appropriate bubbling step to satisfy the heap-order property.

Python Implementation

Code Fragments 9.8 and 9.9 present a Python implementation of an adaptable priority queue, as a subclass of the HeapPriorityQueue class from Section 9.3.4. Our modifications to the original class are relatively minor. We define a public Locator class that inherits from the nonpublic _Item class and augments it with an additional _index field. We make it a public class because we will be using locators as return values and parameters; however, the public interface for the locator class does not include any other functionality for the user.

To update locators during the flow of our heap operations, we rely on an intentional design decision that our original class uses a nonpublic _swap method for all data movement. We override that utility to execute the additional step of updating the stored indices within the two swapped locator instances.

We provide a new _bubble utility that manages the reinstatement of the heap-order property when a key has changed at an arbitrary position within the heap, either due to a key update, or the blind replacement of a removed element with the item from the last position of the tree. The _bubble utility determines whether to apply up-heap or down-heap bubbling, depending on whether the given location has a parent with a smaller key. (If an updated key coincidentally remains valid for its current location, we technically call _downheap but no swaps result.)

The public methods are provided in Code Fragment 9.9. The existing add method is overridden, both to make use of a Locator instance rather than an _Item instance for storage of the new element, and to return the locator to the caller. The remainder of that method is similar to the original, with the management of locator indices enacted by the use of the new version of _swap. There is no reason to override the remove_min method because the only change in behavior for the adaptable priority queue is again provided by the overridden _swap method.

The update and remove methods provide the core new functionality for the adaptable priority queue. We perform robust checking of the validity of a locator that is sent by a caller (although in the interest of space, our displayed code does not do preliminary type-checking to ensure that the parameter is indeed a Locator instance). To ensure that a locator is associated with a current element of the given priority queue, we examine the index that is encapsulated within the locator object, and then verify that the entry of the list at that index is the very same locator.

In conclusion, the adaptable priority queue provides the same asymptotic efficiency and space usage as the nonadaptive version, and provides logarithmic performance for the new locator-based update and remove methods. A summary of the performance is given in Table 9.4.

```
1  class AdaptableHeapPriorityQueue(HeapPriorityQueue):
2    """A locator-based priority queue implemented with a binary heap."""
3
4    #------------------------------ nested Locator class ------------------------------
5    class Locator(HeapPriorityQueue._Item):
6      """Token for locating an entry of the priority queue."""
7      __slots__ = '_index'               # add index as additional field
8
9      def __init__(self, k, v, j):
10       super().__init__(k,v)
11       self._index = j
12
13   #------------------------------ nonpublic behaviors ------------------------------
14   # override swap to record new indices
15   def _swap(self, i, j):
16     super()._swap(i,j)                  # perform the swap
17     self._data[i]._index = i            # reset locator index (post-swap)
18     self._data[j]._index = j            # reset locator index (post-swap)
19
20   def _bubble(self, j):
21     if j > 0 and self._data[j] < self._data[self._parent(j)]:
22       self._upheap(j)
23     else:
24       self._downheap(j)
```

Code Fragment 9.8: An implementation of an adaptable priority queue (continued in Code Fragment 9.9). This extends the HeapPriorityQueue class of Code Fragments 9.4 and 9.5

```python
25    def add(self, key, value):
26        """Add a key-value pair."""
27        token = self.Locator(key, value, len(self._data))   # initiaize locator index
28        self._data.append(token)
29        self._upheap(len(self._data) - 1)
30        return token
31
32    def update(self, loc, newkey, newval):
33        """Update the key and value for the entry identified by Locator loc."""
34        j = loc._index
35        if not (0 <= j < len(self) and self._data[j] is loc):
36            raise ValueError('Invalid locator')
37        loc._key = newkey
38        loc._value = newval
39        self._bubble(j)
40
41    def remove(self, loc):
42        """Remove and return the (k,v) pair identified by Locator loc."""
43        j = loc._index
44        if not (0 <= j < len(self) and self._data[j] is loc):
45            raise ValueError('Invalid locator')
46        if j == len(self) - 1:                 # item at last position
47            self._data.pop( )                   # just remove it
48        else:
49            self._swap(j, len(self)-1)          # swap item to the last position
50            self._data.pop( )                   # remove it from the list
51            self._bubble(j)                     # fix item displaced by the swap
52        return (loc._key, loc._value)
```

Code Fragment 9.9: An implementation of an adaptable priority queue (continued from Code Fragment 9.8).

Operation	Running Time
len(P), P.is_empty( ), P.min( )	$O(1)$
P.add(k,v)	$O(\log n)^*$
P.update(loc, k, v)	$O(\log n)$
P.remove(loc)	$O(\log n)^*$
P.remove_min( )	$O(\log n)^*$

*amortized with dynamic array

Table 9.4: Running times of the methods of an adaptable priority queue, P, of size n, realized by means of our array-based heap representation. The space requirement is $O(n)$.

9.6 Exercises

For help with exercises, please visit the site, www.wiley.com/college/goodrich.

Reinforcement

R-9.1 How long would it take to remove the $\lceil \log n \rceil$ smallest elements from a heap that contains n entries, using the remove_min operation?

R-9.2 Suppose you label each position p of a binary tree T with a key equal to its preorder rank. Under what circumstances is T a heap?

R-9.3 What does each remove_min call return within the following sequence of priority queue ADT methods: add(5,A), add(4,B), add(7,F), add(1,D), remove_min( ), add(3,J), add(6,L), remove_min( ), remove_min( ), add(8,G), remove_min( ), add(2,H), remove_min( ), remove_min( )?

R-9.4 An airport is developing a computer simulation of air-traffic control that handles events such as landings and takeoffs. Each event has a *time stamp* that denotes the time when the event will occur. The simulation program needs to efficiently perform the following two fundamental operations:

- Insert an event with a given time stamp (that is, add a future event).
- Extract the event with smallest time stamp (that is, determine the next event to process).

Which data structure should be used for the above operations? Why?

R-9.5 The min method for the UnsortedPriorityQueue class executes in $O(n)$ time, as analyzed in Table 9.2. Give a simple modification to the class so that min runs in $O(1)$ time. Explain any necessary modifications to other methods of the class.

R-9.6 Can you adapt your solution to the previous problem to make remove_min run in $O(1)$ time for the UnsortedPriorityQueue class? Explain your answer.

R-9.7 Illustrate the execution of the selection-sort algorithm on the following input sequence: $(22, 15, 36, 44, 10, 3, 9, 13, 29, 25)$.

R-9.8 Illustrate the execution of the insertion-sort algorithm on the input sequence of the previous problem.

R-9.9 Give an example of a worst-case sequence with n elements for insertion-sort, and show that insertion-sort runs in $\Omega(n^2)$ time on such a sequence.

R-9.10 At which positions of a heap might the third smallest key be stored?

R-9.11 At which positions of a heap might the largest key be stored?

R-9.12 Consider a situation in which a user has numeric keys and wishes to have a priority queue that is *maximum-oriented*. How could a standard (min-oriented) priority queue be used for such a purpose?

R-9.13 Illustrate the execution of the in-place heap-sort algorithm on the following input sequence: $(2, 5, 16, 4, 10, 23, 39, 18, 26, 15)$.

R-9.14 Let T be a complete binary tree such that position p stores an element with key $f(p)$, where $f(p)$ is the level number of p (see Section 8.3.2). Is tree T a heap? Why or why not?

R-9.15 Explain why the description of down-heap bubbling does not consider the case in which position p has a right child but not a left child.

R-9.16 Is there a heap H storing seven entries with distinct keys such that a pre-order traversal of H yields the entries of H in increasing or decreasing order by key? How about an inorder traversal? How about a postorder traversal? If so, give an example; if not, say why.

R-9.17 Let H be a heap storing 15 entries using the array-based representation of a complete binary tree. What is the sequence of indices of the array that are visited in a preorder traversal of H? What about an inorder traversal of H? What about a postorder traversal of H?

R-9.18 Show that the sum

$$\sum_{i=1}^{n} \log i,$$

which appears in the analysis of heap-sort, is $\Omega(n \log n)$.

R-9.19 Bill claims that a preorder traversal of a heap will list its keys in nonde-creasing order. Draw an example of a heap that proves him wrong.

R-9.20 Hillary claims that a postorder traversal of a heap will list its keys in non-increasing order. Draw an example of a heap that proves her wrong.

R-9.21 Show all the steps of the algorithm for removing the entry $(16, X)$ from the heap of Figure 9.1, assuming the entry had been identified with a locator.

R-9.22 Show all the steps of the algorithm for replacing key of entry $(5, A)$ with 18 in the heap of Figure 9.1, assuming the entry had been identified with a locator.

R-9.23 Draw an example of a heap whose keys are all the odd numbers from 1 to 59 (with no repeats), such that the insertion of an entry with key 32 would cause up-heap bubbling to proceed all the way up to a child of the root (replacing that child's key with 32).

R-9.24 Describe a sequence of n insertions in a heap that requires $\Omega(n \log n)$ time to process.

R-9.25 Complete Figure 9.9 by showing all the steps of the in-place heap-sort algorithm. Show both the array and the associated heap at the end of each step.

Creativity

C-9.26 Show how to implement the stack ADT using only a priority queue and one additional integer instance variable.

C-9.27 Show how to implement the FIFO queue ADT using only a priority queue and one additional integer instance variable.

C-9.28 Professor Idle suggests the following solution to the previous problem. Whenever an item is inserted into the queue, it is assigned a key that is equal to the current size of the queue. Does such a strategy result in FIFO semantics? Prove that it is so or provide a counterexample.

C-9.29 Reimplement the SortedPriorityQueue using a Python list. Make sure to maintain remove_min's $O(1)$ performance.

C-9.30 Give a nonrecursive implementation of the _upheap method for the class HeapPriorityQueue.

C-9.31 Give a nonrecursive implementation of the _downheap method for the class HeapPriorityQueue.

C-9.32 Assume that we are using a linked representation of a complete binary tree T, and an extra reference to the last node of that tree. Show how to update the reference to the last node after operations add or remove_min in $O(\log n)$ time, where n is the current number of nodes of T. Be sure and handle all possible cases, as illustrated in Figure 9.12.

C-9.33 When using a linked-tree representation for a heap, an alternative method for finding the last node during an insertion in a heap T is to store, in the last node and each leaf node of T, a reference to the leaf node immediately to its right (wrapping to the first node in the next lower level for the rightmost leaf node). Show how to maintain such references in $O(1)$ time per operation of the priority queue ADT assuming that T is implemented with a linked structure.

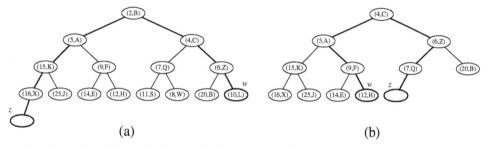

(a) (b)

Figure 9.12: Updating the last node in a complete binary tree after operation add or remove. Node w is the last node before operation add or after operation remove. Node z is the last node after operation add or before operation remove.

C-9.34 We can represent a path from the root to a given node of a binary tree by means of a binary string, where 0 means "go to the left child" and 1 means "go to the right child." For example, the path from the root to the node storing $(8,W)$ in the heap of Figure 9.12a is represented by "101." Design an $O(\log n)$-time algorithm for finding the last node of a complete binary tree with n nodes, based on the above representation. Show how this algorithm can be used in the implementation of a complete binary tree by means of a linked structure that does not keep a reference to the last node.

C-9.35 Given a heap T and a key k, give an algorithm to compute all the entries in T having a key less than or equal to k. For example, given the heap of Figure 9.12a and query $k = 7$, the algorithm should report the entries with keys 2, 4, 5, 6, and 7 (but not necessarily in this order). Your algorithm should run in time proportional to the number of entries returned, and should *not* modify the heap

C-9.36 Provide a justification of the time bounds in Table 9.4.

C-9.37 Give an alternative analysis of bottom-up heap construction by showing the following summation is $O(1)$, for any positive integer h:

$$\sum_{i=1}^{h} (i/2^i).$$

C-9.38 Suppose two binary trees, T_1 and T_2, hold entries satisfying the heap-order property (but not necessarily the complete binary tree property). Describe a method for combining T_1 and T_2 into a binary tree T, whose nodes hold the union of the entries in T_1 and T_2 and also satisfy the heap-order property. Your algorithm should run in time $O(h_1 + h_2)$ where h_1 and h_2 are the respective heights of T_1 and T_2.

C-9.39 Implement a heappushpop method for the HeapPriorityQueue class, with semantics akin to that described for the heapq module in Section 9.3.7.

C-9.40 Implement a heapreplace method for the HeapPriorityQueue class, with semantics akin to that described for the heapq module in Section 9.3.7.

C-9.41 Tamarindo Airlines wants to give a first-class upgrade coupon to their top $\log n$ frequent flyers, based on the number of miles accumulated, where n is the total number of the airlines' frequent flyers. The algorithm they currently use, which runs in $O(n \log n)$ time, sorts the flyers by the number of miles flown and then scans the sorted list to pick the top $\log n$ flyers. Describe an algorithm that identifies the top $\log n$ flyers in $O(n)$ time.

C-9.42 Explain how the k largest elements from an unordered collection of size n can be found in time $O(n + k \log n)$ using a maximum-oriented heap.

C-9.43 Explain how the k largest elements from an unordered collection of size n can be found in time $O(n \log k)$ using $O(k)$ auxiliary space.

C-9.44 Given a class, PriorityQueue, that implements the minimum-oriented priority queue ADT, provide an implementation of a MaxPriorityQueue class that adapts to provide a maximum-oriented abstraction with methods add, max, and remove_max. Your implementation should not make any assumption about the internal workings of the original PriorityQueue class, nor the type of keys that might be used.

C-9.45 Write a key function for nonnegative integers that determines order based on the number of 1's in each integer's binary expansion.

C-9.46 Give an alternative implementation of the pq_sort function, from Code Fragment 9.7, that accepts a key function as an optional parameter.

C-9.47 Describe an in-place version of the selection-sort algorithm for an array that uses only $O(1)$ space for instance variables in addition to the array.

C-9.48 Assuming the input to the sorting problem is given in an array A, describe how to implement the insertion-sort algorithm using only the array A and at most a constant number of additional variables.

C-9.49 Give an alternate description of the in-place heap-sort algorithm using the standard minimum-oriented priority queue (instead of a maximum-oriented one).

C-9.50 An online computer system for trading stocks needs to process orders of the form "buy 100 shares at $x each" or "sell 100 shares at $y each." A buy order for $x can only be processed if there is an existing sell order with price $y such that $y \leq x$. Likewise, a sell order for $y can only be processed if there is an existing buy order with price $x such that $y \leq x$. If a buy or sell order is entered but cannot be processed, it must wait for a future order that allows it to be processed. Describe a scheme that allows buy and sell orders to be entered in $O(\log n)$ time, independent of whether or not they can be immediately processed.

C-9.51 Extend a solution to the previous problem so that users are allowed to update the prices for their buy or sell orders that have yet to be processed.

C-9.52 A group of children want to play a game, called *Unmonopoly*, where in each turn the player with the most money must give half of his/her money to the player with the least amount of money. What data structure(s) should be used to play this game efficiently? Why?

Projects

P-9.53 Implement the in-place heap-sort algorithm. Experimentally compare its running time with that of the standard heap-sort that is not in-place.

P-9.54 Use the approach of either Exercise C-9.42 or C-9.43 to reimplement the top method of the FavoritesListMTF class from Section 7.6.2. Make sure that results are generated from largest to smallest.

P-9.55 Write a program that can process a sequence of stock buy and sell orders as described in Exercise C-9.50.

P-9.56 Let S be a set of n points in the plane with distinct integer x- and y-coordinates. Let T be a complete binary tree storing the points from S at its external nodes, such that the points are ordered left to right by increasing x-coordinates. For each node v in T, let $S(v)$ denote the subset of S consisting of points stored in the subtree rooted at v. For the root r of T, define $top(r)$ to be the point in $S = S(r)$ with maximum y-coordinate. For every other node v, define $top(r)$ to be the point in S with highest y-coordinate in $S(v)$ that is not also the highest y-coordinate in $S(u)$, where u is the parent of v in T (if such a point exists). Such labeling turns T into a *priority search tree*. Describe a linear-time algorithm for turning T into a priority search tree. Implement this approach.

P-9.57 One of the main applications of priority queues is in operating systems—for *scheduling jobs* on a CPU. In this project you are to build a program that schedules simulated CPU jobs. Your program should run in a loop, each iteration of which corresponds to a *time slice* for the CPU. Each job is assigned a priority, which is an integer between -20 (highest priority) and 19 (lowest priority), inclusive. From among all jobs waiting to be processed in a time slice, the CPU must work on a job with highest priority. In this simulation, each job will also come with a *length* value, which is an integer between 1 and 100, inclusive, indicating the number of time slices that are needed to process this job. For simplicity, you may assume jobs cannot be interrupted—once it is scheduled on the CPU, a job runs for a number of time slices equal to its length. Your simulator must output the name of the job running on the CPU in each time slice and must process a sequence of commands, one per time slice, each of which is of the form "add job *name* with length n and priority p" or "no new job this slice".

P-9.58 Develop a Python implementation of an adaptable priority queue that is based on an unsorted list and supports location-aware entries.

Chapter Notes

Knuth's book on sorting and searching [65] describes the motivation and history for the selection-sort, insertion-sort, and heap-sort algorithms. The heap-sort algorithm is due to Williams [103], and the linear-time heap construction algorithm is due to Floyd [39]. Additional algorithms and analyses for heaps and heap-sort variations can be found in papers by Bentley [15], Carlsson [24], Gonnet and Munro [45], McDiarmid and Reed [74], and Schaffer and Sedgewick [88].

Chapter

10 Maps, Hash Tables, and Skip Lists

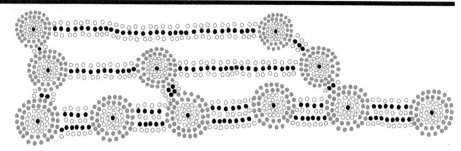

Contents

10.1   Maps and Dictionaries

Python's **dict** class is arguably the most significant data structure in the language. It represents an abstraction known as a **dictionary** in which unique **keys** are mapped to associated **values**. Because of the relationship they express between keys and values, dictionaries are commonly known as **associative arrays** or **maps**. In this book, we use the term *dictionary* when specifically discussing Python's dict class, and the term *map* when discussing the more general notion of the abstract data type.

As a simple example, Figure 10.1 illustrates a map from the names of countries to their associated units of currency.

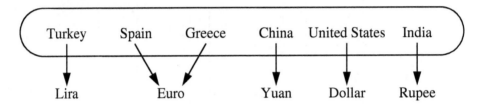

Figure 10.1: A map from countries (the keys) to their units of currency (the values).

We note that the keys (the country names) are assumed to be unique, but the values (the currency units) are not necessarily unique. For example, we note that Spain and Greece both use the euro for currency. Maps use an array-like syntax for indexing, such as currency['Greece'] to access a value associated with a given key or currency['Greece'] = 'Drachma' to remap it to a new value. Unlike a standard array, indices for a map need not be consecutive nor even numeric. Common applications of maps include the following.

- A university's information system relies on some form of a student ID as a key that is mapped to that student's associated record (such as the student's name, address, and course grades) serving as the value.
- The domain-name system (DNS) maps a host name, such as www.wiley.com, to an Internet-Protocol (IP) address, such as 208.215.179.146.
- A social media site typically relies on a (nonnumeric) username as a key that can be efficiently mapped to a particular user's associated information.
- A computer graphics system may map a color name, such as 'turquoise', to the triple of numbers that describes the color's RGB (red-green-blue) representation, such as (64,224,208).
- Python uses a dictionary to represent each namespace, mapping an identifying string, such as 'pi', to an associated object, such as 3.14159.

In this chapter and the next we demonstrate that a map may be implemented so that a search for a key, and its associated value, can be performed very efficiently, thereby supporting fast lookup in such applications.

10.1.1   The Map ADT

In this section, we introduce the ***map ADT***, and define its behaviors to be consistent with those of Python's built-in dict class. We begin by listing what we consider the most significant five behaviors of a map M as follows:

M[k]: Return the value v associated with key k in map M, if one exists; otherwise raise a KeyError. In Python, this is implemented with the special method __getitem__.

M[k] = v: Associate value v with key k in map M, replacing the existing value if the map already contains an item with key equal to k. In Python, this is implemented with the special method __setitem__.

del M[k]: Remove from map M the item with key equal to k; if M has no such item, then raise a KeyError. In Python, this is implemented with the special method __delitem__.

len(M): Return the number of items in map M. In Python, this is implemented with the special method __len__.

iter(M): The default iteration for a map generates a sequence of *keys* in the map. In Python, this is implemented with the special method __iter__, and it allows loops of the form, **for** k **in** M.

We have highlighted the above five behaviors because they demonstrate the core functionality of a map—namely, the ability to query, add, modify, or delete a key-value pair, and the ability to report all such pairs. For additional convenience, map M should also support the following behaviors:

k in M: Return True if the map contains an item with key k. In Python, this is implemented with the special __contains__ method.

M.get(k, d=None): Return M[k] if key k exists in the map; otherwise return default value d. This provides a form to query M[k] without risk of a KeyError.

M.setdefault(k, d): If key k exists in the map, simply return M[k]; if key k does not exist, set M[k] = d and return that value.

M.pop(k, d=None): Remove the item associated with key k from the map and return its associated value v. If key k is not in the map, return default value d (or raise KeyError if parameter d is None).

M.popitem(): Remove an arbitrary key-value pair from the map, and return a (k,v) tuple representing the removed pair. If map is empty, raise a KeyError.

M.clear(): Remove all key-value pairs from the map.

M.keys(): Return a set-like view of all keys of M.

M.values(): Return a set-like view of all values of M.

M.items(): Return a set-like view of (k,v) tuples for all entries of M.

M.update(M2): Assign M[k] = v for every (k,v) pair in map M2.

M == M2: Return True if maps M and M2 have identical key-value associations.

M != M2: Return True if maps M and M2 do not have identical key-value associations.

Example 10.1: *In the following, we show the effect of a series of operations on an initially empty map storing items with integer keys and single-character values. We use the literal syntax for Python's dict class to describe the map contents.*

Operation	Return Value	Map
len(M)	0	{ }
M['K'] = 2	–	{'K': 2}
M['B'] = 4	–	{'K': 2, 'B': 4}
M['U'] = 2	–	{'K': 2, 'B': 4, 'U': 2}
M['V'] = 8	–	{'K': 2, 'B': 4, 'U': 2, 'V': 8}
M['K'] = 9	–	{'K': 9, 'B': 4, 'U': 2, 'V': 8}
M['B']	4	{'K': 9, 'B': 4, 'U': 2, 'V': 8}
M['X']	KeyError	{'K': 9, 'B': 4, 'U': 2, 'V': 8}
M.get('F')	None	{'K': 9, 'B': 4, 'U': 2, 'V': 8}
M.get('F', 5)	5	{'K': 9, 'B': 4, 'U': 2, 'V': 8}
M.get('K', 5)	9	{'K': 9, 'B': 4, 'U': 2, 'V': 8}
len(M)	4	{'K': 9, 'B': 4, 'U': 2, 'V': 8}
del M['V']	–	{'K': 9, 'B': 4, 'U': 2}
M.pop('K')	9	{'B': 4, 'U': 2}
M.keys()	'B', 'U'	{'B': 4, 'U': 2}
M.values()	4, 2	{'B': 4, 'U': 2}
M.items()	('B', 4), ('U', 2)	{'B': 4, 'U': 2}
M.setdefault('B', 1)	4	{'B': 4, 'U': 2}
M.setdefault('A', 1)	1	{'A': 1, 'B': 4, 'U': 2}
M.popitem()	('B', 4)	{'A': 1, 'U': 2}

10.1.2 Application: Counting Word Frequencies

As a case study for using a map, consider the problem of counting the number of occurrences of words in a document. This is a standard task when performing a statistical analysis of a document, for example, when categorizing an email or news article. A map is an ideal data structure to use here, for we can use words as keys and word counts as values. We show such an application in Code Fragment 10.1.

We break apart the original document using a combination of file and string methods that results in a loop over a lowercased version of all whitespace separated pieces of the document. We omit all nonalphabetic characters so that parentheses, apostrophes, and other such punctuation are not considered part of a word.

In terms of map operations, we begin with an empty Python dictionary named freq. During the first phase of the algorithm, we execute the command

$$\text{freq[word]} = 1 + \text{freq.get(word, 0)}$$

for each word occurrence. We use the get method on the right-hand side because the current word might not exist in the dictionary; the default value of 0 is appropriate in that case.

During the second phase of the algorithm, after the full document has been processed, we examine the contents of the frequency map, looping over freq.items( ) to determine which word has the most occurrences.

```
1  freq = { }
2  for piece in open(filename).read( ).lower( ).split( ):
3      # only consider alphabetic characters within this piece
4      word = ''.join(c for c in piece if c.isalpha( ))
5      if word:    # require at least one alphabetic character
6          freq[word] = 1 + freq.get(word, 0)
7
8  max_word = ''
9  max_count = 0
10 for (w,c) in freq.items( ):        # (key, value) tuples represent (word, count)
11     if c > max_count:
12         max_word = w
13         max_count = c
14 print('The most frequent word is', max_word)
15 print('Its number of occurrences is', max_count)
```

Code Fragment 10.1: A program for counting word frequencies in a document, and reporting the most frequent word. We use Python's dict class for the map. We convert the input to lowercase and ignore any nonalphabetic characters.

10.1.3   Python's MutableMapping Abstract Base Class

Section 2.4.3 provides an introduction to the concept of an ***abstract base class*** and the role of such classes in Python's collections module. Methods that are declared to be abstract in such a base class must be implemented by concrete subclasses. However, an abstract base class may provide *concrete* implementation of other methods that depend upon use of the presumed abstract methods. (This is an example of the ***template method design pattern***.)

The collections module provides two abstract base classes that are relevant to our current discussion: the Mapping and MutableMapping classes. The Mapping class includes all nonmutating methods supported by Python's dict class, while the MutableMapping class extends that to include the mutating methods. What we define as the map ADT in Section 10.1.1 is akin to the MutableMapping abstract base class in Python's collections module.

The significance of these abstract base classes is that they provide a framework to assist in creating a user-defined map class. In particular, the MutableMapping class provides *concrete* implementations for all behaviors other than the first five outlined in Section 10.1.1: __getitem__, __setitem__, __delitem__, __len__, and __iter__. As we implement the map abstraction with various data structures, as long as we provide the five core behaviors, we can inherit all other derived behaviors by simply declaring MutableMapping as a parent class.

To better understand the MutableMapping class, we provide a few examples of how concrete behaviors can be derived from the five core abstractions. For example, the __contains__ method, supporting the syntax k in M, could be implemented by making a guarded attempt to retrieve self[k] to determine if the key exists.

```
def __contains__(self, k):
  try:
    self[k]                    # access via __getitem__ (ignore result)
    return True
  except KeyError:
    return False               # attempt failed
```

A similar approach might be used to provide the logic of the setdefault method.

```
def setdefault(self, k, d):
  try:
    return self[k]             # if __getitem__ succeeds, return value
  except KeyError:             # otherwise:
    self[k] = d                # set default value with __setitem__
    return d                   # and return that newly assigned value
```

We leave as exercises the implementations of the remaining concrete methods of the MutableMapping class.

10.1.4 Our MapBase Class

We will be providing many different implementations of the map ADT, in the remainder of this chapter and next, using a variety of data structures demonstrating a trade-off of advantages and disadvantages. Figure 10.2 provides a preview of those classes.

The MutableMapping abstract base class, from Python's collections module and discussed in the preceding pages, is a valuable tool when implementing a map. However, in the interest of greater code reuse, we define our own MapBase class, which is itself a subclass of the MutableMapping class. Our MapBase class provides additional support for the composition design pattern. This is a technique we introduced when implementing a priority queue (see Section 9.2.1) in order to group a key-value pair as a single instance for internal use.

More formally, our MapBase class is defined in Code Fragment 10.2, extending the existing MutableMapping abstract base class so that we inherit the many useful concrete methods that class provides. We then define a nonpublic nested _Item class, whose instances are able to store both a key and value. This nested class is reasonably similar in design to the _Item class that was defined within our PriorityQueueBase class in Section 9.2.1, except that for a map we provide support for both equality tests and comparisons, both of which rely on the item's key. The notion of equality is necessary for all of our map implementations, as a way to determine whether a key given as a parameter is equivalent to one that is already stored in the map. The notion of comparisons between keys, using the < operator, will become relevant when we later introduce a *sorted map ADT* (Section 10.3).

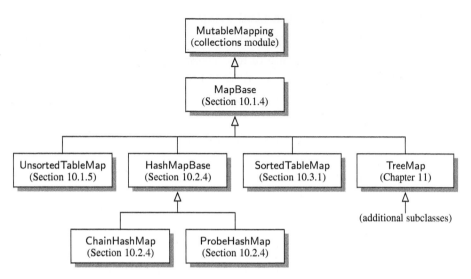

Figure 10.2: Our hierarchy of map types (with references to where they are defined).

```
1  class MapBase(MutableMapping):
2    """Our own abstract base class that includes a nonpublic _Item class."""
3
4    #----------------------------- nested _Item class -----------------------------
5    class _Item:
6      """Lightweight composite to store key-value pairs as map items."""
7      __slots__ = '_key', '_value'
8
9      def __init__(self, k, v):
10       self._key = k
11       self._value = v
12
13     def __eq__(self, other):
14       return self._key == other._key     # compare items based on their keys
15
16     def __ne__(self, other):
17       return not (self == other)         # opposite of __eq__
18
19     def __lt__(self, other):
20       return self._key < other._key      # compare items based on their keys
```

Code Fragment 10.2: Extending the MutableMapping abstract base class to provide a nonpublic _Item class for use in our various map implementations.

10.1.5 Simple Unsorted Map Implementation

We demonstrate the use of the MapBase class with a very simple concrete implementation of the map ADT. Code Fragment 10.3 presents an UnsortedTableMap class that relies on storing key-value pairs in arbitrary order within a Python list.

An empty table is initialized as self._table within the constructor for our map. When a new key is entered into the map, via line 22 of the __setitem__ method, we create a new instance of the nested _Item class, which is inherited from our MapBase class.

This list-based map implementation is simple, but it is not particularly efficient. Each of the fundamental methods, __getitem__, __setitem__, and __delitem__, relies on a for loop to scan the underlying list of items in search of a matching key. In a best-case scenario, such a match may be found near the beginning of the list, in which case the loop terminates; in the worst case, the entire list will be examined. Therefore, each of these methods runs in $O(n)$ time on a map with n items.

```
1   class UnsortedTableMap(MapBase):
2     """Map implementation using an unordered list."""
3
4     def __init__(self):
5       """Create an empty map."""
6       self._table = [ ]                              # list of _Item's
7
8     def __getitem__(self, k):
9       """Return value associated with key k (raise KeyError if not found)."""
10      for item in self._table:
11        if k == item._key:
12          return item._value
13      raise KeyError('Key Error: ' + repr(k))
14
15    def __setitem__(self, k, v):
16      """Assign value v to key k, overwriting existing value if present."""
17      for item in self._table:
18        if k == item._key:                           # Found a match:
19          item._value = v                            # reassign value
20          return                                     # and quit
21      # did not find match for key
22      self._table.append(self._Item(k,v))
23
24    def __delitem__(self, k):
25      """Remove item associated with key k (raise KeyError if not found)."""
26      for j in range(len(self._table)):
27        if k == self._table[j]._key:                 # Found a match:
28          self._table.pop(j)                         # remove item
29          return                                     # and quit
30      raise KeyError('Key Error: ' + repr(k))
31
32    def __len__(self):
33      """Return number of items in the map."""
34      return len(self._table)
35
36    def __iter__(self):
37      """Generate iteration of the map's keys."""
38      for item in self._table:
39        yield item._key                              # yield the KEY
```

Code Fragment 10.3: An implementation of a map using a Python list as an unsorted table. Parent class MapBase is given in Code Fragment 10.2.

10.2   Hash Tables

In this section, we introduce one of the most practical data structures for implementing a map, and the one that is used by Python's own implementation of the dict class. This structure is known as a ***hash table***.

Intuitively, a map M supports the abstraction of using keys as indices with a syntax such as M[k]. As a mental warm-up, consider a restricted setting in which a map with n items uses keys that are known to be integers in a range from 0 to $N-1$ for some $N \geq n$. In this case, we can represent the map using a ***lookup table*** of length N, as diagrammed in Figure 10.3.

0	1	2	3	4	5	6	7	8	9	10
	D		Z			C	Q			

Figure 10.3: A lookup table with length 11 for a map containing items (1,D), (3,Z), (6,C), and (7,Q).

In this representation, we store the value associated with key k at index k of the table (presuming that we have a distinct way to represent an empty slot). Basic map operations of __getitem__, __setitem__, and __delitem__ can be implemented in $O(1)$ worst-case time.

There are two challenges in extending this framework to the more general setting of a map. First, we may not wish to devote an array of length N if it is the case that $N \gg n$. Second, we do not in general require that a map's keys be integers. The novel concept for a hash table is the use of a ***hash function*** to map general keys to corresponding indices in a table. Ideally, keys will be well distributed in the range from 0 to $N-1$ by a hash function, but in practice there may be two or more distinct keys that get mapped to the same index. As a result, we will conceptualize our table as a ***bucket array***, as shown in Figure 10.4, in which each bucket may manage a collection of items that are sent to a specific index by the hash function. (To save space, an empty bucket may be replaced by None.)

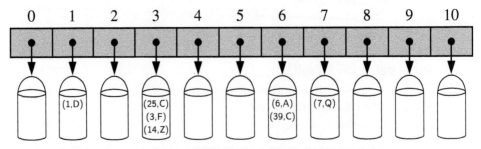

Figure 10.4: A bucket array of capacity 11 with items (1,D), (25,C), (3,F), (14,Z), (6,A), (39,C), and (7,Q), using a simple hash function.

10.2.1   Hash Functions

The goal of a ***hash function***, h, is to map each key k to an integer in the range $[0, N-1]$, where N is the capacity of the bucket array for a hash table. Equipped with such a hash function, h, the main idea of this approach is to use the hash function value, $h(k)$, as an index into our bucket array, A, instead of the key k (which may not be appropriate for direct use as an index). That is, we store the item (k, v) in the bucket $A[h(k)]$.

If there are two or more keys with the same hash value, then two different items will be mapped to the same bucket in A. In this case, we say that a ***collision*** has occurred. To be sure, there are ways of dealing with collisions, which we will discuss later, but the best strategy is to try to avoid them in the first place. We say that a hash function is "good" if it maps the keys in our map so as to sufficiently minimize collisions. For practical reasons, we also would like a hash function to be fast and easy to compute.

It is common to view the evaluation of a hash function, $h(k)$, as consisting of two portions—a ***hash code*** that maps a key k to an integer, and a ***compression function*** that maps the hash code to an integer within a range of indices, $[0, N-1]$, for a bucket array. (See Figure 10.5.)

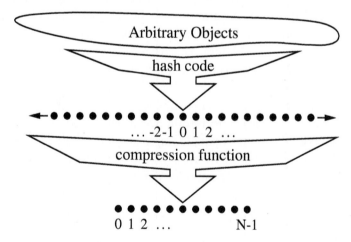

Figure 10.5: Two parts of a hash function: a hash code and a compression function.

The advantage of separating the hash function into two such components is that the hash code portion of that computation is independent of a specific hash table size. This allows the development of a general hash code for each object that can be used for a hash table of any size; only the compression function depends upon the table size. This is particularly convenient, because the underlying bucket array for a hash table may be dynamically resized, depending on the number of items currently stored in the map. (See Section 10.2.3.)

Hash Codes

The first action that a hash function performs is to take an arbitrary key k in our map and compute an integer that is called the **hash code** for k; this integer need not be in the range $[0, N-1]$, and may even be negative. We desire that the set of hash codes assigned to our keys should avoid collisions as much as possible. For if the hash codes of our keys cause collisions, then there is no hope for our compression function to avoid them. In this subsection, we begin by discussing the theory of hash codes. Following that, we discuss practical implementations of hash codes in Python.

Treating the Bit Representation as an Integer

To begin, we note that, for any data type X that is represented using at most as many bits as our integer hash codes, we can simply take as a hash code for X an integer interpretation of its bits. For example, the hash code for key 314 could simply be 314. The hash code for a floating-point number such as 3.14 could be based upon an interpretation of the bits of the floating-point representation as an integer.

For a type whose bit representation is longer than a desired hash code, the above scheme is not immediately applicable. For example, Python relies on 32-bit hash codes. If a floating-point number uses a 64-bit representation, its bits cannot be viewed directly as a hash code. One possibility is to use only the high-order 32 bits (or the low-order 32 bits). This hash code, of course, ignores half of the information present in the original key, and if many of the keys in our map only differ in these bits, then they will collide using this simple hash code.

A better approach is to combine in some way the high-order and low-order portions of a 64-bit key to form a 32-bit hash code, which takes all the original bits into consideration. A simple implementation is to add the two components as 32-bit numbers (ignoring overflow), or to take the exclusive-or of the two components. These approaches of combining components can be extended to any object x whose binary representation can be viewed as an n-tuple $(x_0, x_1, \ldots, x_{n-1})$ of 32-bit integers, for example, by forming a hash code for x as $\sum_{i=0}^{n-1} x_i$, or as $x_0 \oplus x_1 \oplus \cdots \oplus x_{n-1}$, where the $\oplus$ symbol represents the bitwise exclusive-or operation (which is ^ in Python).

Polynomial Hash Codes

The summation and exclusive-or hash codes, described above, are not good choices for character strings or other variable-length objects that can be viewed as tuples of the form $(x_0, x_1, \ldots, x_{n-1})$, where the order of the x_i's is significant. For example, consider a 16-bit hash code for a character string s that sums the Unicode values of the characters in s. This hash code unfortunately produces lots of unwanted collisions for common groups of strings. In particular, `"temp01"` and `"temp10"` collide using this function, as do `"stop"`, `"tops"`, `"pots"`, and `"spot"`. A better hash code should somehow take into consideration the positions of the x_i's. An alternative hash code, which does exactly this, is to choose a nonzero constant, $a \neq 1$, and use as a hash code the value

$$x_0 a^{n-1} + x_1 a^{n-2} + \cdots + x_{n-2} a + x_{n-1}.$$

Mathematically speaking, this is simply a polynomial in a that takes the components $(x_0, x_1, \ldots, x_{n-1})$ of an object x as its coefficients. This hash code is therefore called a ***polynomial hash code***. By Horner's rule (see Exercise C-3.50), this polynomial can be computed as

$$x_{n-1} + a(x_{n-2} + a(x_{n-3} + \cdots + a(x_2 + a(x_1 + ax_0))\cdots)).$$

Intuitively, a polynomial hash code uses multiplication by different powers as a way to spread out the influence of each component across the resulting hash code.

Of course, on a typical computer, evaluating a polynomial will be done using the finite bit representation for a hash code; hence, the value will periodically overflow the bits used for an integer. Since we are more interested in a good spread of the object x with respect to other keys, we simply ignore such overflows. Still, we should be mindful that such overflows are occurring and choose the constant a so that it has some nonzero, low-order bits, which will serve to preserve some of the information content even as we are in an overflow situation.

We have done some experimental studies that suggest that 33, 37, 39, and 41 are particularly good choices for a when working with character strings that are English words. In fact, in a list of over 50,000 English words formed as the union of the word lists provided in two variants of Unix, we found that taking a to be 33, 37, 39, or 41 produced less than 7 collisions in each case!

Cyclic-Shift Hash Codes

A variant of the polynomial hash code replaces multiplication by a with a cyclic shift of a partial sum by a certain number of bits. For example, a 5-bit cyclic shift of the 32-bit value 00111101100101101010100010101000 is achieved by taking the leftmost five bits and placing those on the rightmost side of the representation, resulting in 10110010110101010001010100000111. While this operation has little natural meaning in terms of arithmetic, it accomplishes the goal of varying the bits of the calculation. In Python, a cyclic shift of bits can be accomplished through careful use of the bitwise operators $<<$ and $>>$, taking care to truncate results to 32-bit integers.

An implementation of a cyclic-shift hash code computation for a character string in Python appears as follows:

```python
def hash_code(s):
    mask = (1 << 32) - 1                    # limit to 32-bit integers
    h = 0
    for character in s:
        h = (h << 5 & mask) | (h >> 27)     # 5-bit cyclic shift of running sum
        h += ord(character)                 # add in value of next character
    return h
```

As with the traditional polynomial hash code, fine-tuning is required when using a cyclic-shift hash code, as we must wisely choose the amount to shift by for each new character. Our choice of a 5-bit shift is justified by experiments run on a list of just over 230,000 English words, comparing the number of collisions for various shift amounts (see Table 10.1).

	Collisions	
Shift	**Total**	**Max**
0	234735	623
1	165076	43
2	38471	13
3	7174	5
4	1379	3
5	190	3
6	502	2
7	560	2
8	5546	4
9	393	3
10	5194	5
11	11559	5
12	822	2
13	900	4
14	2001	4
15	19251	8
16	211781	37

Table 10.1: Comparison of collision behavior for the cyclic-shift hash code as applied to a list of 230,000 English words. The "Total" column records the total number of words that collide with at least one other, and the "Max" column records the maximum number of words colliding at any one hash code. Note that with a cyclic shift of 0, this hash code reverts to the one that simply sums all the characters.

Hash Codes in Python

The standard mechanism for computing hash codes in Python is a built-in function with signature hash(x) that returns an integer value that serves as the hash code for object x. However, only *immutable* data types are deemed hashable in Python. This restriction is meant to ensure that a particular object's hash code remains constant during that object's lifespan. This is an important property for an object's use as a key in a hash table. A problem could occur if a key were inserted into the hash table, yet a later search were performed for that key based on a different hash code than that which it had when inserted; the wrong bucket would be searched.

Among Python's built-in data types, the immutable int, float, str, tuple, and frozenset classes produce robust hash codes, via the hash function, using techniques similar to those discussed earlier in this section. Hash codes for character strings are well crafted based on a technique similar to polynomial hash codes, except using exclusive-or computations rather than additions. If we repeat the experiment described in Table 10.1 using Python's built-in hash codes, we find that only 8 strings out of the set of more than 230,000 collide with another. Hash codes for tuples are computed with a similar technique based upon a combination of the hash codes of the individual elements of the tuple. When hashing a frozenset, the order of the elements should be irrelevant, and so a natural option is to compute the exclusive-or of the individual hash codes without any shifting. If hash(x) is called for an instance x of a mutable type, such as a list, a TypeError is raised.

Instances of user-defined classes are treated as unhashable by default, with a TypeError raised by the hash function. However, a function that computes hash codes can be implemented in the form of a special method named __hash__ within a class. The returned hash code should reflect the immutable attributes of an instance. It is common to return a hash code that is itself based on the computed hash of the combination of such attributes. For example, a Color class that maintains three numeric red, green, and blue components might implement the method as:

```
def __hash__(self):
    return hash( (self._red, self._green, self._blue) )   # hash combined tuple
```

An important rule to obey is that if a class defines equivalence through __eq__, then any implementation of __hash__ must be consistent, in that if x == y, then hash(x) == hash(y). This is important because if two instances are considered to be equivalent and one is used as a key in a hash table, a search for the second instance should result in the discovery of the first. It is therefore important that the hash code for the second match the hash code for the first, so that the proper bucket is examined. This rule extends to any well-defined comparisons between objects of different classes. For example, since Python treats the expression 5 == 5.0 as true, it ensures that hash(5) and hash(5.0) are the same.

Compression Functions

The hash code for a key k will typically not be suitable for immediate use with a bucket array, because the integer hash code may be negative or may exceed the capacity of the bucket array. Thus, once we have determined an integer hash code for a key object k, there is still the issue of mapping that integer into the range $[0, N-1]$. This computation, known as a *compression function*, is the second action performed as part of an overall hash function. A good compression function is one that minimizes the number of collisions for a given set of distinct hash codes.

The Division Method

A simple compression function is the *division method*, which maps an integer i to

$$i \bmod N,$$

where N, the size of the bucket array, is a fixed positive integer. Additionally, if we take N to be a prime number, then this compression function helps "spread out" the distribution of hashed values. Indeed, if N is not prime, then there is greater risk that patterns in the distribution of hash codes will be repeated in the distribution of hash values, thereby causing collisions. For example, if we insert keys with hash codes $\{200, 205, 210, 215, 220, \ldots, 600\}$ into a bucket array of size 100, then each hash code will collide with three others. But if we use a bucket array of size 101, then there will be no collisions. If a hash function is chosen well, it should ensure that the probability of two different keys getting hashed to the same bucket is $1/N$. Choosing N to be a prime number is not always enough, however, for if there is a repeated pattern of hash codes of the form $pN + q$ for several different p's, then there will still be collisions.

The MAD Method

A more sophisticated compression function, which helps eliminate repeated patterns in a set of integer keys, is the *Multiply-Add-and-Divide* (or "MAD") method. This method maps an integer i to

$$[(ai+b) \bmod p] \bmod N,$$

where N is the size of the bucket array, p is a prime number larger than N, and a and b are integers chosen at random from the interval $[0, p-1]$, with $a > 0$. This compression function is chosen in order to eliminate repeated patterns in the set of hash codes and get us closer to having a "good" hash function, that is, one such that the probability any two different keys collide is $1/N$. This good behavior would be the same as we would have if these keys were "thrown" into A uniformly at random.

10.2.2 Collision-Handling Schemes

The main idea of a hash table is to take a bucket array, A, and a hash function, h, and use them to implement a map by storing each item (k, v) in the "bucket" $A[h(k)]$. This simple idea is challenged, however, when we have two distinct keys, k_1 and k_2, such that $h(k_1) = h(k_2)$. The existence of such *collisions* prevents us from simply inserting a new item (k, v) directly into the bucket $A[h(k)]$. It also complicates our procedure for performing insertion, search, and deletion operations.

Separate Chaining

A simple and efficient way for dealing with collisions is to have each bucket $A[j]$ store its own secondary container, holding items (k, v) such that $h(k) = j$. A natural choice for the secondary container is a small map instance implemented using a list, as described in Section 10.1.5. This *collision resolution* rule is known as *separate chaining*, and is illustrated in Figure 10.6.

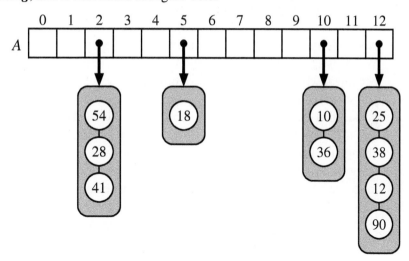

Figure 10.6: A hash table of size 13, storing 10 items with integer keys, with collisions resolved by separate chaining. The compression function is $h(k) = k \bmod 13$. For simplicity, we do not show the values associated with the keys.

In the worst case, operations on an individual bucket take time proportional to the size of the bucket. Assuming we use a good hash function to index the n items of our map in a bucket array of capacity N, the expected size of a bucket is n/N. Therefore, if given a good hash function, the core map operations run in $O(\lceil n/N \rceil)$. The ratio $\lambda = n/N$, called the *load factor* of the hash table, should be bounded by a small constant, preferably below 1. As long as λ is $O(1)$, the core operations on the hash table run in $O(1)$ expected time.

Open Addressing

The separate chaining rule has many nice properties, such as affording simple implementations of map operations, but it nevertheless has one slight disadvantage: It requires the use of an auxiliary data structure—a list—to hold items with colliding keys. If space is at a premium (for example, if we are writing a program for a small handheld device), then we can use the alternative approach of always storing each item directly in a table slot. This approach saves space because no auxiliary structures are employed, but it requires a bit more complexity to deal with collisions. There are several variants of this approach, collectively referred to as *open addressing* schemes, which we discuss next. Open addressing requires that the load factor is always at most 1 and that items are stored directly in the cells of the bucket array itself.

Linear Probing and Its Variants

A simple method for collision handling with open addressing is *linear probing*. With this approach, if we try to insert an item (k, v) into a bucket $A[j]$ that is already occupied, where $j = h(k)$, then we next try $A[(j+1) \bmod N]$. If $A[(j+1) \bmod N]$ is also occupied, then we try $A[(j+2) \bmod N]$, and so on, until we find an empty bucket that can accept the new item. Once this bucket is located, we simply insert the item there. Of course, this collision resolution strategy requires that we change the implementation when searching for an existing key—the first step of all __getitem__, __setitem__, or __delitem__ operations. In particular, to attempt to locate an item with key equal to k, we must examine consecutive slots, starting from $A[h(k)]$, until we either find an item with that key or we find an empty bucket. (See Figure 10.7.) The name "linear probing" comes from the fact that accessing a cell of the bucket array can be viewed as a "probe."

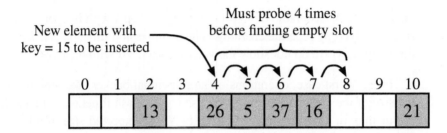

Figure 10.7: Insertion into a hash table with integer keys using linear probing. The hash function is $h(k) = k \bmod 11$. Values associated with keys are not shown.

To implement a deletion, we cannot simply remove a found item from its slot in the array. For example, after the insertion of key 15 portrayed in Figure 10.7, if the item with key 37 were trivially deleted, a subsequent search for 15 would fail because that search would start by probing at index 4, then index 5, and then index 6, at which an empty cell is found. A typical way to get around this difficulty is to replace a deleted item with a special "available" marker object. With this special marker possibly occupying spaces in our hash table, we modify our search algorithm so that the search for a key k will skip over cells containing the available marker and continue probing until reaching the desired item or an empty bucket (or returning back to where we started from). Additionally, our algorithm for __setitem__ should remember an available cell encountered during the search for k, since this is a valid place to put a new item (k, v), if no existing item is found.

Although use of an open addressing scheme can save space, linear probing suffers from an additional disadvantage. It tends to cluster the items of a map into contiguous runs, which may even overlap (particularly if more than half of the cells in the hash table are occupied). Such contiguous runs of occupied hash cells cause searches to slow down considerably.

Another open addressing strategy, known as **quadratic probing**, iteratively tries the buckets $A[(h(k) + f(i)) \bmod N]$, for $i = 0, 1, 2, \ldots$, where $f(i) = i^2$, until finding an empty bucket. As with linear probing, the quadratic probing strategy complicates the removal operation, but it does avoid the kinds of clustering patterns that occur with linear probing. Nevertheless, it creates its own kind of clustering, called **secondary clustering**, where the set of filled array cells still has a non-uniform pattern, even if we assume that the original hash codes are distributed uniformly. When N is prime and the bucket array is less than half full, the quadratic probing strategy is guaranteed to find an empty slot. However, this guarantee is not valid once the table becomes at least half full, or if N is not chosen as a prime number; we explore the cause of this type of clustering in an exercise (C-10.36).

An open addressing strategy that does not cause clustering of the kind produced by linear probing or the kind produced by quadratic probing is the **double hashing** strategy. In this approach, we choose a secondary hash function, h', and if h maps some key k to a bucket $A[h(k)]$ that is already occupied, then we iteratively try the buckets $A[(h(k) + f(i)) \bmod N]$ next, for $i = 1, 2, 3, \ldots$, where $f(i) = i \cdot h'(k)$. In this scheme, the secondary hash function is not allowed to evaluate to zero; a common choice is $h'(k) = q - (k \bmod q)$, for some prime number $q < N$. Also, N should be a prime.

Another approach to avoid clustering with open addressing is to iteratively try buckets $A[(h(k) + f(i)) \bmod N]$ where $f(i)$ is based on a pseudo-random number generator, providing a repeatable, but somewhat arbitrary, sequence of subsequent probes that depends upon bits of the original hash code. This is the approach currently used by Python's dictionary class.

10.2.3   Load Factors, Rehashing, and Efficiency

In the hash table schemes described thus far, it is important that the load factor, $\lambda = n/N$, be kept below 1. With separate chaining, as λ gets very close to 1, the probability of a collision greatly increases, which adds overhead to our operations, since we must revert to linear-time list-based methods in buckets that have collisions. Experiments and average-case analyses suggest that we should maintain $\lambda < 0.9$ for hash tables with separate chaining.

With open addressing, on the other hand, as the load factor λ grows beyond 0.5 and starts approaching 1, clusters of entries in the bucket array start to grow as well. These clusters cause the probing strategies to "bounce around" the bucket array for a considerable amount of time before they find an empty slot. In Exercise C-10.36, we explore the degradation of quadratic probing when $\lambda \geq 0.5$. Experiments suggest that we should maintain $\lambda < 0.5$ for an open addressing scheme with linear probing, and perhaps only a bit higher for other open addressing schemes (for example, Python's implementation of open addressing enforces that $\lambda < 2/3$).

If an insertion causes the load factor of a hash table to go above the specified threshold, then it is common to resize the table (to regain the specified load factor) and to reinsert all objects into this new table. Although we need not define a new hash code for each object, we do need to reapply a new compression function that takes into consideration the size of the new table. Each ***rehashing*** will generally scatter the items throughout the new bucket array. When rehashing to a new table, it is a good requirement for the new array's size to be at least double the previous size. Indeed, if we always double the size of the table with each rehashing operation, then we can amortize the cost of rehashing all the entries in the table against the time used to insert them in the first place (as with dynamic arrays; see Section 5.3).

Efficiency of Hash Tables

Although the details of the average-case analysis of hashing are beyond the scope of this book, its probabilistic basis is quite intuitive. If our hash function is good, then we expect the entries to be uniformly distributed in the N cells of the bucket array. Thus, to store n entries, the expected number of keys in a bucket would be $\lceil n/N \rceil$, which is $O(1)$ if n is $O(N)$.

The costs associated with a periodic rehashing, to resize a table after occasional insertions or deletions can be accounted for separately, leading to an additional $O(1)$ amortized cost for __setitem__ and __getitem__.

In the worst case, a poor hash function could map every item to the same bucket. This would result in linear-time performance for the core map operations with separate chaining, or with any open addressing model in which the secondary sequence of probes depends only on the hash code. A summary of these costs is given in Table 10.2.

Operation	List	Hash Table	
		expected	worst case
__getitem__	$O(n)$	$O(1)$	$O(n)$
__setitem__	$O(n)$	$O(1)$	$O(n)$
__delitem__	$O(n)$	$O(1)$	$O(n)$
__len__	$O(1)$	$O(1)$	$O(1)$
__iter__	$O(n)$	$O(n)$	$O(n)$

Table 10.2: Comparison of the running times of the methods of a map realized by means of an unsorted list (as in Section 10.1.5) or a hash table. We let n denote the number of items in the map, and we assume that the bucket array supporting the hash table is maintained such that its capacity is proportional to the number of items in the map.

In practice, hash tables are among the most efficient means for implementing a map, and it is essentially taken for granted by programmers that their core operations run in constant time. Python's dict class is implemented with hashing, and the Python interpreter relies on dictionaries to retrieve an object that is referenced by an identifier in a given namespace. (See Sections 1.10 and 2.5.) The basic command c = a + b involves two calls to __getitem__ in the dictionary for the local namespace to retrieve the values identified as a and b, and a call to __setitem__ to store the result associated with name c in that namespace. In our own algorithm analysis, we simply presume that such dictionary operations run in constant time, independent of the number of entries in the namespace. (Admittedly, the number of entries in a typical namespace can almost surely be bounded by a constant.)

In a 2003 academic paper [31], researchers discuss the possibility of exploiting a hash table's worst-case performance to cause a denial-of-service (DoS) attack of Internet technologies. For many published algorithms that compute hash codes, they note that an attacker could precompute a very large number of moderate-length strings that all hash to the identical 32-bit hash code. (Recall that by any of the hashing schemes we describe, other than double hashing, if two keys are mapped to the same hash code, they will be inseparable in the collision resolution.)

In late 2011, another team of researchers demonstrated an implementation of just such an attack [61]. Web servers allow a series of key-value parameters to be embedded in a URL using a syntax such as ?key1=val1&key2=val2&key3=val3. Typically, those key-value pairs are immediately stored in a map by the server, and a limit is placed on the length and number of such parameters presuming that storage time in the map will be linear in the number of entries. If all keys were to collide, that storage requires quadratic time (causing the server to perform an inordinate amount of work). In spring of 2012, Python developers distributed a security patch that introduces randomization into the computation of hash codes for strings, making it less tractable to reverse engineer a set of colliding strings.

10.2.4 Python Hash Table Implementation

In this section, we develop two implementations of a hash table, one using separate chaining and the other using open addressing with linear probing. While these approaches to collision resolution are quite different, there are a great many commonalities to the hashing algorithms. For that reason, we extend the MapBase class (from Code Fragment 10.2), to define a new HashMapBase class (see Code Fragment 10.4), providing much of the common functionality to our two hash table implementations. The main design elements of the HashMapBase class are:

- The bucket array is represented as a Python list, named self._table, with all entries initialized to None.

- We maintain an instance variable self._n that represents the number of distinct items that are currently stored in the hash table.

- If the load factor of the table increases beyond 0.5, we double the size of the table and rehash all items into the new table.

- We define a _hash_function utility method that relies on Python's built-in hash function to produce hash codes for keys, and a randomized Multiply-Add-and-Divide (MAD) formula for the compression function.

What is not implemented in the base class is any notion of how a "bucket" should be represented. With separate chaining, each bucket will be an independent structure. With open addressing, however, there is no tangible container for each bucket; the "buckets" are effectively interleaved due to the probing sequences.

In our design, the HashMapBase class presumes the following to be abstract methods, which must be implemented by each concrete subclass:

- _bucket_getitem(j, k)
  This method should search bucket j for an item having key k, returning the associated value, if found, or else raising a KeyError.

- _bucket_setitem(j, k, v)
  This method should modify bucket j so that key k becomes associated with value v. If the key already exists, the new value overwrites the existing value. Otherwise, a new item is inserted and *this method is responsible for incrementing* self._n.

- _bucket_delitem(j, k)
  This method should remove the item from bucket j having key k, or raise a KeyError if no such item exists. (self._n is decremented *after* this method.)

- __iter__
  This is the standard map method to iterate through all keys of the map. Our base class does not delegate this on a per-bucket basis because "buckets" in open addressing are not inherently disjoint.

```
1   class HashMapBase(MapBase):
2     """Abstract base class for map using hash-table with MAD compression."""
3
4     def __init__(self, cap=11, p=109345121):
5       """Create an empty hash-table map."""
6       self._table = cap * [ None ]
7       self._n = 0                               # number of entries in the map
8       self._prime = p                           # prime for MAD compression
9       self._scale = 1 + randrange(p-1)          # scale from 1 to p-1 for MAD
10      self._shift = randrange(p)                # shift from 0 to p-1 for MAD
11
12    def _hash_function(self, k):
13      return (hash(k)*self._scale + self._shift) % self._prime % len(self._table)
14
15    def __len__(self):
16      return self._n
17
18    def __getitem__(self, k):
19      j = self._hash_function(k)
20      return self._bucket_getitem(j, k)         # may raise KeyError
21
22    def __setitem__(self, k, v):
23      j = self._hash_function(k)
24      self._bucket_setitem(j, k, v)             # subroutine maintains self._n
25      if self._n > len(self._table) // 2:       # keep load factor <= 0.5
26        self._resize(2 * len(self._table) - 1)  # number 2^x - 1 is often prime
27
28    def __delitem__(self, k):
29      j = self._hash_function(k)
30      self._bucket_delitem(j, k)                # may raise KeyError
31      self._n -= 1
32
33    def _resize(self, c):                       # resize bucket array to capacity c
34      old = list(self.items())                  # use iteration to record existing items
35      self._table = c * [None]                  # then reset table to desired capacity
36      self._n = 0                               # n recomputed during subsequent adds
37      for (k,v) in old:
38        self[k] = v                             # reinsert old key-value pair
```

Code Fragment 10.4: A base class for our hash table implementations, extending our MapBase class from Code Fragment 10.2.

Separate Chaining

Code Fragment 10.5 provides a concrete implementation of a hash table with separate chaining, in the form of the ChainHashMap class. To represent a single bucket, it relies on an instance of the UnsortedTableMap class from Code Fragment 10.3.

The first three methods in the class use index j to access the potential bucket in the bucket array, and a check for the special case in which that table entry is None. The only time we need a new bucket structure is when _bucket_setitem is called on an otherwise empty slot. The remaining functionality relies on map behaviors that are already supported by the individual UnsortedTableMap instances. We need a bit of forethought to determine whether the application of __setitem__ on the chain causes a net increase in the size of the map (that is, whether the given key is new).

```
 1  class ChainHashMap(HashMapBase):
 2    """Hash map implemented with separate chaining for collision resolution."""
 3
 4    def _bucket_getitem(self, j, k):
 5      bucket = self._table[j]
 6      if bucket is None:
 7        raise KeyError('Key Error: ' + repr(k))       # no match found
 8      return bucket[k]                                 # may raise KeyError
 9
10    def _bucket_setitem(self, j, k, v):
11      if self._table[j] is None:
12        self._table[j] = UnsortedTableMap( )          # bucket is new to the table
13      oldsize = len(self._table[j])
14      self._table[j][k] = v
15      if len(self._table[j]) > oldsize:               # key was new to the table
16        self._n += 1                                  # increase overall map size
17
18    def _bucket_delitem(self, j, k):
19      bucket = self._table[j]
20      if bucket is None:
21        raise KeyError('Key Error: ' + repr(k))       # no match found
22      del bucket[k]                                    # may raise KeyError
23
24    def __iter__(self):
25      for bucket in self._table:
26        if bucket is not None:                         # a nonempty slot
27          for key in bucket:
28            yield key
```

Code Fragment 10.5: Concrete hash map class with separate chaining.

Linear Probing

Our implementation of a ProbeHashMap class, using open addressing with linear probing, is given in Code Fragments 10.6 and 10.7. In order to support deletions, we use a technique described in Section 10.2.2 in which we place a special marker in a table location at which an item has been deleted, so that we can distinguish between it and a location that has always been empty. In our implementation, we declare a class-level attribute, _AVAIL, as a sentinel. (We use an instance of the built-in object class because we do not care about any behaviors of the sentinel, just our ability to differentiate it from other objects.)

The most challenging aspect of open addressing is to properly trace the series of probes when collisions occur during an insertion or search for an item. To this end, we define a nonpublic utility, _find_slot, that searches for an item with key k in "bucket" j (that is, where j is the index returned by the hash function for key k).

```
1  class ProbeHashMap(HashMapBase):
2    """Hash map implemented with linear probing for collision resolution."""
3    _AVAIL = object( )        # sentinal marks locations of previous deletions
4
5    def _is_available(self, j):
6      """Return True if index j is available in table."""
7      return self._table[j] is None or self._table[j] is ProbeHashMap._AVAIL
8
9    def _find_slot(self, j, k):
10     """Search for key k in bucket at index j.
11
12     Return (success, index) tuple, described as follows:
13     If match was found, success is True and index denotes its location.
14     If no match found, success is False and index denotes first available slot.
15     """
16     firstAvail = None
17     while True:
18       if self._is_available(j):
19         if firstAvail is None:
20           firstAvail = j                  # mark this as first avail
21         if self._table[j] is None:
22           return (False, firstAvail)       # search has failed
23       elif k == self._table[j]._key:
24         return (True, j)                   # found a match
25       j = (j + 1) % len(self._table)       # keep looking (cyclically)
```

Code Fragment 10.6: Concrete ProbeHashMap class that uses linear probing for collision resolution (continued in Code Fragment 10.7).

```
26    def _bucket_getitem(self, j, k):
27      found, s = self._find_slot(j, k)
28      if not found:
29        raise KeyError('Key Error: ' + repr(k))          # no match found
30      return self._table[s]._value
31
32    def _bucket_setitem(self, j, k, v):
33      found, s = self._find_slot(j, k)
34      if not found:
35        self._table[s] = self._Item(k,v)                  # insert new item
36        self._n += 1                                       # size has increased
37      else:
38        self._table[s]._value = v                          # overwrite existing
39
40    def _bucket_delitem(self, j, k):
41      found, s = self._find_slot(j, k)
42      if not found:
43        raise KeyError('Key Error: ' + repr(k))          # no match found
44      self._table[s] = ProbeHashMap._AVAIL                 # mark as vacated
45
46    def __iter__(self):
47      for j in range(len(self._table)):                    # scan entire table
48        if not self._is_available(j):
49          yield self._table[j]._key
```

Code Fragment 10.7: Concrete ProbeHashMap class that uses linear probing for collision resolution (continued from Code Fragment 10.6).

The three primary map operations each rely on the _find_slot utility. When attempting to retrieve the value associated with a given key, we must continue probing until we find the key, or until we reach a table slot with the None value. We cannot stop the search upon reaching an _AVAIL sentinel, because it represents a location that may have been filled when the desired item was once inserted.

When a key-value pair is being assigned in the map, we must attempt to find an existing item with the given key, so that we might overwrite its value, before adding a new item to the map. Therefore, we must search beyond any occurrences of the _AVAIL sentinel when inserting. However, if no match is found, we prefer to repurpose the first slot marked with _AVAIL, if any, when placing the new element in the table. The _find_slot method enacts this logic, continuing the search until a truly empty slot, but returning the index of the first available slot for an insertion.

When deleting an existing item within _bucket_delitem, we intentionally set the table entry to the _AVAIL sentinel in accordance with our strategy.

10.3 Sorted Maps

The traditional map ADT allows a user to look up the value associated with a given key, but the search for that key is a form known as an ***exact search***.

For example, computer systems often maintain information about events that have occurred (such as financial transactions), organizing such events based upon what are known as ***time stamps***. If we can assume that time stamps are unique for a particular system, then we might organize a map with a time stamp serving as the key, and a record about the event that occurred at that time as the value. A particular time stamp could serve as a reference ID for an event, in which case we can quickly retrieve information about that event from the map. However, the map ADT does not provide any way to get a list of all events ordered by the time at which they occur, or to search for which event occurred closest to a particular time. In fact, the fast performance of hash-based implementations of the map ADT relies on the intentionally scattering of keys that may seem very "near" to each other in the original domain, so that they are more uniformly distributed in a hash table.

In this section, we introduce an extension known as the ***sorted map*** ADT that includes all behaviors of the standard map, plus the following:

M.find_min( ): Return the (key,value) pair with minimum key (or None, if map is empty).

M.find_max( ): Return the (key,value) pair with maximum key (or None, if map is empty).

M.find_lt(k): Return the (key,value) pair with the greatest key that is strictly less than k (or None, if no such item exists).

M.find_le(k): Return the (key,value) pair with the greatest key that is less than or equal to k (or None, if no such item exists).

M.find_gt(k): Return the (key,value) pair with the least key that is strictly greater than k (or None, if no such item exists).

M.find_ge(k): Return the (key,value) pair with the least key that is greater than or equal to k (or None, if no such item).

M.find_range(start, stop): Iterate all (key,value) pairs with start $<=$ key $<$ stop. If start is None, iteration begins with minimum key; if stop is None, iteration concludes with maximum key.

iter(M): Iterate all keys of the map according to their natural order, from smallest to largest.

reversed(M): Iterate all keys of the map in reverse order; in Python, this is implemented with the __reversed__ method.

10.3.1 Sorted Search Tables

Several data structures can efficiently support the sorted map ADT, and we will examine some advanced techniques in Section 10.4 and Chapter 11. In this section, we begin by exploring a simple implementation of a sorted map. We store the map's items in an array-based sequence A so that they are in increasing order of their keys, assuming the keys have a naturally defined order. (See Figure 10.8.) We refer to this implementation of a map as a ***sorted search table***.

0	1	2	3	4	5	6	7	8	9	10	11	12	13	14	15
2	4	5	7	8	9	12	14	17	19	22	25	27	28	33	37

Figure 10.8: Realization of a map by means of a sorted search table. We show only the keys for this map, so as to highlight their ordering.

As was the case with the unsorted table map of Section 10.1.5, the sorted search table has a space requirement that is $O(n)$, assuming we grow and shrink the array to keep its size proportional to the number of items in the map. The primary advantage of this representation, and our reason for insisting that A be array-based, is that it allows us to use the ***binary search*** algorithm for a variety of efficient operations.

Binary Search and Inexact Searches

We originally presented the binary search algorithm in Section 4.1.3, as a means for detecting whether a given target is stored within a sorted sequence. In our original presentation (Code Fragment 4.3 on page 156), a binary_search function returned True of False to designate whether the desired target was found. While such an approach could be used to implement the __contains__ method of the map ADT, we can adapt the binary search algorithm to provide far more useful information when performing forms of inexact search in support of the sorted map ADT.

The important realization is that while performing a binary search, we can determine the index at or near where a target might be found. During a successful search, the standard implementation determines the precise index at which the target is found. During an unsuccessful search, although the target is not found, the algorithm will effectively determine a pair of indices designating elements of the collection that are just less than or just greater than the missing target.

As a motivating example, our original simulation from Figure 4.5 on page 156 shows a successful binary search for a target of 22, using the same data we portray in Figure 10.8. Had we instead been searching for 21, the first four steps of the algorithm would be the same. The subsequent difference is that we would make an additional call with inverted parameters high=9 and low=10, effectively concluding that the missing target lies in the gap between values 19 and 22 in that example.

Implementation

In Code Fragments 10.8 through 10.10, we present a complete implementation of a class, SortedTableMap, that supports the sorted map ADT. The most notable feature of our design is the inclusion of a _find_index utility function. This method using the binary search algorithm, but by convention returns the *index* of the leftmost item in the search interval having key greater than or equal to k. Therefore, if the key is present, it will return the index of the item having that key. (Recall that keys are unique in a map.) When the key is missing, the function returns the index of the item in the search interval that is just beyond where the key would have been located. As a technicality, the method returns index $high + 1$ to indicate that no items of the interval had a key greater than k.

We rely on this utility method when implementing the traditional map operations and the new sorted map operations. The body of each of the __getitem__, __setitem__, and __delitem__ methods begins with a call to _find_index to determine a candidate index at which a matching key might be found. For __getitem__, we simply check whether that is a valid index containing the target to determine the result. For __setitem__, recall that the goal is to replace the value of an existing item, if one with key k is found, but otherwise to insert a new item into the map. The index returned by _find_index will be the index of the match, if one exists, or otherwise the exact index at which the new item should be inserted. For __delitem__, we again rely on the convenience of _find_index to determine the location of the item to be popped, if any.

Our _find_index utility is equally valuable when implementing the various inexact search methods given in Code Fragment 10.10. For each of the methods find_lt, find_le, find_gt, and find_ge, we begin with a call to _find_index utility, which locates the first index at which there is an element with key $\geq k$, if any. This is precisely what we want for find_ge, if valid, and just beyond the index we want for find_lt. For find_gt and find_le we need some extra case analysis to distinguish whether the indicated index has a key equal to k. For example, if the indicated item has a matching key, our find_gt implementation increments the index before continuing with the process. (We omit the implementation of find_le, for brevity.) In all cases, we must properly handle boundary cases, reporting None when unable to find a key with the desired property.

Our strategy for implementing find_range is to use the _find_index utility to locate the first item with key $\geq$ start (assuming start is not None). With that knowledge, we use a while loop to sequentially report items until reaching one that has a key greater than or equal to the stopping value (or until reaching the end of the table). It is worth noting that the while loop may trivially iterate zero items if the first key that is greater than or equal to start also happens to be greater than or equal to stop. This represents an empty range in the map.

```
 1  class SortedTableMap(MapBase):
 2    """Map implementation using a sorted table."""
 3
 4    #----------------------------- nonpublic behaviors -----------------------------
 5    def _find_index(self, k, low, high):
 6      """Return index of the leftmost item with key greater than or equal to k.
 7
 8      Return high + 1 if no such item qualifies.
 9
10      That is, j will be returned such that:
11          all items of slice table[low:j] have key < k
12          all items of slice table[j:high+1] have key >= k
13      """
14      if high < low:
15        return high + 1                          # no element qualifies
16      else:
17        mid = (low + high) // 2
18        if k == self._table[mid]._key:
19          return mid                             # found exact match
20        elif k < self._table[mid]._key:
21          return self._find_index(k, low, mid - 1)    # Note: may return mid
22        else:
23          return self._find_index(k, mid + 1, high)   # answer is right of mid
24
25    #----------------------------- public behaviors -----------------------------
26    def __init__(self):
27      """Create an empty map."""
28      self._table = [ ]
29
30    def __len__(self):
31      """Return number of items in the map."""
32      return len(self._table)
33
34    def __getitem__(self, k):
35      """Return value associated with key k (raise KeyError if not found)."""
36      j = self._find_index(k, 0, len(self._table) - 1)
37      if j == len(self._table) or self._table[j]._key != k:
38        raise KeyError('Key Error: ' + repr(k))
39      return self._table[j]._value
```

Code Fragment 10.8: An implementation of a SortedTableMap class (continued in Code Fragments 10.9 and 10.10).

```
40    def __setitem__(self, k, v):
41      """Assign value v to key k, overwriting existing value if present."""
42      j = self._find_index(k, 0, len(self._table) − 1)
43      if j < len(self._table) and self._table[j]._key == k:
44        self._table[j]._value = v                        # reassign value
45      else:
46        self._table.insert(j, self._Item(k,v))           # adds new item
47
48    def __delitem__(self, k):
49      """Remove item associated with key k (raise KeyError if not found)."""
50      j = self._find_index(k, 0, len(self._table) − 1)
51      if j == len(self._table) or self._table[j]._key != k:
52        raise KeyError('Key Error: ' + repr(k))
53      self._table.pop(j)                                 # delete item
54
55    def __iter__(self):
56      """Generate keys of the map ordered from minimum to maximum."""
57      for item in self._table:
58        yield item._key
59
60    def __reversed__(self):
61      """Generate keys of the map ordered from maximum to minimum."""
62      for item in reversed(self._table):
63        yield item._key
64
65    def find_min(self):
66      """Return (key,value) pair with minimum key (or None if empty)."""
67      if len(self._table) > 0:
68        return (self._table[0]._key, self._table[0]._value)
69      else:
70        return None
71
72    def find_max(self):
73      """Return (key,value) pair with maximum key (or None if empty)."""
74      if len(self._table) > 0:
75        return (self._table[−1]._key, self._table[−1]._value)
76      else:
77        return None
```

Code Fragment 10.9: An implementation of a SortedTableMap class (together with Code Fragments 10.8 and 10.10).

```
78    def find_ge(self, k):
79      """Return (key,value) pair with least key greater than or equal to k."""
80      j = self._find_index(k, 0, len(self._table) − 1)         # j's key >= k
81      if j < len(self._table):
82        return (self._table[j]._key, self._table[j]._value)
83      else:
84        return None
85
86    def find_lt(self, k):
87      """Return (key,value) pair with greatest key strictly less than k."""
88      j = self._find_index(k, 0, len(self._table) − 1)         # j's key >= k
89      if j > 0:
90        return (self._table[j−1]._key, self._table[j−1]._value) # Note use of j-1
91      else:
92        return None
93
94    def find_gt(self, k):
95      """Return (key,value) pair with least key strictly greater than k."""
96      j = self._find_index(k, 0, len(self._table) − 1)         # j's key >= k
97      if j < len(self._table) and self._table[j]._key == k:
98        j += 1                                                 # advanced past match
99      if j < len(self._table):
100       return (self._table[j]._key, self._table[j]._value)
101     else:
102       return None
103
104   def find_range(self, start, stop):
105     """Iterate all (key,value) pairs such that start <= key < stop.
106
107     If start is None, iteration begins with minimum key of map.
108     If stop is None, iteration continues through the maximum key of map.
109     """
110     if start is None:
111       j = 0
112     else:
113       j = self._find_index(start, 0, len(self._table)−1)     # find first result
114     while j < len(self._table) and (stop is None or self._table[j]._key < stop):
115       yield (self._table[j]._key, self._table[j]._value)
116       j += 1
```

Code Fragment 10.10: An implementation of a SortedTableMap class (continued from Code Fragments 10.9 and 10.10). We omit the find_le method due to space.

Analysis

We conclude by analyzing the performance of our SortedTableMap implementation. A summary of the running times for all methods of the sorted map ADT (including the traditional map operations) is given in Table 10.3. It should be clear that the __len__, find_min, and find_max methods run in $O(1)$ time, and that iterating the keys of the table in either direction can be peformed in $O(n)$ time.

The analysis for the various forms of search all depend on the fact that a binary search on a table with n entries runs in $O(\log n)$ time. This claim was originally shown as Proposition 4.2 in Section 4.2, and that analysis clearly applies to our _find_index method as well. We therefore claim an $O(\log n)$ worst-case running time for methods __getitem__, find_lt, find_gt, find_le, and find_ge. Each of these makes a single call to _find_index, followed by a constant number of additional steps to determine the appropriate answer based on the index. The analysis of find_range is a bit more interesting. It begins with a binary search to find the first item within the range (if any). After that, it executes a loop that takes $O(1)$ time per iteration to report subsequent values until reaching the end of the range. If there are s items reported in the range, the total running time is $O(s + \log n)$.

In contrast to the efficient search operations, update operations for a sorted table may take considerable time. Although binary search can help identify the index at which an update occurs, both insertions and deletions require, in the worst case, that linearly many existing elements be shifted in order to maintain the sorted order of the table. Specifically, the potential call to _table.insert from within __setitem__ and _table.pop from within __delitem__ lead to $O(n)$ worst-case time. (See the discussion of corresponding operations of the list class in Section 5.4.1.)

In conclusion, sorted tables are primarily used in situations where we expect many searches but relatively few updates.

Operation	Running Time
len(M)	$O(1)$
k in M	$O(\log n)$
M[k] = v	$O(n)$ worst case; $O(\log n)$ if existing k
del M[k]	$O(n)$ worst case
M.find_min( ), M.find_max( )	$O(1)$
M.find_lt(k), M.find_gt(k) M.find_le(k), M.find_ge(k)	$O(\log n)$
M.find_range(start, stop)	$O(s + \log n)$ where s items are reported
iter(M), reversed(M)	$O(n)$

Table 10.3: Performance of a sorted map, as implemented with SortedTableMap. We use n to denote the number of items in the map at the time the operation is performed. The space requirement is $O(n)$.

10.3.2   Two Applications of Sorted Maps

In this section, we explore applications in which there is particular advantage to using a *sorted* map rather than a traditional (unsorted) map. To apply a sorted map, keys must come from a domain that is totally ordered. Furthermore, to take advantage of the inexact or range searches afforded by a sorted map, there should be some reason why nearby keys have relevance to a search.

Flight Databases

There are several Web sites on the Internet that allow users to perform queries on flight databases to find flights between various cities, typically with the intent to buy a ticket. To make a query, a user specifies origin and destination cities, a departure date, and a departure time. To support such queries, we can model the flight database as a map, where keys are Flight objects that contain fields corresponding to these four parameters. That is, a key is a tuple

$$k = (\text{origin}, \text{destination}, \text{date}, \text{time}).$$

Additional information about a flight, such as the flight number, the number of seats still available in first (F) and coach (Y) class, the flight duration, and the fare, can be stored in the value object.

Finding a requested flight is not simply a matter of finding an exact match for a requested query. Although a user typically wants to exactly match the origin and destination cities, he or she may have flexibility for the departure date, and certainly will have some flexibility for the departure time on a specific day. We can handle such a query by ordering our keys lexicographically. Then, an efficient implementation for a sorted map would be a good way to satisfy users' queries. For instance, given a user query key k, we could call find_ge(k) to return the first flight between the desired cities, having a departure date and time matching the desired query or later. Better yet, with well-constructed keys, we could use find_range(k1, k2) to find all flights within a given range of times. For example, if $k1 = (\text{ORD}, \text{PVD}, \text{05May}, 09{:}30)$, and $k2 = (\text{ORD}, \text{PVD}, \text{05May}, 20{:}00)$, a respective call to find_range(k1, k2) might result in the following sequence of key-value pairs:

```
(ORD, PVD, 05May, 09:53)   :   (AA 1840, F5, Y15, 02:05, $251),
(ORD, PVD, 05May, 13:29)   :   (AA 600, F2, Y0, 02:16, $713),
(ORD, PVD, 05May, 17:39)   :   (AA 416, F3, Y9, 02:09, $365),
(ORD, PVD, 05May, 19:50)   :   (AA 1828, F9, Y25, 02:13, $186)
```

Maxima Sets

Life is full of trade-offs. We often have to trade off a desired performance measure against a corresponding cost. Suppose, for the sake of an example, we are interested in maintaining a database rating automobiles by their maximum speeds and their cost. We would like to allow someone with a certain amount of money to query our database to find the fastest car they can possibly afford.

We can model such a trade-off problem as this by using a key-value pair to model the two parameters that we are trading off, which in this case would be the pair (cost, speed) for each car. Notice that some cars are strictly better than other cars using this measure. For example, a car with cost-speed pair $(20000, 100)$ is strictly better than a car with cost-speed pair $(30000, 90)$. At the same time, there are some cars that are not strictly dominated by another car. For example, a car with cost-speed pair $(20000, 100)$ may be better or worse than a car with cost-speed pair $(30000, 120)$, depending on how much money we have to spend. (See Figure 10.9.)

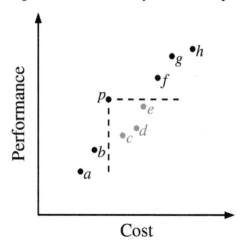

Figure 10.9: Illustrating the cost-performance trade-off with pairs represented by points in the plane. Notice that point p is strictly better than points c, d, and e, but may be better or worse than points a, b, f, g, and h, depending on the price we are willing to pay. Thus, if we were to add p to our set, we could remove the points c, d, and e, but not the others.

Formally, we say a cost-performance pair (a, b) ***dominates*** pair $(c, d) \neq (a, b)$ if $a \leq c$ and $b \geq d$, that is, if the first pair has no greater cost and at least as good performance. A pair (a, b) is called a ***maximum*** pair if it is not dominated by any other pair. We are interested in maintaining the set of maxima of a collection of cost-performance pairs. That is, we would like to add new pairs to this collection (for example, when a new car is introduced), and to query this collection for a given dollar amount, d, to find the fastest car that costs no more than d dollars.

Maintaining a Maxima Set with a Sorted Map

We can store the set of maxima pairs in a sorted map, M, so that the cost is the key field and performance (speed) is the value field. We can then implement operations $add(c, p)$, which adds a new cost-performance pair (c, p), and $best(c)$, which returns the best pair with cost at most c, as shown in Code Fragment 10.11.

```
 1  class CostPerformanceDatabase:
 2    """Maintain a database of maximal (cost,performance) pairs."""
 3
 4    def __init__(self):
 5      """Create an empty database."""
 6      self._M = SortedTableMap( )            # or a more efficient sorted map
 7
 8    def best(self, c):
 9      """Return (cost,performance) pair with largest cost not exceeding c.
10
11      Return None if there is no such pair.
12      """
13      return self._M.find_le(c)
14
15    def add(self, c, p):
16      """Add new entry with cost c and performance p."""
17      # determine if (c,p) is dominated by an existing pair
18      other = self._M.find_le(c)             # other is at least as cheap as c
19      if other is not None and other[1] >= p:   # if its performance is as good,
20        return                               # (c,p) is dominated, so ignore
21      self._M[c] = p                         # else, add (c,p) to database
22      # and now remove any pairs that are dominated by (c,p)
23      other = self._M.find_gt(c)             # other more expensive than c
24      while other is not None and other[1] <= p:
25        del self._M[other[0]]
26        other = self._M.find_gt(c)
```

Code Fragment 10.11: An implementation of a class maintaining a set of maxima cost-performance pairs using a sorted map.

Unfortunately, if we implement M using the SortedTableMap, the add behavior has $O(n)$ worst-case running time. If, on the other hand, we implement M using a skip list, which we next describe, we can perform $best(c)$ queries in $O(\log n)$ expected time and $add(c, p)$ updates in $O((1 + r) \log n)$ expected time, where r is the number of points removed.

10.4 Skip Lists

An interesting data structure for realizing the sorted map ADT is the ***skip list***. In Section 10.3.1, we saw that a sorted array will allow $O(\log n)$-time searches via the binary search algorithm. Unfortunately, update operations on a sorted array have $O(n)$ worst-case running time because of the need to shift elements. In Chapter 7 we demonstrated that linked lists support very efficient update operations, as long as the position within the list is identified. Unfortunately, we cannot perform fast searches on a standard linked list; for example, the binary search algorithm requires an efficient means for direct accessing an element of a sequence by index.

Skip lists provide a clever compromise to efficiently support search and update operations. A ***skip list*** S for a map M consists of a series of lists $\{S_0, S_1, \ldots, S_h\}$. Each list S_i stores a subset of the items of M sorted by increasing keys, plus items with two sentinel keys denoted $-\infty$ and $+\infty$, where $-\infty$ is smaller than every possible key that can be inserted in M and $+\infty$ is larger than every possible key that can be inserted in M. In addition, the lists in S satisfy the following:

- List S_0 contains every item of the map M (plus sentinels $-\infty$ and $+\infty$).
- For $i = 1, \ldots, h-1$, list S_i contains (in addition to $-\infty$ and $+\infty$) a randomly generated subset of the items in list S_{i-1}.
- List S_h contains only $-\infty$ and $+\infty$.

An example of a skip list is shown in Figure 10.10. It is customary to visualize a skip list S with list S_0 at the bottom and lists $S_1, \ldots, S_h$ above it. Also, we refer to h as the ***height*** of skip list S.

Intuitively, the lists are set up so that S_{i+1} contains more or less alternate items of S_i. As we shall see in the details of the insertion method, the items in S_{i+1} are chosen at random from the items in S_i by picking each item from S_i to also be in S_{i+1} with probability $1/2$. That is, in essence, we "flip a coin" for each item in S_i

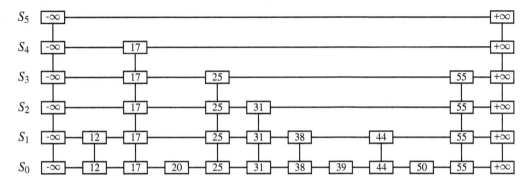

Figure 10.10: Example of a skip list storing 10 items. For simplicity, we show only the items' keys, not their associated values.

and place that item in S_{i+1} if the coin comes up "heads." Thus, we expect S_1 to have about $n/2$ items, S_2 to have about $n/4$ items, and, in general, S_i to have about $n/2^i$ items. In other words, we expect the height h of S to be about $\log n$. The halving of the number of items from one list to the next is not enforced as an explicit property of skip lists, however. Instead, randomization is used.

Functions that generate numbers that can be viewed as random numbers are built into most modern computers, because they are used extensively in computer games, cryptography, and computer simulations, Some functions, called *pseudo-random number generators*, generate random-like numbers, starting with an initial *seed*. (See discusion of random module in Section 1.11.1.) Other methods use hardware devices to extract "true" random numbers from nature. In any case, we will assume that our computer has access to numbers that are sufficiently random for our analysis.

The main advantage of using *randomization* in data structure and algorithm design is that the structures and functions that result are usually simple and efficient. The skip list has the same logarithmic time bounds for searching as is achieved by the binary search algorithm, yet it extends that performance to update methods when inserting or deleting items. Nevertheless, the bounds are *expected* for the skip list, while binary search has a *worst-case* bound with a sorted table.

A skip list makes random choices in arranging its structure in such a way that search and update times are $O(\log n)$ *on average*, where n is the number of items in the map. Interestingly, the notion of average time complexity used here does not depend on the probability distribution of the keys in the input. Instead, it depends on the use of a random-number generator in the implementation of the insertions to help decide where to place the new item. The running time is averaged over all possible outcomes of the random numbers used when inserting entries.

Using the position abstraction used for lists and trees, we view a skip list as a two-dimensional collection of positions arranged horizontally into *levels* and vertically into *towers*. Each level is a list S_i and each tower contains positions storing the same item across consecutive lists. The positions in a skip list can be traversed using the following operations:

> **next(p):** Return the position following p on the same level.
>
> **prev(p):** Return the position preceding p on the same level.
>
> **below(p):** Return the position below p in the same tower.
>
> **above(p):** Return the position above p in the same tower.

We conventionally assume that the above operations return None if the position requested does not exist. Without going into the details, we note that we can easily implement a skip list by means of a linked structure such that the individual traversal methods each take $O(1)$ time, given a skip-list position p. Such a linked structure is essentially a collection of h doubly linked lists aligned at towers, which are also doubly linked lists.

10.4.1   Search and Update Operations in a Skip List

The skip-list structure affords simple map search and update algorithms. In fact, all of the skip-list search and update algorithms are based on an elegant SkipSearch method that takes a key k and finds the position p of the item in list S_0 that has the largest key less than or equal to k (which is possibly $-\infty$).

Searching in a Skip List

Suppose we are given a search key k. We begin the SkipSearch method by setting a position variable p to the topmost, left position in the skip list S, called the **start position** of S. That is, the start position is the position of S_h storing the special entry with key $-\infty$. We then perform the following steps (see Figure 10.11), where key(p) denotes the key of the item at position p:

1. If S.below(p) is None, then the search terminates—we are **at the bottom** and have located the item in S with the largest key less than or equal to the search key k. Otherwise, we **drop down** to the next lower level in the present tower by setting $p = S$.below(p).
2. Starting at position p, we move p forward until it is at the rightmost position on the present level such that key$(p) \le k$. We call this the **scan forward** step. Note that such a position always exists, since each level contains the keys $+\infty$ and $-\infty$. It may be that p remains where it started after we perform such a forward scan for this level.
3. Return to step 1.

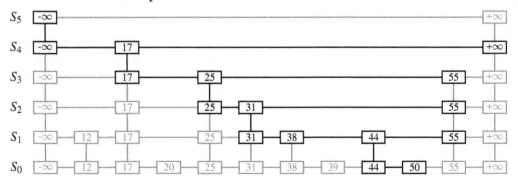

Figure 10.11: Example of a search in a skip list. The positions examined when searching for key 50 are highlighted.

We give a pseudo-code description of the skip-list search algorithm, SkipSearch, in Code Fragment 10.12. Given this method, the map operation $M[k]$ is performed by computing $p = \mathsf{SkipSearch}(k)$ and testing whether or not key$(p) = k$. If these two keys are equal, we return the associated value; otherwise, we raise a KeyError.

Algorithm SkipSearch(k):

    Input: A search key k

    Output: Position p in the bottom list S_0 with the largest key such that key(p) $\leq$ k

      p = start   {begin at start position}

      while below(p) $\neq$ **None do**

        p = below(p)   {drop down}

        while k $\geq$ key(next(p)) **do**

          p = next(p)   {scan forward}

    return p.

Code Fragment 10.12: Algorthm to search a skip list S for key k.

As it turns out, the expected running time of algorithm SkipSearch on a skip list with n entries is $O(\log n)$. We postpone the justification of this fact, however, until after we discuss the implementation of the update methods for skip lists. Navigation starting at the position identified by SkipSearch(k) can be easily used to provide the additional forms of searches in the sorted map ADT (e.g., find_gt, find_range).

Insertion in a Skip List

The execution of the map operation M[k] = v begins with a call to SkipSearch(k). This gives us the position p of the bottom-level item with the largest key less than or equal to k (note that p may hold the special item with key $-\infty$). If key(p) = k, the associated value is overwritten with v. Otherwise, we need to create a new tower for item (k,v). We insert (k,v) immediately after position p within S_0. After inserting the new item at the bottom level, we use randomization to decide the height of the tower for the new item. We "flip" a coin, and if the flip comes up tails, then we stop here. Else (the flip comes up heads), we backtrack to the previous (next higher) level and insert (k,v) in this level at the appropriate position. We again flip a coin; if it comes up heads, we go to the next higher level and repeat. Thus, we continue to insert the new item (k,v) in lists until we finally get a flip that comes up tails. We link together all the references to the new item (k,v) created in this process to create its tower. A coin flip can be simulated with Python's built-in pseudo-random number generator from the random module by calling randrange(2), which returns 0 or 1, each with probability $1/2$.

We give the insertion algorithm for a skip list S in Code Fragment 10.13 and we illustrate it in Figure 10.12. The algorithm uses an insertAfterAbove($p,q,(k,v)$) method that inserts a position storing the item (k,v) after position p (on the same level as p) and above position q, returning the new position r (and setting internal references so that next, prev, above, and below methods will work correctly for p, q, and r). The expected running time of the insertion algorithm on a skip list with n entries is $O(\log n)$, which we show in Section 10.4.2.

Algorithm SkipInsert(k,v):

    Input: Key k and value v

    Output: Topmost position of the item inserted in the skip list

    p = SkipSearch(k)

    q = **None**   {q will represent top node in new item's tower}

    i = −1

    repeat

       i = i + 1

       if i ≥ h **then**

          h = h + 1   {add a new level to the skip list}

          t = next(s)

          s = insertAfterAbove(**None**, s, (−∞, **None**))   {grow leftmost tower}

          insertAfterAbove(s, t, (+∞, **None**))   {grow rightmost tower}

       while above(p) is **None do**

          p = prev(p)   {scan backward}

       p = above(p)   {jump up to higher level}

       q = insertAfterAbove(p, q, (k, v))   {increase height of new item's tower}

    until coinFlip() == tails

    n = n + 1

    return q

Code Fragment 10.13: Insertion in a skip list. Method coinFlip() returns "heads" or "tails", each with probability 1/2. Instance variables n, h, and s hold the number of entries, the height, and the start node of the skip list.

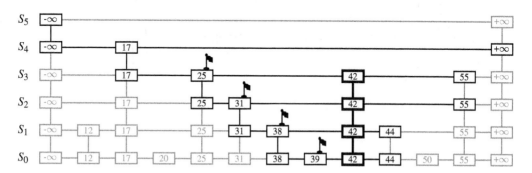

Figure 10.12: Insertion of an entry with key 42 into the skip list of Figure 10.10. We assume that the random "coin flips" for the new entry came up heads three times in a row, followed by tails. The positions visited are highlighted. The positions inserted to hold the new entry are drawn with thick lines, and the positions preceding them are flagged.

Removal in a Skip List

Like the search and insertion algorithms, the removal algorithm for a skip list is quite simple. In fact, it is even easier than the insertion algorithm. That is, to perform the map operation del M[k] we begin by executing method SkipSearch(k). If the position p stores an entry with key different from k, we raise a KeyError. Otherwise, we remove p and all the positions above p, which are easily accessed by using above operations to climb up the tower of this entry in S starting at position p. While removing levels of the tower, we reestablish links between the horizontal neighbors of each removed position. The removal algorithm is illustrated in Figure 10.13 and a detailed description of it is left as an exercise (R-10.24). As we show in the next subsection, deletion operation in a skip list with n entries has $O(\log n)$ expected running time.

Before we give this analysis, however, there are some minor improvements to the skip-list data structure we would like to discuss. First, we do not actually need to store references to values at the levels of the skip list above the bottom level, because all that is needed at these levels are references to keys. In fact, we can more efficiently represent a tower as a single object, storing the key-value pair, and maintaining j previous references and j next references if the tower reaches level S_j. Second, for the horizontal axes, it is possible to keep the list singly linked, storing only the next references. We can perform insertions and removals in strictly a top-down, scan-forward fashion. We explore the details of this optimization in Exercise C-10.44. Neither of these optimizations improve the asymptotic performance of skip lists by more than a constant factor, but these improvements can, nevertheless, be meaningful in practice. In fact, experimental evidence suggests that optimized skip lists are faster in practice than AVL trees and other balanced search trees, which are discussed in Chapter 11.

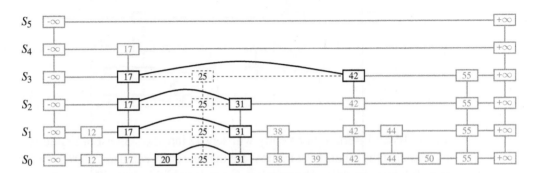

Figure 10.13: Removal of the entry with key 25 from the skip list of Figure 10.12. The positions visited after the search for the position of S_0 holding the entry are highlighted. The positions removed are drawn with dashed lines.

Maintaining the Topmost Level

A skip list S must maintain a reference to the start position (the topmost, left position in S) as an instance variable, and must have a policy for any insertion that wishes to continue inserting a new entry past the top level of S. There are two possible courses of action we can take, both of which have their merits.

One possibility is to restrict the top level, h, to be kept at some fixed value that is a function of n, the number of entries currently in the map (from the analysis we will see that $h = \max\{10, 2\lceil \log n \rceil\}$ is a reasonable choice, and picking $h = 3\lceil \log n \rceil$ is even safer). Implementing this choice means that we must modify the insertion algorithm to stop inserting a new position once we reach the topmost level (unless $\lceil \log n \rceil < \lceil \log(n+1) \rceil$, in which case we can now go at least one more level, since the bound on the height is increasing).

The other possibility is to let an insertion continue inserting a new position as long as heads keeps getting returned from the random number generator. This is the approach taken by algorithm SkipInsert of Code Fragment 10.13. As we show in the analysis of skip lists, the probability that an insertion will go to a level that is more than $O(\log n)$ is very low, so this design choice should also work.

Either choice will still result in the expected $O(\log n)$ time to perform search, insertion, and removal, however, which we show in the next section.

10.4.2 Probabilistic Analysis of Skip Lists ⋆

As we have shown above, skip lists provide a simple implementation of a sorted map. In terms of worst-case performance, however, skip lists are not a superior data structure. In fact, if we do not officially prevent an insertion from continuing significantly past the current highest level, then the insertion algorithm can go into what is almost an infinite loop (it is not actually an infinite loop, however, since the probability of having a fair coin repeatedly come up heads forever is 0). Moreover, we cannot infinitely add positions to a list without eventually running out of memory. In any case, if we terminate position insertion at the highest level h, then the ***worst-case*** running time for performing the _ _getitem_ _, _ _setitem_ _, and _ _delitem_ _ map operations in a skip list S with n entries and height h is $O(n+h)$. This worst-case performance occurs when the tower of every entry reaches level $h-1$, where h is the height of S. However, this event has very low probability. Judging from this worst case, we might conclude that the skip-list structure is strictly inferior to the other map implementations discussed earlier in this chapter. But this would not be a fair analysis, for this worst-case behavior is a gross overestimate.

Bounding the Height of a Skip List

Because the insertion step involves randomization, a more accurate analysis of skip lists involves a bit of probability. At first, this might seem like a major undertaking, for a complete and thorough probabilistic analysis could require deep mathematics (and, indeed, there are several such deep analyses that have appeared in data structures research literature). Fortunately, such an analysis is not necessary to understand the expected asymptotic behavior of skip lists. The informal and intuitive probabilistic analysis we give below uses only basic concepts of probability theory.

Let us begin by determining the expected value of the height h of a skip list S with n entries (assuming that we do not terminate insertions early). The probability that a given entry has a tower of height $i \geq 1$ is equal to the probability of getting i consecutive heads when flipping a coin, that is, this probability is $1/2^i$. Hence, the probability P_i that level i has at least one position is at most

$$P_i \leq \frac{n}{2^i},$$

for the probability that any one of n different events occurs is at most the sum of the probabilities that each occurs.

The probability that the height h of S is larger than i is equal to the probability that level i has at least one position, that is, it is no more than P_i. This means that h is larger than, say, $3\log n$ with probability at most

$$
\begin{aligned}
P_{3\log n} \quad &\leq \quad \frac{n}{2^{3\log n}} \\
&= \quad \frac{n}{n^3} = \frac{1}{n^2}.
\end{aligned}
$$

For example, if $n = 1000$, this probability is a one-in-a-million long shot. More generally, given a constant $c > 1$, h is larger than $c\log n$ with probability at most $1/n^{c-1}$. That is, the probability that h is smaller than $c\log n$ is at least $1 - 1/n^{c-1}$. Thus, with high probability, the height h of S is $O(\log n)$.

Analyzing Search Time in a Skip List

Next, consider the running time of a search in skip list S, and recall that such a search involves two nested **while** loops. The inner loop performs a scan forward on a level of S as long as the next key is no greater than the search key k, and the outer loop drops down to the next level and repeats the scan forward iteration. Since the height h of S is $O(\log n)$ with high probability, the number of drop-down steps is $O(\log n)$ with high probability.

So we have yet to bound the number of scan-forward steps we make. Let n_i be the number of keys examined while scanning forward at level i. Observe that, after the key at the starting position, each additional key examined in a scan-forward at level i cannot also belong to level $i+1$. If any of these keys were on the previous level, we would have encountered them in the previous scan-forward step. Thus, the probability that any key is counted in n_i is $1/2$. Therefore, the expected value of n_i is exactly equal to the expected number of times we must flip a fair coin before it comes up heads. This expected value is 2. Hence, the expected amount of time spent scanning forward at any level i is $O(1)$. Since S has $O(\log n)$ levels with high probability, a search in S takes expected time $O(\log n)$. By a similar analysis, we can show that the expected running time of an insertion or a removal is $O(\log n)$.

Space Usage in a Skip List

Finally, let us turn to the space requirement of a skip list S with n entries. As we observed above, the expected number of positions at level i is $n/2^i$, which means that the expected total number of positions in S is

$$\sum_{i=0}^{h} \frac{n}{2^i} = n \sum_{i=0}^{h} \frac{1}{2^i}.$$

Using Proposition 3.5 on geometric summations, we have

$$\sum_{i=0}^{h} \frac{1}{2^i} = \frac{\left(\frac{1}{2}\right)^{h+1} - 1}{\frac{1}{2} - 1} = 2 \cdot \left(1 - \frac{1}{2^{h+1}}\right) < 2 \quad \text{for all } h \geq 0.$$

Hence, the expected space requirement of S is $O(n)$.

Table 10.4 summarizes the performance of a sorted map realized by a skip list.

Operation	Running Time
len(M)	$O(1)$
k in M	$O(\log n)$ expected
M[k] = v	$O(\log n)$ expected
del M[k]	$O(\log n)$ expected
M.find_min( ), M.find_max( )	$O(1)$
M.find_lt(k), M.find_gt(k) M.find_le(k), M.find_ge(k)	$O(\log n)$ expected
M.find_range(start, stop)	$O(s + \log n)$ expected, with s items reported
iter(M), reversed(M)	$O(n)$

Table 10.4: Performance of a sorted map implemented with a skip list. We use n to denote the number of entries in the dictionary at the time the operation is performed. The expected space requirement is $O(n)$.

10.5 Sets, Multisets, and Multimaps

We conclude this chapter by examining several additional abstractions that are closely related to the map ADT, and that can be implemented using data structures similar to those for a map.

- A *set* is an unordered collection of elements, without duplicates, that typically supports efficient membership tests. In essence, elements of a set are like keys of a map, but without any auxiliary values.

- A *multiset* (also known as a *bag*) is a set-like container that allows duplicates.

- A *multimap* is similar to a traditional map, in that it associates values with keys; however, in a multimap the same key can be mapped to multiple values. For example, the index of this book maps a given term to one or more locations at which the term occurs elsewhere in the book.

10.5.1 The Set ADT

Python provides support for representing the mathematical notion of a set through the built-in classes **frozenset** and **set**, as originally discussed in Chapter 1, with frozenset being an immutable form. Both of those classes are implemented using hash tables in Python.

Python's collections module defines abstract base classes that essentially mirror these built-in classes. Although the choice of names is counterintuitive, the abstract base class collections.Set matches the concrete frozenset class, while the abstract base class collections.MutableSet is akin to the concrete set class.

In our own discussion, we equate the "set ADT" with the behavior of the built-in set class (and thus, the collections.MutableSet base class). We begin by listing what we consider to be the five most fundamental behaviors for a set S:

S.add(e): Add element e to the set. This has no effect if the set already contains e.

S.discard(e): Remove element e from the set, if present. This has no effect if the set does not contain e.

e in S: Return True if the set contains element e. In Python, this is implemented with the special _ _contains_ _ method.

len(S): Return the number of elements in set S. In Python, this is implemented with the special method _ _len_ _.

iter(S): Generate an iteration of all elements of the set. In Python, this is implemented with the special method _ _iter_ _.

In the next section, we will see that the above five methods suffice for deriving all other behaviors of a set. Those remaining behaviors can be naturally grouped as follows. We begin by describing the following additional operations for removing one or more elements from a set:

S.remove(e): Remove element e from the set. If the set does not contain e, raise a KeyError.

S.pop( ): Remove and return an arbitrary element from the set. If the set is empty, raise a KeyError.

S.clear( ): Remove all elements from the set.

The next group of behaviors perform Boolean comparisons between two sets.

S == T: Return True if sets S and T have identical contents.

S != T: Return True if sets S and T are not equivalent.

S <= T: Return True if set S is a subset of set T.

S < T: Return True if set S is a *proper* subset of set T.

S >= T: Return True if set S is a superset of set T.

S > T: Return True if set S is a *proper* superset of set T.

S.isdisjoint(T): Return True if sets S and T have no common elements.

Finally, there exists a variety of behaviors that either update an existing set, or compute a new set instance, based on classical set theory operations.

S | T: Return a new set representing the union of sets S and T.

S |= T: Update set S to be the union of S and set T.

S & T: Return a new set representing the intersection of sets S and T.

S &= T: Update set S to be the intersection of S and set T.

S ^ T: Return a new set representing the symmetric difference of sets S and T, that is, a set of elements that are in precisely one of S or T.

S ^= T: Update set S to become the symmetric difference of itself and set T.

S − T: Return a new set containing elements in S but not T.

S −= T: Update set S to remove all common elements with set T.

10.5.2   Python's MutableSet Abstract Base Class

To aid in the creation of user-defined set classes, Python's collections module provides a MutableSet abstract base class (just as it provides the MutableMapping abstract base class discussed in Section 10.1.3). The MutableSet base class provides concrete implementations for all methods described in Section 10.5.1, except for five core behaviors (add, discard, __contains__, __len__, and __iter__) that must be implemented by any concrete subclass. This design is an example of what is known as the *template method pattern*, as the concrete methods of the MutableSet class rely on the presumed abstract methods that will subsequently be provided by a subclass.

For the purpose of illustration, we examine algorithms for implementing several of the derived methods of the MutableSet base class. For example, to determine if one set is a proper subset of another, we must verify two conditions: a proper subset must have size strictly smaller than that of its superset, and each element of a subset must be contained in the superset. An implementation of the corresponding __lt__ method based on this logic is given in Code Fragment 10.14.

```python
def __lt__(self, other):       # supports syntax S < T
    """Return true if this set is a proper subset of other."""
    if len(self) >= len(other):
        return False           # proper subset must have strictly smaller size
    for e in self:
        if e not in other:
            return False       # not a subset since element missing from other
    return True                # success; all conditions are met
```

Code Fragment 10.14:   A possible implementation of the MutableSet.__lt__ method, which tests if one set is a proper subset of another.

As another example, we consider the computation of the union of two sets. The set ADT includes two forms for computing a union. The syntax S | T should produce a new set that has contents equal to the union of existing sets S and T. This operation is implemented through the special method __or__ in Python. Another syntax, S |= T is used to *update* existing set S to become the union of itself and set T. Therefore, all elements of T that are not already contained in S should be added to S. We note that this "in-place" operation may be implemented more efficiently than if we were to rely on the first form, using the syntax S = S | T, in which identifier S is reassigned to a new set instance that represents the union. For convenience, Python's built-in set class supports named version of these behaviors, with S.union(T) equivalent to S | T, and S.update(T) equivalent to S |= T (yet, those named versions are not formally provided by the MutableSet abstract base class).

```
def __or__(self, other):                    # supports syntax S | T
  """Return a new set that is the union of two existing sets."""
  result = type(self)( )                     # create new instance of concrete class
  for e in self:
    result.add(e)
  for e in other:
    result.add(e)
  return result
```

Code Fragment 10.15: An implementation of the MutableSet.__or__ method, which computes the union of two existing sets.

An implementation of the behavior that computes a new set as a union of two others is given in the form of the __or__ special method, in Code Fragment 10.15. An important subtlety in this implementation is the instantiation of the resulting set. Since the MutableSet class is designed as an abstract base class, instances must belong to a concrete subclass. When computing the union of two such concrete instances, the result should presumably be an instance of the same class as the operands. The function type(self) returns a reference to the actual class of the instance identified as self, and the subsequent parentheses in expression type(self)( ) call the default constructor for that class.

In terms of efficiency, we analyze such set operations while letting n denote the size of S and m denote the size of set T for an operation such as S | T. If the concrete sets are implemented with hashing, the expected running time of the implementation in Code Fragment 10.15 is $O(m+n)$, because it loops over both sets, performing constant-time operations in the form of a containment check and a possible insertion into the result.

Our implementation of the in-place version of a union is given in Code Fragment 10.16, in the form of the __ior__ special method that supports syntax S |= T. Notice that in this case, we do not create a new set instance, instead we modify and return the existing set, after updating its contents to reflect the union operation. The in-place version of the union has expected running time $O(m)$ where m is the size of the second set, because we only have to loop through that second set.

```
def __ior__(self, other):         # supports syntax S |= T
  """Modify this set to be the union of itself an another set."""
  for e in other:
    self.add(e)
  return self                      # technical requirement of in-place operator
```

Code Fragment 10.16: An implementation of the MutableSet.__ior__ method, which performs an in-place union of one set with another.

10.5.3   Implementing Sets, Multisets, and Multimaps

Sets

Although sets and maps have very different public interfaces, they are really quite similar. A set is simply a map in which keys do not have associated values. Any data structure used to implement a map can be modified to implement the set ADT with similar performance guarantees. We could trivially adapt any map class by storing set elements as keys, and using None as an irrelevant value, but such an implementation is unnecessarily wasteful. An efficient set implementation should abandon the _Item composite that we use in our MapBase class and instead store set elements directly in a data structure.

Multisets

The same element may occur several times in a multiset. All of the data structures we have seen can be reimplemented to allow for duplicates to appear as separate elements. However, another way to implement a multiset is by using a *map* in which the map key is a (distinct) element of the multiset, and the associated value is a count of the number of occurrences of that element within the multiset. In fact, that is essentially what we did in Section 10.1.2 when computing the frequency of words within a document.

Python's standard collections module includes a definition for a class named Counter that is in essence a multiset. Formally, the Counter class is a subclass of dict, with the expectation that values are integers, and with additional functionality like a most_common(n) method that returns a list of the *n* most common elements. The standard __iter__ reports each element only once (since those are formally the keys of the dictionary). There is another method named elements( ) that iterates through the multiset with each element being repeated according to its count.

Multimaps

Although there is no multimap in Python's standard libraries, a common implementation approach is to use a standard map in which the value associated with a key is itself a container class storing any number of associated values. We give an example of such a MultiMap class in Code Fragment 10.17. Our implementation uses the standard dict class as the map, and a list of values as a composite value in the dictionary. We have designed the class so that a different map implementation can easily be substituted by overriding the class-level _MapType attribute at line 3.

```
1   class MultiMap:
2     """A multimap class built upon use of an underlying map for storage."""
3     _MapType = dict                  # Map type; can be redefined by subclass
4
5     def __init__(self):
6       """Create a new empty multimap instance."""
7       self._map = self._MapType( )          # create map instance for storage
8       self._n = 0
9
10    def __iter__(self):
11      """Iterate through all (k,v) pairs in multimap."""
12      for k,secondary in self._map.items( ):
13        for v in secondary:
14          yield (k,v)
15
16    def add(self, k, v):
17      """Add pair (k,v) to multimap."""
18      container = self._map.setdefault(k, [ ])     # create empty list, if needed
19      container.append(v)
20      self._n += 1
21
22    def pop(self, k):
23      """Remove and return arbitrary (k,v) with key k (or raise KeyError)."""
24      secondary = self._map[k]               # may raise KeyError
25      v = secondary.pop( )
26      if len(secondary) == 0:
27        del self._map[k]                     # no pairs left
28      self._n -= 1
29      return (k, v)
30
31    def find(self, k):
32      """Return arbitrary (k,v) pair with given key (or raise KeyError)."""
33      secondary = self._map[k]               # may raise KeyError
34      return (k, secondary[0])
35
36    def find_all(self, k):
37      """Generate iteration of all (k,v) pairs with given key."""
38      secondary = self._map.get(k, [ ])          # empty list, by default
39      for v in secondary:
40        yield (k,v)
```

Code Fragment 10.17: An implementation of a MultiMap using a dict for storage. The __len__ method, which returns self._n, is omitted from this listing.

10.6   Exercises

For help with exercises, please visit the site, www.wiley.com/college/goodrich.

Reinforcement

R-10.1 Give a concrete implementation of the pop method in the context of the MutableMapping class, relying only on the five primary abstract methods of that class.

R-10.2 Give a concrete implementation of the items( ) method in the context of the MutableMapping class, relying only on the five primary abstract methods of that class. What would its running time be if directly applied to the UnsortedTableMap subclass?

R-10.3 Give a concrete implementation of the items( ) method directly within the UnsortedTableMap class, ensuring that the entire iteration runs in $O(n)$ time.

R-10.4 What is the worst-case running time for inserting n key-value pairs into an initially empty map M that is implemented with the UnsortedTableMap class?

R-10.5 Reimplement the UnsortedTableMap class from Section 10.1.5, using the PositionalList class from Section 7.4 rather than a Python list.

R-10.6 Which of the hash table collision-handling schemes could tolerate a load factor above 1 and which could not?

R-10.7 Our Position classes for lists and trees support the __eq__ method so that two distinct position instances are considered equivalent if they refer to the same underlying node in a structure. For positions to be allowed as keys in a hash table, there must be a definition for the __hash__ method that is consistent with this notion of equivalence. Provide such a __hash__ method.

R-10.8 What would be a good hash code for a vehicle identification number that is a string of numbers and letters of the form "9X9XX99X9XX999999," where a "9" represents a digit and an "X" represents a letter?

R-10.9 Draw the 11-entry hash table that results from using the hash function, $h(i) = (3i+5) \mod 11$, to hash the keys 12, 44, 13, 88, 23, 94, 11, 39, 20, 16, and 5, assuming collisions are handled by chaining.

R-10.10 What is the result of the previous exercise, assuming collisions are handled by linear probing?

R-10.11 Show the result of Exercise R-10.9, assuming collisions are handled by quadratic probing, up to the point where the method fails.

R-10.12 What is the result of Exercise R-10.9 when collisions are handled by double hashing using the secondary hash function $h'(k) = 7 - (k \bmod 7)$?

R-10.13 What is the worst-case time for putting n entries in an initially empty hash table, with collisions resolved by chaining? What is the best case?

R-10.14 Show the result of rehashing the hash table shown in Figure 10.6 into a table of size 19 using the new hash function $h(k) = 3k \bmod 17$.

R-10.15 Our HashMapBase class maintains a load factor $\lambda \le 0.5$. Reimplement that class to allow the user to specify the maximum load, and adjust the concrete subclasses accordingly.

R-10.16 Give a pseudo-code description of an insertion into a hash table that uses quadratic probing to resolve collisions, assuming we also use the trick of replacing deleted entries with a special "deactivated entry" object.

R-10.17 Modify our ProbeHashMap to use quadratic probing.

R-10.18 Explain why a hash table is not suited to implement a sorted map.

R-10.19 Describe how a sorted list implemented as a doubly linked list could be used to implement the sorted map ADT.

R-10.20 What is the worst-case asymptotic running time for performing n deletions from a SortedTableMap instance that initially contains $2n$ entries?

R-10.21 Consider the following variant of the _find_index method from Code Fragment 10.8, in the context of the SortedTableMap class:

```
def _find_index(self, k, low, high):
  if high < low:
    return high + 1
  else:
    mid = (low + high) // 2
    if self._table[mid]._key < k:
      return self._find_index(k, mid + 1, high)
    else:
      return self._find_index(k, low, mid − 1)
```

Does this always produce the same result as the original version? Justify your answer.

R-10.22 What is the expected running time of the methods for maintaining a maxima set if we insert n pairs such that each pair has lower cost and performance than one before it? What is contained in the sorted map at the end of this series of operations? What if each pair had a lower cost and higher performance than the one before it?

R-10.23 Draw an example skip list S that results from performing the following series of operations on the skip list shown in Figure 10.13: del S[38], S[48] = 'x', S[24] = 'y', del S[55]. Record your coin flips, as well.

R-10.24 Give a pseudo-code description of the __delitem__ map operation when using a skip list.

R-10.25 Give a concrete implementation of the pop method, in the context of a MutableSet abstract base class, that relies only on the five core set behaviors described in Section 10.5.2.

R-10.26 Give a concrete implementation of the isdisjoint method in the context of the MutableSet abstract base class, relying only on the five primary abstract methods of that class. Your algorithm should run in $O(\min(n,m))$ where n and m denote the respective cardinalities of the two sets.

R-10.27 What abstraction would you use to manage a database of friends' birthdays in order to support efficient queries such as "find all friends whose birthday is today" and "find the friend who will be the next to celebrate a birthday"?

Creativity

C-10.28 On page 406 of Section 10.1.3, we give an implementation of the method setdefault as it might appear in the MutableMapping abstract base class. While that method accomplishes the goal in a general fashion, its efficiency is less than ideal. In particular, when the key is new, there will be a failed search due to the initial use of __getitem__, and then a subsequent insertion via __setitem__. For a concrete implementation, such as the UnsortedTableMap, this is twice the work because a complete scan of the table will take place during the failed __getitem__, and then another complete scan of the table takes place due to the implementation of __setitem__. A better solution is for the UnsortedTableMap class to override setdefault to provide a direct solution that performs a single search. Give such an implementation of UnsortedTableMap.setdefault.

C-10.29 Repeat Exercise C-10.28 for the ProbeHashMap class.

C-10.30 Repeat Exercise C-10.28 for the ChainHashMap class.

C-10.31 For an ideal compression function, the capacity of the bucket array for a hash table should be a prime number. Therefore, we consider the problem of locating a prime number in a range $[M, 2M]$. Implement a method for finding such a prime by using the *sieve algorithm*. In this algorithm, we allocate a $2M$ cell Boolean array A, such that cell i is associated with the integer i. We then initialize the array cells to all be "true" and we "mark off" all the cells that are multiples of 2, 3, 5, 7, and so on. This process can stop after it reaches a number larger than $\sqrt{2M}$. (Hint: Consider a bootstrapping method for finding the primes up to $\sqrt{2M}$.)

C-10.32 Perform experiments on our ChainHashMap and ProbeHashMap classes to measure its efficiency using random key sets and varying limits on the load factor (see Exercise R-10.15).

C-10.33 Our implementation of separate chaining in ChainHashMap conserves memory by representing empty buckets in the table as None, rather than as empty instances of a secondary structure. Because many of these buckets will hold a single item, a better optimization is to have those slots of the table directly reference the _Item instance, and to reserve use of secondary containers for buckets that have two or more items. Modify our implementation to provide this additional optimization.

C-10.34 Computing a hash code can be expensive, especially for lengthy keys. In our hash table implementations, we compute the hash code when first inserting an item, and recompute each item's hash code each time we resize our table. Python's dict class makes an interesting trade-off. The hash code is computed once, when an item is inserted, and the hash code is stored as an extra field of the item composite, so that it need not be recomputed. Reimplement our HashTableBase class to use such an approach.

C-10.35 Describe how to perform a removal from a hash table that uses linear probing to resolve collisions where we do not use a special marker to represent deleted elements. That is, we must rearrange the contents so that it appears that the removed entry was never inserted in the first place.

C-10.36 The quadratic probing strategy has a clustering problem related to the way it looks for open slots. Namely, when a collision occurs at bucket $h(k)$, it checks buckets $A[(h(k)+i^2) \bmod N]$, for $i = 1, 2, \ldots, N-1$.

     a. Show that $i^2 \bmod N$ will assume at most $(N+1)/2$ distinct values, for N prime, as i ranges from 1 to $N-1$. As a part of this justification, note that $i^2 \bmod N = (N-i)^2 \bmod N$ for all i.

     b. A better strategy is to choose a prime N such that $N \bmod 4 = 3$ and then to check the buckets $A[(h(k) \pm i^2) \bmod N]$ as i ranges from 1 to $(N-1)/2$, alternating between plus and minus. Show that this alternate version is guaranteed to check every bucket in A.

C-10.37 Refactor our ProbeHashMap design so that the sequence of secondary probes for collision resolution can be more easily customized. Demonstrate your new framework by providing separate concrete subclasses for linear probing and quadratic probing.

C-10.38 Design a variation of binary search for performing the multimap operation find_all(k) implemented with a sorted search table that includes duplicates, and show that it runs in time $O(s + \log n)$, where n is the number of elements in the dictionary and s is the number of items with given key k.

C-10.39 Although keys in a map are distinct, the binary search algorithm can be applied in a more general setting in which an array stores possibly duplicative elements in nondecreasing order. Consider the goal of identifying the index of the *leftmost* element with key greater than or equal to given k. Does the _find_index method as given in Code Fragment 10.8 guarantee such a result? Does the _find_index method as given in Exercise R-10.21 guarantee such a result? Justify your answers.

C-10.40 Suppose we are given two sorted search tables S and T, each with n entries (with S and T being implemented with arrays). Describe an $O(\log^2 n)$-time algorithm for finding the kth smallest key in the union of the keys from S and T (assuming no duplicates).

C-10.41 Give an $O(\log n)$-time solution for the previous problem.

C-10.42 Suppose that each row of an $n \times n$ array A consists of 1's and 0's such that, in any row of A, all the 1's come before any 0's in that row. Assuming A is already in memory, describe a method running in $O(n \log n)$ time (not $O(n^2)$ time!) for counting the number of 1's in A.

C-10.43 Given a collection C of n cost-performance pairs (c, p), describe an algorithm for finding the maxima pairs of C in $O(n \log n)$ time.

C-10.44 Show that the methods above(p) and prev(p) are not actually needed to efficiently implement a map using a skip list. That is, we can implement insertions and deletions in a skip list using a strictly top-down, scan-forward approach, without ever using the above or prev methods. (Hint: In the insertion algorithm, first repeatedly flip the coin to determine the level where you should start inserting the new entry.)

C-10.45 Describe how to modify a skip-list representation so that index-based operations, such as retrieving the item at index j, can be performed in $O(\log n)$ expected time.

C-10.46 For sets S and T, the syntax S ^ T returns a new set that is the symmetric difference, that is, a set of elements that are in precisely one of S or T. This syntax is supported by the special __xor__ method. Provide an implementation of that method in the context of the MutableSet abstract base class, relying only on the five primary abstract methods of that class.

C-10.47 In the context of the MutableSet abstract base class, describe a concrete implementation of the __and__ method, which supports the syntax S & T for computing the intersection of two existing sets.

C-10.48 An *inverted file* is a critical data structure for implementing a search engine or the index of a book. Given a document D, which can be viewed as an unordered, numbered list of words, an inverted file is an ordered list of words, L, such that, for each word w in L, we store the indices of the places in D where w appears. Design an efficient algorithm for constructing L from D.

C-10.49 Python's collections module provides an OrderedDict class that is unrelated to our sorted map abstraction. An OrderedDict is a subclass of the standard hash-based dict class that retains the expected $O(1)$ performance for the primary map operations, but that also guarantees that the __iter__ method reports items of the map according to first-in, first-out (FIFO) order. That is, the key that has been in the dictionary the longest is reported first. (The order is unaffected when the value for an existing key is overwritten.) Describe an algorithmic approach for achieving such performance.

Projects

P-10.50 Perform a comparative analysis that studies the collision rates for various hash codes for character strings, such as various polynomial hash codes for different values of the parameter a. Use a hash table to determine collisions, but only count collisions where different strings map to the same hash code (not if they map to the same location in this hash table). Test these hash codes on text files found on the Internet.

P-10.51 Perform a comparative analysis as in the previous exercise, but for 10-digit telephone numbers instead of character strings.

P-10.52 Implement an OrderedDict class, as described in Exercise C-10.49, ensuring that the primary map operations run in $O(1)$ expected time.

P-10.53 Design a Python class that implements the skip-list data structure. Use this class to create a complete implementation of the sorted map ADT.

P-10.54 Extend the previous project by providing a graphical animation of the skip-list operations. Visualize how entries move up the skip list during insertions and are linked out of the skip list during removals. Also, in a search operation, visualize the scan-forward and drop-down actions.

P-10.55 Write a spell-checker class that stores a lexicon of words, W, in a Python set, and implements a method, check(s), which performs a *spell check* on the string s with respect to the set of words, W. If s is in W, then the call to check(s) returns a list containing only s, as it is assumed to be spelled correctly in this case. If s is not in W, then the call to check(s) returns a list of every word in W that might be a correct spelling of s. Your program should be able to handle all the common ways that s might be a misspelling of a word in W, including swapping adjacent characters in a word, inserting a single character in between two adjacent characters in a word, deleting a single character from a word, and replacing a character in a word with another character. For an extra challenge, consider phonetic substitutions as well.

Chapter Notes

Hashing is a well-studied technique. The reader interested in further study is encouraged to explore the book by Knuth [65], as well as the book by Vitter and Chen [100]. Skip lists were introduced by Pugh [86]. Our analysis of skip lists is a simplification of a presentation given by Motwani and Raghavan [80]. For a more in-depth analysis of skip lists, please see the various research papers on skip lists that have appeared in the data structures literature [59, 81, 84]. Exercise C-10.36 was contributed by James Lee.

Chapter

11

Search Trees

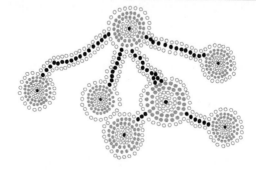

Contents

11.1   Binary Search Trees

In Chapter 8 we introduced the tree data structure and demonstrated a variety of applications. One important use is as a *search tree* (as described on page 332). In this chapter, we use a search tree structure to efficiently implement a *sorted map*. The three most fundamental methods of a map M (see Section 10.1.1) are:

M[k]: Return the value v associated with key k in map M, if one exists; otherwise raise a KeyError; implemented with __getitem__ method.

M[k] = v: Associate value v with key k in map M, replacing the existing value if the map already contains an item with key equal to k; implemented with __setitem__ method.

del M[k]: Remove from map M the item with key equal to k; if M has no such item, then raise a KeyError; implemented with __delitem__ method.

The sorted map ADT includes additional functionality (see Section 10.3), guaranteeing that an iteration reports keys in sorted order, and supporting additional searches such as find_gt(k) and find_range(start, stop).

Binary trees are an excellent data structure for storing items of a map, assuming we have an order relation defined on the keys. In this context, a *binary search tree* is a binary tree T with each position p storing a key-value pair (k,v) such that:

- Keys stored in the left subtree of p are less than k.
- Keys stored in the right subtree of p are greater than k.

An example of such a binary search tree is given in Figure 11.1. As a matter of convenience, we will not diagram the values associated with keys in this chapter, since those values do not affect the placement of items within a search tree.

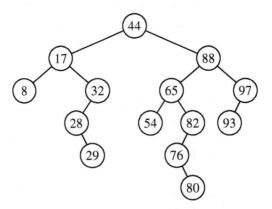

Figure 11.1: A binary search tree with integer keys. We omit the display of associated values in this chapter, since they are not relevant to the order of items within a search tree.

11.1.1 Navigating a Binary Search Tree

We begin by demonstrating that a binary search tree hierarchically represents the sorted order of its keys. In particular, the structural property regarding the placement of keys within a binary search tree assures the following important consequence regarding an ***inorder traversal*** (Section 8.4.3) of the tree.

Proposition 11.1: *An inorder traversal of a binary search tree visits positions in increasing order of their keys.*

Justification: We prove this by induction on the size of a subtree. If a subtree has at most one item, its keys are trivially visited in order. More generally, an inorder traversal of a (sub)tree consists of a recursive traversal of the (possibly empty) left subtree, followed by a visit of the root, and then a recursive traversal of the (possibly empty) right subtree. By induction, a recursive inorder traversal of the left subtree will produce an iteration of the keys in that subtree in increasing order. Furthermore, by the binary search tree property, all keys in the left subtree have keys strictly smaller than that of the root. Therefore, visiting the root just after that subtree extends the increasing order of keys. Finally, by the search tree property, all keys in the right subtree are strictly greater than the root, and by induction, an inorder traversal of that subtree will visit those keys in increasing order. ∎

Since an inorder traversal can be executed in linear time, a consequence of this proposition is that we can produce a sorted iteration of the keys of a map in linear time, when represented as a binary search tree.

Although an inorder traversal is typically expressed using a top-down recursion, we can provide nonrecursive descriptions of operations that allow more fine-grained navigation among the positions of a binary search relative to the order of their keys. Our generic binary tree ADT from Chapter 8 is defined as a positional structure, allowing direct navigation using methods such as parent(p), left(p), and right(p). With a binary *search* tree, we can provide additional navigation based on the natural order of the keys stored in the tree. In particular, we can support the following methods, akin to those provided by a PositionalList (Section 7.4.1).

first( ): Return the position containing the least key, or None if the tree is empty.

last( ): Return the position containing the greatest key, or None if empty tree.

before(p): Return the position containing the greatest key that is less than that of position p (i.e., the position that would be visited immediately before p in an inorder traversal), or None if p is the first position.

after(p): Return the position containing the least key that is greater than that of position p (i.e., the position that would be visited immediately after p in an inorder traversal), or None if p is the last position.

The "first" position of a binary search tree can be located by starting a walk at the root and continuing to the left child, as long as a left child exists. By symmetry, the last position is reached by repeated steps rightward starting at the root.

The successor of a position, after(p), is determined by the following algorithm.

Algorithm after(p):
    if right(p) is not None **then** {successor is leftmost position in p's right subtree}
        walk = right(p)
        while left(walk) is not None **do**
          walk = left(walk)
        return walk
    else {successor is nearest ancestor having p in its left subtree}
        walk = p
        ancestor = parent(walk)
        while ancestor is not None **and** walk == right(ancestor) **do**
          walk = ancestor
          ancestor = parent(walk)
        return ancestor

Code Fragment 11.1: Computing the successor of a position in a binary search tree.

The rationale for this process is based purely on the workings of an inorder traversal, given the correspondence of Proposition 11.1. If p has a right subtree, that right subtree is recursively traversed immediately after p is visited, and so the first position to be visited after p is the *leftmost* position within the right subtree. If p does not have a right subtree, then the flow of control of an inorder traversal returns to p's parent. If p were in the *right* subtree of that parent, then the parent's subtree traversal is complete and the flow of control progresses to its parent and so on. Once an ancestor is reached in which the recursion is returning from its *left* subtree, then that ancestor becomes the next position visited by the inorder traversal, and thus is the successor of p. Notice that the only case in which no such ancestor is found is when p was the rightmost (last) position of the full tree, in which case there is no successor.

A symmetric algorithm can be defined to determine the predecessor of a position, before(p). At this point, we note that the running time of single call to after(p) or before(p) is bounded by the height h of the full tree, because it is found after either a single downward walk or a single upward walk. While the worst-case running time is $O(h)$, we note that either of these methods run in $O(1)$ *amortized* time, in that series of n calls to after(p) starting at the first position will execute in a total of $O(n)$ time. We leave a formal justification of this fact to Exercise C-11.34, but intuitively the upward and downward paths mimic steps of the inorder traversal (a related argument was made in the justification of Proposition 9.3).

11.1.2 Searches

The most important consequence of the structural property of a binary search tree is its namesake search algorithm. We can attempt to locate a particular key in a binary search tree by viewing it as a decision tree (recall Figure 8.7). In this case, the question asked at each position p is whether the desired key k is less than, equal to, or greater than the key stored at position p, which we denote as p.key( ). If the answer is "less than," then the search continues in the left subtree. If the answer is "equal," then the search terminates successfully. If the answer is "greater than," then the search continues in the right subtree. Finally, if we reach an empty subtree, then the search terminates unsuccessfully. (See Figure 11.2.)

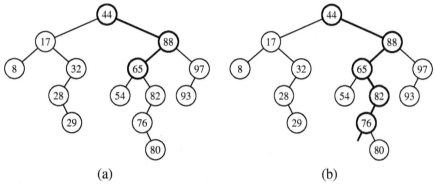

(a)   (b)

Figure 11.2: (a) A successful search for key 65 in a binary search tree; (b) an unsuccessful search for key 68 that terminates because there is no subtree to the left of the key 76.

We describe this approach in Code Fragment 11.2. If key k occurs in a subtree rooted at p, a call to TreeSearch(T, p, k) results in the position at which the key is found; in this case, the __getitem__ map operation would return the associated value at that position. In the event of an unsuccessful search, the TreeSearch algorithm returns the final position explored on the search path (which we will later make use of when determining where to insert a new item in a search tree).

Algorithm TreeSearch(T, p, k):
    if k == p.key( ) **then**
        return *p*   {successful search}
    else if k < p.key( ) and T.left(p) is not None **then**
        return TreeSearch(T, T.left(p), k)   {recur on left subtree}
    else if k > p.key( ) and T.right(p) is not None **then**
        return TreeSearch(T, T.right(p), k)   {recur on right subtree}
    return p   {unsuccessful search}

Code Fragment 11.2: Recursive search in a binary search tree.

Analysis of Binary Tree Searching

The analysis of the worst-case running time of searching in a binary search tree T is simple. Algorithm TreeSearch is recursive and executes a constant number of primitive operations for each recursive call. Each recursive call of TreeSearch is made on a child of the previous position. That is, TreeSearch is called on the positions of a path of T that starts at the root and goes down one level at a time. Thus, the number of such positions is bounded by $h+1$, where h is the height of T. In other words, since we spend $O(1)$ time per position encountered in the search, the overall search runs in $O(h)$ time, where h is the height of the binary search tree T. (See Figure 11.3.)

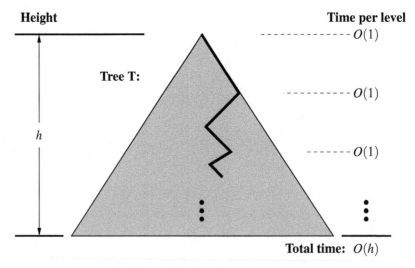

Figure 11.3: Illustrating the running time of searching in a binary search tree. The figure uses standard caricature of a binary search tree as a big triangle and a path from the root as a zig-zag line.

In the context of the sorted map ADT, the search will be used as a subroutine for implementing the __getitem__ method, as well as for the __setitem__ and __delitem__ methods, since each of these begins by trying to locate an existing item with a given key. To implement sorted map operations such as find_lt and find_gt, we will combine this search with traversal methods before and after. All of these operations will run in worst-case $O(h)$ time for a tree with height h. We can use a variation of this technique to implement the find_range method in time $O(s+h)$, where s is the number of items reported (see Exercise C-11.34).

Admittedly, the height h of T can be as large as the number of entries, n, but we expect that it is usually much smaller. Indeed, later in this chapter we show various strategies to maintain an upper bound of $O(\log n)$ on the height of a search tree T.

11.1.3 Insertions and Deletions

Algorithms for inserting or deleting entries of a binary search tree are fairly straightforward, although not trivial.

Insertion

The map command $M[k] = v$, as supported by the __setitem__ method, begins with a search for key k (assuming the map is nonempty). If found, that item's existing value is reassigned. Otherwise, a node for the new item can be inserted into the underlying tree T in place of the empty subtree that was reached at the end of the failed search. The binary search tree property is sustained by that placement (note that it is placed exactly where a search would expect it). Pseudo-code for such a TreeInsert algorithm is given in in Code Fragment 11.3.

Algorithm TreeInsert(T, k, v):
    Input: A search key k to be associated with value v
    $p = $ TreeSearch(T, T.root(), k)
    if k == p.key() **then**
        Set p's value to v
    else if k < p.key() **then**
        add node with item (k,v) as left child of p
    else
        add node with item (k,v) as right child of p

Code Fragment 11.3: Algorithm for inserting a key-value pair into a map that is represented as a binary search tree.

An example of insertion into a binary search tree is shown in Figure 11.4.

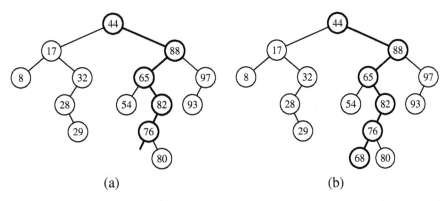

        (a)   (b)

Figure 11.4: Insertion of an item with key 68 into the search tree of Figure 11.2. Finding the position to insert is shown in (a), and the resulting tree is shown in (b).

Deletion

Deleting an item from a binary search tree T is a bit more complex than inserting a new item because the location of the deletion might be anywhere in the tree. (In contrast, insertions are always enacted at the bottom of a path.) To delete an item with key k, we begin by calling TreeSearch(T, T.root( ), k) to find the position p of T storing an item with key equal to k. If the search is successful, we distinguish between two cases (of increasing difficulty):

- If p has at most one child, the deletion of the node at position p is easily implemented. When introducing update methods for the LinkedBinaryTree class in Section 8.3.1, we declared a nonpublic utility, _delete(p), that deletes a node at position p and replaces it with its child (if any), presuming that p has at most one child. That is precisely the desired behavior. It removes the item with key k from the map while maintaining all other ancestor-descendant relationships in the tree, thereby assuring the upkeep of the binary search tree property. (See Figure 11.5.)

- If position p has two children, we cannot simply remove the node from T since this would create a "hole" and two orphaned children. Instead, we proceed as follows (see Figure 11.6):

  o We locate position r containing the item having the greatest key that is strictly less than that of position p, that is, r = before(p) by the notation of Section 11.1.1. Because p has two children, its predecessor is the rightmost position of the left subtree of p.

  o We use r's item as a replacement for the one being deleted at position p. Because r has the immediately preceding key in the map, any items in p's right subtree will have keys greater than r and any other items in p's left subtree will have keys less than r. Therefore, the binary search tree property is satisfied after the replacement.

  o Having used r's as a replacement for p, we instead delete the node at position r from the tree. Fortunately, since r was located as the rightmost position in a subtree, r does not have a right child. Therefore, its deletion can be performed using the first (and simpler) approach.

As with searching and insertion, this algorithm for a deletion involves the traversal of a single path downward from the root, possibly moving an item between two positions of this path, and removing a node from that path and promoting its child. Therefore, it executes in time $O(h)$ where h is the height of the tree.

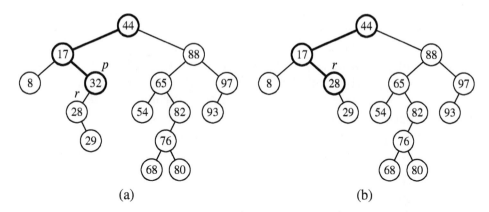

Figure 11.5: Deletion from the binary search tree of Figure 11.4b, where the item to delete (with key 32) is stored at a position p with one child r: (a) before the deletion; (b) after the deletion.

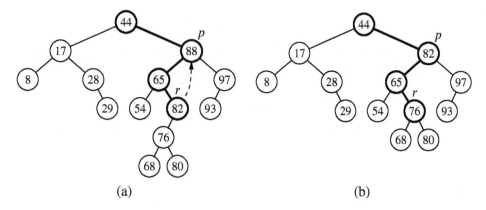

Figure 11.6: Deletion from the binary search tree of Figure 11.5b, where the item to delete (with key 88) is stored at a position p with two children, and replaced by its predecessor r: (a) before the deletion; (b) after the deletion.

11.1.4   Python Implementation

In Code Fragments 11.4 through 11.8 we define a TreeMap class that implements the sorted map ADT using a binary search tree. In fact, our implementation is more general. We support all of the standard map operations (Section 10.1.1), all additional sorted map operations (Section 10.3), and positional operations including first( ), last( ), find_position(k), before(p), after(p), and delete(p).

Our TreeMap class takes advantage of *multiple inheritance* for code reuse, inheriting from the LinkedBinaryTree class of Section 8.3.1 for our representation as a positional binary tree, and from the MapBase class from Code Fragment 10.2 of Section 10.1.4 to provide us with the key-value composite item and the concrete behaviors from the collections.MutableMapping abstract base class. We subclass the nested Position class to support more specific p.key( ) and p.value( ) accessors for our map, rather than the p.element( ) syntax inherited from the tree ADT.

We define several nonpublic utilities, most notably a _subtree_search(p, k) method that corresponds to the TreeSearch algorithm of Code Fragment 11.2. That returns a position, ideally one that contains the key k, or otherwise the last position that is visited on the search path. We rely on the fact that the final position during an unsuccessful search is either the nearest key less than k or the nearest key greater than k. This search utility becomes the basis for the public find_position(k) method, and also for internal use when searching, inserting, or deleting items from a map, as well as for the robust searches of the sorted map ADT.

When making structural modifications to the tree, we rely on nonpublic update methods, such as _add_right, that are inherited from the LinkedBinaryTree class (see Section 8.3.1). It is important that these inherited methods remain nonpublic, as the search tree property could be violated through misuse of such operations.

Finally, we note that our code is peppered with calls to presumed methods named _rebalance_insert, _rebalance_delete, and _rebalance_access. These methods serve as *hooks* for future use when balancing search trees; we discuss them in Section 11.2. We conclude with a brief guide to the organization of our code.

Code Fragment 11.4: Beginning of TreeMap class including redefined Position class and nonpublic search utilities.

Code Fragment 11.5: Positional methods first( ), last( ), before(p), after(p), and find_position(p) accessor.

Code Fragment 11.6: Selected methods of the sorted map ADT: find_min( ), find_ge(k), and find_range(start, stop); related methods are omitted for the sake of brevity.

Code Fragment 11.7: __getitem__(k), __setitem__(k, v), and __iter__( ).

Code Fragment 11.8: Deletion either by position, as delete(p), or by key, as __delitem__(k).

```
1   class TreeMap(LinkedBinaryTree, MapBase):
2     """Sorted map implementation using a binary search tree."""
3
4     #--------------------------- override Position class ---------------------------
5     class Position(LinkedBinaryTree.Position):
6       def key(self):
7         """Return key of map's key-value pair."""
8         return self.element()._key
9
10      def value(self):
11        """Return value of map's key-value pair."""
12        return self.element()._value
13
14    #--------------------------- nonpublic utilities ---------------------------
15    def _subtree_search(self, p, k):
16      """Return Position of p's subtree having key k, or last node searched."""
17      if k == p.key():                              # found match
18        return p
19      elif k < p.key():                             # search left subtree
20        if self.left(p) is not None:
21          return self._subtree_search(self.left(p), k)
22      else:                                         # search right subtree
23        if self.right(p) is not None:
24          return self._subtree_search(self.right(p), k)
25      return p                                      # unsucessful search
26
27    def _subtree_first_position(self, p):
28      """Return Position of first item in subtree rooted at p."""
29      walk = p
30      while self.left(walk) is not None:            # keep walking left
31        walk = self.left(walk)
32      return walk
33
34    def _subtree_last_position(self, p):
35      """Return Position of last item in subtree rooted at p."""
36      walk = p
37      while self.right(walk) is not None:           # keep walking right
38        walk = self.right(walk)
39      return walk
```

Code Fragment 11.4: Beginning of a TreeMap class based on a binary search tree.

```
40    def first(self):
41      """Return the first Position in the tree (or None if empty)."""
42      return self._subtree_first_position(self.root()) if len(self) > 0 else None
43
44    def last(self):
45      """Return the last Position in the tree (or None if empty)."""
46      return self._subtree_last_position(self.root()) if len(self) > 0 else None
47
48    def before(self, p):
49      """Return the Position just before p in the natural order.
50
51      Return None if p is the first position.
52      """
53      self._validate(p)                      # inherited from LinkedBinaryTree
54      if self.left(p):
55        return self._subtree_last_position(self.left(p))
56      else:
57        # walk upward
58        walk = p
59        above = self.parent(walk)
60        while above is not None and walk == self.left(above):
61          walk = above
62          above = self.parent(walk)
63        return above
64
65    def after(self, p):
66      """Return the Position just after p in the natural order.
67
68      Return None if p is the last position.
69      """
70      # symmetric to before(p)
71
72    def find_position(self, k):
73      """Return position with key k, or else neighbor (or None if empty)."""
74      if self.is_empty():
75        return None
76      else:
77        p = self._subtree_search(self.root(), k)
78        self._rebalance_access(p)            # hook for balanced tree subclasses
79        return p
```

Code Fragment 11.5: Navigational methods of the TreeMap class.

```
80    def find_min(self):
81      """Return (key,value) pair with minimum key (or None if empty)."""
82      if self.is_empty():
83        return None
84      else:
85        p = self.first()
86        return (p.key(), p.value())
87
88    def find_ge(self, k):
89      """Return (key,value) pair with least key greater than or equal to k.
90
91      Return None if there does not exist such a key.
92      """
93      if self.is_empty():
94        return None
95      else:
96        p = self.find_position(k)              # may not find exact match
97        if p.key() < k:                        # p's key is too small
98          p = self.after(p)
99        return (p.key(), p.value()) if p is not None else None
100
101   def find_range(self, start, stop):
102     """Iterate all (key,value) pairs such that start <= key < stop.
103
104     If start is None, iteration begins with minimum key of map.
105     If stop is None, iteration continues through the maximum key of map.
106     """
107     if not self.is_empty():
108       if start is None:
109         p = self.first()
110       else:
111         # we initialize p with logic similar to find_ge
112         p = self.find_position(start)
113         if p.key() < start:
114           p = self.after(p)
115       while p is not None and (stop is None or p.key() < stop):
116         yield (p.key(), p.value())
117         p = self.after(p)
```

Code Fragment 11.6: Some of the sorted map operations for the TreeMap class.

```
118    def __getitem__(self, k):
119      """Return value associated with key k (raise KeyError if not found)."""
120      if self.is_empty():
121        raise KeyError('Key Error: ' + repr(k))
122      else:
123        p = self._subtree_search(self.root(), k)
124        self._rebalance_access(p)              # hook for balanced tree subclasses
125        if k != p.key():
126          raise KeyError('Key Error: ' + repr(k))
127        return p.value()
128
129    def __setitem__(self, k, v):
130      """Assign value v to key k, overwriting existing value if present."""
131      if self.is_empty():
132        leaf = self._add_root(self._Item(k,v))      # from LinkedBinaryTree
133      else:
134        p = self._subtree_search(self.root(), k)
135        if p.key() == k:
136          p.element()._value = v             # replace existing item's value
137          self._rebalance_access(p)          # hook for balanced tree subclasses
138          return
139        else:
140          item = self._Item(k,v)
141          if p.key() < k:
142            leaf = self._add_right(p, item)  # inherited from LinkedBinaryTree
143          else:
144            leaf = self._add_left(p, item)   # inherited from LinkedBinaryTree
145      self._rebalance_insert(leaf)           # hook for balanced tree subclasses
146
147    def __iter__(self):
148      """Generate an iteration of all keys in the map in order."""
149      p = self.first()
150      while p is not None:
151        yield p.key()
152        p = self.after(p)
```

Code Fragment 11.7: Map operations for accessing and inserting items in the TreeMap class. Reverse iteration can be implemented with __reverse__, using symmetric approach to __iter__.

```
153    def delete(self, p):
154      """Remove the item at given Position."""
155      self._validate(p)                              # inherited from LinkedBinaryTree
156      if self.left(p) and self.right(p):             # p has two children
157        replacement = self._subtree_last_position(self.left(p))
158        self._replace(p, replacement.element())      # from LinkedBinaryTree
159        p = replacement
160      # now p has at most one child
161      parent = self.parent(p)
162      self._delete(p)                                # inherited from LinkedBinaryTree
163      self._rebalance_delete(parent)                 # if root deleted, parent is None
164
165    def __delitem__(self, k):
166      """Remove item associated with key k (raise KeyError if not found)."""
167      if not self.is_empty():
168        p = self._subtree_search(self.root(), k)
169        if k == p.key():
170          self.delete(p)                             # rely on positional version
171          return                                     # successful deletion complete
172        self._rebalance_access(p)                     # hook for balanced tree subclasses
173      raise KeyError('Key Error: ' + repr(k))
```

Code Fragment 11.8: Support for deleting an item from a TreeMap, located either by position or by key.

11.1.5 Performance of a Binary Search Tree

An analysis of the operations of our TreeMap class is given in Table 11.1. Almost all operations have a worst-case running time that depends on h, where h is the height of the current tree. This is because most operations rely on a constant amount of work for each node along a particular path of the tree, and the maximum path length within a tree is proportional to the height of the tree. Most notably, our implementations of map operations __getitem__, __setitem__, and __delitem__ each begin with a call to the _subtree_search utility which traces a path downward from the root of the tree, using $O(1)$ time at each node to determine how to continue the search. Similar paths are traced when looking for a replacement during a deletion, or when computing a position's inorder predecessor or successor. We note that although a single call to the after method has worst-case running time of $O(h)$, the n successive calls made during a call to __iter__ require a total of $O(n)$ time, since each edge is traced at most twice; in a sense, those calls have $O(1)$ amortized time bounds. A similar argument can be used to prove the $O(s+h)$ worst-case bound for a call to find_range that reports s results (see Exercise C-11.34).

Operation	Running Time
k in T	$O(h)$
T[k], T[k] = v	$O(h)$
T.delete(p), del T[k]	$O(h)$
T.find_position(k)	$O(h)$
T.first( ), T.last( ), T.find_min( ), T.find_max( )	$O(h)$
T.before(p), T.after(p)	$O(h)$
T.find_lt(k), T.find_le(k), T.find_gt(k), T.find_ge(k)	$O(h)$
T.find_range(start, stop)	$O(s+h)$
iter(T), reversed(T)	$O(n)$

Table 11.1: Worst-case running times of the operations for a TreeMap T. We denote the current height of the tree with h, and the number of items reported by find_range as s. The space usage is $O(n)$, where n is the number of items stored in the map.

A binary search tree T is therefore an efficient implementation of a map with n entries only if its height is small. In the best case, T has height $h = \lceil \log(n+1) \rceil - 1$, which yields logarithmic-time performance for all the map operations. In the worst case, however, T has height n, in which case it would look and feel like an ordered list implementation of a map. Such a worst-case configuration arises, for example, if we insert items with keys in increasing or decreasing order. (See Figure 11.7.)

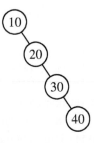

Figure 11.7: Example of a binary search tree with linear height, obtained by inserting entries with keys in increasing order.

We can nevertheless take comfort that, on average, a binary search tree with n keys generated from a random series of insertions and removals of keys has expected height $O(\log n)$; the justification of this statement is beyond the scope of the book, requiring careful mathematical language to precisely define what we mean by a random series of insertions and removals, and sophisticated probability theory.

In applications where one cannot guarantee the random nature of updates, it is better to rely on variations of search trees, presented in the remainder of this chapter, that guarantee a ***worst-case*** height of $O(\log n)$, and thus $O(\log n)$ worst-case time for searches, insertions, and deletions.

11.2 Balanced Search Trees

In the closing of the previous section, we noted that if we could assume a random series of insertions and removals, the standard binary search tree supports $O(\log n)$ expected running times for the basic map operations. However, we may only claim $O(n)$ worst-case time, because some sequences of operations may lead to an unbalanced tree with height proportional to n.

In the remainder of this chapter, we explore four search tree algorithms that provide stronger performance guarantees. Three of the four data structures (AVL trees, splay trees, and red-black trees) are based on augmenting a standard binary search tree with occasional operations to reshape the tree and reduce its height.

The primary operation to rebalance a binary search tree is known as a ***rotation***. During a rotation, we "rotate" a child to be above its parent, as diagrammed in Figure 11.8.

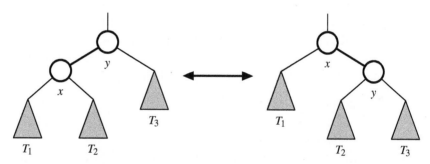

Figure 11.8: A rotation operation in a binary search tree. A rotation can be performed to transform the left formation into the right, or the right formation into the left. Note that all keys in subtree T_1 have keys less than that of position x, all keys in subtree T_2 have keys that are between those of positions x and y, and all keys in subtree T_3 have keys that are greater than that of position y.

To maintain the binary search tree property through a rotation, we note that if position x was a left child of position y prior to a rotation (and therefore the key of x is less than the key of y), then y becomes the *right* child of x after the rotation, and vice versa. Furthermore, we must relink the subtree of items with keys that lie between the keys of the two positions that are being rotated. For example, in Figure 11.8 the subtree labeled T_2 represents items with keys that are known to be greater than that of position x and less than that of position y. In the first configuration of that figure, T_2 is the right subtree of position x; in the second configuration, it is the left subtree of position y.

Because a single rotation modifies a constant number of parent-child relationships, it can be implemented in $O(1)$ time with a linked binary tree representation.

In the context of a tree-balancing algorithm, a rotation allows the shape of a tree to be modified while maintaining the search tree property. If used wisely, this operation can be performed to avoid highly unbalanced tree configurations. For example, a rightward rotation from the first formation of Figure 11.8 to the second reduces the depth of each node in subtree T_1 by one, while increasing the depth of each node in subtree T_3 by one. (Note that the depth of nodes in subtree T_2 are unaffected by the rotation.)

One or more rotations can be combined to provide broader rebalancing within a tree. One such compound operation we consider is a ***trinode restructuring***. For this manipulation, we consider a position x, its parent y, and its grandparent z. The goal is to restructure the subtree rooted at z in order to reduce the overall path length to x and its subtrees. Pseudo-code for a restructure(x) method is given in Code Fragment 11.9 and illustrated in Figure 11.9. In describing a trinode restructuring, we temporarily rename the positions x, y, and z as a, b, and c, so that a precedes b and b precedes c in an inorder traversal of T. There are four possible orientations mapping x, y, and z to a, b, and c, as shown in Figure 11.9, which are unified into one case by our relabeling. The trinode restructuring replaces z with the node identified as b, makes the children of this node be a and c, and makes the children of a and c be the four previous children of x, y, and z (other than x and y), while maintaining the inorder relationships of all the nodes in T.

Algorithm restructure(x):

   Input: A position x of a binary search tree T that has both a parent y and a grandparent z

   Output: Tree T after a trinode restructuring (which corresponds to a single or double rotation) involving positions x, y, and z

1: Let (a, b, c) be a left-to-right (inorder) listing of the positions x, y, and z, and let (T_1, T_2, T_3, T_4) be a left-to-right (inorder) listing of the four subtrees of x, y, and z not rooted at x, y, or z.

2: Replace the subtree rooted at z with a new subtree rooted at b.

3: Let a be the left child of b and let T_1 and T_2 be the left and right subtrees of a, respectively.

4: Let c be the right child of b and let T_3 and T_4 be the left and right subtrees of c, respectively.

Code Fragment 11.9: The trinode restructuring operation in a binary search tree.

In practice, the modification of a tree T caused by a trinode restructuring operation can be implemented through case analysis either as a single rotation (as in Figure 11.9a and b) or as a double rotation (as in Figure 11.9c and d). The double rotation arises when position x has the middle of the three relevant keys and is first rotated above its parent, and then above what was originally its grandparent. In any of the cases, the trinode restructuring is completed with $O(1)$ running time.

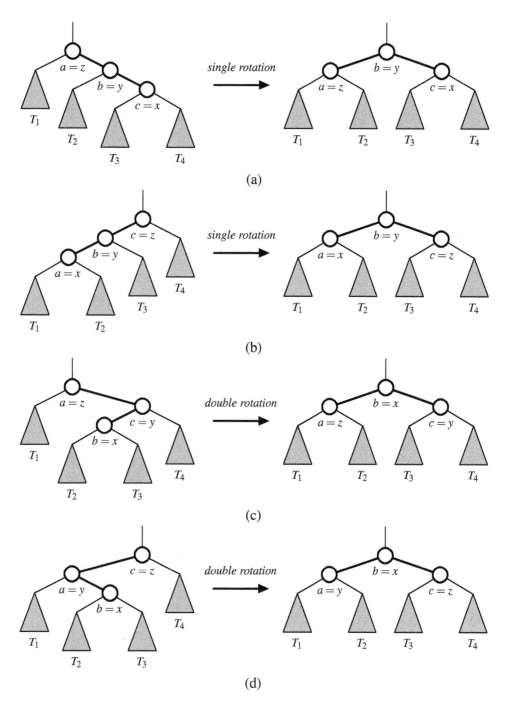

Figure 11.9: Schematic illustration of a trinode restructuring operation: (a and b) require a single rotation; (c and d) require a double rotation.

11.2.1   Python Framework for Balancing Search Trees

Our TreeMap class, introduced in Section 11.1.4, is a concrete map implementation that does not perform any explicit balancing operations. However, we designed that class to also serve as a base class for other subclasses that implement more advanced tree-balancing algorithms. A summary of our inheritance hierarchy is shown in Figure 11.10.

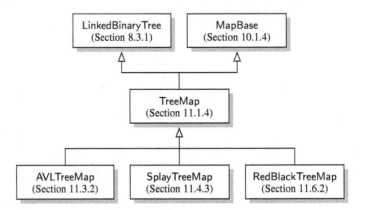

Figure 11.10: Our hierarchy of balanced search trees (with references to where they are defined). Recall that TreeMap inherits multiply from LinkedBinaryTree and MapBase.

Hooks for Rebalancing Operations

Our implementation of the basic map operations in Section 11.1.4 includes strategic calls to three nonpublic methods that serve as *hooks* for rebalancing algorithms:

- A call to _rebalance_insert(p) is made from within the __setitem__ method immediately after a new node is added to the tree at position *p*.
- A call to _rebalance_delete(p) is made each time a node has been deleted from the tree, with position *p* identifying the *parent* of the node that has just been removed. Formally, this hook is called from within the public delete(p) method, which is indirectly invoked by the public __delitem__(k) behavior.
- We also provide a hook, _rebalance_access(p), that is called when an item at position *p* of a tree is accessed through a public method such as __getitem__. This hook is used by the *splay tree* structure (see Section 11.4) to restructure a tree so that more frequently accessed items are brought closer to the root.

We provide trivial declarations of these three methods, in Code Fragment 11.10, having bodies that do nothing (using the **pass** statement). A subclass of TreeMap may override any of these methods to implement a nontrivial action to rebalance a tree. This is another example of the *template method design pattern*, as seen in Section 8.4.6.

```
174    def _rebalance_insert(self, p): pass
175    def _rebalance_delete(self, p): pass
176    def _rebalance_access(self, p): pass
```

Code Fragment 11.10: Additional code for the TreeMap class (continued from Code Fragment 11.8), providing stubs for the rebalancing hooks.

Nonpublic Methods for Rotating and Restructuring

A second form of support for balanced search trees is our inclusion of nonpublic utility methods _rotate and _restructure that, respectively, implement a single rotation and a trinode restructuring (described at the beginning of Section 11.2). Although these methods are not invoked by the public TreeMap operations, we promote code reuse by providing these implementation in this class so that they are inherited by all balanced-tree subclasses.

Our implementations are provided in Code Fragment 11.11. To simplify the code, we define an additional _relink utility that properly links parent and child nodes to each other, including the special case in which a "child" is a None reference. The focus of the _rotate method then becomes redefining the relationship between the parent and child, relinking a rotated node directly to its original grandparent, and shifting the "middle" subtree (that labeled as T_2 in Figure 11.8) between the rotated nodes. For the trinode restructuring, we determine whether to perform a single or double rotation, as originally described in Figure 11.9.

Factory for Creating Tree Nodes

We draw attention to an important subtlety in the design of both our TreeMap class and the original LinkedBinaryTree subclass. The low-level definition of a node is provided by the nested _Node class within LinkedBinaryTree. Yet, several of our tree-balancing strategies require that auxiliary information be stored at each node to guide the balancing process. Those classes will override the nested _Node class to provide storage for an additional field.

Whenever we add a new node to the tree, as within the _add_right method of the LinkedBinaryTree (originally given in Code Fragment 8.10), we intentionally instantiate the node using the syntax self._Node, rather than the qualified name LinkedBinaryTree._Node. This is vital to our framework! When the expression self._Node is applied to an instance of a tree (sub)class, Python's name resolution follows the inheritance structure (as described in Section 2.5.2). If a subclass has overridden the definition for the _Node class, instantiation of self._Node relies on the newly defined node class. This technique is an example of the ***factory method design pattern***, as we provide a *subclass* the means to control the type of node that is created within methods of the *parent* class.

```
177    def _relink(self, parent, child, make_left_child):
178      """Relink parent node with child node (we allow child to be None)."""
179      if make_left_child:                        # make it a left child
180        parent._left = child
181      else:                                      # make it a right child
182        parent._right = child
183      if child is not None:                      # make child point to parent
184        child._parent = parent
185
186    def _rotate(self, p):
187      """Rotate Position p above its parent."""
188      x = p._node
189      y = x._parent                              # we assume this exists
190      z = y._parent                              # grandparent (possibly None)
191      if z is None:
192        self._root = x                           # x becomes root
193        x._parent = None
194      else:
195        self._relink(z, x, y == z._left)         # x becomes a direct child of z
196      # now rotate x and y, including transfer of middle subtree
197      if x == y._left:
198        self._relink(y, x._right, True)          # x._right becomes left child of y
199        self._relink(x, y, False)                # y becomes right child of x
200      else:
201        self._relink(y, x._left, False)          # x._left becomes right child of y
202        self._relink(x, y, True)                 # y becomes left child of x
203
204    def _restructure(self, x):
205      """Perform trinode restructure of Position x with parent/grandparent."""
206      y = self.parent(x)
207      z = self.parent(y)
208      if (x == self.right(y)) == (y == self.right(z)):  # matching alignments
209        self._rotate(y)                          # single rotation (of y)
210        return y                                 # y is new subtree root
211      else:                                      # opposite alignments
212        self._rotate(x)                          # double rotation (of x)
213        self._rotate(x)
214        return x                                 # x is new subtree root
```

Code Fragment 11.11: Additional code for the TreeMap class (continued from Code Fragment 11.10), to provide nonpublic utilities for balanced search tree subclasses.

11.3 AVL Trees

The TreeMap class, which uses a standard binary search tree as its data structure, should be an efficient map data structure, but its worst-case performance for the various operations is linear time, because it is possible that a series of operations results in a tree with linear height. In this section, we describe a simple balancing strategy that guarantees worst-case logarithmic running time for all the fundamental map operations.

Definition of an AVL Tree

The simple correction is to add a rule to the binary search tree definition that will maintain a logarithmic height for the tree. Although we originally defined the height of a subtree rooted at position p of a tree to be the number of *edges* on the longest path from p to a leaf (see Section 8.1.3), it is easier for explanation in this section to consider the height to be the number of *nodes* on such a longest path. By this definition, a leaf position has height 1, while we trivially define the height of a "null" child to be 0.

In this section, we consider the following ***height-balance property***, which characterizes the structure of a binary search tree T in terms of the heights of its nodes.

Height-Balance Property: For every position p of T, the heights of the children of p differ by at most 1.

Any binary search tree T that satisfies the height-balance property is said to be an ***AVL tree***, named after the initials of its inventors: Adel'son-Vel'skii and Landis. An example of an AVL tree is shown in Figure 11.11.

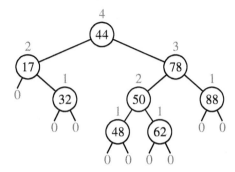

Figure 11.11: An example of an AVL tree. The keys of the items are shown inside the nodes, and the heights of the nodes are shown above the nodes (with empty subtrees having height 0).

An immediate consequence of the height-balance property is that a subtree of an AVL tree is itself an AVL tree. The height-balance property has also the important consequence of keeping the height small, as shown in the following proposition.

Proposition 11.2: *The height of an AVL tree storing n entries is* $O(\log n)$.

Justification: Instead of trying to find an upper bound on the height of an AVL tree directly, it turns out to be easier to work on the "inverse problem" of finding a lower bound on the minimum number of nodes $n(h)$ of an AVL tree with height h. We will show that $n(h)$ grows at least exponentially. From this, it will be an easy step to derive that the height of an AVL tree storing n entries is $O(\log n)$.

We begin by noting that $n(1) = 1$ and $n(2) = 2$, because an AVL tree of height 1 must have exactly one node and an AVL tree of height 2 must have at least two nodes. Now, an AVL tree with the minimum number of nodes having height h for $h \geq 3$, is such that both its subtrees are AVL trees with the minimum number of nodes: one with height $h-1$ and the other with height $h-2$. Taking the root into account, we obtain the following formula that relates $n(h)$ to $n(h-1)$ and $n(h-2)$, for $h \geq 3$:

$$n(h) = 1 + n(h-1) + n(h-2). \tag{11.1}$$

At this point, the reader familiar with the properties of Fibonacci progressions (Section 1.8 and Exercise C-3.49) will already see that $n(h)$ is a function exponential in h. To formalize that observation, we proceed as follows.

Formula 11.1 implies that $n(h)$ is a strictly increasing function of h. Thus, we know that $n(h-1) > n(h-2)$. Replacing $n(h-1)$ with $n(h-2)$ in Formula 11.1 and dropping the 1, we get, for $h \geq 3$,

$$n(h) > 2 \cdot n(h-2). \tag{11.2}$$

Formula 11.2 indicates that $n(h)$ at least doubles each time h increases by 2, which intuitively means that $n(h)$ grows exponentially. To show this fact in a formal way, we apply Formula 11.2 repeatedly, yielding the following series of inequalities:

$$
\begin{aligned}
n(h) \;&>\; 2 \cdot n(h-2)\\
&>\; 4 \cdot n(h-4)\\
&>\; 8 \cdot n(h-6)\\
&\;\;\vdots\\
&>\; 2^i \cdot n(h-2i).
\end{aligned}
\tag{11.3}
$$

That is, $n(h) > 2^i \cdot n(h-2i)$, for any integer i, such that $h-2i \geq 1$. Since we already know the values of $n(1)$ and $n(2)$, we pick i so that $h-2i$ is equal to either 1 or 2. That is, we pick

$$i = \left\lceil \frac{h}{2} \right\rceil - 1.$$

By substituting the above value of i in Formula 11.3, we obtain, for $h \geq 3$,

$$
\begin{aligned}
n(h) \ &> \ 2^{\lceil \frac{h}{2} \rceil - 1} \cdot n\left(h - 2\left\lceil \frac{h}{2} \right\rceil + 2\right) \\
&\geq \ 2^{\lceil \frac{h}{2} \rceil - 1} n(1) \\
&\geq \ 2^{\frac{h}{2} - 1}.
\end{aligned}
\tag{11.4}
$$

By taking logarithms of both sides of Formula 11.4, we obtain

$$
\log(n(h)) \ > \ \frac{h}{2} - 1,
$$

from which we get

$$
h \ < \ 2\log(n(h)) + 2,
\tag{11.5}
$$

which implies that an AVL tree storing n entries has height at most $2\log n + 2$. ∎

By Proposition 11.2 and the analysis of binary search trees given in Section 11.1, the operation __getitem__, in a map implemented with an AVL tree, runs in time $O(\log n)$, where n is the number of items in the map. Of course, we still have to show how to maintain the height-balance property after an insertion or deletion.

11.3.1 Update Operations

Given a binary search tree T, we say that a position is **balanced** if the absolute value of the difference between the heights of its children is at most 1, and we say that it is **unbalanced** otherwise. Thus, the height-balance property characterizing AVL trees is equivalent to saying that every position is balanced.

The insertion and deletion operations for AVL trees begin similarly to the corresponding operations for (standard) binary search trees, but with post-processing for each operation to restore the balance of any portions of the tree that are adversely affected by the change.

Insertion

Suppose that tree T satisfies the height-balance property, and hence is an AVL tree, prior to the insertion of a new item. An insertion of a new item in a binary search tree, as described in Section 11.1.3, results in a new node at a leaf position p. This action may violate the height-balance property (see, for example, Figure 11.12a), yet the only positions that may become unbalanced are ancestors of p, because those are the only positions whose subtrees have changed. Therefore, let us describe how to restructure T to fix any unbalance that may have occurred.

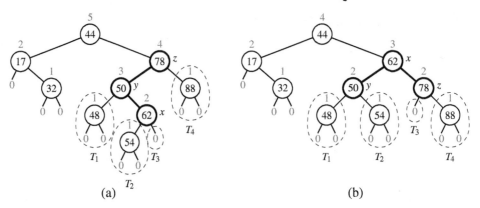

Figure 11.12: An example insertion of an item with key 54 in the AVL tree of Figure 11.11: (a) after adding a new node for key 54, the nodes storing keys 78 and 44 become unbalanced; (b) a trinode restructuring restores the height-balance property. We show the heights of nodes above them, and we identify the nodes x, y, and z and subtrees T_1, T_2, T_3, and T_4 participating in the trinode restructuring.

We restore the balance of the nodes in the binary search tree T by a simple "search-and-repair" strategy. In particular, let z be the first position we encounter in going up from p toward the root of T such that z is unbalanced (see Figure 11.12a.) Also, let y denote the child of z with higher height (and note that y must be an ancestor of p). Finally, let x be the child of y with higher height (there cannot be a tie and position x must also be an ancestor of p, possibly p itself). We rebalance the subtree rooted at z by calling the ***trinode restructuring*** method, restructure(x), originally described in Section 11.2. An example of such a restructuring in the context of an AVL insertion is portrayed in Figure 11.12.

To formally argue the correctness of this process in reestablishing the AVL height-balance property, we consider the implication of z being the nearest ancestor of p that became unbalanced after the insertion of p. It must be that the height of y increased by one due to the insertion and that it is now 2 greater than its sibling. Since y remains balanced, it must be that it formerly had subtrees with equal heights, and that the subtree containing x has increased its height by one. That subtree increased either because $x = p$, and thus its height changed from 0 to 1, or because x previously had equal-height subtrees and the height of the one containing p has increased by 1. Letting $h \geq 0$ denote the height of the tallest child of x, this scenario might be portrayed as in Figure 11.13.

After the trinode restructuring, we see that each of x, y, and z has become balanced. Furthermore, the node that becomes the root of the subtree after the restructuring has height $h + 2$, which is precisely the height that z had before the insertion of the new item. Therefore, any ancestor of z that became temporarily unbalanced becomes balanced again, and this one restructuring restores the height-balance property ***globally***.

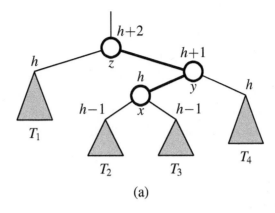

(a)

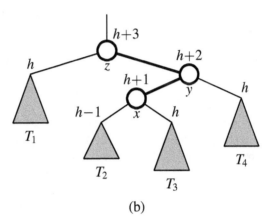

(b)

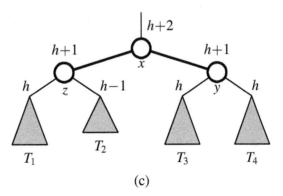

(c)

Figure 11.13: Rebalancing of a subtree during a typical insertion into an AVL tree: (a) before the insertion; (b) after an insertion in subtree T_3 causes imbalance at z; (c) after restoring balance with trinode restructuring. Notice that the overall height of the subtree after the insertion is the same as before the insertion.

Deletion

Recall that a deletion from a regular binary search tree results in the structural removal of a node having either zero or one children. Such a change may violate the height-balance property in an AVL tree. In particular, if position p represents the parent of the removed node in tree T, there may be an unbalanced node on the path from p to the root of T. (See Figure 11.14a.) In fact, there can be at most one such unbalanced node. (The justification of this fact is left as Exercise C-11.49.)

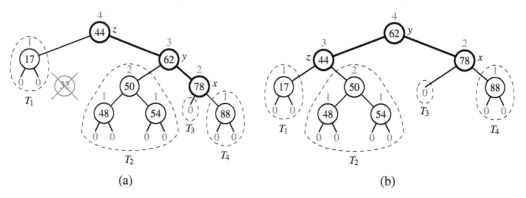

(a)   (b)

Figure 11.14: Deletion of the item with key 32 from the AVL tree of Figure 11.12b: (a) after removing the node storing key 32, the root becomes unbalanced; (b) a (single) rotation restores the height-balance property.

As with insertion, we use trinode restructuring to restore balance in the tree T. In particular, let z be the first unbalanced position encountered going up from p toward the root of T. Also, let y be the child of z with larger height (note that position y is the child of z that is not an ancestor of p), and let x be the child of y defined as follows: If one of the children of y is taller than the other, let x be the taller child of y; else (both children of y have the same height), let x be the child of y on the same side as y (that is, if y is the left child of z, let x be the left child of y, else let x be the right child of y). In any case, we then perform a restructure(x) operation. (See Figure 11.14b.)

The restructured subtree is rooted at the middle position denoted as b in the description of the trinode restructuring operation. The height-balance property is guaranteed to be *locally* restored within the subtree of b. (See Exercises R-11.11 and R-11.12). Unfortunately, this trinode restructuring may reduce the height of the subtree rooted at b by 1, which may cause an ancestor of b to become unbalanced. So, after rebalancing z, we continue walking up T looking for unbalanced positions. If we find another, we perform a restructure operation to restore its balance, and continue marching up T looking for more, all the way to the root. Still, since the height of T is $O(\log n)$, where n is the number of entries, by Proposition 11.2, $O(\log n)$ trinode restructurings are sufficient to restore the height-balance property.

Performance of AVL Trees

By Proposition 11.2, the height of an AVL tree with n items is guaranteed to be $O(\log n)$. Because the standard binary search tree operation had running times bounded by the height (see Table 11.1), and because the additional work in maintaining balance factors and restructuring an AVL tree can be bounded by the length of a path in the tree, the traditional map operations run in worst-case logarithmic time with an AVL tree. We summarize these results in Table 11.2, and illustrate this performance in Figure 11.15.

Operation	Running Time
k in T	$O(\log n)$
T[k] = v	$O(\log n)$
T.delete(p), del T[k]	$O(\log n)$
T.find_position(k)	$O(\log n)$
T.first( ), T.last( ), T.find_min( ), T.find_max( )	$O(\log n)$
T.before(p), T.after(p)	$O(\log n)$
T.find_lt(k), T.find_le(k), T.find_gt(k), T.find_ge(k)	$O(\log n)$
T.find_range(start, stop)	$O(s + \log n)$
iter(T), reversed(T)	$O(n)$

Table 11.2: Worst-case running times of operations for an n-item sorted map realized as an AVL tree T, with s denoting the number of items reported by find_range.

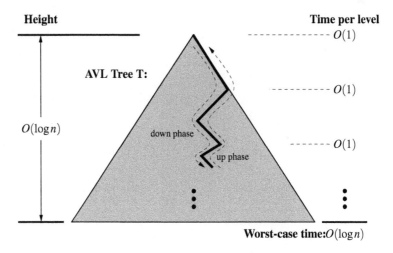

Figure 11.15: Illustrating the running time of searches and updates in an AVL tree. The time performance is $O(1)$ per level, broken into a down phase, which typically involves searching, and an up phase, which typically involves updating height values and performing local trinode restructurings (rotations).

11.3.2   Python Implementation

A complete implementation of an AVLTreeMap class is provided in Code Fragments 11.12 and 11.13. It inherits from the standard TreeMap class and relies on the balancing framework described in Section 11.2.1. We highlight two important aspects of our implementation. First, the AVLTreeMap overrides the definition of the nested _Node class, as shown in Code Fragment 11.12, in order to provide support for storing the height of the subtree stored at a node. We also provide several utilities involving heights of nodes, and the corresponding positions.

To implement the core logic of the AVL balancing strategy, we define a utility, named _rebalance, that suffices as a hook for restoring the height-balance property after an insertion or a deletion. Although the inherited behaviors for insertion and deletion are quite different, the necessary post-processing for an AVL tree can be unified. In both cases, we trace an upward path from the position p at which the change took place, recalculating the height of each position based on the (updated) heights of its children, and using a trinode restructuring operation if an imbalanced position is reached. If we reach an ancestor with height that is unchanged by the overall map operation, or if we perform a trinode restructuring that results in the subtree having the same height it had before the map operation, we stop the process; no further ancestor's height will change. To detect the stopping condition, we record the "old" height of each node and compare it to the newly calculated height.

```python
 1  class AVLTreeMap(TreeMap):
 2    """Sorted map implementation using an AVL tree."""
 3
 4    #-------------------------- nested _Node class --------------------------
 5    class _Node(TreeMap._Node):
 6      """Node class for AVL maintains height value for balancing."""
 7      __slots__ = '_height'         # additional data member to store height
 8
 9      def __init__(self, element, parent=None, left=None, right=None):
10        super().__init__(element, parent, left, right)
11        self._height = 0              # will be recomputed during balancing
12
13      def left_height(self):
14        return self._left._height if self._left is not None else 0
15
16      def right_height(self):
17        return self._right._height if self._right is not None else 0
```

Code Fragment 11.12: AVLTreeMap class (continued in Code Fragment 11.13).

```
18    #-------------------------- positional-based utility methods --------------------------
19    def _recompute_height(self, p):
20      p._node._height = 1 + max(p._node.left_height( ), p._node.right_height( ))
21
22    def _isbalanced(self, p):
23      return abs(p._node.left_height( ) − p._node.right_height( )) <= 1
24
25    def _tall_child(self, p, favorleft=False):  # parameter controls tiebreaker
26      if p._node.left_height( ) + (1 if favorleft else 0) > p._node.right_height( ):
27        return self.left(p)
28      else:
29        return self.right(p)
30
31    def _tall_grandchild(self, p):
32      child = self._tall_child(p)
33      # if child is on left, favor left grandchild; else favor right grandchild
34      alignment = (child == self.left(p))
35      return self._tall_child(child, alignment)
36
37    def _rebalance(self, p):
38      while p is not None:
39        old_height = p._node._height          # trivially 0 if new node
40        if not self._isbalanced(p):            # imbalance detected!
41          # perform trinode restructuring, setting p to resulting root,
42          # and recompute new local heights after the restructuring
43          p = self._restructure(self._tall_grandchild(p))
44          self._recompute_height(self.left(p))
45          self._recompute_height(self.right(p))
46        self._recompute_height(p)              # adjust for recent changes
47        if p._node._height == old_height:      # has height changed?
48          p = None                             # no further changes needed
49        else:
50          p = self.parent(p)                   # repeat with parent
51
52    #-------------------------- override balancing hooks --------------------------
53    def _rebalance_insert(self, p):
54      self._rebalance(p)
55
56    def _rebalance_delete(self, p):
57      self._rebalance(p)
```

Code Fragment 11.13: AVLTreeMap class (continued from Code Fragment 11.12).

11.4   Splay Trees

The next search tree structure we study is known as a a ***splay tree***. This structure is conceptually quite different from the other balanced search trees we discuss in this chapter, for a splay tree does not strictly enforce a logarithmic upper bound on the height of the tree. In fact, there are no additional height, balance, or other auxiliary data associated with the nodes of this tree.

The efficiency of splay trees is due to a certain move-to-root operation, called ***splaying***, that is performed at the bottommost position p reached during every insertion, deletion, or even a search. (In essence, this is a tree variant of the move-to-front heuristic that we explored for lists in Section 7.6.2.) Intuitively, a splay operation causes more frequently accessed elements to remain nearer to the root, thereby reducing the typical search times. The surprising thing about splaying is that it allows us to guarantee a logarithmic amortized running time, for insertions, deletions, and searches.

11.4.1   Splaying

Given a node x of a binary search tree T, we ***splay*** x by moving x to the root of T through a sequence of restructurings. The particular restructurings we perform are important, for it is not sufficient to move x to the root of T by just any sequence of restructurings. The specific operation we perform to move x up depends upon the relative positions of x, its parent y, and (if it exists) x's grandparent z. There are three cases that we consider.

zig-zig: The node x and its parent y are both left children or both right children. (See Figure 11.16.) We promote x, making y a child of x and z a child of y, while maintaining the inorder relationships of the nodes in T.

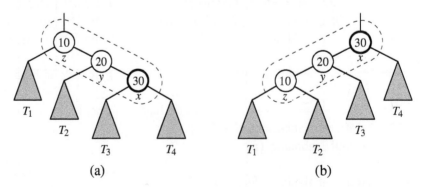

(a)   (b)

Figure 11.16: Zig-zig: (a) before; (b) after. There is another symmetric configuration where x and y are left children.

zig-zag: One of x and y is a left child and the other is a right child. (See Figure 11.17.) In this case, we promote x by making x have y and z as its children, while maintaining the inorder relationships of the nodes in T.

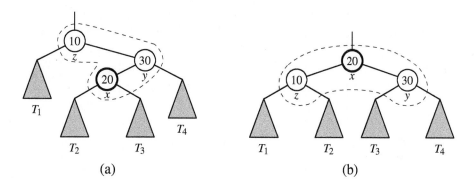

(a)   (b)

Figure 11.17: Zig-zag: (a) before; (b) after. There is another symmetric configuration where x is a right child and y is a left child.

zig: x does not have a grandparent. (See Figure 11.18.) In this case, we perform a single rotation to promote x over y, making y a child of x, while maintaining the relative inorder relationships of the nodes in T.

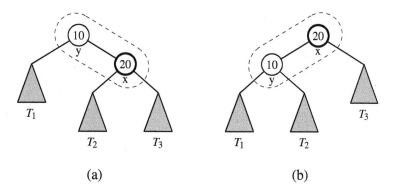

(a)   (b)

Figure 11.18: Zig: (a) before; (b) after. There is another symmetric configuration where x is originally a left child of y.

We perform a zig-zig or a zig-zag when x has a grandparent, and we perform a zig when x has a parent but not a grandparent. A **splaying** step consists of repeating these restructurings at x until x becomes the root of T. An example of the splaying of a node is shown in Figures 11.19 and 11.20.

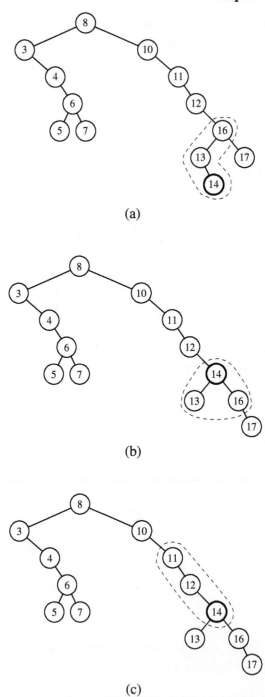

(a)

(b)

(c)

Figure 11.19: Example of splaying a node: (a) splaying the node storing 14 starts with a zig-zag; (b) after the zig-zag; (c) the next step will be a zig-zig. (Continues in Figure 11.20.)

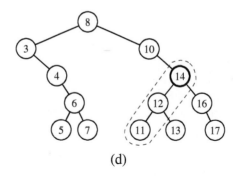

(d)

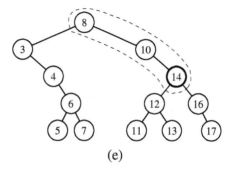

(e)

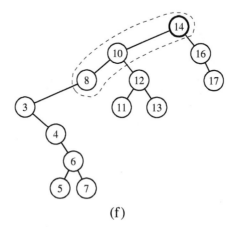

(f)

Figure 11.20: Example of splaying a node:(d) after the zig-zig; (e) the next step is again a zig-zig; (f) after the zig-zig. (Continued from Figure 11.19.)

11.4.2 When to Splay

The rules that dictate when splaying is performed are as follows:

- When searching for key k, if k is found at position p, we splay p, else we splay the leaf position at which the search terminates unsuccessfully. For example, the splaying in Figures 11.19 and 11.20 would be performed after searching successfully for key 14 or unsuccessfully for key 15.

- When inserting key k, we splay the newly created internal node where k gets inserted. For example, the splaying in Figures 11.19 and 11.20 would be performed if 14 were the newly inserted key. We show a sequence of insertions in a splay tree in Figure 11.21.

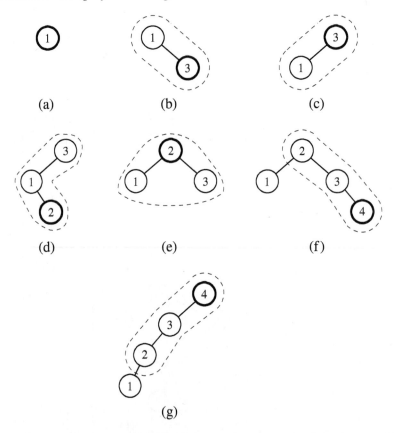

Figure 11.21: A sequence of insertions in a splay tree: (a) initial tree; (b) after inserting 3, but before a zig step; (c) after splaying; (d) after inserting 2, but before a zig-zag step; (e) after splaying; (f) after inserting 4, but before a zig-zig step; (g) after splaying.

- When deleting a key k, we splay the position p that is the parent of the removed node; recall that by the removal algorithm for binary search trees, the removed node may be that originally containing k, or a descendant node with a replacement key. An example of splaying following a deletion is shown in Figure 11.22.

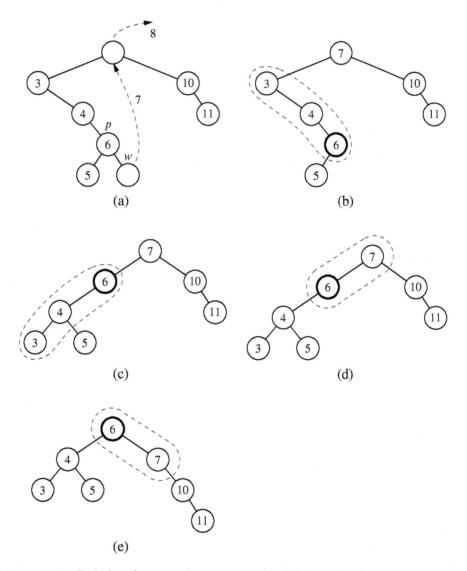

Figure 11.22: Deletion from a splay tree: (a) the deletion of 8 from the root node is performed by moving to the root the key of its inorder predecessor w, deleting w, and splaying the parent p of w; (b) splaying p starts with a zig-zig; (c) after the zig-zig; (d) the next step is a zig; (e) after the zig.

11.4.3   Python Implementation

Although the mathematical analysis of a splay tree's performance is complex (see Section 11.4.4), the *implementation* of splay trees is a rather simple adaptation to a standard binary search tree. Code Fragment 11.14 provides a complete implementation of a SplayTreeMap class, based upon the underlying TreeMap class and use of the balancing framework described in Section 11.2.1. It is important to note that our original TreeMap class makes calls to the _rebalance_access method, not just from within the __getitem__ method, but also during __setitem__ when modifying the value associated with an existing key, and after any map operations that result in a failed search.

```
 1  class SplayTreeMap(TreeMap):
 2    """Sorted map implementation using a splay tree."""
 3    #------------------------------- splay operation -------------------------------
 4    def _splay(self, p):
 5      while p != self.root( ):
 6        parent = self.parent(p)
 7        grand = self.parent(parent)
 8        if grand is None:
 9          # zig case
10          self._rotate(p)
11        elif (parent == self.left(grand)) == (p == self.left(parent)):
12          # zig-zig case
13          self._rotate(parent)                    # move PARENT up
14          self._rotate(p)                         # then move p up
15        else:
16          # zig-zag case
17          self._rotate(p)                         # move p up
18          self._rotate(p)                         # move p up again
19
20    #--------------------------- override balancing hooks ---------------------------
21    def _rebalance_insert(self, p):
22      self._splay(p)
23
24    def _rebalance_delete(self, p):
25      if p is not None:
26        self._splay(p)
27
28    def _rebalance_access(self, p):
29      self._splay(p)
```

Code Fragment 11.14: A complete implementation of the SplayTreeMap class.

11.4.4   Amortized Analysis of Splaying ⋆

After a zig-zig or zig-zag, the depth of position p decreases by two, and after a zig the depth of p decreases by one. Thus, if p has depth d, splaying p consists of a sequence of $\lfloor d/2 \rfloor$ zig-zigs and/or zig-zags, plus one final zig if d is odd. Since a single zig-zig, zig-zag, or zig affects a constant number of nodes, it can be done in $O(1)$ time. Thus, splaying a position p in a binary search tree T takes time $O(d)$, where d is the depth of p in T. In other words, the time for performing a splaying step for a position p is asymptotically the same as the time needed just to reach that position in a top-down search from the root of T.

Worst-Case Time

In the worst case, the overall running time of a search, insertion, or deletion in a splay tree of height h is $O(h)$, since the position we splay might be the deepest position in the tree. Moreover, it is possible for h to be as large as n, as shown in Figure 11.21. Thus, from a worst-case point of view, a splay tree is not an attractive data structure.

In spite of its poor worst-case performance, a splay tree performs well in an amortized sense. That is, in a sequence of intermixed searches, insertions, and deletions, each operation takes on average logarithmic time. We perform the amortized analysis of splay trees using the accounting method.

Amortized Performance of Splay Trees

For our analysis, we note that the time for performing a search, insertion, or deletion is proportional to the time for the associated splaying. So let us consider only splaying time.

Let T be a splay tree with n keys, and let w be a node of T. We define the *size* $n(w)$ of w as the number of nodes in the subtree rooted at w. Note that this definition implies that the size of a nonleaf node is one more than the sum of the sizes of its children. We define the *rank* $r(w)$ of a node w as the logarithm in base 2 of the size of w, that is, $r(w) = \log(n(w))$. Clearly, the root of T has the maximum size, n, and the maximum rank, $\log n$, while each leaf has size 1 and rank 0.

We use cyber-dollars to pay for the work we perform in splaying a position p in T, and we assume that one cyber-dollar pays for a zig, while two cyber-dollars pay for a zig-zig or a zig-zag. Hence, the cost of splaying a position at depth d is d cyber-dollars. We keep a virtual account storing cyber-dollars at each position of T. Note that this account exists only for the purpose of our amortized analysis, and does not need to be included in a data structure implementing the splay tree T.

An Accounting Analysis of Splaying

When we perform a splaying, we pay a certain number of cyber-dollars (the exact value of the payment will be determined at the end of our analysis). We distinguish three cases:

- If the payment is equal to the splaying work, then we use it all to pay for the splaying.

- If the payment is greater than the splaying work, we deposit the excess in the accounts of several nodes.

- If the payment is less than the splaying work, we make withdrawals from the accounts of several nodes to cover the deficiency.

We show below that a payment of $O(\log n)$ cyber-dollars per operation is sufficient to keep the system working, that is, to ensure that each node keeps a nonnegative account balance.

An Accounting Invariant for Splaying

We use a scheme in which transfers are made between the accounts of the nodes to ensure that there will always be enough cyber-dollars to withdraw for paying for splaying work when needed.

In order to use the accounting method to perform our analysis of splaying, we maintain the following invariant:

> *Before and after a splaying, each node w of T has $r(w)$ cyber-dollars in its account.*

Note that the invariant is "financially sound," since it does not require us to make a preliminary deposit to endow a tree with zero keys.

Let $r(T)$ be the sum of the ranks of all the nodes of T. To preserve the invariant after a splaying, we must make a payment equal to the splaying work plus the total change in $r(T)$. We refer to a single zig, zig-zig, or zig-zag operation in a splaying as a splaying *substep*. Also, we denote the rank of a node w of T before and after a splaying substep with $r(w)$ and $r'(w)$, respectively. The following proposition gives an upper bound on the change of $r(T)$ caused by a single splaying substep. We will repeatedly use this lemma in our analysis of a full splaying of a node to the root.

Proposition 11.3: *Let δ be the variation of $r(T)$ caused by a single splaying substep (a zig, zig-zig, or zig-zag) for a node x in T. We have the following:*

- $\delta \leq 3(r'(x) - r(x)) - 2$ *if the substep is a zig-zig or zig-zag.*
- $\delta \leq 3(r'(x) - r(x))$ *if the substep is a zig.*

Justification: We use the fact (see Proposition B.1, Appendix A) that, if $a > 0$, $b > 0$, and $c > a + b$,

$$\log a + \log b < 2\log c - 2. \tag{11.6}$$

Let us consider the change in $r(T)$ caused by each type of splaying substep.

zig-zig: (Recall Figure 11.16.) Since the size of each node is one more than the size of its two children, note that only the ranks of x, y, and z change in a zig-zig operation, where y is the parent of x and z is the parent of y. Also, $r'(x) = r(z)$, $r'(y) \leq r'(x)$, and $r(x) \leq r(y)$. Thus,

$$\begin{aligned} \delta &= r'(x) + r'(y) + r'(z) - r(x) - r(y) - r(z) \\ &= r'(y) + r'(z) - r(x) - r(y) \\ &\leq r'(x) + r'(z) - 2r(x). \end{aligned} \tag{11.7}$$

Note that $n(x) + n'(z) < n'(x)$. Thus, $r(x) + r'(z) < 2r'(x) - 2$, as per Formula 11.6; that is,

$$r'(z) < 2r'(x) - r(x) - 2.$$

This inequality and Formula 11.7 imply

$$\begin{aligned} \delta &\leq r'(x) + (2r'(x) - r(x) - 2) - 2r(x) \\ &\leq 3(r'(x) - r(x)) - 2. \end{aligned}$$

zig-zag: (Recall Figure 11.17.) Again, by the definition of size and rank, only the ranks of x, y, and z change, where y denotes the parent of x and z denotes the parent of y. Also, $r(x) < r(y) < r(z) = r'(x)$. Thus,

$$\begin{aligned} \delta &= r'(x) + r'(y) + r'(z) - r(x) - r(y) - r(z) \\ &= r'(y) + r'(z) - r(x) - r(y) \\ &\leq r'(y) + r'(z) - 2r(x). \end{aligned} \tag{11.8}$$

Note that $n'(y) + n'(z) < n'(x)$; hence, $r'(y) + r'(z) < 2r'(x) - 2$, as per Formula 11.6. Thus,

$$\begin{aligned} \delta &\leq 2r'(x) - 2 - 2r(x) \\ &= 2(r'(x) - r(x)) - 2 \leq 3(r'(x) - r(x)) - 2. \end{aligned}$$

zig: (Recall Figure 11.18.) In this case, only the ranks of x and y change, where y denotes the parent of x. Also, $r'(y) \leq r(y)$ and $r'(x) \geq r(x)$. Thus,

$$\begin{aligned} \delta &= r'(y) + r'(x) - r(y) - r(x) \\ &\leq r'(x) - r(x) \\ &\leq 3(r'(x) - r(x)). \end{aligned}$$

■

Proposition 11.4: *Let T be a splay tree with root t, and let Δ be the total variation of $r(T)$ caused by splaying a node x at depth d. We have*

$$\Delta \le 3(r(t) - r(x)) - d + 2.$$

Justification: Splaying node x consists of $c = \lceil d/2 \rceil$ splaying substeps, each of which is a zig-zig or a zig-zag, except possibly the last one, which is a zig if d is odd. Let $r_0(x) = r(x)$ be the initial rank of x, and for $i = 1, \ldots, c$, let $r_i(x)$ be the rank of x after the ith substep and δ_i be the variation of $r(T)$ caused by the ith substep. By Proposition 11.3, the total variation Δ of $r(T)$ caused by splaying x is

$$
\begin{aligned}
\Delta &= \sum_{i=1}^{c} \delta_i \\
&\le 2 + \sum_{i=1}^{c} 3(r_i(x) - r_{i-1}(x)) - 2 \\
&= 3(r_c(x) - r_0(x)) - 2c + 2 \\
&\le 3(r(t) - r(x)) - d + 2.
\end{aligned}
$$
∎

By Proposition 11.4, if we make a payment of $3(r(t) - r(x)) + 2$ cyber-dollars towards the splaying of node x, we have enough cyber-dollars to maintain the invariant, keeping $r(w)$ cyber-dollars at each node w in T, and pay for the entire splaying work, which costs d cyber-dollars. Since the size of the root t is n, its rank $r(t) = \log n$. Given that $r(x) \ge 0$, the payment to be made for splaying is $O(\log n)$ cyber-dollars. To complete our analysis, we have to compute the cost for maintaining the invariant when a node is inserted or deleted.

When inserting a new node w into a splay tree with n keys, the ranks of all the ancestors of w are increased. Namely, let $w_0, w_i, \ldots, w_d$ be the ancestors of w, where $w_0 = w$, w_i is the parent of w_{i-1}, and w_d is the root. For $i = 1, \ldots, d$, let $n'(w_i)$ and $n(w_i)$ be the size of w_i before and after the insertion, respectively, and let $r'(w_i)$ and $r(w_i)$ be the rank of w_i before and after the insertion. We have

$$n'(w_i) = n(w_i) + 1.$$

Also, since $n(w_i) + 1 \le n(w_{i+1})$, for $i = 0, 1, \ldots, d-1$, we have the following for each i in this range:

$$r'(w_i) = \log(n'(w_i)) = \log(n(w_i) + 1) \le \log(n(w_{i+1})) = r(w_{i+1}).$$

Thus, the total variation of $r(T)$ caused by the insertion is

$$
\begin{aligned}
\sum_{i=1}^{d} \left(r'(w_i) - r(w_i) \right) &\le r'(w_d) + \sum_{i=1}^{d-1} \left(r(w_{i+1}) - r(w_i) \right) \\
&= r'(w_d) - r(w_0) \\
&\le \log n.
\end{aligned}
$$

Therefore, a payment of $O(\log n)$ cyber-dollars is sufficient to maintain the invariant when a new node is inserted.

When deleting a node w from a splay tree with n keys, the ranks of all the ancestors of w are decreased. Thus, the total variation of $r(T)$ caused by the deletion is negative, and we do not need to make any payment to maintain the invariant when a node is deleted. Therefore, we may summarize our amortized analysis in the following proposition (which is sometimes called the "balance proposition" for splay trees):

Proposition 11.5: *Consider a sequence of m operations on a splay tree, each one a search, insertion, or deletion, starting from a splay tree with zero keys. Also, let n_i be the number of keys in the tree after operation i, and n be the total number of insertions. The total running time for performing the sequence of operations is*

$$O\left(m + \sum_{i=1}^{m} \log n_i \right),$$

which is $O(m \log n)$.

In other words, the amortized running time of performing a search, insertion, or deletion in a splay tree is $O(\log n)$, where n is the size of the splay tree at the time. Thus, a splay tree can achieve logarithmic-time amortized performance for implementing a sorted map ADT. This amortized performance matches the worst-case performance of AVL trees, $(2,4)$ trees, and red-black trees, but it does so using a simple binary tree that does not need any extra balance information stored at each of its nodes. In addition, splay trees have a number of other interesting properties that are not shared by these other balanced search trees. We explore one such additional property in the following proposition (which is sometimes called the "Static Optimality" proposition for splay trees):

Proposition 11.6: *Consider a sequence of m operations on a splay tree, each one a search, insertion, or deletion, starting from a splay tree T with zero keys. Also, let $f(i)$ denote the number of times the entry i is accessed in the splay tree, that is, its frequency, and let n denote the total number of entries. Assuming that each entry is accessed at least once, then the total running time for performing the sequence of operations is*

$$O\left(m + \sum_{i=1}^{n} f(i) \log(m/f(i)) \right).$$

We omit the proof of this proposition, but it is not as hard to justify as one might imagine. The remarkable thing is that this proposition states that the amortized running time of accessing an entry i is $O(\log(m/f(i)))$.

11.5 (2,4) Trees

In this section, we consider a data structure known as a *(2,4) tree*. It is a particular example of a more general structure known as a *multiway search tree*, in which internal nodes may have more than two children. Other forms of multiway search trees will be discussed in Section 15.3.

11.5.1 Multiway Search Trees

Recall that general trees are defined so that internal nodes may have many children. In this section, we discuss how general trees can be used as multiway search trees. Map items stored in a search tree are pairs of the form (k, v), where k is the *key* and v is the *value* associated with the key.

Definition of a Multiway Search Tree

Let w be a node of an ordered tree. We say that w is a *d-node* if w has d children. We define a multiway search tree to be an ordered tree T that has the following properties, which are illustrated in Figure 11.23a:

- Each internal node of T has at least two children. That is, each internal node is a d-node such that $d \geq 2$.
- Each internal d-node w of T with children $c_1, \ldots, c_d$ stores an ordered set of $d-1$ key-value pairs $(k_1, v_1), \ldots, (k_{d-1}, v_{d-1})$, where $k_1 \leq \cdots \leq k_{d-1}$.
- Let us conventionally define $k_0 = -\infty$ and $k_d = +\infty$. For each item (k, v) stored at a node in the subtree of w rooted at c_i, $i = 1, \ldots, d$, we have that $k_{i-1} \leq k \leq k_i$.

That is, if we think of the set of keys stored at w as including the special fictitious keys $k_0 = -\infty$ and $k_d = +\infty$, then a key k stored in the subtree of T rooted at a child node c_i must be "in between" two keys stored at w. This simple viewpoint gives rise to the rule that a d-node stores $d-1$ regular keys, and it also forms the basis of the algorithm for searching in a multiway search tree.

By the above definition, the external nodes of a multiway search do not store any data and serve only as "placeholders." These external nodes can be efficiently represented by None references, as has been our convention with binary search trees (Section 11.1). However, for the sake of exposition, we will discuss these as actual nodes that do not store anything. Based on this definition, there is an interesting relationship between the number of key-value pairs and the number of external nodes in a multiway search tree.

Proposition 11.7: *An n-item multiway search tree has $n+1$ external nodes.*

We leave the justification of this proposition as an exercise (C-11.52).

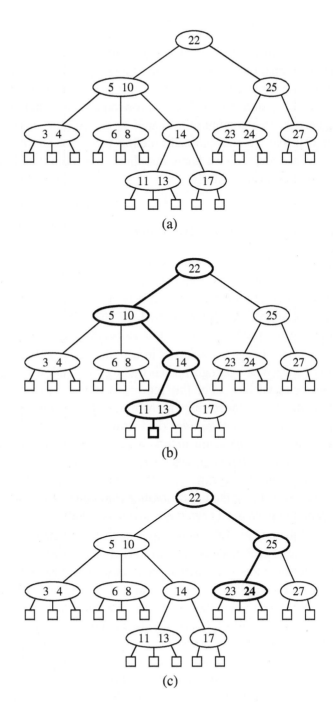

Figure 11.23: (a) A multiway search tree T; (b) search path in T for key 12 (unsuccessful search); (c) search path in T for key 24 (successful search).

Searching in a Multiway Tree

Searching for an item with key k in a multiway search tree T is simple. We perform such a search by tracing a path in T starting at the root. (See Figure 11.23b and c.) When we are at a d-node w during this search, we compare the key k with the keys $k_1, \ldots, k_{d-1}$ stored at w. If $k = k_i$ for some i, the search is successfully completed. Otherwise, we continue the search in the child c_i of w such that $k_{i-1} < k < k_i$. (Recall that we conventionally define $k_0 = -\infty$ and $k_d = +\infty$.) If we reach an external node, then we know that there is no item with key k in T, and the search terminates unsuccessfully.

Data Structures for Representing Multiway Search Trees

In Section 8.3.3, we discuss a linked data structure for representing a general tree. This representation can also be used for a multiway search tree. When using a general tree to implement a multiway search tree, we must store at each node one or more key-value pairs associated with that node. That is, we need to store with w a reference to some collection that stores the items for w.

During a search for key k in a multiway search tree, the primary operation needed when navigating a node is finding the smallest key at that node that is greater than or equal to k. For this reason, it is natural to model the information at a node itself as a sorted map, allowing use of the find_ge(k) method. We say such a map serves as a *secondary* data structure to support the *primary* data structure represented by the entire multiway search tree. This reasoning may at first seem like a circular argument, since we need a representation of a (secondary) ordered map to represent a (primary) ordered map. We can avoid any circular dependence, however, by using the *bootstrapping* technique, where we use a simple solution to a problem to create a new, more advanced solution.

In the context of a multiway search tree, a natural choice for the secondary structure at each node is the SortedTableMap of Section 10.3.1. Because we want to determine the associated value in case of a match for key k, and otherwise the corresponding child c_i such that $k_{i-1} < k < k_i$, we recommend having each key k_i in the secondary structure map to the pair (v_i, c_i). With such a realization of a multiway search tree T, processing a d-node w while searching for an item of T with key k can be performed using a binary search operation in $O(\log d)$ time. Let $d_{\max}$ denote the maximum number of children of any node of T, and let h denote the height of T. The search time in a multiway search tree is therefore $O(h \log d_{\max})$. If $d_{\max}$ is a constant, the running time for performing a search is $O(h)$.

The primary efficiency goal for a multiway search tree is to keep the height as small as possible. We next discuss a strategy that caps $d_{\max}$ at 4 while guaranteeing a height h that is logarithmic in n, the total number of items stored in the map.

11.5.2 (2,4)-Tree Operations

A multiway search tree that keeps the secondary data structures stored at each node small and also keeps the primary multiway tree balanced is the **(2, 4)** *tree*, which is sometimes called a 2-4 tree or 2-3-4 tree. This data structure achieves these goals by maintaining two simple properties (see Figure 11.24):

Size Property: Every internal node has at most four children.

Depth Property: All the external nodes have the same depth.

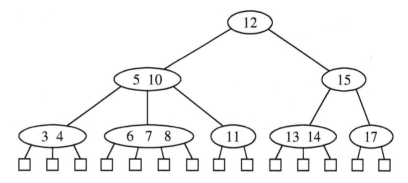

Figure 11.24: A $(2,4)$ tree.

Again, we assume that external nodes are empty and, for the sake of simplicity, we describe our search and update methods assuming that external nodes are real nodes, although this latter requirement is not strictly needed.

Enforcing the size property for $(2,4)$ trees keeps the nodes in the multiway search tree simple. It also gives rise to the alternative name "2-3-4 tree," since it implies that each internal node in the tree has 2, 3, or 4 children. Another implication of this rule is that we can represent the secondary map stored at each internal node using an unordered list or an ordered array, and still achieve $O(1)$-time performance for all operations (since $d_{max} = 4$). The depth property, on the other hand, enforces an important bound on the height of a $(2,4)$ tree.

Proposition 11.8: *The height of a $(2,4)$ tree storing n items is $O(\log n)$.*

Justification: Let h be the height of a $(2,4)$ tree T storing n items. We justify the proposition by showing the claim

$$\frac{1}{2}\log(n+1) \le h \le \log(n+1). \tag{11.9}$$

To justify this claim note first that, by the size property, we can have at most 4 nodes at depth 1, at most 4^2 nodes at depth 2, and so on. Thus, the number of external nodes in T is at most 4^h. Likewise, by the depth property and the definition of a $(2,4)$ tree, we must have at least 2 nodes at depth 1, at least 2^2 nodes at depth 2, and so on. Thus, the number of external nodes in T is at least 2^h. In addition, by Proposition 11.7, the number of external nodes in T is $n+1$. Therefore, we obtain

$$2^h \le n+1 \le 4^h.$$

Taking the logarithm in base 2 of the terms for the above inequalities, we get that

$$h \le \log(n+1) \le 2h,$$

which justifies our claim (Formula 11.9) when terms are rearranged.   ■

Proposition 11.8 states that the size and depth properties are sufficient for keeping a multiway tree balanced. Moreover, this proposition implies that performing a search in a $(2,4)$ tree takes $O(\log n)$ time and that the specific realization of the secondary structures at the nodes is not a crucial design choice, since the maximum number of children $d_{\max}$ is a constant.

Maintaining the size and depth properties requires some effort after performing insertions and deletions in a $(2,4)$ tree, however. We discuss these operations next.

Insertion

To insert a new item (k,v), with key k, into a $(2,4)$ tree T, we first perform a search for k. Assuming that T has no item with key k, this search terminates unsuccessfully at an external node z. Let w be the parent of z. We insert the new item into node w and add a new child y (an external node) to w on the left of z.

Our insertion method preserves the depth property, since we add a new external node at the same level as existing external nodes. Nevertheless, it may violate the size property. Indeed, if a node w was previously a 4-node, then it would become a 5-node after the insertion, which causes the tree T to no longer be a $(2,4)$ tree. This type of violation of the size property is called an ***overflow*** at node w, and it must be resolved in order to restore the properties of a $(2,4)$ tree. Let $c_1,\dots,c_5$ be the children of w, and let $k_1,\dots,k_4$ be the keys stored at w. To remedy the overflow at node w, we perform a ***split*** operation on w as follows (see Figure 11.25):

- Replace w with two nodes w' and w'', where
    - w' is a 3-node with children c_1,c_2,c_3 storing keys k_1 and k_2
    - w'' is a 2-node with children c_4,c_5 storing key k_4.
- If w is the root of T, create a new root node u; else, let u be the parent of w.
- Insert key k_3 into u and make w' and w'' children of u, so that if w was child i of u, then w' and w'' become children i and $i+1$ of u, respectively.

As a consequence of a split operation on node w, a new overflow may occur at the parent u of w. If such an overflow occurs, it triggers in turn a split at node u. (See Figure 11.26.) A split operation either eliminates the overflow or propagates it into the parent of the current node. We show a sequence of insertions in a $(2,4)$ tree in Figure 11.27.

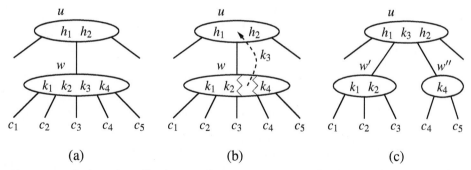

Figure 11.25: A node split: (a) overflow at a 5-node w; (b) the third key of w inserted into the parent u of w; (c) node w replaced with a 3-node w' and a 2-node w''.

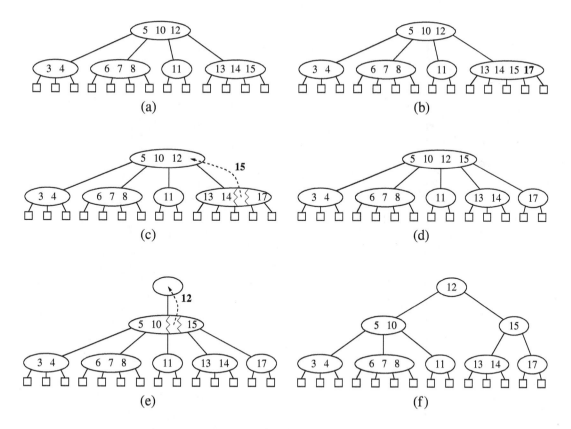

Figure 11.26: An insertion in a $(2,4)$ tree that causes a cascading split: (a) before the insertion; (b) insertion of 17, causing an overflow; (c) a split; (d) after the split a new overflow occurs; (e) another split, creating a new root node; (f) final tree.

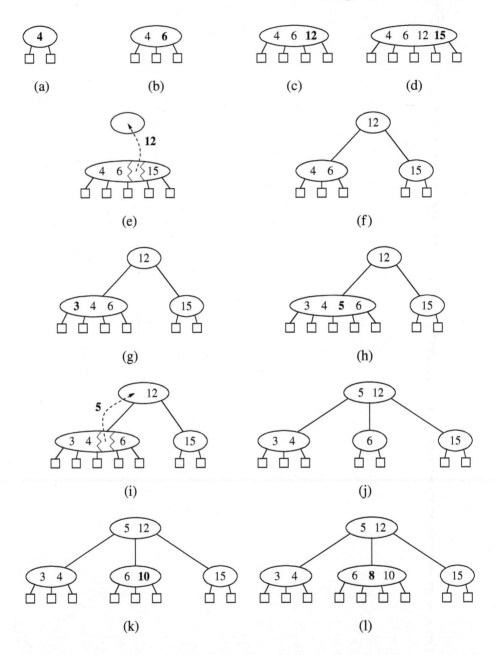

Figure 11.27: A sequence of insertions into a $(2,4)$ tree: (a) initial tree with one item; (b) insertion of 6; (c) insertion of 12; (d) insertion of 15, which causes an overflow; (e) split, which causes the creation of a new root node; (f) after the split; (g) insertion of 3; (h) insertion of 5, which causes an overflow; (i) split; (j) after the split; (k) insertion of 10; (l) insertion of 8.

Analysis of Insertion in a (2,4) Tree

Because $d_{\max}$ is at most 4, the original search for the placement of new key k uses $O(1)$ time at each level, and thus $O(\log n)$ time overall, since the height of the tree is $O(\log n)$ by Proposition 11.8.

The modifications to a single node to insert a new key and child can be implemented to run in $O(1)$ time, as can a single split operation. The number of cascading split operations is bounded by the height of the tree, and so that phase of the insertion process also runs in $O(\log n)$ time. Therefore, the total time to perform an insertion in a $(2,4)$ tree is $O(\log n)$.

Deletion

Let us now consider the removal of an item with key k from a $(2,4)$ tree T. We begin such an operation by performing a search in T for an item with key k. Removing an item from a $(2,4)$ tree can always be reduced to the case where the item to be removed is stored at a node w whose children are external nodes. Suppose, for instance, that the item with key k that we wish to remove is stored in the ith item (k_i, v_i) at a node z that has only internal-node children. In this case, we swap the item (k_i, v_i) with an appropriate item that is stored at a node w with external-node children as follows (see Figure 11.28d):

1. We find the rightmost internal node w in the subtree rooted at the ith child of z, noting that the children of node w are all external nodes.
2. We swap the item (k_i, v_i) at z with the last item of w.

Once we ensure that the item to remove is stored at a node w with only external-node children (because either it was already at w or we swapped it into w), we simply remove the item from w and remove the ith external node of w.

Removing an item (and a child) from a node w as described above preserves the depth property, for we always remove an external child from a node w with only external children. However, in removing such an external node, we may violate the size property at w. Indeed, if w was previously a 2-node, then it becomes a 1-node with no items after the removal (Figure 11.28a and d), which is not allowed in a $(2,4)$ tree. This type of violation of the size property is called an **underflow** at node w. To remedy an underflow, we check whether an immediate sibling of w is a 3-node or a 4-node. If we find such a sibling s, then we perform a **transfer** operation, in which we move a child of s to w, a key of s to the parent u of w and s, and a key of u to w. (See Figure 11.28b and c.) If w has only one sibling, or if both immediate siblings of w are 2-nodes, then we perform a **fusion** operation, in which we merge w with a sibling, creating a new node w', and move a key from the parent u of w to w'. (See Figure 11.28e and f.)

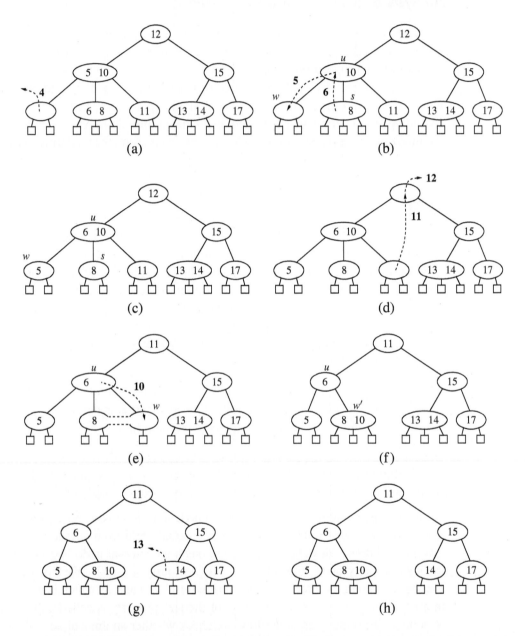

Figure 11.28: A sequence of removals from a $(2,4)$ tree: (a) removal of 4, causing an underflow; (b) a transfer operation; (c) after the transfer operation; (d) removal of 12, causing an underflow; (e) a fusion operation; (f) after the fusion operation; (g) removal of 13; (h) after removing 13.

A fusion operation at node w may cause a new underflow to occur at the parent u of w, which in turn triggers a transfer or fusion at u. (See Figure 11.29.) Hence, the number of fusion operations is bounded by the height of the tree, which is $O(\log n)$ by Proposition 11.8. If an underflow propagates all the way up to the root, then the root is simply deleted. (See Figure 11.29c and d.)

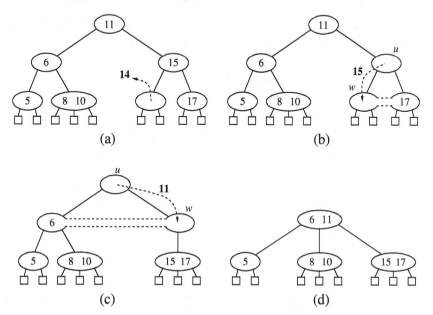

Figure 11.29: A propagating sequence of fusions in a $(2,4)$ tree: (a) removal of 14, which causes an underflow; (b) fusion, which causes another underflow; (c) second fusion operation, which causes the root to be removed; (d) final tree.

Performance of (2,4) Trees

The asymptotic performance of a $(2,4)$ tree is identical to that of an AVL tree (see Table 11.2) in terms of the sorted map ADT, with guaranteed logarithmic bounds for most operations. The time complexity analysis for a $(2,4)$ tree having n key-value pairs is based on the following:

- The height of a $(2,4)$ tree storing n entries is $O(\log n)$, by Proposition 11.8.
- A split, transfer, or fusion operation takes $O(1)$ time.
- A search, insertion, or removal of an entry visits $O(\log n)$ nodes.

Thus, $(2,4)$ trees provide for fast map search and update operations. $(2,4)$ trees also have an interesting relationship to the data structure we discuss next.

11.6   Red-Black Trees

Although AVL trees and $(2,4)$ trees have a number of nice properties, they also have some disadvantages. For instance, AVL trees may require many restructure operations (rotations) to be performed after a deletion, and $(2,4)$ trees may require many split or fusing operations to be performed after an insertion or removal. The data structure we discuss in this section, the red-black tree, does not have these drawbacks; it uses $O(1)$ structural changes after an update in order to stay balanced.

Formally, a ***red-black tree*** is a binary search tree (see Section 11.1) with nodes colored red and black in a way that satisfies the following properties:

Root Property: The root is black.

Red Property: The children of a red node (if any) are black.

Depth Property: All nodes with zero or one children have the same ***black depth***, defined as the number of black ancestors. (Recall that a node is its own ancestor).

An example of a red-black tree is shown in Figure 11.30.

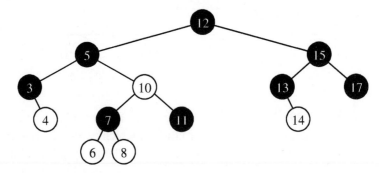

Figure 11.30: An example of a red-black tree, with "red" nodes drawn in white. The common black depth for this tree is 3.

We can make the red-black tree definition more intuitive by noting an interesting correspondence between red-black trees and $(2,4)$ trees (excluding their trivial external nodes). Namely, given a red-black tree, we can construct a corresponding $(2,4)$ tree by merging every red node w into its parent, storing the entry from w at its parent, and with the children of w becoming ordered children of the parent. For example, the red-black tree in Figure 11.30 corresponds to the $(2,4)$ tree from Figure 11.24, as illustrated in Figure 11.31. The depth property of the red-black tree corresponds to the depth property of the $(2,4)$ tree since exactly one black node of the red-black tree contributes to each node of the corresponding $(2,4)$ tree.

Conversely, we can transform any $(2,4)$ tree into a corresponding red-black tree by coloring each node w black and then performing the following transformations, as illustrated in Figure 11.32.

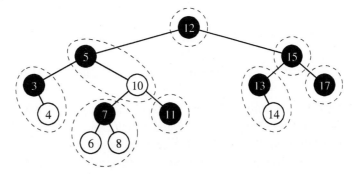

Figure 11.31: An illustration that the red-black tree of Figure 11.30 corresponds to the $(2,4)$ tree of Figure 11.24, based on the highlighted grouping of red nodes with their black parents.

- If w is a 2-node, then keep the (black) children of w as is.

- If w is a 3-node, then create a new red node y, give w's last two (black) children to y, and make the first child of w and y be the two children of w.

- If w is a 4-node, then create two new red nodes y and z, give w's first two (black) children to y, give w's last two (black) children to z, and make y and z be the two children of w.

Notice that a red node always has a black parent in this construction.

Proposition 11.9: *The height of a red-black tree storing n entries is $O(\log n)$.*

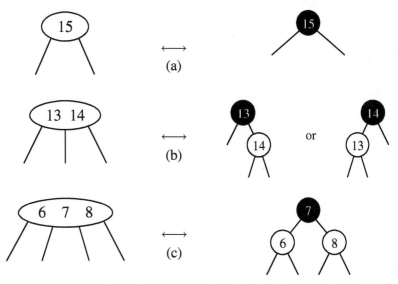

Figure 11.32: Correspondence between nodes of a $(2,4)$ tree and a red-black tree: (a) 2-node; (b) 3-node; (c) 4-node.

Justification: Let T be a red-black tree storing n entries, and let h be the height of T. We justify this proposition by establishing the following fact:

$$\log(n+1) - 1 \le h \le 2\log(n+1) - 2.$$

Let d be the common black depth of all nodes of T having zero or one children. Let T' be the $(2,4)$ tree associated with T, and let h' be the height of T' (excluding trivial leaves). Because of the correspondence between red-black trees and $(2,4)$ trees, we know that $h' = d$. Hence, by Proposition 11.8, $d = h' \le \log(n+1) - 1$. By the red property, $h \le 2d$. Thus, we obtain $h \le 2\log(n+1) - 2$. The other inequality, $\log(n+1) - 1 \le h$, follows from Proposition 8.8 and the fact that T has n nodes. ∎

11.6.1   Red-Black Tree Operations

The algorithm for searching in a red-black tree T is the same as that for a standard binary search tree (Section 11.1). Thus, searching in a red-black tree takes time proportional to the height of the tree, which is $O(\log n)$ by Proposition 11.9.

The correspondence between $(2,4)$ trees and red-black trees provides important intuition that we will use in our discussion of how to perform updates in red-black trees; in fact, the update algorithms for red-black trees can seem mysteriously complex without this intuition. Split and fuse operations of a $(2,4)$ tree will be effectively mimicked by recoloring neighboring red-black tree nodes. A rotation within a red-black tree will be used to change orientations of a 3-node between the two forms shown in Figure 11.32(b).

Insertion

Now consider the insertion of a key-value pair (k,v) into a red-black tree T. The algorithm initially proceeds as in a standard binary search tree (Section 11.1.3). Namely, we search for k in T until we reach a null subtree, and we introduce a new leaf x at that position, storing the item. In the special case that x is the only node of T, and thus the root, we color it black. In all other cases, we color x red. This action corresponds to inserting (k,v) into a node of the $(2,4)$ tree T' with external children. The insertion preserves the root and depth properties of T, but it may violate the red property. Indeed, if x is not the root of T and the parent y of x is red, then we have a parent and a child (namely, y and x) that are both red. Note that by the root property, y cannot be the root of T, and by the red property (which was previously satisfied), the parent z of y must be black. Since x and its parent are red, but x's grandparent z is black, we call this violation of the red property a *double red* at node x. To remedy a double red, we consider two cases.

Case 1: *The Sibling s of y Is Black (or None).* (See Figure 11.33.) In this case, the double red denotes the fact that we have added the new node to a corresponding 3-node of the $(2,4)$ tree T', effectively creating a malformed 4-node. This formation has one red node (y) that is the parent of another red node (x), while we want it to have the two red nodes as siblings instead. To fix this problem, we perform a ***trinode restructuring*** of T. The trinode restructuring is done by the operation restructure(x), which consists of the following steps (see again Figure 11.33; this operation is also discussed in Section 11.2):

- Take node x, its parent y, and grandparent z, and temporarily relabel them as a, b, and c, in left-to-right order, so that a, b, and c will be visited in this order by an inorder tree traversal.
- Replace the grandparent z with the node labeled b, and make nodes a and c the children of b, keeping inorder relationships unchanged.

After performing the restructure(x) operation, we color b black and we color a and c red. Thus, the restructuring eliminates the double-red problem. Notice that the portion of any path through the restructured part of the tree is incident to exactly one black node, both before and after the trinode restructuring. Therefore, the black depth of the tree is unaffected.

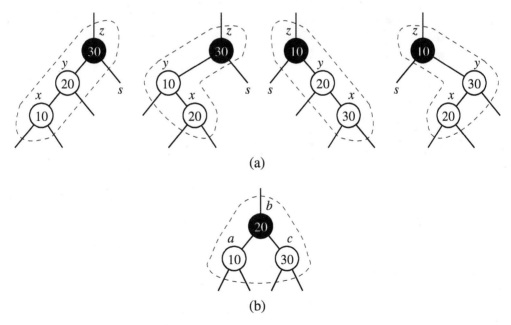

(a)

(b)

Figure 11.33: Restructuring a red-black tree to remedy a double red: (a) the four configurations for x, y, and z before restructuring; (b) after restructuring.

Case 2: ***The Sibling s of y Is Red.*** (See Figure 11.34.) In this case, the double red denotes an overflow in the corresponding $(2,4)$ tree T'. To fix the problem, we perform the equivalent of a split operation. Namely, we do a ***recoloring***: we color y and s black and their parent z red (unless z is the root, in which case, it remains black). Notice that unless z is the root, the portion of any path through the affected part of the tree is incident to exactly one black node, both before and after the recoloring. Therefore, the black depth of the tree is unaffected by the recoloring unless z is the root, in which case it is increased by one.

However, it is possible that the double-red problem reappears after such a recoloring, albeit higher up in the tree T, since z may have a red parent. If the double-red problem reappears at z, then we repeat the consideration of the two cases at z. Thus, a recoloring either eliminates the double-red problem at node x, or propagates it to the grandparent z of x. We continue going up T performing recolorings until we finally resolve the double-red problem (with either a final recoloring or a trinode restructuring). Thus, the number of recolorings caused by an insertion is no more than half the height of tree T, that is, $O(\log n)$ by Proposition 11.9.

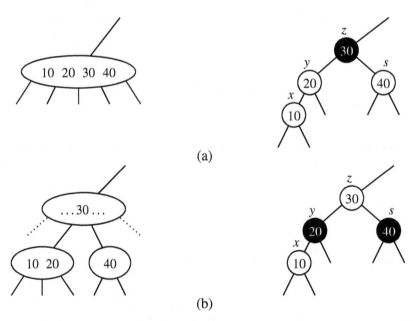

Figure 11.34: Recoloring to remedy the double-red problem: (a) before recoloring and the corresponding 5-node in the associated $(2,4)$ tree before the split; (b) after recoloring and the corresponding nodes in the associated $(2,4)$ tree after the split.

As further examples, Figures 11.35 and 11.36 show a sequence of insertion operations in a red-black tree.

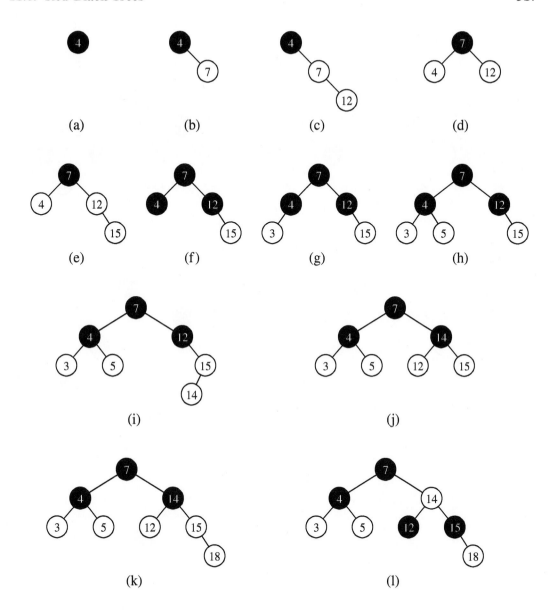

Figure 11.35: A sequence of insertions in a red-black tree: (a) initial tree; (b) insertion of 7; (c) insertion of 12, which causes a double red; (d) after restructuring; (e) insertion of 15, which causes a double red; (f) after recoloring (the root remains black); (g) insertion of 3; (h) insertion of 5; (i) insertion of 14, which causes a double red; (j) after restructuring; (k) insertion of 18, which causes a double red; (l) after recoloring. (Continues in Figure 11.36.)

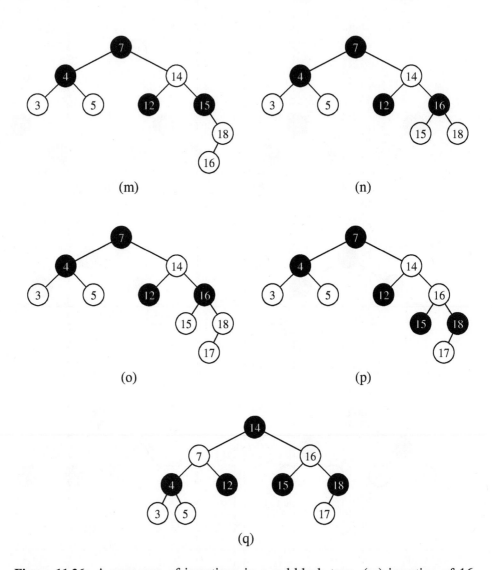

Figure 11.36: A sequence of insertions in a red-black tree: (m) insertion of 16, which causes a double red; (n) after restructuring; (o) insertion of 17, which causes a double red; (p) after recoloring there is again a double red, to be handled by a restructuring; (q) after restructuring. (Continued from Figure 11.35.)

Deletion

Deleting an item with key k from a red-black tree T initially proceeds as for a binary search tree (Section 11.1.3). Structurally, the process results in the removal a node that has at most one child (either that originally containing key k or its inorder predecessor) and the promotion of its remaining child (if any).

If the removed node was red, this structural change does not affect the black depths of any paths in the tree, nor introduce any red violations, and so the resulting tree remains a valid red-black tree. In the corresponding $(2,4)$ tree T', this case denotes the shrinking of a 3-node or 4-node. If the removed node was black, then it either had zero children or it had one child that was a red leaf (because the null subtree of the removed node has black height 0). In the latter case, the removed node represents the black part of a corresponding 3-node, and we restore the red-black properties by recoloring the promoted child to black.

The more complex case is when a (nonroot) black leaf is removed. In the corresponding $(2,4)$ tree, this denotes the removal of an item from a 2-node. Without rebalancing, such a change results in a deficit of one for the black depth along the path leading to the deleted item. By necessity, the removed node must have a sibling whose subtree has black height 1 (given that this was a valid red-black tree prior to the deletion of the black leaf).

To remedy this scenario, we consider a more general setting with a node z that is known to have two subtrees, T_{heavy} and T_{light}, such that the root of T_{light} (if any) is black and such that the black depth of T_{heavy} is exactly one more than that of T_{light}, as portrayed in Figure 11.37. In the case of a removed black leaf, z is the parent of that leaf and T_{light} is trivially the empty subtree that remains after the deletion. We describe the more general case of a deficit because our algorithm for rebalancing the tree will, in some cases, push the deficit higher in the tree (just as the resolution of a deletion in a $(2,4)$ tree sometimes cascades upward). We let y denote the root of T_{heavy}. (Such a node exists because T_{heavy} has black height at least one.)

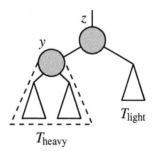

Figure 11.37: Portrayal of a deficit between the black heights of subtrees of node z. The gray color in illustrating y and z denotes the fact that these nodes may be colored either black or red.

We consider three possible cases to remedy a deficit.

Case 1: *Node y Is Black and Has a Red Child x.* (See Figure 11.38.)

We perform a ***trinode restructuring***, as originally described in Section 11.2. The operation restructure(x) takes the node x, its parent y, and grandparent z, labels them temporarily left to right as a, b, and c, and replaces z with the node labeled b, making it the parent of the other two. We color a and c black, and give b the former color of z.

Notice that the path to T_{light} in the result includes one additional black node after the restructure, thereby resolving its deficit. In contrast, the number of black nodes on paths to any of the other three subtrees illustrated in Figure 11.38 remains unchanged.

Resolving this case corresponds to a transfer operation in the $(2,4)$ tree T' between the two children of the node with z. The fact that y has a red child assures us that it represents either a 3-node or a 4-node. In effect, the item previously stored at z is demoted to become a new 2-node to resolve the deficiency, while an item stored at y or its child is promoted to take the place of the item previously stored at z.

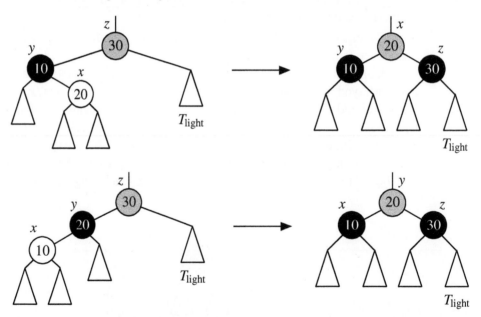

Figure 11.38: Resolving a black deficit in T_{light} by performing a trinode restructuring as restructure(x). Two possible configurations are shown (two other configurations are symmetric). The gray color of z in the left figures denotes the fact that this node may be colored either red or black. The root of the restructured portion is given that same color, while the children of that node are both colored black in the result.

Case 2: *Node y Is Black and Both Children of y Are Black (or None).*

Resolving this case corresponds to a fusion operation in the corresponding $(2,4)$ tree T', as y must represent a 2-node. We do a ***recoloring***; we color y red, and, if z is red, we color it black. (See Figure 11.39). This does not introduce any red violation, because y does not have a red child.

In the case that z was originally red, and thus the parent in the corresponding $(2,4)$ tree is a 3-node or 4-node, this recoloring resolves the deficit. (See Figure 11.39a.) The path leading to T_{light} includes one additional black node in the result, while the recoloring did not affect the number of black nodes on the path to the subtrees of T_{heavy}.

In the case that z was originally black, and thus the parent in the corresponding $(2,4)$ tree is a 2-node, the recoloring has not increased the number of black nodes on the path to T_{light}; in fact, it has *reduced* the number of black nodes on the path to T_{heavy}. (See Figure 11.39b.) After this step, the two children of z will have the same black height. However, the entire tree rooted at z has become deficient, thereby propogating the problem higher in the tree; we must repeat consideration of all three cases at the parent of z as a remedy.

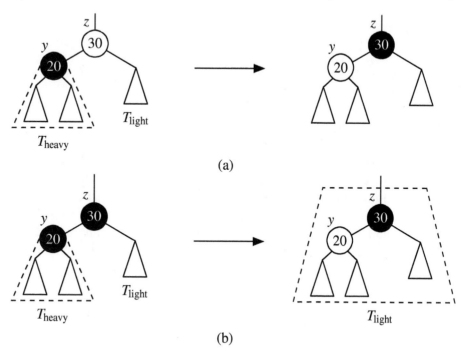

Figure 11.39: Resolving a black deficit in T_{light} by a recoloring operation: (a) when z is originally red, reversing the colors of y and z resolves the black deficit in T_{light}, ending the process; (b) when z is originally black, recoloring y causes the entire subtree of z to have a black deficit, requiring a cascading remedy.

Case 3: *Node y Is Red.* (See Figure 11.40.)

Because y is red and T_{heavy} has black depth at least 1, z must be black and the two subtrees of y must each have a black root and a black depth equal to that of T_{heavy}. In this case, we perform a rotation about y and z, and then recolor y black and z red. This denotes a reorientation of a 3-node in the corresponding (2,4) tree T'.

This does not immediately resolve the deficit, as the new subtree of z is an old subtree of y with black root y' and black height equal to that of the original T_{heavy}. We reapply the algorithm to resolve the deficit at z, knowing that the new child y', that is the root of T_{heavy} is now black, and therefore that either Case 1 applies or Case 2 applies. Furthermore, the next application will be the last, because Case 1 is always terminal and Case 2 will be terminal given that z is red.

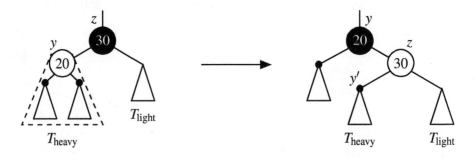

Figure 11.40: A rotation and recoloring about red node y and black node z, assuming a black deficit at z. This amounts to a change of orientation in the corresponding 3-node of a (2,4) tree. This operation does not affect the black depth of any paths through this portion of the tree. Furthermore, because y was originally red, the new subtree of z must have a black root y' and must have black height equal to the original T_{heavy}. Therefore, a black deficit remains at node z after the transformation.

In Figure 11.41, we show a sequence of deletions on a red-black tree. A dashed edge in those figures, such as to the right of 7 in part (c), represents a branch with a black deficiency that has not yet been resolved. We illustrate a Case 1 restructuring in parts (c) and (d). We illustrate a Case 2 recoloring in parts (f) and (g). Finally, we show an example of a Case 3 rotation between parts (i) and (j), concluding with a Case 2 recoloring in part (k).

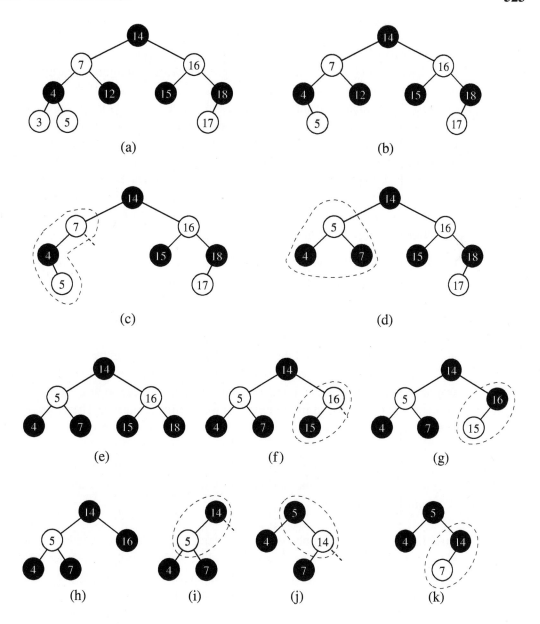

Figure 11.41: A sequence of deletions from a red-black tree: (a) initial tree; (b) removal of 3; (c) removal of 12, causing a black deficit to the right of 7 (handled by restructuring); (d) after restructuring; (e) removal of 17; (f) removal of 18, causing a black deficit to the right of 16 (handled by recoloring); (g) after recoloring; (h) removal of 15; (i) removal of 16, causing a black deficit to the right of 14 (handled initially by a rotation); (j) after the rotation the black deficit needs to be handled by a recoloring; (k) after the recoloring.

Performance of Red-Black Trees

The asymptotic performance of a red-black tree is identical to that of an AVL tree or a $(2,4)$ tree in terms of the sorted map ADT, with guaranteed logarithmic time bounds for most operations. (See Table 11.2 for a summary of the AVL performance.) The primary advantage of a red-black tree is that an insertion or deletion requires only a ***constant number of restructuring operations***. (This is in contrast to AVL trees and $(2,4)$ trees, both of which require a logarithmic number of structural changes per map operation in the worst case.) That is, an insertion or deletion in a red-black tree requires logarithmic time for a search, and may require a logarithmic number of recoloring operations that cascade upward. Yet we show, in the following propositions, that there are a constant number of rotations or restructure operations for a single map operation.

Proposition 11.10: *The insertion of an item in a red-black tree storing n items can be done in $O(\log n)$ time and requires $O(\log n)$ recolorings and at most one trinode restructuring.*

Justification: Recall that an insertion begins with a downward search, the creation of a new leaf node, and then a potential upward effort to remedy a double-red violation. There may be logarithmically many recoloring operations due to an upward cascading of Case 2 applications, but a single application of the Case 1 action eliminates the double-red problem with a trinode restructuring. Therefore, at most one restructuring operation is needed for a red-black tree insertion.   ∎

Proposition 11.11: *The algorithm for deleting an item from a red-black tree with n items takes $O(\log n)$ time and performs $O(\log n)$ recolorings and at most two restructuring operations.*

Justification: A deletion begins with the standard binary search tree deletion algorithm, which requires time proportional to the height of the tree; for red-black trees, that height is $O(\log n)$. The subsequent rebalancing takes place along an upward path from the parent of a deleted node.

We considered three cases to remedy a resulting black deficit. Case 1 requires a trinode restructuring operation, yet completes the process, so this case is applied at most once. Case 2 may be applied logarithmically many times, but it only involves a recoloring of up to two nodes per application. Case 3 requires a rotation, but this case can only apply once, because if the rotation does not resolve the problem, the very next action will be a terminal application of either Case 1 or Case 2.

In the worst case, there will be $O(\log n)$ recolorings from Case 2, a single rotation from Case 3, and a trinode restructuring from Case 1.   ∎

11.6.2 Python Implementation

A complete implementation of a RedBlackTreeMap class is provided in Code Fragments 11.15 through 11.17. It inherits from the standard TreeMap class and relies on the balancing framework described in Section 11.2.1.

We begin, in Code Fragment 11.15, by overriding the definition of the nested _Node class to introduce an additional Boolean field to denote the current color of a node. Our constructor intentionally sets the color of a new node to red to be consistent with our approach for inserting items. We define several additional utility functions, at the top of Code Fragment 11.16, that aid in setting the color of nodes and querying various conditions.

When an element has been inserted as a leaf in the tree, the _rebalance_insert hook is called, allowing us the opportunity to modify the tree. The new node is red by default, so we need only look for the special case of the new node being the root (in which case it should be colored black), or the possibility that we have a double-red violation because the new node's parent is also red. To remedy such violations, we closely follow the case analysis described in Section 11.6.1.

The rebalancing after a deletion also follows the case analysis described in Section 11.6.1. An additional challenge is that by the time the _rebalance_hook is called, the old node has already been removed from the tree. That hook is invoked on the *parent* of the removed node. Some of the case analysis depends on knowing about the properties of the removed node. Fortunately, we can reverse engineer that information by relying on the red-black tree properties. In particular, if p denotes the parent of the removed node, it must be that:

- If p has no children, the removed node was a red leaf. (Exercise R-11.26.)
- If p has one child, the removed node was a black leaf, causing a deficit, unless that one remaining child is a red leaf. (Exercise R-11.27.)
- If p has two children, the removed node was a black node with one red child, which was promoted. (Exercise R-11.28.)

```python
1  class RedBlackTreeMap(TreeMap):
2    """Sorted map implementation using a red-black tree."""
3    class _Node(TreeMap._Node):
4      """Node class for red-black tree maintains bit that denotes color."""
5      __slots__ = '_red'      # add additional data member to the Node class
6
7      def __init__(self, element, parent=None, left=None, right=None):
8        super().__init__(element, parent, left, right)
9        self._red = True        # new node red by default
```

Code Fragment 11.15: Beginning of the RedBlackTreeMap class. (Continued in Code Fragment 11.16.)

```
10    #------------------------ positional-based utility methods ------------------------
11    # we consider a nonexistent child to be trivially black
12    def _set_red(self, p): p._node._red = True
13    def _set_black(self, p): p._node._red = False
14    def _set_color(self, p, make_red): p._node._red = make_red
15    def _is_red(self, p): return p is not None and p._node._red
16    def _is_red_leaf(self, p): return self._is_red(p) and self.is_leaf(p)
17
18    def _get_red_child(self, p):
19      """Return a red child of p (or None if no such child)."""
20      for child in (self.left(p), self.right(p)):
21        if self._is_red(child):
22          return child
23      return None
24
25    #------------------------ support for insertions ------------------------
26    def _rebalance_insert(self, p):
27      self._resolve_red(p)                          # new node is always red
28
29    def _resolve_red(self, p):
30      if self.is_root(p):
31        self._set_black(p)                          # make root black
32      else:
33        parent = self.parent(p)
34        if self._is_red(parent):                    # double red problem
35          uncle = self.sibling(parent)
36          if not self._is_red(uncle):               # Case 1: misshapen 4-node
37            middle = self._restructure(p)           # do trinode restructuring
38            self._set_black(middle)                 # and then fix colors
39            self._set_red(self.left(middle))
40            self._set_red(self.right(middle))
41          else:                                     # Case 2: overfull 5-node
42            grand = self.parent(parent)
43            self._set_red(grand)                    # grandparent becomes red
44            self._set_black(self.left(grand))       # its children become black
45            self._set_black(self.right(grand))
46            self._resolve_red(grand)                # recur at red grandparent
```

Code Fragment 11.16: Continuation of the RedBlackTreeMap class. (Continued from Code Fragment 11.15, and concluded in Code Fragment 11.17.)

```
47    #------------------------ support for deletions ------------------------
48    def _rebalance_delete(self, p):
49      if len(self) == 1:
50        self._set_black(self.root())         # special case: ensure that root is black
51      elif p is not None:
52        n = self.num_children(p)
53        if n == 1:                           # deficit exists unless child is a red leaf
54          c = next(self.children(p))
55          if not self._is_red_leaf(c):
56            self._fix_deficit(p, c)
57        elif n == 2:                         # removed black node with red child
58          if self._is_red_leaf(self.left(p)):
59            self._set_black(self.left(p))
60          else:
61            self._set_black(self.right(p))
62
63    def _fix_deficit(self, z, y):
64      """Resolve black deficit at z, where y is the root of z's heavier subtree."""
65      if not self._is_red(y):   # y is black; will apply Case 1 or 2
66        x = self._get_red_child(y)
67        if x is not None:       # Case 1: y is black and has red child x; do "transfer"
68          old_color = self._is_red(z)
69          middle = self._restructure(x)
70          self._set_color(middle, old_color)   # middle gets old color of z
71          self._set_black(self.left(middle))   # children become black
72          self._set_black(self.right(middle))
73        else:                   # Case 2: y is black, but no red children; recolor as "fusion"
74          self._set_red(y)
75          if self._is_red(z):
76            self._set_black(z)                 # this resolves the problem
77          elif not self.is_root(z):
78            self._fix_deficit(self.parent(z), self.sibling(z))  # recur upward
79      else:   # Case 3: y is red; rotate misaligned 3-node and repeat
80        self._rotate(y)
81        self._set_black(y)
82        self._set_red(z)
83        if z == self.right(y):
84          self._fix_deficit(z, self.left(z))
85        else:
86          self._fix_deficit(z, self.right(z))
```

Code Fragment 11.17: Conclusion of the RedBlackTreeMap class. (Continued from Code Fragment 11.16.)

11.7   Exercises

For help with exercises, please visit the site, www.wiley.com/college/goodrich.

Reinforcement

R-11.1 If we insert the entries $(1,A)$, $(2,B)$, $(3,C)$, $(4,D)$, and $(5,E)$, in this order, into an initially empty binary search tree, what will it look like?

R-11.2 Insert, into an empty binary search tree, entries with keys 30, 40, 24, 58, 48, 26, 11, 13 (in this order). Draw the tree after each insertion.

R-11.3 How many different binary search trees can store the keys $\{1,2,3\}$?

R-11.4 Dr. Amongus claims that the order in which a fixed set of entries is inserted into a binary search tree does not matter—the same tree results every time. Give a small example that proves he is wrong.

R-11.5 Dr. Amongus claims that the order in which a fixed set of entries is inserted into an AVL tree does not matter—the same AVL tree results every time. Give a small example that proves he is wrong.

R-11.6 Our implementation of the TreeMap._subtree_search utility, from Code Fragment 11.4, relies on recursion. For a large unbalanced tree, Python's default limit on recursive depth may be prohibitive. Give an alternative implementation of that method that does not rely on the use of recursion.

R-11.7 Do the trinode restructurings in Figures 11.12 and 11.14 result in single or double rotations?

R-11.8 Draw the AVL tree resulting from the insertion of an entry with key 52 into the AVL tree of Figure 11.14b.

R-11.9 Draw the AVL tree resulting from the removal of the entry with key 62 from the AVL tree of Figure 11.14b.

R-11.10 Explain why performing a rotation in an n-node binary tree when using the array-based representation of Section 8.3.2 takes $\Omega(n)$ time.

R-11.11 Give a schematic figure, in the style of Figure 11.13, showing the heights of subtrees during a deletion operation in an AVL tree that triggers a trinode restructuring for the case in which the two children of the node denoted as y start with equal heights. What is the net effect of the height of the rebalanced subtree due to the deletion operation?

R-11.12 Repeat the previous problem, considering the case in which y's children start with different heights.

R-11.13 The rules for a deletion in an AVL tree specifically require that when the two subtrees of the node denoted as y have equal height, child x should be chosen to be "aligned" with y (so that x and y are both left children or both right children). To better understand this requirement, repeat Exercise R-11.11 assuming we picked the misaligned choice of x. Why might there be a problem in restoring the AVL property with that choice?

R-11.14 Perform the following sequence of operations in an initially empty splay tree and draw the tree after each set of operations.

    a. Insert keys 0, 2, 4, 6, 8, 10, 12, 14, 16, 18, in this order.
    b. Search for keys 1, 3, 5, 7, 9, 11, 13, 15, 17, 19, in this order.
    c. Delete keys 0, 2, 4, 6, 8, 10, 12, 14, 16, 18, in this order.

R-11.15 What does a splay tree look like if its entries are accessed in increasing order by their keys?

R-11.16 Is the search tree of Figure 11.23(a) a $(2,4)$ tree? Why or why not?

R-11.17 An alternative way of performing a split at a node w in a $(2,4)$ tree is to partition w into w' and w'', with w' being a 2-node and w'' a 3-node. Which of the keys k_1, k_2, k_3, or k_4 do we store at w's parent? Why?

R-11.18 Dr. Amongus claims that a $(2,4)$ tree storing a set of entries will always have the same structure, regardless of the order in which the entries are inserted. Show that he is wrong.

R-11.19 Draw four different red-black trees that correspond to the same $(2,4)$ tree.

R-11.20 Consider the set of keys $K = \{1,2,3,4,5,6,7,8,9,10,11,12,13,14,15\}$.

    a. Draw a $(2,4)$ tree storing K as its keys using the fewest number of nodes.
    b. Draw a $(2,4)$ tree storing K as its keys using the maximum number of nodes.

R-11.21 Consider the sequence of keys $(5,16,22,45,2,10,18,30,50,12,1)$. Draw the result of inserting entries with these keys (in the given order) into

    a. An initially empty $(2,4)$ tree.
    b. An initially empty red-black tree.

R-11.22 For the following statements about red-black trees, provide a justification for each true statement and a counterexample for each false one.

    a. A subtree of a red-black tree is itself a red-black tree.
    b. A node that does not have a sibling is red.
    c. There is a unique $(2,4)$ tree associated with a given red-black tree.
    d. There is a unique red-black tree associated with a given $(2,4)$ tree.

R-11.23 Explain why you would get the same output in an inorder listing of the entries in a binary search tree, T, independent of whether T is maintained to be an AVL tree, splay tree, or red-black tree.

R-11.24 Consider a tree T storing 100,000 entries. What is the worst-case height of T in the following cases?

  a. T is a binary search tree.
  b. T is an AVL tree.
  c. T is a splay tree.
  d. T is a $(2,4)$ tree.
  e. T is a red-black tree.

R-11.25 Draw an example of a red-black tree that is not an AVL tree.

R-11.26 Let T be a red-black tree and let p be the position of the *parent* of the original node that is deleted by the standard search tree deletion algorithm. Prove that if p has zero children, the removed node was a red leaf.

R-11.27 Let T be a red-black tree and let p be the position of the *parent* of the original node that is deleted by the standard search tree deletion algorithm. Prove that if p has one child, the deletion has caused a black deficit at p, except for the case when the one remaining child is a red leaf.

R-11.28 Let T be a red-black tree and let p be the position of the *parent* of the original node that is deleted by the standard search tree deletion algorithm. Prove that if p has two children, the removed node was black and had one red child.

Creativity

C-11.29 Explain how to use an AVL tree or a red-black tree to sort n comparable elements in $O(n \log n)$ time in the worst case.

C-11.30 Can we use a splay tree to sort n comparable elements in $O(n \log n)$ time in the ***worst case***? Why or why not?

C-11.31 Repeat Exercise C-10.28 for the TreeMap class.

C-11.32 Show that any n-node binary tree can be converted to any other n-node binary tree using $O(n)$ rotations.

C-11.33 For a key k that is not found in binary search tree T, prove that both the greatest key less than k and the least key greater than k lie on the path traced by the search for k.

C-11.34 In Section 11.1.2 we claim that the find_range method of a binary search tree executes in $O(s+h)$ time where s is the number of items found within the range and h is the height of the tree. Our implementation, in Code Fragment 11.6 begins by searching for the starting key, and then repeatedly calling the after method until reaching the end of the range. Each call to after is guaranteed to run in $O(h)$ time. This suggests a weaker $O(sh)$ bound for find_range, since it involves $O(s)$ calls to after. Prove that this implementation achieves the stronger $O(s+h)$ bound.

C-11.35 Describe how to perform an operation remove_range(start, stop) that removes all the items whose keys fall within range(start, stop) in a sorted map that is implemented with a binary search tree T, and show that this method runs in time $O(s+h)$, where s is the number of items removed and h is the height of T.

C-11.36 Repeat the previous problem using an AVL tree, achieving a running time of $O(s\log n)$. Why doesn't the solution to the previous problem trivially result in an $O(s+\log n)$ algorithm for AVL trees?

C-11.37 Suppose we wish to support a new method count_range(start, stop) that determines how many keys of a sorted map fall in the specified range. We could clearly implement this in $O(s+h)$ time by adapting our approach to find_range. Describe how to modify the search tree structure to support $O(h)$ worst-case time for count_range.

C-11.38 If the approach described in the previous problem were implemented as part of the TreeMap class, what additional modifications (if any) would be necessary to a subclass such as AVLTreeMap in order to maintain support for the new method?

C-11.39 Draw a schematic of an AVL tree such that a single remove operation could require $\Omega(\log n)$ trinode restructurings (or rotations) from a leaf to the root in order to restore the height-balance property.

C-11.40 In our AVL implementation, each node stores the height of its subtree, which is an arbitrarily large integer. The space usage for an AVL tree can be reduced by instead storing the **balance factor** of a node, which is defined as the height of its left subtree minus the height of its right subtree. Thus, the balance factor of a node is always equal to -1, 0, or 1, except during an insertion or removal, when it may become **temporarily** equal to -2 or $+2$. Reimplement the AVLTreeMap class storing balance factors rather than subtree heights.

C-11.41 If we maintain a reference to the position of the leftmost node of a binary search tree, then operation find_min can be performed in $O(1)$ time. Describe how the implementation of the other map methods need to be modified to maintain a reference to the leftmost position.

C-11.42 If the approach described in the previous problem were implemented as part of the TreeMap class, what additional modifications (if any) would be necessary to a subclass such as AVLTreeMap in order to accurately maintain the reference to the leftmost position?

C-11.43 Describe a modification to the binary search tree implementation having worst-case $O(1)$-time performance for methods after(p) and before(p) without adversely affecting the asymptotics of any other methods.

C-11.44 If the approach described in the previous problem were implemented as part of the TreeMap class, what additional modifications (if any) would be necessary to a subclass such as AVLTreeMap in order to maintain the efficiency?

C-11.45 For a standard binary search tree, Table 11.1 claims $O(h)$-time performance for the delete(p) method. Explain why delete(p) would run in $O(1)$ time if given a solution to Exercise C-11.43.

C-11.46 Describe a modification to the binary search tree data structure that would support the following two index-based operations for a sorted map in $O(h)$ time, where h is the height of the tree.

at_index(i): Return the position p of the item at index i of a sorted map.

index_of(p): Return the index i of the item at position p of a sorted map.

C-11.47 Draw a splay tree, T_1, together with the sequence of updates that produced it, and a red-black tree, T_2, on the same set of ten entries, such that a preorder traversal of T_1 would be the same as a preorder traversal of T_2.

C-11.48 Show that the nodes that become temporarily unbalanced in an AVL tree during an insertion may be nonconsecutive on the path from the newly inserted node to the root.

C-11.49 Show that at most one node in an AVL tree becomes temporarily unbalanced after the immediate deletion of a node as part of the standard __delitem__ map operation.

C-11.50 Let T and U be $(2,4)$ trees storing n and m entries, respectively, such that all the entries in T have keys less than the keys of all the entries in U. Describe an $O(\log n + \log m)$-time method for *joining* T and U into a single tree that stores all the entries in T and U.

C-11.51 Repeat the previous problem for red-black trees T and U.

C-11.52 Justify Proposition 11.7.

C-11.53 The Boolean indicator used to mark nodes in a red-black tree as being "red" or "black" is not strictly needed when we have distinct keys. Describe a scheme for implementing a red-black tree without adding any extra space to standard binary search tree nodes.

C-11.54 Let T be a red-black tree storing n entries, and let k be the key of an entry in T. Show how to construct from T, in $O(\log n)$ time, two red-black trees T' and T'', such that T' contains all the keys of T less than k, and T'' contains all the keys of T greater than k. This operation destroys T.

C-11.55 Show that the nodes of any AVL tree T can be colored "red" and "black" so that T becomes a red-black tree.

C-11.56 The standard splaying step requires two passes, one downward pass to find the node x to splay, followed by an upward pass to splay the node x. Describe a method for splaying and searching for x in one downward pass. Each substep now requires that you consider the next two nodes in the path down to x, with a possible zig substep performed at the end. Describe how to perform the zig-zig, zig-zag, and zig steps.

C-11.57 Consider a variation of splay trees, called *half-splay trees*, where splaying a node at depth d stops as soon as the node reaches depth $\lfloor d/2 \rfloor$. Perform an amortized analysis of half-splay trees.

C-11.58 Describe a sequence of accesses to an n-node splay tree T, where n is odd, that results in T consisting of a single chain of nodes such that the path down T alternates between left children and right children.

C-11.59 As a positional structure, our TreeMap implementation has a subtle flaw. A position instance p associated with an key-value pair (k, v) should remain valid as long as that item remains in the map. In particular, that position should be unaffected by calls to insert or delete other items in the collection. Our algorithm for deleting an item from a binary search tree may fail to provide such a guarantee, in particular because of our rule for using the inorder predecessor of a key as a replacement when deleting a key that is located in a node with two children. Given an explicit series of Python commands that demonstrates such a flaw.

C-11.60 How might the TreeMap implementation be changed to avoid the flaw described in the previous problem?

Projects

P-11.61 Perform an experimental study to compare the speed of our AVL tree, splay tree, and red-black tree implementations for various sequences of operations.

P-11.62 Redo the previous exercise, including an implementation of skip lists. (See Exercise P-10.53.)

P-11.63 Implement the Map ADT using a $(2, 4)$ tree. (See Section 10.1.1.)

P-11.64 Redo the previous exercise, including all methods of the Sorted Map ADT. (See Section 10.3.)

P-11.65 Redo Exercise P-11.63 providing *positional* support, as we did for binary search trees (Section 11.1.1), so as to include methods first( ), last( ), before(p), after(p), and find_position(k). Each item should have a distinct position in this abstraction, even though several items may be stored at a single node of a tree.

P-11.66 Write a Python class that can take any red-black tree and convert it into its corresponding $(2,4)$ tree and can take any $(2,4)$ tree and convert it into its corresponding red-black tree.

P-11.67 In describing multisets and multimaps in Section 10.5.3, we describe a general approach for adapting a traditional map by storing all duplicates within a secondary container as a value in the map. Give an alternative implementation of a multimap using a binary search tree such that each entry of the map is stored at a distinct node of the tree. With the existence of duplicates, we redefine the search tree property so that all items in the left subtree of a position p with key k have keys that are less than *or equal to k*, while all items in the right subtree of p have keys that are greater than *or equal to k*. Use the public interface given in Code Fragment 10.17.

P-11.68 Prepare an implementation of splay trees that uses top-down splaying as described in Exercise C-11.56. Perform extensive experimental studies to compare its performance to the standard bottom-up splaying implemented in this chapter.

P-11.69 The *mergeable heap* ADT is an extension of the priority queue ADT consisting of operations add(k, v), min( ), remove_min( ) and merge(h), where the merge(h) operations performs a union of the mergeable heap h with the present one, incorporating all items into the current one while emptying h. Describe a concrete implementation of the mergeable heap ADT that achieves $O(\log n)$ performance for all its operations, where n denotes the size of the resulting heap for the merge operation.

P-11.70 Write a program that performs a simple n-body simulation, called "Jumping Leprechauns." This simulation involves n leprechauns, numbered 1 to n. It maintains a gold value g_i for each leprechaun i, which begins with each leprechaun starting out with a million dollars worth of gold, that is, $g_i = 1\,000\,000$ for each $i = 1, 2, \ldots, n$. In addition, the simulation also maintains, for each leprechaun, i, a place on the horizon, which is represented as a double-precision floating-point number, x_i. In each iteration of the simulation, the simulation processes the leprechauns in order. Processing a leprechaun i during this iteration begins by computing a new place on the horizon for i, which is determined by the assignment

$$x_i = x_i + rg_i,$$

where r is a random floating-point number between -1 and 1. The leprechaun i then steals half the gold from the nearest leprechauns on either side of him and adds this gold to his gold value, g_i. Write a program that can perform a series of iterations in this simulation for a given number, n, of leprechauns. You must maintain the set of horizon positions using a sorted map data structure described in this chapter.

Chapter Notes

Some of the data structures discussed in this chapter are extensively covered by Knuth in his *Sorting and Searching* book [65], and by Mehlhorn in [76]. AVL trees are due to Adel'son-Vel'skii and Landis [2], who invented this class of balanced search trees in 1962. Binary search trees, AVL trees, and hashing are described in Knuth's *Sorting and Searching* [65] book. Average-height analyses for binary search trees can be found in the books by Aho, Hopcroft, and Ullman [6] and Cormen, Leiserson, Rivest and Stein [29]. The handbook by Gonnet and Baeza-Yates [44] contains a number of theoretical and experimental comparisons among map implementations. Aho, Hopcroft, and Ullman [5] discuss $(2,3)$ trees, which are similar to $(2,4)$ trees. Red-black trees were defined by Bayer [10]. Variations and interesting properties of red-black trees are presented in a paper by Guibas and Sedgewick [48]. The reader interested in learning more about different balanced tree data structures is referred to the books by Mehlhorn [76] and Tarjan [95], and the book chapter by Mehlhorn and Tsakalidis [78]. Knuth [65] is excellent additional reading that includes early approaches to balancing trees. Splay trees were invented by Sleator and Tarjan [89] (see also [95]).

Chapter 12. Sorting and Selection

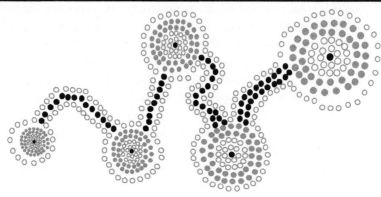

Contents

12.1 Why Study Sorting Algorithms?

Much of this chapter focuses on algorithms for sorting a collection of objects. Given a collection, the goal is to rearrange the elements so that they are ordered from smallest to largest (or to produce a new copy of the sequence with such an order). As we did when studying priority queues (see Section 9.4), we assume that such a consistent order exists. In Python, the natural order of objects is typically[1] defined using the $<$ operator having following properties:

- **Irreflexive property**: $k \not< k$.
- **Transitive property**: if $k_1 < k_2$ and $k_2 < k_3$, then $k_1 < k_3$.

The transitive property is important as it allows us to infer the outcome of certain comparisons without taking the time to perform those comparisons, thereby leading to more efficient algorithms.

Sorting is among the most important, and well studied, of computing problems. Data sets are often stored in sorted order, for example, to allow for efficient searches with the binary search algorithm (see Section 4.1.3). Many advanced algorithms for a variety of problems rely on sorting as a subroutine.

Python has built-in support for sorting data, in the form of the sort method of the list class that rearranges the contents of a list, and the built-in sorted function that produces a new list containing the elements of an arbitrary collection in sorted order. Those built-in functions use advanced algorithms (some of which we will describe in this chapter), and they are highly optimized. A programmer should typically rely on calls to the built-in sorting functions, as it is rare to have a special enough circumstance to warrant implementing a sorting algorithm from scratch.

With that said, it remains important to have a deep understanding of sorting algorithms. Most immediately, when calling the built-in function, it is good to know what to expect in terms of efficiency and how that may depend upon the initial order of elements or the type of objects that are being sorted. More generally, the ideas and approaches that have led to advances in the development of sorting algorithm carry over to algorithm development in many other areas of computing.

We have introduced several sorting algorithms already in this book:

- Insertion-sort (see Sections 5.5.2, 7.5, and 9.4.1)
- Selection-sort (see Section 9.4.1)
- Bubble-sort (see Exercise C-7.38)
- Heap-sort (see Section 9.4.2)

In this chapter, we present four other sorting algorithms, called ***merge-sort***, ***quick-sort***, ***bucket-sort***, and ***radix-sort***, and then discuss the advantages and disadvantages of the various algorithms in Section 12.5.

---

[1]In Section 12.6.1, we will explore another technique used in Python for sorting data according to an order other than the natural order defined by the $<$ operator.

12.2   Merge-Sort

12.2.1   Divide-and-Conquer

The first two algorithms we describe in this chapter, merge-sort and quick-sort, use recursion in an algorithmic design pattern called ***divide-and-conquer***. We have already seen the power of recursion in describing algorithms in an elegant manner (see Chapter 4). The divide-and-conquer pattern consists of the following three steps:

1. ***Divide:*** If the input size is smaller than a certain threshold (say, one or two elements), solve the problem directly using a straightforward method and return the solution so obtained. Otherwise, divide the input data into two or more disjoint subsets.

2. ***Conquer:*** Recursively solve the subproblems associated with the subsets.

3. ***Combine:*** Take the solutions to the subproblems and merge them into a solution to the original problem.

Using Divide-and-Conquer for Sorting

We will first describe the merge-sort algorithm at a high level, without focusing on whether the data is an array-based (Python) list or a linked list; we will soon give concrete implementations for each. To sort a sequence S with n elements using the three divide-and-conquer steps, the merge-sort algorithm proceeds as follows:

1. ***Divide:*** If S has zero or one element, return S immediately; it is already sorted. Otherwise (S has at least two elements), remove all the elements from S and put them into two sequences, S_1 and S_2, each containing about half of the elements of S; that is, S_1 contains the first $\lfloor n/2 \rfloor$ elements of S, and S_2 contains the remaining $\lceil n/2 \rceil$ elements.

2. ***Conquer:*** Recursively sort sequences S_1 and S_2.

3. ***Combine:*** Put back the elements into S by merging the sorted sequences S_1 and S_2 into a sorted sequence.

In reference to the divide step, we recall that the notation $\lfloor x \rfloor$ indicates the ***floor*** of x, that is, the largest integer k, such that $k \leq x$. Similarly, the notation $\lceil x \rceil$ indicates the ***ceiling*** of x, that is, the smallest integer m, such that $x \leq m$.

We can visualize an execution of the merge-sort algorithm by means of a binary tree T, called the ***merge-sort tree***. Each node of T represents a recursive invocation (or call) of the merge-sort algorithm. We associate with each node v of T the sequence S that is processed by the invocation associated with v. The children of node v are associated with the recursive calls that process the subsequences S_1 and S_2 of S. The external nodes of T are associated with individual elements of S, corresponding to instances of the algorithm that make no recursive calls.

Figure 12.1 summarizes an execution of the merge-sort algorithm by showing the input and output sequences processed at each node of the merge-sort tree. The step-by-step evolution of the merge-sort tree is shown in Figures 12.2 through 12.4.

This algorithm visualization in terms of the merge-sort tree helps us analyze the running time of the merge-sort algorithm. In particular, since the size of the input sequence roughly halves at each recursive call of merge-sort, the height of the merge-sort tree is about $\log n$ (recall that the base of log is 2 if omitted).

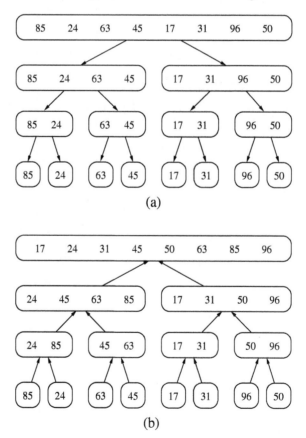

Figure 12.1: Merge-sort tree T for an execution of the merge-sort algorithm on a sequence with 8 elements: (a) input sequences processed at each node of T; (b) output sequences generated at each node of T.

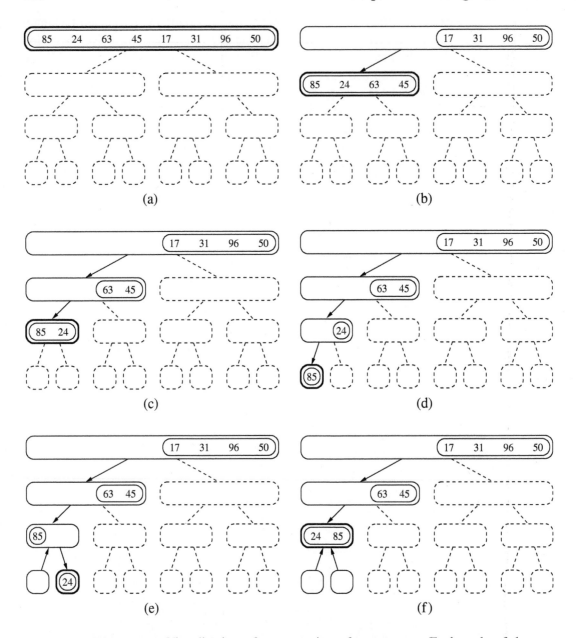

Figure 12.2: Visualization of an execution of merge-sort. Each node of the tree represents a recursive call of merge-sort. The nodes drawn with dashed lines represent calls that have not been made yet. The node drawn with thick lines represents the current call. The empty nodes drawn with thin lines represent completed calls. The remaining nodes (drawn with thin lines and not empty) represent calls that are waiting for a child invocation to return. (Continues in Figure 12.3.)

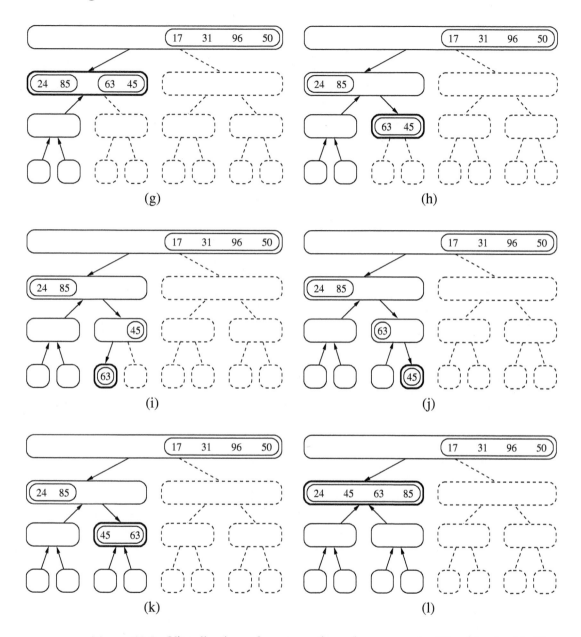

Figure 12.3: Visualization of an execution of merge-sort. (Combined with Figures 12.2 and 12.4.)

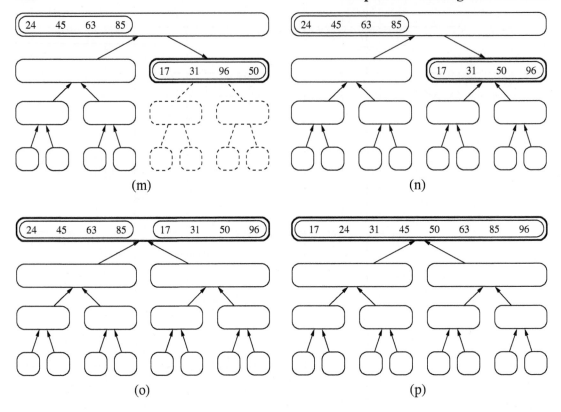

Figure 12.4: Visualization of an execution of merge-sort (continued from Figure 12.3). Several invocations are omitted between (m) and (n). Note the merging of two halves performed in step (p).

Proposition 12.1: *The merge-sort tree associated with an execution of merge-sort on a sequence of size n has height* $\lceil \log n \rceil$.

We leave the justification of Proposition 12.1 as a simple exercise (R-12.1). We will use this proposition to analyze the running time of the merge-sort algorithm.

Having given an overview of merge-sort and an illustration of how it works, let us consider each of the steps of this divide-and-conquer algorithm in more detail. Dividing a sequence of size n involves separating it at the element with index $\lceil n/2 \rceil$, and recursive calls can be started by passing these smaller sequences as parameters. The difficult step is combining the two sorted sequences into a single sorted sequence. Thus, before we present our analysis of merge-sort, we need to say more about how this is done.

12.2.2 Array-Based Implementation of Merge-Sort

We begin by focusing on the case when a sequence of items is represented as an (array-based) Python list. The merge function (Code Fragment 12.1) is responsible for the subtask of merging two previously sorted sequences, S_1 and S_2, with the output copied into S. We copy one element during each pass of the while loop, conditionally determining whether the next element should be taken from S_1 or S_2. The divide-and-conquer merge-sort algorithm is given in Code Fragment 12.2.

We illustrate a step of the merge process in Figure 12.5. During the process, index i represents the number of elements of S_1 that have been copied to S, while index j represents the number of elements of S_2 that have been copied to S. Assuming S_1 and S_2 both have at least one uncopied element, we copy the smaller of the two elements being considered. Since $i + j$ objects have been previously copied, the next element is placed in $S[i + j]$. (For example, when $i + j$ is 0, the next element is copied to $S[0]$). If we reach the end of one of the sequences, we must copy the next element from the other.

```
1  def merge(S1, S2, S):
2    """Merge two sorted Python lists S1 and S2 into properly sized list S."""
3    i = j = 0
4    while i + j < len(S):
5      if j == len(S2) or (i < len(S1) and S1[i] < S2[j]):
6        S[i+j] = S1[i]           # copy ith element of S1 as next item of S
7        i += 1
8      else:
9        S[i+j] = S2[j]           # copy jth element of S2 as next item of S
10       j += 1
```

Code Fragment 12.1: An implementation of the merge operation for Python's array-based list class.

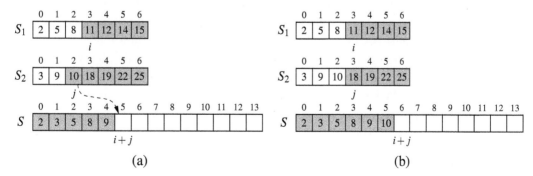

Figure 12.5: A step in the merge of two sorted arrays for which $S_2[j] < S_1[i]$. We show the arrays before the copy step in (a) and after it in (b).

```
1  def merge_sort(S):
2    """Sort the elements of Python list S using the merge-sort algorithm."""
3    n = len(S)
4    if n < 2:
5      return                        # list is already sorted
6    # divide
7    mid = n // 2
8    S1 = S[0:mid]                    # copy of first half
9    S2 = S[mid:n]                    # copy of second half
10   # conquer (with recursion)
11   merge_sort(S1)                   # sort copy of first half
12   merge_sort(S2)                   # sort copy of second half
13   # merge results
14   merge(S1, S2, S)                 # merge sorted halves back into S
```

Code Fragment 12.2: An implementation of the recursive merge-sort algorithm for Python's array-based list class (using the merge function defined in Code Fragment 12.1.

12.2.3   The Running Time of Merge-Sort

We begin by analyzing the running time of the merge algorithm. Let n_1 and n_2 be the number of elements of S_1 and S_2, respectively. It is clear that the operations performed inside each pass of the while loop take $O(1)$ time. The key observation is that during each iteration of the loop, one element is copied from either S_1 or S_2 into S (and that element is considered no further). Therefore, the number of iterations of the loop is $n_1 + n_2$. Thus, the running time of algorithm merge is $O(n_1 + n_2)$.

Having analyzed the running time of the merge algorithm used to combine subproblems, let us analyze the running time of the entire merge-sort algorithm, assuming it is given an input sequence of n elements. For simplicity, we restrict our attention to the case where n is a power of 2. We leave it to an exercise (R-12.3) to show that the result of our analysis also holds when n is not a power of 2.

When evaluating the merge-sort recursion, we rely on the analysis technique introduced in Section 4.2. We account for the amount of time spent within each recursive call, but excluding any time spent waiting for successive recursive calls to terminate. In the case of our merge_sort function, we account for the time to divide the sequence into two subsequences, and the call to merge to combine the two sorted sequences, but we exclude the two recursive calls to merge_sort.

A merge-sort tree T, as portrayed in Figures 12.2 through 12.4, can guide our analysis. Consider a recursive call associated with a node v of the merge-sort tree T. The divide step at node v is straightforward; this step runs in time proportional to the size of the sequence for v, based on the use of slicing to create copies of the two list halves. We have already observed that the merging step also takes time that is linear in the size of the merged sequence. If we let i denote the depth of node v, the time spent at node v is $O(n/2^i)$, since the size of the sequence handled by the recursive call associated with v is equal to $n/2^i$.

Looking at the tree T more globally, as shown in Figure 12.6, we see that, given our definition of "time spent at a node," the running time of merge-sort is equal to the sum of the times spent at the nodes of T. Observe that T has exactly 2^i nodes at depth i. This simple observation has an important consequence, for it implies that the overall time spent at all the nodes of T at depth i is $O(2^i \cdot n/2^i)$, which is $O(n)$. By Proposition 12.1, the height of T is $\lceil \log n \rceil$. Thus, since the time spent at each of the $\lceil \log n \rceil + 1$ levels of T is $O(n)$, we have the following result:

Proposition 12.2: *Algorithm merge-sort sorts a sequence S of size n in $O(n \log n)$ time, assuming two elements of S can be compared in $O(1)$ time.*

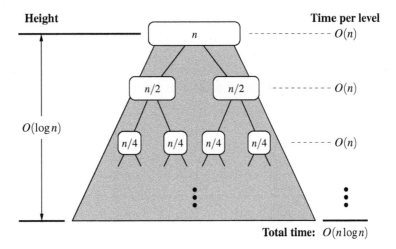

Figure 12.6: A visual analysis of the running time of merge-sort. Each node represents the time spent in a particular recursive call, labeled with the size of its subproblem.

12.2.4 Merge-Sort and Recurrence Equations ⋆

There is another way to justify that the running time of the merge-sort algorithm is $O(n\log n)$ (Proposition 12.2). Namely, we can deal more directly with the recursive nature of the merge-sort algorithm. In this section, we present such an analysis of the running time of merge-sort, and in so doing, introduce the mathematical concept of a ***recurrence equation*** (also known as ***recurrence relation***).

Let the function $t(n)$ denote the worst-case running time of merge-sort on an input sequence of size n. Since merge-sort is recursive, we can characterize function $t(n)$ by means of an equation where the function $t(n)$ is recursively expressed in terms of itself. In order to simplify our characterization of $t(n)$, let us restrict our attention to the case when n is a power of 2. (We leave the problem of showing that our asymptotic characterization still holds in the general case as an exercise.) In this case, we can specify the definition of $t(n)$ as

$$t(n) = \begin{cases} b & \text{if } n \leq 1 \\ 2t(n/2) + cn & \text{otherwise.} \end{cases}$$

An expression such as the one above is called a recurrence equation, since the function appears on both the left- and right-hand sides of the equal sign. Although such a characterization is correct and accurate, what we really desire is a big-Oh type of characterization of $t(n)$ that does not involve the function $t(n)$ itself. That is, we want a ***closed-form*** characterization of $t(n)$.

We can obtain a closed-form solution by applying the definition of a recurrence equation, assuming n is relatively large. For example, after one more application of the equation above, we can write a new recurrence for $t(n)$ as

$$\begin{aligned} t(n) &= 2(2t(n/2^2) + (cn/2)) + cn \\ &= 2^2 t(n/2^2) + 2(cn/2) + cn = 2^2 t(n/2^2) + 2cn. \end{aligned}$$

If we apply the equation again, we get $t(n) = 2^3 t(n/2^3) + 3cn$. At this point, we should see a pattern emerging, so that after applying this equation i times, we get

$$t(n) = 2^i t(n/2^i) + icn.$$

The issue that remains, then, is to determine when to stop this process. To see when to stop, recall that we switch to the closed form $t(n) = b$ when $n \leq 1$, which will occur when $2^i = n$. In other words, this will occur when $i = \log n$. Making this substitution, then, yields

$$\begin{aligned} t(n) &= 2^{\log n} t(n/2^{\log n}) + (\log n)cn \\ &= nt(1) + cn\log n \\ &= nb + cn\log n. \end{aligned}$$

That is, we get an alternative justification of the fact that $t(n)$ is $O(n\log n)$.

12.2.5 Alternative Implementations of Merge-Sort

Sorting Linked Lists

The merge-sort algorithm can easily be adapted to use any form of a basic queue as its container type. In Code Fragment 12.3, we provide such an implementation, based on use of the LinkedQueue class from Section 7.1.2. The $O(n \log n)$ bound for merge-sort from Proposition 12.2 applies to this implementation as well, since each basic operation runs in $O(1)$ time when implemented with a linked list. We show an example execution of this version of the merge algorithm in Figure 12.7.

```
 1  def merge(S1, S2, S):
 2      """Merge two sorted queue instances S1 and S2 into empty queue S."""
 3      while not S1.is_empty( ) and not S2.is_empty():
 4          if S1.first( ) < S2.first():
 5              S.enqueue(S1.dequeue())
 6          else:
 7              S.enqueue(S2.dequeue())
 8      while not S1.is_empty():              # move remaining elements of S1 to S
 9          S.enqueue(S1.dequeue())
10      while not S2.is_empty():              # move remaining elements of S2 to S
11          S.enqueue(S2.dequeue())
12
13  def merge_sort(S):
14      """Sort the elements of queue S using the merge-sort algorithm."""
15      n = len(S)
16      if n < 2:
17          return                           # list is already sorted
18      # divide
19      S1 = LinkedQueue( )                   # or any other queue implementation
20      S2 = LinkedQueue()
21      while len(S1) < n // 2:              # move the first n//2 elements to S1
22          S1.enqueue(S.dequeue())
23      while not S.is_empty():              # move the rest to S2
24          S2.enqueue(S.dequeue())
25      # conquer (with recursion)
26      merge_sort(S1)                       # sort first half
27      merge_sort(S2)                       # sort second half
28      # merge results
29      merge(S1, S2, S)                     # merge sorted halves back into S
```

Code Fragment 12.3: An implementation of merge-sort using a basic queue.

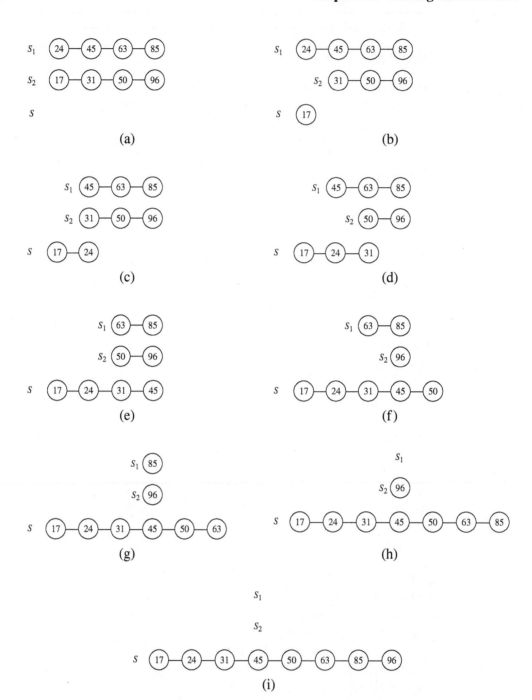

Figure 12.7: Example of an execution of the merge algorithm, as implemented in Code Fragment 12.3 using queues.

A Bottom-Up (Nonrecursive) Merge-Sort

There is a nonrecursive version of array-based merge-sort, which runs in $O(n \log n)$ time. It is a bit faster than recursive merge-sort in practice, as it avoids the extra overheads of recursive calls and temporary memory at each level. The main idea is to perform merge-sort bottom-up, performing the merges level by level going up the merge-sort tree. Given an input array of elements, we begin by merging every successive pair of elements into sorted runs of length two. We merge these runs into runs of length four, merge these new runs into runs of length eight, and so on, until the array is sorted. To keep the space usage reasonable, we deploy a second array that stores the merged runs (swapping input and output arrays after each iteration). We give a Python implementation in Code Fragment 12.4. A similar bottom-up approach can be used for sorting linked lists. (See Exercise C-12.29.)

```python
 1  def merge(src, result, start, inc):
 2    """Merge src[start:start+inc] and src[start+inc:start+2*inc] into result."""
 3    end1 = start+inc                   # boundary for run 1
 4    end2 = min(start+2*inc, len(src))  # boundary for run 2
 5    x, y, z = start, start+inc, start  # index into run 1, run 2, result
 6    while x < end1 and y < end2:
 7      if src[x] < src[y]:
 8        result[z] = src[x]; x += 1     # copy from run 1 and increment x
 9      else:
10        result[z] = src[y]; y += 1     # copy from run 2 and increment y
11      z += 1                           # increment z to reflect new result
12    if x < end1:
13      result[z:end2] = src[x:end1]     # copy remainder of run 1 to output
14    elif y < end2:
15      result[z:end2] = src[y:end2]     # copy remainder of run 2 to output
16
17  def merge_sort(S):
18    """Sort the elements of Python list S using the merge-sort algorithm."""
19    n = len(S)
20    logn = math.ceil(math.log(n,2))
21    src, dest = S, [None] * n          # make temporary storage for dest
22    for i in (2**k for k in range(logn)):  # pass i creates all runs of length 2i
23      for j in range(0, n, 2*i):       # each pass merges two length i runs
24        merge(src, dest, j, i)
25      src, dest = dest, src            # reverse roles of lists
26    if S is not src:
27      S[0:n] = src[0:n]                # additional copy to get results to S
```

Code Fragment 12.4: An implementation of the nonrecursive merge-sort algorithm.

12.3 Quick-Sort

The next sorting algorithm we discuss is called *quick-sort*. Like merge-sort, this algorithm is also based on the *divide-and-conquer* paradigm, but it uses this technique in a somewhat opposite manner, as all the hard work is done *before* the recursive calls.

High-Level Description of Quick-Sort

The quick-sort algorithm sorts a sequence S using a simple recursive approach. The main idea is to apply the divide-and-conquer technique, whereby we divide S into subsequences, recur to sort each subsequence, and then combine the sorted subsequences by a simple concatenation. In particular, the quick-sort algorithm consists of the following three steps (see Figure 12.8):

1. *Divide:* If S has at least two elements (nothing needs to be done if S has zero or one element), select a specific element x from S, which is called the *pivot*. As is common practice, choose the pivot x to be the last element in S. Remove all the elements from S and put them into three sequences:
   - L, storing the elements in S less than x
   - E, storing the elements in S equal to x
   - G, storing the elements in S greater than x
   Of course, if the elements of S are distinct, then E holds just one element—the pivot itself.
2. *Conquer:* Recursively sort sequences L and G.
3. *Combine:* Put back the elements into S in order by first inserting the elements of L, then those of E, and finally those of G.

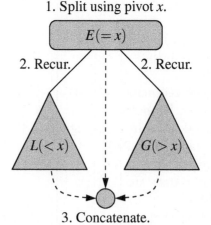

Figure 12.8: A visual schematic of the quick-sort algorithm.

Like merge-sort, the execution of quick-sort can be visualized by means of a binary recursion tree, called the ***quick-sort tree***. Figure 12.9 summarizes an execution of the quick-sort algorithm by showing the input and output sequences processed at each node of the quick-sort tree. The step-by-step evolution of the quick-sort tree is shown in Figures 12.10, 12.11, and 12.12.

Unlike merge-sort, however, the height of the quick-sort tree associated with an execution of quick-sort is linear in the worst case. This happens, for example, if the sequence consists of n distinct elements and is already sorted. Indeed, in this case, the standard choice of the last element as pivot yields a subsequence L of size $n-1$, while subsequence E has size 1 and subsequence G has size 0. At each invocation of quick-sort on subsequence L, the size decreases by 1. Hence, the height of the quick-sort tree is $n-1$.

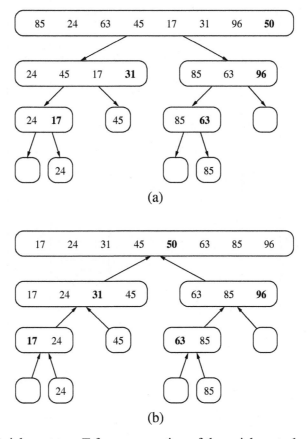

Figure 12.9: Quick-sort tree T for an execution of the quick-sort algorithm on a sequence with 8 elements: (a) input sequences processed at each node of T; (b) output sequences generated at each node of T. The pivot used at each level of the recursion is shown in bold.

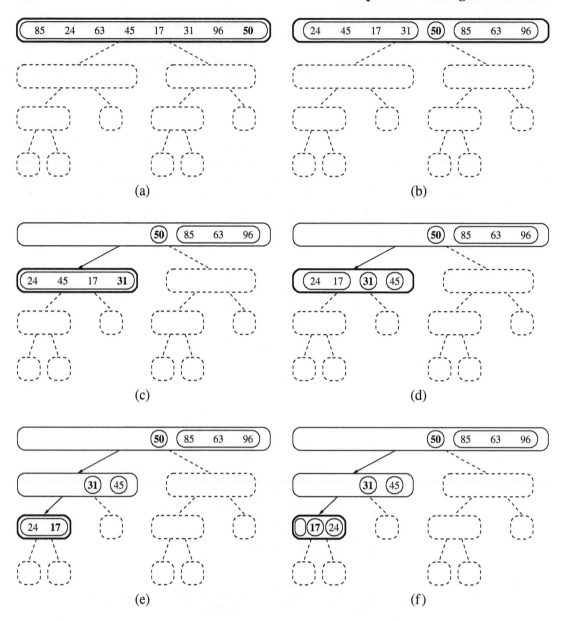

Figure 12.10: Visualization of quick-sort. Each node of the tree represents a recursive call. The nodes drawn with dashed lines represent calls that have not been made yet. The node drawn with thick lines represents the running invocation. The empty nodes drawn with thin lines represent terminated calls. The remaining nodes represent suspended calls (that is, active invocations that are waiting for a child invocation to return). Note the divide steps performed in (b), (d), and (f). (Continues in Figure 12.11.)

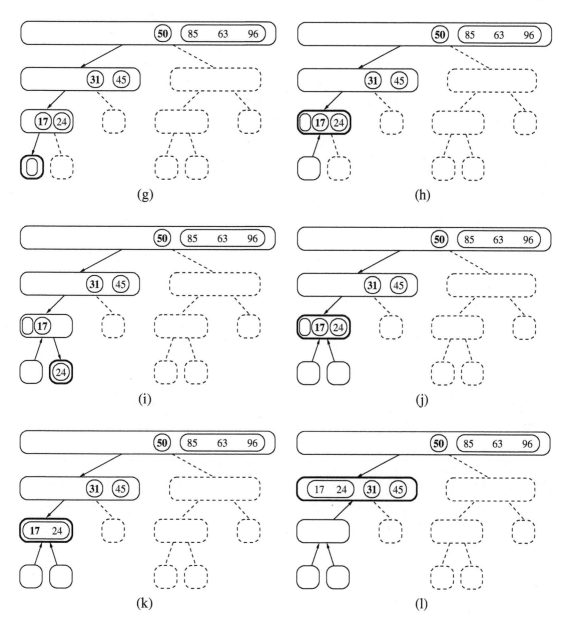

Figure 12.11: Visualization of an execution of quick-sort. Note the concatenation step performed in (k). (Continues in Figure 12.12.)

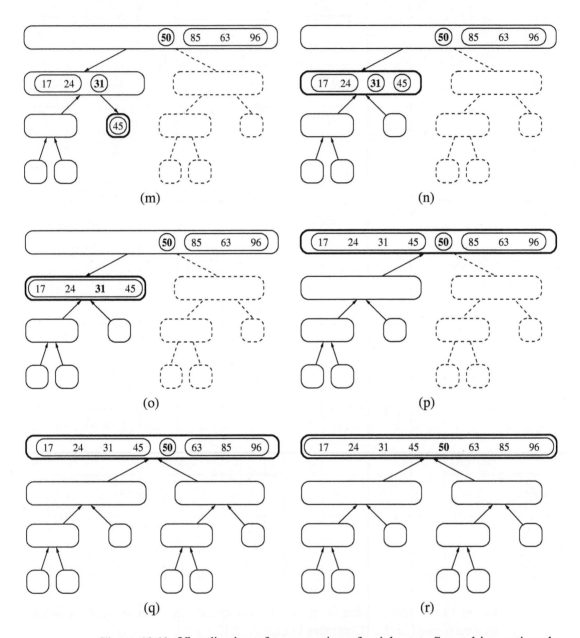

Figure 12.12: Visualization of an execution of quick-sort. Several invocations between (p) and (q) have been omitted. Note the concatenation steps performed in (o) and (r). (Continued from Figure 12.11.)

Performing Quick-Sort on General Sequences

In Code Fragment 12.5, we give an implementation of the quick-sort algorithm that works on any sequence type that operates as a queue. This particular version relies on the LinkedQueue class from Section 7.1.2; we provide a more streamlined implementation of quick-sort using an array-based sequence in Section 12.3.2.

Our implementation chooses the first item of the queue as the pivot (since it is easily accessible), and then it divides sequence S into queues L, E, and G of elements that are respectively less than, equal to, and greater than the pivot. We then recur on the L and G lists, and transfer elements from the sorted lists L, E, and G back to S. All of the queue operations run in $O(1)$ worst-case time when implemented with a linked list.

```
1  def quick_sort(S):
2    """Sort the elements of queue S using the quick-sort algorithm."""
3    n = len(S)
4    if n < 2:
5      return                            # list is already sorted
6    # divide
7    p = S.first( )                      # using first as arbitrary pivot
8    L = LinkedQueue()
9    E = LinkedQueue()
10   G = LinkedQueue()
11   while not S.is_empty():             # divide S into L, E, and G
12     if S.first( ) < p:
13       L.enqueue(S.dequeue())
14     elif p < S.first():
15       G.enqueue(S.dequeue())
16     else:                            # S.first() must equal pivot
17       E.enqueue(S.dequeue())
18   # conquer (with recursion)
19   quick_sort(L)                       # sort elements less than p
20   quick_sort(G)                       # sort elements greater than p
21   # concatenate results
22   while not L.is_empty():
23     S.enqueue(L.dequeue())
24   while not E.is_empty():
25     S.enqueue(E.dequeue())
26   while not G.is_empty():
27     S.enqueue(G.dequeue())
```

Code Fragment 12.5: Quick-sort for a sequence S implemented as a queue.

Running Time of Quick-Sort

We can analyze the running time of quick-sort with the same technique used for merge-sort in Section 12.2.3. Namely, we can identify the time spent at each node of the quick-sort tree T and sum up the running times for all the nodes.

Examining Code Fragment 12.5, we see that the divide step and the final concatenation of quick-sort can be implemented in linear time. Thus, the time spent at a node v of T is proportional to the **input size** $s(v)$ of v, defined as the size of the sequence handled by the invocation of quick-sort associated with node v. Since subsequence E has at least one element (the pivot), the sum of the input sizes of the children of v is at most $s(v) - 1$.

Let s_i denote the sum of the input sizes of the nodes at depth i for a particular quick-sort tree T. Clearly, $s_0 = n$, since the root r of T is associated with the entire sequence. Also, $s_1 \le n - 1$, since the pivot is not propagated to the children of r. More generally, it must be that $s_i < s_{i-1}$ since the elements of the subsequences at depth i all come from distinct subsequences at depth $i - 1$, and at least one element from depth $i - 1$ does not propagate to depth i because it is in a set E (in fact, one element from *each node* at depth $i - 1$ does not propagate to depth i).

We can therefore bound the overall running time of an execution of quick-sort as $O(n \cdot h)$ where h is the overall height of the quick-sort tree T for that execution. Unfortunately, in the worst case, the height of a quick-sort tree is $\Theta(n)$, as observed in Section 12.3. Thus, quick-sort runs in $O(n^2)$ worst-case time. Paradoxically, if we choose the pivot as the last element of the sequence, this worst-case behavior occurs for problem instances when sorting should be easy—if the sequence is already sorted.

Given its name, we would expect quick-sort to run quickly, and it often does in practice. The best case for quick-sort on a sequence of distinct elements occurs when subsequences L and G have roughly the same size. In that case, as we saw with merge-sort, the tree has height $O(\log n)$ and therefore quick-sort runs in $O(n \log n)$ time; we leave the justification of this fact as an exercise (R-12.10). More so, we can observe an $O(n \log n)$ running time even if the split between L and G is not as perfect. For example, if every divide step caused one subsequence to have one-fourth of those elements and the other to have three-fourths of the elements, the height of the tree would remain $O(\log n)$ and thus the overall performance $O(n \log n)$.

We will see in the next section that introducing randomization in the choice of a pivot will makes quick-sort essentially behave in this way on average, with an expected running time that is $O(n \log n)$.

12.3.1 Randomized Quick-Sort

One common method for analyzing quick-sort is to assume that the pivot will always divide the sequence in a reasonably balanced manner. We feel such an assumption would presuppose knowledge about the input distribution that is typically not available, however. For example, we would have to assume that we will rarely be given "almost" sorted sequences to sort, which are actually common in many applications. Fortunately, this assumption is not needed in order for us to match our intuition to quick-sort's behavior.

In general, we desire some way of getting close to the best-case running time for quick-sort. The way to get close to the best-case running time, of course, is for the pivot to divide the input sequence S almost equally. If this outcome were to occur, then it would result in a running time that is asymptotically the same as the best-case running time. That is, having pivots close to the "middle" of the set of elements leads to an $O(n \log n)$ running time for quick-sort.

Picking Pivots at Random

Since the goal of the partition step of the quick-sort method is to divide the sequence S with sufficient balance, let us introduce randomization into the algorithm and pick as the pivot a ***random element*** of the input sequence. That is, instead of picking the pivot as the first or last element of S, we pick an element of S at random as the pivot, keeping the rest of the algorithm unchanged. This variation of quick-sort is called ***randomized quick-sort***. The following proposition shows that the expected running time of randomized quick-sort on a sequence with n elements is $O(n \log n)$. This expectation is taken over all the possible random choices the algorithm makes, and is independent of any assumptions about the distribution of the possible input sequences the algorithm is likely to be given.

Proposition 12.3: *The expected running time of randomized quick-sort on a sequence S of size n is $O(n \log n)$.*

Justification: We assume two elements of S can be compared in $O(1)$ time. Consider a single recursive call of randomized quick-sort, and let n denote the size of the input for this call. Say that this call is "good" if the pivot chosen is such that subsequences L and G have size at least $n/4$ and at most $3n/4$ each; otherwise, a call is "bad."

Now, consider the implications of our choosing a pivot uniformly at random. Note that there are $n/2$ possible good choices for the pivot for any given call of size n of the randomized quick-sort algorithm. Thus, the probability that any call is good is $1/2$. Note further that a good call will at least partition a list of size n into two lists of size $3n/4$ and $n/4$, and a bad call could be as bad as producing a single call of size $n-1$.

Now consider a recursion trace for randomized quick-sort. This trace defines a binary tree, T, such that each node in T corresponds to a different recursive call on a subproblem of sorting a portion of the original list.

Say that a node v in T is in *size group* i if the size of v's subproblem is greater than $(3/4)^{i+1}n$ and at most $(3/4)^i n$. Let us analyze the expected time spent working on all the subproblems for nodes in size group i. By the linearity of expectation (Proposition B.19), the expected time for working on all these subproblems is the sum of the expected times for each one. Some of these nodes correspond to good calls and some correspond to bad calls. But note that, since a good call occurs with probability $1/2$, the expected number of consecutive calls we have to make before getting a good call is 2. Moreover, notice that as soon as we have a good call for a node in size group i, its children will be in size groups higher than i. Thus, for any element x from in the input list, the expected number of nodes in size group i containing x in their subproblems is 2. In other words, the expected total size of all the subproblems in size group i is $2n$. Since the nonrecursive work we perform for any subproblem is proportional to its size, this implies that the total expected time spent processing subproblems for nodes in size group i is $O(n)$.

The number of size groups is $\log_{4/3} n$, since repeatedly multiplying by $3/4$ is the same as repeatedly dividing by $4/3$. That is, the number of size groups is $O(\log n)$. Therefore, the total expected running time of randomized quick-sort is $O(n \log n)$. (See Figure 12.13.) ∎

If fact, we can show that the running time of randomized quick-sort is $O(n \log n)$ with high probability. (See Exercise C-12.54.)

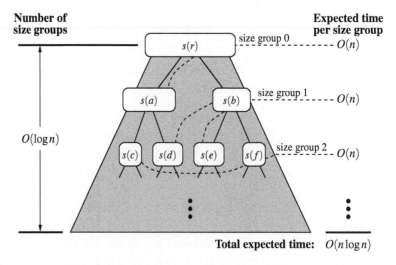

Figure 12.13: A visual time analysis of the quick-sort tree T. Each node is shown labeled with the size of its subproblem.

12.3.2   Additional Optimizations for Quick-Sort

An algorithm is ***in-place*** if it uses only a small amount of memory in addition to that needed for the original input. Our implementation of heap-sort, from Section 9.4.2, is an example of such an in-place sorting algorithm. Our implementation of quick-sort from Code Fragment 12.5 does not qualify as in-place because we use additional containers L, E, and G when dividing a sequence S within each recursive call. Quick-sort of an array-based sequence can be adapted to be in-place, and such an optimization is used in most deployed implementations.

Performing the quick-sort algorithm in-place requires a bit of ingenuity, however, for we must use the input sequence itself to store the subsequences for all the recursive calls. We show algorithm inplace_quick_sort, which performs in-place quick-sort, in Code Fragment 12.6. Our implementation assumes that the input sequence, S, is given as a Python list of elements. In-place quick-sort modifies the input sequence using element swapping and does not explicitly create subsequences. Instead, a subsequence of the input sequence is implicitly represented by a range of positions specified by a leftmost index a and a rightmost index b. The

```
1  def inplace_quick_sort(S, a, b):
2    """Sort the list from S[a] to S[b] inclusive using the quick-sort algorithm."""
3    if a >= b: return                        # range is trivially sorted
4    pivot = S[b]                             # last element of range is pivot
5    left = a                                 # will scan rightward
6    right = b−1                              # will scan leftward
7    while left <= right:
8      # scan until reaching value equal or larger than pivot (or right marker)
9      while left <= right and S[left] < pivot:
10       left += 1
11     # scan until reaching value equal or smaller than pivot (or left marker)
12     while left <= right and pivot < S[right]:
13       right −= 1
14     if left <= right:                      # scans did not strictly cross
15       S[left], S[right] = S[right], S[left]         # swap values
16       left, right = left + 1, right − 1             # shrink range
17
18   # put pivot into its final place (currently marked by left index)
19   S[left], S[b] = S[b], S[left]
20   # make recursive calls
21   inplace_quick_sort(S, a, left − 1)
22   inplace_quick_sort(S, left + 1, b)
```

Code Fragment 12.6: In-place quick-sort for a Python list S.

divide step is performed by scanning the array simultaneously using local variables left, which advances forward, and right, which advances backward, swapping pairs of elements that are in reverse order, as shown in Figure 12.14. When these two indices pass each other, the division step is complete and the algorithm completes by recurring on these two sublists. There is no explicit "combine" step, because the concatenation of the two sublists is implicit to the in-place use of the original list.

It is worth noting that if a sequence has duplicate values, we are not explicitly creating three sublists L, E, and G, as in our original quick-sort description. We instead allow elements equal to the pivot (other than the pivot itself) to be dispersed across the two sublists. Exercise R-12.11 explores the subtlety of our implementation in the presence of duplicate keys, and Exercise C-12.33 describes an in-place algorithm that strictly partitions into three sublists L, E, and G.

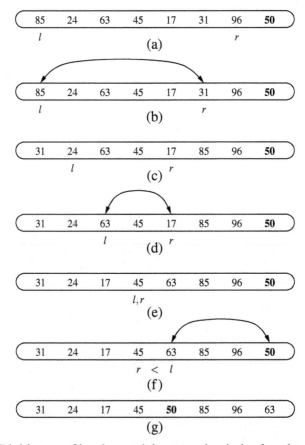

Figure 12.14: Divide step of in-place quick-sort, using index l as shorthand for identifier left, and index r as shorthand for identifier right. Index l scans the sequence from left to right, and index r scans the sequence from right to left. A swap is performed when l is at an element as large as the pivot and r is at an element as small as the pivot. A final swap with the pivot, in part (f), completes the divide step.

Although the implementation we describe in this section for dividing the sequence into two pieces is in-place, we note that the complete quick-sort algorithm needs space for a stack proportional to the depth of the recursion tree, which in this case can be as large as $n - 1$. Admittedly, the expected stack depth is $O(\log n)$, which is small compared to n. Nevertheless, a simple trick lets us guarantee the stack size is $O(\log n)$. The main idea is to design a nonrecursive version of in-place quick-sort using an explicit stack to iteratively process subproblems (each of which can be represented with a pair of indices marking subarray boundaries). Each iteration involves popping the top subproblem, splitting it in two (if it is big enough), and pushing the two new subproblems. The trick is that when pushing the new subproblems, we should first push the larger subproblem and then the smaller one. In this way, the sizes of the subproblems will at least double as we go down the stack; hence, the stack can have depth at most $O(\log n)$. We leave the details of this implementation as an exercise (P-12.56).

Pivot Selection

Our implementation in this section blindly picks the last element as the pivot at each level of the quick-sort recursion. This leaves it susceptible to the $\Theta(n^2)$-time worst case, most notably when the original sequence is already sorted, reverse sorted, or nearly sorted.

As described in Section 12.3.1, this can be improved upon by using a randomly chosen pivot for each partition step. In practice, another common technique for choosing a pivot is to use the median of tree values, taken respectively from the front, middle, and tail of the array. This ***median-of-three*** heuristic will more often choose a good pivot and computing a median of three may require lower overhead than selecting a pivot with a random number generator. For larger data sets, the median of more than three potential pivots might be computed.

Hybrid Approaches

Although quick-sort has very good performance on large data sets, it has rather high overhead on relatively small data sets. For example, the process of quick-sorting a sequence of eight elements, as illustrated in Figures 12.10 through 12.12, involves considerable bookkeeping. In practice, a simple algorithm like insertion-sort (Section 7.5) will execute faster when sorting such a short sequence.

It is therefore common, in optimized sorting implementations, to use a hybrid approach, with a divide-and-conquer algorithm used until the size of a subsequence falls below some threshold (perhaps 50 elements); insertion-sort can be directly invoked upon portions with length below the threshold. We will further discuss such practical considerations in Section 12.5, when comparing the performance of various sorting algorithms.

12.4   Studying Sorting through an Algorithmic Lens

Recapping our discussions on sorting to this point, we have described several methods with either a worst case or expected running time of $O(n \log n)$ on an input sequence of size n. These methods include merge-sort and quick-sort, described in this chapter, as well as heap-sort (Section 9.4.2). In this section, we study sorting as an algorithmic problem, addressing general issues about sorting algorithms.

12.4.1   Lower Bound for Sorting

A natural first question to ask is whether we can sort any faster than $O(n \log n)$ time. Interestingly, if the computational primitive used by a sorting algorithm is the comparison of two elements, this is in fact the best we can do—comparison-based sorting has an $\Omega(n \log n)$ worst-case lower bound on its running time. (Recall the notation $\Omega(\cdot)$ from Section 3.3.1.) To focus on the main cost of comparison-based sorting, let us only count comparisons, for the sake of a lower bound.

Suppose we are given a sequence $S = (x_0, x_1, \ldots, x_{n-1})$ that we wish to sort, and assume that all the elements of S are distinct (this is not really a restriction since we are deriving a lower bound). We do not care if S is implemented as an array or a linked list, for the sake of our lower bound, since we are only counting comparisons. Each time a sorting algorithm compares two elements x_i and x_j (that is, it asks, "is $x_i < x_j$?"), there are two outcomes: "yes" or "no." Based on the result of this comparison, the sorting algorithm may perform some internal calculations (which we are not counting here) and will eventually perform another comparison between two other elements of S, which again will have two outcomes. Therefore, we can represent a comparison-based sorting algorithm with a decision tree T (recall Example 8.6). That is, each internal node v in T corresponds to a comparison and the edges from position v to its children correspond to the computations resulting from either a "yes" or "no" answer. It is important to note that the hypothetical sorting algorithm in question probably has no explicit knowledge of the tree T. The tree simply represents all the possible sequences of comparisons that a sorting algorithm might make, starting from the first comparison (associated with the root) and ending with the last comparison (associated with the parent of an external node).

Each possible initial order, or ***permutation***, of the elements in S will cause our hypothetical sorting algorithm to execute a series of comparisons, traversing a path in T from the root to some external node. Let us associate with each external node v in T, then, the set of permutations of S that cause our sorting algorithm to end up in v. The most important observation in our lower-bound argument is that each external node v in T can represent the sequence of comparisons for at most one permutation of S. The justification for this claim is simple: If two different permutations P_1 and P_2 of S are associated with the same external node, then there are at least two objects x_i and x_j, such that x_i is before x_j in P_1 but x_i is after x_j in P_2. At the same time, the output associated with v must be a specific reordering of S, with either x_i or x_j appearing before the other. But if P_1 and P_2 both cause the sorting algorithm to output the elements of S in this order, then that implies there is a way to trick the algorithm into outputting x_i and x_j in the wrong order. Since this cannot be allowed by a correct sorting algorithm, each external node of T must be associated with exactly one permutation of S. We use this property of the decision tree associated with a sorting algorithm to prove the following result:

Proposition 12.4: *The running time of any comparison-based algorithm for sorting an n-element sequence is $\Omega(n \log n)$ in the worst case.*

Justification: The running time of a comparison-based sorting algorithm must be greater than or equal to the height of the decision tree T associated with this algorithm, as described above. (See Figure 12.15.) By the argument above, each external node in T must be associated with one permutation of S. Moreover, each permutation of S must result in a different external node of T. The number of permutations of n objects is $n! = n(n-1)(n-2)\cdots 2 \cdot 1$. Thus, T must have at least $n!$ external nodes. By Proposition 8.8, the height of T is at least $\log(n!)$. This immediately justifies the proposition, because there are at least $n/2$ terms that are greater than or equal to $n/2$ in the product $n!$; hence,

$$\log(n!) \geq \log\left(\left(\frac{n}{2}\right)^{\frac{n}{2}}\right) = \frac{n}{2}\log\frac{n}{2},$$

which is $\Omega(n \log n)$. ■

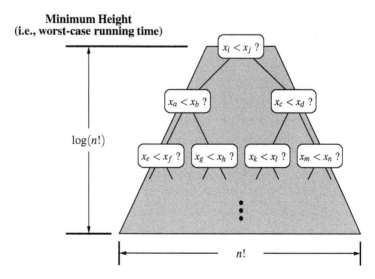

Figure 12.15: Visualizing the lower bound for comparison-based sorting.

12.4.2   Linear-Time Sorting: Bucket-Sort and Radix-Sort

In the previous section, we showed that $\Omega(n \log n)$ time is necessary, in the worst case, to sort an n-element sequence with a comparison-based sorting algorithm. A natural question to ask, then, is whether there are other kinds of sorting algorithms that can be designed to run asymptotically faster than $O(n \log n)$ time. Interestingly, such algorithms exist, but they require special assumptions about the input sequence to be sorted. Even so, such scenarios often arise in practice, such as when sorting integers from a known range or sorting character strings, so discussing them is worthwhile. In this section, we consider the problem of sorting a sequence of entries, each a key-value pair, where the keys have a restricted type.

Bucket-Sort

Consider a sequence S of n entries whose keys are integers in the range $[0, N-1]$, for some integer $N \geq 2$, and suppose that S should be sorted according to the keys of the entries. In this case, it is possible to sort S in $O(n+N)$ time. It might seem surprising, but this implies, for example, that if N is $O(n)$, then we can sort S in $O(n)$ time. Of course, the crucial point is that, because of the restrictive assumption about the format of the elements, we can avoid using comparisons.

The main idea is to use an algorithm called ***bucket-sort***, which is not based on comparisons, but on using keys as indices into a bucket array B that has cells indexed from 0 to $N-1$. An entry with key k is placed in the "bucket" $B[k]$, which itself is a sequence (of entries with key k). After inserting each entry of the input sequence S into its bucket, we can put the entries back into S in sorted order by enumerating the contents of the buckets $B[0], B[1], \ldots, B[N-1]$ in order. We describe the bucket-sort algorithm in Code Fragment 12.7.

Algorithm bucketSort(S):
>   ***Input:*** Sequence S of entries with integer keys in the range $[0, N-1]$
>   ***Output:*** Sequence S sorted in nondecreasing order of the keys
>
>   let B be an array of N sequences, each of which is initially empty
>   **for** each entry e in S **do**
>   k = the key of e
>   remove e from S and insert it at the end of bucket (sequence) B[k]
>   **for** i = 0 to N−1 **do**
>   **for** each entry e in sequence B[i] **do**
>   remove e from B[i] and insert it at the end of S

Code Fragment 12.7: Bucket-sort.

It is easy to see that bucket-sort runs in $O(n+N)$ time and uses $O(n+N)$ space. Hence, bucket-sort is efficient when the range N of values for the keys is small compared to the sequence size n, say $N = O(n)$ or $N = O(n\log n)$. Still, its performance deteriorates as N grows compared to n.

An important property of the bucket-sort algorithm is that it works correctly even if there are many different elements with the same key. Indeed, we described it in a way that anticipates such occurrences.

Stable Sorting

When sorting key-value pairs, an important issue is how equal keys are handled. Let $S = ((k_0, v_0), \ldots, (k_{n-1}, v_{n-1}))$ be a sequence of such entries. We say that a sorting algorithm is *stable* if, for any two entries (k_i, v_i) and (k_j, v_j) of S such that $k_i = k_j$ and (k_i, v_i) precedes (k_j, v_j) in S before sorting (that is, $i < j$), entry (k_i, v_i) also precedes entry (k_j, v_j) after sorting. Stability is important for a sorting algorithm because applications may want to preserve the initial order of elements with the same key.

Our informal description of bucket-sort in Code Fragment 12.7 guarantees stability as long as we ensure that all sequences act as queues, with elements processed and removed from the front of a sequence and inserted at the back. That is, when initially placing elements of S into buckets, we should process S from front to back, and add each element to the end of its bucket. Subsequently, when transferring elements from the buckets back to S, we should process each $B[i]$ from front to back, with those elements added to the end of S.

Radix-Sort

One of the reasons that stable sorting is so important is that it allows the bucket-sort approach to be applied to more general contexts than to sort integers. Suppose, for example, that we want to sort entries with keys that are pairs (k, l), where k and l are integers in the range $[0, N-1]$, for some integer $N \geq 2$. In a context such as this, it is common to define an order on these keys using the *lexicographic* (dictionary) convention, where $(k_1, l_1) < (k_2, l_2)$ if $k_1 < k_2$ or if $k_1 = k_2$ and $l_1 < l_2$ (see page 15). This is a pairwise version of the lexicographic comparison function, which can be applied to equal-length character strings, or to tuples of length d.

The *radix-sort* algorithm sorts a sequence S of entries with keys that are pairs, by applying a stable bucket-sort on the sequence twice; first using one component of the pair as the key when ordering and then using the second component. But which order is correct? Should we first sort on the k's (the first component) and then on the l's (the second component), or should it be the other way around?

To gain intuition before answering this question, we consider the following example.

Example 12.5: *Consider the following sequence S (we show only the keys):*

$$S = ((3,3),(1,5),(2,5),(1,2),(2,3),(1,7),(3,2),(2,2)).$$

If we sort S stably on the first component, then we get the sequence

$$S_1 = ((1,5),(1,2),(1,7),(2,5),(2,3),(2,2),(3,3),(3,2)).$$

If we then stably sort this sequence S_1 using the second component, we get the sequence

$$S_{1,2} = ((1,2),(2,2),(3,2),(2,3),(3,3),(1,5),(2,5),(1,7)),$$

which is unfortunately not a sorted sequence. On the other hand, if we first stably sort S using the second component, then we get the sequence

$$S_2 = ((1,2),(3,2),(2,2),(3,3),(2,3),(1,5),(2,5),(1,7)).$$

If we then stably sort sequence S_2 using the first component, we get the sequence

$$S_{2,1} = ((1,2),(1,5),(1,7),(2,2),(2,3),(2,5),(3,2),(3,3)),$$

which is indeed sequence S lexicographically ordered.

So, from this example, we are led to believe that we should first sort using the second component and then again using the first component. This intuition is exactly right. By first stably sorting by the second component and then again by the first component, we guarantee that if two entries are equal in the second sort (by the first component), then their relative order in the starting sequence (which is sorted by the second component) is preserved. Thus, the resulting sequence is guaranteed to be sorted lexicographically every time. We leave to a simple exercise (R-12.18) the determination of how this approach can be extended to triples and other d-tuples of numbers. We can summarize this section as follows:

Proposition 12.6: *Let S be a sequence of n key-value pairs, each of which has a key $(k_1, k_2, \ldots, k_d)$, where k_i is an integer in the range $[0, N-1]$ for some integer $N \geq 2$. We can sort S lexicographically in time $O(d(n+N))$ using radix-sort.*

Radix sort can be applied to any key that can be viewed as a composite of smaller pieces that are to be sorted lexicographically. For example, we can apply it to sort character strings of moderate length, as each individual character can be represented as an integer value. (Some care is needed to properly handle strings with varying lengths.)

12.5 Comparing Sorting Algorithms

At this point, it might be useful for us to take a moment and consider all the algorithms we have studied in this book to sort an n-element sequence.

Considering Running Time and Other Factors

We have studied several methods, such as insertion-sort, and selection-sort, that have $O(n^2)$-time behavior in the average and worst case. We have also studied several methods with $O(n \log n)$-time behavior, including heap-sort, merge-sort, and quick-sort. Finally, the bucket-sort and radix-sort methods run in linear time for certain types of keys. Certainly, the selection-sort algorithm is a poor choice in any application, since it runs in $O(n^2)$ time even in the best case. But, of the remaining sorting algorithms, which is the best?

As with many things in life, there is no clear "best" sorting algorithm from the remaining candidates. There are trade-offs involving efficiency, memory usage, and stability. The sorting algorithm best suited for a particular application depends on the properties of that application. In fact, the default sorting algorithm used by computing languages and systems has evolved greatly over time. We can offer some guidance and observations, therefore, based on the known properties of the "good" sorting algorithms.

Insertion-Sort

If implemented well, the running time of *insertion-sort* is $O(n + m)$, where m is the number of *inversions* (that is, the number of pairs of elements out of order). Thus, insertion-sort is an excellent algorithm for sorting small sequences (say, less than 50 elements), because insertion-sort is simple to program, and small sequences necessarily have few inversions. Also, insertion-sort is quite effective for sorting sequences that are already "almost" sorted. By "almost," we mean that the number of inversions is small. But the $O(n^2)$-time performance of insertion-sort makes it a poor choice outside of these special contexts.

Heap-Sort

Heap-sort, on the other hand, runs in $O(n \log n)$ time in the worst case, which is optimal for comparison-based sorting methods. Heap-sort can easily be made to execute in-place, and is a natural choice on small- and medium-sized sequences, when input data can fit into main memory. However, heap-sort tends to be outperformed by both quick-sort and merge-sort on larger sequences. A standard heap-sort does not provide a stable sort, because of the swapping of elements.

Quick-Sort

Although its $O(n^2)$-time worst-case performance makes *quick-sort* susceptible in real-time applications where we must make guarantees on the time needed to complete a sorting operation, we expect its performance to be $O(n \log n)$-time, and experimental studies have shown that it outperforms both heap-sort and merge-sort on many tests. Quick-sort does not naturally provide a stable sort, due to the swapping of elements during the partitioning step.

For decades quick-sort was the default choice for a general-purpose, in-memory sorting algorithm. Quick-sort was included as the qsort sorting utility provided in C language libraries, and was the basis for sorting utilities on Unix operating systems for many years. It was also the standard algorithm for sorting arrays in Java through version 6 of that language. (We discuss Java7 below.)

Merge-Sort

Merge-sort runs in $O(n \log n)$ time in the worst case. It is quite difficult to make merge-sort run in-place for arrays, and without that optimization the extra overhead of allocate a temporary array, and copying between the arrays is less attractive than in-place implementations of heap-sort and quick-sort for sequences that can fit entirely in a computer's main memory. Even so, merge-sort is an excellent algorithm for situations where the input is stratified across various levels of the computer's memory hierarchy (e.g., cache, main memory, external memory). In these contexts, the way that merge-sort processes runs of data in long merge streams makes the best use of all the data brought as a block into a level of memory, thereby reducing the total number of memory transfers.

The GNU sorting utility (and most current versions of the Linux operating system) relies on a multiway merge-sort variant. Since 2003, the standard sort method of Python's list class has been a hybrid approach named *Tim-sort* (designed by Tim Peters), which is essentially a bottom-up merge-sort that takes advantage of some initial runs in the data while using insertion-sort to build additional runs. Tim-sort has also become the default algorithm for sorting arrays in Java7.

Bucket-Sort and Radix-Sort

Finally, if an application involves sorting entries with small integer keys, character strings, or d-tuples of keys from a discrete range, then *bucket-sort* or *radix-sort* is an excellent choice, for it runs in $O(d(n+N))$ time, where $[0, N-1]$ is the range of integer keys (and $d = 1$ for bucket sort). Thus, if $d(n+N)$ is significantly "below" the $n \log n$ function, then this sorting method should run faster than even quick-sort, heap-sort, or merge-sort.

12.6 Python's Built-In Sorting Functions

Python provides two built-in ways to sort data. The first is the sort method of the list class. As an example, suppose that we define the following list:

colors = ['red', 'green', 'blue', 'cyan', 'magenta', 'yellow']

That method has the effect of reordering the elements of the list into order, as defined by the natural meaning of the < operator for those elements. In the above example, within elements that are strings, the natural order is defined alphabetically. Therefore, after a call to colors.sort( ), the order of the list would become:

['blue', 'cyan', 'green', 'magenta', 'red', 'yellow']

Python also supports a built-in function, named sorted, that can be used to produce a new ordered list containing the elements of any existing iterable container. Going back to our original example, the syntax sorted(colors) would return a new list of those colors, in alphabetical order, while leaving the contents of the original list unchanged. This second form is more general because it can be applied to any iterable object as a parameter; for example, sorted('green') returns ['e', 'e', 'g', 'n', 'r'].

12.6.1 Sorting According to a Key Function

There are many situations in which we wish to sort a list of elements, but according to some order other than the natural order defined by the < operator. For example, we might wish to sort a list of strings from shortest to longest (rather than alphabetically). Both of Python's built-in sort functions allow a caller to control the notion of order that is used when sorting. This is accomplished by providing, as an optional keyword parameter, a reference to a secondary function that computes a *key* for each element of the primary sequence; then the primary elements are sorted based on the natural order of their keys. (See pages 27 and 28 of Section 1.5.1 for a discussion of this technique in the context of the built-in min and max functions.)

A key function must be a one-parameter function that accepts an element as a parameter and returns a key. For example, we could use the built-in len function when sorting strings by length, as a call len(s) for string s returns its length. To sort our colors list based on length, we use the syntax colors.sort(key=len) to mutate the list or sorted(colors, key=len) to generate a new ordered list, while leaving the original alone. When sorted with the length function as a key, the contents are:

['red', 'blue', 'cyan', 'green', 'yellow', 'magenta']

These built-in functions also support a keyword parameter, reverse, that can be set to True to cause the sort order to be from largest to smallest.

Decorate-Sort-Undecorate Design Pattern

Python's support for a key function when sorting is implemented using what is known as the ***decorate-sort-undecorate design pattern***. It proceeds in 3 steps:

1. Each element of the list is temporarily replaced with a "decorated" version that includes the result of the key function applied to the element.
2. The list is sorted based upon the natural order of the keys (Figure 12.16).
3. The decorated elements are replaced by the original elements.

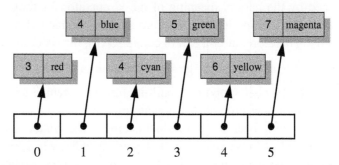

Figure 12.16: A list of "decorated" strings, using their lengths as decoration. This list has been sorted by those keys.

Although there is already built-in support for Python, if we were to implement such a strategy ourselves, a natural way to represent a "decorated" element is using the same composition strategy that we used for representing key-value pairs within a priority queue. Code Fragment 9.1 of Section 9.2.1 includes just such an _Item class, defined so that the < operator for items relies upon the given keys. With such a composition, we could trivially adapt any sorting algorithm to use the decorate-sort-undecorate pattern, as demonstrated in Code Fragment 12.8 with merge-sort.

```
1  def decorated_merge_sort(data, key=None):
2    """Demonstration of the decorate-sort-undecorate pattern."""
3    if key is not None:
4      for j in range(len(data)):
5        data[j] = _Item(key(data[j]), data[j])      # decorate each element
6    merge_sort(data)                                 # sort with existing algorithm
7    if key is not None:
8      for j in range(len(data)):
9        data[j] = data[j]._value                     # undecorate each element
```

Code Fragment 12.8: An approach for implementing the decorate-sort-undecorate pattern based upon the array-based merge-sort of Code Fragment 12.1. The _Item class is identical to that which was used in the PriorityQueueBase class. (See Code Fragment 9.1.)

12.7 Selection

As important as it is, sorting is not the only interesting problem dealing with a total order relation on a set of elements. There are a number of applications in which we are interested in identifying a single element in terms of its rank relative to the sorted order of the entire set. Examples include identifying the minimum and maximum elements, but we may also be interested in, say, identifying the ***median*** element, that is, the element such that half of the other elements are smaller and the remaining half are larger. In general, queries that ask for an element with a given rank are called ***order statistics***.

Defining the Selection Problem

In this section, we discuss the general order-statistic problem of selecting the kth smallest element from an unsorted collection of n comparable elements. This is known as the ***selection*** problem. Of course, we can solve this problem by sorting the collection and then indexing into the sorted sequence at index $k - 1$. Using the best comparison-based sorting algorithms, this approach would take $O(n \log n)$ time, which is obviously an overkill for the cases where $k = 1$ or $k = n$ (or even $k = 2$, $k = 3$, $k = n - 1$, or $k = n - 5$), because we can easily solve the selection problem for these values of k in $O(n)$ time. Thus, a natural question to ask is whether we can achieve an $O(n)$ running time for all values of k (including the interesting case of finding the median, where $k = \lfloor n/2 \rfloor$).

12.7.1 Prune-and-Search

We can indeed solve the selection problem in $O(n)$ time for any value of k. Moreover, the technique we use to achieve this result involves an interesting algorithmic design pattern. This design pattern is known as ***prune-and-search*** or ***decrease-and-conquer***. In applying this design pattern, we solve a given problem that is defined on a collection of n objects by pruning away a fraction of the n objects and recursively solving the smaller problem. When we have finally reduced the problem to one defined on a constant-sized collection of objects, we then solve the problem using some brute-force method. Returning back from all the recursive calls completes the construction. In some cases, we can avoid using recursion, in which case we simply iterate the prune-and-search reduction step until we can apply a brute-force method and stop. Incidentally, the binary search method described in Section 4.1.3 is an example of the prune-and-search design pattern.

12.7.2   Randomized Quick-Select

In applying the prune-and-search pattern to finding the kth smallest element in an unordered sequence of n elements, we describe a simple and practical algorithm, known as *randomized quick-select*. This algorithm runs in $O(n)$ *expected* time, taken over all possible random choices made by the algorithm; this expectation does not depend whatsoever on any randomness assumptions about the input distribution. We note though that randomized quick-select runs in $O(n^2)$ time in the *worst case*, the justification of which is left as an exercise (R-12.24). We also provide an exercise (C-12.55) for modifying randomized quick-select to define a *deterministic* selection algorithm that runs in $O(n)$ *worst-case* time. The existence of this deterministic algorithm is mostly of theoretical interest, however, since the constant factor hidden by the big-Oh notation is relatively large in that case.

Suppose we are given an unsorted sequence S of n comparable elements together with an integer $k \in [1,n]$. At a high level, the quick-select algorithm for finding the kth smallest element in S is similar to the randomized quick-sort algorithm described in Section 12.3.1. We pick a "pivot" element from S at random and use this to subdivide S into three subsequences L, E, and G, storing the elements of S less than, equal to, and greater than the pivot, respectively. In the prune step, we determine which of these subsets contains the desired element, based on the value of k and the sizes of those subsets. We then recur on the appropriate subset, noting that the desired element's rank in the subset may differ from its rank in the full set. An implementation of randomized quick-select is shown in Code Fragment 12.9.

```
1   def quick_select(S, k):
2     """Return the kth smallest element of list S, for k from 1 to len(S)."""
3     if len(S) == 1:
4       return S[0]
5     pivot = random.choice(S)              # pick random pivot element from S
6     L = [x for x in S if x < pivot]       # elements less than pivot
7     E = [x for x in S if x == pivot]      # elements equal to pivot
8     G = [x for x in S if pivot < x]       # elements greater than pivot
9     if k <= len(L):
10      return quick_select(L, k)           # kth smallest lies in L
11    elif k <= len(L) + len(E):
12      return pivot                        # kth smallest equal to pivot
13    else:
14      j = k − len(L) − len(E)             # new selection parameter
15      return quick_select(G, j)           # kth smallest is jth in G
```

Code Fragment 12.9: Randomized quick-select algorithm.

12.7.3 Analyzing Randomized Quick-Select

Showing that randomized quick-select runs in $O(n)$ time requires a simple probabilistic argument. The argument is based on the *linearity of expectation*, which states that if X and Y are random variables and c is a number, then

$$E(X+Y) = E(X) + E(Y) \qquad \text{and} \qquad E(cX) = cE(X),$$

where we use $E(\mathcal{Z})$ to denote the expected value of the expression $\mathcal{Z}$.

Let $t(n)$ be the running time of randomized quick-select on a sequence of size n. Since this algorithm depends on random events, its running time, $t(n)$, is a random variable. We want to bound $E(t(n))$, the expected value of $t(n)$. Say that a recursive invocation of our algorithm is "good" if it partitions S so that the size of each of L and G is at most $3n/4$. Clearly, a recursive call is good with probability at least $1/2$. Let $g(n)$ denote the number of consecutive recursive calls we make, including the present one, before we get a good one. Then we can characterize $t(n)$ using the following *recurrence equation*:

$$t(n) \leq bn \cdot g(n) + t(3n/4),$$

where $b \geq 1$ is a constant. Applying the linearity of expectation for $n > 1$, we get

$$E(t(n)) \leq E(bn \cdot g(n) + t(3n/4)) = bn \cdot E(g(n)) + E(t(3n/4)).$$

Since a recursive call is good with probability at least $1/2$, and whether a recursive call is good or not is independent of its parent call being good, the expected value of $g(n)$ is at most the expected number of times we must flip a fair coin before it comes up "heads." That is, $E(g(n)) \leq 2$. Thus, if we let $T(n)$ be shorthand for $E(t(n))$, then we can write the case for $n > 1$ as

$$T(n) \leq T(3n/4) + 2bn.$$

To convert this relation into a closed form, let us iteratively apply this inequality assuming n is large. So, for example, after two applications,

$$T(n) \leq T((3/4)^2 n) + 2b(3/4)n + 2bn.$$

At this point, we should see that the general case is

$$T(n) \leq 2bn \cdot \sum_{i=0}^{\lceil \log_{4/3} n \rceil} (3/4)^i.$$

In other words, the expected running time is at most $2bn$ times a geometric sum whose base is a positive number less than 1. Thus, by Proposition 3.5, $T(n)$ is $O(n)$.

Proposition 12.7: *The expected running time of randomized quick-select on a sequence S of size n is $O(n)$, assuming two elements of S can be compared in $O(1)$ time.*

12.8   Exercises

For help with exercises, please visit the site, www.wiley.com/college/goodrich.

Reinforcement

R-12.1 Give a complete justification of Proposition 12.1.

R-12.2 In the merge-sort tree shown in Figures 12.2 through 12.4, some edges are drawn as arrows. What is the meaning of a downward arrow? How about an upward arrow?

R-12.3 Show that the running time of the merge-sort algorithm on an n-element sequence is $O(n \log n)$, even when n is not a power of 2.

R-12.4 Is our array-based implementation of merge-sort given in Section 12.2.2 stable? Explain why or why not.

R-12.5 Is our linked-list-based implementation of merge-sort given in Code Fragment 12.3 stable? Explain why or why not.

R-12.6 An algorithm that sorts key-value entries by key is said to be *straggling* if, any time two entries e_i and e_j have equal keys, but e_i appears before e_j in the input, then the algorithm places e_i after e_j in the output. Describe a change to the merge-sort algorithm in Section 12.2 to make it straggling.

R-12.7 Suppose we are given two n-element sorted sequences A and B each with distinct elements, but potentially some elements that are in both sequences. Describe an $O(n)$-time method for computing a sequence representing the union $A \cup B$ (with no duplicates) as a sorted sequence.

R-12.8 Suppose we modify the deterministic version of the quick-sort algorithm so that, instead of selecting the last element in an n-element sequence as the pivot, we choose the element at index $\lfloor n/2 \rfloor$. What is the running time of this version of quick-sort on a sequence that is already sorted?

R-12.9 Consider a modification of the deterministic version of the quick-sort algorithm where we choose the element at index $\lfloor n/2 \rfloor$ as our pivot. Describe the kind of sequence that would cause this version of quick-sort to run in $\Omega(n^2)$ time.

R-12.10 Show that the best-case running time of quick-sort on a sequence of size n with distinct elements is $\Omega(n \log n)$.

R-12.11 Suppose function inplace_quick_sort is executed on a sequence with duplicate elements. Prove that the algorithm still correctly sorts the input sequence. What happens in the partition step when there are elements equal to the pivot? What is the running time of the algorithm if all the input elements are equal?

R-12.12 If the outermost while loop of our implementation of inplace_quick_sort (line 7 of Code Fragment 12.6) were changed to use condition left < right (rather than left <= right), there would be a flaw. Explain the flaw and give a specific input sequence on which such an implementation fails.

R-12.13 If the conditional at line 14 of our inplace_quick_sort implementation of Code Fragment 12.6 were changed to use condition left < right (rather than left <= right), there would be a flaw. Explain the flaw and give a specific input sequence on which such an implementation fails.

R-12.14 Following our analysis of randomized quick-sort in Section 12.3.1, show that the probability that a given input element x belongs to more than $2 \log n$ subproblems in size group i is at most $1/n^2$.

R-12.15 Of the $n!$ possible inputs to a given comparison-based sorting algorithm, what is the absolute maximum number of inputs that could be correctly sorted with just n comparisons?

R-12.16 Jonathan has a comparison-based sorting algorithm that sorts the first k elements of a sequence of size n in $O(n)$ time. Give a big-Oh characterization of the biggest that k can be?

R-12.17 Is the bucket-sort algorithm in-place? Why or why not?

R-12.18 Describe a radix-sort method for lexicographically sorting a sequence S of triplets (k, l, m), where k, l, and m are integers in the range $[0, N-1]$, for some $N \geq 2$. How could this scheme be extended to sequences of d-tuples $(k_1, k_2, \ldots, k_d)$, where each k_i is an integer in the range $[0, N-1]$?

R-12.19 Suppose S is a sequence of n values, each equal to 0 or 1. How long will it take to sort S with the merge-sort algorithm? What about quick-sort?

R-12.20 Suppose S is a sequence of n values, each equal to 0 or 1. How long will it take to sort S stably with the bucket-sort algorithm?

R-12.21 Given a sequence S of n values, each equal to 0 or 1, describe an in-place method for sorting S.

R-12.22 Give an example input list that requires merge-sort and heap-sort to take $O(n \log n)$ time to sort, but insertion-sort runs in $O(n)$ time. What if you reverse this list?

R-12.23 What is the best algorithm for sorting each of the following: general comparable objects, long character strings, 32-bit integers, double-precision floating-point numbers, and bytes? Justify your answer.

R-12.24 Show that the worst-case running time of quick-select on an n-element sequence is $\Omega(n^2)$.

Creativity

C-12.25 Linda claims to have an algorithm that takes an input sequence S and produces an output sequence T that is a sorting of the n elements in S.

    a. Give an algorithm, is_sorted, that tests in $O(n)$ time if T is sorted.

    b. Explain why the algorithm is_sorted is not sufficient to prove a particular output T to Linda's algorithm is a sorting of S.

    c. Describe what additional information Linda's algorithm could output so that her algorithm's correctness could be established on any given S and T in $O(n)$ time.

C-12.26 Describe and analyze an efficient method for removing all duplicates from a collection A of n elements.

C-12.27 Augment the PositionalList class (see Section 7.4) to support a method named merge with the following behavior. If A and B are PositionalList instances whose elements are sorted, the syntax A.merge(B) should merge all elements of B into A so that A remains sorted and B becomes empty. Your implementation must accomplish the merge by relinking existing nodes; you are not to create any new nodes.

C-12.28 Augment the PositionalList class (see Section 7.4) to support a method named sort that sorts the elements of a list by relinking existing nodes; you are not to create any new nodes. You may use your choice of sorting algorithm.

C-12.29 Implement a bottom-up merge-sort for a collection of items by placing each item in its own queue, and then repeatedly merging pairs of queues until all items are sorted within a single queue.

C-12.30 Modify our in-place quick-sort implementation of Code Fragment 12.6 to be a *randomized* version of the algorithm, as discussed in Section 12.3.1.

C-12.31 Consider a version of deterministic quick-sort where we pick as our pivot the median of the d last elements in the input sequence of n elements, for a fixed, constant odd number $d \geq 3$. What is the asymptotic worst-case running time of quick-sort in this case?

C-12.32 Another way to analyze randomized quick-sort is to use a *recurrence equation*. In this case, we let $T(n)$ denote the expected running time of randomized quick-sort, and we observe that, because of the worst-case partitions for good and bad splits, we can write

$$T(n) \leq \frac{1}{2}\left(T(3n/4) + T(n/4)\right) + \frac{1}{2}\left(T(n-1)\right) + bn,$$

where bn is the time needed to partition a list for a given pivot and concatenate the result sublists after the recursive calls return. Show, by induction, that $T(n)$ is $O(n\log n)$.

C-12.33 Our high-level description of quick-sort describes partitioning the elements into three sets L, E, and G, having keys less than, equal to, or greater than the pivot, respectively. However, our in-place quick-sort implementation of Code Fragment 12.6 does not gather all elements equal to the pivot into a set E. An alternative strategy for an in-place, three-way partition is as follows. Loop through the elements from left to right maintaining indices i, j, and k and the invariant that all elements of slice S[0:i] are strictly less than the pivot, all elements of slice S[i:j] are equal to the pivot, and all elements of slice S[j:k] are strictly greater than the pivot; elements of S[k:n] are yet unclassified. In each pass of the loop, classify one additional element, performing a constant number of swaps as needed. Implement an in-place quick-sort using this strategy.

C-12.34 Suppose we are given an n-element sequence S such that each element in S represents a different vote for president, where each vote is given as an integer representing a particular candidate, yet the integers may be arbitrarily large (even if the number of candidates is not). Design an $O(n \log n)$-time algorithm to see who wins the election S represents, assuming the candidate with the most votes wins.

C-12.35 Consider the voting problem from Exercise C-12.34, but now suppose that we know the number $k < n$ of candidates running, even though the integer IDs for those candidates can be arbitrarily large. Describe an $O(n \log k)$-time algorithm for determining who wins the election.

C-12.36 Consider the voting problem from Exercise C-12.34, but now suppose the integers 1 to k are used to identify $k < n$ candidates. Design an $O(n)$-time algorithm to determine who wins the election.

C-12.37 Show that any comparison-based sorting algorithm can be made to be stable without affecting its asymptotic running time.

C-12.38 Suppose we are given two sequences A and B of n elements, possibly containing duplicates, on which a total order relation is defined. Describe an efficient algorithm for determining if A and B contain the same set of elements. What is the running time of this method?

C-12.39 Given an array A of n integers in the range $[0, n^2 - 1]$, describe a simple method for sorting A in $O(n)$ time.

C-12.40 Let $S_1, S_2, \ldots, S_k$ be k different sequences whose elements have integer keys in the range $[0, N - 1]$, for some parameter $N \geq 2$. Describe an algorithm that produces k respective sorted sequences in $O(n + N)$ time, were n denotes the sum of the sizes of those sequences.

C-12.41 Given a sequence S of n elements, on which a total order relation is defined, describe an efficient method for determining whether there are two equal elements in S. What is the running time of your method?

C-12.42 Let S be a sequence of n elements on which a total order relation is defined. Recall that an *inversion* in S is a pair of elements x and y such that x appears before y in S but $x > y$. Describe an algorithm running in $O(n\log n)$ time for determining the *number* of inversions in S.

C-12.43 Let S be a sequence of n integers. Describe a method for printing out all the pairs of inversions in S in $O(n+k)$ time, where k is the number of such inversions.

C-12.44 Let S be a random permutation of n distinct integers. Argue that the expected running time of insertion-sort on S is $\Omega(n^2)$. (Hint: Note that half of the elements ranked in the top half of a sorted version of S are expected to be in the first half of S.)

C-12.45 Let A and B be two sequences of n integers each. Given an integer m, describe an $O(n\log n)$-time algorithm for determining if there is an integer a in A and an integer b in B such that $m = a+b$.

C-12.46 Given a set of n integers, describe and analyze a fast method for finding the $\lceil \log n \rceil$ integers closest to the median.

C-12.47 Bob has a set A of n nuts and a set B of n bolts, such that each nut in A has a unique matching bolt in B. Unfortunately, the nuts in A all look the same, and the bolts in B all look the same as well. The only kind of a comparison that Bob can make is to take a nut-bolt pair (a,b), such that a is in A and b is in B, and test it to see if the threads of a are larger, smaller, or a perfect match with the threads of b. Describe and analyze an efficient algorithm for Bob to match up all of his nuts and bolts.

C-12.48 Our quick-select implementation can be made more space-efficient by initially computing only the *counts* for sets L, E, and G, creating only the new subset that will be needed for recursion. Implement such a version.

C-12.49 Describe an in-place version of the quick-select algorithm in pseudo-code, assuming that you are allowed to modify the order of elements.

C-12.50 Show how to use a deterministic $O(n)$-time selection algorithm to sort a sequence of n elements in $O(n\log n)$ *worst-case* time.

C-12.51 Given an unsorted sequence S of n comparable elements, and an integer k, give an $O(n\log k)$ expected-time algorithm for finding the $O(k)$ elements that have rank $\lceil n/k \rceil$, $2\lceil n/k \rceil$, $3\lceil n/k \rceil$, and so on.

C-12.52 Space aliens have given us a function, alien_split, that can take a sequence S of n integers and partition S in $O(n)$ time into sequences $S_1, S_2, \ldots, S_k$ of size at most $\lceil n/k \rceil$ each, such that the elements in S_i are less than or equal to every element in S_{i+1}, for $i = 1, 2, \ldots, k-1$, for a fixed number, $k < n$. Show how to use alien_split to sort S in $O(n\log n/\log k)$ time.

C-12.53 Read documenation of the reverse keyword parameter of Python's sorting functions, and describe how the decorate-sort-undecorate paradigm could be used to implement it, without assuming anything about the key type.

C-12.54 Show that randomized quick-sort runs in $O(n \log n)$ time with probability at least $1 - 1/n$, that is, with **high probability**, by answering the following:

    a. For each input element x, define $C_{i,j}(x)$ to be a 0/1 random variable that is 1 if and only if element x is in $j + 1$ subproblems that belong to size group i. Argue why we need not define $C_{i,j}$ for $j > n$.

    b. Let $X_{i,j}$ be a 0/1 random variable that is 1 with probability $1/2^j$, independent of any other events, and let $L = \lceil \log_{4/3} n \rceil$. Argue why $\sum_{i=0}^{L-1} \sum_{j=0}^{n} C_{i,j}(x) \leq \sum_{i=0}^{L-1} \sum_{j=0}^{n} X_{i,j}$.

    c. Show that the expected value of $\sum_{i=0}^{L-1} \sum_{j=0}^{n} X_{i,j}$ is $(2 - 1/2^n)L$.

    d. Show that the probability that $\sum_{i=0}^{L} \sum_{j=0}^{n} X_{i,j} > 4L$ is at most $1/n^2$, using the **Chernoff bound** that states that if X is the sum of a finite number of independent 0/1 random variables with expected value $\mu > 0$, then $\Pr(X > 2\mu) < (4/e)^{-\mu}$, where $e = 2.71828128\ldots$.

    e. Argue why the previous claim proves randomized quick-sort runs in $O(n \log n)$ time with probability at least $1 - 1/n$.

C-12.55 We can make the quick-select algorithm deterministic, by choosing the pivot of an n-element sequence as follows:

> Partition the set S into $\lceil n/5 \rceil$ groups of size 5 each (except possibly for one group). Sort each little set and identify the median element in this set. From this set of $\lceil n/5 \rceil$ "baby" medians, apply the selection algorithm recursively to find the median of the baby medians. Use this element as the pivot and proceed as in the quick-select algorithm.

Show that this deterministic quick-select algorithm runs in $O(n)$ time by answering the following questions (please ignore floor and ceiling functions if that simplifies the mathematics, for the asymptotics are the same either way):

    a. How many baby medians are less than or equal to the chosen pivot? How many are greater than or equal to the pivot?

    b. For each baby median less than or equal to the pivot, how many other elements are less than or equal to the pivot? Is the same true for those greater than or equal to the pivot?

    c. Argue why the method for finding the deterministic pivot and using it to partition S takes $O(n)$ time.

    d. Based on these estimates, write a recurrence equation to bound the worst-case running time $t(n)$ for this selection algorithm (note that in the worst case there are two recursive calls—one to find the median of the baby medians and one to recur on the larger of L and G).

    e. Using this recurrence equation, show by induction that $t(n)$ is $O(n)$.

Projects

P-12.56 Implement a nonrecursive, in-place version of the quick-sort algorithm, as described at the end of Section 12.3.2.

P-12.57 Experimentally compare the performance of in-place quick-sort and a version of quick-sort that is not in-place.

P-12.58 Perform a series of benchmarking tests on a version of merge-sort and quick-sort to determine which one is faster. Your tests should include sequences that are "random" as well as "almost" sorted.

P-12.59 Implement deterministic and randomized versions of the quick-sort algorithm and perform a series of benchmarking tests to see which one is faster. Your tests should include sequences that are very "random" looking as well as ones that are "almost" sorted.

P-12.60 Implement an in-place version of insertion-sort and an in-place version of quick-sort. Perform benchmarking tests to determine the range of values of n where quick-sort is on average better than insertion-sort.

P-12.61 Design and implement a version of the bucket-sort algorithm for sorting a list of n entries with integer keys taken from the range $[0, N-1]$, for $N \geq 2$. The algorithm should run in $O(n+N)$ time.

P-12.62 Design and implement an animation for one of the sorting algorithms described in this chapter. Your animation should illustrate the key properties of this algorithm in an intuitive manner.

Chapter Notes

Knuth's classic text on *Sorting and Searching* [65] contains an extensive history of the sorting problem and algorithms for solving it. Huang and Langston [53] show how to merge two sorted lists in-place in linear time. The standard quick-sort algorithm is due to Hoare [51]. Several optimizations for quick-sort are described by Bentley and McIlroy [16]. More information about randomization, including Chernoff bounds, can be found in the appendix and the book by Motwani and Raghavan [80]. The quick-sort analysis given in this chapter is a combination of the analysis given in an earlier Java edition of this book and the analysis of Kleinberg and Tardos [60]. Exercise C-12.32 is due to Littman. Gonnet and Baeza-Yates [44] analyze and compare experimentally several sorting algorithms. The term "prune-and-search" comes originally from the computational geometry literature (such as in the work of Clarkson [26] and Megiddo [75]). The term "decrease-and-conquer" is from Levitin [70].

Chapter

13

Text Processing

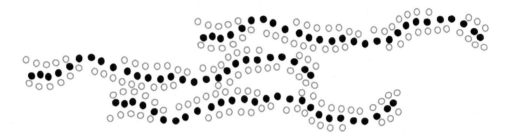

Contents

13.1   Abundance of Digitized Text

Despite the wealth of multimedia information, text processing remains one of the dominant functions of computers. Computer are used to edit, store, and display documents, and to transport documents over the Internet. Furthermore, digital systems are used to archive a wide range of textual information, and new data is being generated at a rapidly increasing pace. A large corpus can readily surpass a petabyte of data (which is equivalent to a thousand terabytes, or a million gigabytes). Common examples of digital collections that include textual information are:

- Snapshots of the World Wide Web, as Internet document formats HTML and XML are primarily text formats, with added tags for multimedia content
- All documents stored locally on a user's computer
- Email archives
- Customer reviews
- Compilations of status updates on social networking sites such as Facebook
- Feeds from microblogging sites such as Twitter and Tumblr

These collections include written text from hundreds of international languages. Furthermore, there are large data sets (such as DNA) that can be viewed computationally as "strings" even though they are not language.

In this chapter we explore some of the fundamental algorithms that can be used to efficiently analyze and process large textual data sets. In addition to having interesting applications, text-processing algorithms also highlight some important algorithmic design patterns.

We begin by examining the problem of searching for a pattern as a substring of a larger piece of text, for example, when searching for a word in a document. The pattern-matching problem gives rise to the ***brute-force method***, which is often inefficient but has wide applicability.

Next, we introduce an algorithmic technique known as ***dynamic programming***, which can be applied in certain settings to solve a problem in polynomial time that appears at first to require exponential time to solve. We demonstrate the application on this technique to the problem of finding partial matches between strings that may be similar but not perfectly aligned. This problem arises when making suggestions for a misspelled word, or when trying to match related genetic samples.

Because of the massive size of textual data sets, the issue of compression is important, both in minimizing the number of bits that need to be communicated through a network and to reduce the long-term storage requirements for archives. For text compression, we can apply the ***greedy method***, which often allows us to approximate solutions to hard problems, and for some problems (such as in text compression) actually gives rise to optimal algorithms.

Finally, we examine several special-purpose data structures that can be used to better organize textual data in order to support more efficient run-time queries.

13.1.1 Notations for Strings and the Python str Class

We use character strings as a model for text when discuss algorithms for text processing. Character strings can come from a wide variety of sources, including scientific, linguistic, and Internet applications. Indeed, the following are examples of such strings:

$$S = \text{"CGTAAACTGCTTTAATCAAACGC"}$$
$$T = \text{"http://www.wiley.com"}$$

The first string, S, comes from DNA applications, and the second string, T, is the Internet address (URL) for the publisher of this book. We refer to Appendix A for an overview of the operations supported by Python's **str** class.

To allow fairly general notions of a string in our algorithm descriptions, we only assume that characters of a string come from a known *alphabet*, which we denote as Σ. For example, in the context of DNA, there are four symbols in the standard alphabet, $\Sigma = \{A, C, G, T\}$. This alphabet Σ can, of course, be a subset of the ASCII or Unicode character sets, but it could also be something more general. Although we assume that an alphabet has a fixed finite size, denoted as $|\Sigma|$, that size can be nontrivial, as with Python's treatment of the Unicode alphabet, which allows for more than a million distinct characters. We therefore consider the impact of $|\Sigma|$ in our asymptotic analysis of text-processing algorithms.

Several string-processing operations involve breaking large strings into smaller strings. In order to be able to speak about the pieces that result from such operations, we will rely on Python's *indexing* and *slicing* notations. For the sake of notation, we let S denote a string of length n. In that case, we let S[j] refer to the character at index j for $0 \leq j \leq n-1$. We let notation S[j:k] for $0 \leq j \leq k \leq n$ denote the slice (or *substring*) of S consisting of characters S[j] up to and including S[k−1], but not S[k]. By this definition, note that substring S[j : j + m] has length m and that substring S[j:j] is trivially the *null string*, having length 0. In accordance with Python conventions, the substring S[j:k] is also the null string when $k < j$.

In order to distinguish some special kinds of substrings, let us refer to any substring of the form S[0:k] for $0 \leq k \leq n$ as a *prefix* of S; such a prefix results in Python when the first index is omitted from slice notation, as in S[:k]. Similarly, any substring of the form S[j:n] for $0 \leq j \leq n$ is a *suffix* of S; such a suffix results in Python when the second index is omitted from slice notation, as in S[j:]. For example, if we again take S to be the string of DNA given above, then "CGTAA" is a prefix of S, "CGC" is a suffix of S, and "C" is both a prefix and suffix of S. Note that the null string is a prefix and a suffix of any string.

13.2   Pattern-Matching Algorithms

In the classic ***pattern-matching*** problem, we are given a ***text*** string T of length n and a ***pattern*** string P of length m, and want to find whether P is a substring of T. If so, we may want to find the lowest index j within T at which P begins, such that T[j:j+m] equals P, or perhaps to find *all* indices of T at which pattern P begins.

The pattern-matching problem is inherent to many behaviors of Python's **str** class, such as P in T, T.find(P), T.index(P), T.count(P), and is a subtask of more complex behaviors such as T.partition(P), T.split(P), and T.replace(P, Q).

In this section, we present three pattern-matching algorithms (with increasing levels of difficulty). For simplicity, we model the outward semantics of our functions upon the find method of the string class, returning the lowest index at which the pattern begins, or -1 if the pattern is not found.

13.2.1   Brute Force

The ***brute-force*** algorithmic design pattern is a powerful technique for algorithm design when we have something we wish to search for or when we wish to optimize some function. When applying this technique in a general situation, we typically enumerate all possible configurations of the inputs involved and pick the best of all these enumerated configurations.

In applying this technique to design a brute-force pattern-matching algorithm, we derive what is probably the first algorithm that we might think of for solving the problem—we simply test all the possible placements of P relative to T. An implementation of this algorithm is shown in Code Fragment 13.1.

```
1  def find_brute(T, P):
2    """Return the lowest index of T at which substring P begins (or else -1)."""
3    n, m = len(T), len(P)              # introduce convenient notations
4    for i in range(n−m+1):            # try every potential starting index within T
5      k = 0                           # an index into pattern P
6      while k < m and T[i + k] == P[k]:        # kth character of P matches
7        k += 1
8      if k == m:                      # if we reached the end of pattern,
9        return i                      # substring T[i:i+m] matches P
10   return −1                         # failed to find a match starting with any i
```

Code Fragment 13.1: An implementation of brute-force pattern-matching algorithm.

Performance

The analysis of the brute-force pattern-matching algorithm could not be simpler. It consists of two nested loops, with the outer loop indexing through all possible starting indices of the pattern in the text, and the inner loop indexing through each character of the pattern, comparing it to its potentially corresponding character in the text. Thus, the correctness of the brute-force pattern-matching algorithm follows immediately from this exhaustive search approach.

The running time of brute-force pattern matching in the worst case is not good, however, because, for each candidate index in T, we can perform up to m character comparisons to discover that P does not match T at the current index. Referring to Code Fragment 13.1, we see that the outer **for** loop is executed at most $n - m + 1$ times, and the inner **while** loop is executed at most m times. Thus, the worst-case running time of the brute-force method is $O(nm)$.

Example 13.1: *Suppose we are given the text string*

$$T = \text{"abacaabaccabacabaabb"}$$

and the pattern string

$$P = \text{"abacab"}$$

Figure 13.1 illustrates the execution of the brute-force pattern-matching algorithm on T and P.

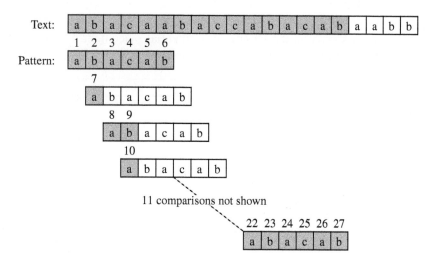

Figure 13.1: Example run of the brute-force pattern-matching algorithm. The algorithm performs 27 character comparisons, indicated above with numerical labels.

13.2.2　The Boyer-Moore Algorithm

At first, it might seem that it is always necessary to examine every character in T in order to locate a pattern P as a substring or to rule out its existence. But this is not always the case. The *Boyer-Moore* pattern-matching algorithm, which we study in this section, can sometimes avoid comparisons between P and a sizable fraction of the characters in T. In this section, we describe a simplified version of the original algorithm by Boyer and Moore.

The main idea of the Boyer-Moore algorithm is to improve the running time of the brute-force algorithm by adding two potentially time-saving heuristics. Roughly stated, these heuristics are as follows:

Looking-Glass Heuristic: When testing a possible placement of P against T, begin the comparisons from the end of P and move backward to the front of P.

Character-Jump Heuristic: During the testing of a possible placement of P within T, a mismatch of text character T[i]=c with the corresponding pattern character P[k] is handled as follows. If c is not contained anywhere in P, then shift P completely past T[i] (for it cannot match any character in P). Otherwise, shift P until an occurrence of character c in P gets aligned with T[i].

We will formalize these heuristics shortly, but at an intuitive level, they work as an integrated team. The looking-glass heuristic sets up the other heuristic to allow us to avoid comparisons between P and whole groups of characters in T. In this case at least, we can get to the destination faster by going backwards, for if we encounter a mismatch during the consideration of P at a certain location in T, then we are likely to avoid lots of needless comparisons by significantly shifting P relative to T using the character-jump heuristic. The character-jump heuristic pays off big if it can be applied early in the testing of a potential placement of P against T. Figure 13.2 demonstrates a few simple applications of these heuristics.

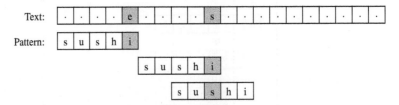

Figure 13.2: A simple example demonstrating the intuition of the Boyer-Moore pattern-matching algorithm. The original comparison results in a mismatch with character e of the text. Because that character is nowhere in the pattern, the entire pattern is shifted beyond its location. The second comparison is also a mismatch, but the mismatched character s occurs elsewhere in the pattern. The pattern is next shifted so that its last occurrence of s is aligned with the corresponding s in the text. The remainder of the process is not illustrated in this figure.

The example of Figure 13.2 is rather basic, because it only involves mismatches with the last character of the pattern. More generally, when a match is found for that last character, the algorithm continues by trying to extend the match with the second-to-last character of the pattern in its current alignment. That process continues until either matching the entire pattern, or finding a mismatch at some interior position of the pattern.

If a mismatch is found, and the mismatched character of the text does not occur in the pattern, we shift the entire pattern beyond that location, as originally illustrated in Figure 13.2. If the mismatched character occurs elsewhere in the pattern, we must consider two possible subcases depending on whether its last occurrence is before or after the character of the pattern that was aligned with the mismatched. Those two cases are illustrated in Figure 13.3.

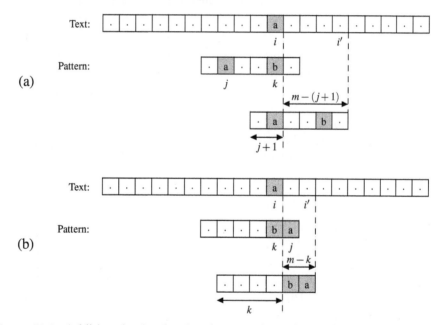

Figure 13.3: Additional rules for the character-jump heuristic of the Boyer-Moore algorithm. We let i represent the index of the mismatched character in the text, k represent the corresponding index in the pattern, and j represent the index of the last occurrence of $T[i]$ within the pattern. We distinguish two cases: (a) $j < k$, in which case we shift the pattern by $k - j$ units, and thus, index i advances by $m - (j+1)$ units; (b) $j > k$, in which case we shift the pattern by one unit, and index i advances by $m - k$ units.

In the case of Figure 13.3(b), we slide the pattern only one unit. It would be more productive to slide it rightward until finding another occurrence of mismatched character $T[i]$ in the pattern, but we do not wish to take time to search for another occurrence. The efficiency of the Boyer-Moore algorithm relies on creating a lookup table that quickly determines where a mismatched character occurs elsewhere in the pattern. In particular, we define a function $last(c)$ as

- If c is in P, $last(c)$ is the index of the last (rightmost) occurrence of c in P. Otherwise, we conventionally define $last(c) = -1$.

If we assume that the alphabet is of fixed, finite size, and that characters can be converted to indices of an array (for example, by using their character code), the last function can be easily implemented as a lookup table with worst-case $O(1)$-time access to the value $last(c)$. However, the table would have length equal to the size of the alphabet (rather than the size of the pattern), and time would be required to initialize the entire table.

We prefer to use a hash table to represent the last function, with only those characters from the pattern occurring in the structure. The space usage for this approach is proportional to the number of distinct alphabet symbols that occur in the pattern, and thus $O(m)$. The expected lookup time remains independent of the problem (although the worst-case bound is $O(m)$). Our complete implementation of the Boyer-Moore pattern-matching algorithm is given in Code Fragment 13.2.

```
1  def find_boyer_moore(T, P):
2    """Return the lowest index of T at which substring P begins (or else -1)."""
3    n, m = len(T), len(P)                    # introduce convenient notations
4    if m == 0: return 0                      # trivial search for empty string
5    last = { }                               # build 'last' dictionary
6    for k in range(m):
7      last[ P[k] ] = k                       # later occurrence overwrites
8    # align end of pattern at index m-1 of text
9    i = m−1                                   # an index into T
10   k = m−1                                   # an index into P
11   while i < n:
12     if T[i] == P[k]:                        # a matching character
13       if k == 0:
14         return i                            # pattern begins at index i of text
15       else:
16         i −= 1                              # examine previous character
17         k −= 1                              # of both T and P
18     else:
19       j = last.get(T[i], −1)                # last(T[i]) is -1 if not found
20       i += m − min(k, j + 1)                # case analysis for jump step
21       k = m − 1                             # restart at end of pattern
22   return −1
```

Code Fragment 13.2: An implementation of the Boyer-Moore algorithm.

The correctness of the Boyer-Moore pattern-matching algorithm follows from the fact that each time the method makes a shift, it is guaranteed not to "skip" over any possible matches. For last(c) is the location of the *last* occurrence of c in P. In Figure 13.4, we illustrate the execution of the Boyer-Moore pattern-matching algorithm on an input string similar to Example 13.1.

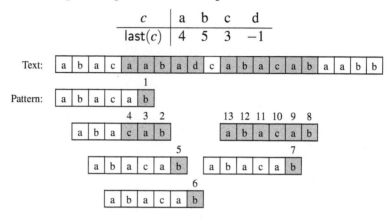

Figure 13.4: An illustration of the Boyer-Moore pattern-matching algorithm, including a summary of the last(c) function. The algorithm performs 13 character comparisons, which are indicated with numerical labels.

Performance

If using a traditional lookup table, the worst-case running time of the Boyer-Moore algorithm is $O(nm + |\Sigma|)$. Namely, the computation of the last function takes time $O(m + |\Sigma|)$, and the actual search for the pattern takes $O(nm)$ time in the worst case, the same as the brute-force algorithm. (With a hash table, the dependence on $|\Sigma|$ is removed.) An example of a text-pattern pair that achieves the worst case is

$$T = \overbrace{aaaaaa \cdots a}^{n}$$
$$P = b\overbrace{aa \cdots a}^{m-1}$$

The worst-case performance, however, is unlikely to be achieved for English text, for, in that case, the Boyer-Moore algorithm is often able to skip large portions of text. Experimental evidence on English text shows that the average number of comparisons done per character is 0.24 for a five-character pattern string.

We have actually presented a simplified version of the Boyer-Moore algorithm. The original algorithm achieves running time $O(n + m + |\Sigma|)$ by using an alternative shift heuristic to the partially matched text string, whenever it shifts the pattern more than the character-jump heuristic. This alternative shift heuristic is based on applying the main idea from the Knuth-Morris-Pratt pattern-matching algorithm, which we discuss next.

13.2.3   The Knuth-Morris-Pratt Algorithm

In examining the worst-case performances of the brute-force and Boyer-Moore pattern-matching algorithms on specific instances of the problem, such as that given in Example 13.1, we should notice a major inefficiency. For a certain alignment of the pattern, if we find several matching characters but then detect a mismatch, we ignore all the information gained by the successful comparisons after restarting with the next incremental placement of the pattern.

The Knuth-Morris-Pratt (or "KMP") algorithm, discussed in this section, avoids this waste of information and, in so doing, it achieves a running time of $O(n+m)$, which is asymptotically optimal. That is, in the worst case any pattern-matching algorithm will have to examine all the characters of the text and all the characters of the pattern at least once. The main idea of the KMP algorithm is to precompute self-overlaps between portions of the pattern so that when a mismatch occurs at one location, we immediately know the maximum amount to shift the pattern before continuing the search. A motivating example is shown in Figure 13.5.

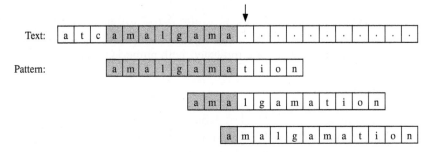

Figure 13.5: A motivating example for the Knuth-Morris-Pratt algorithm. If a mismatch occurs at the indicated location, the pattern could be shifted to the second alignment, without explicit need to recheck the partial match with the prefix ama. If the mismatched character is not an l, then the next potential alignment of the pattern can take advantage of the common a.

The Failure Function

To implement the KMP algorithm, we will precompute a *failure function*, f, that indicates the proper shift of P upon a failed comparison. Specifically, the failure function $f(k)$ is defined as the length of the longest prefix of P that is a suffix of P[1:k+1] (note that we did *not* include P[0] here, since we will shift at least one unit). Intuitively, if we find a mismatch upon character P[k+1], the function $f(k)$ tells us how many of the immediately preceding characters can be reused to restart the pattern. Example 13.2 describes the value of the failure function for the example pattern from Figure 13.5.

Example 13.2: *Consider the pattern* $P =$ *"amalgamation" from Figure 13.5. The Knuth-Morris-Pratt (KMP) failure function,* $f(k)$, *for the string P is as shown in the following table:*

k	0	1	2	3	4	5	6	7	8	9	10	11
$P[k]$	a	m	a	l	g	a	m	a	t	i	o	n
$f(k)$	0	0	1	0	0	1	2	3	0	0	0	0

Implementation

Our implementation of the KMP pattern-matching algorithm is shown in Code Fragment 13.3. It relies on a utility function, compute_kmp_fail, discussed on the next page, to compute the failure function efficiently.

The main part of the KMP algorithm is its **while** loop, each iteration of which performs a comparison between the character at index j in T and the character at index k in P. If the outcome of this comparison is a match, the algorithm moves on to the next characters in both T and P (or reports a match if reaching the end of the pattern). If the comparison failed, the algorithm consults the failure function for a new candidate character in P, or starts over with the next index in T if failing on the first character of the pattern (since nothing can be reused).

```
1  def find_kmp(T, P):
2      """Return the lowest index of T at which substring P begins (or else -1)."""
3      n, m = len(T), len(P)              # introduce convenient notations
4      if m == 0: return 0               # trivial search for empty string
5      fail = compute_kmp_fail(P)        # rely on utility to precompute
6      j = 0                             # index into text
7      k = 0                             # index into pattern
8      while j < n:
9          if T[j] == P[k]:              # P[0:1+k] matched thus far
10             if k == m − 1:            # match is complete
11                 return j − m + 1
12             j += 1                    # try to extend match
13             k += 1
14         elif k > 0:
15             k = fail[k−1]             # reuse suffix of P[0:k]
16         else:
17             j += 1
18     return −1                         # reached end without match
```

Code Fragment 13.3: An implementation of the KMP pattern-matching algorithm. The compute_kmp_fail utility function is given in Code Fragment 13.4.

Constructing the KMP Failure Function

To construct the failure function, we use the method shown in Code Fragment 13.4, which is a "bootstrapping" process that compares the pattern to itself as in the KMP algorithm. Each time we have two characters that match, we set $f(j) = k+1$. Note that since we have $j > k$ throughout the execution of the algorithm, $f(k-1)$ is always well defined when we need to use it.

```
1  def compute_kmp_fail(P):
2      """Utility that computes and returns KMP 'fail' list."""
3      m = len(P)
4      fail = [0] * m              # by default, presume overlap of 0 everywhere
5      j = 1
6      k = 0
7      while j < m:                # compute f(j) during this pass, if nonzero
8          if P[j] == P[k]:        # k + 1 characters match thus far
9              fail[j] = k + 1
10             j += 1
11             k += 1
12         elif k > 0:             # k follows a matching prefix
13             k = fail[k−1]
14         else:                   # no match found starting at j
15             j += 1
16     return fail
```

Code Fragment 13.4: An implementation of the compute_kmp_fail utility in support of the KMP pattern-matching algorithm. Note how the algorithm uses the previous values of the failure function to efficiently compute new values.

Performance

Excluding the computation of the failure function, the running time of the KMP algorithm is clearly proportional to the number of iterations of the **while** loop. For the sake of the analysis, let us define $s = j - k$. Intuitively, s is the total amount by which the pattern P has been shifted with respect to the text T. Note that throughout the execution of the algorithm, we have $s \leq n$. One of the following three cases occurs at each iteration of the loop.

- If $T[j] = P[k]$, then j and k each increase by 1, and thus, s does not change.
- If $T[j] \neq P[k]$ and $k > 0$, then j does not change and s increases by at least 1, since in this case s changes from $j - k$ to $j - f(k-1)$, which is an addition of $k - f(k-1)$, which is positive because $f(k-1) < k$.
- If $T[j] \neq P[k]$ and $k = 0$, then j increases by 1 and s increases by 1, since k does not change.

Thus, at each iteration of the loop, either j or s increases by at least 1 (possibly both); hence, the total number of iterations of the **while** loop in the KMP pattern-matching algorithm is at most $2n$. Achieving this bound, of course, assumes that we have already computed the failure function for P.

The algorithm for computing the failure function runs in $O(m)$ time. Its analysis is analogous to that of the main KMP algorithm, yet with a pattern of length m compared to itself. Thus, we have:

Proposition 13.3: *The Knuth-Morris-Pratt algorithm performs pattern matching on a text string of length n and a pattern string of length m in $O(n+m)$ time.*

The correctness of this algorithm follows from the definition of the failure function. Any comparisons that are skipped are actually unnecessary, for the failure function guarantees that all the ignored comparisons are redundant—they would involve comparing the same matching characters over again.

In Figure 13.6, we illustrate the execution of the KMP pattern-matching algorithm on the same input strings as in Example 13.1. Note the use of the failure function to avoid redoing one of the comparisons between a character of the pattern and a character of the text. Also note that the algorithm performs fewer overall comparisons than the brute-force algorithm run on the same strings (Figure 13.1).

The failure function:

k	0	1	2	3	4	5
$P[k]$	a	b	a	c	a	b
$f(k)$	0	0	1	0	1	2

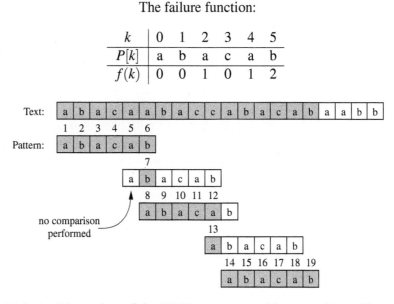

Figure 13.6: An illustration of the KMP pattern-matching algorithm. The primary algorithm performs 19 character comparisons, which are indicated with numerical labels. (Additional comparisons would be performed during the computation of the failure function.)

13.3 Dynamic Programming

In this section, we discuss the *dynamic programming* algorithm-design technique. This technique is similar to the divide-and-conquer technique (Section 12.2.1), in that it can be applied to a wide variety of different problems. Dynamic programming can often be used to take problems that seem to require exponential time and produce polynomial-time algorithms to solve them. In addition, the algorithms that result from applications of the dynamic programming technique are usually quite simple—often needing little more than a few lines of code to describe some nested loops for filling in a table.

13.3.1 Matrix Chain-Product

Rather than starting out with an explanation of the general components of the dynamic programming technique, we begin by giving a classic, concrete example. Suppose we are given a collection of n two-dimensional matrices for which we wish to compute the mathematical product

$$A = A_0 \cdot A_1 \cdot A_2 \cdots A_{n-1},$$

where A_i is a $d_i \times d_{i+1}$ matrix, for $i = 0, 1, 2, \ldots, n-1$. In the standard matrix multiplication algorithm (which is the one we will use), to multiply a $d \times e$-matrix B times an $e \times f$-matrix C, we compute the product, A, as

$$A[i][j] = \sum_{k=0}^{e-1} B[i][k] \cdot C[k][j].$$

This definition implies that matrix multiplication is associative, that is, it implies that $B \cdot (C \cdot D) = (B \cdot C) \cdot D$. Thus, we can parenthesize the expression for A any way we wish and we will end up with the same answer. However, we will not necessarily perform the same number of primitive (that is, scalar) multiplications in each parenthesization, as is illustrated in the following example.

Example 13.4: *Let B be a 2×10-matrix, let C be a 10×50-matrix, and let D be a 50×20-matrix. Computing $B \cdot (C \cdot D)$ requires $2 \cdot 10 \cdot 20 + 10 \cdot 50 \cdot 20 = 10400$ multiplications, whereas computing $(B \cdot C) \cdot D$ requires $2 \cdot 10 \cdot 50 + 2 \cdot 50 \cdot 20 = 3000$ multiplications.*

The *matrix chain-product* problem is to determine the parenthesization of the expression defining the product A that minimizes the total number of scalar multiplications performed. As the example above illustrates, the differences between parenthesizations can be dramatic, so finding a good solution can result in significant speedups.

Defining Subproblems

One way to solve the matrix chain-product problem is to simply enumerate all the possible ways of parenthesizing the expression for A and determine the number of multiplications performed by each one. Unfortunately, the set of all different parenthesizations of the expression for A is equal in number to the set of all different binary trees that have n leaves. This number is exponential in n. Thus, this straightforward ("brute-force") algorithm runs in exponential time, for there are an exponential number of ways to parenthesize an associative arithmetic expression.

We can significantly improve the performance achieved by the brute-force algorithm, however, by making a few observations about the nature of the matrix chain-product problem. The first is that the problem can be split into **subproblems**. In this case, we can define a number of different subproblems, each of which is to compute the best parenthesization for some subexpression $A_i \cdot A_{i+1} \cdots A_j$. As a concise notation, we use $N_{i,j}$ to denote the minimum number of multiplications needed to compute this subexpression. Thus, the original matrix chain-product problem can be characterized as that of computing the value of $N_{0,n-1}$. This observation is important, but we need one more in order to apply the dynamic programming technique.

Characterizing Optimal Solutions

The other important observation we can make about the matrix chain-product problem is that it is possible to characterize an optimal solution to a particular subproblem in terms of optimal solutions to its subproblems. We call this property the **subproblem optimality** condition.

In the case of the matrix chain-product problem, we observe that, no matter how we parenthesize a subexpression, there has to be some final matrix multiplication that we perform. That is, a full parenthesization of a subexpression $A_i \cdot A_{i+1} \cdots A_j$ has to be of the form $(A_i \cdots A_k) \cdot (A_{k+1} \cdots A_j)$, for some $k \in \{i, i+1, \ldots, j-1\}$. Moreover, for whichever k is the correct one, the products $(A_i \cdots A_k)$ and $(A_{k+1} \cdots A_j)$ must also be solved optimally. If this were not so, then there would be a global optimal that had one of these subproblems solved suboptimally. But this is impossible, since we could then reduce the total number of multiplications by replacing the current subproblem solution by an optimal solution for the subproblem. This observation implies a way of explicitly defining the optimization problem for $N_{i,j}$ in terms of other optimal subproblem solutions. Namely, we can compute $N_{i,j}$ by considering each place k where we could put the final multiplication and taking the minimum over all such choices.

Designing a Dynamic Programming Algorithm

We can therefore characterize the optimal subproblem solution, $N_{i,j}$, as

$$N_{i,j} = \min_{i \le k < j} \{N_{i,k} + N_{k+1,j} + d_i d_{k+1} d_{j+1}\},$$

where $N_{i,i} = 0$, since no work is needed for a single matrix. That is, $N_{i,j}$ is the minimum, taken over all possible places to perform the final multiplication, of the number of multiplications needed to compute each subexpression plus the number of multiplications needed to perform the final matrix multiplication.

Notice that there is a *sharing of subproblems* going on that prevents us from dividing the problem into completely independent subproblems (as we would need to do to apply the divide-and-conquer technique). We can, nevertheless, use the equation for $N_{i,j}$ to derive an efficient algorithm by computing $N_{i,j}$ values in a bottom-up fashion, and storing intermediate solutions in a table of $N_{i,j}$ values. We can begin simply enough by assigning $N_{i,i} = 0$ for $i = 0, 1, \ldots, n-1$. We can then apply the general equation for $N_{i,j}$ to compute $N_{i,i+1}$ values, since they depend only on $N_{i,i}$ and $N_{i+1,i+1}$ values that are available. Given the $N_{i,i+1}$ values, we can then compute the $N_{i,i+2}$ values, and so on. Therefore, we can build $N_{i,j}$ values up from previously computed values until we can finally compute the value of $N_{0,n-1}$, which is the number that we are searching for. A Python implementation of this *dynamic programming* solution is given in Code Fragment 13.5; we use techniques from Section 5.6 for representing a multidimensional table in Python.

```
1  def matrix_chain(d):
2      """d is a list of n+1 numbers such that size of kth matrix is d[k]-by-d[k+1].
3
4      Return an n-by-n table such that N[i][j] represents the minimum number of
5      multiplications needed to compute the product of Ai through Aj inclusive.
6      """
7      n = len(d) − 1                        # number of matrices
8      N = [[0] * n for i in range(n)]       # initialize n-by-n result to zero
9      for b in range(1, n):                 # number of products in subchain
10         for i in range(n−b):              # start of subchain
11             j = i + b                     # end of subchain
12             N[i][j] = min(N[i][k]+N[k+1][j]+d[i]*d[k+1]*d[j+1] for k in range(i,j))
13     return N
```

Code Fragment 13.5: Dynamic programming algorithm for the matrix chain-product problem.

Thus, we can compute $N_{0,n-1}$ with an algorithm that consists primarily of three nested loops (the third of which computes the min term). Each of these loops iterates at most n times per execution, with a constant amount of additional work within. Therefore, the total running time of this algorithm is $O(n^3)$.

13.3.2   DNA and Text Sequence Alignment

A common text-processing problem, which arises in genetics and software engineering, is to test the similarity between two text strings. In a genetics application, the two strings could correspond to two strands of DNA, for which we want to compute similarities. Likewise, in a software engineering application, the two strings could come from two versions of source code for the same program, for which we want to determine changes made from one version to the next. Indeed, determining the similarity between two strings is so common that the Unix and Linux operating systems have a built-in program, named `diff`, for comparing text files.

Given a string $X = x_0 x_1 x_2 \cdots x_{n-1}$, a **subsequence** of X is any string that is of the form $x_{i_1} x_{i_2} \cdots x_{i_k}$, where $i_j < i_{j+1}$; that is, it is a sequence of characters that are not necessarily contiguous but are nevertheless taken in order from X. For example, the string *AAAG* is a subsequence of the string *CGATAATTGAGA*.

The DNA and text similarity problem we address here is the **longest common subsequence** (LCS) problem. In this problem, we are given two character strings, $X = x_0 x_1 x_2 \cdots x_{n-1}$ and $Y = y_0 y_1 y_2 \cdots y_{m-1}$, over some alphabet (such as the alphabet $\{A, C, G, T\}$ common in computational genetics) and are asked to find a longest string S that is a subsequence of both X and Y. One way to solve the longest common subsequence problem is to enumerate all subsequences of X and take the largest one that is also a subsequence of Y. Since each character of X is either in or not in a subsequence, there are potentially 2^n different subsequences of X, each of which requires $O(m)$ time to determine whether it is a subsequence of Y. Thus, this brute-force approach yields an exponential-time algorithm that runs in $O(2^n m)$ time, which is very inefficient. Fortunately, the LCS problem is efficiently solvable using **dynamic programming**.

The Components of a Dynamic Programming Solution

As mentioned above, the dynamic programming technique is used primarily for **optimization** problems, where we wish to find the "best" way of doing something. We can apply the dynamic programming technique in such situations if the problem has certain properties:

Simple Subproblems: There has to be some way of repeatedly breaking the global optimization problem into subproblems. Moreover, there should be a way to parameterize subproblems with just a few indices, like i, j, k, and so on.

Subproblem Optimization: An optimal solution to the global problem must be a composition of optimal subproblem solutions.

Subproblem Overlap: Optimal solutions to unrelated subproblems can contain subproblems in common.

Applying Dynamic Programming to the LCS Problem

Recall that in the LCS problem, we are given two character strings, X and Y, of length n and m, respectively, and are asked to find a longest string S that is a subsequence of both X and Y. Since X and Y are character strings, we have a natural set of indices with which to define subproblems—indices into the strings X and Y. Let us define a subproblem, therefore, as that of computing the value $L_{j,k}$, which we will use to denote the length of a longest string that is a subsequence of both prefixes $X[0:j]$ and $Y[0:k]$. This definition allows us to rewrite $L_{j,k}$ in terms of optimal subproblem solutions. This definition depends on which of two cases we are in. (See Figure 13.7.)

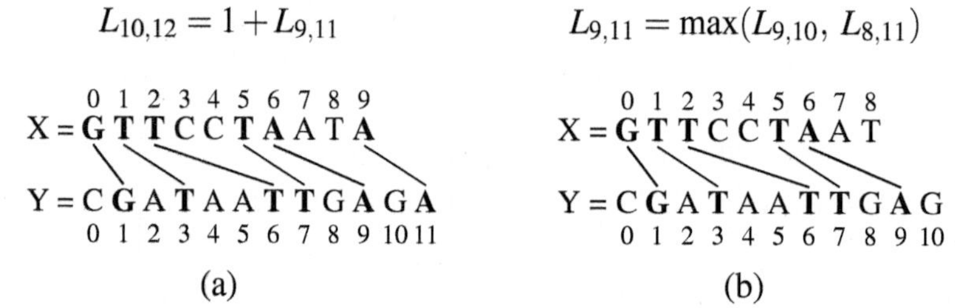

$$L_{10,12} = 1 + L_{9,11} \qquad\qquad\qquad L_{9,11} = \max(L_{9,10}, L_{8,11})$$

$$\text{(a)} \qquad\qquad\qquad\qquad\qquad\qquad \text{(b)}$$

Figure 13.7: The two cases in the longest common subsequence algorithm for computing $L_{j,k}$: (a) $x_{j-1} = y_{k-1}$; (b) $x_{j-1} \neq y_{k-1}$.

- $x_{j-1} = y_{k-1}$. In this case, we have a match between the last character of $X[0:j]$ and the last character of $Y[0:k]$. We claim that this character belongs to a longest common subsequence of $X[0:j]$ and $Y[0:k]$. To justify this claim, let us suppose it is not true. There has to be some longest common subsequence $x_{a_1} x_{a_2} \ldots x_{a_c} = y_{b_1} y_{b_2} \ldots y_{b_c}$. If $x_{a_c} = x_{j-1}$ or $y_{b_c} = y_{k-1}$, then we get the same sequence by setting $a_c = j - 1$ and $b_c = k - 1$. Alternately, if $x_{a_c} \neq x_{j-1}$ and $y_{b_c} \neq y_{k-1}$, then we can get an even longer common subsequence by adding $x_{j-1} = y_{k-1}$ to the end. Thus, a longest common subsequence of $X[0:j]$ and $Y[0:k]$ ends with x_{j-1}. Therefore, we set

$$L_{j,k} = 1 + L_{j-1,k-1} \quad \text{if } x_{j-1} = y_{k-1}.$$

- $x_{j-1} \neq y_{k-1}$. In this case, we cannot have a common subsequence that includes both x_{j-1} and y_{k-1}. That is, we can have a common subsequence end with x_{j-1} or one that ends with y_{k-1} (or possibly neither), but certainly not both. Therefore, we set

$$L_{j,k} = \max\{L_{j-1,k}, L_{j,k-1}\} \quad \text{if } x_{j-1} \neq y_{k-1}.$$

We note that because slice $Y[0:0]$ is the empty string, $L_{j,0} = 0$ for $j = 0, 1, \ldots, n$; similarly, because slice $X[0:0]$ is the empty string, $L_{0,k} = 0$ for $k = 0, 1, \ldots, m$.

The LCS Algorithm

The definition of $L_{j,k}$ satisfies subproblem optimization, for we cannot have a longest common subsequence without also having longest common subsequences for the subproblems. Also, it uses subproblem overlap, because a subproblem solution $L_{j,k}$ can be used in several other problems (namely, the problems $L_{j+1,k}$, $L_{j,k+1}$, and $L_{j+1,k+1}$). Turning this definition of $L_{j,k}$ into an algorithm is actually quite straightforward. We create an $(n+1) \times (m+1)$ array, L, defined for $0 \le j \le n$ and $0 \le k \le m$. We initialize all entries to 0, in particular so that all entries of the form $L_{j,0}$ and $L_{0,k}$ are zero. Then, we iteratively build up values in L until we have $L_{n,m}$, the length of a longest common subsequence of X and Y. We give a Python implementation of this algorithm in Code Fragment 13.6.

```
1  def LCS(X, Y):
2    """Return table such that L[j][k] is length of LCS for X[0:j] and Y[0:k]."""
3    n, m = len(X), len(Y)                       # introduce convenient notations
4    L = [[0] * (m+1) for k in range(n+1)]       # (n+1) x (m+1) table
5    for j in range(n):
6      for k in range(m):
7        if X[j] == Y[k]:                        # align this match
8          L[j+1][k+1] = L[j][k] + 1
9        else:                                   # choose to ignore one character
10         L[j+1][k+1] = max(L[j][k+1], L[j+1][k])
11   return L
```

Code Fragment 13.6: Dynamic programming algorithm for the LCS problem.

The running time of the algorithm of the LCS algorithm is easy to analyze, for it is dominated by two nested **for** loops, with the outer one iterating n times and the inner one iterating m times. Since the if-statement and assignment inside the loop each requires $O(1)$ primitive operations, this algorithm runs in $O(nm)$ time. Thus, the dynamic programming technique can be applied to the longest common subsequence problem to improve significantly over the exponential-time brute-force solution to the LCS problem.

The LCS function of Code Fragment 13.6 computes the length of the longest common subsequence (stored as $L_{n,m}$), but not the subsequence itself. Fortunately, it is easy to extract the actual longest common subsequence if given the complete table of $L_{j,k}$ values computed by the LCS function. The solution can be reconstructed back to front by reverse engineering the calculation of length $L_{n,m}$. At any position $L_{j,k}$, if $x_j = y_k$, then the length is based on the common subsequence associated with length $L_{j-1,k-1}$, followed by common character x_j. We can record x_j as part of the sequence, and then continue the analysis from $L_{j-1,k-1}$. If $x_j \ne y_k$, then we can move to the larger of $L_{j,k-1}$ and $L_{j-1,k}$. We continue this process until reaching some $L_{j,k} = 0$ (for example, if j or k is 0 as a boundary case). A Python implementation of this strategy is given in Code Fragment 13.7. This function constructs a longest common subsequence in $O(n+m)$ additional time, since each pass of the **while** loop decrements either j or k (or both). An illustration of the algorithm for computing the longest common subsequence is given in Figure 13.8.

```
1  def LCS_solution(X, Y, L):
2    """Return the longest common substring of X and Y, given LCS table L."""
3    solution = [ ]
4    j,k = len(X), len(Y)
5    while L[j][k] > 0:                    # common characters remain
6      if X[j−1] == Y[k−1]:
7        solution.append(X[j−1])
8        j −= 1
9        k −= 1
10     elif L[j−1][k] >= L[j][k−1]:
11       j −=1
12     else:
13       k −= 1
14   return ''.join(reversed(solution))    # return left-to-right version
```

Code Fragment 13.7: Reconstructing the longest common subsequence.

	0	1	2	3	4	5	6	7	8	9	10	11	12
0	0	0	0	0	0	0	0	0	0	0	0	0	0
1	0	0	1	1	1	1	1	1	1	1	1	1	1
2	0	0	1	1	2	2	2	2	2	2	2	2	2
3	0	0	1	1	2	2	2	3	3	3	3	3	3
4	0	1	1	1	2	2	2	3	3	3	3	3	3
5	0	1	1	1	2	2	2	3	3	3	3	3	3
6	0	1	1	1	2	2	2	3	4	4	4	4	4
7	0	1	1	2	2	3	3	3	4	4	5	5	5
8	0	1	1	2	2	3	4	4	4	4	5	5	6
9	0	1	1	2	3	3	4	5	5	5	5	5	6
10	0	1	1	2	3	4	4	5	5	5	6	6	6

$$\begin{array}{c} 0\ 1\ 2\ 3\ 4\ 5\ 6\ 7\ 8\ 9 \\ X = G\ T\ T\ C\ C\ T\ A\ A\ T\ A \\ \\ Y = C\ G\ A\ T\ A\ A\ T\ T\ G\ A\ G\ A \\ 0\ 1\ 2\ 3\ 4\ 5\ 6\ 7\ 8\ 9\ 10\ 11 \end{array}$$

Figure 13.8: Illustration of the algorithm for constructing a longest common subsequence from the array L. A diagonal step on the highlighted path represents the use of a common character (with that character's respective indices in the sequences highlighted in the margins).

13.4 Text Compression and the Greedy Method

In this section, we consider an important text-processing task, ***text compression***. In this problem, we are given a string X defined over some alphabet, such as the ASCII or Unicode character sets, and we want to efficiently encode X into a small binary string Y (using only the characters 0 and 1). Text compression is useful in any situation where we wish to reduce bandwidth for digital communications, so as to minimize the time needed to transmit our text. Likewise, text compression is useful for storing large documents more efficiently, so as to allow a fixed-capacity storage device to contain as many documents as possible.

The method for text compression explored in this section is the ***Huffman code***. Standard encoding schemes, such as ASCII, use fixed-length binary strings to encode characters (with 7 or 8 bits in the traditional or extended ASCII systems, respectively). The Unicode system was originally proposed as a 16-bit fixed-length representation, although common encodings reduce the space usage by allowing common groups of characters, such as those from the ASCII system, with fewer bits. The Huffman code saves space over a fixed-length encoding by using short code-word strings to encode high-frequency characters and long code-word strings to encode low-frequency characters. Furthermore, the Huffman code uses a variable-length encoding specifically optimized for a given string X over any alphabet. The optimization is based on the use of character ***frequencies***, where we have, for each character c, a count $f(c)$ of the number of times c appears in the string X.

To encode the string X, we convert each character in X to a variable-length code-word, and we concatenate all these code-words in order to produce the encoding Y for X. In order to avoid ambiguities, we insist that no code-word in our encoding be a prefix of another code-word in our encoding. Such a code is called a ***prefix code***, and it simplifies the decoding of Y to retrieve X. (See Figure 13.9.) Even with this restriction, the savings produced by a variable-length prefix code can be significant, particularly if there is a wide variance in character frequencies (as is the case for natural language text in almost every written language).

Huffman's algorithm for producing an optimal variable-length prefix code for X is based on the construction of a binary tree T that represents the code. Each edge in T represents a bit in a code-word, with an edge to a left child representing a "0" and an edge to a right child representing a "1." Each leaf v is associated with a specific character, and the code-word for that character is defined by the sequence of bits associated with the edges in the path from the root of T to v. (See Figure 13.9.) Each leaf v has a ***frequency***, $f(v)$, which is simply the frequency in X of the character associated with v. In addition, we give each internal node v in T a frequency, $f(v)$, that is the sum of the frequencies of all the leaves in the subtree rooted at v.

(a)

Character	a	b	d	e	f	h	i	k	n	o	r	s	t	u	v
Frequency	9	5	1	3	7	3	1	1	1	4	1	5	1	2	1	1

(b)

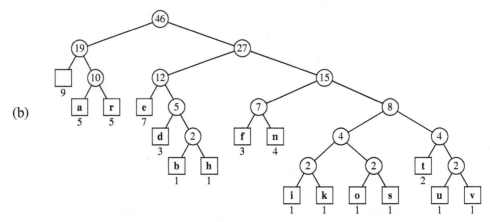

Figure 13.9: An illustration of an example Huffman code for the input string $X =$ "a fast runner need never be afraid of the dark": (a) frequency of each character of X; (b) Huffman tree T for string X. The code for a character c is obtained by tracing the path from the root of T to the leaf where c is stored, and associating a left child with 0 and a right child with 1. For example, the code for "r" is 011, and the code for "h" is 10111.

13.4.1 The Huffman Coding Algorithm

The Huffman coding algorithm begins with each of the d distinct characters of the string X to encode being the root node of a single-node binary tree. The algorithm proceeds in a series of rounds. In each round, the algorithm takes the two binary trees with the smallest frequencies and merges them into a single binary tree. It repeats this process until only one tree is left. (See Code Fragment 13.8.)

Each iteration of the **while** loop in Huffman's algorithm can be implemented in $O(\log d)$ time using a priority queue represented with a heap. In addition, each iteration takes two nodes out of Q and adds one in, a process that will be repeated $d - 1$ times before exactly one node is left in Q. Thus, this algorithm runs in $O(n + d \log d)$ time. Although a full justification of this algorithm's correctness is beyond our scope here, we note that its intuition comes from a simple idea—any optimal code can be converted into an optimal code in which the code-words for the two lowest-frequency characters, a and b, differ only in their last bit. Repeating the argument for a string with a and b replaced by a character c, gives the following:

Proposition 13.5: *Huffman's algorithm constructs an optimal prefix code for a string of length n with d distinct characters in $O(n + d \log d)$ time.*

Algorithm Huffman(X):

    Input: String X of length n with d distinct characters

    Output: Coding tree for X

    Compute the frequency $f(c)$ of each character c of X.

    Initialize a priority queue Q.

    for each character c in X **do**

        Create a single-node binary tree T storing c.

        Insert T into Q with key $f(c)$.

    while len(Q) > 1 **do**

        $(f_1, T_1) = Q$.remove_min()

        $(f_2, T_2) = Q$.remove_min()

        Create a new binary tree T with left subtree T_1 and right subtree T_2.

        Insert T into Q with key $f_1 + f_2$.

    $(f, T) = Q$.remove_min()

    return tree T

Code Fragment 13.8: Huffman coding algorithm.

13.4.2 The Greedy Method

Huffman's algorithm for building an optimal encoding is an example application of an algorithmic design pattern called the ***greedy method***. This design pattern is applied to optimization problems, where we are trying to construct some structure while minimizing or maximizing some property of that structure.

The general formula for the greedy method pattern is almost as simple as that for the brute-force method. In order to solve a given optimization problem using the greedy method, we proceed by a sequence of choices. The sequence starts from some well-understood starting condition, and computes the cost for that initial condition. The pattern then asks that we iteratively make additional choices by identifying the decision that achieves the best cost improvement from all of the choices that are currently possible. This approach does not always lead to an optimal solution.

But there are several problems that it does work for, and such problems are said to possess the ***greedy-choice*** property. This is the property that a global optimal condition can be reached by a series of locally optimal choices (that is, choices that are each the current best from among the possibilities available at the time), starting from a well-defined starting condition. The problem of computing an optimal variable-length prefix code is just one example of a problem that possesses the greedy-choice property.

13.5   Tries

The pattern-matching algorithms presented in Section 13.2 speed up the search in a text by preprocessing the pattern (to compute the failure function in the Knuth-Morris-Pratt algorithm or the last function in the Boyer-Moore algorithm). In this section, we take a complementary approach, namely, we present string searching algorithms that preprocess the text. This approach is suitable for applications where a series of queries is performed on a fixed text, so that the initial cost of preprocessing the text is compensated by a speedup in each subsequent query (for example, a Web site that offers pattern matching in Shakespeare's *Hamlet* or a search engine that offers Web pages on the *Hamlet* topic).

A *trie* (pronounced "try") is a tree-based data structure for storing strings in order to support fast pattern matching. The main application for tries is in information retrieval. Indeed, the name "trie" comes from the word "re*trie*val." In an information retrieval application, such as a search for a certain DNA sequence in a genomic database, we are given a collection S of strings, all defined using the same alphabet. The primary query operations that tries support are pattern matching and *prefix matching*. The latter operation involves being given a string X, and looking for all the strings in S that contain X as a prefix.

13.5.1   Standard Tries

Let S be a set of s strings from alphabet Σ such that no string in S is a prefix of another string. A *standard trie* for S is an ordered tree T with the following properties (see Figure 13.10):

- Each node of T, except the root, is labeled with a character of Σ.
- The children of an internal node of T have distinct labels.
- T has s leaves, each associated with a string of S, such that the concatenation of the labels of the nodes on the path from the root to a leaf v of T yields the string of S associated with v.

Thus, a trie T represents the strings of S with paths from the root to the leaves of T. Note the importance of assuming that no string in S is a prefix of another string. This ensures that each string of S is uniquely associated with a leaf of T. (This is similar to the restriction for prefix codes with Huffman coding, as described in Section 13.4.) We can always satisfy this assumption by adding a special character that is not in the original alphabet Σ at the end of each string.

An internal node in a standard trie T can have anywhere between 1 and $|\Sigma|$ children. There is an edge going from the root r to one of its children for each character that is first in some string in the collection S. In addition, a path from the root of T to an internal node v at depth k corresponds to a k-character prefix $X[0:k]$

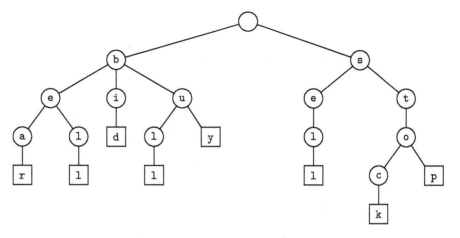

Figure 13.10: Standard trie for the strings {bear, bell, bid, bull, buy, sell, stock, stop}.

of a string X of S. In fact, for each character c that can follow the prefix $X[0:k]$ in a string of the set S, there is a child of v labeled with character c. In this way, a trie concisely stores the common prefixes that exist among a set of strings.

As a special case, if there are only two characters in the alphabet, then the trie is essentially a binary tree, with some internal nodes possibly having only one child (that is, it may be an improper binary tree). In general, although it is possible that an internal node has up to $|\Sigma|$ children, in practice the average degree of such nodes is likely to be much smaller. For example, the trie shown in Figure 13.10 has several internal nodes with only one child. On larger data sets, the average degree of nodes is likely to get smaller at greater depths of the tree, because there may be fewer strings sharing the common prefix, and thus fewer continuations of that pattern. Furthermore, in many languages, there will be character combinations that are unlikely to naturally occur.

The following proposition provides some important structural properties of a standard trie:

Proposition 13.6: *A standard trie storing a collection S of s strings of total length n from an alphabet Σ has the following properties:*

- *The height of T is equal to the length of the longest string in S.*
- *Every internal node of T has at most $|\Sigma|$ children.*
- *T has s leaves*
- *The number of nodes of T is at most $n+1$.*

The worst case for the number of nodes of a trie occurs when no two strings share a common nonempty prefix; that is, except for the root, all internal nodes have one child.

A trie T for a set S of strings can be used to implement a set or map whose keys are the strings of S. Namely, we perform a search in T for a string X by tracing down from the root the path indicated by the characters in X. If this path can be traced and terminates at a leaf node, then we know X is a key in the map. For example, in the trie in Figure 13.10, tracing the path for "bull" ends up at a leaf. If the path cannot be traced or the path can be traced but terminates at an internal node, then X is not a key in the map. In the example in Figure 13.10, the path for "bet" cannot be traced and the path for "be" ends at an internal node. Neither such word is in the map.

It is easy to see that the running time of the search for a string of length m is $O(m \cdot |\Sigma|)$, because we visit at most $m + 1$ nodes of T and we spend $O(|\Sigma|)$ time at each node determining the child having the subsequent character as a label. The $O(|\Sigma|)$ upper bound on the time to locate a child with a given label is achievable, even if the children of a node are unordered, since there are at most $|\Sigma|$ children. We can improve the time spent at a node to be $O(\log |\Sigma|)$ or expected $O(1)$, by mapping characters to children using a secondary search table or hash table at each node, or by using a direct lookup table of size $|\Sigma|$ at each node, if $|\Sigma|$ is sufficiently small (as is the case for DNA strings). For these reasons, we typically expect a search for a string of length m to run in $O(m)$ time.

From the discussion above, it follows that we can use a trie to perform a special type of pattern matching, called ***word matching***, where we want to determine whether a given pattern matches one of the words of the text exactly. Word matching differs from standard pattern matching because the pattern cannot match an arbitrary substring of the text—only one of its words. To accomplish this, each word of the original document must be added to the trie. (See Figure 13.11.) A simple extension of this scheme supports prefix-matching queries. However, arbitrary occurrences of the pattern in the text (for example, the pattern is a proper suffix of a word or spans two words) cannot be efficiently performed.

To construct a standard trie for a set S of strings, we can use an incremental algorithm that inserts the strings one at a time. Recall the assumption that no string of S is a prefix of another string. To insert a string X into the current trie T, we trace the path associated with X in T, creating a new chain of nodes to store the remaining characters of X when we get stuck. The running time to insert X with length m is similar to a search, with worst-case $O(m \cdot |\Sigma|)$ performance, or expected $O(m)$ if using secondary hash tables at each node. Thus, constructing the entire trie for set S takes expected $O(n)$ time, where n is the total length of the strings of S.

There is a potential space inefficiency in the standard trie that has prompted the development of the ***compressed trie***, which is also known (for historical reasons) as the ***Patricia trie***. Namely, there are potentially a lot of nodes in the standard trie that have only one child, and the existence of such nodes is a waste. We discuss the compressed trie next.

0	1	2	3	4	5	6	7	8	9	10	11	12	13	14	15	16	17	18	19	20	21	22
s	e	e		a		b	e	a	r	?		s	e	l	l		s	t	o	c	k	!

23	24	25	26	27	28	29	30	31	32	33	34	35	36	37	38	39	40	41	42	43	44	45
	s	e	e		a		b	u	l	l	?		b	u	y		s	t	o	c	k	!

46	47	48	49	50	51	52	53	54	55	56	57	58	59	60	61	62	63	64	65	66	67	68
	b	i	d		s	t	o	c	k	!		b	i	d		s	t	o	c	k	!	

69	70	71	72	73	74	75	76	77	78	79	80	81	82	83	84	85	86	87	88
h	e	a	r		t	h	e		b	e	l	l	?		s	t	o	p	!

(a)

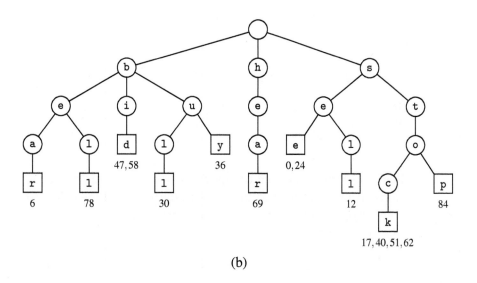

(b)

Figure 13.11: Word matching with a standard trie: (a) text to be searched (articles and prepositions, which are also known as ***stop words***, excluded); (b) standard trie for the words in the text, with leaves augmented with indications of the index at which the given work begins in the text. For example, the leaf for the word stock notes that the word begins at indices 17, 40, 51, and 62 of the text.

13.5.2 Compressed Tries

A *compressed trie* is similar to a standard trie but it ensures that each internal node in the trie has at least two children. It enforces this rule by compressing chains of single-child nodes into individual edges. (See Figure 13.12.) Let T be a standard trie. We say that an internal node v of T is *redundant* if v has one child and is not the root. For example, the trie of Figure 13.10 has eight redundant nodes. Let us also say that a chain of $k \geq 2$ edges,

$$(v_0, v_1)(v_1, v_2) \cdots (v_{k-1}, v_k),$$

is *redundant* if:

- v_i is redundant for $i = 1, \ldots, k-1$.
- v_0 and v_k are not redundant.

We can transform T into a compressed trie by replacing each redundant chain $(v_0, v_1) \cdots (v_{k-1}, v_k)$ of $k \geq 2$ edges into a single edge (v_0, v_k), relabeling v_k with the concatenation of the labels of nodes $v_1, \ldots, v_k$.

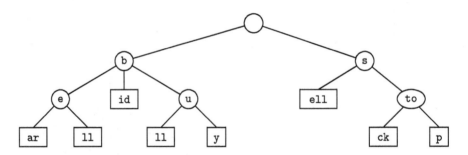

Figure 13.12: Compressed trie for the strings {bear, bell, bid, bull, buy, sell, stock, stop}. (Compare this with the standard trie shown in Figure 13.10.) In addition to compression at the leaves, notice the internal node with label `to` shared by words `stock` and `stop`.

Thus, nodes in a compressed trie are labeled with strings, which are substrings of strings in the collection, rather than with individual characters. The advantage of a compressed trie over a standard trie is that the number of nodes of the compressed trie is proportional to the number of strings and not to their total length, as shown in the following proposition (compare with Proposition 13.6).

Proposition 13.7: *A compressed trie storing a collection S of s strings from an alphabet of size d has the following properties:*

- *Every internal node of T has at least two children and most d children.*
- *T has s leaves nodes.*
- *The number of nodes of T is $O(s)$.*

The attentive reader may wonder whether the compression of paths provides any significant advantage, since it is offset by a corresponding expansion of the node labels. Indeed, a compressed trie is truly advantageous only when it is used as an **auxiliary** index structure over a collection of strings already stored in a primary structure, and is not required to actually store all the characters of the strings in the collection.

Suppose, for example, that the collection S of strings is an array of strings $S[0]$, $S[1]$, ..., $S[s-1]$. Instead of storing the label X of a node explicitly, we represent it implicitly by a combination of three integers $(i, j : k)$, such that $X = S[i][j : k]$; that is, X is the slice of $S[i]$ consisting of the characters from the jth up to but not including the kth. (See the example in Figure 13.13. Also compare with the standard trie of Figure 13.11.)

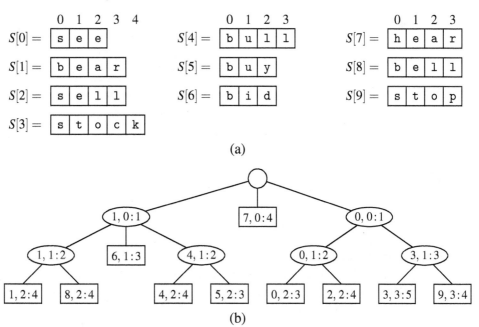

Figure 13.13: (a) Collection S of strings stored in an array. (b) Compact representation of the compressed trie for S.

This additional compression scheme allows us to reduce the total space for the trie itself from $O(n)$ for the standard trie to $O(s)$ for the compressed trie, where n is the total length of the strings in S and s is the number of strings in S. We must still store the different strings in S, of course, but we nevertheless reduce the space for the trie.

Searching in a compressed trie is not necessarily faster than in a standard tree, since there is still need to compare every character of the desired pattern with the potentially multi-character labels while traversing paths in the trie.

13.5.3   Suffix Tries

One of the primary applications for tries is for the case when the strings in the collection S are all the suffixes of a string X. Such a trie is called the *suffix trie* (also known as a *suffix tree* or *position tree*) of string X. For example, Figure 13.14a shows the suffix trie for the eight suffixes of string "minimize." For a suffix trie, the compact representation presented in the previous section can be further simplified. Namely, the label of each vertex is a pair (j,k) indicating the string $X[j:k]$. (See Figure 13.14b.) To satisfy the rule that no suffix of X is a prefix of another suffix, we can add a special character, denoted with $, that is not in the original alphabet Σ at the end of X (and thus to every suffix). That is, if string X has length n, we build a trie for the set of n strings $X[j:n]$, for $j = 0, \ldots, n-1$.

Saving Space

Using a suffix trie allows us to save space over a standard trie by using several space compression techniques, including those used for the compressed trie.

The advantage of the compact representation of tries now becomes apparent for suffix tries. Since the total length of the suffixes of a string X of length n is

$$1 + 2 + \cdots + n = \frac{n(n+1)}{2},$$

storing all the suffixes of X explicitly would take $O(n^2)$ space. Even so, the suffix trie represents these strings implicitly in $O(n)$ space, as formally stated in the following proposition.

Proposition 13.8: *The compact representation of a suffix trie T for a string X of length n uses $O(n)$ space.*

Construction

We can construct the suffix trie for a string of length n with an incremental algorithm like the one given in Section 13.5.1. This construction takes $O(|\Sigma|n^2)$ time because the total length of the suffixes is quadratic in n. However, the (compact) suffix trie for a string of length n can be constructed in $O(n)$ time with a specialized algorithm, different from the one for general tries. This linear-time construction algorithm is fairly complex, however, and is not reported here. Still, we can take advantage of the existence of this fast construction algorithm when we want to use a suffix trie to solve other problems.

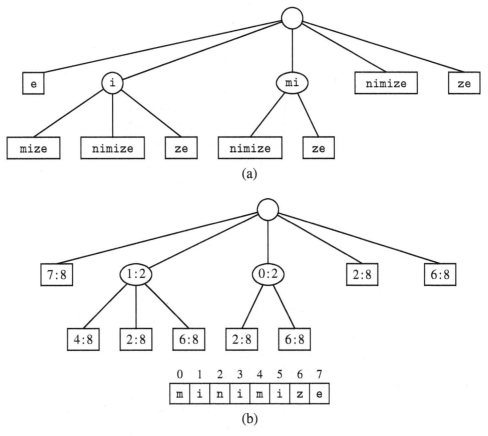

Figure 13.14: (a) Suffix trie T for the string $X =$ "minimize". (b) Compact representation of T, where pair $j:k$ denotes slice $X[j:k]$ in the reference string.

Using a Suffix Trie

The suffix trie T for a string X can be used to efficiently perform pattern-matching queries on text X. Namely, we can determine whether a pattern P is a substring of X by trying to trace a path associated with P in T. P is a substring of X if and only if such a path can be traced. The search down the trie T assumes that nodes in T store some additional information, with respect to the compact representation of the suffix trie:

> If node v has label (j,k) and Y is the string of length y associated with the path from the root to v (included), then $X[k-y:k] = Y$.

This property ensures that we can easily compute the start index of the pattern in the text when a match occurs.

13.5.4   Search Engine Indexing

The World Wide Web contains a huge collection of text documents (Web pages). Information about these pages are gathered by a program called a ***Web crawler***, which then stores this information in a special dictionary database. A Web ***search engine*** allows users to retrieve relevant information from this database, thereby identifying relevant pages on the Web containing given keywords. In this section, we present a simplified model of a search engine.

Inverted Files

The core information stored by a search engine is a dictionary, called an ***inverted index*** or ***inverted file***, storing key-value pairs (w, L), where w is a word and L is a collection of pages containing word w. The keys (words) in this dictionary are called ***index terms*** and should be a set of vocabulary entries and proper nouns as large as possible. The elements in this dictionary are called ***occurrence lists*** and should cover as many Web pages as possible.

We can efficiently implement an inverted index with a data structure consisting of the following:

1. An array storing the occurrence lists of the terms (in no particular order).
2. A compressed trie for the set of index terms, where each leaf stores the index of the occurrence list of the associated term.

The reason for storing the occurrence lists outside the trie is to keep the size of the trie data structure sufficiently small to fit in internal memory. Instead, because of their large total size, the occurrence lists have to be stored on disk.

With our data structure, a query for a single keyword is similar to a word-matching query (Section 13.5.1). Namely, we find the keyword in the trie and we return the associated occurrence list.

When multiple keywords are given and the desired output are the pages containing ***all*** the given keywords, we retrieve the occurrence list of each keyword using the trie and return their intersection. To facilitate the intersection computation, each occurrence list should be implemented with a sequence sorted by address or with a map, to allow efficient set operations.

In addition to the basic task of returning a list of pages containing given keywords, search engines provide an important additional service by ***ranking*** the pages returned by relevance. Devising fast and accurate ranking algorithms for search engines is a major challenge for computer researchers and electronic commerce companies.

13.6 Exercises

For help with exercises, please visit the site, www.wiley.com/college/goodrich.

Reinforcement

R-13.1 List the prefixes of the string $P =$"aaabbaaa" that are also suffixes of P.

R-13.2 What is the longest (proper) prefix of the string "cgtacgttcgtacg" that is also a suffix of this string?

R-13.3 Draw a figure illustrating the comparisons done by brute-force pattern matching for the text "aaabaadaabaaa" and pattern "aabaaa".

R-13.4 Repeat the previous problem for the Boyer-Moore algorithm, not counting the comparisons made to compute the last(c) function.

R-13.5 Repeat Exercise R-13.3 for the Knuth-Morris-Pratt algorithm, not counting the comparisons made to compute the failure function.

R-13.6 Compute a map representing the last function used in the Boyer-Moore pattern-matching algorithm for characters in the pattern string:

"the quick brown fox jumped over a lazy cat".

R-13.7 Compute a table representing the Knuth-Morris-Pratt failure function for the pattern string "cgtacgttcgtac".

R-13.8 What is the best way to multiply a chain of matrices with dimensions that are 10×5, 5×2, 2×20, 20×12, 12×4, and 4×60? Show your work.

R-13.9 In Figure 13.8, we illustrate that GTTTAA is a longest common subsequence for the given strings X and Y. However, that answer is not unique. Give another common subsequence of X and Y having length six.

R-13.10 Show the longest common subsequence array L for the two strings:

$$X = \text{"skullandbones"}$$
$$Y = \text{"lullabybabies"}$$

What is a longest common subsequence between these strings?

R-13.11 Draw the frequency array and Huffman tree for the following string:

"dogs do not spot hot pots or cats".

R-13.12 Draw a standard trie for the following set of strings:

{ abab, baba, ccccc, bbaaaa, caa, bbaacc, cbcc, cbca }.

R-13.13 Draw a compressed trie for the strings given in the previous problem.

R-13.14 Draw the compact representation of the suffix trie for the string:

"minimize minime".

Creativity

C-13.15 Describe an example of a text T of length n and a pattern P of length m such that force the brute-force pattern-matching algorithm achieves a running time that is $\Omega(nm)$.

C-13.16 Adapt the brute-force pattern-matching algorithm in order to implement a function, rfind_brute(T,P), that returns the index at which the *rightmost* occurrence of pattern P within text T, if any.

C-13.17 Redo the previous problem, adapting the Boyer-Moore pattern-matching algorithm appropriately to implement a function rfind_boyer_moore(T,P).

C-13.18 Redo Exercise C-13.16, adapting the Knuth-Morris-Pratt pattern-matching algorithm appropriately to implement a function rfind_kmp(T,P).

C-13.19 The count method of Python's str class reports the maximum number of *nonoverlapping* occurrences of a pattern within a string. For example, the call 'abababa'.count('aba') returns 2 (not 3). Adapt the brute-force pattern-matching algorithm to implement a function, count_brute(T,P), with similar outcome.

C-13.20 Redo the previous problem, adapting the Boyer-Moore pattern-matching algorithm in order to implement a function count_boyer_moore(T,P).

C-13.21 Redo Exercise C-13.19, adapting the Knuth-Morris-Pratt pattern-matching algorithm appropriately to implement a function count_kmp(T,P).

C-13.22 Give a justification of why the compute_kmp_fail function (Code Fragment 13.4) runs in $O(m)$ time on a pattern of length m.

C-13.23 Let T be a text of length n, and let P be a pattern of length m. Describe an $O(n+m)$-time method for finding the longest prefix of P that is a substring of T.

C-13.24 Say that a pattern P of length m is a **circular** substring of a text T of length $n > m$ if P is a (normal) substring of T, or if P is equal to the concatenation of a suffix of T and a prefix of T, that is, if there is an index $0 \le k < m$, such that $P = T[n-m+k:n] + T[0:k]$. Give an $O(n+m)$-time algorithm for determining whether P is a circular substring of T.

C-13.25 The Knuth-Morris-Pratt pattern-matching algorithm can be modified to run faster on binary strings by redefining the failure function as:

$$f(k) = \text{the largest } j < k \text{ such that } P[0:j]\widehat{p}_j \text{ is a suffix of } P[1:k+1],$$

where $\widehat{p}_j$ denotes the complement of the jth bit of P. Describe how to modify the KMP algorithm to be able to take advantage of this new failure function and also give a method for computing this failure function. Show that this method makes at most n comparisons between the text and the pattern (as opposed to the $2n$ comparisons needed by the standard KMP algorithm given in Section 13.2.3).

C-13.26 Modify the simplified Boyer-Moore algorithm presented in this chapter using ideas from the KMP algorithm so that it runs in $O(n+m)$ time.

C-13.27 Design an efficient algorithm for the matrix chain multiplication problem that outputs a fully parenthesized expression for how to multiply the matrices in the chain using the minimum number of operations.

C-13.28 A native Australian named Anatjari wishes to cross a desert carrying only a single water bottle. He has a map that marks all the watering holes along the way. Assuming he can walk k miles on one bottle of water, design an efficient algorithm for determining where Anatjari should refill his bottle in order to make as few stops as possible. Argue why your algorithm is correct.

C-13.29 Describe an efficient greedy algorithm for making change for a specified value using a minimum number of coins, assuming there are four denominations of coins (called quarters, dimes, nickels, and pennies), with values 25, 10, 5, and 1, respectively. Argue why your algorithm is correct.

C-13.30 Give an example set of denominations of coins so that a greedy change-making algorithm will not use the minimum number of coins.

C-13.31 In the *art gallery guarding* problem we are given a line L that represents a long hallway in an art gallery. We are also given a set $X = \{x_0, x_1, \ldots, x_{n-1}\}$ of real numbers that specify the positions of paintings in this hallway. Suppose that a single guard can protect all the paintings within distance at most 1 of his or her position (on both sides). Design an algorithm for finding a placement of guards that uses the minimum number of guards to guard all the paintings with positions in X.

C-13.32 Let P be a convex polygon, a *triangulation* of P is an addition of diagonals connecting the vertices of P so that each interior face is a triangle. The *weight* of a triangulation is the sum of the lengths of the diagonals. Assuming that we can compute lengths and add and compare them in constant time, give an efficient algorithm for computing a minimum-weight triangulation of P.

C-13.33 Let T be a text string of length n. Describe an $O(n)$-time method for finding the longest prefix of T that is a substring of the reversal of T.

C-13.34 Describe an efficient algorithm to find the longest palindrome that is a suffix of a string T of length n. Recall that a *palindrome* is a string that is equal to its reversal. What is the running time of your method?

C-13.35 Given a sequence $S = (x_0, x_1, \ldots, x_{n-1})$ of numbers, describe an $O(n^2)$-time algorithm for finding a longest subsequence $T = (x_{i_0}, x_{i_1}, \ldots, x_{i_{k-1}})$ of numbers, such that $i_j < i_{j+1}$ and $x_{i_j} > x_{i_{j+1}}$. That is, T is a longest decreasing subsequence of S.

C-13.36 Give an efficient algorithm for determining if a pattern P is a subsequence (not substring) of a text T. What is the running time of your algorithm?

C-13.37 Define the *edit distance* between two strings X and Y of length n and m, respectively, to be the number of edits that it takes to change X into Y. An edit consists of a character insertion, a character deletion, or a character replacement. For example, the strings "algorithm" and "rhythm" have edit distance 6. Design an $O(nm)$-time algorithm for computing the edit distance between X and Y.

C-13.38 Let X and Y be strings of length n and m, respectively. Define $B(j,k)$ to be the length of the longest common substring of the suffix $X[n-j:n]$ and the suffix $Y[m-k:m]$. Design an $O(nm)$-time algorithm for computing all the values of $B(j,k)$ for $j = 1,\ldots,n$ and $k = 1,\ldots,m$.

C-13.39 Anna has just won a contest that allows her to take n pieces of candy out of a candy store for free. Anna is old enough to realize that some candy is expensive, while other candy is relatively cheap, costing much less. The jars of candy are numbered 0, 1, ..., $m-1$, so that jar j has n_j pieces in it, with a price of c_j per piece. Design an $O(n+m)$-time algorithm that allows Anna to maximize the value of the pieces of candy she takes for her winnings. Show that your algorithm produces the maximum value for Anna.

C-13.40 Let three integer arrays, A, B, and C, be given, each of size n. Given an arbitrary integer k, design an $O(n^2 \log n)$-time algorithm to determine if there exist numbers, a in A, b in B, and c in C, such that $k = a+b+c$.

C-13.41 Give an $O(n^2)$-time algorithm for the previous problem.

C-13.42 Given a string X of length n and a string Y of length m, describe an $O(n+m)$-time algorithm for finding the longest prefix of X that is a suffix of Y.

C-13.43 Give an efficient algorithm for deleting a string from a standard trie and analyze its running time.

C-13.44 Give an efficient algorithm for deleting a string from a compressed trie and analyze its running time.

C-13.45 Describe an algorithm for constructing the compact representation of a suffix trie, given its noncompact representation, and analyze its running time.

Projects

P-13.46 Use the LCS algorithm to compute the best sequence alignment between some DNA strings, which you can get online from GenBank.

P-13.47 Write a program that takes two character strings (which could be, for example, representations of DNA strands) and computes their edit distance, showing the corresponding pieces. (See Exercise C-13.37.)

P-13.48 Perform an experimental analysis of the efficiency (number of character comparisons performed) of the brute-force and KMP pattern-matching algorithms for varying-length patterns.

P-13.49 Perform an experimental analysis of the efficiency (number of character comparisons performed) of the brute-force and Boyer-Moore pattern-matching algorithms for varying-length patterns.

P-13.50 Perform an experimental comparison of the relative speeds of the brute-force, KMP, and Boyer-Moore pattern-matching algorithms. Document the relative running times on large text documents that are then searched using varying-length patterns.

P-13.51 Experiment with the efficiency of the find method of Python's str class and develop a hypothesis about which pattern-matching algorithm it uses. Try using inputs that are likely to cause both best-case and worst-case running times for various algorithms. Describe your experiments and your conclusions.

P-13.52 Implement a compression and decompression scheme that is based on Huffman coding.

P-13.53 Create a class that implements a standard trie for a set of ASCII strings. The class should have a constructor that takes a list of strings as an argument, and the class should have a method that tests whether a given string is stored in the trie.

P-13.54 Create a class that implements a compressed trie for a set of ASCII strings. The class should have a constructor that takes a list of strings as an argument, and the class should have a method that tests whether a given string is stored in the trie.

P-13.55 Create a class that implements a prefix trie for an ASCII string. The class should have a constructor that takes a string as an argument, and a method for pattern matching on the string.

P-13.56 Implement the simplified search engine described in Section 13.5.4 for the pages of a small Web site. Use all the words in the pages of the site as index terms, excluding stop words such as articles, prepositions, and pronouns.

P-13.57 Implement a search engine for the pages of a small Web site by adding a page-ranking feature to the simplified search engine described in Section 13.5.4. Your page-ranking feature should return the most relevant pages first. Use all the words in the pages of the site as index terms, excluding stop words, such as articles, prepositions, and pronouns.

Chapter Notes

The KMP algorithm is described by Knuth, Morris, and Pratt in their journal article [66], and Boyer and Moore describe their algorithm in a journal article published the same year [18]. In their article, however, Knuth *et al.* [66] also prove that the Boyer-Moore algorithm runs in linear time. More recently, Cole [27] shows that the Boyer-Moore algorithm makes at most $3n$ character comparisons in the worst case, and this bound is tight. All of the algorithms discussed above are also discussed in the book chapter by Aho [4], albeit in a more theoretical framework, including the methods for regular-expression pattern matching. The reader interested in further study of string pattern-matching algorithms is referred to the book by Stephen [90] and the book chapters by Aho [4], and Crochemore and Lecroq [30].

Dynamic programming was developed in the operations research community and formalized by Bellman [13].

The trie was invented by Morrison [79] and is discussed extensively in the classic *Sorting and Searching* book by Knuth [65]. The name "Patricia" is short for "Practical Algorithm to Retrieve Information Coded in Alphanumeric" [79]. McCreight [73] shows how to construct suffix tries in linear time. An introduction to the field of information retrieval, which includes a discussion of search engines for the Web, is provided in the book by Baeza-Yates and Ribeiro-Neto [8].

Chapter

14

Graph Algorithms

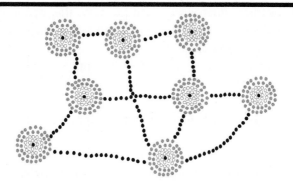

Contents

14.1   Graphs

A **graph** is a way of representing relationships that exist between pairs of objects. That is, a graph is a set of objects, called vertices, together with a collection of pairwise connections between them, called edges. Graphs have applications in modeling many domains, including mapping, transportation, computer networks, and electrical engineering. By the way, this notion of a "graph" should not be confused with bar charts and function plots, as these kinds of "graphs" are unrelated to the topic of this chapter.

Viewed abstractly, a **graph** G is simply a set V of **vertices** and a collection E of pairs of vertices from V, called **edges**. Thus, a graph is a way of representing connections or relationships between pairs of objects from some set V. Incidentally, some books use different terminology for graphs and refer to what we call vertices as **nodes** and what we call edges as **arcs**. We use the terms "vertices" and "edges."

Edges in a graph are either **directed** or **undirected**. An edge (u,v) is said to be **directed** from u to v if the pair (u,v) is ordered, with u preceding v. An edge (u,v) is said to be **undirected** if the pair (u,v) is not ordered. Undirected edges are sometimes denoted with set notation, as $\{u,v\}$, but for simplicity we use the pair notation (u,v), noting that in the undirected case (u,v) is the same as (v,u). Graphs are typically visualized by drawing the vertices as ovals or rectangles and the edges as segments or curves connecting pairs of ovals and rectangles. The following are some examples of directed and undirected graphs.

Example 14.1: *We can visualize collaborations among the researchers of a certain discipline by constructing a graph whose vertices are associated with the researchers themselves, and whose edges connect pairs of vertices associated with researchers who have coauthored a paper or book. (See Figure 14.1.) Such edges are undirected because coauthorship is a* **symmetric** *relation; that is, if A has coauthored something with B, then B necessarily has coauthored something with A.*

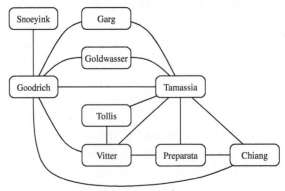

Figure 14.1: Graph of coauthorship among some authors.

Example 14.2: *We can associate with an object-oriented program a graph whose vertices represent the classes defined in the program, and whose edges indicate inheritance between classes. There is an edge from a vertex v to a vertex u if the class for v inherits from the class for u. Such edges are directed because the inheritance relation only goes in one direction (that is, it is* **asymmetric***).*

If all the edges in a graph are undirected, then we say the graph is an ***undirected graph***. Likewise, a ***directed graph***, also called a ***digraph***, is a graph whose edges are all directed. A graph that has both directed and undirected edges is often called a ***mixed graph***. Note that an undirected or mixed graph can be converted into a directed graph by replacing every undirected edge (u,v) by the pair of directed edges (u,v) and (v,u). It is often useful, however, to keep undirected and mixed graphs represented as they are, for such graphs have several applications, as in the following example.

Example 14.3: *A city map can be modeled as a graph whose vertices are intersections or dead ends, and whose edges are stretches of streets without intersections. This graph has both undirected edges, which correspond to stretches of two-way streets, and directed edges, which correspond to stretches of one-way streets. Thus, in this way, a graph modeling a city map is a mixed graph.*

Example 14.4: *Physical examples of graphs are present in the electrical wiring and plumbing networks of a building. Such networks can be modeled as graphs, where each connector, fixture, or outlet is viewed as a vertex, and each uninterrupted stretch of wire or pipe is viewed as an edge. Such graphs are actually components of much larger graphs, namely the local power and water distribution networks. Depending on the specific aspects of these graphs that we are interested in, we may consider their edges as undirected or directed, for, in principle, water can flow in a pipe and current can flow in a wire in either direction.*

The two vertices joined by an edge are called the ***end vertices*** (or ***endpoints***) of the edge. If an edge is directed, its first endpoint is its ***origin*** and the other is the ***destination*** of the edge. Two vertices u and v are said to be ***adjacent*** if there is an edge whose end vertices are u and v. An edge is said to be ***incident*** to a vertex if the vertex is one of the edge's endpoints. The ***outgoing edges*** of a vertex are the directed edges whose origin is that vertex. The ***incoming edges*** of a vertex are the directed edges whose destination is that vertex. The ***degree*** of a vertex v, denoted $\deg(v)$, is the number of incident edges of v. The ***in-degree*** and ***out-degree*** of a vertex v are the number of the incoming and outgoing edges of v, and are denoted $\text{indeg}(v)$ and $\text{outdeg}(v)$, respectively.

Example 14.5: *We can study air transportation by constructing a graph G, called a* **flight network**, *whose vertices are associated with airports, and whose edges are associated with flights. (See Figure 14.2.) In graph G, the edges are directed because a given flight has a specific travel direction. The endpoints of an edge e in G correspond respectively to the origin and destination of the flight corresponding to e. Two airports are adjacent in G if there is a flight that flies between them, and an edge e is incident to a vertex v in G if the flight for e flies to or from the airport for v. The outgoing edges of a vertex v correspond to the outbound flights from v's airport, and the incoming edges correspond to the inbound flights to v's airport. Finally, the in-degree of a vertex v of G corresponds to the number of inbound flights to v's airport, and the out-degree of a vertex v in G corresponds to the number of outbound flights.*

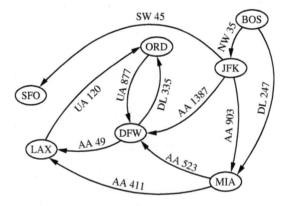

Figure 14.2: Example of a directed graph representing a flight network. The endpoints of edge UA 120 are LAX and ORD; hence, LAX and ORD are adjacent. The in-degree of DFW is 3, and the out-degree of DFW is 2.

The definition of a graph refers to the group of edges as a ***collection***, not a ***set***, thus allowing two undirected edges to have the same end vertices, and for two directed edges to have the same origin and the same destination. Such edges are called ***parallel edges*** or ***multiple edges***. A flight network can contain parallel edges (Example 14.5), such that multiple edges between the same pair of vertices could indicate different flights operating on the same route at different times of the day. Another special type of edge is one that connects a vertex to itself. Namely, we say that an edge (undirected or directed) is a ***self-loop*** if its two endpoints coincide. A self-loop may occur in a graph associated with a city map (Example 14.3), where it would correspond to a "circle" (a curving street that returns to its starting point).

With few exceptions, graphs do not have parallel edges or self-loops. Such graphs are said to be ***simple***. Thus, we can usually say that the edges of a simple graph are a ***set*** of vertex pairs (and not just a collection). Throughout this chapter, we assume that a graph is simple unless otherwise specified.

A *path* is a sequence of alternating vertices and edges that starts at a vertex and ends at a vertex such that each edge is incident to its predecessor and successor vertex. A *cycle* is a path that starts and ends at the same vertex, and that includes at least one edge. We say that a path is *simple* if each vertex in the path is distinct, and we say that a cycle is *simple* if each vertex in the cycle is distinct, except for the first and last one. A *directed path* is a path such that all edges are directed and are traversed along their direction. A *directed cycle* is similarly defined. For example, in Figure 14.2, (BOS, NW 35, JFK, AA 1387, DFW) is a directed simple path, and (LAX, UA 120, ORD, UA 877, DFW, AA 49, LAX) is a directed simple cycle. Note that a directed graph may have a cycle consisting of two edges with opposite direction between the same pair of vertices, for example (ORD, UA 877, DFW, DL 335, ORD) in Figure 14.2. A directed graph is *acyclic* if it has no directed cycles. For example, if we were to remove the edge UA 877 from the graph in Figure 14.2, the remaining graph is acyclic. If a graph is simple, we may omit the edges when describing path P or cycle C, as these are well defined, in which case P is a list of adjacent vertices and C is a cycle of adjacent vertices.

Example 14.6: *Given a graph G representing a city map (see Example 14.3), we can model a couple driving to dinner at a recommended restaurant as traversing a path though G. If they know the way, and do not accidentally go through the same intersection twice, then they traverse a simple path in G. Likewise, we can model the entire trip the couple takes, from their home to the restaurant and back, as a cycle. If they go home from the restaurant in a completely different way than how they went, not even going through the same intersection twice, then their entire round trip is a simple cycle. Finally, if they travel along one-way streets for their entire trip, we can model their night out as a directed cycle.*

Given vertices u and v of a (directed) graph G, we say that u *reaches* v, and that v is *reachable* from u, if G has a (directed) path from u to v. In an undirected graph, the notion of *reachability* is symmetric, that is to say, u reaches v if an only if v reaches u. However, in a directed graph, it is possible that u reaches v but v does not reach u, because a directed path must be traversed according to the respective directions of the edges. A graph is *connected* if, for any two vertices, there is a path between them. A directed graph $\vec{G}$ is *strongly connected* if for any two vertices u and v of $\vec{G}$, u reaches v and v reaches u. (See Figure 14.3 for some examples.)

A *subgraph* of a graph G is a graph H whose vertices and edges are subsets of the vertices and edges of G, respectively. A *spanning subgraph* of G is a subgraph of G that contains all the vertices of the graph G. If a graph G is not connected, its maximal connected subgraphs are called the *connected components* of G. A *forest* is a graph without cycles. A *tree* is a connected forest, that is, a connected graph without cycles. A *spanning tree* of a graph is a spanning subgraph that is a tree. (Note that this definition of a tree is somewhat different from the one given in Chapter 8, as there is not necessarily a designated root.)

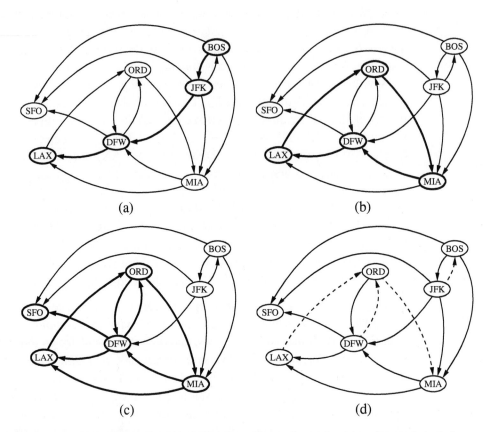

(a)   (b)

(c)   (d)

Figure 14.3: Examples of reachability in a directed graph: (a) a directed path from BOS to LAX is highlighted; (b) a directed cycle (ORD, MIA, DFW, LAX, ORD) is highlighted; its vertices induce a strongly connected subgraph; (c) the subgraph of the vertices and edges reachable from ORD is highlighted; (d) the removal of the dashed edges results in an acyclic directed graph.

Example 14.7: *Perhaps the most talked about graph today is the Internet, which can be viewed as a graph whose vertices are computers and whose (undirected) edges are communication connections between pairs of computers on the Internet. The computers and the connections between them in a single domain, like wiley.com, form a subgraph of the Internet. If this subgraph is connected, then two users on computers in this domain can send email to one another without having their information packets ever leave their domain. Suppose the edges of this subgraph form a spanning tree. This implies that, if even a single connection goes down (for example, because someone pulls a communication cable out of the back of a computer in this domain), then this subgraph will no longer be connected.*

In the propositions that follow, we explore a few important properties of graphs.

Proposition 14.8: *If G is a graph with m edges and vertex set V, then*

$$\sum_{v \ in \ V} deg(v) = 2m.$$

Justification: An edge (u,v) is counted twice in the summation above; once by its endpoint u and once by its endpoint v. Thus, the total contribution of the edges to the degrees of the vertices is twice the number of edges. ■

Proposition 14.9: *If G is a directed graph with m edges and vertex set V, then*

$$\sum_{v \ in \ V} indeg(v) = \sum_{v \ in \ V} outdeg(v) = m.$$

Justification: In a directed graph, an edge (u,v) contributes one unit to the out-degree of its origin u and one unit to the in-degree of its destination v. Thus, the total contribution of the edges to the out-degrees of the vertices is equal to the number of edges, and similarly for the in-degrees. ■

We next show that a simple graph with n vertices has $O(n^2)$ edges.

Proposition 14.10: *Let G be a simple graph with n vertices and m edges. If G is undirected, then $m \leq n(n-1)/2$, and if G is directed, then $m \leq n(n-1)$.*

Justification: Suppose that G is undirected. Since no two edges can have the same endpoints and there are no self-loops, the maximum degree of a vertex in G is $n-1$ in this case. Thus, by Proposition 14.8, $2m \leq n(n-1)$. Now suppose that G is directed. Since no two edges can have the same origin and destination, and there are no self-loops, the maximum in-degree of a vertex in G is $n-1$ in this case. Thus, by Proposition 14.9, $m \leq n(n-1)$. ■

There are a number of simple properties of trees, forests, and connected graphs.

Proposition 14.11: *Let G be an undirected graph with n vertices and m edges.*

- *If G is connected, then $m \geq n-1$.*
- *If G is a tree, then $m = n-1$.*
- *If G is a forest, then $m \leq n-1$.*

14.1.1 The Graph ADT

A graph is a collection of vertices and edges. We model the abstraction as a combination of three data types: Vertex, Edge, and Graph. A Vertex is a lightweight object that stores an arbitrary element provided by the user (e.g., an airport code); we assume it supports a method, element( ), to retrieve the stored element. An Edge also stores an associated object (e.g., a flight number, travel distance, cost), retrieved with the element( ) method. In addition, we assume that an Edge supports the following methods:

endpoints( ): Return a tuple (u, v) such that vertex u is the origin of the edge and vertex v is the destination; for an undirected graph, the orientation is arbitrary.

opposite(v): Assuming vertex v is one endpoint of the edge (either origin or destination), return the other endpoint.

The primary abstraction for a graph is the Graph ADT. We presume that a graph can be either *undirected* or *directed*, with the designation declared upon construction; recall that a mixed graph can be represented as a directed graph, modeling edge $\{u, v\}$ as a pair of directed edges (u, v) and (v, u). The Graph ADT includes the following methods:

vertex_count( ): Return the number of vertices of the graph.

vertices( ): Return an iteration of all the vertices of the graph.

edge_count( ): Return the number of edges of the graph.

edges( ): Return an iteration of all the edges of the graph.

get_edge(u,v): Return the edge from vertex u to vertex v, if one exists; otherwise return None. For an undirected graph, there is no difference between get_edge(u,v) and get_edge(v,u).

degree(v, out=True): For an undirected graph, return the number of edges incident to vertex v. For a directed graph, return the number of outgoing (resp. incoming) edges incident to vertex v, as designated by the optional parameter.

incident_edges(v, out=True): Return an iteration of all edges incident to vertex v. In the case of a directed graph, report outgoing edges by default; report incoming edges if the optional parameter is set to False.

insert_vertex(x=None): Create and return a new Vertex storing element x.

insert_edge(u, v, x=None): Create and return a new Edge from vertex u to vertex v, storing element x (None by default).

remove_vertex(v): Remove vertex v and all its incident edges from the graph.

remove_edge(e): Remove edge e from the graph.

14.2 Data Structures for Graphs

In this section, we introduce four data structures for representing a graph. In each representation, we maintain a collection to store the vertices of a graph. However, the four representations differ greatly in the way they organize the edges.

- In an *edge list*, we maintain an unordered list of all edges. This minimally suffices, but there is no efficient way to locate a particular edge (u,v), or the set of all edges incident to a vertex v.
- In an *adjacency list*, we maintain, for each vertex, a separate list containing those edges that are incident to the vertex. The complete set of edges can be determined by taking the union of the smaller sets, while the organization allows us to more efficiently find all edges incident to a given vertex.
- An *adjacency map* is very similar to an adjacency list, but the secondary container of all edges incident to a vertex is organized as a map, rather than as a list, with the adjacent vertex serving as a key. This allows for access to a specific edge (u,v) in $O(1)$ expected time.
- An *adjacency matrix* provides worst-case $O(1)$ access to a specific edge (u,v) by maintaining an $n \times n$ matrix, for a graph with n vertices. Each entry is dedicated to storing a reference to the edge (u,v) for a particular pair of vertices u and v; if no such edge exists, the entry will be None.

A summary of the performance of these structures is given in Table 14.1. We give further explanation of the structures in the remainder of this section.

Operation	Edge List	Adj. List	Adj. Map	Adj. Matrix
vertex_count( )	$O(1)$	$O(1)$	$O(1)$	$O(1)$
edge_count( )	$O(1)$	$O(1)$	$O(1)$	$O(1)$
vertices( )	$O(n)$	$O(n)$	$O(n)$	$O(n)$
edges( )	$O(m)$	$O(m)$	$O(m)$	$O(m)$
get_edge(u,v)	$O(m)$	$O(\min(d_u,d_v))$	$O(1)$ exp.	$O(1)$
degree(v)	$O(m)$	$O(1)$	$O(1)$	$O(n)$
incident_edges(v)	$O(m)$	$O(d_v)$	$O(d_v)$	$O(n)$
insert_vertex(x)	$O(1)$	$O(1)$	$O(1)$	$O(n^2)$
remove_vertex(v)	$O(m)$	$O(d_v)$	$O(d_v)$	$O(n^2)$
insert_edge(u,v,x)	$O(1)$	$O(1)$	$O(1)$ exp.	$O(1)$
remove_edge(e)	$O(1)$	$O(1)$	$O(1)$ exp.	$O(1)$

Table 14.1: A summary of the running times for the methods of the graph ADT, using the graph representations discussed in this section. We let n denote the number of vertices, m the number of edges, and d_v the degree of vertex v. Note that the adjacency matrix uses $O(n^2)$ space, while all other structures use $O(n+m)$ space.

14.2.1   Edge List Structure

The *edge list* structure is possibly the simplest, though not the most efficient, representation of a graph G. All vertex objects are stored in an unordered list V, and all edge objects are stored in an unordered list E. We illustrate an example of the edge list structure for a graph G in Figure 14.4.

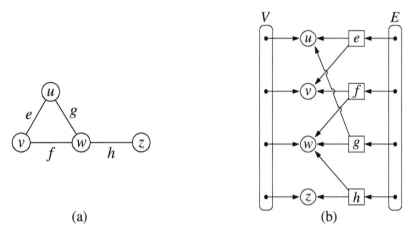

(a)   (b)

Figure 14.4: (a) A graph G; (b) schematic representation of the edge list structure for G. Notice that an edge object refers to the two vertex objects that correspond to its endpoints, but that vertices do not refer to incident edges.

To support the many methods of the Graph ADT (Section 14.1), we assume the following additional features of an edge list representation. Collections V and E are represented with doubly linked lists using our PositionalList class from Chapter 7.

Vertex Objects

The vertex object for a vertex v storing element x has instance variables for:

- A reference to element x, to support the element( ) method.
- A reference to the position of the vertex instance in the list V, thereby allowing v to be efficiently removed from V if it were removed from the graph.

Edge Objects

The edge object for an edge e storing element x has instance variables for:

- A reference to element x, to support the element( ) method.
- References to the vertex objects associated with the endpoint vertices of e. These allow the edge instance to provide constant-time support for methods endpoints( ) and opposite(v).
- A reference to the position of the edge instance in list E, thereby allowing e to be efficiently removed from E if it were removed from the graph.

Performance of the Edge List Structure

The performance of an edge list structure in fulfilling the graph ADT is summarized in Table 14.2. We begin by discussing the space usage, which is $O(n+m)$ for representing a graph with n vertices and m edges. Each individual vertex or edge instance uses $O(1)$ space, and the additional lists V and E use space proportional to their number of entries.

In terms of running time, the edge list structure does as well as one could hope in terms of reporting the number of vertices or edges, or in producing an iteration of those vertices or edges. By querying the respective list V or E, the vertex_count and edge_count methods run in $O(1)$ time, and by iterating through the appropriate list, the methods vertices and edges run respectively in $O(n)$ and $O(m)$ time.

The most significant limitations of an edge list structure, especially when compared to the other graph representations, are the $O(m)$ running times of methods get_edge(u,v), degree(v), and incident_edges(v). The problem is that with all edges of the graph in an unordered list E, the only way to answer those queries is through an exhaustive inspection of all edges. The other data structures introduced in this section will implement these methods more efficiently.

Finally, we consider the methods that update the graph. It is easy to add a new vertex or a new edge to the graph in $O(1)$ time. For example, a new edge can be added to the graph by creating an Edge instance storing the given element as data, adding that instance to the positional list E, and recording its resulting Position within E as an attribute of the edge. That stored position can later be used to locate and remove this edge from E in $O(1)$ time, and thus implement the method remove_edge(e)

It is worth discussing why the remove_vertex(v) method has a running time of $O(m)$. As stated in the graph ADT, when a vertex v is removed from the graph, all edges incident to v must also be removed (otherwise, we would have a contradiction of edges that refer to vertices that are not part of the graph). To locate the incident edges to the vertex, we must examine all edges of E.

Operation	Running Time
vertex_count( ), edge_count( )	$O(1)$
vertices( )	$O(n)$
edges( )	$O(m)$
get_edge(u,v), degree(v), incident_edges(v)	$O(m)$
insert_vertex(x), insert_edge(u,v,x), remove_edge(e)	$O(1)$
remove_vertex(v)	$O(m)$

Table 14.2: Running times of the methods of a graph implemented with the edge list structure. The space used is $O(n+m)$, where n is the number of vertices and m is the number of edges.

14.2.2   Adjacency List Structure

In contrast to the edge list representation of a graph, the *adjacency list* structure groups the edges of a graph by storing them in smaller, secondary containers that are associated with each individual vertex. Specifically, for each vertex v, we maintain a collection $I(v)$, called the *incidence collection* of v, whose entries are edges incident to v. (In the case of a directed graph, outgoing and incoming edges can be respectively stored in two separate collections, $I_{out}(v)$ and $I_{in}(v)$.) Traditionally, the incidence collection $I(v)$ for a vertex v is a list, which is why we call this way of representing a graph the *adjacency list* structure.

We require that the primary structure for an adjacency list maintain the collection V of vertices in a way so that we can locate the secondary structure $I(v)$ for a given vertex v in $O(1)$ time. This could be done by using a positional list to represent V, with each Vertex instance maintaining a direct reference to its $I(v)$ incidence collection; we illustrate such an adjacency list structure of a graph in Figure 14.5. If vertices can be uniquely numbered from 0 to $n-1$, we could instead use a primary array-based structure to access the appropriate secondary lists.

The primary benefit of an adjacency list is that the collection $I(v)$ contains exactly those edges that should be reported by the method incident_edges(v). Therefore, we can implement this method by iterating the edges of $I(v)$ in $O(\deg(v))$ time, where $\deg(v)$ is the degree of vertex v. This is the best possible outcome for any graph representation, because there are $\deg(v)$ edges to be reported.

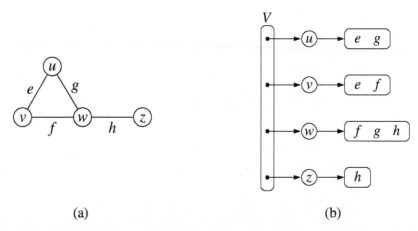

(a)   (b)

Figure 14.5: (a) An undirected graph G; (b) a schematic representation of the adjacency list structure for G. Collection V is the primary list of vertices, and each vertex has an associated list of incident edges. Although not diagrammed as such, we presume that each edge of the graph is represented with a unique Edge instance that maintains references to its endpoint vertices.

Performance of the Adjacency List Structure

Table 14.3 summarizes the performance of the adjacency list structure implementation of a graph, assuming that the primary collection V and all secondary collections $I(v)$ are implemented with doubly linked lists.

Asymptotically, the space requirements for an adjacency list are the same as an edge list structure, using $O(n+m)$ space for a graph with n vertices and m edges. The primary list of vertices uses $O(n)$ space. The sum of the lengths of all secondary lists is $O(m)$, for reasons that were formalized in Propositions 14.8 and 14.9. In short, an undirected edge (u,v) is referenced in both $I(u)$ and $I(v)$, but its presence in the graph results in only a constant amount of additional space.

We have already noted that the incident_edges(v) method can be achieved in $O(\deg(v))$ time based on use of $I(v)$. We can achieve the degree(v) method of the graph ADT to use $O(1)$ time, assuming collection $I(v)$ can report its size in similar time. To locate a specific edge for implementing get_edge(u,v), we can search through either $I(u)$ and $I(v)$. By choosing the smaller of the two, we get $O(\min(\deg(u),\deg(v)))$ running time.

The rest of the bounds in Table 14.3 can be achieved with additional care. To efficiently support deletions of edges, an edge (u,v) would need to maintain a reference to its positions within both $I(u)$ and $I(v)$, so that it could be deleted from those collections in $O(1)$ time. To remove a vertex v, we must also remove any incident edges, but at least we can locate those edges in $O(\deg(v))$ time.

The easiest way to support edges() in $O(m)$ and count_edges() in $O(1)$ is to maintain an auxiliary list E of edges, as in the edge list representation. Otherwise, we can implement the edges method in $O(n+m)$ time by accessing each secondary list and reporting its edges, taking care not to report an undirected edge (u,v) twice.

Operation	Running Time
vertex_count( ), edge_count( )	$O(1)$
vertices( )	$O(n)$
edges( )	$O(m)$
get_edge(u,v)	$O(\min(\deg(u),\deg(v)))$
degree(v)	$O(1)$
incident_edges(v)	$O(\deg(v))$
insert_vertex(x), insert_edge(u,v,x)	$O(1)$
remove_edge(e)	$O(1)$
remove_vertex(v)	$O(\deg(v))$

Table 14.3: Running times of the methods of a graph implemented with the adjacency list structure. The space used is $O(n+m)$, where n is the number of vertices and m is the number of edges.

14.2.3 Adjacency Map Structure

In the adjacency list structure, we assume that the secondary incidence collections are implemented as unordered linked lists. Such a collection $I(v)$ uses space proportional to $O(\deg(v))$, allows an edge to be added or removed in $O(1)$ time, and allows an iteration of all edges incident to vertex v in $O(\deg(v))$ time. However, the best implementation of get_edge(u,v) requires $O(\min(\deg(u), \deg(v)))$ time, because we must search through either $I(u)$ or $I(v)$.

We can improve the performance by using a hash-based map to implement $I(v)$ for each vertex v. Specifically, we let the opposite endpoint of each incident edge serve as a key in the map, with the edge structure serving as the value. We call such a graph representation an ***adjacency map***. (See Figure 14.6.) The space usage for an adjacency map remains $O(n+m)$, because $I(v)$ uses $O(\deg(v))$ space for each vertex v, as with the adjacency list.

The advantage of the adjacency map, relative to an adjacency list, is that the get_edge(u,v) method can be implemented in ***expected*** $O(1)$ time by searching for vertex u as a key in $I(v)$, or vice versa. This provides a likely improvement over the adjacency list, while retaining the worst-case bound of $O(\min(\deg(u), \deg(v)))$.

In comparing the performance of adjacency map to other representations (see Table 14.1), we find that it essentially achieves optimal running times for all methods, making it an excellent all-purpose choice as a graph representation.

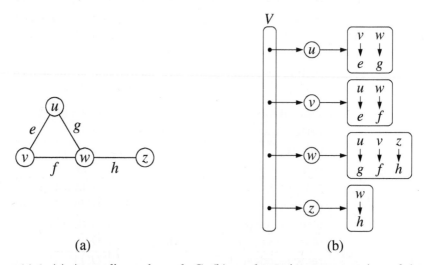

<table>
<tr><td>(a)</td><td>(b)</td></tr>
</table>

Figure 14.6: (a) An undirected graph G; (b) a schematic representation of the adjacency map structure for G. Each vertex maintains a secondary map in which neighboring vertices serve as keys, with the connecting edges as associated values. Although not diagrammed as such, we presume that there is a unique Edge instance for each edge of the graph, and that it maintains references to its endpoint vertices.

14.2.4 Adjacency Matrix Structure

The **adjacency matrix** structure for a graph G augments the edge list structure with a matrix A (that is, a two-dimensional array, as in Section 5.6), which allows us to locate an edge between a given pair of vertices in *worst-case* constant time. In the adjacency matrix representation, we think of the vertices as being the integers in the set $\{0, 1, \ldots, n-1\}$ and the edges as being pairs of such integers. This allows us to store references to edges in the cells of a two-dimensional $n \times n$ array A. Specifically, the cell $A[i, j]$ holds a reference to the edge (u, v), if it exists, where u is the vertex with index i and v is the vertex with index j. If there is no such edge, then $A[i, j] = $ None. We note that array A is symmetric if graph G is undirected, as $A[i, j] = A[j, i]$ for all pairs i and j. (See Figure 14.7.)

The most significant advantage of an adjacency matrix is that any edge (u, v) can be accessed in worst-case $O(1)$ time; recall that the adjacency map supports that operation in $O(1)$ *expected* time. However, several operation are less efficient with an adjacency matrix. For example, to find the edges incident to vertex v, we must presumably examine all n entries in the row associated with v; recall that an adjacency list or map can locate those edges in optimal $O(\deg(v))$ time. Adding or removing vertices from a graph is problematic, as the matrix must be resized.

Furthermore, the $O(n^2)$ space usage of an adjacency matrix is typically far worse than the $O(n+m)$ space required of the other representations. Although, in the worst case, the number of edges in a **dense** graph will be proportional to n^2, most real-world graphs are **sparse**. In such cases, use of an adjacency matrix is inefficient. However, if a graph is dense, the constants of proportionality of an adjacency matrix can be smaller than that of an adjacency list or map. In fact, if edges do not have auxiliary data, a Boolean adjacency matrix can use one bit per edge slot, such that $A[i, j] = $ True if and only if associated (u, v) is an edge.

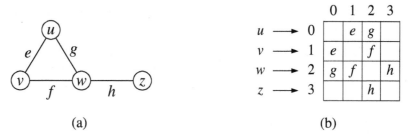

(a)   (b)

Figure 14.7: (a) An undirected graph G; (b) a schematic representation of the auxiliary adjacency matrix structure for G, in which n vertices are mapped to indices 0 to $n-1$. Although not diagrammed as such, we presume that there is a unique Edge instance for each edge, and that it maintains references to its endpoint vertices. We also assume that there is a secondary edge list (not pictured), to allow the edges( ) method to run in $O(m)$ time, for a graph with m edges.

14.2.5 Python Implementation

In this section, we provide an implementation of the Graph ADT. Our implementation will support directed or undirected graphs, but for ease of explanation, we first describe it in the context of an undirected graph.

We use a variant of the ***adjacency map*** representation. For each vertex v, we use a Python dictionary to represent the secondary incidence map $I(v)$. However, we do not explicitly maintain lists V and E, as originally described in the edge list representation. The list V is replaced by a top-level dictionary D that maps each vertex v to its incidence map $I(v)$; note that we can iterate through all vertices by generating the set of keys for dictionary D. By using such a dictionary D to map vertices to the secondary incidence maps, we need not maintain references to those incidence maps as part of the vertex structures. Also, a vertex does not need to explicitly maintain a reference to its position in D, because it can be determined in $O(1)$ expected time. This greatly simplifies our implementation. However, a consequence of our design is that some of the worst-case running time bounds for the graph ADT operations, given in Table 14.1, become ***expected*** bounds. Rather than maintain list E, we are content with taking the union of the edges found in the various incidence maps; technically, this runs in $O(n+m)$ time rather than strictly $O(m)$ time, as the dictionary D has n keys, even if some incidence maps are empty.

Our implementation of the graph ADT is given in Code Fragments 14.1 through 14.3. Classes Vertex and Edge, given in Code Fragment 14.1, are rather simple, and can be nested within the more complex Graph class. Note that we define the __hash__ method for both Vertex and Edge so that those instances can be used as keys in Python's hash-based sets and dictionaries. The rest of the Graph class is given in Code Fragments 14.2 and 14.3. Graphs are undirected by default, but can be declared as directed with an optional parameter to the constructor.

Internally, we manage the directed case by having two different top-level dictionary instances, _outgoing and _incoming, such that _outgoing[v] maps to another dictionary representing $I_{\text{out}}(v)$, and _incoming[v] maps to a representation of $I_{\text{in}}(v)$. In order to unify our treatment of directed and undirected graphs, we continue to use the _outgoing and _incoming identifiers in the undirected case, yet as aliases to the same dictionary. For convenience, we define a utility named is_directed to allow us to distinguish between the two cases.

For methods degree and incident_edges, which each accept an optional parameter to differentiate between the outgoing and incoming orientations, we choose the appropriate map before proceeding. For method insert_vertex, we always initialize _outgoing[v] to an empty dictionary for new vertex v. In the directed case, we independently initialize _incoming[v] as well. For the undirected case, that step is unnecessary as _outgoing and _incoming are aliases. We leave the implementations of methods remove_vertex and remove_edge as exercises (C-14.37 and C-14.38).

```
1    #------------------------ nested Vertex class ------------------------
2    class Vertex:
3      """Lightweight vertex structure for a graph."""
4      __slots__ = '_element'
5
6      def __init__(self, x):
7        """Do not call constructor directly. Use Graph's insert_vertex(x)."""
8        self._element = x
9
10     def element(self):
11       """Return element associated with this vertex."""
12       return self._element
13
14     def __hash__(self):          # will allow vertex to be a map/set key
15       return hash(id(self))
16
17   #------------------------ nested Edge class ------------------------
18   class Edge:
19     """Lightweight edge structure for a graph."""
20     __slots__ = '_origin', '_destination', '_element'
21
22     def __init__(self, u, v, x):
23       """Do not call constructor directly. Use Graph's insert_edge(u,v,x)."""
24       self._origin = u
25       self._destination = v
26       self._element = x
27
28     def endpoints(self):
29       """Return (u,v) tuple for vertices u and v."""
30       return (self._origin, self._destination)
31
32     def opposite(self, v):
33       """Return the vertex that is opposite v on this edge."""
34       return self._destination if v is self._origin else self._origin
35
36     def element(self):
37       """Return element associated with this edge."""
38       return self._element
39
40     def __hash__(self):          # will allow edge to be a map/set key
41       return hash( (self._origin, self._destination) )
```

Code Fragment 14.1: Vertex and Edge classes (to be nested within Graph class).

```
1   class Graph:
2     """Representation of a simple graph using an adjacency map."""
3
4     def __init__(self, directed=False):
5       """Create an empty graph (undirected, by default).
6
7       Graph is directed if optional paramter is set to True.
8       """
9       self._outgoing = { }
10      # only create second map for directed graph; use alias for undirected
11      self._incoming = { } if directed else self._outgoing
12
13    def is_directed(self):
14      """Return True if this is a directed graph; False if undirected.
15
16      Property is based on the original declaration of the graph, not its contents.
17      """
18      return self._incoming is not self._outgoing  # directed if maps are distinct
19
20    def vertex_count(self):
21      """Return the number of vertices in the graph."""
22      return len(self._outgoing)
23
24    def vertices(self):
25      """Return an iteration of all vertices of the graph."""
26      return self._outgoing.keys( )
27
28    def edge_count(self):
29      """Return the number of edges in the graph."""
30      total = sum(len(self._outgoing[v]) for v in self._outgoing)
31      # for undirected graphs, make sure not to double-count edges
32      return total if self.is_directed( ) else total // 2
33
34    def edges(self):
35      """Return a set of all edges of the graph."""
36      result = set( )          # avoid double-reporting edges of undirected graph
37      for secondary_map in self._outgoing.values( ):
38        result.update(secondary_map.values( ))       # add edges to resulting set
39      return result
```

Code Fragment 14.2: Graph class definition (continued in Code Fragment 14.3).

```
40    def get_edge(self, u, v):
41      """Return the edge from u to v, or None if not adjacent."""
42      return self._outgoing[u].get(v)              # returns None if v not adjacent
43
44    def degree(self, v, outgoing=True):
45      """Return number of (outgoing) edges incident to vertex v in the graph.
46
47      If graph is directed, optional parameter used to count incoming edges.
48      """
49      adj = self._outgoing if outgoing else self._incoming
50      return len(adj[v])
51
52    def incident_edges(self, v, outgoing=True):
53      """Return all (outgoing) edges incident to vertex v in the graph.
54
55      If graph is directed, optional parameter used to request incoming edges.
56      """
57      adj = self._outgoing if outgoing else self._incoming
58      for edge in adj[v].values():
59        yield edge
60
61    def insert_vertex(self, x=None):
62      """Insert and return a new Vertex with element x."""
63      v = self.Vertex(x)
64      self._outgoing[v] = { }
65      if self.is_directed():
66        self._incoming[v] = { }         # need distinct map for incoming edges
67      return v
68
69    def insert_edge(self, u, v, x=None):
70      """Insert and return a new Edge from u to v with auxiliary element x."""
71      e = self.Edge(u, v, x)
72      self._outgoing[u][v] = e
73      self._incoming[v][u] = e
```

Code Fragment 14.3: Graph class definition (continued from Code Fragment 14.2). We omit error-checking of parameters for brevity.

14.3   Graph Traversals

Greek mythology tells of an elaborate labyrinth that was built to house the monstrous Minotaur, which was part bull and part man. This labyrinth was so complex that neither beast nor human could escape it. No human, that is, until the Greek hero, Theseus, with the help of the king's daughter, Ariadne, decided to implement a *graph traversal* algorithm. Theseus fastened a ball of thread to the door of the labyrinth and unwound it as he traversed the twisting passages in search of the monster. Theseus obviously knew about good algorithm design, for, after finding and defeating the beast, Theseus easily followed the string back out of the labyrinth to the loving arms of Ariadne.

Formally, a *traversal* is a systematic procedure for exploring a graph by examining all of its vertices and edges. A traversal is efficient if it visits all the vertices and edges in time proportional to their number, that is, in linear time.

Graph traversal algorithms are key to answering many fundamental questions about graphs involving the notion of *reachability*, that is, in determining how to travel from one vertex to another while following paths of a graph. Interesting problems that deal with reachability in an undirected graph G include the following:

- Computing a path from vertex u to vertex v, or reporting that no such path exists.

- Given a start vertex s of G, computing, for every vertex v of G, a path with the minimum number of edges between s and v, or reporting that no such path exists.

- Testing whether G is connected.

- Computing a spanning tree of G, if G is connected.

- Computing the connected components of G.

- Computing a cycle in G, or reporting that G has no cycles.

Interesting problems that deal with reachability in a directed graph $\vec{G}$ include the following:

- Computing a directed path from vertex u to vertex v, or reporting that no such path exists.

- Finding all the vertices of $\vec{G}$ that are reachable from a given vertex s.

- Determine whether $\vec{G}$ is acyclic.

- Determine whether $\vec{G}$ is strongly connected.

In the remainder of this section, we present two efficient graph traversal algorithms, called *depth-first search* and *breadth-first search*, respectively.

14.3.1   Depth-First Search

The first traversal algorithm we consider in this section is ***depth-first search*** (DFS). Depth-first search is useful for testing a number of properties of graphs, including whether there is a path from one vertex to another and whether or not a graph is connected.

Depth-first search in a graph G is analogous to wandering in a labyrinth with a string and a can of paint without getting lost. We begin at a specific starting vertex s in G, which we initialize by fixing one end of our string to s and painting s as "visited." The vertex s is now our "current" vertex—call our current vertex u. We then traverse G by considering an (arbitrary) edge (u,v) incident to the current vertex u. If the edge (u,v) leads us to a vertex v that is already visited (that is, painted), we ignore that edge. If, on the other hand, (u,v) leads to an unvisited vertex v, then we unroll our string, and go to v. We then paint v as "visited," and make it the current vertex, repeating the computation above. Eventually, we will get to a "dead end," that is, a current vertex v such that all the edges incident to v lead to vertices already visited. To get out of this impasse, we roll our string back up, backtracking along the edge that brought us to v, going back to a previously visited vertex u. We then make u our current vertex and repeat the computation above for any edges incident to u that we have not yet considered. If all of u's incident edges lead to visited vertices, then we again roll up our string and backtrack to the vertex we came from to get to u, and repeat the procedure at that vertex. Thus, we continue to backtrack along the path that we have traced so far until we find a vertex that has yet unexplored edges, take one such edge, and continue the traversal. The process terminates when our backtracking leads us back to the start vertex s, and there are no more unexplored edges incident to s.

The pseudo-code for a depth-first search traversal starting at a vertex u (see Code Fragment 14.4) follows our analogy with string and paint. We use recursion to implement the string analogy, and we assume that we have a mechanism (the paint analogy) to determine whether a vertex or edge has been previously explored.

Algorithm DFS(G,u):   {We assume u has already been marked as visited}
    Input: A graph G and a vertex u of G
    Output: A collection of vertices reachable from u, with their discovery edges
    for each outgoing edge e $= (u,v)$ of u **do**
        if vertex v has not been visited **then**
            Mark vertex v as visited (via edge e).
            Recursively call DFS(G,v).

Code Fragment 14.4: The DFS algorithm.

Classifying Graph Edges with DFS

An execution of depth-first search can be used to analyze the structure of a graph, based upon the way in which edges are explored during the traversal. The DFS process naturally identifies what is known as the *depth-first search tree* rooted at a starting vertex *s*. Whenever an edge $e = (u, v)$ is used to discover a new vertex *v* during the DFS algorithm of Code Fragment 14.4, that edge is known as a *discovery edge* or *tree edge*, as oriented from *u* to *v*. All other edges that are considered during the execution of DFS are known as *nontree edges*, which take us to a previously visited vertex. In the case of an undirected graph, we will find that all nontree edges that are explored connect the current vertex to one that is an ancestor of it in the DFS tree. We will call such an edge a *back edge*. When performing a DFS on a directed graph, there are three possible kinds of nontree edges:

- *back edges*, which connect a vertex to an ancestor in the DFS tree
- *forward edges*, which connect a vertex to a descendant in the DFS tree
- *cross edges*, which connect a vertex to a vertex that is neither its ancestor nor its descendant.

An example application of the DFS algorithm on a directed graph is shown in Figure 14.8, demonstrating each type of nontree edge. An example application of the DFS algorithm on an undirected graph is shown in Figure 14.9.

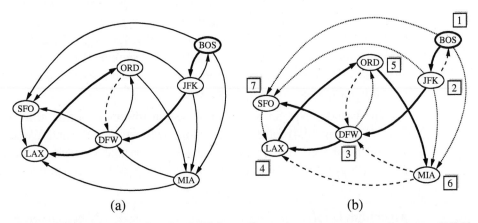

(a)   (b)

Figure 14.8: An example of a DFS in a directed graph, starting at vertex (BOS): (a) intermediate step, where, for the first time, a considered edge leads to an already visited vertex (DFW); (b) the completed DFS. The tree edges are shown with thick lines, the back edges are shown with dashed lines, and the forward and cross edges are shown with dotted lines. The order in which the vertices are visited is indicated by a label next to each vertex. The edge (ORD,DFW) is a back edge, but (DFW,ORD) is a forward edge. Edge (BOS,SFO) is a forward edge, and (SFO,LAX) is a cross edge.

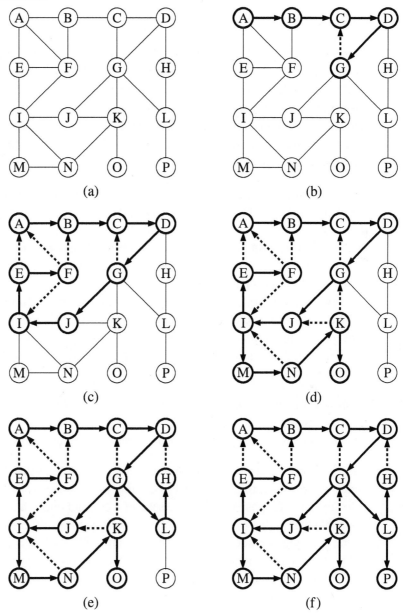

Figure 14.9: Example of depth-first search traversal on an undirected graph starting at vertex *A*. We assume that a vertex's adjacencies are considered in alphabetical order. Visited vertices and explored edges are highlighted, with discovery edges drawn as solid lines and nontree (back) edges as dashed lines: (a) input graph; (b) path of tree edges, traced from A until back edge (G,C) is examined; (c) reaching F, which is a dead end; (d) after backtracking to I, resuming with edge (I,M), and hitting another dead end at O; (e) after backtracking to G, continuing with edge (G,L), and hitting another dead end at H; (f) final result.

Properties of a Depth-First Search

There are a number of observations that we can make about the depth-first search algorithm, many of which derive from the way the DFS algorithm partitions the edges of a graph G into groups. We begin with the most significant property.

Proposition 14.12: *Let G be an undirected graph on which a DFS traversal starting at a vertex s has been performed. Then the traversal visits all vertices in the connected component of s, and the discovery edges form a spanning tree of the connected component of s.*

Justification: Suppose there is at least one vertex w in s's connected component not visited, and let v be the first unvisited vertex on some path from s to w (we may have $v = w$). Since v is the first unvisited vertex on this path, it has a neighbor u that was visited. But when we visited u, we must have considered the edge (u, v); hence, it cannot be correct that v is unvisited. Therefore, there are no unvisited vertices in s's connected component.

Since we only follow a discovery edge when we go to an unvisited vertex, we will never form a cycle with such edges. Therefore, the discovery edges form a connected subgraph without cycles, hence a tree. Moreover, this is a spanning tree because, as we have just seen, the depth-first search visits each vertex in the connected component of s.   ■

Proposition 14.13: *Let $\vec{G}$ be a directed graph. Depth-first search on $\vec{G}$ starting at a vertex s visits all the vertices of $\vec{G}$ that are reachable from s. Also, the DFS tree contains directed paths from s to every vertex reachable from s.*

Justification: Let V_s be the subset of vertices of $\vec{G}$ visited by DFS starting at vertex s. We want to show that V_s contains s and every vertex reachable from s belongs to V_s. Suppose now, for the sake of a contradiction, that there is a vertex w reachable from s that is not in V_s. Consider a directed path from s to w, and let (u, v) be the first edge on such a path taking us out of V_s, that is, u is in V_s but v is not in V_s. When DFS reaches u, it explores all the outgoing edges of u, and thus must reach also vertex v via edge (u, v). Hence, v should be in V_s, and we have obtained a contradiction. Therefore, V_s must contain every vertex reachable from s.

We prove the second fact by induction on the steps of the algorithm. We claim that each time a discovery edge (u, v) is identified, there exists a directed path from s to v in the DFS tree. Since u must have previously been discovered, there exists a path from s to u, so by appending the edge (u, v) to that path, we have a directed path from s to v.   ■

Note that since back edges always connect a vertex v to a previously visited vertex u, each back edge implies a cycle in G, consisting of the discovery edges from u to v plus the back edge (u, v).

Running Time of Depth-First Search

In terms of its running time, depth-first search is an efficient method for traversing a graph. Note that DFS is called at most once on each vertex (since it gets marked as visited), and therefore every edge is examined at most twice for an undirected graph, once from each of its end vertices, and at most once in a directed graph, from its origin vertex. If we let $n_s \leq n$ be the number of vertices reachable from a vertex s, and $m_s \leq m$ be the number of incident edges to those vertices, a DFS starting at s runs in $O(n_s + m_s)$ time, provided the following conditions are satisfied:

- The graph is represented by a data structure such that creating and iterating through the incident_edges(v) takes $O(\deg(v))$ time, and the e.opposite(v) method takes $O(1)$ time. The adjacency list structure is one such structure, but the adjacency matrix structure is not.
- We have a way to "mark" a vertex or edge as explored, and to test if a vertex or edge has been explored in $O(1)$ time. We discuss ways of implementing DFS to achieve this goal in the next section.

Given the assumptions above, we can solve a number of interesting problems.

Proposition 14.14: *Let G be an undirected graph with n vertices and m edges. A DFS traversal of G can be performed in $O(n + m)$ time, and can be used to solve the following problems in $O(n + m)$ time:*

- *Computing a path between two given vertices of G, if one exists.*
- *Testing whether G is connected.*
- *Computing a spanning tree of G, if G is connected.*
- *Computing the connected components of G.*
- *Computing a cycle in G, or reporting that G has no cycles.*

Proposition 14.15: *Let $\vec{G}$ be a directed graph with n vertices and m edges. A DFS traversal of $\vec{G}$ can be performed in $O(n + m)$ time, and can be used to solve the following problems in $O(n + m)$ time:*

- *Computing a directed path between two given vertices of $\vec{G}$, if one exists.*
- *Computing the set of vertices of $\vec{G}$ that are reachable from a given vertex s.*
- *Testing whether $\vec{G}$ is strongly connected.*
- *Computing a directed cycle in $\vec{G}$, or reporting that $\vec{G}$ is acyclic.*
- *Computing the **transitive closure** of $\vec{G}$ (see Section 14.4).*

The justification of Propositions 14.14 and 14.15 is based on algorithms that use slightly modified versions of the DFS algorithm as subroutines. We will explore some of those extensions in the remainder of this section.

14.3.2   DFS Implementation and Extensions

We begin by providing a Python implementation of the basic depth-first search algorithm, originally described with pseudo-code in Code Fragment 14.4. Our DFS function is presented in Code Fragment 14.5.

```
1  def DFS(g, u, discovered):
2    """Perform DFS of the undiscovered portion of Graph g starting at Vertex u.
3
4    discovered is a dictionary mapping each vertex to the edge that was used to
5    discover it during the DFS. (u should be "discovered" prior to the call.)
6    Newly discovered vertices will be added to the dictionary as a result.
7    """
8    for e in g.incident_edges(u):          # for every outgoing edge from u
9      v = e.opposite(u)
10     if v not in discovered:              # v is an unvisited vertex
11       discovered[v] = e                  # e is the tree edge that discovered v
12       DFS(g, v, discovered)              # recursively explore from v
```

Code Fragment 14.5: Recursive implementation of depth-first search on a graph, starting at a designated vertex u.

In order to track which vertices have been visited, and to build a representation of the resulting DFS tree, our implementation introduces a third parameter, named discovered. This parameter should be a Python dictionary that maps a vertex of the graph to the tree edge that was used to discover that vertex. As a technicality, we assume that the source vertex u occurs as a key of the dictionary, with None as its value. Thus, a caller might start the traversal as follows:

```
result = {u : None}        # a new dictionary, with u trivially discovered
DFS(g, u, result)
```

The dictionary serves two purposes. Internally, the dictionary provides a mechanism for recognizing visited vertices, as they will appear as keys in the dictionary. Externally, the DFS function augments this dictionary as it proceeds, and thus the values within the dictionary are the DFS tree edges at the conclusion of the process.

Because the dictionary is hash-based, the test, "**if** v **not in** discovered," and the record-keeping step, "discovered[v] = e," run in $O(1)$ *expected* time, rather than worst-case time. In practice, this is a compromise we are willing to accept, but it does violate the formal analysis of the algorithm, as given on page 643. If we could assume that vertices could be numbered from 0 to $n-1$, then those numbers could be used as indices into an array-based lookup table rather than a hash-based map. Alternatively, we could store each vertex's discovery status and associated tree edge directly as part of the vertex instance.

Reconstructing a Path from *u* to *v*

We can use the basic DFS function as a tool to identify the (directed) path leading from vertex *u* to *v*, if *v* is reachable from *u*. This path can easily be reconstructed from the information that was recorded in the discovery dictionary during the traversal. Code Fragment 14.6 provides an implementation of a secondary function that produces an ordered list of vertices on the path from *u* to *v*.

To reconstruct the path, we begin at the *end* of the path, examining the discovery dictionary to determine what edge was used to reach vertex *v*, and then what the other endpoint of that edge is. We add that vertex to a list, and then repeat the process to determine what edge was used to discover it. Once we have traced the path all the way back to the starting vertex *u*, we can reverse the list so that it is properly oriented from *u* to *v*, and return it to the caller. This process takes time proportional to the length of the path, and therefore it runs in $O(n)$ time (in addition to the time originally spent calling DFS).

```
 1  def construct_path(u, v, discovered):
 2    path = [ ]                                 # empty path by default
 3    if v in discovered:
 4      # we build list from v to u and then reverse it at the end
 5      path.append(v)
 6      walk = v
 7      while walk is not u:
 8        e = discovered[walk]                   # find edge leading to walk
 9        parent = e.opposite(walk)
10        path.append(parent)
11        walk = parent
12      path.reverse( )                          # reorient path from u to v
13    return path
```

Code Fragment 14.6: Function to reconstruct a directed path from *u* to *v*, given the trace of discovery from a DFS started at *u*. The function returns an ordered list of vertices on the path.

Testing for Connectivity

We can use the basic DFS function to determine whether a graph is connected. In the case of an undirected graph, we simply start a depth-first search at an arbitrary vertex and then test whether len(discovered) equals *n* at the conclusion. If the graph is connected, then by Proposition 14.12, all vertices will have been discovered; conversely, if the graph is not connected, there must be at least one vertex *v* that is not reachable from *u*, and that will not be discovered.

For directed graph, $\vec{G}$, we may wish to test whether it is ***strongly connected***, that is, whether for every pair of vertices u and v, both u reaches v and v reaches u. If we start an independent call to DFS from each vertex, we could determine whether this was the case, but those n calls when combined would run in $O(n(n+m))$. However, we can determine if $\vec{G}$ is strongly connected much faster than this, requiring only two depth-first searches.

We begin by performing a depth-first search of our directed graph $\vec{G}$ starting at an arbitrary vertex s. If there is any vertex of $\vec{G}$ that is not visited by this traversal, and is not reachable from s, then the graph is not strongly connected. If this first depth-first search visits each vertex of $\vec{G}$, we need to then check whether s is reachable from all other vertices. Conceptually, we can accomplish this by making a copy of graph $\vec{G}$, but with the orientation of all edges reversed. A depth-first search starting at s in the reversed graph will reach every vertex that could reach s in the original. In practice, a better approach than making a new graph is to reimplement a version of the DFS method that loops through all ***incoming*** edges to the current vertex, rather than all ***outgoing*** edges. Since this algorithm makes just two DFS traversals of $\vec{G}$, it runs in $O(n+m)$ time.

Computing all Connected Components

When a graph is not connected, the next goal we may have is to identify all of the ***connected components*** of an undirected graph, or the ***strongly connected components*** of a directed graph. We begin by discussing the undirected case.

If an initial call to DFS fails to reach all vertices of a graph, we can restart a new call to DFS at one of those unvisited vertices. An implementation of such a comprehensive DFS_all method is given in Code Fragment 14.7.

```
1   def DFS_complete(g):
2     """Perform DFS for entire graph and return forest as a dictionary.
3
4     Result maps each vertex v to the edge that was used to discover it.
5     (Vertices that are roots of a DFS tree are mapped to None.)
6     """
7     forest = { }
8     for u in g.vertices( ):
9       if u not in forest:
10        forest[u] = None                  # u will be the root of a tree
11        DFS(g, u, forest)
12    return forest
```

Code Fragment 14.7: Top-level function that returns a DFS forest for an entire graph.

Although the DFS_complete function makes multiple calls to the original DFS function, the total time spent by a call to DFS_complete is $O(n+m)$. For an undirected graph, recall from our original analysis on page 643 that a single call to DFS starting at vertex s runs in time $O(n_s + m_s)$ where n_s is the number of vertices reachable from s, and m_s is the number of incident edges to those vertices. Because each call to DFS explores a different component, the sum of $n_s + m_s$ terms is $n+m$. The $O(n+m)$ total bound applies to the directed case as well, even though the sets of reachable vertices are not necessarily disjoint. However, because the same discovery dictionary is passed as a parameter to all DFS calls, we know that the DFS subroutine is called once on each vertex, and then each outgoing edge is explored only once during the process.

The DFS_complete function can be used to analyze the connected components of an undirected graph. The discovery dictionary it returns represents a *DFS forest* for the entire graph. We say this is a forest rather than a tree, because the graph may not be connected. The number of connected components can be determined by the number of vertices in the discovery dictionary that have None as their discovery edge (those are roots of DFS trees). A minor modification to the core DFS method could be used to tag each vertex with a component number when it is discovered. (See Exercise C-14.44.)

The situation is more complex for finding strongly connected components of a directed graph. There exists an approach for computing those components in $O(n+m)$ time, making use of two separate depth-first search traversals, but the details are beyond the scope of this book.

Detecting Cycles with DFS

For both undirected and directed graphs, a cycle exists if and only if a *back edge* exists relative to the DFS traversal of that graph. It is easy to see that if a back edge exists, a cycle exists by taking the back edge from the descendant to its ancestor and then following the tree edges back to the descendant. Conversely, if a cycle exists in the graph, there must be a back edge relative to a DFS (although we do not prove this fact here).

Algorithmically, detecting a back edge in the undirected case is easy, because all edges are either tree edges or back edges. In the case of a directed graph, additional modifications to the core DFS implementation are needed to properly categorize a nontree edge as a back edge. When a directed edge is explored leading to a previously visited vertex, we must recognize whether that vertex is an ancestor of the current vertex. This requires some additional bookkeeping, for example, by tagging vertices upon which a recursive call to DFS is still active. We leave details as an exercise (C-14.43).

14.3.3 Breadth-First Search

The advancing and backtracking of a depth-first search, as described in the previous section, defines a traversal that could be physically traced by a single person exploring a graph. In this section, we consider another algorithm for traversing a connected component of a graph, known as a *breadth-first search* (BFS). The BFS algorithm is more akin to sending out, in all directions, many explorers who collectively traverse a graph in coordinated fashion.

A BFS proceeds in rounds and subdivides the vertices into *levels*. BFS starts at vertex s, which is at level 0. In the first round, we paint as "visited," all vertices adjacent to the start vertex s—these vertices are one step away from the beginning and are placed into level 1. In the second round, we allow all explorers to go two steps (i.e., edges) away from the starting vertex. These new vertices, which are adjacent to level 1 vertices and not previously assigned to a level, are placed into level 2 and marked as "visited." This process continues in similar fashion, terminating when no new vertices are found in a level.

A Python implementation of BFS is given in Code Fragment 14.8. We follow a convention similar to that of DFS (Code Fragment 14.5), using a discovered dictionary both to recognize visited vertices, and to record the discovery edges of the BFS tree. We illustrate a BFS traversal in Figure 14.10.

```
1  def BFS(g, s, discovered):
2    """Perform BFS of the undiscovered portion of Graph g starting at Vertex s.
3
4    discovered is a dictionary mapping each vertex to the edge that was used to
5    discover it during the BFS (s should be mapped to None prior to the call).
6    Newly discovered vertices will be added to the dictionary as a result.
7    """
8    level = [s]                          # first level includes only s
9    while len(level) > 0:
10     next_level = [ ]                   # prepare to gather newly found vertices
11     for u in level:
12       for e in g.incident_edges(u):   # for every outgoing edge from u
13         v = e.opposite(u)
14         if v not in discovered:        # v is an unvisited vertex
15           discovered[v] = e            # e is the tree edge that discovered v
16           next_level.append(v)         # v will be further considered in next pass
17     level = next_level                 # relabel 'next' level to become current
```

Code Fragment 14.8: Implementation of breadth-first search on a graph, starting at a designated vertex s.

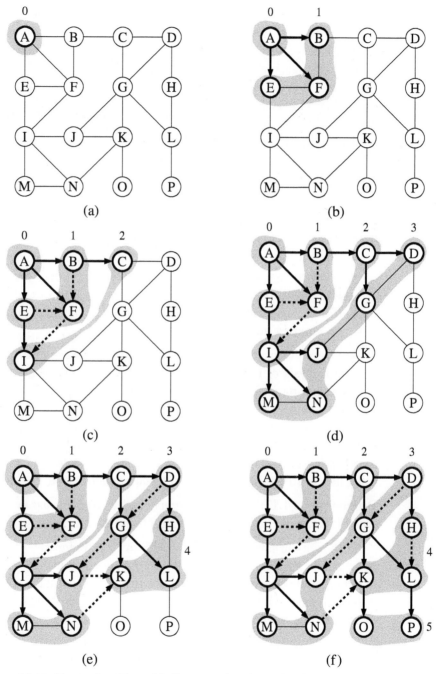

Figure 14.10: Example of breadth-first search traversal, where the edges incident to a vertex are considered in alphabetical order of the adjacent vertices. The discovery edges are shown with solid lines and the nontree (cross) edges are shown with dashed lines: (a) starting the search at A; (b) discovery of level 1; (c) discovery of level 2; (d) discovery of level 3; (e) discovery of level 4; (f) discovery of level 5.

When discussing DFS, we described a classification of nontree edges being either ***back edges***, which connect a vertex to one of its ancestors, ***forward edges***, which connect a vertex to one of its descendants, or ***cross edges***, which connect a vertex to another vertex that is neither its ancestor nor its descendant. For BFS on an undirected graph, all nontree edges are cross edges (see Exercise C-14.47), and for BFS on a directed graph, all nontree edges are either back edges or cross edges (see Exercise C-14.48).

The BFS traversal algorithm has a number of interesting properties, some of which we explore in the proposition that follows. Most notably, a path in a breadth-first search tree rooted at vertex s to any other vertex v is guaranteed to be the shortest such path from s to v in terms of the number of edges.

Proposition 14.16: *Let G be an undirected or directed graph on which a BFS traversal starting at vertex s has been performed. Then*

- *The traversal visits all vertices of G that are reachable from s.*
- *For each vertex v at level i, the path of the BFS tree T between s and v has i edges, and any other path of G from s to v has at least i edges.*
- *If (u,v) is an edge that is not in the BFS tree, then the level number of v can be at most 1 greater than the level number of u.*

We leave the justification of this proposition as an exercise (C-14.50).

The analysis of the running time of BFS is similar to the one of DFS, with the algorithm running in $O(n+m)$ time, or more specifically, in $O(n_s+m_s)$ time if n_s is the number of vertices reachable from vertex s, and $m_s \leq m$ is the number of incident edges to those vertices. To explore the entire graph, the process can be restarted at another vertex, akin to the DFS_complete function of Code Fragment 14.7. Also, the actual path from vertex s to vertex v can be reconstructed using the construct_path function of Code Fragment 14.6

Proposition 14.17: *Let G be a graph with n vertices and m edges represented with the adjacency list structure. A BFS traversal of G takes $O(n+m)$ time.*

Although our implementation of BFS in Code Fragment 14.8 progresses level by level, the BFS algorithm can also be implemented using a single FIFO queue to represent the current fringe of the search. Starting with the source vertex in the queue, we repeatedly remove the vertex from the front of the queue and insert any of its unvisited neighbors to the back of the queue. (See Exercise C-14.51.)

In comparing the capabilities of DFS and BFS, both can be used to efficiently find the set of vertices that are reachable from a given source, and to determine paths to those vertices. However, BFS guarantees that those paths use as few edges as possible. For an undirected graph, both algorithms can be used to test connectivity, to identify connected components, or to locate a cycle. For directed graphs, the DFS algorithm is better suited for certain tasks, such as finding a directed cycle in the graph, or in identifying the strongly connected components.

14.4 Transitive Closure

We have seen that graph traversals can be used to answer basic questions of reachability in a directed graph. In particular, if we are interested in knowing whether there is a path from vertex u to vertex v in a graph, we can perform a DFS or BFS traversal starting at u and observe whether v is discovered. If representing a graph with an adjacency list or adjacency map, we can answer the question of reachability for u and v in $O(n+m)$ time (see Propositions 14.15 and 14.17).

In certain applications, we may wish to answer many reachability queries more efficiently, in which case it may be worthwhile to precompute a more convenient representation of a graph. For example, the first step for a service that computes driving directions from an origin to a destination might be to assess whether the destination is reachable. Similarly, in an electricity network, we may wish to be able to quickly determine whether current flows from one particular vertex to another. Motivated by such applications, we introduce the following definition. The ***transitive closure*** of a directed graph $\vec{G}$ is itself a directed graph $\vec{G}^*$ such that the vertices of $\vec{G}^*$ are the same as the vertices of $\vec{G}$, and $\vec{G}^*$ has an edge (u,v), whenever $\vec{G}$ has a directed path from u to v (including the case where (u,v) is an edge of the original $\vec{G}$).

If a graph is represented as an adjacency list or adjacency map, we can compute its transitive closure in $O(n(n+m))$ time by making use of n graph traversals, one from each starting vertex. For example, a DFS starting at vertex u can be used to determine all vertices reachable from u, and thus a collection of edges originating with u in the transitive closure.

In the remainder of this section, we explore an alternative technique for computing the transitive closure of a directed graph that is particularly well suited for when a directed graph is represented by a data structure that supports $O(1)$-time lookup for the get_edge(u,v) method (for example, the adjacency-matrix structure). Let $\vec{G}$ be a directed graph with n vertices and m edges. We compute the transitive closure of $\vec{G}$ in a series of rounds. We initialize $\vec{G}_0 = \vec{G}$. We also arbitrarily number the vertices of $\vec{G}$ as $v_1, v_2, \ldots, v_n$. We then begin the computation of the rounds, beginning with round 1. In a generic round k, we construct directed graph $\vec{G}_k$ starting with $\vec{G}_k = \vec{G}_{k-1}$ and adding to $\vec{G}_k$ the directed edge (v_i, v_j) if directed graph $\vec{G}_{k-1}$ contains both the edges (v_i, v_k) and (v_k, v_j). In this way, we will enforce a simple rule embodied in the proposition that follows.

Proposition 14.18: *For $i = 1, \ldots, n$, directed graph $\vec{G}_k$ has an edge (v_i, v_j) if and only if directed graph $\vec{G}$ has a directed path from v_i to v_j, whose intermediate vertices (if any) are in the set $\{v_1, \ldots, v_k\}$. In particular, $\vec{G}_n$ is equal to $\vec{G}^*$, the transitive closure of $\vec{G}$.*

Proposition 14.18 suggests a simple algorithm for computing the transitive closure of $\vec{G}$ that is based on the series of rounds to compute each $\vec{G}_k$. This algorithm is known as the ***Floyd-Warshall algorithm***, and its pseudo-code is given in Code Fragment 14.9. We illustrate an example run of the Floyd-Warshall algorithm in Figure 14.11.

Algorithm FloydWarshall($\vec{G}$):
    Input: A directed graph $\vec{G}$ with n vertices
    Output: The transitive closure $\vec{G}^*$ of $\vec{G}$

    let $v_1, v_2, \ldots, v_n$ be an arbitrary numbering of the vertices of $\vec{G}$
    $\vec{G}_0 = \vec{G}$
    for $k = 1$ to n **do**
        $\vec{G}_k = \vec{G}_{k-1}$
        for all i, j in $\{1, \ldots, n\}$ with $i \neq j$ and $i, j \neq k$ **do**
            if both edges (v_i, v_k) and (v_k, v_j) are in $\vec{G}_{k-1}$ **then**
                add edge (v_i, v_j) to $\vec{G}_k$ (if it is not already present)
    return $\vec{G}_n$

Code Fragment 14.9: Pseudo-code for the Floyd-Warshall algorithm. This algorithm computes the transitive closure $\vec{G}^*$ of G by incrementally computing a series of directed graphs $\vec{G}_0, \vec{G}_1, \ldots, \vec{G}_n$, for $k = 1, \ldots, n$.

From this pseudo-code, we can easily analyze the running time of the Floyd-Warshall algorithm assuming that the data structure representing G supports methods get_edge and insert_edge in $O(1)$ time. The main loop is executed n times and the inner loop considers each of $O(n^2)$ pairs of vertices, performing a constant-time computation for each one. Thus, the total running time of the Floyd-Warshall algorithm is $O(n^3)$. From the description and analysis above we may immediately derive the following proposition.

Proposition 14.19: *Let $\vec{G}$ be a directed graph with n vertices, and let $\vec{G}$ be represented by a data structure that supports lookup and update of adjacency information in $O(1)$ time. Then the Floyd-Warshall algorithm computes the transitive closure $\vec{G}^*$ of $\vec{G}$ in $O(n^3)$ time.*

Performance of the Floyd-Warshall Algorithm

Asymptotically, the $O(n^3)$ running time of the Floyd-Warshall algorithm is no better than that achieved by repeatedly running DFS, once from each vertex, to compute the reachability. However, the Floyd-Warshall algorithm matches the asymptotic bounds of the repeated DFS when a graph is dense, or when a graph is sparse but represented as an adjacency matrix. (See Exercise R-14.12.)

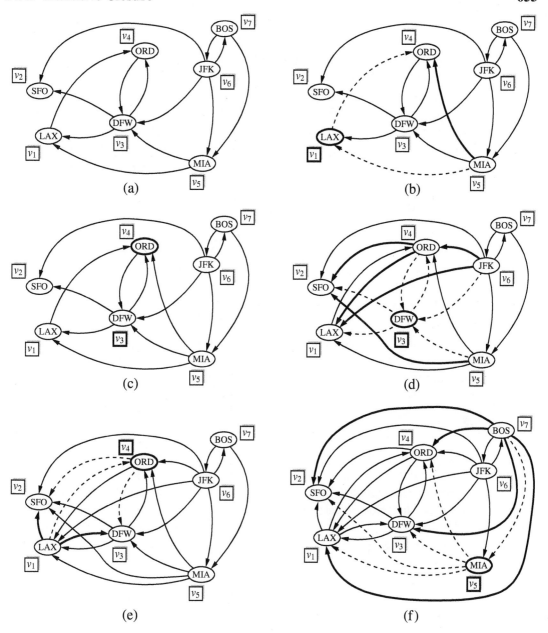

Figure 14.11: Sequence of directed graphs computed by the Floyd-Warshall algorithm: (a) initial directed graph $\vec{G} = \vec{G}_0$ and numbering of the vertices; (b) directed graph $\vec{G}_1$; (c) $\vec{G}_2$; (d) $\vec{G}_3$; (e) $\vec{G}_4$; (f) $\vec{G}_5$. Note that $\vec{G}_5 = \vec{G}_6 = \vec{G}_7$. If directed graph $\vec{G}_{k-1}$ has the edges (v_i, v_k) and (v_k, v_j), but not the edge (v_i, v_j), in the drawing of directed graph $\vec{G}_k$, we show edges (v_i, v_k) and (v_k, v_j) with dashed lines, and edge (v_i, v_j) with a thick line. For example, in (b) existing edges (MIA,LAX) and (LAX,ORD) result in new edge (MIA,ORD).

The importance of the Floyd-Warshall algorithm is that it is much easier to implement than DFS, and much faster in practice because there are relatively few low-level operations hidden within the asymptotic notation. The algorithm is particularly well suited for the use of an adjacency matrix, as a single bit can be used to designate the reachability modeled as an edge (u,v) in the transitive closure.

However, note that repeated calls to DFS results in better asymptotic performance when the graph is sparse and represented using an adjacency list or adjacency map. In that case, a single DFS runs in $O(n+m)$ time, and so the transitive closure can be computed in $O(n^2 + nm)$ time, which is preferable to $O(n^3)$.

Python Implementation

We conclude with a Python implementation of the Floyd-Warshall algorithm, as presented in Code Fragment 14.10. Although the original algorithm is described using a series of directed graphs $\vec{G}_0, \vec{G}_1, \ldots, \vec{G}_n$, we create a single copy of the original graph (using the deepcopy method of Python's copy module) and then repeatedly add new edges to the closure as we progress through rounds of the Floyd-Warshall algorithm.

The algorithm requires a canonical numbering of the graph's vertices; therefore, we create a list of the vertices in the closure graph, and subsequently index that list for our order. Within the outermost loop, we must consider all pairs i and j. Finally, we optimize by only iterating through all values of j after we have verified that i has been chosen such that (v_i, v_k) exists in the current version of our closure.

```
1  def floyd_warshall(g):
2    """Return a new graph that is the transitive closure of g."""
3    closure = deepcopy(g)                          # imported from copy module
4    verts = list(closure.vertices())               # make indexable list
5    n = len(verts)
6    for k in range(n):
7      for i in range(n):
8        # verify that edge (i,k) exists in the partial closure
9        if i != k and closure.get_edge(verts[i],verts[k]) is not None:
10         for j in range(n):
11           # verify that edge (k,j) exists in the partial closure
12           if i != j != k and closure.get_edge(verts[k],verts[j]) is not None:
13             # if (i,j) not yet included, add it to the closure
14             if closure.get_edge(verts[i],verts[j]) is None:
15               closure.insert_edge(verts[i],verts[j])
16    return closure
```

Code Fragment 14.10: Python implementation of the Floyd-Warshall algorithm.

14.5 Directed Acyclic Graphs

Directed graphs without directed cycles are encountered in many applications. Such a directed graph is often referred to as a ***directed acyclic graph***, or ***DAG***, for short. Applications of such graphs include the following:

- Prerequisites between courses of a degree program.
- Inheritance between classes of an object-oriented program.
- Scheduling constraints between the tasks of a project.

We explore this latter application further in the following example:

Example 14.20: *In order to manage a large project, it is convenient to break it up into a collection of smaller tasks. The tasks, however, are rarely independent, because scheduling constraints exist between them. (For example, in a house building project, the task of ordering nails obviously precedes the task of nailing shingles to the roof deck.) Clearly, scheduling constraints cannot have circularities, because they would make the project impossible. (For example, in order to get a job you need to have work experience, but in order to get work experience you need to have a job.) The scheduling constraints impose restrictions on the order in which the tasks can be executed. Namely, if a constraint says that task a must be completed before task b is started, then a must precede b in the order of execution of the tasks. Thus, if we model a feasible set of tasks as vertices of a directed graph, and we place a directed edge from u to v whenever the task for u must be executed before the task for v, then we define a directed acyclic graph.*

14.5.1 Topological Ordering

The example above motivates the following definition. Let $\vec{G}$ be a directed graph with n vertices. A ***topological ordering*** of $\vec{G}$ is an ordering $v_1, \ldots, v_n$ of the vertices of $\vec{G}$ such that for every edge (v_i, v_j) of $\vec{G}$, it is the case that $i < j$. That is, a topological ordering is an ordering such that any directed path in $\vec{G}$ traverses vertices in increasing order. Note that a directed graph may have more than one topological ordering. (See Figure 14.12.)

Proposition 14.21: $\vec{G}$ *has a topological ordering if and only if it is acyclic.*

Justification: The necessity (the "only if" part of the statement) is easy to demonstrate. Suppose $\vec{G}$ is topologically ordered. Assume, for the sake of a contradiction, that $\vec{G}$ has a cycle consisting of edges $(v_{i_0}, v_{i_1}), (v_{i_1}, v_{i_2}), \ldots, (v_{i_{k-1}}, v_{i_0})$. Because of the topological ordering, we must have $i_0 < i_1 < \cdots < i_{k-1} < i_0$, which is clearly impossible. Thus, $\vec{G}$ must be acyclic.

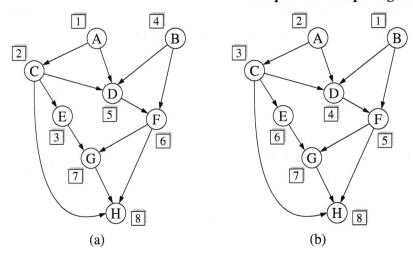

(a)   (b)

Figure 14.12: Two topological orderings of the same acyclic directed graph.

We now argue the sufficiency of the condition (the "if" part). Suppose $\vec{G}$ is acyclic. We will give an algorithmic description of how to build a topological ordering for $\vec{G}$. Since $\vec{G}$ is acyclic, $\vec{G}$ must have a vertex with no incoming edges (that is, with in-degree 0). Let v_1 be such a vertex. Indeed, if v_1 did not exist, then in tracing a directed path from an arbitrary start vertex, we would eventually encounter a previously visited vertex, thus contradicting the acyclicity of $\vec{G}$. If we remove v_1 from $\vec{G}$, together with its outgoing edges, the resulting directed graph is still acyclic. Hence, the resulting directed graph also has a vertex with no incoming edges, and we let v_2 be such a vertex. By repeating this process until the directed graph becomes empty, we obtain an ordering $v_1, \ldots, v_n$ of the vertices of $\vec{G}$. Because of the construction above, if (v_i, v_j) is an edge of $\vec{G}$, then v_i must be deleted before v_j can be deleted, and thus, $i < j$. Therefore, $v_1, \ldots, v_n$ is a topological ordering. ∎

Proposition 14.21's justification suggests an algorithm for computing a topological ordering of a directed graph, which we call *topological sorting*. We present a Python implementation of the technique in Code Fragment 14.11, and an example execution of the algorithm in Figure 14.13. Our implementation uses a dictionary, named incount, to map each vertex v to a counter that represents the current number of incoming edges to v, excluding those coming from vertices that have previously been added to the topological order. Technically, a Python dictionary provides $O(1)$ expected time access to entries, rather than worst-case time; as was the case with our graph traversals, this could be converted to worst-case time if vertices could be indexed from 0 to $n-1$, or if we store the counter as an element of a vertex.

As a side effect, the topological sorting algorithm of Code Fragment 14.11 also tests whether the given directed graph $\vec{G}$ is acyclic. Indeed, if the algorithm terminates without ordering all the vertices, then the subgraph of the vertices that have not been ordered must contain a directed cycle.

```
1   def topological_sort(g):
2     """Return a list of verticies of directed acyclic graph g in topological order.
3
4     If graph g has a cycle, the result will be incomplete.
5     """
6     topo = [ ]                    # a list of vertices placed in topological order
7     ready = [ ]                   # list of vertices that have no remaining constraints
8     incount = { }                 # keep track of in-degree for each vertex
9     for u in g.vertices():
10      incount[u] = g.degree(u, False)      # parameter requests incoming degree
11      if incount[u] == 0:                   # if u has no incoming edges,
12        ready.append(u)                     # it is free of constraints
13    while len(ready) > 0:
14      u = ready.pop( )                      # u is free of constraints
15      topo.append(u)                        # add u to the topological order
16      for e in g.incident_edges(u):         # consider all outgoing neighbors of u
17        v = e.opposite(u)
18        incount[v] −= 1                      # v has one less constraint without u
19        if incount[v] == 0:
20          ready.append(v)
21    return topo
```

Code Fragment 14.11: Python implementation for the topological sorting algorithm. (We show an example execution of this algorithm in Figure 14.13.)

Performance of Topological Sorting

Proposition 14.22: *Let $\vec{G}$ be a directed graph with n vertices and m edges, using an adjacency list representation. The topological sorting algorithm runs in $O(n+m)$ time using $O(n)$ auxiliary space, and either computes a topological ordering of $\vec{G}$ or fails to include some vertices, which indicates that $\vec{G}$ has a directed cycle.*

Justification: The initial recording of the n in-degrees uses $O(n)$ time based on the degree method. Say that a vertex u is *visited* by the topological sorting algorithm when u is removed from the ready list. A vertex u can be visited only when incount(u) is 0, which implies that all its predecessors (vertices with outgoing edges into u) were previously visited. As a consequence, any vertex that is on a directed cycle will never be visited, and any other vertex will be visited exactly once. The algorithm traverses all the outgoing edges of each visited vertex once, so its running time is proportional to the number of outgoing edges of the visited vertices. In accordance with Proposition 14.9, the running time is $(n+m)$. Regarding the space usage, observe that containers topo, ready, and incount have at most one entry per vertex, and therefore use $O(n)$ space. ∎

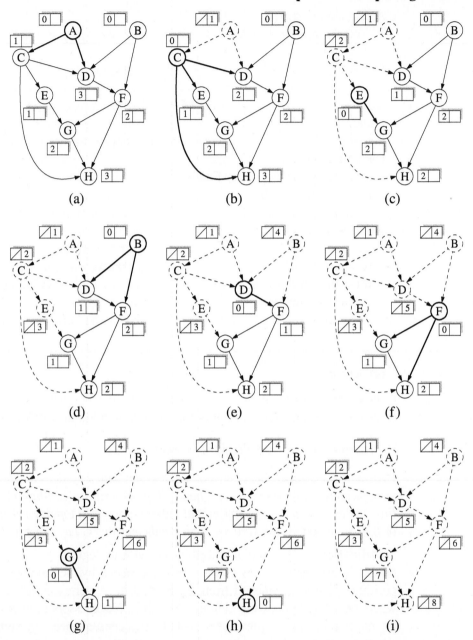

Figure 14.13: Example of a run of algorithm topological_sort (Code Fragment 14.11). The label near a vertex shows its current incount value, and its eventual rank in the resulting topological order. The highlighted vertex is one with incount equal to zero that will become the next vertex in the topological order. Dashed lines denote edges that have already been examined and which are no longer reflected in the incount values.

14.6 Shortest Paths

As we saw in Section 14.3.3, the breadth-first search strategy can be used to find a shortest path from some starting vertex to every other vertex in a connected graph. This approach makes sense in cases where each edge is as good as any other, but there are many situations where this approach is not appropriate.

For example, we might want to use a graph to represent the roads between cities, and we might be interested in finding the fastest way to travel cross-country. In this case, it is probably not appropriate for all the edges to be equal to each other, for some inter-city distances will likely be much larger than others. Likewise, we might be using a graph to represent a computer network (such as the Internet), and we might be interested in finding the fastest way to route a data packet between two computers. In this case, it again may not be appropriate for all the edges to be equal to each other, for some connections in a computer network are typically much faster than others (for example, some edges might represent low-bandwidth connections, while others might represent high-speed, fiber-optic connections). It is natural, therefore, to consider graphs whose edges are not weighted equally.

14.6.1 Weighted Graphs

A ***weighted graph*** is a graph that has a numeric (for example, integer) label $w(e)$ associated with each edge e, called the ***weight*** of edge e. For $e = (u,v)$, we let notation $w(u,v) = w(e)$. We show an example of a weighted graph in Figure 14.14.

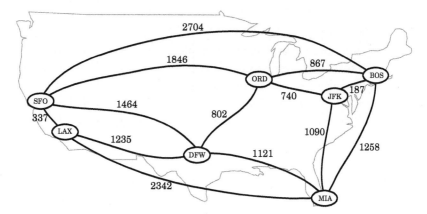

Figure 14.14: A weighted graph whose vertices represent major U.S. airports and whose edge weights represent distances in miles. This graph has a path from JFK to LAX of total weight 2,777 (going through ORD and DFW). This is the minimum-weight path in the graph from JFK to LAX.

Defining Shortest Paths in a Weighted Graph

Let G be a weighted graph. The *length* (or weight) of a path is the sum of the weights of the edges of P. That is, if $P = ((v_0, v_1), (v_1, v_2), \ldots, (v_{k-1}, v_k))$, then the length of P, denoted $w(P)$, is defined as

$$w(P) = \sum_{i=0}^{k-1} w(v_i, v_{i+1}).$$

The *distance* from a vertex u to a vertex v in G, denoted $d(u, v)$, is the length of a minimum-length path (also called *shortest path*) from u to v, if such a path exists.

People often use the convention that $d(u, v) = \infty$ if there is no path at all from u to v in G. Even if there is a path from u to v in G, however, if there is a cycle in G whose total weight is negative, the distance from u to v may not be defined. For example, suppose vertices in G represent cities, and the weights of edges in G represent how much money it costs to go from one city to another. If someone were willing to actually pay us to go from say JFK to ORD, then the "cost" of the edge (JFK,ORD) would be negative. If someone else were willing to pay us to go from ORD to JFK, then there would be a negative-weight cycle in G and distances would no longer be defined. That is, anyone could now build a path (with cycles) in G from any city A to another city B that first goes to JFK and then cycles as many times as he or she likes from JFK to ORD and back, before going on to B. The existence of such paths would allow us to build arbitrarily low negative-cost paths (and, in this case, make a fortune in the process). But distances cannot be arbitrarily low negative numbers. Thus, any time we use edge weights to represent distances, we must be careful not to introduce any negative-weight cycles.

Suppose we are given a weighted graph G, and we are asked to find a shortest path from some vertex s to each other vertex in G, viewing the weights on the edges as distances. In this section, we explore efficient ways of finding all such shortest paths, if they exist. The first algorithm we discuss is for the simple, yet common, case when all the edge weights in G are nonnegative (that is, $w(e) \geq 0$ for each edge e of G); hence, we know in advance that there are no negative-weight cycles in G. Recall that the special case of computing a shortest path when all weights are equal to one was solved with the BFS traversal algorithm presented in Section 14.3.3.

There is an interesting approach for solving this *single-source* problem based on the *greedy method* design pattern (Section 13.4.2). Recall that in this pattern we solve the problem at hand by repeatedly selecting the best choice from among those available in each iteration. This paradigm can often be used in situations where we are trying to optimize some cost function over a collection of objects. We can add objects to our collection, one at a time, always picking the next one that optimizes the function from among those yet to be chosen.

14.6.2 Dijkstra's Algorithm

The main idea in applying the greedy method pattern to the single-source shortest-path problem is to perform a "weighted" breadth-first search starting at the source vertex s. In particular, we can use the greedy method to develop an algorithm that iteratively grows a "cloud" of vertices out of s, with the vertices entering the cloud in order of their distances from s. Thus, in each iteration, the next vertex chosen is the vertex outside the cloud that is closest to s. The algorithm terminates when no more vertices are outside the cloud (or when those outside the cloud are not connected to those within the cloud), at which point we have a shortest path from s to every vertex of G that is reachable from s. This approach is a simple, but nevertheless powerful, example of the greedy method design pattern. Applying the greedy method to the single-source, shortest-path problem, results in an algorithm known as ***Dijkstra's algorithm***.

Edge Relaxation

Let us define a label $D[v]$ for each vertex v in V, which we use to approximate the distance in G from s to v. The meaning of these labels is that $D[v]$ will always store the length of the best path we have found *so far* from s to v. Initially, $D[s] = 0$ and $D[v] = \infty$ for each $v \neq s$, and we define the set C, which is our "*cloud*" of vertices, to initially be the empty set. At each iteration of the algorithm, we select a vertex u not in C with smallest $D[u]$ label, and we pull u into C. (In general, we will use a priority queue to select among the vertices outside the cloud.) In the very first iteration we will, of course, pull s into C. Once a new vertex u is pulled into C, we then update the label $D[v]$ of each vertex v that is adjacent to u and is outside of C, to reflect the fact that there may be a new and better way to get to v via u. This update operation is known as a ***relaxation*** procedure, for it takes an old estimate and checks if it can be improved to get closer to its true value. The specific edge relaxation operation is as follows:

> **Edge Relaxation:**
> $$\textbf{if } D[u] + w(u,v) < D[v] \textbf{ then}$$
> $$D[v] = D[u] + w(u,v)$$

Algorithm Description and Example

We give the pseudo-code for Dijkstra's algorithm in Code Fragment 14.12, and illustrate several iterations of Dijkstra's algorithm in Figures 14.15 through 14.17.

Algorithm ShortestPath(G, s):

    Input: A weighted graph G with nonnegative edge weights, and a distinguished vertex s of G.

    Output: The length of a shortest path from s to v for each vertex v of G.

    Initialize $D[s] = 0$ and $D[v] = \infty$ for each vertex $v \neq s$.

    Let a priority queue Q contain all the vertices of G using the D labels as keys.

    while Q is not empty **do**

        {pull a new vertex u into the cloud}

        $u =$ value returned by Q.remove_min()

        for each vertex v adjacent to u such that v is in Q **do**

            {perform the *relaxation* procedure on edge (u, v)}

            if $D[u] + w(u, v) < D[v]$ **then**

                $D[v] = D[u] + w(u, v)$

                Change to $D[v]$ the key of vertex v in Q.

    return the label $D[v]$ of each vertex v

Code Fragment 14.12: Pseudo-code for Dijkstra's algorithm, solving the single-source shortest-path problem.

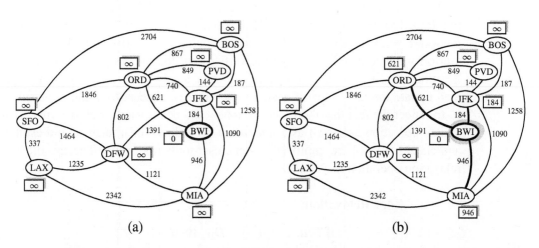

(a)   (b)

Figure 14.15: An execution of Dijkstra's algorithm on a weighted graph. The start vertex is BWI. A box next to each vertex v stores the label $D[v]$. The edges of the shortest-path tree are drawn as thick arrows, and for each vertex u outside the "cloud" we show the current best edge for pulling in u with a thick line. (Continues in Figure 14.16.)

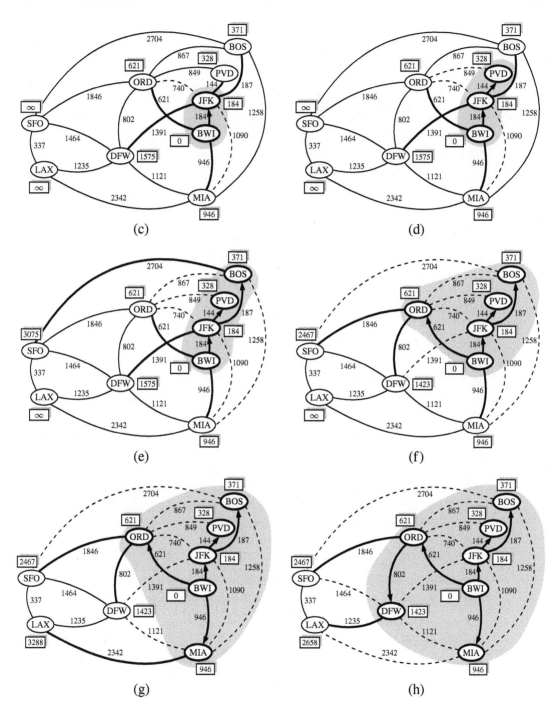

Figure 14.16: An example execution of Dijkstra's algorithm. (Continued from Figure 14.15; continued in Figure 14.17.)

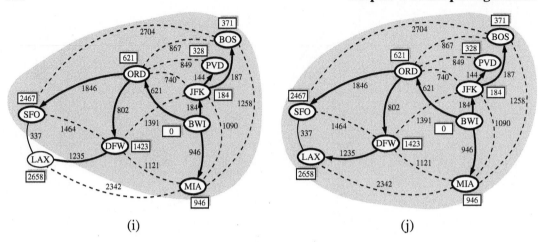

(i)   (j)

Figure 14.17: An example execution of Dijkstra's algorithm. (Continued from Figure 14.16.)

Why It Works

The interesting aspect of the Dijkstra algorithm is that, at the moment a vertex u is pulled into C, its label $D[u]$ stores the correct length of a shortest path from v to u. Thus, when the algorithm terminates, it will have computed the shortest-path distance from s to every vertex of G. That is, it will have solved the single-source shortest-path problem.

It is probably not immediately clear why Dijkstra's algorithm correctly finds the shortest path from the start vertex s to each other vertex u in the graph. Why is it that the distance from s to u is equal to the value of the label $D[u]$ at the time vertex u is removed from the priority queue Q and added to the cloud C? The answer to this question depends on there being no negative-weight edges in the graph, for it allows the greedy method to work correctly, as we show in the proposition that follows.

Proposition 14.23: *In Dijkstra's algorithm, whenever a vertex v is pulled into the cloud, the label $D[v]$ is equal to $d(s,v)$, the length of a shortest path from s to v.*

Justification: Suppose that $D[v] > d(s,v)$ for some vertex v in V, and let z be the **first** vertex the algorithm pulled into the cloud C (that is, removed from Q) such that $D[z] > d(s,z)$. There is a shortest path P from s to z (for otherwise $d(s,z) = \infty = D[z]$). Let us therefore consider the moment when z is pulled into C, and let y be the first vertex of P (when going from s to z) that is not in C at this moment. Let x be the predecessor of y in path P (note that we could have $x = s$). (See Figure 14.18.) We know, by our choice of y, that x is already in C at this point.

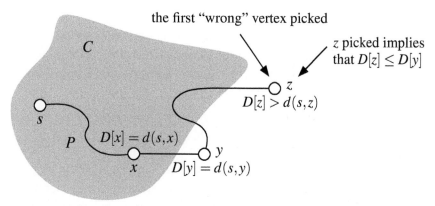

Figure 14.18: A schematic illustration for the justification of Proposition 14.23.

Moreover, $D[x] = d(s,x)$, since z is the **first** incorrect vertex. When x was pulled into C, we tested (and possibly updated) $D[y]$ so that we had at that point

$$D[y] \leq D[x] + w(x,y) = d(s,x) + w(x,y).$$

But since y is the next vertex on the shortest path from s to z, this implies that

$$D[y] = d(s,y).$$

But we are now at the moment when we are picking z, not y, to join C; hence,

$$D[z] \leq D[y].$$

It should be clear that a subpath of a shortest path is itself a shortest path. Hence, since y is on the shortest path from s to z,

$$d(s,y) + d(y,z) = d(s,z).$$

Moreover, $d(y,z) \geq 0$ because there are no negative-weight edges. Therefore,

$$D[z] \leq D[y] = d(s,y) \leq d(s,y) + d(y,z) = d(s,z).$$

But this contradicts the definition of z; hence, there can be no such vertex z. ∎

The Running Time of Dijkstra's Algorithm

In this section, we analyze the time complexity of Dijkstra's algorithm. We denote with n and m the number of vertices and edges of the input graph G, respectively. We assume that the edge weights can be added and compared in constant time. Because of the high level of the description we gave for Dijkstra's algorithm in Code Fragment 14.12, analyzing its running time requires that we give more details on its implementation. Specifically, we should indicate the data structures used and how they are implemented.

Let us first assume that we are representing the graph G using an adjacency list or adjacency map structure. This data structure allows us to step through the vertices adjacent to u during the relaxation step in time proportional to their number. Therefore, the time spent in the management of the nested **for** loop, and the number of iterations of that loop, is

$$\sum_{u \text{ in } V_G} \text{outdeg}(u),$$

which is $O(m)$ by Proposition 14.9. The outer **while** loop executes $O(n)$ times, since a new vertex is added to the cloud during each iteration. This still does not settle all the details for the algorithm analysis, however, for we must say more about how to implement the other principal data structure in the algorithm—the priority queue Q.

Referring back to Code Fragment 14.12 in search of priority queue operations, we find that n vertices are originally inserted into the priority queue; since these are the only insertions, the maximum size of the queue is n. In each of n iterations of the **while** loop, a call to remove_min is made to extract the vertex u with smallest D label from Q. Then, for each neighbor v of u, we perform an edge relaxation, and may potentially update the key of v in the queue. Thus, we actually need an implementation of an *adaptable priority queue* (Section 9.5), in which case the key of a vertex v is changed using the method update(ℓ, k), where ℓ is the locator for the priority queue entry associated with vertex v. In the worst case, there could be one such update for each edge of the graph. Overall, the running time of Dijkstra's algorithm is bounded by the sum of the following:

- n insertions into Q.
- n calls to the remove_min method on Q.
- m calls to the update method on Q.

If Q is an adaptable priority queue implemented as a heap, then each of the above operations run in $O(\log n)$, and so the overall running time for Dijkstra's algorithm is $O((n+m)\log n)$. Note that if we wish to express the running time as a function of n only, then it is $O(n^2 \log n)$ in the worst case.

Let us now consider an alternative implementation for the adaptable priority queue Q using an unsorted sequence. (See Exercise P-9.58.) This, of course, requires that we spend $O(n)$ time to extract the minimum element, but it affords very fast key updates, provided Q supports location-aware entries (Section 9.5.1). Specifically, we can implement each key update done in a relaxation step in $O(1)$ time—we simply change the key value once we locate the entry in Q to update. Hence, this implementation results in a running time that is $O(n^2 + m)$, which can be simplified to $O(n^2)$ since G is simple.

Comparing the Two Implementations

We have two choices for implementing the adaptable priority queue with location-aware entries in Dijkstra's algorithm: a heap implementation, which yields a running time of $O((n+m)\log n)$, and an unsorted sequence implementation, which yields a running time of $O(n^2)$. Since both implementations would be fairly simple to code, they are about equal in terms of the programming sophistication needed. These two implementations are also about equal in terms of the constant factors in their worst-case running times. Looking only at these worst-case times, we prefer the heap implementation when the number of edges in the graph is small (that is, when $m < n^2/\log n$), and we prefer the sequence implementation when the number of edges is large (that is, when $m > n^2/\log n$).

Proposition 14.24: *Given a weighted graph G with n vertices and m edges, such that the weight of each edge is nonnegative, and a vertex s of G, Dijkstra's algorithm can compute the distance from s to all other vertices of G in the better of $O(n^2)$ or $O((n+m)\log n)$ time.*

We note that an advanced priority queue implementation, known as a **_Fibonacci heap_**, can be used to implement Dijkstra's algorithm in $O(m+n\log n)$ time.

Programming Dijkstra's Algorithm in Python

Having given a pseudo-code description of Dijkstra's algorithm, let us now present Python code for performing Dijkstra's algorithm, assuming we are given a graph whose edge elements are nonnegative integer weights. Our implementation of the algorithm is in the form of a function, shortest_path_lengths, that takes a graph and a designated source vertex as parameters. (See Code Fragment 14.13.) It returns a dictionary, named cloud, mapping each vertex v that is reachable from the source to its shortest-path distance $d(s,v)$. We rely on our AdaptableHeapPriorityQueue developed in Section 9.5.2 as an adaptable priority queue.

As we have done with other algorithms in this chapter, we rely on dictionaries to map vertices to associated data (in this case, mapping v to its distance bound $D[v]$ and its adaptable priority queue locator). The expected $O(1)$-time access to elements of these dictionaries could be converted to worst-case bounds, either by numbering vertices from 0 to $n-1$ to use as indices into a list, or by storing the information within each vertex's element.

The pseudo-code for Dijkstra's algorithm begins by assigning $d[v] = \infty$ for each v other than the source. We rely on the special value **float**('inf') in Python to provide a numeric value that represents positive infinity. However, we avoid including vertices with this "infinite" distance in the resulting cloud that is returned by the function. The use of this numeric limit could be avoided altogether by waiting to add a vertex to the priority queue until after an edge that reaches it is relaxed. (See Exercise C-14.64.)

```
1   def shortest_path_lengths(g, src):
2     """Compute shortest-path distances from src to reachable vertices of g.
3
4     Graph g can be undirected or directed, but must be weighted such that
5     e.element() returns a numeric weight for each edge e.
6
7     Return dictionary mapping each reachable vertex to its distance from src.
8     """
9     d = { }                                # d[v] is upper bound from s to v
10    cloud = { }                            # map reachable v to its d[v] value
11    pq = AdaptableHeapPriorityQueue( )     # vertex v will have key d[v]
12    pqlocator = { }                        # map from vertex to its pq locator
13
14    # for each vertex v of the graph, add an entry to the priority queue, with
15    # the source having distance 0 and all others having infinite distance
16    for v in g.vertices( ):
17      if v is src:
18        d[v] = 0
19      else:
20        d[v] = float('inf')                # syntax for positive infinity
21      pqlocator[v] = pq.add(d[v], v)       # save locator for future updates
22
23    while not pq.is_empty( ):
24      key, u = pq.remove_min( )
25      cloud[u] = key                       # its correct d[u] value
26      del pqlocator[u]                     # u is no longer in pq
27      for e in g.incident_edges(u):        # outgoing edges (u,v)
28        v = e.opposite(u)
29        if v not in cloud:
30          # perform relaxation step on edge (u,v)
31          wgt = e.element( )
32          if d[u] + wgt < d[v]:            # better path to v?
33            d[v] = d[u] + wgt              # update the distance
34            pq.update(pqlocator[v], d[v], v)   # update the pq entry
35
36    return cloud                           # only includes reachable vertices
```

Code Fragment 14.13: Python implementation of Dijkstra's algorithm for comput-ing the shortest-path distances from a single source. We assume that e.element( ) for edge e represents the weight of that edge.

Reconstructing the Shortest-Path Tree

Our pseudo-code description of Dijkstra's algorithm in Code Fragment 14.12, and our implementation in Code Fragment 14.13, computes the value $d[v]$, for each vertex v, that is the length of the shortest path from the source vertex s to v. However, those forms of the algorithm do not explicitly compute the actual paths that achieve those distances. The collection of all shortest paths emanating from source s can be compactly represented by what is known as the ***shortest-path tree***. The paths form a rooted tree because if a shortest path from s to v passes through an intermediate vertex u, it must begin with a shortest path from s to u.

In this section, we demonstrate that the shortest-path tree rooted at source s can be reconstructed in $O(n+m)$ time, given the set of $d[v]$ values produced by Dijkstra's algorithm using s as the source. As we did when representing the DFS and BFS trees, we will map each vertex $v \neq s$ to a parent u (possibly, $u = s$), such that u is the vertex immediately before v on a shortest path from s to v. If u is the vertex just before v on the shortest path from s to v, it must be that

$$d[u] + w(u,v) = d[v].$$

Conversely, if the above equation is satisfied, then the shortest path from s to u, followed by the edge (u,v) is a shortest path to v.

Our implementation in Code Fragment 14.14 reconstructs the tree based on this logic, testing all *incoming* edges to each vertex v, looking for a (u,v) that satisfies the key equation. The running time is $O(n+m)$, as we consider each vertex and all incoming edges to those vertices. (See Proposition 14.9.)

```
1  def shortest_path_tree(g, s, d):
2    """Reconstruct shortest-path tree rooted at vertex s, given distance map d.
3
4    Return tree as a map from each reachable vertex v (other than s) to the
5    edge e=(u,v) that is used to reach v from its parent u in the tree.
6    """
7    tree = { }
8    for v in d:
9      if v is not s:
10        for e in g.incident_edges(v, False):      # consider INCOMING edges
11          u = e.opposite(v)
12          wgt = e.element( )
13          if d[v] == d[u] + wgt:
14            tree[v] = e                           # edge e is used to reach v
15    return tree
```

Code Fragment 14.14: Python function that reconstructs the shortest paths, based on knowledge of the single-source distances.

14.7   Minimum Spanning Trees

Suppose we wish to connect all the computers in a new office building using the least amount of cable. We can model this problem using an undirected, weighted graph G whose vertices represent the computers, and whose edges represent all the possible pairs (u,v) of computers, where the weight $w(u,v)$ of edge (u,v) is equal to the amount of cable needed to connect computer u to computer v. Rather than computing a shortest-path tree from some particular vertex v, we are interested instead in finding a tree T that contains all the vertices of G and has the minimum total weight over all such trees. Algorithms for finding such a tree are the focus of this section.

Problem Definition

Given an undirected, weighted graph G, we are interested in finding a tree T that contains all the vertices in G and minimizes the sum

$$w(T) = \sum_{(u,v) \text{ in } T} w(u,v).$$

A tree, such as this, that contains every vertex of a connected graph G is said to be a *spanning tree*, and the problem of computing a spanning tree T with smallest total weight is known as the *minimum spanning tree* (or *MST*) problem.

The development of efficient algorithms for the minimum spanning tree problem predates the modern notion of computer science itself. In this section, we discuss two classic algorithms for solving the MST problem. These algorithms are both applications of the *greedy method*, which, as was discussed briefly in the previous section, is based on choosing objects to join a growing collection by iteratively picking an object that minimizes some cost function. The first algorithm we discuss is the Prim-Jarník algorithm, which grows the MST from a single root vertex, much in the same way as Dijkstra's shortest-path algorithm. The second algorithm we discuss is Kruskal's algorithm, which "grows" the MST in clusters by considering edges in nondecreasing order of their weights.

In order to simplify the description of the algorithms, we assume, in the following, that the input graph G is undirected (that is, all its edges are undirected) and simple (that is, it has no self-loops and no parallel edges). Hence, we denote the edges of G as unordered vertex pairs (u,v).

Before we discuss the details of these algorithms, however, let us give a crucial fact about minimum spanning trees that forms the basis of the algorithms.

A Crucial Fact about Minimum Spanning Trees

The two MST algorithms we discuss are based on the greedy method, which in this case depends crucially on the following fact. (See Figure 14.19.)

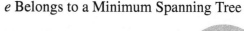

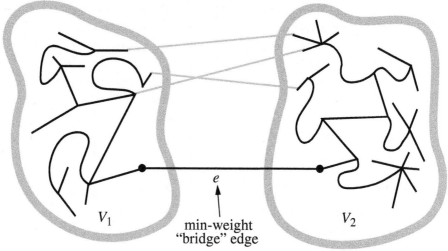

Figure 14.19: An illustration of the crucial fact about minimum spanning trees.

Proposition 14.25: *Let G be a weighted connected graph, and let V_1 and V_2 be a partition of the vertices of G into two disjoint nonempty sets. Furthermore, let e be an edge in G with minimum weight from among those with one endpoint in V_1 and the other in V_2. There is a minimum spanning tree T that has e as one of its edges.*

Justification: Let T be a minimum spanning tree of G. If T does not contain edge e, the addition of e to T must create a cycle. Therefore, there is some edge $f \neq e$ of this cycle that has one endpoint in V_1 and the other in V_2. Moreover, by the choice of e, $w(e) \leq w(f)$. If we remove f from $T \cup \{e\}$, we obtain a spanning tree whose total weight is no more than before. Since T was a minimum spanning tree, this new tree must also be a minimum spanning tree. ∎

In fact, if the weights in G are distinct, then the minimum spanning tree is unique; we leave the justification of this less crucial fact as an exercise (C-14.65). In addition, note that Proposition 14.25 remains valid even if the graph G contains negative-weight edges or negative-weight cycles, unlike the algorithms we presented for shortest paths.

14.7.1   Prim-Jarník Algorithm

In the Prim-Jarník algorithm, we grow a minimum spanning tree from a single cluster starting from some "root" vertex s. The main idea is similar to that of Dijkstra's algorithm. We begin with some vertex s, defining the initial "cloud" of vertices C. Then, in each iteration, we choose a minimum-weight edge $e = (u,v)$, connecting a vertex u in the cloud C to a vertex v outside of C. The vertex v is then brought into the cloud C and the process is repeated until a spanning tree is formed. Again, the crucial fact about minimum spanning trees comes into play, for by always choosing the smallest-weight edge joining a vertex inside C to one outside C, we are assured of always adding a valid edge to the MST.

To efficiently implement this approach, we can take another cue from Dijkstra's algorithm. We maintain a label $D[v]$ for each vertex v outside the cloud C, so that $D[v]$ stores the weight of the minimum observed edge for joining v to the cloud C. (In Dijkstra's algorithm, this label measured the full path length from starting vertex s to v, including an edge (u,v).) These labels serve as keys in a priority queue used to decide which vertex is next in line to join the cloud. We give the pseudo-code in Code Fragment 14.15.

Algorithm PrimJarnik(G):

> *Input:* An undirected, weighted, connected graph G with n vertices and m edges
> *Output:* A minimum spanning tree T for G
>
> Pick any vertex s of G
> $D[s] = 0$
> **for** each vertex $v \neq s$ **do**
> > $D[v] = \infty$
>
> Initialize $T = \emptyset$.
> Initialize a priority queue Q with an entry $(D[v], (v, \text{None}))$ for each vertex v, where $D[v]$ is the key in the priority queue, and (v, None) is the associated value.
> **while** Q is not empty **do**
> > $(u,e) = $ value returned by Q.remove_min()
> > Connect vertex u to T using edge e.
> > **for** each edge $e' = (u,v)$ such that v is in Q **do**
> > > {check if edge (u,v) better connects v to T}
> > > **if** $w(u,v) < D[v]$ **then**
> > > > $D[v] = w(u,v)$
> > > > Change the key of vertex v in Q to $D[v]$.
> > > > Change the value of vertex v in Q to (v,e').
>
> **return** the tree T

Code Fragment 14.15: The Prim-Jarník algorithm for the MST problem.

Analyzing the Prim-Jarník Algorithm

The implementation issues for the Prim-Jarník algorithm are similar to those for Dijkstra's algorithm, relying on an adaptable priority queue Q (Section 9.5.1). We initially perform n insertions into Q, later perform n extract-min operations, and may update a total of m priorities as part of the algorithm. Those steps are the primary contributions to the overall running time. With a heap-based priority queue, each operation runs in $O(\log n)$ time, and the overall time for the algorithm is $O((n+m)\log n)$, which is $O(m\log n)$ for a connected graph. Alternatively, we can achieve $O(n^2)$ running time by using an unsorted list as a priority queue.

Illustrating the Prim-Jarník Algorithm

We illustrate the Prim-Jarník algorithm in Figures 14.20 through 14.21.

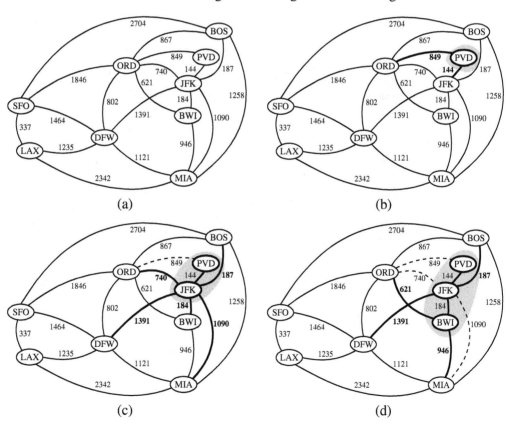

Figure 14.20: An illustration of the Prim-Jarník MST algorithm, starting with vertex PVD. (Continues in Figure 14.21.)

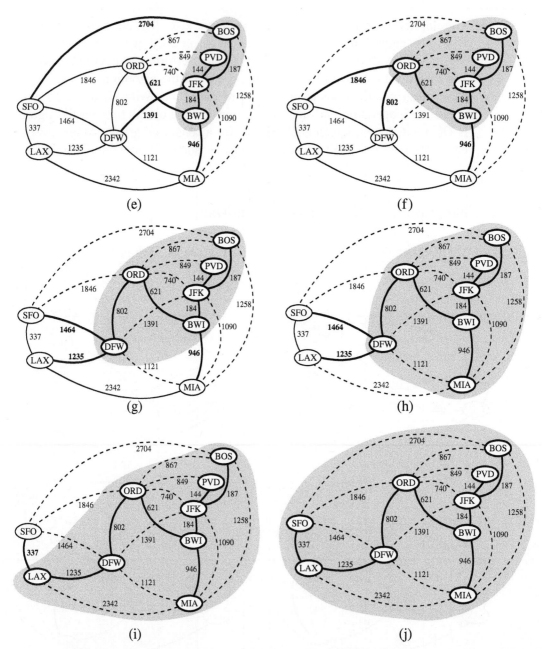

Figure 14.21: An illustration of the Prim-Jarník MST algorithm. (Continued from Figure 14.20.)

Python Implementation

Code Fragment 14.16 presents a Python implementation of the Prim-Jarník algorithm. The MST is returned as an unordered list of edges.

```
1  def MST_PrimJarnik(g):
2    """Compute a minimum spanning tree of weighted graph g.
3
4    Return a list of edges that comprise the MST (in arbitrary order).
5    """
6    d = { }                               # d[v] is bound on distance to tree
7    tree = [ ]                            # list of edges in spanning tree
8    pq = AdaptableHeapPriorityQueue( )    # d[v] maps to value (v, e=(u,v))
9    pqlocator = { }                       # map from vertex to its pq locator
10
11   # for each vertex v of the graph, add an entry to the priority queue, with
12   # the source having distance 0 and all others having infinite distance
13   for v in g.vertices( ):
14     if len(d) == 0:                     # this is the first node
15       d[v] = 0                          # make it the root
16     else:
17       d[v] = float('inf')               # positive infinity
18     pqlocator[v] = pq.add(d[v], (v,None))
19
20   while not pq.is_empty( ):
21     key,value = pq.remove_min( )
22     u,edge = value                      # unpack tuple from pq
23     del pqlocator[u]                    # u is no longer in pq
24     if edge is not None:
25       tree.append(edge)                 # add edge to tree
26     for link in g.incident_edges(u):
27       v = link.opposite(u)
28       if v in pqlocator:                # thus v not yet in tree
29         # see if edge (u,v) better connects v to the growing tree
30         wgt = link.element( )
31         if wgt < d[v]:                  # better edge to v?
32           d[v] = wgt                    # update the distance
33           pq.update(pqlocator[v], d[v], (v, link))  # update the pq entry
34   return tree
```

Code Fragment 14.16: Python implementation of the Prim-Jarník algorithm for the minimum spanning tree problem.

14.7.2 Kruskal's Algorithm

In this section, we introduce ***Kruskal's algorithm*** for constructing a minimum spanning tree. While the Prim-Jarník algorithm builds the MST by growing a single tree until it spans the graph, Kruskal's algorithm maintains a ***forest*** of clusters, repeatedly merging pairs of clusters until a single cluster spans the graph.

Initially, each vertex is by itself in a singleton cluster. The algorithm then considers each edge in turn, ordered by increasing weight. If an edge e connects two different clusters, then e is added to the set of edges of the minimum spanning tree, and the two clusters connected by e are merged into a single cluster. If, on the other hand, e connects two vertices that are already in the same cluster, then e is discarded. Once the algorithm has added enough edges to form a spanning tree, it terminates and outputs this tree as the minimum spanning tree.

We give pseudo-code for Kruskal's MST algorithm in Code Fragment 14.17 and we show an example of this algorithm in Figures 14.22, 14.23, and 14.24.

Algorithm Kruskal(G):
    Input: A simple connected weighted graph G with n vertices and m edges
    Output: A minimum spanning tree T for G
    for each vertex v in G **do**
      Define an elementary cluster $C(v) = \{v\}$.
    Initialize a priority queue Q to contain all edges in G, using the weights as keys.
    $T = \emptyset$ {T will ultimately contain the edges of the MST}
    while T has fewer than $n-1$ edges **do**
      (u,v) = value returned by Q.remove_min()
      Let $C(u)$ be the cluster containing u, and let $C(v)$ be the cluster containing v.
      if $C(u) \neq C(v)$ **then**
        Add edge (u,v) to T.
        Merge $C(u)$ and $C(v)$ into one cluster.
    return tree T

Code Fragment 14.17: Kruskal's algorithm for the MST problem.

As was the case with the Prim-Jarník algorithm, the correctness of Kruskal's algorithm is based upon the crucial fact about minimum spanning trees from Proposition 14.25. Each time Kruskal's algorithm adds an edge (u,v) to the minimum spanning tree T, we can define a partitioning of the set of vertices V (as in the proposition) by letting V_1 be the cluster containing v and letting V_2 contain the rest of the vertices in V. This clearly defines a disjoint partitioning of the vertices of V and, more importantly, since we are extracting edges from Q in order by their weights, e must be a minimum-weight edge with one vertex in V_1 and the other in V_2. Thus, Kruskal's algorithm always adds a valid minimum spanning tree edge.

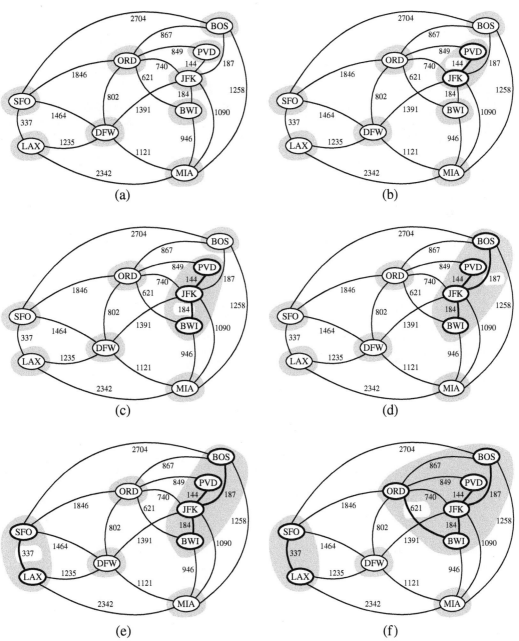

Figure 14.22: Example of an execution of Kruskal's MST algorithm on a graph with integer weights. We show the clusters as shaded regions and we highlight the edge being considered in each iteration. (Continues in Figure 14.23.)

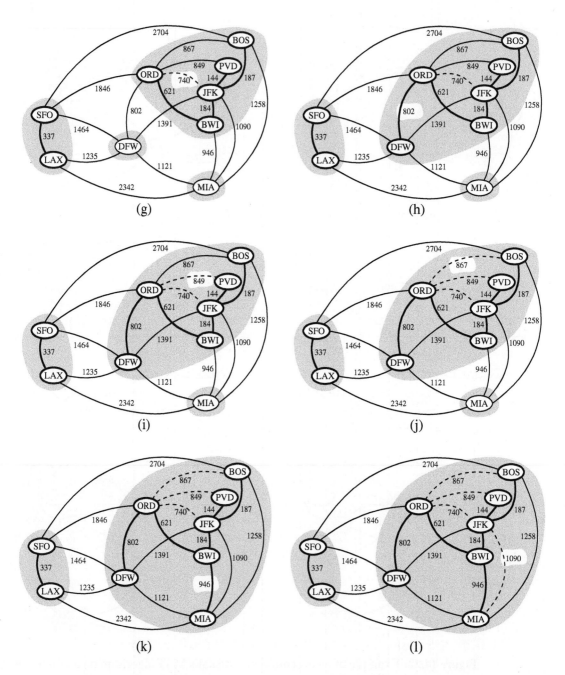

Figure 14.23: An example of an execution of Kruskal's MST algorithm. Rejected edges are shown dashed. (Continues in Figure 14.24.)

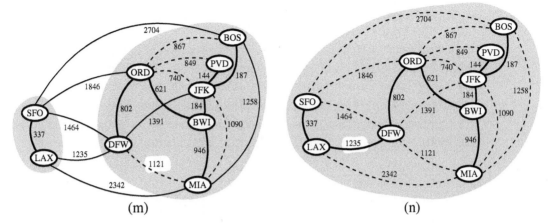

Figure 14.24: Example of an execution of Kruskal's MST algorithm (continued). The edge considered in (n) merges the last two clusters, which concludes this execution of Kruskal's algorithm. (Continued from Figure 14.23.)

The Running Time of Kruskal's Algorithm

There are two primary contributions to the running time of Kruskal's algorithm. The first is the need to consider the edges in nondecreasing order of their weights, and the second is the management of the cluster partition. Analyzing its running time requires that we give more details on its implementation.

The ordering of edges by weight can be implemented in $O(m \log m)$, either by use of a sorting algorithm or a priority queue Q. If that queue is implemented with a heap, we can initialize Q in $O(m \log m)$ time by repeated insertions, or in $O(m)$ time using bottom-up heap construction (see Section 9.3.6), and the subsequent calls to remove_min each run in $O(\log m)$ time, since the queue has size $O(m)$. We note that since m is $O(n^2)$ for a simple graph, $O(\log m)$ is the same as $O(\log n)$. Therefore, the running time due to the ordering of edges is $O(m \log n)$.

The remaining task is the management of clusters. To implement Kruskal's algorithm, we must be able to find the clusters for vertices u and v that are endpoints of an edge e, to test whether those two clusters are distinct, and if so, to merge those two clusters into one. None of the data structures we have studied thus far are well suited for this task. However, we conclude this chapter by formalizing the problem of managing *disjoint partitions*, and introducing efficient *union-find* data structures. In the context of Kruskal's algorithm, we perform at most $2m$ find operations and $n - 1$ union operations. We will see that a simple union-find structure can perform that combination of operations in $O(m + n \log n)$ time (see Proposition 14.26), and a more advanced structure can support an even faster time.

For a connected graph, $m \geq n - 1$, and therefore, the bound of $O(m \log n)$ time for ordering the edges dominates the time for managing the clusters. We conclude that the running time of Kruskal's algorithm is $O(m \log n)$.

Python Implementation

Code Fragment 14.18 presents a Python implementation of Kruskal's algorithm. As with our implementation of the Prim-Jarník algorithm, the minimum spanning tree is returned in the form of a list of edges. As a consequence of Kruskal's algorithm, those edges will be reported in nondecreasing order of their weights.

Our implementation assumes use of a Partition class for managing the cluster partition. An implementation of the Partition class is presented in Section 14.7.3.

```
 1  def MST_Kruskal(g):
 2    """Compute a minimum spanning tree of a graph using Kruskal's algorithm.
 3
 4    Return a list of edges that comprise the MST.
 5
 6    The elements of the graph's edges are assumed to be weights.
 7    """
 8    tree = [ ]                          # list of edges in spanning tree
 9    pq = HeapPriorityQueue( )           # entries are edges in G, with weights as key
10    forest = Partition( )               # keeps track of forest clusters
11    position = { }                      # map each node to its Partition entry
12
13    for v in g.vertices( ):
14      position[v] = forest.make_group(v)
15
16    for e in g.edges( ):
17      pq.add(e.element( ), e)           # edge's element is assumed to be its weight
18
19    size = g.vertex_count( )
20    while len(tree) != size − 1 and not pq.is_empty( ):
21      # tree not spanning and unprocessed edges remain
22      weight,edge = pq.remove_min( )
23      u,v = edge.endpoints( )
24      a = forest.find(position[u])
25      b = forest.find(position[v])
26      if a != b:
27        tree.append(edge)
28        forest.union(a,b)
29
30    return tree
```

Code Fragment 14.18: Python implementation of Kruskal's algorithm for the minimum spanning tree problem.

14.7.3 Disjoint Partitions and Union-Find Structures

In this section, we consider a data structure for managing a *partition* of elements into a collection of disjoint sets. Our initial motivation is in support of Kruskal's minimum spanning tree algorithm, in which a forest of disjoint trees is maintained, with occasional merging of neighboring trees. More generally, the disjoint partition problem can be applied to various models of discrete growth.

We formalize the problem with the following model. A partition data structure manages a universe of elements that are organized into disjoint sets (that is, an element belongs to one and only one of these sets). Unlike with the Set ADT or Python's set class, we do not expect to be able to iterate through the contents of a set, nor to efficiently test whether a given set includes a given element. To avoid confusion with such notions of a set, we will refer to the clusters of our partition as *groups*. However, we will not require an explicit structure for each group, instead allowing the organization of groups to be implicit. To differentiate between one group and another, we assume that at any point in time, each group has a designated entry that we refer to as the *leader* of the group.

Formally, we define the methods of a *partition ADT* using position objects, each of which stores an element x. The partition ADT supports the following methods.

> **make_group(x):** Create a singleton group containing new element x and return the position storing x.
>
> **union(p, q):** Merge the groups containing positions p and q.
>
> **find(p):** Return the position of the leader of the group containing position p.

Sequence Implementation

A simple implementation of a partition with a total of n elements uses a collection of sequences, one for each group, where the sequence for a group A stores element positions. Each position object stores a variable, element, which references its associated element x and allows the execution of an element() method in $O(1)$ time. In addition, each position stores a variable, group, that references the sequence storing p, since this sequence is representing the group containing p's element. (See Figure 14.25.)

With this representation, we can easily perform the make_group(x) and find(p) operations in $O(1)$ time, allowing the first position in a sequence to serve as the "leader." Operation union(p,q) requires that we join two sequences into one and update the group references of the positions in one of the two. We choose to implement this operation by removing all the positions from the sequence with smaller

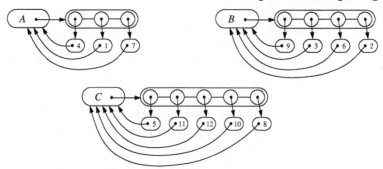

Figure 14.25: Sequence-based implementation of a partition consisting of three groups: $A = \{1,4,7\}$, $B = \{2,3,6,9\}$, and $C = \{5,8,10,11,12\}$.

size, and inserting them in the sequence with larger size. Each time we take a position from the smaller group a and insert it into the larger group b, we update the group reference for that position to now point to b. Hence, the operation union(p,q) takes time $O(\min(n_p,n_q))$, where n_p (resp. n_q) is the cardinality of the group containing position p (resp. q). Clearly, this time is $O(n)$ if there are n elements in the partition universe. However, we next present an amortized analysis that shows this implementation to be much better than appears from this worst-case analysis.

Proposition 14.26: *When using the above sequence-based partition implementation, performing a series of k make_group, union, and find operations on an initially empty partition involving at most n elements takes $O(k + n \log n)$ time.*

Justification: We use the accounting method and assume that one cyber-dollar can pay for the time to perform a find operation, a make_group operation, or the movement of a position object from one sequence to another in a union operation. In the case of a find or make_group operation, we charge the operation itself 1 cyber-dollar. In the case of a union operation, we assume that 1 cyber-dollar pays for the constant-time work in comparing the sizes of the two sequences, and that we charge 1 cyber-dollar to each position that we move from the smaller group to the larger group. Clearly, the 1 cyber-dollar charged for each find and make_group operation, together with the first cyber-dollar collected for each union operation, accounts for a total of k cyber-dollars.

  Consider, then, the number of charges made to positions on behalf of union operations. The important observation is that each time we move a position from one group to another, the size of that position's group at least doubles. Thus, each position is moved from one group to another at most $\log n$ times; hence, each position can be charged at most $O(\log n)$ times. Since we assume that the partition is initially empty, there are $O(n)$ different elements referenced in the given series of operations, which implies that the total time for moving elements during the union operations is $O(n \log n)$.   ■

A Tree-Based Partition Implementation ⋆

An alternative data structure for representing a partition uses a collection of trees to store the *n* elements, where each tree is associated with a different group. (See Figure 14.26.) In particular, we implement each tree with a linked data structure whose nodes are themselves the group position objects. We view each position *p* as being a node having an instance variable, element, referring to its element *x*, and an instance variable, parent, referring to its parent node. By convention, if *p* is the ***root*** of its tree, we set *p*'s parent reference to itself.

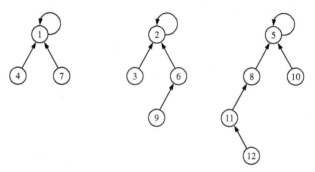

Figure 14.26: Tree-based implementation of a partition consisting of three groups: $A = \{1,4,7\}$, $B = \{2,3,6,9\}$, and $C = \{5,8,10,11,12\}$.

With this partition data structure, operation find(*p*) is performed by walking up from position *p* to the root of its tree, which takes $O(n)$ time in the worst case. Operation union(*p*,*q*) can be implemented by making one of the trees a subtree of the other. This can be done by first locating the two roots, and then in $O(1)$ additional time by setting the parent reference of one root to point to the other root. See Figure 14.27 for an example of both operations.

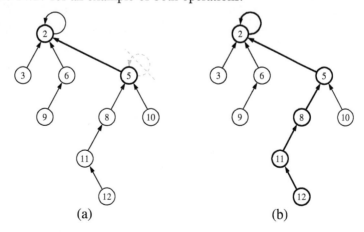

(a)   (b)

Figure 14.27: Tree-based implementation of a partition: (a) operation union(*p*,*q*); (b) operation find(*p*), where *p* denotes the position object for element 12.

At first, this implementation may seem to be no better than the sequence-based data structure, but we add the following two simple heuristics to make it run faster.

Union-by-Size: With each position p, store the number of elements in the subtree rooted at p. In a union operation, make the root of the smaller group become a child of the other root, and update the size field of the larger root.

Path Compression: In a find operation, for each position q that the find visits, reset the parent of q to the root. (See Figure 14.28.)

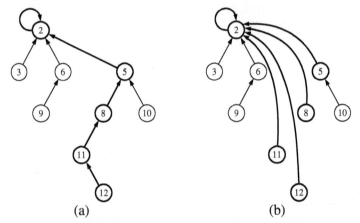

(a)   (b)

Figure 14.28: Path-compression heuristic: (a) path traversed by operation find on element 12; (b) restructured tree.

A surprising property of this data structure, when implemented using the union-by-size and path-compression heuristics, is that performing a series of k operations involving n elements takes $O(k\log^* n)$ time, where $\log^* n$ is the *log-star* function, which is the inverse of the *tower-of-twos* function. Intuitively, $\log^* n$ is the number of times that one can iteratively take the logarithm (base 2) of a number before getting a number smaller than 2. Table 14.4 shows a few sample values.

minimum n	2	$2^2 = 4$	$2^{2^2} = 16$	$2^{2^{2^2}} = 65,536$	$2^{2^{2^{2^2}}} = 2^{65,536}$
$\log^* n$	1	2	3	4	5

Table 14.4: Some values of $\log^* n$ and critical values for its inverse.

Proposition 14.27: *When using the tree-based partition representation with both union-by-size and path compression, performing a series of k make_group, union, and find operations on an initially empty partition involving at most n elements takes $O(k\log^* n)$ time.*

Although the analysis for this data structure is rather complex, its implementation is quite straightforward. We conclude with complete Python code for the structure, given in Code Fragment 14.19.

```
1  class Partition:
2    """Union-find structure for maintaining disjoint sets."""
3
4    #------------------------ nested Position class ------------------------
5    class Position:
6      __slots__ = '_container', '_element', '_size', '_parent'
7
8      def __init__(self, container, e):
9        """Create a new position that is the leader of its own group."""
10       self._container = container      # reference to Partition instance
11       self._element = e
12       self._size = 1
13       self._parent = self              # convention for a group leader
14
15     def element(self):
16       """Return element stored at this position."""
17       return self._element
18
19   #------------------------ public Partition methods ------------------------
20   def make_group(self, e):
21     """Makes a new group containing element e, and returns its Position."""
22     return self.Position(self, e)
23
24   def find(self, p):
25     """Finds the group containing p and return the position of its leader."""
26     if p._parent != p:
27       p._parent = self.find(p._parent)   # overwrite p._parent after recursion
28     return p._parent
29
30   def union(self, p, q):
31     """Merges the groups containing elements p and q (if distinct)."""
32     a = self.find(p)
33     b = self.find(q)
34     if a is not b:                        # only merge if different groups
35       if a._size > b._size:
36         b._parent = a
37         a._size += b._size
38       else:
39         a._parent = b
40         b._size += a._size
```

Code Fragment 14.19: Python implementation of a Partition class using union-by-size and path compression.

14.8   Exercises

For help with exercises, please visit the site, www.wiley.com/college/goodrich.

Reinforcement

R-14.1 Draw a simple undirected graph G that has 12 vertices, 18 edges, and 3 connected components.

R-14.2 If G is a simple undirected graph with 12 vertices and 3 connected components, what is the largest number of edges it might have?

R-14.3 Draw an adjacency matrix representation of the undirected graph shown in Figure 14.1.

R-14.4 Draw an adjacency list representation of the undirected graph shown in Figure 14.1.

R-14.5 Draw a simple, connected, directed graph with 8 vertices and 16 edges such that the in-degree and out-degree of each vertex is 2. Show that there is a single (nonsimple) cycle that includes all the edges of your graph, that is, you can trace all the edges in their respective directions without ever lifting your pencil. (Such a cycle is called an *Euler tour*.)

R-14.6 Suppose we represent a graph G having n vertices and m edges with the edge list structure. Why, in this case, does the insert_vertex method run in $O(1)$ time while the remove_vertex method runs in $O(m)$ time?

R-14.7 Give pseudo-code for performing the operation insert_edge(u,v,x) in $O(1)$ time using the adjacency matrix representation.

R-14.8 Repeat Exercise R-14.7 for the adjacency list representation, as described in the chapter.

R-14.9 Can edge list E be omitted from the adjacency matrix representation while still achieving the time bounds given in Table 14.1? Why or why not?

R-14.10 Can edge list E be omitted from the adjacency list representation while still achieving the time bounds given in Table 14.3? Why or why not?

R-14.11 Would you use the adjacency matrix structure or the adjacency list structure in each of the following cases? Justify your choice.

    a. The graph has 10,000 vertices and 20,000 edges, and it is important to use as little space as possible.

    b. The graph has 10,000 vertices and 20,000,000 edges, and it is important to use as little space as possible.

    c. You need to answer the query get_edge(u,v) as fast as possible, no matter how much space you use.

R-14.12 Explain why the DFS traversal runs in $O(n^2)$ time on an n-vertex simple graph that is represented with the adjacency matrix structure.

R-14.13 In order to verify that all of its nontree edges are back edges, redraw the graph from Figure 14.8b so that the DFS tree edges are drawn with solid lines and oriented downward, as in a standard portrayal of a tree, and with all nontree edges drawn using dashed lines.

R-14.14 A simple undirected graph is ***complete*** if it contains an edge between every pair of distinct vertices. What does a depth-first search tree of a complete graph look like?

R-14.15 Recalling the definition of a complete graph from Exercise R-14.14, what does a breadth-first search tree of a complete graph look like?

R-14.16 Let G be an undirected graph whose vertices are the integers 1 through 8, and let the adjacent vertices of each vertex be given by the table below:

vertex	adjacent vertices
1	(2, 3, 4)
2	(1, 3, 4)
3	(1, 2, 4)
4	(1, 2, 3, 6)
5	(6, 7, 8)
6	(4, 5, 7)
7	(5, 6, 8)
8	(5, 7)

Assume that, in a traversal of G, the adjacent vertices of a given vertex are returned in the same order as they are listed in the table above.

a. Draw G.

b. Give the sequence of vertices of G visited using a DFS traversal starting at vertex 1.

c. Give the sequence of vertices visited using a BFS traversal starting at vertex 1.

R-14.17 Draw the transitive closure of the directed graph shown in Figure 14.2.

R-14.18 If the vertices of the graph from Figure 14.11 are numbered as ($v_1 =$ JFK, $v_2 =$ LAX, $v_3 =$ MIA, $v_4 =$ BOS, $v_5 =$ ORD, $v_6 =$ SFO, $v_7 =$ DFW), in what order would edges be added to the transitive closure during the Floyd-Warshall algorithm?

R-14.19 How many edges are in the transitive closure of a graph that consists of a simple directed path of n vertices?

R-14.20 Given an n-node complete binary tree T, rooted at a given position, consider a directed graph $\vec{G}$ having the nodes of T as its vertices. For each parent-child pair in T, create a directed edge in $\vec{G}$ from the parent to the child. Show that the transitive closure of $\vec{G}$ has $O(n \log n)$ edges.

R-14.21 Compute a topological ordering for the directed graph drawn with solid edges in Figure 14.3d.

R-14.22 Bob loves foreign languages and wants to plan his course schedule for the following years. He is interested in the following nine language courses: LA15, LA16, LA22, LA31, LA32, LA126, LA127, LA141, and LA169. The course prerequisites are:

- LA15: (none)
- LA16: LA15
- LA22: (none)
- LA31: LA15
- LA32: LA16, LA31
- LA126: LA22, LA32
- LA127: LA16
- LA141: LA22, LA16
- LA169: LA32

In what order can Bob take these courses, respecting the prerequisites?

R-14.23 Draw a simple, connected, weighted graph with 8 vertices and 16 edges, each with unique edge weights. Identify one vertex as a "start" vertex and illustrate a running of Dijkstra's algorithm on this graph.

R-14.24 Show how to modify the pseudo-code for Dijkstra's algorithm for the case when the graph is directed and we want to compute shortest directed paths from the source vertex to all the other vertices.

R-14.25 Draw a simple, connected, undirected, weighted graph with 8 vertices and 16 edges, each with unique edge weights. Illustrate the execution of the Prim-Jarník algorithm for computing the minimum spanning tree of this graph.

R-14.26 Repeat the previous problem for Kruskal's algorithm.

R-14.27 There are eight small islands in a lake, and the state wants to build seven bridges to connect them so that each island can be reached from any other one via one or more bridges. The cost of constructing a bridge is proportional to its length. The distances between pairs of islands are given in the following table.

	1	2	3	4	5	6	7	8
1	-	240	210	340	280	200	345	120
2	-	-	265	175	215	180	185	155
3	-	-	-	260	115	350	435	195
4	-	-	-	-	160	330	295	230
5	-	-	-	-	-	360	400	170
6	-	-	-	-	-	-	175	205
7	-	-	-	-	-	-	-	305
8	-	-	-	-	-	-	-	-

Find which bridges to build to minimize the total construction cost.

R-14.28 Describe the meaning of the graphical conventions used in Figure 14.9 illustrating a DFS traversal. What do the line thicknesses signify? What do the arrows signify? How about dashed lines?

R-14.29 Repeat Exercise R-14.28 for Figure 14.8 that illustrates a directed DFS traversal.

R-14.30 Repeat Exercise R-14.28 for Figure 14.10 that illustrates a BFS traversal.

R-14.31 Repeat Exercise R-14.28 for Figure 14.11 illustrating the Floyd-Warshall algorithm.

R-14.32 Repeat Exercise R-14.28 for Figure 14.13 that illustrates the topological sorting algorithm.

R-14.33 Repeat Exercise R-14.28 for Figures 14.15 and 14.16 illustrating Dijkstra's algorithm.

R-14.34 Repeat Exercise R-14.28 for Figures 14.20 and 14.21 that illustrate the Prim-Jarník algorithm.

R-14.35 Repeat Exercise R-14.28 for Figures 14.22 through 14.24 that illustrate Kruskal's algorithm.

R-14.36 George claims he has a fast way to do path compression in a partition structure, starting at a position p. He puts p into a list L, and starts following parent pointers. Each time he encounters a new position, q, he adds q to L and updates the parent pointer of each node in L to point to q's parent. Show that George's algorithm runs in $\Omega(h^2)$ time on a path of length h.

Creativity

C-14.37 Give a Python implementation of the remove_vertex(v) method for our adjacency map implementation of Section 14.2.5, making sure your implementation works for both directed and undirected graphs. Your method should run in $O(\deg(v))$ time.

C-14.38 Give a Python implementation of the remove_edge(e) method for our adjacency map implementation of Section 14.2.5, making sure your implementation works for both directed and undirected graphs. Your method should run in $O(1)$ time.

C-14.39 Suppose we wish to represent an n-vertex graph G using the edge list structure, assuming that we identify the vertices with the integers in the set $\{0, 1, \ldots, n-1\}$. Describe how to implement the collection E to support $O(\log n)$-time performance for the get_edge(u, v) method. How are you implementing the method in this case?

C-14.40 Let T be the spanning tree rooted at the start vertex produced by the depth-first search of a connected, undirected graph G. Argue why every edge of G not in T goes from a vertex in T to one of its ancestors, that is, it is a *back edge*.

C-14.41 Our solution to reporting a path from u to v in Code Fragment 14.6 could be made more efficient in practice if the DFS process ended as soon as v is discovered. Describe how to modify our code base to implement this optimization.

C-14.42 Let G be an undirected graph G with n vertices and m edges. Describe an $O(n+m)$-time algorithm for traversing each edge of G exactly once in each direction.

C-14.43 Implement an algorithm that returns a cycle in a directed graph $\vec{G}$, if one exists.

C-14.44 Write a function, components(g), for undirected graph g, that returns a dictionary mapping each vertex to an integer that serves as an identifier for its connected component. That is, two vertices should be mapped to the same identifier if and only if they are in the same connected component.

C-14.45 Say that a maze is *constructed correctly* if there is one path from the start to the finish, the entire maze is reachable from the start, and there are no loops around any portions of the maze. Given a maze drawn in an $n \times n$ grid, how can we determine if it is constructed correctly? What is the running time of this algorithm?

C-14.46 Computer networks should avoid single points of failure, that is, network vertices that can disconnect the network if they fail. We say an undirected, connected graph G is *biconnected* if it contains no vertex whose removal would divide G into two or more connected components. Give an algorithm for adding at most n edges to a connected graph G, with $n \geq 3$ vertices and $m \geq n-1$ edges, to guarantee that G is biconnected. Your algorithm should run in $O(n+m)$ time.

C-14.47 Explain why all nontree edges are cross edges, with respect to a BFS tree constructed for an undirected graph.

C-14.48 Explain why there are no forward nontree edges with respect to a BFS tree constructed for a directed graph.

C-14.49 Show that if T is a BFS tree produced for a connected graph G, then, for each vertex v at level i, the path of T between s and v has i edges, and any other path of G between s and v has at least i edges.

C-14.50 Justify Proposition 14.16.

C-14.51 Provide an implementation of the BFS algorithm that uses a FIFO queue, rather than a level-by-level formulation, to manage vertices that have been discovered until the time when their neighbors are considered.

C-14.52 A graph G is *bipartite* if its vertices can be partitioned into two sets X and Y such that every edge in G has one end vertex in X and the other in Y. Design and analyze an efficient algorithm for determining if an undirected graph G is bipartite (without knowing the sets X and Y in advance).

C-14.53 An *Euler tour* of a directed graph $\vec{G}$ with n vertices and m edges is a cycle that traverses each edge of $\vec{G}$ exactly once according to its direction. Such a tour always exists if $\vec{G}$ is connected and the in-degree equals the out-degree of each vertex in $\vec{G}$. Describe an $O(n+m)$-time algorithm for finding an Euler tour of such a directed graph $\vec{G}$.

C-14.54 A company named RT&T has a network of n switching stations connected by m high-speed communication links. Each customer's phone is directly connected to one station in his or her area. The engineers of RT&T have developed a prototype video-phone system that allows two customers to see each other during a phone call. In order to have acceptable image quality, however, the number of links used to transmit video signals between the two parties cannot exceed 4. Suppose that RT&T's network is represented by a graph. Design an efficient algorithm that computes, for each station, the set of stations it can reach using no more than 4 links.

C-14.55 The time delay of a long-distance call can be determined by multiplying a small fixed constant by the number of communication links on the telephone network between the caller and callee. Suppose the telephone network of a company named RT&T is a tree. The engineers of RT&T want to compute the maximum possible time delay that may be experienced in a long-distance call. Given a tree T, the *diameter* of T is the length of a longest path between two nodes of T. Give an efficient algorithm for computing the diameter of T.

C-14.56 Tamarindo University and many other schools worldwide are doing a joint project on multimedia. A computer network is built to connect these schools using communication links that form a tree. The schools decide to install a file server at one of the schools to share data among all the schools. Since the transmission time on a link is dominated by the link setup and synchronization, the cost of a data transfer is proportional to the number of links used. Hence, it is desirable to choose a "central" location for the file server. Given a tree T and a node v of T, the *eccentricity* of v is the length of a longest path from v to any other node of T. A node of T with minimum eccentricity is called a *center* of T.

    a. Design an efficient algorithm that, given an n-node tree T, computes a center of T.

    b. Is the center unique? If not, how many distinct centers can a tree have?

C-14.57 Say that an n-vertex directed acyclic graph $\vec{G}$ is *compact* if there is some way of numbering the vertices of $\vec{G}$ with the integers from 0 to $n-1$ such that $\vec{G}$ contains the edge (i,j) if and only if $i < j$, for all i,j in $[0,n-1]$. Give an $O(n^2)$-time algorithm for detecting if $\vec{G}$ is compact.

C-14.58 Let $\vec{G}$ be a weighted directed graph with n vertices. Design a variation of Floyd-Warshall's algorithm for computing the lengths of the shortest paths from each vertex to every other vertex in $O(n^3)$ time.

C-14.59 Design an efficient algorithm for finding a *longest* directed path from a vertex s to a vertex t of an acyclic weighted directed graph $\vec{G}$. Specify the graph representation used and any auxiliary data structures used. Also, analyze the time complexity of your algorithm.

C-14.60 An independent set of an undirected graph $G = (V,E)$ is a subset I of V such that no two vertices in I are adjacent. That is, if u and v are in I, then (u,v) is not in E. A *maximal independent set M* is an independent set such that, if we were to add any additional vertex to M, then it would not be independent any more. Every graph has a maximal independent set. (Can you see this? This question is not part of the exercise, but it is worth thinking about.) Give an efficient algorithm that computes a maximal independent set for a graph G. What is this method's running time?

C-14.61 Give an example of an n-vertex simple graph G that causes Dijkstra's algorithm to run in $\Omega(n^2 \log n)$ time when its implemented with a heap.

C-14.62 Give an example of a weighted directed graph $\vec{G}$ with negative-weight edges, but no negative-weight cycle, such that Dijkstra's algorithm incorrectly computes the shortest-path distances from some start vertex s.

C-14.63 Consider the following greedy strategy for finding a shortest path from vertex *start* to vertex *goal* in a given connected graph.

1: Initialize *path* to *start*.
2: Initialize set *visited* to {*start*}.
3: If *start*=*goal*, return *path* and exit. Otherwise, continue.
4: Find the edge (*start*,*v*) of minimum weight such that v is adjacent to *start* and v is not in *visited*.
5: Add v to *path*.
6: Add v to *visited*.
7: Set *start* equal to v and go to step 3.

Does this greedy strategy always find a shortest path from *start* to *goal*? Either explain intuitively why it works, or give a counterexample.

C-14.64 Our implementation of shortest_path_lengths in Code Fragment 14.13 relies on use of "infinity" as a numeric value, to represent the distance bound for vertices that are not (yet) known to be reachable from the source. Reimplement that function without such a sentinel, so that vertices, other than the source, are not added to the priority queue until it is evident that they are reachable.

C-14.65 Show that if all the weights in a connected weighted graph G are distinct, then there is exactly one minimum spanning tree for G.

C-14.66 An old MST method, called *Barůvka's algorithm*, works as follows on a graph G having n vertices and m edges with distinct weights:

> Let T be a subgraph of G initially containing just the vertices in V.
> **while** T has fewer than $n-1$ edges **do**
> > **for** each connected component C_i of T **do**
> > > Find the lowest-weight edge (u,v) in E with u in C_i and v not in C_i.
> > > Add (u,v) to T (unless it is already in T).
> > **return** T

Prove that this algorithm is correct and that it runs in $O(m \log n)$ time.

C-14.67 Let G be a graph with n vertices and m edges such that all the edge weights in G are integers in the range $[1,n]$. Give an algorithm for finding a minimum spanning tree for G in $O(m \log^* n)$ time.

C-14.68 Consider a diagram of a telephone network, which is a graph G whose vertices represent switching centers, and whose edges represent communication lines joining pairs of centers. Edges are marked by their bandwidth, and the bandwidth of a path is equal to the lowest bandwidth among the path's edges. Give an algorithm that, given a network and two switching centers a and b, outputs the maximum bandwidth of a path between a and b.

C-14.69 NASA wants to link n stations spread over the country using communication channels. Each pair of stations has a different bandwidth available, which is known a priori. NASA wants to select $n-1$ channels (the minimum possible) in such a way that all the stations are linked by the channels and the total bandwidth (defined as the sum of the individual bandwidths of the channels) is maximum. Give an efficient algorithm for this problem and determine its worst-case time complexity. Consider the weighted graph $G = (V,E)$, where V is the set of stations and E is the set of channels between the stations. Define the weight $w(e)$ of an edge e in E as the bandwidth of the corresponding channel.

C-14.70 Inside the Castle of Asymptopia there is a maze, and along each corridor of the maze there is a bag of gold coins. The amount of gold in each bag varies. A noble knight, named Sir Paul, will be given the opportunity to walk through the maze, picking up bags of gold. He may enter the maze only through a door marked "ENTER" and exit through another door marked "EXIT." While in the maze he may not retrace his steps. Each corridor of the maze has an arrow painted on the wall. Sir Paul may only go down the corridor in the direction of the arrow. There is no way to traverse a "loop" in the maze. Given a map of the maze, including the amount of gold in each corridor, describe an algorithm to help Sir Paul pick up the most gold.

C-14.71 Suppose you are given a *timetable*, which consists of:

- A set $\mathcal{A}$ of n airports, and for each airport a in $\mathcal{A}$, a minimum connecting time $c(a)$.
- A set $\mathcal{F}$ of m flights, and the following, for each flight f in $\mathcal{F}$:
  - Origin airport $a_1(f)$ in $\mathcal{A}$
  - Destination airport $a_2(f)$ in $\mathcal{A}$
  - Departure time $t_1(f)$
  - Arrival time $t_2(f)$

Describe an efficient algorithm for the flight scheduling problem. In this problem, we are given airports a and b, and a time t, and we wish to compute a sequence of flights that allows one to arrive at the earliest possible time in b when departing from a at or after time t. Minimum connecting times at intermediate airports must be observed. What is the running time of your algorithm as a function of n and m?

C-14.72 Suppose we are given a directed graph $\vec{G}$ with n vertices, and let M be the $n \times n$ adjacency matrix corresponding to $\vec{G}$.

  a. Let the product of M with itself (M^2) be defined, for $1 \le i, j \le n$, as follows:

$$M^2(i,j) = M(i,1) \odot M(1,j) \oplus \cdots \oplus M(i,n) \odot M(n,j),$$

  where "$\oplus$" is the Boolean **or** operator and "$\odot$" is Boolean **and**. Given this definition, what does $M^2(i,j) = 1$ imply about the vertices i and j? What if $M^2(i,j) = 0$?

  b. Suppose M^4 is the product of M^2 with itself. What do the entries of M^4 signify? How about the entries of $M^5 = (M^4)(M)$? In general, what information is contained in the matrix M^p?

  c. Now suppose that $\vec{G}$ is weighted and assume the following:
  1: for $1 \le i \le n$, $M(i,i) = 0$.
  2: for $1 \le i, j \le n$, $M(i,j) = weight(i,j)$ if (i,j) is in E.
  3: for $1 \le i, j \le n$, $M(i,j) = \infty$ if (i,j) is not in E.
  Also, let M^2 be defined, for $1 \le i, j \le n$, as follows:

$$M^2(i,j) = \min\{M(i,1) + M(1,j), \ldots, M(i,n) + M(n,j)\}.$$

  If $M^2(i,j) = k$, what may we conclude about the relationship between vertices i and j?

C-14.73 Karen has a new way to do path compression in a tree-based union/find partition data structure starting at a position p. She puts all the positions that are on the path from p to the root in a set S. Then she scans through S and sets the parent pointer of each position in S to its parent's parent pointer (recall that the parent pointer of the root points to itself). If this pass changed the value of any position's parent pointer, then she repeats this process, and goes on repeating this process until she makes a scan through S that does not change any position's parent value. Show that Karen's algorithm is correct and analyze its running time for a path of length h.

Projects

P-14.74 Use an adjacency matrix to implement a class supporting a simplified graph ADT that does not include update methods. Your class should include a constructor method that takes two collections—a collection V of vertex elements and a collection E of pairs of vertex elements—and produces the graph G that these two collections represent.

P-14.75 Implement the simplified graph ADT described in Project P-14.74, using the edge list structure.

P-14.76 Implement the simplified graph ADT described in Project P-14.74, using the adjacency list structure.

P-14.77 Extend the class of Project P-14.76 to support the update methods of the graph ADT.

P-14.78 Design an experimental comparison of repeated DFS traversals versus the Floyd-Warshall algorithm for computing the transitive closure of a directed graph.

P-14.79 Perform an experimental comparison of two of the minimum spanning tree algorithms discussed in this chapter (Kruskal and Prim-Jarník). Develop an extensive set of experiments to test the running times of these algorithms using randomly generated graphs.

P-14.80 One way to construct a *maze* starts with an $n \times n$ grid such that each grid cell is bounded by four unit-length walls. We then remove two boundary unit-length walls, to represent the start and finish. For each remaining unit-length wall not on the boundary, we assign a random value and create a graph G, called the *dual*, such that each grid cell is a vertex in G and there is an edge joining the vertices for two cells if and only if the cells share a common wall. The weight of each edge is the weight of the corresponding wall. We construct the maze by finding a minimum spanning tree T for G and removing all the walls corresponding to edges in T. Write a program that uses this algorithm to generate mazes and then solves them. Minimally, your program should draw the maze and, ideally, it should visualize the solution as well.

P-14.81 Write a program that builds the routing tables for the nodes in a computer network, based on shortest-path routing, where path distance is measured by hop count, that is, the number of edges in a path. The input for this problem is the connectivity information for all the nodes in the network, as in the following example:

241.12.31.14: 241.12.31.15 241.12.31.18 241.12.31.19

which indicates three network nodes that are connected to 241.12.31.14, that is, three nodes that are one hop away. The routing table for the node at address A is a set of pairs (B,C), which indicates that, to route a message from A to B, the next node to send to (on the shortest path from A to B) is C. Your program should output the routing table for each node in the network, given an input list of node connectivity lists, each of which is input in the syntax as shown above, one per line.

Chapter Notes

The depth-first search method is a part of the "folklore" of computer science, but Hopcroft and Tarjan [52, 94] are the ones who showed how useful this algorithm is for solving several different graph problems. Knuth [64] discusses the topological sorting problem. The simple linear-time algorithm that we describe for determining if a directed graph is strongly connected is due to Kosaraju. The Floyd-Warshall algorithm appears in a paper by Floyd [38] and is based upon a theorem of Warshall [102].

The first known minimum spanning tree algorithm is due to Barůvka [9], and was published in 1926. The Prim-Jarník algorithm was first published in Czech by Jarník [55] in 1930 and in English in 1957 by Prim [85]. Kruskal published his minimum spanning tree algorithm in 1956 [67]. The reader interested in further study of the history of the minimum spanning tree problem is referred to the paper by Graham and Hell [47]. The current asymptotically fastest minimum spanning tree algorithm is a randomized method of Karger, Klein, and Tarjan [57] that runs in $O(m)$ expected time. Dijkstra [35] published his single-source, shortest-path algorithm in 1959. The running time for the Prim-Jarník algorithm, and also that of Dijkstra's algorithm, can actually be improved to be $O(n \log n + m)$ by implementing the queue Q with either of two more sophisticated data structures, the "Fibonacci Heap" [40] or the "Relaxed Heap" [37].

To learn about different algorithms for drawing graphs, please see the book chapter by Tamassia and Liotta [92] and the book by Di Battista, Eades, Tamassia and Tollis [34]. The reader interested in further study of graph algorithms is referred to the books by Ahuja, Magnanti, and Orlin [7], Cormen, Leiserson, Rivest and Stein [29], Mehlhorn [77], and Tarjan [95], and the book chapter by van Leeuwen [98].

Chapter

15

Memory Management and B-Trees

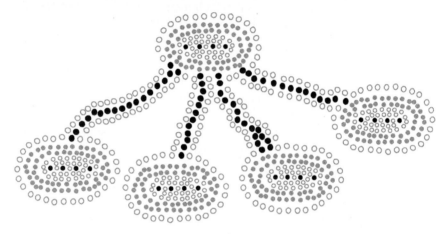

Contents

Our study of data structures thus far has focused primarily upon the efficiency of computations, as measured by the number of primitive operations that are executed on a central processing unit (CPU). In practice, the performance of a computer system is also greatly impacted by the management of the computer's memory systems. In our analysis of data structures, we have provided asymptotic bounds for the overall amount of memory used by a data structure. In this chapter, we consider more subtle issues involving the use of a computer's memory system.

We first discuss ways in which memory is allocated and deallocated during the execution of a computer program, and the impact that this has on the program's performance. Second, we discuss the complexity of multilevel memory hierarchies in today's computer systems. Although we often abstract a computer's memory as consisting of a single pool of interchangeable locations, in practice, the data used by an executing program is stored and transferred between a combination of physical memories (e.g., CPU registers, caches, internal memory, and external memory). We consider the use of classic data structures in the algorithms used to manage memory, and how the use of memory hierarchies impacts the choice of data structures and algorithms for classic problems such as searching and sorting.

15.1   Memory Management

In order to implement any data structure on an actual computer, we need to use computer memory. Computer memory is organized into a sequence of *words*, each of which typically consists of 4, 8, or 16 bytes (depending on the computer). These memory words are numbered from 0 to $N - 1$, where N is the number of memory words available to the computer. The number associated with each memory word is known as its *memory address*. Thus, the memory in a computer can be viewed as basically one giant array of memory words. For example, in Figure 5.1 of Section 5.2, we portrayed a section of the computer's memory as follows:

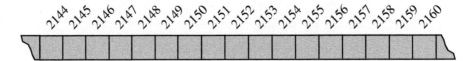

In order to run programs and store information, the computer's memory must be *managed* so as to determine what data is stored in what memory cells. In this section, we discuss the basics of memory management, most notably describing the way in which memory is allocated to store new objects, the way in which portions of memory are deallocated and reclaimed, when no longer needed, and the way in which the Python interpreter uses memory in completing its tasks.

15.1.1 Memory Allocation

With Python, all objects are stored in a pool of memory, known as the ***memory heap*** or ***Python heap*** (which should not be confused with the "heap" data structure presented in Chapter 9). When a command such as

w = Widget( )

is executed, assuming Widget is the name of a class, a new instance of the class is created and stored somewhere within the memory heap. The Python interpreter is responsible for negotiating the use of space with the operating system and for managing the use of the memory heap when executing a Python program.

The storage available in the memory heap is divided into ***blocks***, which are contiguous array-like "chunks" of memory that may be of variable or fixed sizes. The system must be implemented so that it can quickly allocate memory for new objects. One popular method is to keep contiguous "holes" of available free memory in a linked list, called the ***free list***. The links joining these holes are stored inside the holes themselves, since their memory is not being used. As memory is allocated and deallocated, the collection of holes in the free lists changes, with the unused memory being separated into disjoint holes divided by blocks of used memory. This separation of unused memory into separate holes is known as ***fragmentation***. The problem is that it becomes more difficult to find large continuous chunks of memory, when needed, even though an equivalent amount of memory may be unused (yet fragmented). Therefore, we would like to minimize fragmentation as much as possible.

There are two kinds of fragmentation that can occur. ***Internal fragmentation*** occurs when a portion of an allocated memory block is unused. For example, a program may request an array of size 1000, but only use the first 100 cells of this array. There is not much that a run-time environment can do to reduce internal fragmentation. ***External fragmentation***, on the other hand, occurs when there is a significant amount of unused memory between several contiguous blocks of allocated memory. Since the run-time environment has control over where to allocate memory when it is requested, the run-time environment should allocate memory in a way to try to reduce external fragmentation as much as reasonably possible.

Several heuristics have been suggested for allocating memory from the heap so as to minimize external fragmentation. The ***best-fit algorithm*** searches the entire free list to find the hole whose size is closest to the amount of memory being requested. The ***first-fit algorithm*** searches from the beginning of the free list for the first hole that is large enough. The ***next-fit algorithm*** is similar, in that it also searches the free list for the first hole that is large enough, but it begins its search from where it left off previously, viewing the free list as a circularly linked list (Section 7.2). The ***worst-fit algorithm*** searches the free list to find the largest hole of available memory, which might be done faster than a search of the entire free list if this list were maintained as a priority queue (Chapter 9). In each algorithm, the requested amount of memory is subtracted from the chosen memory hole and the leftover part of that hole is returned to the free list.

Although it might sound good at first, the best-fit algorithm tends to produce the worst external fragmentation, since the leftover parts of the chosen holes tend to be small. The first-fit algorithm is fast, but it tends to produce a lot of external fragmentation at the front of the free list, which slows down future searches. The next-fit algorithm spreads fragmentation more evenly throughout the memory heap, thus keeping search times low. This spreading also makes it more difficult to allocate large blocks, however. The worst-fit algorithm attempts to avoid this problem by keeping contiguous sections of free memory as large as possible.

15.1.2 Garbage Collection

In some languages, like C and C++, the memory space for objects must be explicitly deallocated by the programmer, which is a duty often overlooked by beginning programmers and is the source of frustrating programming errors even for experienced programmers. The designers of Python instead placed the burden of memory management entirely on the interpreter. The process of detecting "stale" objects, deallocating the space devoted to those objects, and returning the reclaimed space to the free list is known as ***garbage collection***.

To perform automated garbage collection, there must first be a way to detect those objects that are no longer necessary. Since the interpreter cannot feasibly analyze the semantics of an arbitrary Python program, it relies on the following conservative rule for reclaiming objects. In order for a program to access an object, it must have a direct or indirect reference to that object. We will define such objects to be ***live objects***. In defining a live object, a ***direct reference*** to an object is in the form of an identifier in an active namespace (i.e., the global namespace, or the local namespace for any active function). For example, immediately after the command w = Widget( ) is executed, identifier w will be defined in the current namespace as a reference to the new widget object. We refer to all such objects with direct references as ***root objects***. An ***indirect reference*** to a live object is a reference that occurs within the state of some other live object. For example, if the widget instance in our earlier example maintains a list as an attribute, that list is also a live object (as it can be reached indirectly through use of identifier w). The set of live objects are defined recursively; thus, any objects that are referenced within the list that is referenced by the widget are also classified as live objects.

The Python interpreter assumes that live objects are the active objects currently being used by the running program; these objects should ***not*** be deallocated. Other objects can be garbage collected. Python relies on the following two strategies for determining which objects are live.

Reference Counts

Within the state of every Python object is an integer known as its ***reference count***. This is the count of how many references to the object exist anywhere in the system. Every time a reference is assigned to this object, its reference count is incremented, and every time one of those references is reassigned to something else, the reference count for the former object is decremented. The maintenance of a reference count for each object adds $O(1)$ space per object, and the increments and decrements to the count add $O(1)$ additional computation time per such operations.

The Python interpreter allows a running program to examine an object's reference count. Within the sys module there is a function named getrefcount that returns an integer equal to the reference count for the object sent as a parameter. It is worth noting that because the formal parameter of that function is assigned to the actual parameter sent by the caller, there is temporarily one additional reference to that object in the local namespace of the function at the time the count is reported.

The advantage of having a reference count for each object is that if an object's count is ever decremented to zero, that object cannot possibly be a live object and therefore the system can immediately deallocate the object (or place it in a queue of objects that are ready to be deallocated).

Cycle Detection

Although it is clear that an object with a reference count of zero cannot be a live object, it is important to recognize that an object with a nonzero reference count need not qualify as live. There may exist a group of objects that have references to each other, even though none of those objects are reachable from a root object.

For example, a running Python program may have an identifier, data, that is a reference to a sequence implemented using a doubly linked list. In this case, the list referenced by data is a root object, the header and trailer nodes that are stored as attributes of the list are live objects, as are all the intermediate nodes of the list that are indirectly referenced and all the elements that are referenced as elements of those nodes. If the identifier, data, were to go out of scope, or to be reassigned to some other object, the reference count for the list instance may go to zero and be garbage collected, but the reference counts for all of the nodes would remain nonzero, stopping them from being garbage collected by the simple rule above.

Every so often, in particular when the available space in the memory heap is becoming scarce, the Python interpreter uses a more advanced form of garbage collection to reclaim objects that are unreachable, despite their nonzero reference counts. There are different algorithms for implementing cycle detection. (The mechanics of garbage collection in Python are abstracted in the gc module, and may vary depending on the implementation of the interpreter.) A classic algorithm for garbage collection is the ***mark-sweep algorithm***, which we next discuss.

The Mark-Sweep Algorithm

In the mark-sweep garbage collection algorithm, we associate a "mark" bit with each object that identifies whether that object is live. When we determine at some point that garbage collection is needed, we suspend all other activity and clear the mark bits of all the objects currently allocated in the memory heap. We then trace through the active namespaces and we mark all the root objects as "live." We must then determine all the other live objects—the ones that are reachable from the root objects. To do this efficiently, we can perform a depth-first search (see Section 14.3.1) on the directed graph that is defined by objects reference other objects. In this case, each object in the memory heap is viewed as a vertex in a directed graph, and the reference from one object to another is viewed as a directed edge. By performing a directed DFS from each root object, we can correctly identify and mark each live object. This process is known as the "mark" phase. Once this process has completed, we then scan through the memory heap and reclaim any space that is being used for an object that has not been marked. At this time, we can also optionally coalesce all the allocated space in the memory heap into a single block, thereby eliminating external fragmentation for the time being. This scanning and reclamation process is known as the "sweep" phase, and when it completes, we resume running the suspended program. Thus, the mark-sweep garbage collection algorithm will reclaim unused space in time proportional to the number of live objects and their references plus the size of the memory heap.

Performing DFS In-Place

The mark-sweep algorithm correctly reclaims unused space in the memory heap, but there is an important issue we must face during the mark phase. Since we are reclaiming memory space at a time when available memory is scarce, we must take care not to use extra space during the garbage collection itself. The trouble is that the DFS algorithm, in the recursive way we have described it in Section 14.3.1, can use space proportional to the number of vertices in the graph. In the case of garbage collection, the vertices in our graph are the objects in the memory heap; hence, we probably do not have this much memory to use. So our only alternative is to find a way to perform DFS in-place rather than recursively, that is, we must perform DFS using only a constant amount of additional storage.

The main idea for performing DFS in-place is to simulate the recursion stack using the edges of the graph (which in the case of garbage collection correspond to object references). When we traverse an edge from a visited vertex v to a new vertex w, we change the edge (v, w) stored in v's adjacency list to point back to v's parent in the DFS tree. When we return back to v (simulating the return from the "recursive" call at w), we can then switch the edge we modified to point back to w, assuming we have some way to identify which edge we need to change back.

15.1.3   Additional Memory Used by the Python Interpreter

We have discussed, in Section 15.1.1, how the Python interpreter allocates memory for objects within a memory heap. However, this is not the only memory that is used when executing a Python program. In this section, we discuss some other important uses of memory.

The Run-Time Call Stack

Stacks have a most important application to the run-time environment of Python programs. A running Python program has a private stack, known as the ***call stack*** or ***Python interpreter stack***, that is used to keep track of the nested sequence of currently active (that is, nonterminated) invocations of functions. Each entry of the stack is a structure known as an ***activation record*** or ***frame***, storing important information about an invocation of a function.

At the top of the call stack is the activation record of the ***running call***, that is, the function activation that currently has control of the execution. The remaining elements of the stack are activation records of the ***suspended calls***, that is, functions that have invoked another function and are currently waiting for that other function to return control when it terminates. The order of the elements in the stack corresponds to the chain of invocations of the currently active functions. When a new function is called, an activation record for that call is pushed onto the stack. When it terminates, its activation record is popped from the stack and the Python interpreter resumes the processing of the previously suspended call.

Each activation record includes a dictionary representing the local namespace for the function call. (See Sections 1.10 and 2.5 for further discussion of namespaces). The namespace maps identifiers, which serve as parameters and local variables, to object values, although the objects being referenced still reside in the memory heap. The activation record for a function call also includes a reference to the function definition itself, and a special variable, known as the ***program counter***, to maintain the address of the statement within the function that is currently executing. When one function returns control to another, the stored program counter for the suspended function allows the interpreter to properly continue execution of that function.

Implementing Recursion

One of the benefits of using a stack to implement the nesting of function calls is that it allows programs to use ***recursion***. That is, it allows a function to call itself, as discussed in Chapter 4. We implicitly described the concept of the call stack and the use of activation records within our portrayal of ***recursion traces*** in that chapter. Interestingly, early programming languages, such as Cobol and Fortran, did not originally use call stacks to implement function calls. But because of the elegance and efficiency that recursion allows, almost all modern programming languages utilize a call stack for function calls, including the current versions of classic languages like Cobol and Fortran.

Each box of a recursive trace corresponds to an activation record that is placed on the call stack during the execution of a recursive function. At any point in time, the content of the call stack corresponds to the chain of boxes from the initial function invocation to the current one. To better illustrate how a call stack is used by recursive functions, we refer back to the Python implementation of the classic recursive definition of the factorial function,

$$n! = n(n-1)(n-2)\cdots 1,$$

with the code originally given in Code Fragment 4.1, and the recursive trace in Figure 4.1. The first time we call factorial, its activation record includes a namespace storing the parameter value n. The function recursively calls itself to compute $(n-1)!$, causing a new activation record, with its own namespace and parameter, to be pushed onto the call stack. In turn, this recursive invocation calls itself to compute $(n-2)!$, and so on. The chain of recursive invocations, and thus the call stack, grows up to size $n+1$, with the most deeply nested call being factorial(0), which returns 1 without any further recursion. The run-time stack allows several invocations of the factorial function to exist simultaneously. Each has an activation record that stores the value of its parameter, and eventually the value to be returned. When the first recursive call eventually terminates, it returns $(n-1)!$, which is then multiplied by n to compute $n!$ for the original call of the factorial method.

The Operand Stack

Interestingly, there is actually another place where the Python interpreter uses a stack. Arithmetic expressions, such as $((a+b)*(c+d))/e$, are evaluated by the interpreter using an *operand stack*. In Section 8.5 we described how to evaluate an arithmetic expression using a postorder traversal of an explicit expression tree. We described that algorithm in a recursive way; however, this recursive description can be simulated using a nonrecursive process that maintains an explicit operand stack. A simple binary operation, such as $a+b$, is computed by pushing a on the stack, pushing b on the stack, and then calling an instruction that pops the top two items from the stack, performs the binary operation on them, and pushes the result back onto the stack. Likewise, instructions for writing and reading elements to and from memory involve the use of pop and push methods for the operand stack.

15.2   Memory Hierarchies and Caching

With the increased use of computing in society, software applications must manage extremely large data sets. Such applications include the processing of online financial transactions, the organization and maintenance of databases, and analyses of customers' purchasing histories and preferences. The amount of data can be so large that the overall performance of algorithms and data structures sometimes depends more on the time to access the data than on the speed of the CPU.

15.2.1   Memory Systems

In order to accommodate large data sets, computers have a *hierarchy* of different kinds of memories, which vary in terms of their size and distance from the CPU. Closest to the CPU are the internal registers that the CPU itself uses. Access to such locations is very fast, but there are relatively few such locations. At the second level in the hierarchy are one or more memory *caches*. This memory is considerably larger than the register set of a CPU, but accessing it takes longer. At the third level in the hierarchy is the *internal memory*, which is also known as *main memory* or *core memory*. The internal memory is considerably larger than the cache memory, but also requires more time to access. Another level in the hierarchy is the *external memory*, which usually consists of disks, CD drives, DVD drives, and/or tapes. This memory is very large, but it is also very slow. Data stored through an external network can be viewed as yet another level in this hierarchy, with even greater storage capacity, but even slower access. Thus, the memory hierarchy for computers can be viewed as consisting of five or more levels, each of which is larger and slower than the previous level. (See Figure 15.1.) During the execution of a program, data is routinely copied from one level of the hierarchy to a neighboring level, and these transfers can become a computational bottleneck.

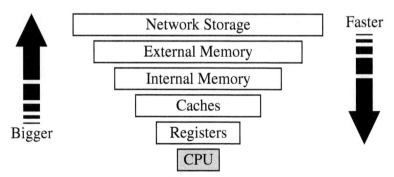

Figure 15.1: The memory hierarchy.

15.2.2   Caching Strategies

The significance of the memory hierarchy on the performance of a program depends greatly upon the size of the problem we are trying to solve and the physical characteristics of the computer system. Often, the bottleneck occurs between two levels of the memory hierarchy—the one that can hold all data items and the level just below that one. For a problem that can fit entirely in main memory, the two most important levels are the cache memory and the internal memory. Access times for internal memory can be as much as 10 to 100 times longer than those for cache memory. It is desirable, therefore, to be able to perform most memory accesses in cache memory. For a problem that does not fit entirely in main memory, on the other hand, the two most important levels are the internal memory and the external memory. Here the differences are even more dramatic, for access times for disks, the usual general-purpose external-memory device, are typically as much as 100000 to 1000000 times longer than those for internal memory.

To put this latter figure into perspective, imagine there is a student in Baltimore who wants to send a request-for-money message to his parents in Chicago. If the student sends his parents an email message, it can arrive at their home computer in about five seconds. Think of this mode of communication as corresponding to an internal-memory access by a CPU. A mode of communication corresponding to an external-memory access that is 500,000 times slower would be for the student to walk to Chicago and deliver his message in person, which would take about a month if he can average 20 miles per day. Thus, we should make as few accesses to external memory as possible.

Most algorithms are not designed with the memory hierarchy in mind, in spite of the great variance between access times for the different levels. Indeed, all of the algorithm analyses described in this book so far have assumed that all memory accesses are equal. This assumption might seem, at first, to be a great oversight—and one we are only addressing now in the final chapter—but there are good reasons why it is actually a reasonable assumption to make.

One justification for this assumption is that it is often necessary to assume that all memory accesses take the same amount of time, since specific device-dependent information about memory sizes is often hard to come by. In fact, information about memory size may be difficult to get. For example, a Python program that is designed to run on many different computer platforms cannot easily be defined in terms of a specific computer architecture configuration. We can certainly use architecture-specific information, if we have it (and we will show how to exploit such information later in this chapter). But once we have optimized our software for a certain architecture configuration, our software will no longer be device-independent. Fortunately, such optimizations are not always necessary, primarily because of the second justification for the equal-time memory-access assumption.

Caching and Blocking

Another justification for the memory-access equality assumption is that operating system designers have developed general mechanisms that allow most memory accesses to be fast. These mechanisms are based on two important *locality-of-reference* properties that most software possesses:

- **Temporal locality**: If a program accesses a certain memory location, then there is increased likelihood that it accesses that same location again in the near future. For example, it is common to use the value of a counter variable in several different expressions, including one to increment the counter's value. In fact, a common adage among computer architects is that a program spends 90 percent of its time in 10 percent of its code.

- **Spatial locality**: If a program accesses a certain memory location, then there is increased likelihood that it soon accesses other locations that are near this one. For example, a program using an array may be likely to access the locations of this array in a sequential or near-sequential manner.

Computer scientists and engineers have performed extensive software profiling experiments to justify the claim that most software possesses both of these kinds of locality of reference. For example, a nested for loop used to repeatedly scan through an array will exhibit both kinds of locality.

Temporal and spatial localities have, in turn, given rise to two fundamental design choices for multilevel computer memory systems (which are present in the interface between cache memory and internal memory, and also in the interface between internal memory and external memory).

The first design choice is called *virtual memory*. This concept consists of providing an address space as large as the capacity of the secondary-level memory, and of transferring data located in the secondary level into the primary level, when they are addressed. Virtual memory does not limit the programmer to the constraint of the internal memory size. The concept of bringing data into primary memory is called *caching*, and it is motivated by temporal locality. By bringing data into primary memory, we are hoping that it will be accessed again soon, and we will be able to respond quickly to all the requests for this data that come in the near future.

The second design choice is motivated by spatial locality. Specifically, if data stored at a secondary-level memory location ℓ is accessed, then we bring into primary-level memory a large block of contiguous locations that include the location ℓ. (See Figure 15.2.) This concept is known as *blocking*, and it is motivated by the expectation that other secondary-level memory locations close to ℓ will soon be accessed. In the interface between cache memory and internal memory, such blocks are often called *cache lines*, and in the interface between internal memory and external memory, such blocks are often called *pages*.

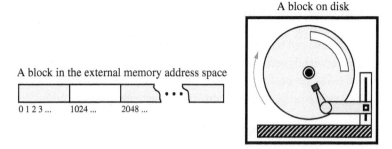

Figure 15.2: Blocks in external memory.

When implemented with caching and blocking, virtual memory often allows us to perceive secondary-level memory as being faster than it really is. There is still a problem, however. Primary-level memory is much smaller than secondary-level memory. Moreover, because memory systems use blocking, any program of substance will likely reach a point where it requests data from secondary-level memory, but the primary memory is already full of blocks. In order to fulfill the request and maintain our use of caching and blocking, we must remove some block from primary memory to make room for a new block from secondary memory in this case. Deciding which block to evict brings up a number of interesting data structure and algorithm design issues.

Caching in Web Browsers

For motivation, we consider a related problem that arises when revisiting information presented in Web pages. To exploit temporal locality of reference, it is often advantageous to store copies of Web pages in a *cache* memory, so these pages can be quickly retrieved when requested again. This effectively creates a two-level memory hierarchy, with the cache serving as the smaller, quicker internal memory, and the network being the external memory. In particular, suppose we have a cache memory that has m "slots" that can contain Web pages. We assume that a Web page can be placed in any slot of the cache. This is known as a *fully associative* cache.

As a browser executes, it requests different Web pages. Each time the browser requests such a Web page p, the browser determines (using a quick test) if p is unchanged and currently contained in the cache. If p is contained in the cache, then the browser satisfies the request using the cached copy. If p is not in the cache, however, the page for p is requested over the Internet and transferred into the cache. If one of the m slots in the cache is available, then the browser assigns p to one of the empty slots. But if all the m cells of the cache are occupied, then the computer must determine which previously viewed Web page to evict before bringing in p to take its place. There are, of course, many different policies that can be used to determine the page to evict.

Page Replacement Algorithms

Some of the better-known page replacement policies include the following (see Figure 15.3):

- **First-in, first-out (FIFO)**: Evict the page that has been in the cache the longest, that is, the page that was transferred to the cache furthest in the past.

- **Least recently used (LRU)**: Evict the page whose last request occurred furthest in the past.

In addition, we can consider a simple and purely random strategy:

- **Random**: Choose a page at random to evict from the cache.

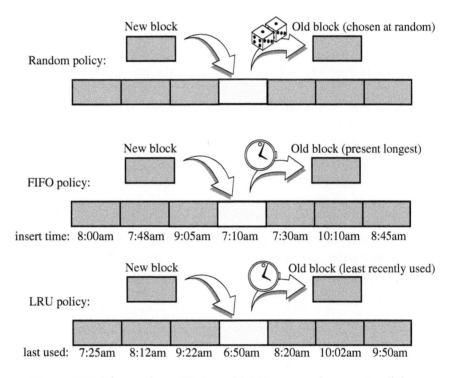

Figure 15.3: The random, FIFO, and LRU page replacement policies.

The random strategy is one of the easiest policies to implement, for it only requires a random or pseudo-random number generator. The overhead involved in implementing this policy is an $O(1)$ additional amount of work per page replacement. Moreover, there is no additional overhead for each page request, other than to determine whether a page request is in the cache or not. Still, this policy makes no attempt to take advantage of any temporal locality exhibited by a user's browsing.

The FIFO strategy is quite simple to implement, as it only requires a queue Q to store references to the pages in the cache. Pages are enqueued in Q when they are referenced by a browser, and then are brought into the cache. When a page needs to be evicted, the computer simply performs a dequeue operation on Q to determine which page to evict. Thus, this policy also requires $O(1)$ additional work per page replacement. Also, the FIFO policy incurs no additional overhead for page requests. Moreover, it tries to take some advantage of temporal locality.

The LRU strategy goes a step further than the FIFO strategy, for the LRU strategy explicitly takes advantage of temporal locality as much as possible, by always evicting the page that was least-recently used. From a policy point of view, this is an excellent approach, but it is costly from an implementation point of view. That is, its way of optimizing temporal and spatial locality is fairly costly. Implementing the LRU strategy requires the use of an adaptable priority queue Q that supports updating the priority of existing pages. If Q is implemented with a sorted sequence based on a linked list, then the overhead for each page request and page replacement is $O(1)$. When we insert a page in Q or update its key, the page is assigned the highest key in Q and is placed at the end of the list, which can also be done in $O(1)$ time. Even though the LRU strategy has constant-time overhead, using the implementation above, the constant factors involved, in terms of the additional time overhead and the extra space for the priority queue Q, make this policy less attractive from a practical point of view.

Since these different page replacement policies have different trade-offs between implementation difficulty and the degree to which they seem to take advantage of localities, it is natural for us to ask for some kind of comparative analysis of these methods to see which one, if any, is the best.

From a worst-case point of view, the FIFO and LRU strategies have fairly unattractive competitive behavior. For example, suppose we have a cache containing m pages, and consider the FIFO and LRU methods for performing page replacement for a program that has a loop that repeatedly requests $m + 1$ pages in a cyclic order. Both the FIFO and LRU policies perform badly on such a sequence of page requests, because they perform a page replacement on every page request. Thus, from a worst-case point of view, these policies are almost the worst we can imagine—they require a page replacement on every page request.

This worst-case analysis is a little too pessimistic, however, for it focuses on each protocol's behavior for one bad sequence of page requests. An ideal analysis would be to compare these methods over all possible page-request sequences. Of course, this is impossible to do exhaustively, but there have been a great number of experimental simulations done on page-request sequences derived from real programs. Based on these experimental comparisons, the LRU strategy has been shown to be usually superior to the FIFO strategy, which is usually better than the random strategy.

15.3 External Searching and B-Trees

Consider the problem of maintaining a large collection of items that does not fit in main memory, such as a typical database. In this context, we refer to the secondary-memory blocks as *disk blocks*. Likewise, we refer to the transfer of a block between secondary memory and primary memory as a *disk transfer*. Recalling the great time difference that exists between main memory accesses and disk accesses, the main goal of maintaining such a collection in external memory is to minimize the number of disk transfers needed to perform a query or update. We refer to this count as the *I/O complexity* of the algorithm involved.

Some Inefficient External-Memory Representations

A typical operation we would like to support is the search for a key in a map. If we were to store n items unordered in a doubly linked list, searching for a particular key within the list requires n transfers in the worst case, since each link hop we perform on the linked list might access a different block of memory.

We can reduce the number of block transfers by using an array-based sequence. A sequential search of an array can be performed using only $O(n/B)$ block transfers because of spatial locality of reference, where B denotes the number of elements that fit into a block. This is because the block transfer when accessing the first element of the array actually retrieves the first B elements, and so on with each successive block. It is worth noting that the bound of $O(n/B)$ transfers is only achieved when using a *compact array representation* (see Section 5.2.2). The standard Python list class is a referential container, and so even though the sequence of references are stored in an array, the actual elements that must be examined during a search are not generally stored sequentially in memory, resulting in n transfers in the worst case.

We could alternately store a sequence using a *sorted* array. In this case, a search performs $O(\log_2 n)$ transfers, via binary search, which is a nice improvement. But we do not get significant benefit from block transfers because each query during a binary search is likely in a different block of the sequence. As usual, update operations are expensive for a sorted array.

Since these simple implementations are I/O inefficient, we should consider the logarithmic-time internal-memory strategies that use balanced binary trees (for example, AVL trees or red-black trees) or other search structures with logarithmic average-case query and update times (for example, skip lists or splay trees). Typically, each node accessed for a query or update in one of these structures will be in a different block. Thus, these methods all require $O(\log_2 n)$ transfers in the worst case to perform a query or update operation. But we can do better! We can perform map queries and updates using only $O(\log_B n) = O(\log n/\log B)$ transfers.

15.3.1 (a,b) Trees

To reduce the number of external-memory accesses when searching, we can represent our map using a multiway search tree (Section 11.5.1). This approach gives rise to a generalization of the $(2,4)$ tree data structure known as the (a,b) tree.

An (a,b) tree is a multiway search tree such that each node has between a and b children and stores between $a-1$ and $b-1$ entries. The algorithms for searching, inserting, and removing entries in an (a,b) tree are straightforward generalizations of the corresponding ones for $(2,4)$ trees. The advantage of generalizing $(2,4)$ trees to (a,b) trees is that a generalized class of trees provides a flexible search structure, where the size of the nodes and the running time of the various map operations depends on the parameters a and b. By setting the parameters a and b appropriately with respect to the size of disk blocks, we can derive a data structure that achieves good external-memory performance.

Definition of an (a,b) Tree

An **(a,b) tree**, where parameters a and b are integers such that $2 \le a \le (b+1)/2$, is a multiway search tree T with the following additional restrictions:

Size Property: Each internal node has at least a children, unless it is the root, and has at most b children.

Depth Property: All the external nodes have the same depth.

Proposition 15.1: *The height of an (a,b) tree storing n entries is $\Omega(\log n/\log b)$ and $O(\log n/\log a)$.*

Justification: Let T be an (a,b) tree storing n entries, and let h be the height of T. We justify the proposition by establishing the following bounds on h:

$$\frac{1}{\log b}\log(n+1) \le h \le \frac{1}{\log a}\log\frac{n+1}{2}+1.$$

By the size and depth properties, the number n'' of external nodes of T is at least $2a^{h-1}$ and at most b^h. By Proposition 11.7, $n'' = n+1$. Thus,

$$2a^{h-1} \le n+1 \le b^h.$$

Taking the logarithm in base 2 of each term, we get

$$(h-1)\log a+1 \le \log(n+1) \le h\log b.$$

An algebraic manipulation of these inequalities completes the justification. ∎

Search and Update Operations

We recall that in a multiway search tree T, each node v of T holds a secondary structure $M(v)$, which is itself a map (Section 11.5.1). If T is an (a,b) tree, then $M(v)$ stores at most b entries. Let $f(b)$ denote the time for performing a search in a map, $M(v)$. The search algorithm in an (a,b) tree is exactly like the one for multiway search trees given in Section 11.5.1. Hence, searching in an (a,b) tree T with n entries takes $O(\frac{f(b)}{\log a}\log n)$ time. Note that if b is considered a constant (and thus a is also), then the search time is $O(\log n)$.

The main application of (a,b) trees is for maps stored in external memory. Namely, to minimize disk accesses, we select the parameters a and b so that each tree node occupies a single disk block (so that $f(b) = 1$ if we wish to simply count block transfers). Providing the right a and b values in this context gives rise to a data structure known as the B-tree, which we will describe shortly. Before we describe this structure, however, let us discuss how insertions and removals are handled in (a,b) trees.

The insertion algorithm for an (a,b) tree is similar to that for a $(2,4)$ tree. An overflow occurs when an entry is inserted into a b-node w, which becomes an illegal $(b+1)$-node. (Recall that a node in a multiway tree is a d-node if it has d children.) To remedy an overflow, we split node w by moving the median entry of w into the parent of w and replacing w with a $\lceil (b+1)/2\rceil$-node w' and a $\lfloor (b+1)/2\rfloor$-node w''. We can now see the reason for requiring $a \le (b+1)/2$ in the definition of an (a,b) tree. Note that as a consequence of the split, we need to build the secondary structures $M(w')$ and $M(w'')$.

Removing an entry from an (a,b) tree is similar to what was done for $(2,4)$ trees. An underflow occurs when a key is removed from an a-node w, distinct from the root, which causes w to become an illegal $(a-1)$-node. To remedy an underflow, we perform a transfer with a sibling of w that is not an a-node or we perform a fusion of w with a sibling that is an a-node. The new node w' resulting from the fusion is a $(2a-1)$-node, which is another reason for requiring $a \le (b+1)/2$.

Table 15.1 shows the performance of a map realized with an (a,b) tree.

Operation	Running Time
M[k]	$O\left(\frac{f(b)}{\log a}\log n\right)$
M[k] = v	$O\left(\frac{g(b)}{\log a}\log n\right)$
del M[k]	$O\left(\frac{g(b)}{\log a}\log n\right)$

Table 15.1: Time bounds for an n-entry map realized by an (a,b) tree T. We assume the secondary structure of the nodes of T support search in $f(b)$ time, and split and fusion operations in $g(b)$ time, for some functions $f(b)$ and $g(b)$, which can be made to be $O(1)$ when we are only counting disk transfers.

15.3.2 B-Trees

A version of the (a,b) tree data structure, which is the best-known method for maintaining a map in external memory, is called the "B-tree." (See Figure 15.4.) A **B-tree of order** d is an (a,b) tree with $a = \lceil d/2 \rceil$ and $b = d$. Since we discussed the standard map query and update methods for (a,b) trees above, we restrict our discussion here to the I/O complexity of B-trees.

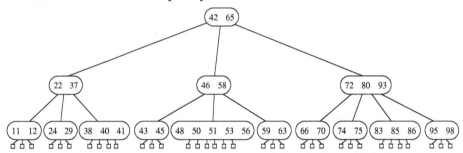

Figure 15.4: A B-tree of order 6.

An important property of B-trees is that we can choose d so that the d children references and the $d-1$ keys stored at a node can fit compactly into a single disk block, implying that d is proportional to B. This choice allows us to assume that a and b are also proportional to B in the analysis of the search and update operations on (a,b) trees. Thus, $f(b)$ and $g(b)$ are both $O(1)$, for each time we access a node to perform a search or an update operation, we need only perform a single disk transfer.

As we have already observed above, each search or update requires that we examine at most $O(1)$ nodes for each level of the tree. Therefore, any map search or update operation on a B-tree requires only $O(\log_{\lceil d/2 \rceil} n)$, that is, $O(\log n / \log B)$, disk transfers. For example, an insert operation proceeds down the B-tree to locate the node in which to insert the new entry. If the node would **overflow** (to have $d+1$ children) because of this addition, then this node is **split** into two nodes that have $\lfloor (d+1)/2 \rfloor$ and $\lceil (d+1)/2 \rceil$ children, respectively. This process is then repeated at the next level up, and will continue for at most $O(\log_B n)$ levels.

Likewise, if a remove operation results in a node **underflow** (to have $\lceil d/2 \rceil - 1$ children), then we move references from a sibling node with at least $\lceil d/2 \rceil + 1$ children or we perform a **fusion** operation of this node with its sibling (and repeat this computation at the parent). As with the insert operation, this will continue up the B-tree for at most $O(\log_B n)$ levels. The requirement that each internal node have at least $\lceil d/2 \rceil$ children implies that each disk block used to support a B-tree is at least half full. Thus, we have the following:

Proposition 15.2: *A B-tree with* n *entries has I/O complexity* $O(\log_B n)$ *for search or update operation, and uses* $O(n/B)$ *blocks, where* B *is the size of a block.*

15.4 External-Memory Sorting

In addition to data structures, such as maps, that need to be implemented in external memory, there are many algorithms that must also operate on input sets that are too large to fit entirely into internal memory. In this case, the objective is to solve the algorithmic problem using as few block transfers as possible. The most classic domain for such external-memory algorithms is the sorting problem.

Multiway Merge-Sort

An efficient way to sort a set S of n objects in external memory amounts to a simple external-memory variation on the familiar merge-sort algorithm. The main idea behind this variation is to merge many recursively sorted lists at a time, thereby reducing the number of levels of recursion. Specifically, a high-level description of this *multiway merge-sort* method is to divide S into d subsets $S_1, S_2, \ldots, S_d$ of roughly equal size, recursively sort each subset S_i, and then simultaneously merge all d sorted lists into a sorted representation of S. If we can perform the merge process using only $O(n/B)$ disk transfers, then, for large enough values of n, the total number of transfers performed by this algorithm satisfies the following recurrence:

$$t(n) = d \cdot t(n/d) + cn/B,$$

for some constant $c \geq 1$. We can stop the recursion when $n \leq B$, since we can perform a single block transfer at this point, getting all of the objects into internal memory, and then sort the set with an efficient internal-memory algorithm. Thus, the stopping criterion for $t(n)$ is

$$t(n) = 1 \quad \text{if } n/B \leq 1.$$

This implies a closed-form solution that $t(n)$ is $O((n/B)\log_d(n/B))$, which is

$$O((n/B)\log(n/B)/\log d).$$

Thus, if we can choose d to be $\Theta(M/B)$, where M is the size of the internal memory, then the worst-case number of block transfers performed by this multiway merge-sort algorithm will be quite low. For reasons given in the next section, we choose

$$d = (M/B) - 1.$$

The only aspect of this algorithm left to specify, then, is how to perform the d-way merge using only $O(n/B)$ block transfers.

15.4.1 Multiway Merging

In a standard merge-sort (Section 12.2), the merge process combines two sorted sequences into one by repeatedly taking the smaller of the items at the front of the two respective lists. In a d-way merge, we repeatedly find the smallest among the items at the front of the d sequences and place it as the next element of the merged sequence. We continue until all elements are included.

In the context of an external-memory sorting algorithm, if main memory has size M and each block has size B, we can store up to M/B blocks within main memory at any given time. We specifically choose $d = (M/B) - 1$ so that we can afford to keep one block from each input sequence in main memory at any given time, and to have one additional block to use as a buffer for the merged sequence. (See Figure 15.5.)

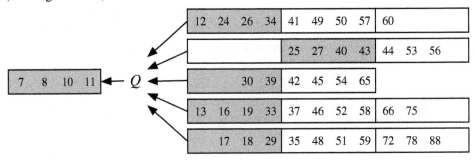

Figure 15.5: A d-way merge with $d = 5$ and $B = 4$. Blocks that currently reside in main memory are shaded.

We maintain the smallest unprocessed element from each input sequence in main memory, requesting the next block from a sequence when the preceding block has been exhausted. Similarly, we use one block of internal memory to buffer the merged sequence, flushing that block to external memory when full. In this way, the total number of transfers performed during a single d-way merge is $O(n/B)$, since we scan each block of list S_i once, and we write out each block of the merged list S' once. In terms of computation time, choosing the smallest of d values can trivially be performed using $O(d)$ operations. If we are willing to devote $O(d)$ internal memory, we can maintain a priority queue identifying the smallest element from each sequence, thereby performing each step of the merge in $O(\log d)$ time by removing the minimum element and replacing it with the next element from the same sequence. Hence, the internal time for the d-way merge is $O(n \log d)$.

Proposition 15.3: *Given an array-based sequence S of n elements stored compactly in external memory, we can sort S with $O((n/B) \log(n/B)/\log(M/B))$ block transfers and $O(n \log n)$ internal computations, where M is the size of the internal memory and B is the size of a block.*

15.5 Exercises

For help with exercises, please visit the site, www.wiley.com/college/goodrich.

Reinforcement

R-15.1 Julia just bought a new computer that uses 64-bit integers to address memory cells. Argue why Julia will never in her life be able to upgrade the main memory of her computer so that it is the maximum-size possible, assuming that you have to have distinct atoms to represent different bits.

R-15.2 Describe, in detail, algorithms for adding an item to, or deleting an item from, an (a,b) tree.

R-15.3 Suppose T is a multiway tree in which each internal node has at least five and at most eight children. For what values of a and b is T a valid (a,b) tree?

R-15.4 For what values of d is the tree T of the previous exercise an order-d B-tree?

R-15.5 Consider an initially empty memory cache consisting of four pages. How many page misses does the LRU algorithm incur on the following page request sequence: $(2,3,4,1,2,5,1,3,5,4,1,2,3)$?

R-15.6 Consider an initially empty memory cache consisting of four pages. How many page misses does the FIFO algorithm incur on the following page request sequence: $(2,3,4,1,2,5,1,3,5,4,1,2,3)$?

R-15.7 Consider an initially empty memory cache consisting of four pages. What is the maximum number of page misses that the random algorithm incurs on the following page request sequence: $(2,3,4,1,2,5,1,3,5,4,1,2,3)$? Show all of the random choices the algorithm made in this case.

R-15.8 Draw the result of inserting, into an initially empty order-7 B-tree, entries with keys $(4,40,23,50,11,34,62,78,66,22,90,59,25,72,64,77,39,12)$, in this order.

Creativity

C-15.9 Describe an efficient external-memory algorithm for removing all the duplicate entries in an array list of size n.

C-15.10 Describe an external-memory data structure to implement the stack ADT so that the total number of disk transfers needed to process a sequence of k push and pop operations is $O(k/B)$.

C-15.11 Describe an external-memory data structure to implement the queue ADT so that the total number of disk transfers needed to process a sequence of k enqueue and dequeue operations is $O(k/B)$.

C-15.12 Describe an external-memory version of the PositionalList ADT (Section 7.4), with block size B, such that an iteration of a list of length n is completed using $O(n/B)$ transfers in the worst case, and all other methods of the ADT require only $O(1)$ transfers.

C-15.13 Change the rules that define red-black trees so that each red-black tree T has a corresponding $(4,8)$ tree, and vice versa.

C-15.14 Describe a modified version of the B-tree insertion algorithm so that each time we create an overflow because of a split of a node w, we redistribute keys among all of w's siblings, so that each sibling holds roughly the same number of keys (possibly cascading the split up to the parent of w). What is the minimum fraction of each block that will always be filled using this scheme?

C-15.15 Another possible external-memory map implementation is to use a skip list, but to collect consecutive groups of $O(B)$ nodes, in individual blocks, on any level in the skip list. In particular, we define an ***order-d B-skip list*** to be such a representation of a skip list structure, where each block contains at least $\lceil d/2 \rceil$ list nodes and at most d list nodes. Let us also choose d in this case to be the maximum number of list nodes from a level of a skip list that can fit into one block. Describe how we should modify the skip-list insertion and removal algorithms for a B-skip list so that the expected height of the structure is $O(\log n / \log B)$.

C-15.16 Describe how to use a B-tree to implement the partition (union-find) ADT (from Section 14.7.3) so that the union and find operations each use at most $O(\log n / \log B)$ disk transfers.

C-15.17 Suppose we are given a sequence S of n elements with integer keys such that some elements in S are colored "blue" and some elements in S are colored "red." In addition, say that a red element e **pairs** with a blue element f if they have the same key value. Describe an efficient external-memory algorithm for finding all the red-blue pairs in S. How many disk transfers does your algorithm perform?

C-15.18 Consider the page caching problem where the memory cache can hold m pages, and we are given a sequence P of n requests taken from a pool of $m+1$ possible pages. Describe the optimal strategy for the offline algorithm and show that it causes at most $m+n/m$ page misses in total, starting from an empty cache.

C-15.19 Describe an efficient external-memory algorithm that determines whether an array of n integers contains a value occurring more than $n/2$ times.

C-15.20 Consider the page caching strategy based on the *least frequently used* (LFU) rule, where the page in the cache that has been accessed the least often is the one that is evicted when a new page is requested. If there are ties, LFU evicts the least frequently used page that has been in the cache the longest. Show that there is a sequence P of n requests that causes LFU to miss $\Omega(n)$ times for a cache of m pages, whereas the optimal algorithm will miss only $O(m)$ times.

C-15.21 Suppose that instead of having the node-search function $f(d) = 1$ in an order-d B-tree T, we have $f(d) = \log d$. What does the asymptotic running time of performing a search in T now become?

Projects

P-15.22 Write a Python class that simulates the best-fit, worst-fit, first-fit, and next-fit algorithms for memory management. Determine experimentally which method is the best under various sequences of memory requests.

P-15.23 Write a Python class that implements all the methods of the ordered map ADT by means of an (a,b) tree, where a and b are integer constants passed as parameters to a constructor.

P-15.24 Implement the B-tree data structure, assuming a block size of 1024 and integer keys. Test the number of "disk transfers" needed to process a sequence of map operations.

Chapter Notes

The reader interested in the study of the architecture of hierarchical memory systems is referred to the book chapter by Burger *et al.* [21] or the book by Hennessy and Patterson [50]. The mark-sweep garbage collection method we describe is one of many different algorithms for performing garbage collection. We encourage the reader interested in further study of garbage collection to examine the book by Jones and Lins [56]. Knuth [62] has very nice discussions about external-memory sorting and searching, and Ullman [97] discusses external memory structures for database systems. The handbook by Gonnet and Baeza-Yates [44] compares the performance of a number of different sorting algorithms, many of which are external-memory algorithms. B-trees were invented by Bayer and Mc-Creight [11] and Comer [28] provides a very nice overview of this data structure. The books by Mehlhorn [76] and Samet [87] also have nice discussions about B-trees and their variants. Aggarwal and Vitter [3] study the I/O complexity of sorting and related problems, establishing upper and lower bounds. Goodrich *et al.* [46] study the I/O complexity of several computational geometry problems. The reader interested in further study of I/O-efficient algorithms is encouraged to examine the survey paper of Vitter [99].

Appendix

 A

Character Strings in Python

A string is a sequence of characters that come from some **_alphabet_**. In Python, the built-in **str** class represents strings based upon the Unicode international character set, a 16-bit character encoding that covers most written languages. Unicode is an extension of the 7-bit ASCII character set that includes the basic Latin alphabet, numerals, and common symbols. Strings are particularly important in most programming applications, as text is often used for input and output.

A basic introduction to the str class was provided in Section 1.2.3, including use of string literals, such as 'hello', and the syntax str(obj) that is used to construct a string representation of a typical object. Common operators that are supported by strings, such as the use of + for concatenation, were further discussed in Section 1.3. This appendix serves as a more detailed reference, describing convenient behaviors that strings support for the processing of text. To organize our overview of the str class behaviors, we group them into the following broad categories of functionality.

Searching for Substrings

The operator syntax, pattern **in** s, can be used to determine if the given pattern occurs as a substring of string s. Table A.1 describes several related methods that determine the number of such occurrences, and the index at which the leftmost or rightmost such occurrence begins. Each of the functions in this table accepts two optional parameters, start and end, which are indices that effectively restrict the search to the implicit slice s[start:end]. For example, the call s.find(pattern, 5) restricts the search to s[5:].

Calling Syntax	Description
s.count(pattern)	Return the number of non-overlapping occurrences of pattern
s.find(pattern)	Return the index starting the leftmost occurrence of pattern; else -1
s.index(pattern)	Similar to find, but raise ValueError if not found
s.rfind(pattern)	Return the index starting the rightmost occurrence of pattern; else -1
s.rindex(pattern)	Similar to rfind, but raise ValueError if not found

Table A.1: Methods that search for substrings.

Constructing Related Strings

Strings in Python are immutable, so none of their methods modify an existing string instance. However, many methods return a newly constructed string that is closely related to an existing one. Table A.2 provides a summary of such methods, including those that replace a given pattern with another, that vary the case of alphabetic characters, that produce a fixed-width string with desired justification, and that produce a copy of a string with extraneous characters stripped from either end.

Calling Syntax	Description
s.replace(old, new)	Return a copy of s with all occurrences of old replaced by new
s.capitalize( )	Return a copy of s with its first character having uppercase
s.upper( )	Return a copy of s with all alphabetic characters in uppercase
s.lower( )	Return a copy of s with all alphabetic characters in lowercase
s.center(width)	Return a copy of s, padded to width, centered among spaces
s.ljust(width)	Return a copy of s, padded to width with trailing spaces
s.rjust(width)	Return a copy of s, padded to width with leading spaces
s.zfill(width)	Return a copy of s, padded to width with leading zeros
s.strip( )	Return a copy of s, with leading and trailing whitespace removed
s.lstrip( )	Return a copy of s, with leading whitespace removed
s.rstrip( )	Return a copy of s, with trailing whitespace removed

Table A.2: String methods that produce related strings.

Several of these methods accept optional parameters not detailed in the table. For example, the replace method replaces all nonoverlapping occurrences of the old pattern by default, but an optional parameter can limit the number of replacements that are performed. The methods that center or justify a text use spaces as the default fill character when padding, but an alternate fill character can be specified as an optional parameter. Similarly, all variants of the strip methods remove leading and trailing whitespace by default, but an optional string parameter designates the choice of characters that should be removed from the ends.

Testing Boolean Conditions

Table A.3 includes methods that test for a Boolean property of a string, such as whether it begins or ends with a pattern, or whether its characters qualify as being alphabetic, numeric, whitespace, etc. For the standard ASCII character set, alphabetic characters are the uppercase A–Z, and lowercase a–z, numeric digits are 0–9, and whitespace includes the space character, tab character, newline, and carriage return. Conventions for what are considered alphabetic and numeric character codes are extended to more general Unicode character sets.

Calling Syntax	Description
s.startswith(pattern)	Return True if pattern is a prefix of string s
s.endswith(pattern)	Return True if pattern is a suffix of string s
s.isspace()	Return True if all characters of nonempty string are whitespace
s.isalpha()	Return True if all characters of nonempty string are alphabetic
s.islower()	Return True if there are one or more alphabetic characters, all of which are lowercased
s.isupper()	Return True if there are one or more alphabetic characters, all of which are uppercased
s.isdigit()	Return True if all characters of nonempty string are in 0–9
s.isdecimal()	Return True if all characters of nonempty string represent digits 0–9, including Unicode equivalents
s.isnumeric()	Return True if all characters of nonempty string are numeric Unicode characters (e.g., 0–9, equivalents, fraction characters)
s.isalnum()	Return True if all characters of nonempty string are either alphabetic or numeric (as per above definitions)

Table A.3: Methods that test Boolean properties of strings.

Splitting and Joining Strings

Table A.4 describes several important methods of Python's string class, used to compose a sequence of strings together using a delimiter to separate each pair, or to take an existing string and determine a decomposition of that string based upon existence of a given separating pattern.

Calling Syntax	Description
sep.join(strings)	Return the composition of the given sequence of strings, inserting sep as delimiter between each pair
s.splitlines()	Return a list of substrings of s, as delimited by newlines
s.split(sep, count)	Return a list of substrings of s, as delimited by the first count occurrences of sep. If count is not specified, split on all occurrences. If sep is not specified, use whitespace as delimiter.
s.rsplit(sep, count)	Similar to split, but using the rightmost occurrences of sep
s.partition(sep)	Return (head, sep, tail) such that s = head + sep + tail, using leftmost occurrence of sep, if any; else return (s, '', '')
s.rpartition(sep)	Return (head, sep, tail) such that s = head + sep + tail, using rightmost occurrence of sep, if any; else return ('', '', s)

Table A.4: Methods for splitting and joining strings.

The join method is used to assemble a string from a series of pieces. An example of its usage is ' and '.join(['red', 'green', 'blue']), which produces the result 'red and green and blue'. Note well that spaces were embedded in the separator string. In contrast, the command 'and'.join(['red', 'green', 'blue']) produces the result 'redandgreenandblue'.

The other methods discussed in Table A.4 serve a dual purpose to join, as they begin with a string and produce a sequence of substrings based upon a given delimiter. For example, the call `'red and green and blue'.split(' and ')` produces the result `['red', 'green', 'blue']`. If no delimiter (or None) is specified, split uses whitespace as a delimiter; thus, `'red and green and blue'.split()` produces `['red', 'and', 'green', 'and', 'blue']`.

String Formatting

The format method of the str class composes a string that includes one or more formatted arguments. The method is invoked with a syntax s.format(arg0, arg1, ...), where s serves as a *formatting string* that expresses the desired result with one or more placeholders in which the arguments will be substituted. As a simple example, the expression `'{} had a little {}'.format('Mary', 'lamb')` produces the result `'Mary had a little lamb'`. The pairs of curly braces in the formatting string are the placeholders for fields that will be substituted into the result. By default, the arguments sent to the function are substituted using positional order; hence, `'Mary'` was the first substitute and `'lamb'` the second. However, the substitution patterns may be explicitly numbered to alter the order, or to use a single argument in more than one location. For example, the expression `'{0}, {0}, {0} your {1}'.format('row', 'boat')` produces the result `'row, row, row your boat'`.

All substitution patterns allow use of annotations to pad an argument to a particular width, using a choice of fill character and justification mode. An example of such an annotation is `'{:-^20}'.format('hello')`. In this example, the hyphen (-) serves as a fill character, the caret (^) designates a desire for the string to be centered, and 20 is the desired width for the argument. This example results in the string `'-------hello--------'`. By default, space is used as a fill character and an implied < character dictates left-justification; an explicit > character would dictate right-justification.

There are additional formatting options for numeric types. A number will be padded with zeros rather than spaces if its width description is prefaced with a zero. For example, a date can be formatted in traditional "YYYY/MM/DD" form as `'{}/{:02}/{:02}'.format(year, month, day)`. Integers can be converted to binary, octal, or hexadecimal by respectively adding the character b, o, or x as a suffix to the annotation. The displayed precision of a floating-point number is specified with a decimal point and the subsequent number of desired digits. For example, the expression `'{:.3}.format(2/3)'` produces the string `'0.667'`, rounded to three digits after the decimal point. A programmer can explicitly designate use of fixed-point representation (e.g., `'0.667'`) by adding the character f as a suffix, or scientific notation (e.g., `'6.667e-01'`) by adding the character e as a suffix.

Appendix

B — Useful Mathematical Facts

In this appendix we give several useful mathematical facts. We begin with some combinatorial definitions and facts.

Logarithms and Exponents

The logarithm function is defined as

$$\log_b a = c \qquad \text{if} \qquad a = b^c.$$

The following identities hold for logarithms and exponents:

1. $\log_b ac = \log_b a + \log_b c$
2. $\log_b a/c = \log_b a - \log_b c$
3. $\log_b a^c = c \log_b a$
4. $\log_b a = (\log_c a)/\log_c b$
5. $b^{\log_c a} = a^{\log_c b}$
6. $(b^a)^c = b^{ac}$
7. $b^a b^c = b^{a+c}$
8. $b^a/b^c = b^{a-c}$

In addition, we have the following:

Proposition B.1: *If $a > 0$, $b > 0$, and $c > a + b$, then*

$$\log a + \log b < 2 \log c - 2.$$

Justification: It is enough to show that $ab < c^2/4$. We can write

$$
\begin{aligned}
ab &= \frac{a^2 + 2ab + b^2 - a^2 + 2ab - b^2}{4} \\
&= \frac{(a+b)^2 - (a-b)^2}{4} \leq \frac{(a+b)^2}{4} < \frac{c^2}{4}.
\end{aligned}
$$

∎

The ***natural logarithm*** function $\ln x = \log_e x$, where $e = 2.71828\ldots$, is the value of the following progression:

$$e = 1 + \frac{1}{1!} + \frac{1}{2!} + \frac{1}{3!} + \cdots.$$

In addition,

$$e^x = 1 + \frac{x}{1!} + \frac{x^2}{2!} + \frac{x^3}{3!} + \cdots$$

$$\ln(1+x) = x - \frac{x^2}{2!} + \frac{x^3}{3!} - \frac{x^4}{4!} + \cdots .$$

There are a number of useful inequalities relating to these functions (which derive from these definitions).

Proposition B.2: *If $x > -1$,*

$$\frac{x}{1+x} \leq \ln(1+x) \leq x.$$

Proposition B.3: *For $0 \leq x < 1$,*

$$1 + x \leq e^x \leq \frac{1}{1-x}.$$

Proposition B.4: *For any two positive real numbers x and n,*

$$\left(1 + \frac{x}{n}\right)^n \leq e^x \leq \left(1 + \frac{x}{n}\right)^{n+x/2} .$$

Integer Functions and Relations

The "floor" and "ceiling" functions are defined respectively as follows:

1. $\lfloor x \rfloor$ = the largest integer less than or equal to x.
2. $\lceil x \rceil$ = the smallest integer greater than or equal to x.

The ***modulo*** operator is defined for integers $a \geq 0$ and $b > 0$ as

$$a \bmod b = a - \left\lfloor \frac{a}{b} \right\rfloor b.$$

The ***factorial*** function is defined as

$$n! = 1 \cdot 2 \cdot 3 \cdot \cdots \cdot (n-1)n.$$

The binomial coefficient is

$$\binom{n}{k} = \frac{n!}{k!(n-k)!},$$

which is equal to the number of different ***combinations*** one can define by choosing k different items from a collection of n items (where the order does not matter). The name "binomial coefficient" derives from the ***binomial expansion***:

$$(a+b)^n = \sum_{k=0}^{n} \binom{n}{k} a^k b^{n-k}.$$

We also have the following relationships.

Proposition B.5: *If* $0 \le k \le n$, *then*

$$\left(\frac{n}{k}\right)^k \le \binom{n}{k} \le \frac{n^k}{k!}.$$

Proposition B.6 (Stirling's Approximation):

$$n! = \sqrt{2\pi n}\left(\frac{n}{e}\right)^n\left(1 + \frac{1}{12n} + \varepsilon(n)\right),$$

where $\varepsilon(n)$ *is* $O(1/n^2)$.

The *Fibonacci progression* is a numeric progression such that $F_0 = 0$, $F_1 = 1$, and $F_n = F_{n-1} + F_{n-2}$ for $n \ge 2$.

Proposition B.7: *If* F_n *is defined by the Fibonacci progression, then* F_n *is* $\Theta(g^n)$, *where* $g = (1 + \sqrt{5})/2$ *is the so-called* **golden ratio**.

Summations

There are a number of useful facts about summations.

Proposition B.8: *Factoring summations:*

$$\sum_{i=1}^{n} af(i) = a\sum_{i=1}^{n} f(i),$$

provided a *does not depend upon* i.

Proposition B.9: *Reversing the order:*

$$\sum_{i=1}^{n}\sum_{j=1}^{m} f(i,j) = \sum_{j=1}^{m}\sum_{i=1}^{n} f(i,j).$$

One special form of is a *telescoping sum*:

$$\sum_{i=1}^{n}(f(i) - f(i-1)) = f(n) - f(0),$$

which arises often in the amortized analysis of a data structure or algorithm.

The following are some other facts about summations that arise often in the analysis of data structures and algorithms.

Proposition B.10: $\sum_{i=1}^{n} i = n(n+1)/2$.

Proposition B.11: $\sum_{i=1}^{n} i^2 = n(n+1)(2n+1)/6$.

Proposition B.12: *If $k \geq 1$ is an integer constant, then*

$$\sum_{i=1}^{n} i^k \text{ is } \Theta(n^{k+1}).$$

Another common summation is the **geometric sum**, $\sum_{i=0}^{n} a^i$, for any fixed real number $0 < a \neq 1$.

Proposition B.13:

$$\sum_{i=0}^{n} a^i = \frac{a^{n+1} - 1}{a - 1},$$

for any real number $0 < a \neq 1$.

Proposition B.14:

$$\sum_{i=0}^{\infty} a^i = \frac{1}{1 - a}$$

for any real number $0 < a < 1$.

There is also a combination of the two common forms, called the **linear exponential** summation, which has the following expansion:

Proposition B.15: *For $0 < a \neq 1$, and $n \geq 2$,*

$$\sum_{i=1}^{n} ia^i = \frac{a - (n+1)a^{(n+1)} + na^{(n+2)}}{(1-a)^2}.$$

The nth **Harmonic number** H_n is defined as

$$H_n = \sum_{i=1}^{n} \frac{1}{i}.$$

Proposition B.16: *If H_n is the nth harmonic number, then H_n is $\ln n + \Theta(1)$.*

Basic Probability

We review some basic facts from probability theory. The most basic is that any statement about a probability is defined upon a **sample space** S, which is defined as the set of all possible outcomes from some experiment. We leave the terms "outcomes" and "experiment" undefined in any formal sense.

Example B.17: *Consider an experiment that consists of the outcome from flipping a coin five times. This sample space has 2^5 different outcomes, one for each different ordering of possible flips that can occur.*

Sample spaces can also be infinite, as the following example illustrates.

Example B.18: *Consider an experiment that consists of flipping a coin until it comes up heads. This sample space is infinite, with each outcome being a sequence of i tails followed by a single flip that comes up heads, for $i = 1, 2, 3, \ldots$.*

A **probability space** is a sample space S together with a probability function Pr that maps subsets of S to real numbers in the interval $[0, 1]$. It captures mathematically the notion of the probability of certain "events" occurring. Formally, each subset A of S is called an **event**, and the probability function Pr is assumed to possess the following basic properties with respect to events defined from S:

1. $\Pr(\emptyset) = 0$.
2. $\Pr(S) = 1$.
3. $0 \le \Pr(A) \le 1$, for any $A \subseteq S$.
4. If $A, B \subseteq S$ and $A \cap B = \emptyset$, then $\Pr(A \cup B) = \Pr(A) + \Pr(B)$.

Two events A and B are **independent** if

$$\Pr(A \cap B) = \Pr(A) \cdot \Pr(B).$$

A collection of events $\{A_1, A_2, \ldots, A_n\}$ is **mutually independent** if

$$\Pr(A_{i_1} \cap A_{i_2} \cap \cdots \cap A_{i_k}) = \Pr(A_{i_1}) \Pr(A_{i_2}) \cdots \Pr(A_{i_k}).$$

for any subset $\{A_{i_1}, A_{i_2}, \ldots, A_{i_k}\}$.

The **conditional probability** that an event A occurs, given an event B, is denoted as $\Pr(A|B)$, and is defined as the ratio

$$\frac{\Pr(A \cap B)}{\Pr(B)},$$

assuming that $\Pr(B) > 0$.

An elegant way for dealing with events is in terms of **random variables**. Intuitively, random variables are variables whose values depend upon the outcome of some experiment. Formally, a **random variable** is a function X that maps outcomes from some sample space S to real numbers. An **indicator random variable** is a random variable that maps outcomes to the set $\{0, 1\}$. Often in data structure and algorithm analysis we use a random variable X to characterize the running time of a randomized algorithm. In this case, the sample space S is defined by all possible outcomes of the random sources used in the algorithm.

We are most interested in the typical, average, or "expected" value of such a random variable. The **expected value** of a random variable X is defined as

$$\mathbf{E}(X) = \sum_x x \Pr(X = x),$$

where the summation is defined over the range of X (which in this case is assumed to be discrete).

Proposition B.19 (The Linearity of Expectation): *Let X and Y be two random variables and let c be a number. Then*

$$E(X+Y) = E(X)+E(Y) \qquad \text{and} \qquad E(cX) = cE(X).$$

Example B.20: *Let X be a random variable that assigns the outcome of the roll of two fair dice to the sum of the number of dots showing. Then* $E(X) = 7$.

Justification: To justify this claim, let X_1 and X_2 be random variables corresponding to the number of dots on each die. Thus, $X_1 = X_2$ (i.e., they are two instances of the same function) and $E(X) = E(X_1 + X_2) = E(X_1) + E(X_2)$. Each outcome of the roll of a fair die occurs with probability $1/6$. Thus,

$$E(X_i) = \frac{1}{6} + \frac{2}{6} + \frac{3}{6} + \frac{4}{6} + \frac{5}{6} + \frac{6}{6} = \frac{7}{2},$$

for $i = 1, 2$. Therefore, $E(X) = 7$.   ∎

Two random variables X and Y are ***independent*** if

$$\Pr(X = x | Y = y) = \Pr(X = x),$$

for all real numbers x and y.

Proposition B.21: *If two random variables X and Y are independent, then*

$$E(XY) = E(X)E(Y).$$

Example B.22: *Let X be a random variable that assigns the outcome of a roll of two fair dice to the product of the number of dots showing. Then* $E(X) = 49/4$.

Justification: Let X_1 and X_2 be random variables denoting the number of dots on each die. The variables X_1 and X_2 are clearly independent; hence

$$E(X) = E(X_1 X_2) = E(X_1)E(X_2) = (7/2)^2 = 49/4.$$ ∎

The following bound and corollaries that follow from it are known as ***Chernoff bounds***.

Proposition B.23: *Let X be the sum of a finite number of independent 0/1 random variables and let $\mu > 0$ be the expected value of X. Then, for $\delta > 0$,*

$$\Pr(X > (1+\delta)\mu) < \left[\frac{e^{\delta}}{(1+\delta)^{(1+\delta)}} \right]^{\mu}.$$

Useful Mathematical Techniques

To compare the growth rates of different functions, it is sometimes helpful to apply the following rule.

Proposition B.24 (L'Hôpital's Rule): *If we have* $\lim_{n\to\infty} f(n) = +\infty$ *and we have* $\lim_{n\to\infty} g(n) = +\infty$, *then* $\lim_{n\to\infty} f(n)/g(n) = \lim_{n\to\infty} f'(n)/g'(n)$, *where* $f'(n)$ *and* $g'(n)$ *respectively denote the derivatives of* $f(n)$ *and* $g(n)$.

In deriving an upper or lower bound for a summation, it is often useful to *split a summation* as follows:

$$\sum_{i=1}^{n} f(i) = \sum_{i=1}^{j} f(i) + \sum_{i=j+1}^{n} f(i).$$

Another useful technique is to **bound a sum by an integral**. If f is a nondecreasing function, then, assuming the following terms are defined,

$$\int_{a-1}^{b} f(x)\,dx \le \sum_{i=a}^{b} f(i) \le \int_{a}^{b+1} f(x)\,dx.$$

There is a general form of recurrence relation that arises in the analysis of divide-and-conquer algorithms:

$$T(n) = aT(n/b) + f(n),$$

for constants $a \ge 1$ and $b > 1$.

Proposition B.25: *Let* $T(n)$ *be defined as above. Then*
1. *If* $f(n)$ *is* $O(n^{\log_b a - \varepsilon})$, *for some constant* $\varepsilon > 0$, *then* $T(n)$ *is* $\Theta(n^{\log_b a})$.
2. *If* $f(n)$ *is* $\Theta(n^{\log_b a} \log^k n)$, *for a fixed nonnegative integer* $k \ge 0$, *then* $T(n)$ *is* $\Theta(n^{\log_b a} \log^{k+1} n)$.
3. *If* $f(n)$ *is* $\Omega(n^{\log_b a + \varepsilon})$, *for some constant* $\varepsilon > 0$, *and if* $af(n/b) \le cf(n)$, *then* $T(n)$ *is* $\Theta(f(n))$.

This proposition is known as the **master method** for characterizing divide-and-conquer recurrence relations asymptotically.

Bibliography

[1] H. Abelson, G. J. Sussman, and J. Sussman, *Structure and Interpretation of Computer Programs*. Cambridge, MA: MIT Press, 2nd ed., 1996.

[2] G. M. Adel'son-Vel'skii and Y. M. Landis, "An algorithm for the organization of information," *Doklady Akademii Nauk SSSR*, vol. 146, pp. 263–266, 1962. English translation in *Soviet Math. Dokl.*, **3**, 1259–1262.

[3] A. Aggarwal and J. S. Vitter, "The input/output complexity of sorting and related problems," *Commun. ACM*, vol. 31, pp. 1116–1127, 1988.

[4] A. V. Aho, "Algorithms for finding patterns in strings," in *Handbook of Theoretical Computer Science* (J. van Leeuwen, ed.), vol. A. Algorithms and Complexity, pp. 255–300, Amsterdam: Elsevier, 1990.

[5] A. V. Aho, J. E. Hopcroft, and J. D. Ullman, *The Design and Analysis of Computer Algorithms*. Reading, MA: Addison-Wesley, 1974.

[6] A. V. Aho, J. E. Hopcroft, and J. D. Ullman, *Data Structures and Algorithms*. Reading, MA: Addison-Wesley, 1983.

[7] R. K. Ahuja, T. L. Magnanti, and J. B. Orlin, *Network Flows: Theory, Algorithms, and Applications*. Englewood Cliffs, NJ: Prentice Hall, 1993.

[8] R. Baeza-Yates and B. Ribeiro-Neto, *Modern Information Retrieval*. Reading, MA: Addison-Wesley, 1999.

[9] O. Barůvka, "O jistem problemu minimalnim," *Praca Moravske Prirodovedecke Spolecnosti*, vol. 3, pp. 37–58, 1926. (in Czech).

[10] R. Bayer, "Symmetric binary B-trees: Data structure and maintenance," *Acta Informatica*, vol. 1, no. 4, pp. 290–306, 1972.

[11] R. Bayer and McCreight, "Organization of large ordered indexes," *Acta Inform.*, vol. 1, pp. 173–189, 1972.

[12] D. M. Beazley, *Python Essential Reference*. Addison-Wesley Professional, 4th ed., 2009.

[13] R. E. Bellman, *Dynamic Programming*. Princeton, NJ: Princeton University Press, 1957.

[14] J. L. Bentley, "Programming pearls: Writing correct programs," *Communications of the ACM*, vol. 26, pp. 1040–1045, 1983.

[15] J. L. Bentley, "Programming pearls: Thanks, heaps," *Communications of the ACM*, vol. 28, pp. 245–250, 1985.

[16] J. L. Bentley and M. D. McIlroy, "Engineering a sort function," *Software—Practice and Experience*, vol. 23, no. 11, pp. 1249–1265, 1993.

[17] G. Booch, *Object-Oriented Analysis and Design with Applications*. Redwood City, CA: Benjamin/Cummings, 1994.

[18] R. S. Boyer and J. S. Moore, "A fast string searching algorithm," *Communications of the ACM*, vol. 20, no. 10, pp. 762–772, 1977.

[19] G. Brassard, "Crusade for a better notation," *SIGACT News*, vol. 17, no. 1, pp. 60–64, 1985.

[20] T. Budd, *An Introduction to Object-Oriented Programming*. Reading, MA: Addison-Wesley, 1991.

[21] D. Burger, J. R. Goodman, and G. S. Sohi, "Memory systems," in *The Computer Science and Engineering Handbook* (A. B. Tucker, Jr., ed.), ch. 18, pp. 447–461, CRC Press, 1997.

[22] J. Campbell, P. Gries, J. Montojo, and G. Wilson, *Practical Programming: An Introduction to Computer Science*. Pragmatic Bookshelf, 2009.

[23] L. Cardelli and P. Wegner, "On understanding types, data abstraction and polymorphism," *ACM Computing Surveys*, vol. 17, no. 4, pp. 471–522, 1985.

[24] S. Carlsson, "Average case results on heapsort," *BIT*, vol. 27, pp. 2–17, 1987.

[25] V. Cedar, *The Quick Python Book*. Manning Publications, 2nd ed., 2010.

[26] K. L. Clarkson, "Linear programming in $O(n3^{d^2})$ time," *Inform. Process. Lett.*, vol. 22, pp. 21–24, 1986.

[27] R. Cole, "Tight bounds on the complexity of the Boyer-Moore pattern matching algorithm," *SIAM J. Comput.*, vol. 23, no. 5, pp. 1075–1091, 1994.

[28] D. Comer, "The ubiquitous B-tree," *ACM Comput. Surv.*, vol. 11, pp. 121–137, 1979.

[29] T. H. Cormen, C. E. Leiserson, R. L. Rivest, and C. Stein, *Introduction to Algorithms*. Cambridge, MA: MIT Press, 3rd ed., 2009.

[30] M. Crochemore and T. Lecroq, "Pattern matching and text compression algorithms," in *The Computer Science and Engineering Handbook* (A. B. Tucker, Jr., ed.), ch. 8, pp. 162–202, CRC Press, 1997.

[31] S. Crosby and D. Wallach, "Denial of service via algorithmic complexity attacks," in *Proc. 12th Usenix Security Symp.*, pp. 29–44, 2003.

[32] M. Dawson, *Python Programming for the Absolute Beginner*. Course Technology PTR, 3rd ed., 2010.

[33] S. A. Demurjian, Sr., "Software design," in *The Computer Science and Engineering Handbook* (A. B. Tucker, Jr., ed.), ch. 108, pp. 2323–2351, CRC Press, 1997.

[34] G. Di Battista, P. Eades, R. Tamassia, and I. G. Tollis, *Graph Drawing*. Upper Saddle River, NJ: Prentice Hall, 1999.

[35] E. W. Dijkstra, "A note on two problems in connexion with graphs," *Numerische Mathematik*, vol. 1, pp. 269–271, 1959.

[36] E. W. Dijkstra, "Recursive programming," *Numerische Mathematik*, vol. 2, no. 1, pp. 312–318, 1960.

[37] J. R. Driscoll, H. N. Gabow, R. Shrairaman, and R. E. Tarjan, "Relaxed heaps: An alternative to Fibonacci heaps with applications to parallel computation," *Commun. ACM*, vol. 31, pp. 1343–1354, 1988.

[38] R. W. Floyd, "Algorithm 97: Shortest path," *Communications of the ACM*, vol. 5, no. 6, p. 345, 1962.

[39] R. W. Floyd, "Algorithm 245: Treesort 3," *Communications of the ACM*, vol. 7, no. 12, p. 701, 1964.

[40] M. L. Fredman and R. E. Tarjan, "Fibonacci heaps and their uses in improved network optimization algorithms," *J. ACM*, vol. 34, pp. 596–615, 1987.

[41] E. Gamma, R. Helm, R. Johnson, and J. Vlissides, *Design Patterns: Elements of Reusable Object-Oriented Software*. Reading, MA: Addison-Wesley, 1995.

[42] A. Goldberg and D. Robson, *Smalltalk-80: The Language*. Reading, MA: Addison-Wesley, 1989.

[43] M. H. Goldwasser and D. Letscher, *Object-Oriented Programming in Python*. Upper Saddle River, NJ: Prentice Hall, 2008.

[44] G. H. Gonnet and R. Baeza-Yates, *Handbook of Algorithms and Data Structures in Pascal and C*. Reading, MA: Addison-Wesley, 1991.

[45] G. H. Gonnet and J. I. Munro, "Heaps on heaps," *SIAM J. Comput.*, vol. 15, no. 4, pp. 964–971, 1986.

[46] M. T. Goodrich, J.-J. Tsay, D. E. Vengroff, and J. S. Vitter, "External-memory computational geometry," in *Proc. 34th Annu. IEEE Sympos. Found. Comput. Sci.*, pp. 714–723, 1993.

[47] R. L. Graham and P. Hell, "On the history of the minimum spanning tree problem," *Annals of the History of Computing*, vol. 7, no. 1, pp. 43–57, 1985.

[48] L. J. Guibas and R. Sedgewick, "A dichromatic framework for balanced trees," in *Proc. 19th Annu. IEEE Sympos. Found. Comput. Sci.*, Lecture Notes Comput. Sci., pp. 8–21, Springer-Verlag, 1978.

[49] Y. Gurevich, "What does $O(n)$ mean?," *SIGACT News*, vol. 17, no. 4, pp. 61–63, 1986.

[50] J. Hennessy and D. Patterson, *Computer Architecture: A Quantitative Approach*. San Francisco: Morgan Kaufmann, 2nd ed., 1996.

[51] C. A. R. Hoare, "Quicksort," *The Computer Journal*, vol. 5, pp. 10–15, 1962.

[52] J. E. Hopcroft and R. E. Tarjan, "Efficient algorithms for graph manipulation," *Communications of the ACM*, vol. 16, no. 6, pp. 372–378, 1973.

[53] B.-C. Huang and M. Langston, "Practical in-place merging," *Communications of the ACM*, vol. 31, no. 3, pp. 348–352, 1988.

[54] J. JáJá, *An Introduction to Parallel Algorithms*. Reading, MA: Addison-Wesley, 1992.

[55] V. Jarník, "O jistem problemu minimalnim," *Praca Moravske Prirodovedecke Spolecnosti*, vol. 6, pp. 57–63, 1930. (in Czech).

[56] R. Jones and R. Lins, *Garbage Collection: Algorithms for Automatic Dynamic Memory Management*. John Wiley and Sons, 1996.

[57] D. R. Karger, P. Klein, and R. E. Tarjan, "A randomized linear-time algorithm to find minimum spanning trees," *Journal of the ACM*, vol. 42, pp. 321–328, 1995.

[58] R. M. Karp and V. Ramachandran, "Parallel algorithms for shared memory machines," in *Handbook of Theoretical Computer Science* (J. van Leeuwen, ed.), pp. 869–941, Amsterdam: Elsevier/The MIT Press, 1990.

[59] P. Kirschenhofer and H. Prodinger, "The path length of random skip lists," *Acta Informatica*, vol. 31, pp. 775–792, 1994.

[60] J. Kleinberg and É. Tardos, *Algorithm Design*. Reading, MA: Addison-Wesley, 2006.

[61] A. Klink and J. Wälde, "Efficient denial of service attacks on web application platforms." 2011.

[62] D. E. Knuth, *Sorting and Searching*, vol. 3 of *The Art of Computer Programming*. Reading, MA: Addison-Wesley, 1973.

[63] D. E. Knuth, "Big omicron and big omega and big theta," in *SIGACT News*, vol. 8, pp. 18–24, 1976.

[64] D. E. Knuth, *Fundamental Algorithms*, vol. 1 of *The Art of Computer Programming*. Reading, MA: Addison-Wesley, 3rd ed., 1997.

[65] D. E. Knuth, *Sorting and Searching*, vol. 3 of *The Art of Computer Programming*. Reading, MA: Addison-Wesley, 2nd ed., 1998.

[66] D. E. Knuth, J. H. Morris, Jr., and V. R. Pratt, "Fast pattern matching in strings," *SIAM J. Comput.*, vol. 6, no. 1, pp. 323–350, 1977.

[67] J. B. Kruskal, Jr., "On the shortest spanning subtree of a graph and the traveling salesman problem," *Proc. Amer. Math. Soc.*, vol. 7, pp. 48–50, 1956.

[68] R. Lesuisse, "Some lessons drawn from the history of the binary search algorithm," *The Computer Journal*, vol. 26, pp. 154–163, 1983.

[69] N. G. Leveson and C. S. Turner, "An investigation of the Therac-25 accidents," *IEEE Computer*, vol. 26, no. 7, pp. 18–41, 1993.

[70] A. Levitin, "Do we teach the right algorithm design techniques?," in *30th ACM SIGCSE Symp. on Computer Science Education*, pp. 179–183, 1999.

[71] B. Liskov and J. Guttag, *Abstraction and Specification in Program Development*. Cambridge, MA/New York: The MIT Press/McGraw-Hill, 1986.

[72] M. Lutz, *Programming Python*. O'Reilly Media, 4th ed., 2011.

[73] E. M. McCreight, "A space-economical suffix tree construction algorithm," *Journal of Algorithms*, vol. 23, no. 2, pp. 262–272, 1976.

[74] C. J. H. McDiarmid and B. A. Reed, "Building heaps fast," *Journal of Algorithms*, vol. 10, no. 3, pp. 352–365, 1989.

[75] N. Megiddo, "Linear programming in linear time when the dimension is fixed," *J. ACM*, vol. 31, pp. 114–127, 1984.

[76] K. Mehlhorn, *Data Structures and Algorithms 1: Sorting and Searching*, vol. 1 of *EATCS Monographs on Theoretical Computer Science*. Heidelberg, Germany: Springer-Verlag, 1984.

[77] K. Mehlhorn, *Data Structures and Algorithms 2: Graph Algorithms and NP-Completeness*, vol. 2 of *EATCS Monographs on Theoretical Computer Science*. Heidelberg, Germany: Springer-Verlag, 1984.

[78] K. Mehlhorn and A. Tsakalidis, "Data structures," in *Handbook of Theoretical Computer Science* (J. van Leeuwen, ed.), vol. A. Algorithms and Complexity, pp. 301–341, Amsterdam: Elsevier, 1990.

[79] D. R. Morrison, "PATRICIA—practical algorithm to retrieve information coded in alphanumeric," *Journal of the ACM*, vol. 15, no. 4, pp. 514–534, 1968.

[80] R. Motwani and P. Raghavan, *Randomized Algorithms*. New York, NY: Cambridge University Press, 1995.

[81] T. Papadakis, J. I. Munro, and P. V. Poblete, "Average search and update costs in skip lists," *BIT*, vol. 32, pp. 316–332, 1992.

[82] L. Perkovic, *Introduction to Computing Using Python: An Application Development Focus*. Wiley, 2011.

[83] D. Phillips, *Python 3: Object Oriented Programming*. Packt Publishing, 2010.

[84] P. V. Poblete, J. I. Munro, and T. Papadakis, "The binomial transform and its application to the analysis of skip lists," in *Proceedings of the European Symposium on Algorithms (ESA)*, pp. 554–569, 1995.

[85] R. C. Prim, "Shortest connection networks and some generalizations," *Bell Syst. Tech. J.*, vol. 36, pp. 1389–1401, 1957.

[86] W. Pugh, "Skip lists: a probabilistic alternative to balanced trees," *Commun. ACM*, vol. 33, no. 6, pp. 668–676, 1990.

[87] H. Samet, *The Design and Analysis of Spatial Data Structures*. Reading, MA: Addison-Wesley, 1990.

[88] R. Schaffer and R. Sedgewick, "The analysis of heapsort," *Journal of Algorithms*, vol. 15, no. 1, pp. 76–100, 1993.

[89] D. D. Sleator and R. E. Tarjan, "Self-adjusting binary search trees," *J. ACM*, vol. 32, no. 3, pp. 652–686, 1985.

[90] G. A. Stephen, *String Searching Algorithms*. World Scientific Press, 1994.

[91] M. Summerfield, *Programming in Python 3: A Complete Introduction to the Python Language*. Addison-Wesley Professional, 2nd ed., 2009.

[92] R. Tamassia and G. Liotta, "Graph drawing," in *Handbook of Discrete and Computational Geometry* (J. E. Goodman and J. O'Rourke, eds.), ch. 52, pp. 1163–1186, CRC Press LLC, 2nd ed., 2004.

[93] R. Tarjan and U. Vishkin, "An efficient parallel biconnectivity algorithm," *SIAM J. Comput.*, vol. 14, pp. 862–874, 1985.

[94] R. E. Tarjan, "Depth first search and linear graph algorithms," *SIAM J. Comput.*, vol. 1, no. 2, pp. 146–160, 1972.

[95] R. E. Tarjan, *Data Structures and Network Algorithms*, vol. 44 of *CBMS-NSF Regional Conference Series in Applied Mathematics*. Philadelphia, PA: Society for Industrial and Applied Mathematics, 1983.

[96] A. B. Tucker, Jr., *The Computer Science and Engineering Handbook*. CRC Press, 1997.

[97] J. D. Ullman, *Principles of Database Systems*. Potomac, MD: Computer Science Press, 1983.

[98] J. van Leeuwen, "Graph algorithms," in *Handbook of Theoretical Computer Science* (J. van Leeuwen, ed.), vol. A. Algorithms and Complexity, pp. 525–632, Amsterdam: Elsevier, 1990.

[99] J. S. Vitter, "Efficient memory access in large-scale computation," in *Proc. 8th Sympos. Theoret. Aspects Comput. Sci.*, Lecture Notes Comput. Sci., Springer-Verlag, 1991.

[100] J. S. Vitter and W. C. Chen, *Design and Analysis of Coalesced Hashing*. New York: Oxford University Press, 1987.

[101] J. S. Vitter and P. Flajolet, "Average-case analysis of algorithms and data structures," in *Algorithms and Complexity* (J. van Leeuwen, ed.), vol. A of *Handbook of Theoretical Computer Science*, pp. 431–524, Amsterdam: Elsevier, 1990.

[102] S. Warshall, "A theorem on boolean matrices," *Journal of the ACM*, vol. 9, no. 1, pp. 11–12, 1962.

[103] J. W. J. Williams, "Algorithm 232: Heapsort," *Communications of the ACM*, vol. 7, no. 6, pp. 347–348, 1964.

[104] D. Wood, *Data Structures, Algorithms, and Performance*. Reading, MA: Addison-Wesley, 1993.

[105] J. Zelle, *Python Programming: An Introduciton to Computer Science*. Franklin, Beedle & Associates Inc., 2nd ed., 2010.

Index

737